The
Resonant Interface

HCI FOUNDATIONS FOR INTERACTION DESIGN

Steven Heim

Long Island University, C. W. Post

The
Resonant Interface

HCI FOUNDATIONS FOR INTERACTION DESIGN

PEARSON

Addison
Wesley

Boston San Francisco New York
London Toronto Sydney Tokyo Singapore Madrid
Mexico City Munich Paris Cape Town Hong Kong Montreal

Publisher: Greg Tobin
Executive Editor: Michael Hirsch
Assistant Editor: Lindsey Triebel
Associate Managing Editor: Jeffrey Holcomb
Senior Author Support/Technology Specialist: Joe Vetere
Cover Design: Joyce Cosentino Wells
Digital Assets Manager: Marianne Groth
Senior Media Producer: Bethany Tidd
Senior Marketing Manager: Michelle Brown
Marketing Assistant: Sarah Milmore
Senior Manufacturing Buyer: Carol Melville
Production Coordination: Shelley Creager, Techbooks, Inc.
Text Design and Composition: Techbooks, Inc.

Cover Image: © Benot Jeanneton/PhotoAlto: Electric Gibson ES-175D guitar, circa 1960.

About the Cover: Musical instruments, such as the guitar, are an excellent example of user-centered design. They provide an efficient and intuitive interface to complex functionality. They have unmistakable affordances that children grasp immediately. They are also accessible to people with disabilities such as blindness. These are fundamental goals for which interaction designers should strive.

The interior of this book was composed in QuarkXpress using ETM version 2.

Library of Congress Cataloging-in-Publication Data

Heim, Steven G.
    The resonant interface / Steven G. Heim.
        p. cm.
    Includes bibliographical references and index.
    ISBN-13: 978-0-321-37596-4
    ISBN-10: 0-321-37596-3
    1. Human-computer interaction. 2.   User interfaces (Computer systems) I. Title.
    QA76.9.H85H9 2007
    004.01'9—dc22

                                                    2007003079

ISBN-13: 978-0-321-37596-4
ISBN-10: 0-321-37596-3

4 5 6 7 8 9 10—RRDC—11 10

Contents

Preface

Welcome to *The Resonant Interface: HCI Foundations for Interaction Design*. This book is for students or practitioners who want to gain a solid foundation in human–computer interaction (HCI) theory and an understanding of how to apply the theory to interaction design. It takes an integrated approach, blending HCI theory and interaction design practice.

The chapters cover the skills needed in design and the principles that guide the creation of digital user interfaces. Each chapter presents a complete design scenario that affords valuable insights into the discipline.

Guiding Principles of This Book

Interaction design must be grounded in the foundations of HCI. There is a natural synergy between interaction design and HCI. A well-rounded study of HCI research and the practical application of that research can provide a solid foundation for interaction design and can foster the creation of more usable and useful user interfaces. This is the core premise of *The Resonant Interface*.

Active learning leads to a far richer experience. *The Resonant Interface* is structured on the concept of active learning. Each chapter begins with a discussion of a particular HCI topic or concept. These are explored in depth and then applied to interface design. The topics are then set in a design scenario that deals with actual interface issues and problems.

Design projects and research agendas that further emphasize the application of HCI theories to interface design are included on the accompanying Web site. This practical experience is invaluable and enables students to understand more fully the relationship between HCI theory and interaction design. Only through active learning can they gain the experience necessary to truly understand the underlying theory.

Interaction design is a team discipline. Groups of specialists are often brought together by project managers to discuss and develop prototypes and specifications. It is the nature of interaction design that the team members frequently come from diverse backgrounds and do not share the same basic beliefs and ideas; they may even use conflicting terminology when describing the interaction environment.

It is essential that everyone on the team have good communication skills and can present ideas without ambiguous and vague language. This is why *The Resonant Interface* contains many team-oriented assignments. Some incorporate interteam involvement for the purposes of evaluation and usability testing; others require members to function in a specific capacity.

The Resonant Interface is a well-crafted tool for the educator who wants to engage and challenge their students. By following the presentation of HCI theory with clearly defined and progressively more complex interaction design assignments, students see first hand the synergy between theory and practice. A rule is a rule is a rule, until it becomes a real-life experience. From the practice of design, students gain a firm understanding of HCI theory.

Organization of the Text

Section I discusses the various ways in which people interact with computers. We look at the innovations and innovators who have paved the way for the technological advances we experience in our everyday lives. We examine various interaction paradigms such as personal, networked, and mobile computing. This leads to an exploration of the diverse interaction styles that enable us to interact with, and benefit from, contemporary computing technologies.

Section II explores the process of interaction design from the initial phase of discovery through the design and testing phases. We investigate the concepts, procedures, models, and methodologies that interaction designers use to develop and test their design ideas and prototypes. We explore what user-centered design means, and experience first hand the complex process of designing usable and useful interfaces.

Section III discusses various facets of interaction, including an in-depth look at the elements that make up contemporary user interfaces such as color, text, icons, and many others.

We approach human–computer interaction from the viewpoint of the human visual, auditory, and haptic perceptual channels. We apply the knowledge we gain from this discussion to specific aspects of interaction design. This helps us to understand the relationship between human perception and interaction design. This also provides a foundation for better understanding the elements that comprise some of the emerging interactive environments such as virtual reality and ubiquitous computing.

Features

- **Active learning approach.** Readers gain the experience necessary to truly understand the underlying HCI theory. Each chapter covers HCI concepts, applies them to interface design, and explores them in a real-world-oriented design scenario.

- **Design Scenario.** From Chapter 4 on, each chapter ends with a project in the form of a design scenario. The design scenarios use the information and techniques explained in the chapter and apply them to a real-world Web site.
- **Maxims.** Throughout the book, maxims are used to aggregate HCI theory and intuitions into an easy-to-digest format. Presenting these ideas in a small, coherent chunk connects research to learning pedagogy.

SUPPLEMENTS

Student Resources

Resources are available to help further students' learning and understanding of the material in this book. The following supplements are located on the book's companion Web site at www.aw.com/heim:

- Research agendas
- Interaction design projects
- Web-based resources supporting the topics and concepts covered in the chapters

Instructor Resources

The following resource is available for instructors:

- PowerPoint® slides

Visit Addison-Wesley's Instructor Resource Center (www.aw.com/irc) or send an e-mail to computing@aw.com for information about how to access this instructor resource.

Acknowledgments

Special thanks go to the Addison-Wesley team for their help and support with publishing this book: Michael Hirsch, Lindsey Triebel, Jeffrey Holcomb, Joe Vetere, Joyce Wells, Maurene Goo, and Michelle Brown. Thanks also goes to Shelley Creager at Techbooks and Philip Koplin for their wonderful production and editing help.

I thank the following reviewers for their suggestions and expertise, which were helpful in the development of this book:

- Christopher Andrews, Knox College
- Ann Bisantz, University at Buffalo, The State University of New York
- Eli Blevis, Indiana University at Bloomington
- William H. Bowers, Pennsylvania State University, Berks

- Yifei Dong, University of Oklahoma
- Richard W. Egan, New Jersey Institute of Technology
- Carlotta B. Eaton, New River Community College
- Juan E. Gilbert, Auburn University
- Wooseob Jeong, University of Wisconsin–Milwaukee
- Paul F. Marty, Florida State University
- Elouise Oyzon, Rochester Institute of Technology

I would like to take this opportunity to express my appreciation and gratitude to my family and friends who lived through this process with me and gave me the support and encouragement I needed to see it through.

Stefania, you transformed my convoluted ramblings into intelligible and elegant prose. That is a gift few possess. I am in awe of your creative abilities.

Mariapia—what can I say? This would all be meaningless without you.

I owe a special debt of gratitude to my dear friend and colleague Dwight Peltzer, without whom this project never would have even begun; Dwight, thank you for everything. I also thank Dr. Susan Fife-Dorchak for the support and opportunity she has given me to invest the time and energy required by this project. Thank you Susan, I am forever grateful.

SECTION I

Using Computers

This section discusses the various ways in which people interact with computers. It begins by looking at the innovations and innovators that have paved the way for the technological advances we experience in our everyday lives. It then examines various interaction paradigms such as personal, networked, and mobile computing. This leads to an exploration of the diverse interaction styles that enable us to interact with and benefit from contemporary computing technologies.

Interaction Paradigms

An interaction paradigm is basically a conceptual framework that serves as a model for thinking about human–computer interaction. It serves as a broad scaffold for thinking about how, why, and where people use computers. Understanding the various interaction paradigms can help us to frame questions about who uses computers and when they are used. Finally it can help us to explore the various manifestations of computing technologies from mainframes to pocket personal computers.

In this chapter we explore the various interaction paradigms that have evolved over the years. This will form the basis for our study of interaction design and will define the scope of our endeavors.

1.1. Innovation

Innovation involves inventing something new or finding a new way to do something. Interaction design strives for innovation by creating new computing devices and interfaces or by improving the way people interact with existing technologies.

Past innovations in computing technologies, such as the popular MP3 players that have become ubiquitous in a very short time, have made our lives more enjoyable. Innovations in medical technologies such as laparoscopic surgery have increased the quality of our health care practices. These and other innovations have quickly become part of our collective experience. The evolution of technology is proceeding rapidly, and new developments are just around the corner. We must gain a firm understanding of this process of innovation so that we can benefit from the lessons learned.

We have benefited in many ways from the energies and creativity of the various technology professionals who have contributed to this evolution over the years. It will be instructive and inspirational to review the work of some of them who stand out for their accomplishments. Their thoughts and efforts can help to motivate and inspire the innovations of the future so that we can create more useful and more usable computing technologies.

1.1.1. Memex

In 1945 Vannevar Bush published an article in the July issue of the *Atlantic Monthly* entitled "As We May Think." In this article, Bush envisioned a device that would help people organize information in a meaningful way. He called this device the "Memex":

> A Memex is a device in which an individual stores all his books, records, and communications, and which is mechanized so that it may be consulted with exceeding speed and flexibility. It is an enlarged intimate supplement to his memory. (*Bush, 1945, 12*)

Bush did not describe the interface in great detail. The bulk of the human—computer interface was embodied in the physical setup, which incorporated the desk, the screens, the levers, the platen, and the keyboard (Figure 1.1). These were electromechanical components that were familiar to his audience and had somewhat obvious functionality. The Memex was never developed, but the concept of a personal computerized aid served as inspiration for many of the computer pioneers of the period.

1.1.2. Human Augmentation System

Douglas Engelbart was fascinated by Bush's ideas, and he thought about how computers could be used to enhance and augment human intelligence. Engelbart pursued this concept during the 1960s with 17 researchers in the Augmentation Research Center (ARC) of the Stanford Research Institute (SRI) in Menlo Park, CA.

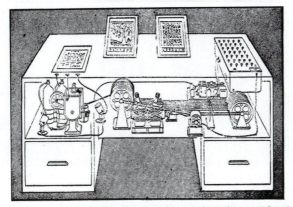

Memex in the form of a desk would instantly bring files and material on any subject to the operator's fingertips. Slanting translucent viewing screens magnify supermicrofilm filed by code numbers. At left is a mechanism which automatically photographs longhand notes, pictures and letters, then files them in the desk for future reference (*LIFE 19*(11), p. 123).

Figure 1.1   The Memex.

The concept of a personal, interactive computer was not common in that age of large-scale mainframe computing:

> It seemed clear to everyone else at the time that nobody would ever take seriously the idea of using computers in direct, immediate interaction with people. The idea of interactive computing—well, it seemed simply ludicrous to most sensible people. (*Engelbart, 1968*)

Engelbart remained dedicated to his vision, and his research team succeeded in developing a human augmentation system based on their oNLine System (NLS), which was unveiled at the Fall Joint Computer Conference in San Francisco in 1968.

The NLS was similar to contemporary desktop computing environments. It had a raster-scan display, a keyboard, and a mouse device. The mouse, invented by Engelbart, was first demonstrated at the 1968 conference. There was also a five-key chorded keyboard. The NLS was a networked system that included e-mail and split-screen videoconferencing (Figure 1.2).

1.1.3. OLIVER

In the same year that Engelbart demonstrated the NLS, J. C. R. Licklider published an article entitled "The Computer as a Communication Device" (Licklider, 1968). In this article, Licklider describes a meeting arranged by Engelbart that involved a team of researchers in a conference room with six television monitors. These monitors displayed the alphanumeric output of a remote computer. Each participant could use a keyboard and a mouse to point to and manipulate text that was visible on all the screens. As each participant presented his or her work, the material was accessed and made visible to the other members of the group.

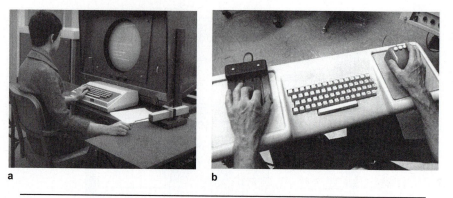

Figure 1.2   (a) The oNLine System (NLS). (b) The NLS chordal keyboard, keyboard, and mouse.
Courtesy Douglas Engelbart and Bootstrap Alliance.

The essential insight of Licklider's article was the potential for advanced modes of communication through a network of computers. The concept of networked computers was not new—a number of institutions already had successfully networked their computers; however, Licklider pointed out that these networks were restricted to groups of similar computers running the same software that resided in the same location. These were basically homogeneous computer networks. Licklider envisioned something more like the current manifestation of the Internet with its diversity of computing technologies and platforms.

Along with the concept of heterogeneous computer networks, Licklider introduced another significant concept in the evolution of human–computer interaction. Because Licklider imagined a high degree of integration in everyday life for networked computing, he saw the need to address the potentially overwhelming nature of the system. His solution was to create an automated assistant, which he called "OLIVER" (online interactive vicarious expediter and responder), an acronym that honors the originator of the concept, Oliver Selfridge.

OLIVER was designed to be a complex of applications, programmed to carry out many low-level tasks, which would serve as an intermediary between the user and his or her online community. OLIVER would manage files and communications, take dictation, and keep track of transactions and appointments.

1.1.4. The Ultimate Display

In 1965 Ivan Sutherland published an article entitled "The Ultimate Display," in which he proposed novel ways of interacting with computers, including the concept of a kinesthetic display. He argued that computers could already use haptic signals to control machinery—there already existed complex hand and arm manipulators—so why not a haptic display that could track eye movement and, therefore, use vision as an input mode? "Eye glance" interaction would involve eye-tracking algorithms that translated eye fixation into commands that would be carried out by the computer.

Sutherland also envisioned a display that would create a realistic environment in which the user would interact with haptic, auditory, and visual stimuli and that was not subject to the physical constraints of the real world:

> The ultimate display would, of course, be a room within which the computer can control the existence of matter. A chair displayed in such a room would be good enough to sit in. Handcuffs displayed in such a room would be confining, and a bullet displayed in such a room would be fatal. With appropriate programming such a display could literally be the Wonderland into which Alice walked. (*Sutherland, 1965, 508*)

1.2. Computing Environments

These three men—Bush, Engelbart, and Sutherland—were innovators and visionaries. They looked at the current state of technology and envisioned what could be. Innovation was and is an important component of interaction design. To find creative solutions to existing problems or to define new potential for computing technologies, we must first understand current technology and the different ways people use computing technologies. We must then apply that knowledge to the design of systems that address human needs, and in the process develop new and novel ways to aid people in their tasks.

To fully understand the complex nature of human–computer interaction we must explore the social, physical, and cognitive environments involved as well as the reasons people have for using computers. If we understand these factors, we will be better able to find new and better computing paradigms for the tasks that people need to accomplish.

1.2.1. Physical Computing Environment

The physical computing environment has evolved from dumb-terminal workstations to any number of public/personal, fixed/mobile configurations. This has increased the potential for computing technologies to enhance the quality of human activities and has also increased the significance of interaction design.

The issues involved in the use of an automated teller machine (ATM) as opposed to a personal digital assistant (PDA) are not drastically different; however, the solutions for their design may vary greatly. ATMs are fixed, public computing stations where people engage in personal computing activities related to financial information. PDAs are mobile, personal information appliances that can be used for a variety of reasons that may also include online banking.

Both systems must have adequate lighting, the input/output (I/O) facilities must be usable and reliable, and there must be enough physical space in which to use the system. The system should not require uncomfortable reaching or difficult movements. Accessibility to people with handicaps must also be considered.

For each of these platforms, the applicability and priority levels of these various requirements may fluctuate, and the solutions in each case may be very different. For instance, lighting for an ATM is designed in a fixed environment. Ambient illumination is stable and screen position can be fixed to avoid glare. PDAs, on the other hand, can be used in many types of environment, from the bright outdoors to dark automotive interiors with intermittent outside illumination. The type of screen, available display settings, use of color, size of type, and design of the icons must be defined by the broad range of possible viewing environments.

> **MAXIM**
>
> Default settings must be carefully thought out.

The physical computing environment will affect many aspects of an interface's design, and some of the requirements may actually contradict each other. For instance, if a system is to be used by many people with different physical attributes, a certain amount of flexibility should be built into the system so that users may adjust it to their own needs. However, because the computer is in a public place, it is possible that one user may adjust certain aspects of the system, such as keyboard height or screen position and angle, which would make it difficult for the next user, who may not know how to change some of these settings. This may mean that certain default settings and adjustments should not be accessible to the general public. This will require tradeoffs and increases the importance of determining the most appropriate and widely accessible default settings through thorough user testing.

The following is a list of some of the issues involved in designing physical computing environments:

- **Safety**—One of the goals of ergonomics is to create a safe computing environment. This can be a significant concern for some systems, especially those used in mission-critical environments. There are, unfortunately, numerous examples of high-risk situations that proved fatal due to computer-related errors. One of the better-known examples involved a computer-controlled radiation device called the Therac-25. Due to an error in the device's design, medical technicians inadvertently subjected certain patients to lethal does of radiation.

- **Efficiency**—Systems should not make the user do more work than is necessary. If the manipulation of a physical device is awkward or not consistent with human capabilities, efficiency will be diminished.

- **User Space**—The user must be able to use the system without discomfort. There must be enough room to stand, sit, or move about comfortably, and there must be enough room to use peripheral devices without difficulty. Some people use computers for long periods of time. If the physical design is not adequate, the user may experience fatigue, pain, or even injury. Public computers and information appliances are used by many people with different physical attributes and must, therefore, be as adjustable as possible to ensure comfort and decrease the risk of pain during long-term use. It must also be possible to easily reset adjustments to default settings. These default settings must be determined as accurately as possible.

- **Work Space**—Users must be able to bring work objects, such as notebooks and other information appliances such as PDAs, to the computing environment and be able to use them comfortably. Users who need to copy text from hard copy should have some type of holder on which to place the source material so that they can easily see both the hard copy and the screen.

- **Lighting**—Ambient illumination can affect the visibility of screen elements. Lighting in outside computing environments can be difficult to control.
- **Noise**—High levels of environmental noise can make auditory interfaces difficult, if not impossible, to use. Some environments, such as libraries and museums, are sensitive to any type of auditory stimuli. Mobile information appliances, such as cell phones and pagers, must have easily accessible audio controls. Many cell phones have vibration settings to avoid annoying ring tones. Other devices, such as wearable computers, also must be designed to address this concern.
- **Pollution**—Some industrial environments, such as factories or warehouses, are difficult to keep clean. Sometimes users must work with machinery that is dirty or greasy. Peripherals such as keyboards and mouse devices can easily become dysfunctional in such environments. Solutions such as plastic keyboard covers, washable touchscreen covers, and auditory interfaces may address some environmental concerns.

1.2.2. Social Computing Environment

Studies have shown that the social environment affects the way people use computers. Computer use has also been shown to affect human social interaction. This is a significant concern for collaborative computing systems. It would be unfortunate if a collaborative system inhibited human–human interactions.

Different computing paradigms imply different social environments. For instance, personal computing is usually a solitary activity done in an office or an isolated corner of the house. This is very different than ubiquitous computing (see later discussion), which implies a more public setting.

Public computers that are used for sensitive personal activities, such as ATMs, should be designed to protect the user's privacy. Audible feedback of personally identifiable information may be embarrassing or even detrimental. Negative auditory feedback that announces when a user makes an error can cause embarrassment for people who work in group settings.

Computers that are used in group settings must afford all members adequate viewing and auditory feedback. Group members may also need to access system functionality through peripheral devices. These must be made available to the group members who need them.

1.2.3. Cognitive Computing Environment

Human cognitive aptitude spans a wide range of capabilities. Interaction design must take into consideration many cognitive factors such as age and conditions relating to disabilities. The computing environment can also affect cognition: some environments involve high cognitive loads, whereas others are less demanding.

Computer system designs must address the relevant issues that arise from these different cognitive and environmental dynamics. The following list covers some of aspects related to the cognitive computing environment:

- **Age**—Some systems are designed specifically for young children who are learning basic skills such as reading or arithmetic. Other systems are designed for scientists and technicians who need to study the human genome. Computing environments that are not age appropriate run the risk of being frustrating or insulting. Technicians may find cute animations annoying, and children may become bored with long lists of hyperlinks.

- **Conditions Related to Disabilities**—Computer systems can be designed specifically for people with conditions related to disabilities. As more public information is being made available through information appliances, the need to make these devices accessible to people with cognitive disabilities is becoming more important. If public information appliances are designed poorly, they may significantly diminish the quality of life for a significant portion of the population.

- **Degree of Technical Knowledge**—Some systems are designed for particular user profiles with specific skills and facilities. These systems can be targeted to the particular needs of the user. Other systems are designed to be used by the general population and must take into consideration a wider range of cognitive abilities. General computing devices are also used by people with diverse technical backgrounds. It may be necessary to afford users different levels of functionality so they can use the system in the most efficient way.

- **Degree of Focus**—Computing systems can be designed for people who are completely focused on the task at hand, such as people playing digital games, or they can be designed for someone who is, say, monitoring many work-related activities that involve heavy machinery in an environment that has excessive noise pollution. The priorities and requirements for the interface design will be different for these two levels of focus.

- **Cognitive Stress**—Computers are used in diverse environments that impose different levels of cognitive stress on the user, from leisure activities such as listening to music to mission-critical environments as in air traffic control. People who use computers in stressful mission-critical environments need clear and unambiguous interface designs. Although this may be an important concern for all computing devices, there is no room for error in fields like medicine, aerospace, or the military. The priority level of certain design criteria may increase in certain situations.

1.3. Analyzing Interaction Paradigms

Since the publication of Vannevar Bush's article describing the Memex, computer scientists and researchers have created numerous and diverse configurations for computing systems. These configurations involve the construction and arrangement of hardware, the development of software applications to control the hardware, the topologies of networked systems, and the components of the human interface that define how people access the system's functionality.

Together these components comprise an interaction paradigm that defines the "who, what, when, where, why, and how" (5W−H) of computer system use. We can use this as a heuristic or procedure to more fully understand interaction paradigms.

1.3.1. 5W+H

We will use the 5W+H heuristic to define existing interaction paradigms and spaces and explore the elements and objects with which the user interacts; this will help to give us an understanding of how these systems work and how to apply that knowledge to the development of future systems.

We will make a slight alteration in the sequence and add a few couplings to the heuristic. Although all of the heuristic's elements are interrelated, some have greater effects on the others. These couplings are, therefore, based on degree of relationship and are not exclusive.

What/How—An in-depth understanding of the physical and virtual interface components of the various computing systems (the what) is essential for the creation of usable systems. We will look at the various physical components of interfaces, such as the I/O devices, and briefly explore the various related interface elements that define how we use these systems (the how), such as windows and icons. The interface components themselves will be more thoroughly explored in Chapter 10.

Where/When—Computer systems can also be defined by their particular physical computing space. This can clearly be seen by comparing the desktop computing space with the wearable computing space. Wearable computing is a result of advances in the fields of mobile and network computing and has given rise to a new network scope: the personal area network (PAN). PAN is defined by the user's ability to access computing functionality remotely (the where) and at any time (the when), regardless of his or her physical location or even while he or she is in transit if desired. This is not something one would attempt with a cathode ray tube (CRT) display.

Who/Why—We will also look at the types of tasks these physical devices and interface components facilitate. These tasks define the reasons why we use computers. This does not disregard the fact that technological developments are often driven by the need to accomplish new tasks or refine the way current solutions are implemented. It simply means that current systems facilitate certain tasks, which create particular motivations for their use. For instance, mainframes were used by highly trained technicians who were well versed in the inner workings of the system. These were often the same people who programmed the computer's various procedures; they understood the logic and syntax intuitively and were involved in large-scale computing for the governmental, industrial, and research communities.

1.3.2. Terms

Advances in technology have brought a broad new range of computer-assisted services to a large portion of the general public. Interaction architectures must now be designed for a greater range of human circumstances and a greater range of potential uses. Before we continue the discussion, let's clarify a few of the terms that have been used to describe these developments.

Information Space—Defined by the information artifacts used and the content included, for example, a book and the topics covered in the book

Interaction Architecture—The structure of an interactive system that describes the relationship and methods of communication between the hardware and software components

Interaction Mode—Refers to perceptual modalities, for example, visual, auditory, or haptic (sometimes used in the literature to refer to interaction styles or particular tasks such as browsing or data entry)

Interaction Paradigm—A model or pattern of human–computer interaction that encompasses all aspects of interaction, including physical, virtual, perceptual, and cognitive

Interaction Space—The abstract space defined by complex computing devices such as displays, sensors, actuators, and processors

Interaction Style—The type of interface and the interaction it implies, for example, command line, graphical user interface (GUI), or speech

Work Space—The place where people carry out work-related activities, which may include virtual as well as physical locations, as in, for example, flight simulation training

1.4. Interaction Paradigms

We will now explore some of the various interaction paradigms and their manifest interaction spaces. In the following sections, we investigate the various components of these systems. We will then, in Chapter 2, look at the various styles of interaction that these spaces involve, from text-based interaction to graphical and multimedia interfaces.

The principal paradigms we will look at include the following (Figure 1.3):

- Large-scale computing
- Personal computing
- Networked computing
- Mobile computing

We will look at some of the significant manifestations of these paradigms and explore the synergies that arise from the confluence of particular paradigms:

- Desktop computing (personal and networked)
- Public-personal computing (personal and networked)
- Information appliances (personal, mobile, and networked)

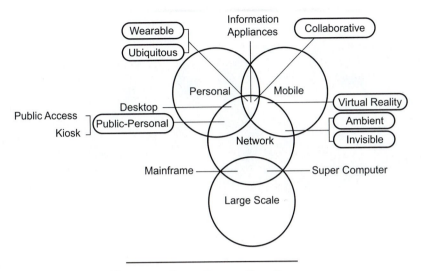

Figure 1.3 Computing paradigm diagram.

Large circles represent principal paradigms. Oblong shapes represent convergent paradigms. Words without surrounding shapes represent specific system architectures (sometimes used for a paradigm reference, as in desktop computing for personal computing).

We will then investigate some of the convergent interaction spaces that have evolved in recent years:

- Collaborative environments (personal, networked, and mobile)
- Embodied virtuality systems:
    - Ubiquitous computing (personal, networked, and mobile)
    - Ambient computing (networked and mobile)
    - Invisible computing (mobile and networked)
    - Wearable computing (personal, networked, and mobile)
- Immersive virtual reality (personal, networked, and mobile)

1.4.1. Large-Scale Computing

What/How—The original mainframe computers were large-scale computing machines, referred to as hosts, which resided in a central location and were accessed by remote alphanumeric terminals equipped with keyboards. The terminals were referred to as "dumb terminals" because they simply reflected the state of the mainframe and had no computing capabilities of their own. These systems are also referred to as host/terminal systems.

Mainframes were originally programmed using punch cards (Figure 1.4). These punch cards were created on a key punch machine and read into the mainframe by a card reader. This was a slow process based on an indirect relationship between

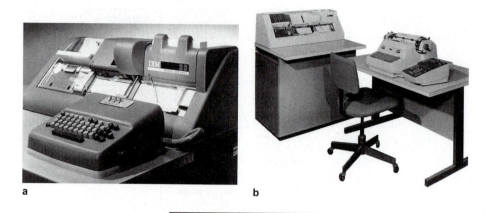

a   b

Figure 1.4   IBM card punch machines.

Courtesy IBM Corporate Archives.

the user and the computer. Large programs were usually processed in batches overnight when the system was not needed for routine daily processing.

Due to the great expense of maintaining mainframe computers, it was not possible to give excessive amounts of time to single users of the system. This led to the development of time-sharing services (TSSs). TSSs were schemes that used the downtime of one user for another user who was currently active. TSSs were generally available during the day.

Smaller, less expensive versions of the mainframe, called minicomputers, eventually became available to companies who could not afford the larger and more powerful mainframes or who simply did not need as much computing power. These minicomputers were structured according to the same interaction architecture as the mainframes.

Concurrent developments in computing for scientific research resulted in the development of high-powered machines, called supercomputers, which were designed to be used for specific computing tasks and to do them as quickly as possible. These highly specialized machines crunched large amounts of data at high speed, as in computing fluid dynamics, weather patterns, seismic activity predictions, and nuclear explosion dynamics.

Supercomputers are used for the very high speed backbone (vBNS) connections that constitute the core of the Internet. Mainframe computing, on the other hand, has often seemed to be on the verge of extinction. However, this is far from the truth. They exist in their current incarnation as so-called enterprise servers that are used in large-scale computing environments such as Wall Street.

When/Where—Most large-scale computers were owned by government agencies and large research institutes that were often affiliated with large universities.

The large-scale computing paradigm fostered a bureaucratic and institutionalized conceptualization of how interaction spaces should be constructed.

Who/Why—Large-scale computing resources were rare and expensive; they were generally only used to carry out government-sponsored research projects and university-based research for large corporate institutions. This was the motivation behind the ARPANET: to connect powerful computers for the purpose of sharing resources within the scientific and military domains. The ARPANET provided the theoretical and practical foundation on which the current Internet was formed.

Mainframes were used by highly trained technicians and scientists in laboratory environments. These research labs, however, also attracted young "hackers" who would sometimes live at these institutes and turn the machines into gaming environments overnight. Some of the earliest computer games originated in this way. Games like Space Wars and Lunar Lander were created by the technicians at the Control Data Corporation to provide incentives to get the system up and running.

1.4.2. Personal Computing

The personal vision of scientists like Douglas Engelbart and the work done by the researchers at the Augmentation Research Center, along with contemporaneous advances in technology, such as the shift from vacuum tubes to integrated circuits, led to the development of smaller, less expensive microcomputers and a new paradigm: personal computing. This new paradigm of personal computing dispersed computing power from a centralized institutional space to a personal space and led to related developments in hardware and software design that involved a greater focus on the human interface.

Computing power was now available to people with little or no technical background, therefore the interaction needed to become more intuitive and less technical. Researchers began exploring the use of graphical representations of computer functionality in the form of symbols and metaphors.

The Alto, developed at the Xerox Palo Alto Research Center in 1973, was the first computer to use a GUI that involved the desktop metaphor: pop-up menus, windows, and icons (Figure 1.5). It is considered to be the first example of a personal computer (PC). Even though the Alto should technically be considered a small minicomputer and not a microcomputer, it served as the profile for the personal computing paradigm: one user sitting at a desk, with uninterrupted access and full responsibility for the functioning and content of the computer's files and programs.

The NLS had a great influence on the development of the Alto (many of the PARC researchers came directly from ARC), which involved Ethernet connections, a CRT display (mounted on its side in portrait orientation), a keyboard, a three-button mouse, and the same five-key chorded keyboard. The system also included a laser printer developed specifically for the Alto. The Alto was never marketed commercially, but its interaction architecture provided the inspiration for the development of the Apple® Lisa, which had a more sophisticated GUI environment.

Figure 1.5   The Xerox Alto computer (1973).
Courtesy Palo Alto Research Center.

Along with the development of PC hardware and operating systems was a parallel evolution in application software. With the development of programs like the VisiCalc spreadsheet program and Lotus 1-2-3, as well as word processing applications and digital games, the PC became a powerful tool for both the office and the newly emerging home office/entertainment center. The PC has gradually become an integral part of our professional and personal lives.

Desktop

What/How—The main interaction architecture for personal computing has traditionally been defined by the desktop environment, which is based on the hardware/software configuration of the PC. This model can be defined as a single user with a keyboard and pointing device interacting with software applications and Internet resources.

The development of the PC meant that users did not have to submit their programs to a system administrator who would place them in a queue to be run when the system was available. Users could now access the computer's functionality continuously without constraint. The software industry boomed by creating programs that ranged from productivity suites, to games, to just about anything people might want.

Numerous storage media options are available for PCs; some are permanent, like CDs and DVD ROMs, and some are updateable, like CDRWs. Storage media technology is becoming cheaper and smaller in size. There is a consistent evolution in storage media that quickly makes today's technology obsolete tomorrow. For instance, the once ubiquitous floppy disk is rapidly joining the mountain of obsolete storage media. This may have consequences in the future for GUIs that traditionally use the image of a floppy disk on the icon for the "Save" function. Portable hard-drive technologies range from the large-capacity arrays used in industry to the pen-sized USB sticks.

Where/When—With the advent of the PC, computing power became available for home use and could address the home/office and entertainment needs of a large segment of the population. Home access was basically unfettered; users could access computing functionality whenever they wanted. The home computer has become a staple in countless households. A generation that takes the presence of a PC for granted has already grown to adulthood; they have never lived in a house without one.

Who/Why—PCs are used for a wide variety of reasons. Applications range from productivity tools that include word processing, spreadsheet, database, and presentation software to communication tools like e-mail and instant messaging software.

Shopping on the Web is becoming an integral part of consumer behavior. People also use the Web for banking and bill paying. Legal and illegal uses of file-sharing technologies have become common. The PC has become a center of activity in the home with applications for both work and play.

Perhaps the more serious question is not who uses personal computers but rather who does not use personal computers. Researchers have begun to explore the ramifications of socioeconomic issues on the information gap—the distance between people who have access to electronic information delivery and those who do not—and education lies at the center of this conversation. PCs, especially those with an Internet connection, are seen as a significant resource for educational institutions. Students in schools that cannot afford to offer this resource are at a disadvantage in a world that increasingly requires basic computer literacy for entry-level employment opportunities.

Public-Personal Computing

Public-personal computing has two distinct manifestations: public-access computing and public information appliances. The Bill & Melinda Gates Foundation has been an active leader in the support and development of public-access computing through the Global Libraries Program, which addresses the need to bridge the information gap, especially in geographic areas that are economically disadvantaged.

Public Access Computing—Public-access computers are generally desktop computers that use software to "lock down" the machine. This means that some users

Figure 1.6 Automated teller machine with touchscreen.
Courtesy BigStockPhoto.com.

lack full privileges and cannot access some operating system functionalities. This is done to ensure the system's proper functioning and protect against malicious or accidental alterations of its settings. There is also a need to make sure that the peripheral devices such as keyboards and pointing devices are not damaged or stolen.

Public Information Appliances—Public information appliances are context- and task-specific devices used by the public to access information or services offered by corporate or governmental agencies. They most often take the form of information kiosks or ticket-dispensing machines.

The most common kiosk-type device is the ATM machine, which basically consists of a touchscreen connected to a network of variable scope (Figure 1.6). The screens comprise buttons, virtual QWERTY keyboards, and number pads, all of which are designed for easy operation and can accommodate different users of varying finger sizes.

Public information appliances are found in both indoor and outdoor installations. It is important that screen visibility remain high. This can be especially difficult in outdoor locations, where lighting conditions can vary according to weather and time of day.

Touchscreens are the preferred form for these kiosks because of the high volume of public use. Peripherals such as keyboards and pointing devices would increase maintenance costs as well as the downtime some systems would incur due to theft and mistreatment.

1.4.3. Networked Computing

Although the personal computing architecture is well suited for the home, it does not entirely address the needs of the office user. Office workers need to communicate and share documents with each other. They require access to corporate documents and databases. It is simply not practical or often possible to maintain individual repositories of corporate information; office and institutional PCs need to be networked. In fact, the Alto was originally designed as a networked office system.

The idea of creating a network of computers that would enable communication between users can be traced to a series of memos written by J. C. R. Licklider in 1962 discussing his concept of the "Galactic Network." Although he did not stay at ARPA long enough to see the project to completion, his vision came to fruition with the launching of the ARPANET at 10:30 pm on October 29, 1969.

What/How—The evolution of the Internet was a direct result of the ARPANET, and it was not long before numerous computer networking technologies revolutionized many industries, such as telecommunications and entertainment.

Networks may differ in scope (e.g., personal area network [PAN], local area network [LAN], metropolitan area network [MAN], or wide area network [WAN]) and connection modality (wired or wireless); however, users generally access the network through a PC. Therefore, the user experience is similar to that in the PC model. There may be limits on file access and restrictions on network locations, but systems often allow for "user profiles" that customize the interface for each individual so that he or she can work in a familiar environment.

Networking does not alter the "what" or the "how" of human–computer interaction to any large degree. The user interacts with more or less the same hardware and software configurations available on a nonnetworked PC and in much the same way. Emerging mobile technologies, on the other hand, are shaping the way networks will be structured in the future and changing the interaction paradigms that will become common for a large portion of the networked population.

Where/When—Networking has revolutionized telecommunications and altered our concepts of place, distance, and time. It has changed our concept of the "where" and the "when." By enabling remote access, networks have freed us from location-based computing, altering our concept of where we use computers. We no longer have to travel to the office to access the company's database; we can do it from any location that has Internet access.

We also can access networked resources at any time. Connections via community antenna television, more commonly known as community access television or cable TV (CATV), allow us to view movies "on demand" according to our personal time schedule. Large corporations with global locations can take advantage of the work cycles on different continents to create work flows that optimize office hours worldwide. Time constraints have been altered; "when" is now a more flexible issue.

Who/Why—The rise of the World Wide Web has created additional avenues for marketing goods and services. Web-based commercial resources have created an entirely new economic space: e-commerce. We now use computers to purchase airplane and movie tickets and to share photos with friends and relatives; activities that we used to do in person.

Networked computers can offer more things to more people and, therefore, have expanded the diversity of the user population. Young people are spending increasing amounts of time playing networked games and instant messaging each other. Older people are enjoying the photos of grandchildren who live far away.

People of all ages and backgrounds with diverse interests and levels of computer literacy are finding reasons to use networked computers (mostly via the Web), such as participating in online auctions and conducting job searches. Networks have significantly altered the face of the user.

1.4.4. Mobile Computing

If we value the pursuit of knowledge, we must be free to follow wherever that search may lead us. The free mind is not a barking dog, to be tethered on a ten-foot chain.

Adlai Stevenson

Data become information when they are organized in a meaningful, actionable way. Knowledge is obtained by the assimilation of that information. In today's world, computers play an important role in the processing of data and the presentation of information.

In the past, computer access to data was restricted by location. In many situations, data had to be gathered and documented on location and transported to the computer. The data would be processed at the central location, and the information gained from that processing would initiate other data-gathering activities. This required time and intermediate steps that could sometimes affect the gathering process as well as the integrity of the data, especially because some data are extremely time sensitive.

That is no longer the case. With mobile and networked computing technologies, computers are no longer "tethered on a ten-foot chain." They can be transported to the remote locations where data are collected. Data can be captured, processed, and presented to the user without his ever leaving the remote site. Mobile technology embodies the essence of Adlai Stevenson's comments on the search for knowledge.

What/How—Mobile computing technologies comprise a very diverse family of devices that have rapidly become ubiquitous in most industrialized societies. There are numerous brands and models of laptop computers, and tablet computers have recently appeared. Digital game and MP3 players represent a thriving commercial segment. Many corporations distribute handheld remote communication and tracking devices to field agents to enhance on-site delivery and maintenance services.

Portable computers ship with embedded touchpads and pointing sticks. Their keyboards range from a bit smaller than desktop keyboards to full size; however, they do not have the added functionality of an extended keyboard with its number pad and additional function keys.

Figure 1.7 (a) Laptop computer. (b) Tablet computer.
Courtesy BigStockPhoto.com.

Laptop and tablet computers use LCD screens (Figure 1.7). Tablets also provide touchscreen interaction and handwriting recognition. Tablets are made in either a "slate format," without a keyboard, or in a laptop design that can be opened into the slate format.

Handheld devices, on the other hand, vary significantly in terms of hardware and software configurations. They can range from small computer–like cell phones with tiny keyboards and screens to MP3 players like the Apple iPod®, which uses a touch wheel and small LCD window (Figure 1.8).

MAXIM

Desktop metaphors do not translate well to mobile devices.

Portable computers have traditionally inherited the desktop metaphor used in contemporary GUI designs. The desktop metaphor is a direct result of the fact that PCs were originally designed for use on or around a physical desk in an office environment. In the desktop paradigm, the relationship between the information space and the work space is direct and, to some degree, intuitive. The desktop metaphor, however, may not always reflect the work space of a person using a portable computer.

Many people use laptop computers as a portable substitute for the desktop model: although they may carry it from the home to the office, they use it exactly as they would a desktop computer. However, others are finding new applications for

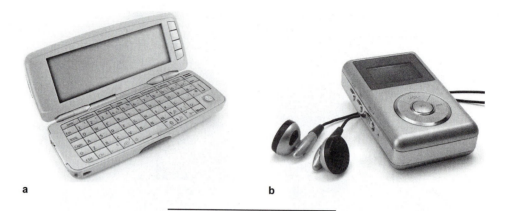

Figure 1.8   (a) Cell phone. (b) MP3 Player.
Courtesy BigStockPhoto.com.

portable computers, and new interaction designs are appearing. The tablet computer with its slate format and handwriting recognition software represents such a new approach to mobile interaction designs.

The most common format for handheld computers is the PDA. These are generally palm-sized devices that run a native operating system (OS), such as the Palm OS® or some version of Microsoft® Windows® like Windows CE®. Some of these interfaces do not differ greatly from their desktop cousins and can become cumbersome due to small screen size. Others, like the Palm OS, that used more innovative designs have become quite popular. In these devices, input is generally accomplished with a stylus using icons, menus, and text entry through miniature soft keyboards. Effective handwriting recognition is not very common, but the calligraphic systems built into the operating systems of these devices are stable, reliable, and relatively intuitive.

MAXIM

Hybrid desktop/mobile environments can afford optimal interaction efficiency.

The small size of these devices, their limited battery life, and the relatively low power of their processors can be problematic for some operations. Therefore, it is advantageous to use a desktop system in tandem with the mobile device for off-loading complex tasks or uploading latest versions of information services. Handhelds can also use flash card technology to store and transfer files and programs to and from their desktop cousins.

Mobile systems can access network resources, such as the Internet, through wireless access points (known as Wi-Fi hot spots) using the IEEE 802.11 family of wireless protocols. Relatively reliable connections and high speeds can be obtained if the signal is strong. Mobile devices can also connect to the Internet through a cell

Figure 1.9 On-board navigation system.
Courtesy BigStockPhoto.com.

phone using Bluetooth or infrared technologies such as IrDA (Infrared Data Association) devices.

Mobile devices can be connected to global positioning systems (GPS), giving them global positioning capabilities with an accuracy of approximately 1 meter. These have become popular in automotive navigation systems that use touchscreens and voice interaction to alleviate potential visual attention problems during driving (Figure 1.9).

One of the most widely adopted mobile computing devices is the cell phone. Cell phones achieved a significant user base in a very short time. It is not uncommon in many developed societies for each member of a family to have a cell phone. Service providers offer incentives for combined family plans and provide inexpensive, if not free, phones.

With the development of more sophisticated cellular networks, cell phones are also evolving into multifunction devices that provide voice, text, and video communications. They are capable of providing entertainment in the form of games and music and are being used to store contact and scheduling information. They are also providing a workout for the often ignored thumb.

Where/When—Mobile technology can be seen as a liberating force, allowing access to information, regardless of location. Wi-Fi hot spots have been made available to the public in coffee shops, airports, and community parks. Business contact information can be shared between two PDAs using infrared technology. Someone stuck in a traffic jam can reschedule appointments with a simple cell phone call.

Due to their mobility, these devices can offer situational computing that can take advantage of location-specific information through location-based mobile services (LMS). LMS can be beneficial for location-sensitive advertisements, public service announcements, social interactions, and location-specific educational information.

The GUIDE system provides visitors to Lancaster, England, with context-sensitive information on a handheld device using 802.11 technology. The system is tailored to the environmental context as well as the visitor's preferences. Base units situated around the city interact with the handheld device by beaming Web pages and positioning information.

Mobile technology can also be perceived as a nuisance. Theatrical performances are often prefaced by an announcement to guests that they turn off all cell phones, pagers, and other mobile telecommunication devices. Social context plays a role in the use of mobile devices.

Who/Why—The reasons why people might use mobile technologies are inexhaustible and range from improvements in medical care, to facilitated learning, to more fulfilling travel and leisure experiences. All of these technologies, however, share one primary benefit: they are designed to be used repetitively for brief and routine tasks. Therefore, they have a different use profile than their desktop cousins, and this should be taken into consideration and reflected in their design.

Mobile technology has become a staple for business people who must keep in touch with the office or with corporate resources while in transit. Mobile technology is also designed for niche applications that are highly technical in nature. Mobile devices with diagnostic applications can facilitate access to large databases linking field workers to more powerful database servers. This enables more immediate assessment of potential problems at remote locations.

Mobile devices can be very useful and offer many advantages; however, they also have disadvantages such as small screens, low bandwidth, and unstable connections and awkward interface interactions as when inputting text.

1.4.5. Collaborative Environments

MAXIM

Networks facilitate collaborative activities.

Networks allow members of a group to interact with other members on shared files and documents, whether the members are in the same room or at remote locations. This creates a virtual space where people can collaborate and work collectively.

Networks can support collaborative work by facilitating tasks such as communication, coordination, organization, and presentation. Computer-mediated communication (CMC) is a general term that describes the way computers are used to support group communication.

The term computer-supported cooperative work (CSCW) was coined by Paul Cashman and Irene Grief to describe technology that supports people who work in groups. Some of the issues that have risen from the research on cooperative work involve the nature of the group tasks, the reasons for group interaction, and the potential tools (groupware) for facilitating the collaborative tasks.

What/How—Computer-mediated communication, as currently practiced, involves networked PCs using familiar desktop environments such as Microsoft Windows® Mac OS X®, or some graphical interface to a Linux system. These systems are often augmented by the addition of audio and video devices such as microphones and Web cams. Engelbart's NLS incorporated many of the components of a CSCW environment, including audio and video conferencing and work flow support.

Current CMC environments may also involve large projected displays that use digital projectors and "smart screens," such as the SMART Board® from SMART Technologies Inc., which can be operated by touch or a computer interface (Figure 1.10).

The Web, with its suite of standardized protocols for network layers, has been a significant force in the development of collaborative environments by allowing greater interoperability in heterogeneous computing environments.

Where/When—CMC has many possible manifestations that cover same- or different-place/time scenarios and involve diverse families of groupware applications and devices. They can be synchronous, as in videoconferencing and instant messaging; or asynchronous, as in the recommender systems built into e-commerce Web sites such as Amazon.com or e-mail systems. They can also involve remote-access white boards, chat rooms, and bulletin board services.

Who/Why—CMC can aid business people who need to collaborate with remote customers or employees. Product development teams involved in product design,

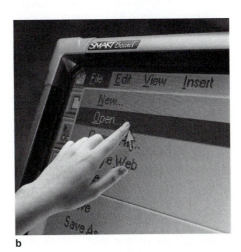

a   b

Figure 1.10 **(a) Actalystä interactive digital signage. (b) SMART Boardä interactive whiteboard.**

software engineering, financial reporting, and so on often require collaboration among distributed resources and personnel. CMC can address this need. Educational institutions have been exploring the use of CMC to build remote-learning environments and enrich learning experiences.

The scientific community has also been interested in CMC: the ARPANET was built to support communication within the scientific and military communities. More recently, "collaboratories" (laboratories without walls) have been developed to allow the scientific community to perform and share research projects and results regardless of physical location. Examples of collaboratories include the following:

- The Research Collaboratory for Structural Bioinformatics (RCSB)—"A non-profit consortium dedicated to improving our understanding of the function of biological systems through the study of the 3-D structure of biological macromolecules" (RCSB, 2005).
- The Chimpanzee Collaboratory—"A collaborative project of attorneys, scientists and public policy experts working to make significant and measurable progress in protecting the lives and establishing the legal rights of chimpanzees and other great apes" (TCC, 2005).
- The National Fusion Grid—"A SciDAC (Scientific Discovery through Advanced Computing Collaboratory) Pilot project that is creating and deploying collaborative software tools throughout the magnetic fusion research community. The goal of the project is to advance scientific understanding and innovation in magnetic fusion research by enabling more efficient use of existing experimental facilities and more effective integration of experiment, theory, and modeling" (FusionGRID, 2005).
- Space Physics and Aeronomy Research Collaboratory (SPARC)—"Allows space physicists to conduct team science on a global scale. It is the realization of the 'net'—real-time access to a world of instruments, models, and colleagues" (SPARC, 2005).

1.4.6. Embodied Virtuality

Some of us use the term "embodied virtuality" to refer to the process of drawing computers out of their electronic shells. The "virtuality" of computer-readable data—all the different ways in which it can be altered, processed and analyzed—is brought into the physical world. (*Weiser, 1991, 95*)

Groupware and CMC applications have facilitated the decoupling of information and location. Information that resides on one machine can be shared across a network and distributed to group members in remote locations. CSCW environments must be designed around the way people normally work on collaborative projects. The diverse nature of CMC applications reflects the complexity of collaborative work.

One of the traditional obstacles in CSCW is the fact that computing power and functionality has traditionally been concentrated inside the physical confines of a computer. Mobile technologies have enabled more flexibility by allowing people to connect to networks without being physically tethered to a specific location; however, portable computers are modeled on the PC interaction architecture, which tries to incorporate as much computing power in one place as possible—the Swiss army knife of computing.

Embodied virtuality (EV), as conceived by Weiser, is focused on decoupling computing power and functionality from "the box." This move is reminiscent of the shift from mainframe computing to personal computing and represents a new paradigm. It can be seen as a sort of "big bang," dispersing computing functionality throughout the environment. EV represents a shift in the way we think about computers; it opens up many new possibilities, but it also raises many questions.

How do we disperse computing functionality throughout the environment? What form should EV computing take? What kind of interface does it require? How much control should we retain, and how much should be automated?

There are a number of different approaches and schools of thought as to how computers should be incorporated into our lives. We will look at a few of the emerging fields in EV:

- Ubiquitous/pervasive computing
- Invisible/transparent computing
- Wearable computing

There are four discernible currents in the field of EV. These are reflected in the location/operation diagram shown in Figure 1.11.

- Side 1—Portable/manual (sometimes wearable) devices such as cell phones, MP3 players, digital cameras, and PDAs offer portable functionality the user can manipulate.
- Side 2—Manual/fixed devices such as ATMs and kiosks are manipulated by the user but are fixed in place.
- Side 3—Portable/automated devices are read by situated sensors, such as the car transceivers used for toll booth payments. There are no possible manual operations.
- Side 4—Automated/fixed devices such as alarm sensors can be used to detect the presence of intruders or industrial hazards.

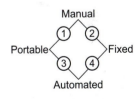

Figure 1.11 Embodied virtuality environments— location/operation.

1.4.7. Contemporary Approaches in Embodied Virtuality

Embodied virtuality concepts are being pursued by researchers at universities and corporate research laboratories under a variety of different designations: ubiquitous (UbiComp), pervasive, wearable, invisible, transparent, ambient, and embedded as well as other, lesser-known designations such as palpable and autonomic computing.

There are often no clear-cut distinctions among the various approaches; they represent a constellation of interaction paradigms, each combining different degrees of user control and embedded architectures. Each approach, however, represents a unique manifestation with particular characteristics that are useful in different circumstances. We will concentrate on three approaches: UbiComp, invisible, and wearable computing. These are the most widely used terms and they cover the overall scope of the EV domain.

Ubiquitous/Pervasive Computing

Where/When—We are already surrounded by computing technologies: they are in our cars regulating the breaking, steering, and engine functions; we carry Web-enabled cell phones and PDAs; we listen to music downloaded from the Web on our MP3 players; and we play massively multiplayer digital games on devices that connect to the Internet. Embedded computing technologies also carry out numerous mission-critical tasks, such as air traffic control and operating room procedures.

Although we live in a world of ubiquitous computing, we are only at the beginning of an evolutionary process. Alan Kay, a contributor to the development of the modern GUI, the Smalltalk computer programming language, and the laptop computer, considers UbiComp (calm technology) to be "third-paradigm" computing, after mainframe and personal computing.

Personal computers are still gaining functionality and complexity. They are not disappearing anytime soon and, in a simplified form, may be well suited to handle certain aspects of a ubiquitous system. However, the new generations of devices are small and portable and facilitate tasks in a way that is simple and intuitive.

Devices like cameras, video recorders, musical instruments, and picture frames are becoming "smart" through the introduction of embedded chips. These devices are now able to communicate with other smart devices and offer all the advantages that computing technologies afford.

The essence of UbiComp is that, to fulfill their potential, computing technologies must be considered a part of the fabric of our lives and not something that resides in a gray box. One manifestation is ambient computing.

Ambient Computing

The concept of a computational grid that is seamlessly integrated into our physical environment is the essence of ambient computing. Smart environments that sense when people are present can be programmed to adjust lighting and heating facilities based on the location and number of people in the room.

These environments can be programmed to identify particular individuals using voice or face recognition as well as wearable identity tags and adjust certain environmental parameters according to specific user preferences. With this technology, public spaces could be made safer through the monitoring of environmental conditions for the detection of gas leaks and other hazards. Such a system could also indicate best possible escape routes in the case of fire.

Commercial enterprises could tailor displays that respond to gender or age and inform customers about the merchandise they pick up and examine. Stores could become more accommodating to tourists who face obstacles because of language or cultural differences. Consider the classic problem of the tourist who wants to buy a souvenir in a country that uses a different currency: he or she must know the exchange rate and do the mental calculation. Alternatively, he or she could use an information appliance that had been set to the exchange rate and would do the calculation. In an invisible computing space, however, the prices would be displayed to the shopper in his or her native currency, based on the most recent exchange rate.

Invisible/Transparent Computing

The most profound technologies are those that disappear. They weave themselves into the fabric of everyday life until they are indistinguishable from it. (*Weiser, 1991, 94*)

What/How—The idea behind invisible computing is the facilitation of tasks without involving the manipulation of a computer interface. The power of computers has traditionally been filtered through the interface. The user must translate a problem into a format that the interface will accept, a task that is usually based on data and file types. The computer processes the data it receives and displays a result. The user must then interpret the results in the context of the problem he or she is trying to solve.

This process involves many interim steps between a problem and its solution—the computer often presents an entirely unrelated set of interim problems to be solved, such as file format and platform compatibility issues—and may result in a mismatch between what is required by the situation and the information that is displayed by the computer.

Invisible computing removes computer interface issues from the process. This can be done in two ways. One can make the interface so simple and intuitive that the user does not have to spend any time or energy on interface-related issues. This would be like driving a car: once we learn to drive, we generally don't think about the basic controls as we drive, right pedal for gas, left pedal for break. Computer interfaces that are that simple and intuitive would virtually disappear; we would not have to think about them, we would just use them.

The second way to make computing invisible is to remove the interface entirely. There are many functions that can be automated and do not require user intervention. We are unaware of the computers that control the steering and breaking mechanisms of our cars; they simply do what they are supposed to do.

Invisible computing can be accomplished by programming devices to carry out specific, well-defined tasks without user intervention. Some practitioners see no difference between UbiComp and invisible computing; however, there are those who focus on the qualities of invisibility to distinguish between the two.

Figure 1.12   A BlackBerry type of device.

Courtesy of
BigStockPhoto.com.

Who/Why—There are many new types of small digital appliances appearing in the market place that are geared to specific work- and entertainment-related activities such as PDAs, BlackBerry® devices (Figure 1.12), digital cameras, MP3 players, and portable game players.

Although PCs are capable of carrying out many of these functions, there is a growing interest in smaller, portable devices that address specific needs in an uncomplicated and easy-to-use way. These devices are referred to as information appliances (IAs), which Donald Norman defines as follows:

> An appliance specializing in information: knowledge, facts, graphics, images, video, or sound. An information appliance is designed to perform a specific activity, such as music, photography, or writing. A distinguishing feature of information appliances is the ability to share information among themselves. (*Norman, 1998, 53*)

Many of these devices retain their native interface elements but have embedded communication, computational, and connectivity enhancements that are invisible to the user. These additional features should not require additional setup or maintenance. As we computerize these devices we must strive to avoid adding unnecessary complexity to the interface. These IAs can be considered nodes in a computational grid that can access resources wirelessly.

Wearable Computing

The underlying principle of wearable computing is the merging of information space with work space, a field called humionics. Researchers at NASA are concerned with creating a seamless integration between these two spaces. Their projects include the Body Wearable Computer (BWC) Project and the Wearable Voice Activated Computer (WEVAC) Project. Similar research is being carried out at the Wearable Group at Carnegie Mellon University and the Wearable Computing project at the MIT Media Lab.

MAXIM

Wearable computing systems require multimodal interfaces.

The goal of humionics is to create an interface that is unobtrusive and easily operated under work-related conditions. Therefore, traditional I/O technologies are generally inadequate for this computing environment. Wearable systems must take advantage of auditory and haptic as well as visual interaction.

What/How—I/O device design for wearable computers depends on the context of use. Because wearable computing involves diverse real-world environments, wearable systems may require custom-designed I/O devices. This can be costly, and their use can present steep learning curves to new users. Therefore, there is a concerted effort in the wearable computing community to create low-cost interfaces that use familiar concepts without resorting to standard mouse and keyboard devices and their related styles of interaction.

One example of a new interaction style is the circular dial on the VuMan developed by the Wearable Group at Carnegie Mellon. The VuMan is a wearable device that allows users access to large amounts of stored information such as manuals, charts, blueprints, or any other information from repositories that might be too heavy or bulky to carry into the field or work site. It uses the concepts of circular input and visualization to map the circular control device with the contents of the screen. This type of navigation has become common to users of the popular iPod music player from Apple Computer.

Wearable computing has created a new scope for network structures—the personal area network (PAN). There are two types of PANs. The first type uses wireless technologies like Bluetooth® to interconnect various wearable devices that may be stitched into the user's clothing or to connect these wearable devices with other information appliances within the personal space near the user or a few meters beyond. An example is a PAN in an automobile that connects a cell phone with an embedded system that facilitates hands-free operation. Standards for wireless PANs (WPANs) are being worked on by the Institute of Electrical and Electronics Engineers (IEEE) 802.15 Working Group for WPAN.

The other type of PAN uses the body's electrical system to transmit network signals. Work is being done on this at the MIT MediaLab with the Personal Information Architecture Group and the Physics and Media Group.

Researchers at IBM's Almaden Research Center are researching PANs and have created a device the size of a deck of cards that allows people to transmit business card information simply by shaking hands. Data can be shared by up to four people simultaneously. Work on PANs has also been done by the Microsoft Corporation, which has registered a patent (no. 6,754,472) for this type of PAN that uses the skin as a power conduit as well as a data bus.

Where/When—To understand the dynamics involved in wearable computing more fully, we define three "spaces" that are involved in the completion of a task: the work space, the information space, and the interaction space:

- An information space is defined by the artifacts people encounter such as documents and schedules.
- An interaction space is defined by the computing technology that is used. There are two components: the physical interaction space and the virtual interaction space. These components can also be understood as the execution space and the evaluation space, respectively. There is a dynamic relationship between the two components that creates the interaction space.
- Work space refers to any physical location that may be involved in a task.

There may or may not be a direct correlation among the different spaces. That is, the interaction space may or may not be the same as a person's work space or information space. In the case of a computer programmer, Web designer, or a professional writer, the information and work spaces are both part of the interaction space created by a PC.

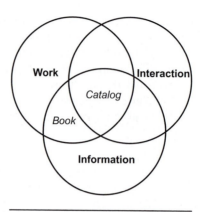

Figure 1.13 Venn diagram of a library space.

Consider the context of library-based research. Many modern libraries use digital card catalogs that contain meta-data about books in the form of abstracts and location indicators, the Dewey Decimal System. The digital catalog constitutes an interaction space, although it is only part of the work space. The book or books in which the researcher is interested reside on a physical shelf that is outside the interaction space. Therefore, while the catalog resides within the information, interaction, and work spaces, the book itself resides outside the interaction space. This creates a gap between parts of the work space and the interaction space (Figure 1.13).

Wearable computing seeks to bridge some of these gaps and make computing functionality more contextual. A possible solution in this scenario might be to embed a chip in the book that communicates meta-data about the book to the researcher's eyeglass-mounted display. The chip could respond to queries entered into a system wearable by the user. Another possibility might be to allow the user to access a digital version of the book on a wearable tablet-type device. In this case, the catalog would interact with the user's wearable system and fetch the contents of the book in digital form.

Who/Why—Wearable interaction devices would be able to make information contextually available, as well as tailor it for specific users. For instance, a student using wearable technology would be able to visit a museum and receive auditory or textual information about works of art based on his or her proximity to distributed sensors; this information would be filtered through personal preference settings such as grade level or course of study parameters.

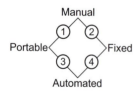

Figure 1.14 Embedded virtuality environments— location/operation.

The military has been involved in a number of research projects involving wearable computers. The systems they are developing are designed to enhance the information processing and communication capabilities of infantry soldiers. Figure 1.14 summarizes the various EV environments and their characteristics based on the location/operation diagram. Table 1.1 outlines various EV environments and their characteristics.

Table 1.1 Embodied Virtuality Environments and Their Characteristics

	Manual	Automated	Fixed	Portable
UbiComp	Some systems are manual	Some systems are automated	Some components are embedded	Some devices are portable
Invisible	User does not interact with computer	System takes care of all computer functionality	Some system components are embedded	Some devices are portable
Wearable	Many of the wearable components allow manual control	Some of the wearable components interact automatically with embedded sensors	Some systems use situated sensors that interact with wearable components	Most system components are portable (wearable)

1.4.8. Virtual Reality

The goals of the virtual reality (VR) community are the direct opposite of the goals of the EV community. EV strives to integrate computer functionality with the real world, whereas VR strives to immerse humans in a virtual world.

Virtual reality technologies can be divided into two distinct groups: immersive and nonimmersive environments. Nonimmersive VR environments can be characterized as screen-based, pointer-driven, three-dimensional (3D) graphical presentations that may involve haptic feedback from a haptic mouse or joystick.

In its simplest form, nonimmersive VR uses development tools and plug-ins for Web browsers to create 3D images that are viewable on a normal computer display. Two examples are the Virtual Reality Modeling Language (VRML), an International Organization for Standardization/International Electrotechnical Commission (ISO/IEC) standard that also can be used to create models for use in fully immersive VR environments, and Apple Computer's QuickTime VR®, which uses two-dimensional (2D) photographs to create interactive 3D models. More-sophisticated systems allow for stereoscopic presentations using special glasses and display systems that involve overlay filters or integrated display functionality.

The goal of immersive virtual reality is the realization of Ivan Sutherland's ultimate display. This goal may remain elusive for the foreseeable future, but progress in that direction continues. Contemporary systems use visual, auditory, and haptic technologies to create as realistic an experience as possible. Even the person's sense of equilibrium is involved in some of the large platform VR devices that offer locomotion simulation. Taste and smell, however, have not yet been addressed.

What/How—Immersive VR environments are designed to create a sense of "being" in a world populated by virtual objects. To create a convincing illusion, they must use as many human perceptual channels as possible. Therefore, sophisticated visual, auditory, and sometimes haptic technologies must be used to create a truly engaging virtual experience.

Visual

One of the most common immersive VR I/O devices is the head-mounted display (HMD). These are relatively large head sets that present stereoscopic images of virtual objects. HMDs can be cumbersome and annoying due to the presence of connecting cables, as well as the insufficient field of view and low resolution capabilities found in the lower-end models. Newer designs that incorporate wearable displays attached to eyeglasses and the emerging laser technologies show promise for lighter, less cumbersome, and more versatile displays.

Another approach to visual displays of VR environments is to use room-size spatial immersive display (SID) technology. SIDs use wall-size visual projections to immerse the user in a panoramic virtual environment. These rooms create a visual and auditory environment in which people can move about and interact with virtual objects. Examples of SIDs are the ImmersaDesk®, PowerWall®, Infinity Wall®, VisionDome®, and Cave Automated Virtual Environment® (CAVE).

There are several CAVE environments in existence around the world. It has been suggested that collaborative work could be done by networking these CAVE systems and creating a tele-immersion environment. Traditional videoconferencing allows people in remote locations to work together as though they were physically in the same location. Tele-immersion would allow people to work together in the same virtual environment, observing and modifying the same virtual objects.

Researchers are exploring ways to exploit the potential of this technology for business and educational applications by making tele-immersion more available and less expensive. New, lower-cost and less space-intensive desktop stereo displays, such as the Totally Active WorkSpace, Personal Penta Panel, and Personal Augmented Reality Immersive System, are being developed. These systems would make tele-immersion more accessible for general computing situations.

Current desktop systems generally use larger-than-desktop displays and HMDs in combination with high-quality audio systems. However, researchers at the Electronic Visualization Laboratory, University of Illinois at Chicago, are exploring the possibility of creating a truly desktop scale tele-Immersion system. The prototype is called the ImmersaDesk3.

Auditory

VR environments should foster a sense of presence that is defined as being immersed in a virtual world. Generally, we rely most heavily on our visual channel; however, the introduction of auditory and haptic stimuli can breathe life into an otherwise detached virtual experience.

High-quality VR simulations use sophisticated audio systems based on head-related transfer functions (HRTF) based on measurements taken of the auditory signals close to the user's eardrum. These systems are capable of creating realistic 3D sound environments by producing auditory feedback in any location within the 3D auditory environment. However, some issues remain involving up–down and front–back localization.

Haptic

Immersive VR environments require some type of user-tracking system that will enable the display to sync with the user's movements. Tracking systems must be able to calculate the position of the user relative to the virtual objects as well as to other users in a networked environment. They must be able to follow the user's point of view and update the imagery to reflect where the user is looking. They must also allow the user to manipulate virtual objects through translational and rotational movements.

Head-movement-tracking systems can be added to the basic stereoscopic image generation capabilities of HMD systems. These tracking devices are usually mounted on the support that holds the HMD. They track the user's location and head movements and relay this information to the display software, which creates dynamically updated depictions of the environment. Tracking systems may also use a dataglove or some type of wand or thong-like device to manipulate the virtual objects.

Movement in a VR environment is often restricted due to the equipment and cables required by the visual and auditory components of the system. There are times, however, when motion is a significant part of the virtual experience. For instance, flight simulations and military training focus on movement as an important part of the environment. These motion systems require more versatile display technologies. These technologies are categorized as passive or active:

- Passive systems, like flight simulators, use a platform device to transport the user within the virtual space and emulate the feeling of being in a real aircraft. The user controls the movement with a joystick or similar device.
- Active locomotion systems allow the user to walk "real" physical distances using a treadmill or pedaling device. These systems are used in military training exercises to simulate real-world physical conditions and test for stamina and endurance.

Where/When—Currently, immersive VR systems are found in large scientific research laboratories. There are commercial applications for VR technologies in the areas of architecture, product design, and engineering. However, only large corporate entities can invest in these technologies with any degree of cost effectiveness. The cost of just the basic system components is prohibitive. Outside of the nonimmersive technologies like VRML and QuickTime VR, there are currently no VR applications for the general computing population.

Who/Why—There are still many issues to resolve in the development of VR systems; a number of application areas for VR technologies already exist, however, such as scientific visualization. VR offers significant benefits in fields like aerospace, aviation, medical, military, and industrial training, and other mission-critical domains that involve work in hazardous or expensive environments.

VR technologies have been used for the visualization of complex data sets. The Visual Human Project (VHP), an outgrowth of the U.S. National Library of Medicine (NLM) 1986 Long-Range Plan, is involved in the creation of a complete digital representation of the human body. A virtual colonoscopy has already been demonstrated, and there are plans for a virtual laparoscopic simulator.

There are applications for engineering—computer-aided design (CAD) and VR. The Clemson Research in Engineering Design and Optimization (CREDO) laboratory is exploring the development of interfaces for virtual reality rapid prototyping. They are also interested in using VR environments in the design process.

The field of education can benefit from the use of VR environments. Due to the overwhelming amount of recent research and investigation, the acquisition of new knowledge and implementation of new concepts is becoming difficult. VR environments can be used to facilitate this process.

The field of psychology has already demonstrated some advantages of VR simulations in the treatment of phobias. Carlin, Hoffman, and Weghorst (1997) were able to treat arachnophobia by using a VR display to simulate a room in which subjects were able to control the number and proximity of virtual spiders. VR has also been used in the treatment of agoraphobia, claustrophobia, and the fear of flying.

1.4.9. Augmented Reality

Augmented reality (AR) is often described as the opposite of VR. VR immerses the user in a virtual environment and supplants reality, whereas the goal of AR is to create a seamless integration between real and virtual objects in a way that augments the user's perception and experience. In AR the user must maintain a sense of presence in the real world.

AR environments have some implied criteria: the virtual information must be relevant to, and in sync with, the real-world environment. This increases the importance of maintaining an accurate connection between virtual and real-world objects. Because the virtual information must be kept in alignment with the real world, the system must efficiently track the user's head movements and maintain a reasonable response time.

What/How—Like VR, AR environments use some type of eyeware however, the eyewear is used to mix views of real-world objects with computer-generated imagery or information. There are also some systems that use screen-based configurations to generate AR environments. The user can view the real world either orthoscopically through special eyewear or by using a video feed from cameras that are attached to the head gear (this is also relevant to teleoperation environments in which the camera is at a remote location).

In both cases, the virtual information can be combined with real objects by being optically superimposed on the screen embedded in the eyewear. It is essential in AR environments that the virtual information be precisely registered with the real-world objects or the user will become confused or disoriented.

There is a natural correlation between AR and invisible computing in the sense that a successful AR environment would integrate virtual and real objects in such a way that it would not be possible to visually distinguish between them. Therefore, the user would not explicitly engage the computer interface; he or she would exist in a "middle ground" between the virtual and the real.

Other embedded virtuality domains such as UbiComp and wearable computing involve AR principles; however, they use computing functionality that is not specifically designed to blend real-world and virtual objects. AR is also referred to by other designations, such as mixed reality, computer-mediated reality, and computer-augmented environments.

There are many different approaches to blending virtual and real-world objects. The virtuality continuum (VC) shown in Figure 1.15 is a spectrum that ranges from real environments to virtual environments and includes views of real objects (either viewed from a video feed or viewed naturally) as well as views of virtual objects.

Environments that fall on the left side of the continuum use virtual information to augment reality. Environments that fall on the right side use real-world stimuli to augment immersive virtual reality environments.

Both VR and AR are generally considered visual environments, although auditory and haptic stimulation can also be used. Real heat, motion, or olfactory stimulation can be used to augment a virtual environment, which would be an example of augmented virtuality (AV).

Some examples of AR systems include the following:

Virtual Glassboat—A cart-mounted computer display that allows views of an underground gas and water piping system.

Outdoor Wearable Augmented Reality Collaboration System (OWARCS)—A class of systems that use wearable technology to facilitate collaboration in outdoor environments.

MagicDesk (Prop-Based Interaction)—A system that uses real objects to accomplish virtual tasks. A 2D desktop environment is superimposed on a real desktop, fusing the virtual and real tools found in each. This allows the user to use, for example, a real stapler to attach two virtual documents.

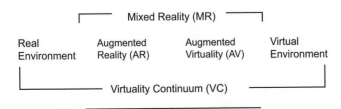

Figure 1.15 Virtuality continuum diagram.

Where/When—In a general sense, AR is beneficial to people who need situated computing functionality that augments their knowledge and understanding of specific places or things.

AR technology is applicable in situations in which people need access to computing functionality and cannot afford to leave their work site: for instance, technicians who need access to large amounts of information such as diagrams and technical charts while they are in the field. This information can be stored electronically and made available through an eyeware system while the technician is working. The diagrams can be superimposed on an actual mechanism, thereby augmenting the technician's knowledge of the object.

Who/Why—AR environments can be beneficial for people whose tasks require a high degree of mobility as well as access to large amounts of information that would be difficult to transport. It can also be appropriate for people who need access to situational information such as the status of an electronic grid within a building.

Summary

As an interaction designer you will need to decide which interaction paradigm best suits the needs of the intended user. In most cases this will be one of the more general computing paradigms such as the personal computing or mobile paradigms. However, the envelope is constantly being pushed, and what was once considered "bleeding edge" technology has often become quite common. Consider the Memex; it was once a dream, but now we carry around technology that is far more advanced in our PDAs and cell phones.

To design a system that is consistent with the user's abilities, limitations, and tasks, you must understand the different paradigms and how they function and the tasks for which they are most suited. The simplest solution is often the best, but a simplistic solution will never be adequate. Study the user's abilities, limitations, tasks, environment, attitudes, and motivations, and then identify the paradigms that best suit their needs. This is the basis for creating an interaction that resonates with the people who use your design.

Resources on the Web

www.aw.com/heim
You will find links to the publications mentioned in the Introduction as well as Web-based resources covering many of the computing paradigms discussed in this chapter.

Suggested Reading

Caroll, J. (Ed.). (2001). *Human-Computer Interaction in the New Millennium* (1 ed.): Addison-Wesley Professional.

Earnshaw, R., Guedj, R., Van Dam, A., & Vince, J. (Eds.). (2001). *Frontiers of Human-Centred Computing, Online Communities and Virtual Environments* (1 ed.): Springer.

Pirhonen, A., Isomäki, H., Roast, C., & Saariluoma, P. (Eds.). (2005). *Future Interaction Design* (1 ed.): Springer.

CHAPTER 2

Interaction Frameworks and Styles

In this chapter we explore the various interaction styles from command-line to natural language. Each type of interaction has inherent attributes that make it suitable for certain computing activities and not for others. We must understand the issues involved with each type of interaction style so that we may craft interfaces that best suit the tasks involved.

We begin by establishing some frameworks in which to explore human–computer interaction (HCI). This will give us a foundation and will help to structure our thinking about the way people interact with computers. Then we will explore each of the established interaction styles and the factors involved in their use. We will also look at some of the evolving interaction styles and see how they might play a larger role in the future.

2.1. Frameworks for Understanding Interaction

A framework is basically a structure that provides a context for conceptualizing something. In this case, the frameworks we will look at describe the way we interact with computers. We can use these frameworks to structure the design process and help us to identify problematic areas within the design. They can also help us to conceptualize the problem space as a whole and not just a conglomeration of individual components that somehow work together to provide a work space and a set of tools.

2.1.1. Execution/Evaluation Action Cycle

Donald Norman's (1990) *The Design of Everyday Things* (originally published in 1988 as *The Psychology of Everyday Things*) is a significant contribution to the field of HCI. One of the important concepts presented in the book is that of the execution/evaluation action cycle (EEAC), which explores the nature of actions and how they are structured. According to Norman, the structure of an action has four basic parts (Figure 2.1):

- **Goals:** We begin with some idea of what we want to happen; this is our goal.
- **Execution:** We must then execute an action in the world.
- **World:** To execute and action, we must manipulate objects in the world.
- **Evaluation:** Finally, we must validate our action and compare the results with our goal.

The execution and evaluation parts each can be broken down into three distinct stages, as will be described.

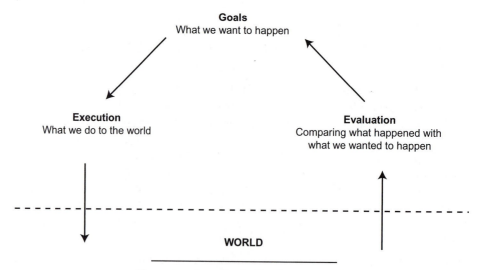

Figure 2.1 Execution/evaluation action cycle.

Seven Stages of Action

Goals do not specify particular actions; they must be translated into intentions that specify the actions that lead to the completion of a goal. Goals and intentions do not have a one-to-one relationship, however; there may be many different ways to achieve a goal, each with its own unique sequence of actions. These actions are the specific tasks that must be accomplished to achieve the user's goals.

For instance, we may decide on a "delete text" goal. That goal can be accomplished by an intention that involves the Edit menu or an intention that involves the Delete key. Each of these intentions involves a sequence of actions that must be specified—click on Edit menu, choose Cut option. These intentions define the tasks to be performed, which require specific actions that must then be executed.

The foregoing description implies the existence of four stages of action (goals plus execution):

- Establishing the goal
- Forming the intention
- Specifying the action sequence
- Executing the action sequence

After the proper actions have been executed, we must evaluate the results. To evaluate the results, we must first perceive the new state that occurs after the action sequence has been executed. We must then interpret what we perceive and then evaluate the relationship between our interpretation of the new state and our original goal.

The evaluation phase, therefore, has three stages:

- Perceiving the world state
- Interpreting the perception
- Evaluating the interpretation (comparing the results with the goal)

This gives us the seven stages of action as depicted in Figure 2.2.

These seven stages form an "approximate model" that manifests itself in numerous variations. Many real-world actions involve iterative loops that cycle through all of the seven stages; others may only involve some of the stages. Norman suggests that many real-world goals and actions are vague and not planned. These are considered opportunistic (data driven): they are formulated ad hoc as the opportunities arise. This is in contrast to the critical goals for which action sequences are thought out in advance. Norman further points out that the cycle can be initiated any place: "In particular, some cycles are data-driven, initiated when an environmental event is perceived, thus starting the cycle. Others are goal-driven, initiated when the person conceives of a new goal to be satisfied" (Norman, 2006).

For instance, I may formulate a goal to create an illustration of the seven stages of action. To accomplish this goal, I will form the intention of launching a drawing

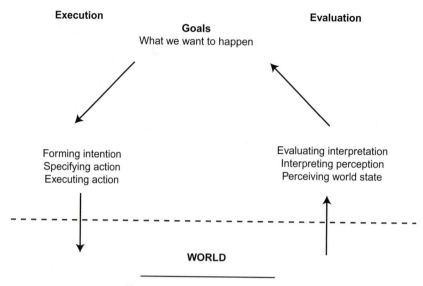

Figure 2.2 Seven stages of action.

program. That intention will require that I specify the action sequence of locating the Applications icon, double-clicking it, and then proceeding to execute all of the subsequent intention/action sequence and evaluation iterations required to complete the goal. That is how my formal goal will be accomplished, and it requires some forethought before I can begin and some rudimentary planning to complete.

During this process I may remember that I wanted to tweak the illustration of the interaction framework given later in Figure 2.3. Because I already have the drawing program open, I take the opportunity to open that illustration, tweak it, and then close it, after which I resume my work on the first illustration. It was not my goal to work on the other illustration; however, I took advantage of having the drawing program open and included that activity in my work process on the spur of the moment.

This is not an uncommon scenario; we take advantage of opportunities as they present themselves every day, and we mix them with our formal goals that are more structured and thought out in advance. This knowledge of how people work encourages an open approach to interaction design. We should always consider the fact that people like to seize opportunities, and we must make sure that our designs do not freeze them into a situation in which they can only carry out their formal thought-out goals.

Gulf of Execution

Norman suggests that many of the difficulties we have in accomplishing our tasks come from the relationship between aspects of execution and aspects of evaluation.

These difficulties arise from the gulfs between the mental representation held in our minds and the physical components and states of the system. We may have formulated a goal, for instance, save a file. We may also have formulated the intention to use the File menu and choose the Save option. The question is whether the interface allows us to carry out the actions required by the intention. Is there a Save option in the File menu? Because this has become a standard, we are inclined to pursue this course of action. If there is no such option in the File menu, there will be a gulf of execution between what we want to accomplish and what the system allows, and therefore our intention will be frustrated.

Gulf of Evaluation

An interface design should allow us to perceive and interpret the state of the system. For instance, the File menu should be clearly visible and located where we expect it to be located. This will decrease the amount of effort we must exert in order to use the interface. Pull-down menus have an intrinsic gulf of evaluation because their options are hidden; therefore, we must use a best-guess method or, if that is unsuccessful, a trial-and-error method to achieve our goals.

Computer programs sometimes use modes. For instance, if you hit the Caps Lock key, all of the characters that you type will be displayed in uppercase. This is not the way the keyboard keys normally work, but it is how they work in Caps Lock mode. Modes are particularly difficult, especially for anyone who is not a frequent user of a particular application. They are often made more difficult because of the paucity of indications given about the state of the system while the mode is active. This can create a significant gulf of evaluation.

Although it may be impossible to avoid such gulfs of evaluation entirely, they should be minimized as much as possible. The seven stages of action can be used to formulate design questions to ensure that the gulfs are kept to a minimum during the design process.

Given a particular interface design, how easily can you (Norman, 1990)

- Determine the function of the device?
- Determine what actions are possible?
- Determine mapping from intention to physical movement?
- Perform the action?
- Determine whether the system is in the desired state?
- Determine the mapping from system state to interpretation?
- Determine what state the system is in?

2.1.2. Interaction Framework

The execution/evaluation action cycle focuses on the user's view of the interaction; it does not consider the system beyond the interface. Abowd and Beale expanded

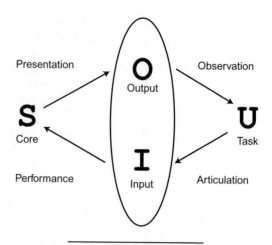

Figure 2.3 Interaction framework.

Courtesy of Cambridge University Press.

this approach explicitly to include the system and the way it communicates with the user by way of the interface (Dix, Finlay, Abowd, & Beale, 1998). Their interaction framework (IF) breaks up the interaction into four main components (Figure 2.3):

- System (S)—Uses its core language (computational attributes related to system state).
- User (U)—Uses its task language (psychological attributes related to user state).
- Input (I)—Uses its input language.
- Output (O)—Uses its output language.

According to this framework, interaction cycles involve two phases: the execution phase, which has three steps, and the evaluation phase, which has four steps.

Execution Phase

- **Articulation**—The user formulates a goal, which is then articulated using the input language.
- **Performance**—The input language is translated into the core language (operations that the system will carry out).
- **Presentation**—The system manifests the result of the core-language operations using the output language.

Evaluation Phase

- **Observation**—The user interprets the results on the screen and reconciles them with the original goal.

During the articulation step the user must reconcile his or her task language, which is based on psychological attributes, with the input language. If there is a clear and unambiguous mapping between these two languages, the articulation step will proceed without difficulty. If there are problems, the user must resolve any incongruities that may exist. This will require more work on the user's part and may lead to frustration.

For instance, if the user wants to draw a circle, he or she will have to translate that task into the input language that is represented by the interface according to the particular interaction style used by the system. This may mean entering commands in a command-line interface or it may mean pointing to an icon and clicking in a GUI. If the icon clearly represents the circle drawing functionality, the user will be able to proceed without difficulty. If the icon is not intelligible (the input language is ambiguous) the user will have trouble accomplishing the task.

During the performance step the system uses the data obtained from the input language to perform operations. Although the user is not involved in this translation, the designer must make sure that the system has the necessary data to perform the operations. In the case of the circle task the system must know what shape to draw, where to draw it, how big it should be, and other properties of the shape such as border and fill colors.

Dix et al. (1998) note that it is important to determine whether the translated input language can reach the required system states. For instance, users should have the ability to change the default settings of an application, such as the default font used to enter text in a drawing program. If the user requires a different font and there is no way to change the default setting, then users must perform the same font selection actions every time they use the program. Because the system is obviously capable of determining what font the user wants to use and is set up to hold a default font setting in memory, there is a gulf in the performance step of the execution phase.

During the presentation step the system must express the altered state of the system in the output language. This is a measure of the expressiveness of the translation. It is also necessary to communicate to the user when the system is involved in the internal processing that occurs before the system state is completely altered. These process are often indicated using a status bar or hourglass icon. This completes the execution phase of the interaction.

During the observation step users must interpret the output and evaluate it against their original goal. This begins the evaluation phase of the interaction. The user must determine whether he or she has accomplished the goal or if any further interaction is required.

Users may not have formulated a precise and complete goal; they also may not know in advance how to accomplish their goals. Human–computer interaction often involves interactive feedback loops that progress from vague ideas about a task to diverse states of completion and even alternate approaches and modified goals. Many goals are also influenced by the observation translation of the output language.

The observation translation can also involve system issues such as system responsiveness, which can be important in common application environments such as word processing. Imagine a word processing application that had a system delay of 1 second between the time you pressed a key and when you saw the character appear on the screen, and you begin to see how important system responsiveness can become.

The frameworks we have just explored will provide us with a structured approach to understanding the way people in which interact with computers. We will apply these frameworks to the various interaction styles such as command-line interfaces and GUIs. This will provide us with a foundation for making determinations about which interaction style is the most appropriate for particular applications.

2.2. Coping with Complexity

Before we look at the interaction styles in depth we must first have a basic understanding of how people approach complex situations. If we wish to create a system that will be easy for people to use, we must understand how they see things; we must see the world through their eyes. To do this we must understand how people cope with the complexities of technologically complex environments.

2.2.1. Mental Models

When we interact with things in the real world we formulate ideas about how they work and assess their potential to assist us in completing our tasks. We try to understand what these things do and how they do it so we can formulate ideas about how to use them.

Some objects are easy to use, for instance, a hammer or a pair of scissors. They pose no difficulties, even for people who have never seen them before. They have affordances that lead to their ease of use such as the handle that fits into the hand and the eye rings of the scissors that are easily grasped.

Other objects are, by their very nature, more complex; it may not be obvious what they are intended to do. They are not transparent in terms of how they function, so we are required to assume many things about their operation. However, if an object is transparent in terms of the way it functions, we can easily formulate a conceptual framework about how it works. This framework will be fairly close to the way the object actually functions.

It has been proposed that the process of trying to create this framework takes the form of a "mental model" of the object or process. A mental model is a cognitive representation of something that defines a logical and believable estimation as to how a thing is constructed or how it functions.

If an object is more opaque and it is not obvious how it functions, our mental model will be derived from our interaction with the object and our past experience with similar objects. In this case our mental model may be only an approximation of the actual functioning of the object. In fact it is not uncommon for people to have completely erroneous mental models and still be able to interact with an object successfully.

Consider the difference between a bicycle and an automobile. A bicycle is transparent in the way it functions. The rider moves the pedals, which turn the front gear. The front gear is connected via a chain to the back gear, which is connected to the back wheel. The rider can easily see the motion of his or her feet being translated into the motion of the back wheel that moves the bicycle forward. Therefore, his or her mental model will be quite accurate.

An automobile, on the other hand, is far more opaque. All drivers understand that to move the car forward you must press the gas pedal; however, the internal functioning of a combustion engine and the subsequent result of movement through the transmission to the wheels is beyond the general driving public's knowledge. People will often have very fuzzy and incomplete ideas as to how the process works, but their mental models are sufficient for normal operation of the vehicle.

Computers often fall into this category. They are complex and do not make their inner processes visible to the user, so people develop mental models that allow them to interact with computers but may be inaccurate if not extremely vague and incoherent.

Mental modes provide a method of understanding interaction that is both predictive and explanatory. Kenneth Craik proposed the concept of mental models in his book *The Nature of Exploration* (Craik, 1943). He described the construction of "small-scale models" that are used to explain and reason about the objects we encounter in the real world.

Mental Models in Interaction Design

Mental models create a framework within which we can function. If our model is sufficiently close to the actual functioning of the system, we can use it without difficulty. However, our model may be based on erroneous assumptions, which may cause us to do more work than is necessary.

For instance, it is not uncommon for novice Web users to think that a search engine needs to be used to access Web sites. This might happen because they have seen other people use the search engine to find Web sites, so they formulate a model that involves the search engine. This erroneous model will cause them to enter valid URLs in the search engine's query box, which causes a needless waste of time—accessing the search engine, entering the URL, and scanning the search results and clicking the appropriate link.

An incomplete mental model might cause users to experience confusion, perhaps leading to frustration. For instance, it is not an easy task for novice users to understand the nature of the different windows that appear on the screen in current

GUIs. They are often unable to distinguish among folders, files, and application environments, not to mention understanding the nature of the desktop. This can make it difficult for them to find files that are saved within folders, and often leads to a very cluttered desktop because that is one of the places from which they can easily retrieve their files and is probably the most accessible part of their mental model of the computer.

Mental models are:

- Unscientific—They are often based on guesswork and approximations.
- Partial—They do not necessarily describe whole systems, just the aspects that are relevant to the persons who formulate them.
- Unstable—They are not concrete formulations, but evolve and adapt to the context.
- Inconsistent—They do not necessarily form a cohesive whole; some parts may be incompatible with other parts of the same model.
- Personal—They are specific to each individual and are not universal concepts that can be applied generically.

People create many mental models and use them when they need them, modifying them as they interact with the interface. These models are used to formulate actions, anticipate system behavior, interpret feedback, and predict future events.

Mental models are crucial to interaction design because computers are complex and opaque; their internal functions are hidden from the user, especially in GUI environments. Users must formulate mental models of the various aspects of the interface so that they can have a framework on which to base their problem-solving approaches.

> **MAXIM**
>
> Designs that align with a user's mental model will be easier for him or her to use.

We can create more-intuitive interfaces if we have some understanding of the mental models that potential users have already constructed. We can gain an understanding of these models during the collection activities in the discovery phase. We can design questions to probe subjects' thoughts about how certain things work, and we can ask them to think out loud as they perform certain tasks.

Understanding mental models is not an exact science, and there are many things about mental models that we do not understand; if we are aware of these models, however, we can provide an interaction design that is more consistent with the mental models of potential users.

Users are not the only ones who create mental models; designers also construct them. They may have mental models of the interface design; they may also have formulated a mental model of the perspective user or the user's tasks.

Problems arise when the designer's model is either not communicated clearly to the user through the interface or diverges from the model the user may have from previous experience. This is the challenge of interaction design: to create an interface that resonates with the user's mental model.

2.2.2. Mapping

The concept of mapping describes how we make connections between things; for instance, we make connections between a stove's burners and their controls so we can light the correct burner and boil water. Mapping is an integral part of the way people interact with their surroundings. Correct mapping can lead to the easy completion of a task. Incorrect mapping can lead to frustration and failure.

Norman presents a very compelling example of the difference between the design of a stove top that is natural and easily understood and an arbitrary design that causes frustration. An arbitrary mapping, such as the one in Figure 2.4a, would require the user to either remember the relationships or else use best-guess or trial-and-error strategies. Figure 2.4b allows a person to relate the controls and burners as sets of two, which is better than the design in Figure 2.4a; however, it still requires some memory tasks. To make the relationships clearer, the designer would be obliged to label the controls, which Norman states is an indication that the design is flawed.

A natural mapping of controls to burners would reflect the layout of the burners, which are usually in a grid formation. If the controls are also laid out in a grid formation, as shown in Figure 2.4c, then people can easily map them to the burners: font/back and left/right.

Let's look another situation in which mapping can become difficult. Consider the lighting system of a room. It is usually installed in the ceiling and is often

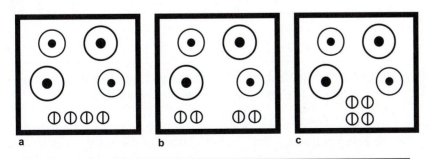

Figure 2.4 (a) Arbitrary mapping. (b) Arbitrary mapping improved. (c) Natural mapping.

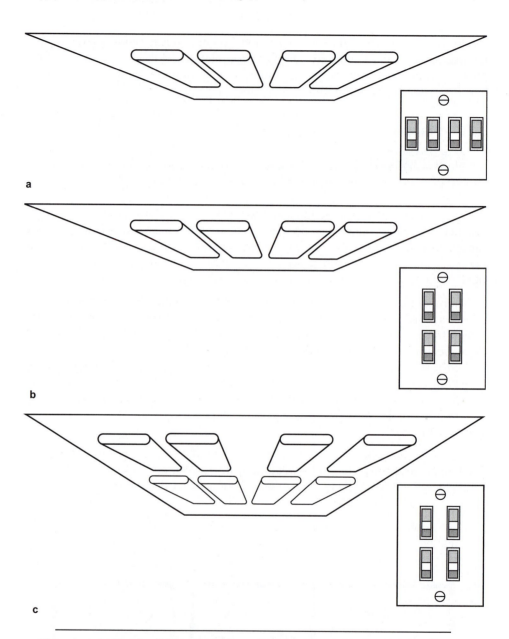

Figure 2.5 (a) Mapping lights and switches—intuitive. (b) Mapping lights and switches—difficult. (c) Mapping lights and switches—translation.

controlled by a panel of switches located somewhere near the entrance doorway. Each of these switches may control one light fixture or they may control a bank of lights. The switches usually do not have any indication as to which lights they control; people must make that determination to the best of their ability. In Figure 2.5a there is a natural inclination to map the switches to the lights from left to right. One can hope that is how they were wired.

To determine the relationship between the switches and the lights they control in less intuitive situations, such as the one in Figure 2.5b, we might attempt to apply some sort of logical connection between the switches and the lights. As we have seen, one of the natural mapping approaches equates physical locations, such as left switches control the lights on the left side of the ceiling and the right switches control the lights on the right side of the ceiling. However, there are a few other possibilities that one might consider, for instance, top–outside/bottom–inside or clockwise–left/right.

The task of mapping the switches to the lights may also require a certain amount of translation between the physical location of the switches and the physical location of the lights (Figure 2.5c). This often requires a translation between different orientations. For example, the switches are usually placed vertically on the wall, which involves left/right–up/down directions, but the lights are located on the ceiling, which involves left/right–front/back directions. We tend to opt for the most straightforward solution by equating similar things and then trying to solve the anomalies. In the foregoing case we would probably assume the left/right similarities and translate the top switches to the front lights.

A one-to-many relationship between switches and lights would further complicate the problem. In complex situations we sometimes revert to trial-and-error strategies. Unless we do this deliberately and pay attention to the results, we will probably not remember the mapping the next time and will have to repeat the process all over again.

> **MAXIM**
>
> Use natural mapping whenever possible.

People are very resourceful, and they will generally find some way of determining the mapping between related objects; in complex environments, however, the confusion created by complex relationships and illogical mapping can lead to errors and frustration. Whenever possible, designers should look for any natural mappings that already exist in the user's world and apply them to the design of the system.

2.2.3. Semantic and Articulatory Distance

When we interact with a device or system we try to reconcile what we want to do with what the device actually does and how it does it. To do this we have to interpret the symbols and components of the system. We can understand these relationships in terms of the distance between the functionality of the device and what we actually want to do. We can consider this to be the semantic distance between ourselves and the system (Hutchins, Hollan, & Norman, 1986).

Semantic Distance
The distance between what people want to do and the meaning of an interface element.

Articulatory Distance

The distance between the physical appearance of an interface element and what it actually means.

Another aspect to this relationship is the distance between the physical appearance of the device controls and their actual functions. This can be considered the articulatory distance.

It is easy for us to go from appearance to meaning when the articulatory distance is small. It is important that we understand this concept because we can use it to improve our designs. By analyzing interface elements in terms of articulatory distance between the object and its meaning, we will have a model with which to determine how difficult it will be for people to understand our designs.

Semantic distance refers to the relationship between the available functionality of the system and the functionality required to complete a task. This is a measure of the usefulness of the design. Interaction designers should strive to minimize both of these distances.

2.2.4. Affordances

The term affordances was created by the psychologist J. J. Gibson and expanded by Donald Norman to apply to interface design. In Norman's *The Design of Everyday Things*, he shows how real-life objects have user interfaces that are sometimes obvious and sometimes confusing.

The affordances of some interfaces can be intuitively understood: a steering wheel affords turning, and a door bell affords pushing. These connections allow us to make predictions about the results of our actions and help us to create usable mental models. When an object does not make its method of functioning visible or when certain aspects do not work in a way in which we assume they should, the object offers little affordance and becomes difficult to learn and use.

One example of affordance confusion arises when text boxes are used as labels as in Figure 2.6. A text box affords text input, and users have grown accustomed to

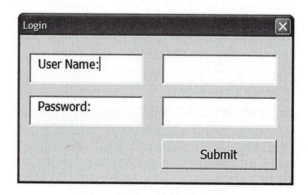

Figure 2.6 Affordance confusion.

this affordance. When a text box is used as a label the affordance it would normally have is contradicted.

Norman (1990) considers an affordance to be a relationship between an object and a user, not a property of an object. What may be an affordance to one person may not be to another. For instance, the affordances an interface has for a blind person are different than those it has for a sighted person. In design, the perception of affordance fosters usability. We must make sure that the affordances a user may need are present and that we do not contradict the user's expectations.

We have explored some of the natural tendencies people have when they relate to the objects in their environment and the complex and multifaceted nature of human activities. Let's now look at some of the ways that people interact with computers and keep in mind the various frameworks we have explored so far.

We need to understand how the existing interaction styles deal with the gulfs and distances identified in the previous frameworks. This will help us to choose the proper styles of interaction and apply them in the most advantageous way.

2.3. Interaction Styles

The term "interaction style" refers to the way in which we interact with computers. For instance, punch cards and card readers were used to interact with mainframe computers; now it is possible to issue spoken commands that initiate menu selections in a telephone-based interface (TBI).

Today, many different types of interaction styles are in use, each with its own inherent advantages and disadvantages. We will now look at some of the more common interaction styles and their attributes and applications.

2.3.1. Command Line

Command-line human–computer interaction is text based. The user types command strings at a prompt (Figure 2.7), and then the computer executes these commands and displays the results. The development of this technology was a great step

Figure 2.7 DOS prompt.

forward in human–computer interaction from the previous punch card interaction. Early command-line interfaces were mainly operated by technicians and computer scientists who became quite efficient at manipulating this powerful new interaction style.

> **MAXIM**
>
> Command-line interfaces are efficient and powerful.

Command-line interfaces are fast and powerful. Many commands are abbreviated, allowing experienced operators to type in a string of commands quickly and efficiently. Commands can be applied to many objects simultaneously and can be combined to allow faster input. Some commands have multiple parameters that can be set and altered, making them precise and flexible.

Command-line interfaces are used by professional technicians who need direct access to system functionality as efficiently as possible. They provide the expert user with a powerful tool that avoids time-consuming pointing and clicking tasks and offers a quick, responsive environment not burdened with the rendering of graphic controls.

If we look at the command-line interaction style from the perspective of the EEAC we see that the intention formation, specification of the action, and the execution stages are complex and require a rather accurate mental model of the computer's internal processing. For instance, to move a file from one folder to another the user would need to know the exact hierarchical directory structure of both the file and the target folder and the proper commands to carry out that intention, and then must enter those commands flawlessly. Compare this with the drag-and-drop operations afforded by direct manipulation interfaces that accomplish the same goal.

Seen from the perspective of the interaction framework, the process involved in translating the user's task language into the input language requires knowledge of the core language, which makes the command-line interaction style difficult for inexperienced users. The output language in a command-line interface can also be confusing for inexperienced users especially because there is very little feedback regarding the results of the intended actions.

The articulatory distance is large in a command-line interface because we are presented with only the command prompt, which gives no indication of functionality, just the affordance of typing at the prompt.

Advantages of command-line interfaces are as follows:

- Suitable for repetitive tasks
- Advantageous for expert users
- Offer direct access to system functionality
- Efficient and powerful

- Not encumbered with graphic controls
  - Low visual load
  - Not taxing on system resources

Due to their large articulatory distance and the fact that the user's mental model must be derived from an accurate understanding of the computer's internal operations, command-line interfaces have steep learning curves. They require a great deal of precision in entering commands and impose a high cognitive load on the user, who is required to remember complex and often cryptic command strings.

Disadvantages of command-line interfaces include the following:

- Low command retention
- Steep learning curve
- High error rates
- Heavy reliance on memory
- Frustrating for novice users

2.3.2. Menu-Based Interface

Although command-line interfaces are efficient and powerful, they do present significant obstacles to the general computing population. To work beyond the limits of human memory, and to make computing functionality accessible to more people, new interaction designs became necessary. The next development in interaction design was the menu-driven interface.

Menu-driven interfaces present users with sequential hierarchal menus that offer lists of functions. The user traverses the various levels, and at each level he or she selects the option that represents the required function. When this is accomplished the user can proceed to the next level.

Menus can be textual, with options presented as numbered choices and chosen by keying in the desired number. They can also be graphical, with options selected by arrow keys or a pointing device or any combination of these styles.

> **MAXIM**
>
> Menus are based on recognition as opposed to recall.

Menu-driven interfaces were considered an improvement in usability over command-line interfaces because they did not require users to recall abstract command strings and enter them without error. Users could now use recognition to search for the proper command from a list of related items.

It can sometimes be difficult to remember all of the options that relate to a specific task, especially if we seldom need to deal with that task. However, if we are

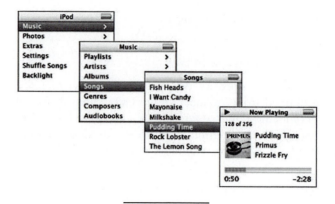

Figure 2.8 iPod menus.

http://www.apple.com/support/ipod101/anatomy/2/

presented with a list of options to choose from, it may be easier to recall the item that fulfils our need. Menus allow users to use recognition rather than recall because all possible menu options are listed and accessible. By showing the range of possible options, they also provide constraints. The user is guided into following a path of operations that will eventually achieve a result. This may or may not be the desired result; however, the user has been constrained during this process to a predefined set of functionality that conforms to the restrictions of the current state of the system.

Menu-based interaction is especially appropriate for small mobile devices such as the iPod (Figure 2.8).

Looking at menu-based interaction from the viewpoint of the EEAC, we see that this style can help the user to form the proper intentions and specify the proper action sequence to achieve his or her goals because he or she is constrained by the choices on each menu. Menu-based interaction also provides a context in which to evaluate the output language. The user chooses a menu option and is presented with a new set of options until the end result is accomplished. The user can evaluate the relative success of any particular action sequence as he or she traverses the menu hierarchy.

The articulatory distance in not as large as that of a command-line interface. System functionality is represented by the options at each level of the menu structure. Each different menu-based interface will present various interaction objects during this process such as buttons, links, or checkboxes that have affordances specific to that class of object. However, menus must be carefully constructed so that the user can develop a coherent mental model of the process. This will enable the user to more easily remember the process and therefore decrease the learning curve of the application.

Menu Types

Most menus are a variation on a few basic categories:

- Single
- Sequential
- Hierarchal
- Networks

Single and Sequential Menus—Single menus present a set of related options. The user may choose one option, multiple options, or no options. When menus allow for only one function choice, the function executes when the option is chosen. When menus allow more than one option to be chosen, a button must be clicked to execute a function.

A sequential menu structure comprising a string of interdependent menus is strictly linear. When the user selects an option in one menu, he or she is presented with a subsequent menu that presents a new set of options (Figure 2.9a,b). This process is continued until the task is completed.

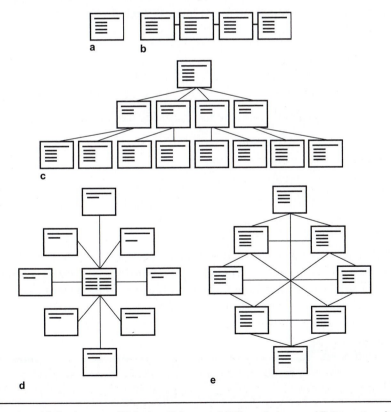

Figure 2.9 (a) Single menu. (b) Sequential menu. (c) Hierarchal menu. (d) Star network menu. (e) Web network menu.

Hierarchal Menus—Hierarchal menus create a "drill-down" structure: a series of choices progressively refines the path to the ultimate option. It is like an inverted tree structure in which the user is presented with various sets of options, each of which leads to another set of options, until the task is completed (Figure 2.9c).

Networked Menus—Networked menus are similar to sequential menus in that they may be a collection of single menus. However, they are loosely structured and not linear. They are also similar to hierarchal menus, except that they sometimes include multiple paths toward the same goal.

A common structure also seen in computer hardware networking is the star structure (Figure 2.9d). Networked systems also may follow a Web format much like the World Wide Web (WWW) (Figure 2.9e). Web networks may have unlimited variations allowing for navigation in multiple directions. In a Web menu structure, the user is free to access any of the grouped menus randomly. Each menu is a complete and independent entity that may allow navigation to other independent menus, or each menu may follow a prescribed path to an ultimate goal, allowing for reversals and parallel navigation.

Advantages of menu-based interfaces include the following:

- Low memory requirements
- Self-explanatory
- Easy to undo errors
- Appropriate for beginners

Disadvantages of menu-based interfaces include the following:

- Rigid and inflexible navigation
- Inefficient for large menu navigation
- Inefficient use of screen real estate
- Slow for expert users

2.3.3. Form Fill-In

Form fill-in interfaces are similar to menu-driven interfaces in that they present the user with a screen of information. The difference is that form fill-ins are used primarily to gather strings of information; they are not related to the navigation of a hierarchical tree structure. Form fill-in interfaces are designed to capture information and proceed in a linear manner.

> **MAXIM**
>
> Always inform the user about the length of paged forms and where they are within the structure.

Digital forms are generally intuitive because they resemble familiar paper forms. Forms may be single screens that require scrolling, or they may be presented in a paged format, with each page related to a coherent topic or containing a group of related fields. It is beneficial to inform the user about the length of the form (how many pages there are) and at what point the user is within the form (e.g., "page 2 out of 4"). This "you are here" information may encourage the user to complete the form. Adding this information to a Web-based form may lower the incidence of aborted online purchases during the form fill-in stage of a transaction (Figure 2.10).

> **MAXIM**
> Form elements must be unambiguously labeled to increase data integrity.

Data integrity is a significant issue and necessitates careful form design. The user must be informed as to precisely what data is required and in what format that information should be entered. For instance, if a date is required, what format should be used, 1/29/2005, 29/1/2005, or January 29, 2005?

Data can be parsed and rejected if they do not conform to requirements; however, this will require the user to re-enter the information, which can become frustrating or annoying. Errors can often be avoided if the form is worded clearly and unambiguously.

Advantages of form fill-in interfaces are as follows:

- Low memory requirements
- Self-explanatory
- Can gather a great deal of information in little space
- Present a context for input information

Disadvantages of form fill-in interfaces include the following:

- Require valid input in valid format
- Require familiarity with interface controls
- Can be tedious to correct mistakes

2.3.4. Question and Answer

> **MAXIM**
> Users must be able to cancel a menu without affecting the state of the computer.

Question and answer interfaces are also called wizards. They take the user through a series of questions to which the user supplies information that will then be used by the computer to set up an application or system environment.

Wizards are restricting and are not generally suitable for expert users. They are, however, easy to use and are quite appropriate for novice users, unless the user is

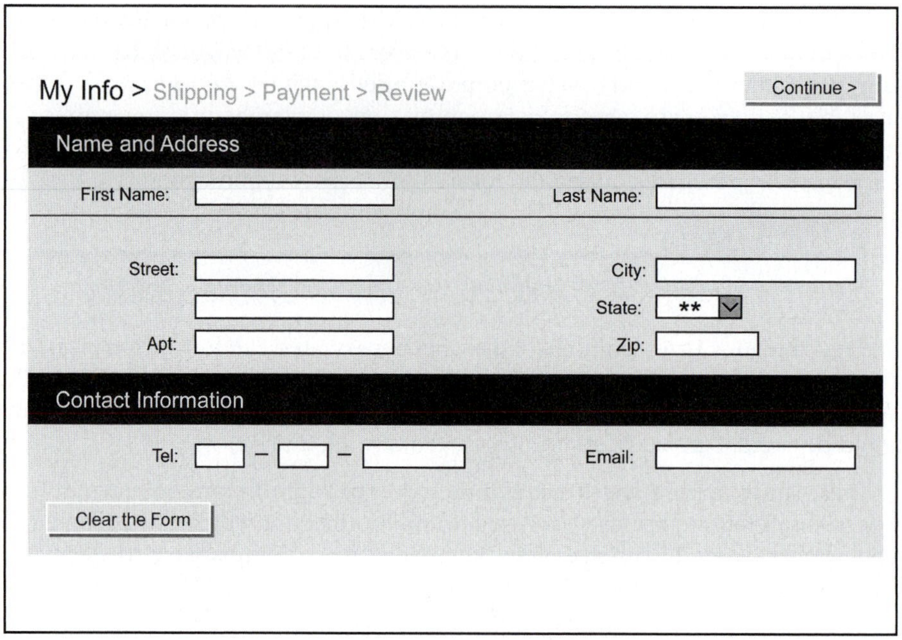

a

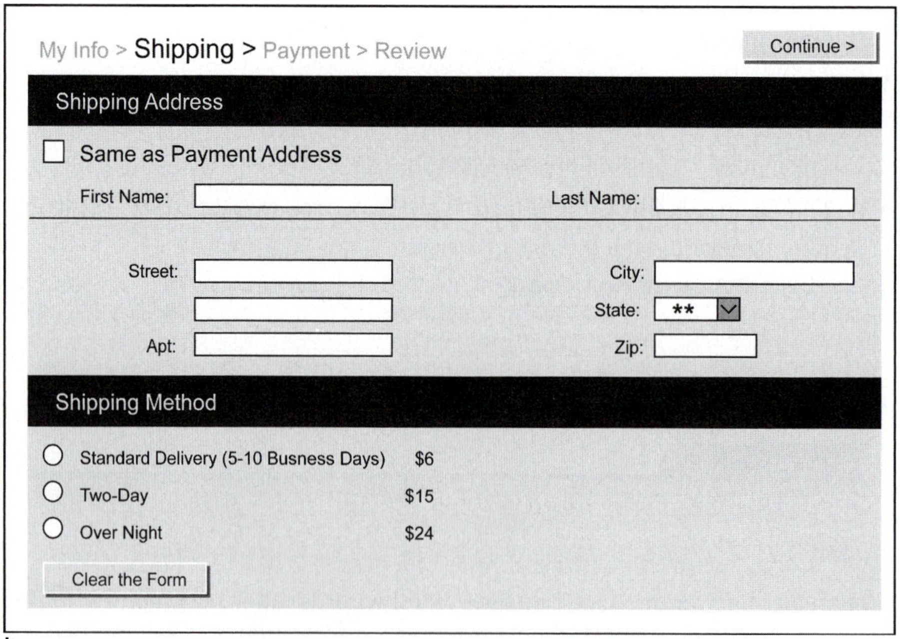

b

Figure 2.10   (a) Order form page 1. (b) Order form page 2.

not familiar with the subject of the questions and cannot supply the relevant answers. These interfaces must, therefore, allow the user to terminate the process without affecting the computer or any relevant software.

Figure 2.11 shows screenshots of the Microsoft Windows Add Network Place wizard. This wizard takes users through the process of creating a new connection to a place on a network. The process is relatively easy; the wizard presents the user with a succession of screens, and the user just fills in the information required.

Appropriately, the buttons on the bottom of the various windows allow the user to go back to previous screens or cancel out completely without any changes being made to the system.

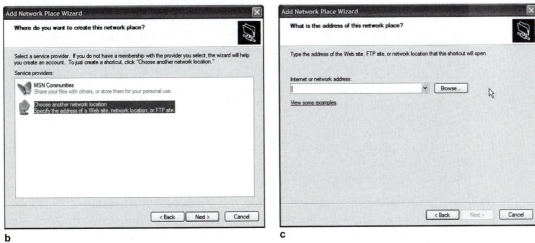

Figure 2.11 (a) Add Network Place wizard. (b) Select a service provider. (c) Address of the network place.

Question and answer interfaces are also similar to menu-based interfaces, but they are generally more restricted than form fill-in interfaces. The execution and evaluation cycles of these three interface styles are quite similar; they differ, however, in the latitude given to the user to form intentions and specify action sequences. The more restricted question and answer interface will present the user with scripted options that are directed to very limited and specific goals and, therefore, will only allow for the formation of limited intentions and action sequences.

Advantages of question and answer interfaces include the following:

- Low memory requirements
- Self-explanatory
- Simple linear presentation
- Easy for beginners

Disadvantages of question and answer interfaces include the following:

- Require valid input supplied by user
- Require familiarity with interface controls
- Can be tedious to correct mistakes

2.3.5. Direct Manipulation

The term "direct manipulation" was coined by Ben Shneiderman in 1982 to describe the emerging graphical user interfaces. It has since been associated with GUIs, such as Microsoft Windows and the Apple operating system (Figure 2.12). We will now explore the concept of direct manipulation.

The term direct manipulation may be a bit misleading because it stresses the user's action of manipulating interface objects and stipulates that it must be direct. This is a bit problematic because most manipulations of interface objects in a GUI are done with a mouse device, which is, strictly speaking, not a direct interaction device. Mouse movements are interpreted by the system and then mapped onto the GUI proportionately.

A touchscreen affords much more direct interaction because the user actually touches the screen objects with his or her hand. This type of interaction, however, is usually confined to touching buttons or virtual keyboards. It can be cumbersome in situations that require manipulating small screen objects like hyperlinks or text characters.

Virtual reality environments, on the other hand, present a more involved type of direct interaction. In a VR environment the user is immersed in a virtual environment that contains objects that he or she can touch, lift, and move around.

These distinctions between direct and proportional/translational interaction may not be relevant to this discussion, however, because Shneiderman's (1982) definition of direct manipulation interfaces is based on the following three criteria:

- Continuous representations of the objects and actions of interest with meaningful visual metaphors.

a

b

Figure 2.12 (a) Microsoft Windows XP®. (b) Mac OS X®.

- Physical actions or presses of labeled buttons instead of complex syntax.
- Rapid, incremental, reversible actions whose effects on the objects of interest are visible immediately.

Only the second of Shneiderman's criteria relates to the user's actions. The other two describe the visual nature and immediacy of direct manipulation interfaces. The term "direct" implies immediate interaction feedback.

From this discussion, we can see that rich visual feedback is at the core of direct manipulation interaction. Users must be informed about system functionality, they must have immediate verification when they carry out an operation, and they must have immediate feedback that an operation terminated, successfully or not.

Cooper and Reimann (2003) propose three phases in a direct manipulation action:

- **Free Phase**—How the screen looks before any user actions.
- **Captive Phase**—How the screen looks during a user action (click, click-drag, etc.).
- **Termination Phase**—How the screen looks after a user action.

Visual feedback is created by a GUI's components. They behave in ways that visually inform the user about the state of the system; for instance, a button's appearance changes to reflect its passive or active states. We must learn how to reflect user's actions in our designs and provide the expected visual feedback from the interface's screen components.

If we look at direct manipulation interfaces through the lens of the EEAC, we see a very rich style of interaction. The range of possible intentions is consistently wide. Users usually have multiple options for specifying action sequences. In fact, beginner users are often overwhelmed by the multitude of possible action sequences. Consider the range of possible action sequences that are available in most commercial operating systems for a simple operation like opening a file:

- The user can double-click the file icon and thereby launch the appropriate application.
- The user can right-click (in Windows) the file icon and select the Open option.
- The user can left-click the file icon and choose the Open option from the folder's File menu
- The user can drag and drop the file icon on top of the application's icon.

These are just a few of the possible action sequences that are available most of the time. Beginners do not usually react enthusiastically to being presented with so many possibilities. But that is not all. Direct manipulation interfaces also provide multiple ways of executing action sequences such as keyboard accelerator and function keys as well as mouse and other pointing-device events.

Advantages of direct manipulation interfaces include the following:

- Easy to learn
- Low memory requirements
- Easy to undo
- Immediate feedback to user actions
- Enables user to use spatial cues
- Easy for beginners

Disadvantages of direct manipulation interfaces include the following:

- Not self-explanatory
- Inefficient use of screen real estate
- High graphical system requirements

2.3.6. Metaphors

The most common form of human–computer interaction is direct manipulation. This is the interaction style found in the popular GUIs such as Windows XP and Mac OS X. GUIs are based on the concept that visual relationships to real-world objects help users to understand complex processes. These relationships are generally manifest in the form of a metaphor. The use of a metaphor can often help people to relate to complex concepts and procedures by drawing on this relationship.

GUIs use metaphors to represent complex procedures that would otherwise require sophisticated knowledge of arcane commands. They allow the designer to capitalize on the relationships implicit in the real-world objects and reinforce the user's familiarity with the system's procedures and functions. They capitalize on the user's intrinsic mental models derived from experience in the real world and apply them to interaction designs.

Real-world affordances can also be carried over into the metaphoric world of direct manipulation. Consider the pushbutton that shows up so often on GUI and Web-based forms. These command buttons often have a 3D appearance that resembles real-world pushbuttons. The raised design of these buttons affords a pushing action that is metaphorically represented by their virtual counterparts.

The metaphors of the desktop, file, and folder emulate real-world concepts that can be carried over into the virtual world of computing. The desktop metaphor was designed so that users with little knowledge of the underlying software could manipulate files in an easy and understandable manner.

The overall metaphor of the desktop with files and folders helps to add cohesiveness to all the various interface components. However, it is debatable whether this kind of metaphor aids or hinders the user in all situations. Although metaphors may initially aid inexperienced users, the scripting of a totally metaphoric environment has some drawbacks.

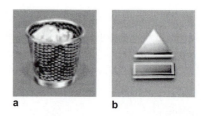

Figure 2.13 (a) The Mac OS X Trash icon. (b) The Mac OS X Eject icon.

Metaphors can be restricting, especially if the tools do not readily relate to anything in the real world. If an object does not perform in a manner consistent with the way it looks and the associations a user has for it in the real world, it will confuse people, and their performance will suffer.

MAXIM

A metaphor's function must be consistent with real-world expectations.

Metaphors should be employed to facilitate learning; they should not contradict the user's previous knowledge. When you create a metaphor that does not behave in the way people expect, not only have you failed to tap into the metaphor's power, you have also confused the user and created needless frustration.

This principle was broken in the original design of the Macintosh trashcan. It served to eject disks as well as delete files. These two operations can hardly be considered related, and the eject function is not something one would associate with a trashcan. In this case the articulatory distance became greater than it needed to be because users were unsure of the underlying functionality of the icon.

This has been corrected by changing the appearance of the Trash icon into an eject symbol when a disk is selected and dragged on the desktop (Figure 2.13). This fosters a more accurate evaluation of the user's perception and decreases the gulf of evaluation.

MAXIM

Don't force a metaphor.

Cooper and Reimann (2003) advise, "Use metaphors if you can find them, but don't bend your interface to fit some arbitrary metaphoric standard." Problems arise in designing an interface when we run out of metaphors or when a situation forces us to stretch and mix metaphors. Metaphors carry intrinsic meaning and associations; this is a two-edged sword, their strength as well as their weakness.

People can use a metaphor's preexisting connotations to their advantage and function with a degree of security in a new and difficult computing situation as long as—and this fact must be perfectly understood—the suggested function is consistent with their expectations.

2.3.7. Web Navigation

The Web has affected us in many ways. It has changed the way we work, and it has had an impact on our leisure activities. The hypertext foundation of the Web has also brought with it unique interaction styles. The Web is a vast repository of information that can be accessed through hyperlinks. We click on a link and are then presented with a new page that, we hope, displays the information we want.

Some Web sites contain a tremendous amount of information related to different products, pricing, and device specifications. It can be a daunting task to navigate to the sought-after information. All too often the links are confusing, which makes finding information a difficult and time-consuming task. Large Web sites will, therefore, generally offer a search function to help people find their way around the site.

This has basically created two distinct interaction styles related to Web navigation: link-based navigation and search. People tend to gravitate to one style or the other as a general rule, but they will resort to searching if the link-based navigation is too confusing or cumbersome.

Link-based navigation is sensitive to articulatory distance. If the Web site's visitor cannot understand the link's label or the meaning of a hyperlinked image, the gulf of evaluation will increase, and the user will have to spend more time thinking about the navigation or may resort to the more time-consuming trial-and-error approach.

Search-based navigation avoids the problems inherent in the more visually oriented link-based navigation; however, if the search engine is not programmed to accept spelling variations and incorrect yet similar search criteria, then the semantic distance will become artificially and unnecessarily large.

Both navigational methods are affected by the user's mental model, although in different ways and to different degrees. A well-constructed search engine may have a slight advantage in this case because the user can first try an inappropriate criterion based on an inaccurate mental model and then be presented with a set of possible results from which he or she may recognize the desired option. This is not possible with the more static navigational method; however, the search engine might present numerous results that could overwhelm the user, who might just quit in frustration.

2.3.8. Three-Dimensional Environments

Researchers and designers have been exploring ways to create more visually engaging and realistic interfaces. Most GUIs are only two-dimensional environments with minimal hints of 3D illusions. This can be seen in the 3D appearance of command buttons and dialogue boxes. Fully 3D environments can more realistically represent real-world metaphors and provide real-world affordances such as moving and rotating virtual objects in 3D spaces.

Maintaining a rich graphical interface is processor intensive; contemporary technology is sufficiently advanced, however, that complex graphical environments are becoming quite common. Much of this progress has been driven by the digital game industry.

Games with rich 3D environments have become the standard for the industry. They require highly dynamic visual environments that update as the action of the game unfolds. The most sophisticated games run on dedicated game consoles that are designed to function under the processor-intensive graphic requirements of digital gaming.

Three-Dimensional Navigation

Navigation in 3D space must address movement and rotation in many different directions. We must be able to move up and down and side to side as well as forward and backward. This is called translation and involves the frontal, transversal, and sagittal planes (Figure 2.14). Translation is often accomplished by using mouse movements, screen arrows, or their keyboard equivalents.

Three-dimensional navigation also means that we must be able to rotate in many directions. Rotation around the different axes is usually confined to pitch (up and down movement) and yaw (side-to-side movement) involving the x and y axes, respectively, and is accomplished by using curved screen arrows or keyboard keys together with function keys (Figure 2.15).

Three-dimensional objects can also be manipulated by grabbing their corners and moving them, resulting in rotational movements. They can also be dragged around and placed anywhere within the virtual space.

Even though 3D interaction may seem more natural—after all, that is how we interact with the real world—it can be quite disorienting on a 2D screen. If we lose orientation, our interpretations of the perceived state of the interface may become inaccurate, leading to misconceptions about the virtual environment. Our mental

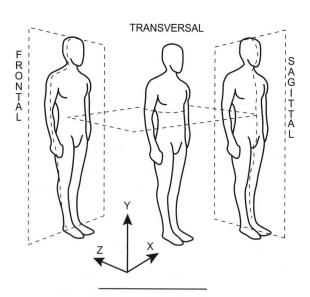

Figure 2.14 Planes and axes.

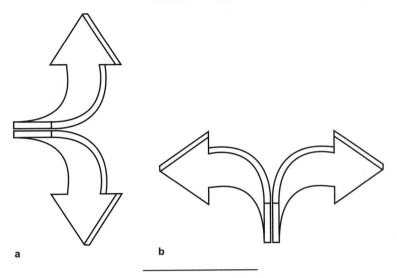

a   b

Figure 2.15   (a) Pitch. (b) Yaw.

models about the way the real world works are not always compatible with 2D representations of 3D environments.

Web-Based Three-Dimensional Interaction

Three-dimensional environments are graphics intensive and therefore result in large files. This poses a problem for Web-based 3D interaction. Internet connections are getting progressively faster, but significant compression algorithms are still required to make 3D interaction viable.

Web-based 3D technologies generally use vector-based graphics because of their small file sizes. Vector graphic formats do not address each pixel in an image like raster graphic formats; instead they use algorithmic descriptions of lines and curves which makes them generally more information efficient.

Virtual Reality Modeling Language—The Virtual Reality Modeling Language (VRML) allows developers to create online 3D environments that can be used for walkthroughs of virtual buildings and environments. VRML uses a text file format with a .wrl extension to describe the characteristics of the virtual environment or world. These worlds can be viewed by anyone with an internet connection and a VRML browser.

VRML worlds are created by using polygons that have parameters, such as transparency, texture maps, and shininess. They can have embedded links to other Web resources and can incorporate scripts written in languages such as JavaScript.

X-3D—XML has had a considerable impact on Web-based applications and services. Traditional markup languages like HTML have migrated to extensible technologies, such as XHTML. Likewise, VRML is being supplanted by the open standard, XML 3D language, or X3-D. X3-D is VRML compatible but offers greater flexibility and control.

Desktop 3D

Researchers have made a number of attempts to create a 3D desktop environment for general computing that would supplant the traditional desktop metaphor. Microsoft explored the possibility, and subsequently abandoned it, in their Task Gallery project, which began in 1999.

The Task Gallery is a 3D interface that incorporates traditional Windows programs and runs on top of the Windows operating system. Although the Task Gallery never left the prototype phase, some of its techniques have migrated to other projects such as Scalable Fabric from Microsoft Research (see later discussion), which is a task management system that addresses some of the problems with multiple window management.

Three-dimensional interfaces are based on the concept that we exist in a 3D world and, therefore, they are more compatible with our normal world view. These interfaces use the illusion of three dimensions to create rooms populated with objects resembling furniture and other household items, which function like traditional interface buttons and icons. For instance, the user may navigate to a room that is used for entertainment. In this room he or she might launch a music application by clicking on a 3D object that resembles a real radio or CD player.

> **MAXIM**
> Three-dimensional navigation can quickly become difficult and confusing.

Navigating through different rooms is like navigating a maze: it can become confusing and requires practice. People can lose their sense of orientation and have difficulty returning to a particular room. The Task Gallery avoids this problem by using only one extendable hallway. The user navigates back and forth in the hallway and interacts with application windows that are placed on stacks distributed around the 3D space.

Navigation is accomplished by a set of simple visual controls comprising arrows that allow straightforward travel, as well as functions that allow the user to rotate the view up, down, and to the sides. Keyboard equivalents are also included.

2.3.9. Zoomable Interface

The concept of zoomable interfaces, or zooming user interfaces (ZUI), can be traced to Jeff Raskin's ZoomWorld, which is based on his zooming interface paradigm (ZIP). Raskin describes his paradigm as analogous to flying, as opposed to the traditional desktop GUI, which he equates to navigating a maze—something that humans are not very good at. A Flash demo of Raskin's ZoomWorld can be seen at http://rchi.raskincenter.org (Figure 2.16).

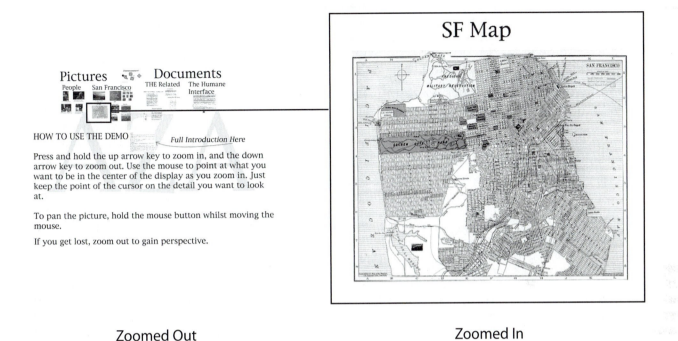

Figure 2.16 Jeff Raskin's ZoomWorld demo.

Courtesy Aza Raskin, Humanized Inc.

In the ZoomWorld interface, the user navigates by climbing higher to get a global view of the interface and diving down to see discrete objects, such as files and charts. The user can then zoom into a specific location within a chart or document. Content searching is also available in ZoomWorld.

> **MAXIM**
>
> Zoomable interfaces allow us to use our sense of relative positioning.

The ZIP is based on our ability to remember landmarks and our sense of relative positioning. It depends, therefore, on organizational cues, such as proportion, color, patterns, proximity, and other visual stimuli as opposed to a rigid hierarchical file structure.

Zooming is not absent in traditional desktop applications, and it does not always require using buttons, toolbars, or menus; it can be accomplished simply using a scrolling mouse. The scroll wheel can be made to zoom by toggling into zoom mode using an accelerator key.

Microsoft Word® allows users to zoom out and see all the pages of a document tiled across the primary window. At this level, the text is unreadable; however, the page layout configuration is clearly discernible: pictures can be located although not easily deciphered, and other page elements, like paragraphs and pull-outs, can be identified. The user can select an approximate location within a desired page and zoom in until only that portion of that specific page is visible.

This is a rather restricted version of a zoomable interface. A true zoomable interface does not use windows to confine document elements, files, or applications. These items simply exist within the zoomable space. Users are free to group documents according to their individual needs. Some examples of existing zoomable interfaces include Piccolo, Pad++, and Scalable Fabric.

Scalable Fabric, an experimental interface developed at Microsoft Research, relates the positioning of windows to the zoom magnification to maximize screen real estate. Active windows occupy the center of the screen at normal size but can be dragged to the periphery and are subsequently resized when they are no longer needed.

2.3.10. Natural Language

Given the ease with which we communicate verbally and our natural inclination to do so, it is understandable that we should try to develop a way to communicate verbally with computers. Could there be some way to tell a computer what we want to accomplish simply by using speech, and would it be possible to communicate using everyday speech or natural language?

Could it be possible to ask a computer to "get the last document I was working on" and have the computer understand the following?

- Who you are—Does it recognize your voice as opposed to your colleague's who is currently using the same machine?
- What you were working on last—Does that mean the last file you modified or the last file you opened or the last file you moved to a different folder?
- What you mean by "get"—Is the file to be opened and displayed on the screen, or should the file icon be placed on the desktop or in the currently active folder?

How wonderful it would be if we could eliminate the need to read through menus of options or remember specific commands just to carry out a rudimentary task. How much time would be saved if we could eliminate the need to navigate labyrinths of hyperlinks just to find a simple piece of information?

To be able to communicate with a computerized entity the way in which the astronauts did with HAL in Arthur C. Clark's *2001: A Space Odyssey* would represent a tremendous evolution in computing technology. After all, language is a relatively simple concept; most children gain a functional mastery of their mother tongue in the first year of life, and can even function in a bilingual environment. Natural language interaction may also be the only viable means of interaction for people with visual handicaps. To create a natural language interaction (NLI) should simply be a matter of entering the vocabulary and programming grammatical rules.

Language, however, is not straightforward; it is often ambiguous and given to misunderstandings. Meaning often depends on context. Words are used as different parts of speech according to context, and therefore have more than one meaning. For example, is the phrase "search results" comprised of two nouns or a verb and a noun? Is it the label for a set of options resulting from a search or is it a command to search the results of a previous search?

Pronouns may also cause confusion. Does the phrase "she said she did not know" refer to two people or just one? In addition, we do not depend on words alone to communicate. Human–human conversation is rich with contextual cues that help to clarify meaning. By eliminating all visual stimuli, language becomes less clear.

Consider a telephone conversation in which you cannot see the other person smile or wink when he or she uses irony or sarcasm. E-mail messages are infamous for the nongrammatical "naturalness" of their language, yet they require little "smiley faces" such as ":-)" to emphasize an emotion or clarify a meaning.

Applications for Natural Language Interaction

Natural language is full of ambiguities and poses considerable complications for automated interaction. However, the potential advantages of a NLI style of computing became the focus of research during the 1980s. There was a great deal of interest in overcoming the obstacles involved in the automation of natural language, and many solutions were proposed.

Some of the researchers involved in this area accepted that the higher levels of linguistic structure would have to be understood and applied to the problem. Natural language is fluid and depends highly on context and nonauditory stimuli, a simple application of vocabulary and rudimentary grammar would be insufficient to achieve adequate robustness for an NLI.

Speech Input—The most common form of NLI research explored text-based applications, but the potential for NLI systems in situations requiring hands-free operation seemed obvious, especially because speech is not a common input channel in human–computer interaction.

Interest in NLIs has not disappeared. The attractiveness of NLIs may even be increasing as more and more people use PDAs and cell phones to access the vast amounts of information published on the Internet. These miniature devices make GUIs less efficient due to their small screens.

Poor Lighting Situations—The advanced color screens on the latest cell phones are almost unusable in bright sun-lit environments. Ironically, these are the places in which the phones get the best reception. These screens work best in dark places, where it also becomes more difficult to see the keypad. A verbal NLI would work well in both situations. It would be a bit more sensitive to background noise, but it would have advantages for use in automobiles and other hands-free environments.

Mobile Applications—Given the ubiquity of the phone system, a NLI would seem an ideal solution for traveling employees who need to have access to online information from distant locations. Contemporary menu-driven telephone systems offer a degree of access but are often tedious and time consuming to use. Access to a phone-based NLI would be a considerable improvement.

In the Home—With the miniaturization of computer technology and the evolution of wired and wireless "home networks," more and more household appliances are manufactured with embedded computer chips that give them a degree of intelligent operation. Like PDAs and cell phones, these appliances also suffer from display limitations due to space or design requirements, which make NLIs seem more appropriate.

As home entertainment technology has evolved, many people have amassed a collection of TVs, cable boxes, VCRs, DVDs, and audio equipment, each with its own remote control. Much of the advanced, time-saving functionality of these devices goes unused because the interfaces do not make them accessible, and many hours are wasted trying to manipulate the controls just to access the basic functionality.

The problem of making functionality visible while maintaining a design look and feel appropriate for a living area, coupled with the difficulties of getting the devices to communicate and interact easily, has led some researchers to suggest that a NLI would be preferable.

Speech Output—The research focus so far has been on verbal input to a NLI. This type of interface requires speech recognition. There has also been research, however, on verbal output. This type of interaction involves speech generation. One application area for this type of interaction involves systems that calculate and report driving directions.

GPS technology has enabled navigational systems to keep track of an automobile's position. These systems calculate constantly updated directions to a requested destination. It is obvious to most people that automobile drivers should attend to the road and traffic conditions more than to the visual controls of the automobile they are driving. It seems natural, therefore, that a hands-free verbal interface to such a navigation system would be preferable to a system with a keyboard and a "silent" screen of text-based directions.

Navigational systems, however, often suffer from a lack of human-like qualities when they report driving directions. It has been shown that people prefer a less precise output that does not give equal weight to all elements of the route. People also prefer to use landmarks and geographical descriptions rather than the overly specific calculations of time and distance more typical of computer-generated output. NLIs could be developed that more closely resemble the language of human-generated directions and deliver them verbally using speech generation.

To realize the dream of a verbal NLI, two distinct areas must be developed. First, the computer must recognize verbal language through speech recognition functionality. If the computer cannot distinguish one word from another, it will never be able to discern meaning from the sounds of human speech. Second, the computer must be able to disambiguate natural language that is grammatically incorrect or semantically vague and contradictory.

MAXIM

NLIs may require constant clarification of linguistic ambiguities.

The idea behind NLIs is that the computer should be able to disambiguate speech by using algorithms that take these aspects into consideration. After an attempt to decode the natural language instructions issued by a user, there may be some lingering ambiguities about which the computer would have to ask for clarification. In these cases a series of dialogues would be required until the computer could narrow down the possible interpretations and act on the command.

This process can become frustrating for users who are not familiar with the system's strengths and weaknesses and therefore must constantly clarify their meaning to the computer through these dialogues.

The numerous problems posed by the ambiguities of natural language have, so far, prevented a feasible solution to the creation of a common NLI. There is no truly universal NLI that can be used by the general population.

Some success has been achieved, however, in the development of NLIs for restricted domains in which the user's language can be confined to a limited set of possibilities. Although this may appear to be a step in the direction of real NLIs, it is actually a regression to the command-line style of interaction with its sets of hidden commands.

In this restricted environment, the user must remember the permitted set of words and phrases, likely reducing his or her vocabulary over time to conform to a succinct set of recognized commands. This may diminish the appeal of limited natural language interaction for the general population.

Natural Language Interaction and Interaction Frameworks

What does auditory NLI look like through the lens of the EEAC? In some ways it seems the polar opposite of command-line interaction, especially during the specification and execution stages. Whereas command-line users are restricted to an arcane set of commands that must be typed without error, the auditory NLI user would simply tell the computer his or her intentions using normal speech.

In auditory NLI, articulatory distance would become irrelevant, as it is in command-line interactions, but for very different reasons. In command-line interaction the articulatory distance is so great that it becomes irrelevant; in auditory NLI, however, the articulatory distance is irrelevant because it is practically nonexistent.

Recall that articulatory distance is the distance between the physical appearance of an interface element and what it actually means. Because the command-line interface presents only the command prompt, which gives no indication of functionality, the articulatory distance is large and cannot be decreased by any adjustment to the interface settings. On the other hand, an auditory NLI (and to some degree text-based NLI) does not involve visual stimuli during the execution part of the interaction; one does not click on buttons or pull-down menu options, so there is nothing to interpret, which eliminates the existence of any type of articulatory distance.

Advantages of NLI include the following:

- Ease of learning
- Low memory requirements
- Flexible interaction
- Low screen requirements
- Appropriate for beginners

Disadvantages of NLI include the following:

- Requires knowledge of the task domain
- May require tedious clarification dialogues
- Complex system development

Summary

As an interaction designer you will need to decide which interaction style best suits the needs of the intended user. You should make no assumptions about existing styles; they all have the potential to satisfy the needs of the user, and it is your job to identify those needs and apply the most appropriate interaction style to the interface.

You must understand the different interaction styles, what they do best, and for whom they are the most suitable. Leaving this part of interaction design to guess work or simply applying the style to which you most easily relate can cause difficulties for your intended users. You must be able to judge the potential benefits of each style with an open mind after a thorough examination of the user's abilities, limitations, goals, and environment.

Resources on the Web

www.aw.com/heim
There are links to websites that discuss the history of user interfaces as well as links to articles on complexity in the interface. You will also find links to websites that discuss and show examples of the various interaction styles discussed in this chapter.

Suggested Reading

Jones, M., & Marsden, G. (2006). *Mobile Interaction Design* John Wiley & Sons.

Milkner, W., Bühler, D., & Dybkjaer, L. (Eds.). (2005). *Spoken Multimodal Human–Computer Dialogue in Mobile Environments* (1 ed.): Springer.

Pitt, I., & Edwards, A. (2002). *Design of Speech Based Devices* (1 ed.): Springer.

Raskin, J. (2000). *The Humane Interface: New Directions for Designing Interactive Systems* (1 ed.): Addison-Wesley Professional.

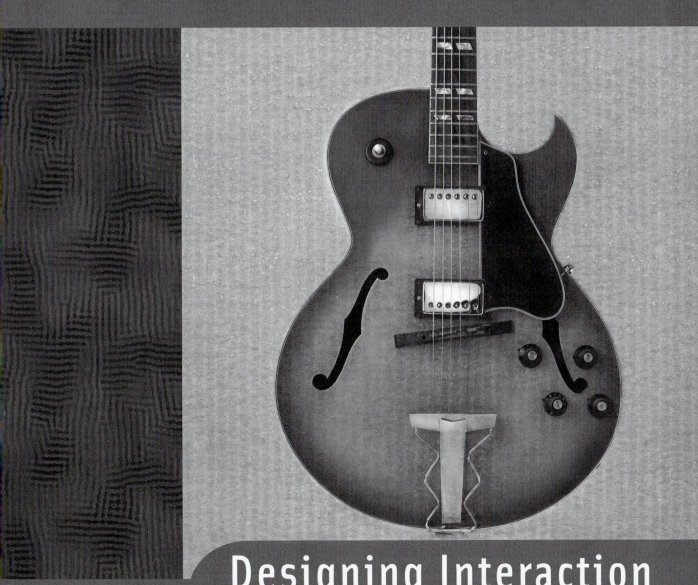

SECTION II

Designing Interaction

This section explores the process of interaction design from the initial phase of discovery through the design and testing phases. It investigates some of the concepts, procedures, models, and methodologies that interaction designers use to develop and test their design ideas and prototypes. It discusses the meaning of user-centered design and affords first-hand experience with the complex process of designing usable and useful interfaces.

Interaction Design Process

Interaction design is an iterative process. Solutions do not happen in a linear way, they evolve during development, which can sometimes be a "one step forward, two steps back" process. Although it might seem counterproductive to step back to a previous stage of development, we are not actually losing ground by doing so because our knowledge path is constantly moving forward (Figure 3.1).

What we learn from the problems we encounter along the way is invaluable and essential for the acquisition of the ultimate design solution. Notice that the knowledge path extends beyond implementation. This represents the fact that, although we strive for the best possible solution, there will always be aspects of a design that can be improved in later versions. We never stop learning, and the public sphere can provide a great deal of information about the usability of our designs.

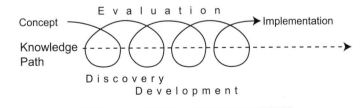

Figure 3.1 The iterative interaction design process.

3.1. Iterative Design

The process of iterative design can be compared to that of writing an essay. You might start with a list of the topics that you want to cover and then arrange them into an outline. You then write a rough draft. This step might take a few attempts before you feel relatively satisfied. In the process, you might think of other ideas that you want to include, which you go back and fit into the outline, a process of iteration between the draft and the outline. The outline now becomes a dynamic tool that can help you to organize new ideas within the existing structure of the essay.

The draft of the essay might then be edited by someone else, and those changes will be an iteration on the draft. The draft now becomes a dynamic tool for further third-party editing until all of the necessary tweaks have been made and the final version is produced. This process as a whole has had a forward momentum even though there were iterations to previous phases along the way.

Final drafts of documents are rarely created on the first attempt; they usually go through a number of iterations starting from the conceptual phase, in which the author determines the topic and content, passing through a number of physical iterations between outlines and rough drafts, and finally reaching the point at which the document is finalized and distributed.

Interaction design follows the same iterative trajectory, constantly moving forward through the different phases but in an iterative framework.

3.2. User-Centered Design

How do designers come up with an interface that's not in your face? That just does what you want, and doesn't make you waste time doing what it wants? (*IBM, 2006*)

User-centered design (UCD) was pioneered by Donald Norman's research laboratory at the University of California at San Diego. The objective of UCD is to develop a design framework that enables interaction designers to build more usable systems. UCD is currently defined in the ISO Standard—Human Centered Design Processes for Interactive Systems.

UCD can be considered a philosophy as well as a process. It is based on the premise that design should emerge from the user's tasks, goals, and environment. The process of UCD focuses on human-centric issues such as cognition, perception, and the physical attributes and conditions of the user and his or her environment.

The central focus of UCD is to acquire a thorough understanding of the people who will use the proposed system. It is essential that the ultimate users, who may or may not be the designer's clients, be formally identified as the "primary users" and that they be intimately involved in the design process from start to finish.

The basic tenants of user-centered design are as follows:

- Early focus on users and their tasks
- Continuous evaluations to determine ease of learning and ease of use
- Iterative design

UCD projects generally involve the following methods:

User Participation—In some projects, particular users become part of the design team. They provide constant contact with the target audience and can be consulted at each step of the design process. If development takes a long time, however, it is possible that these users will begin to affiliate themselves more with the designers than the ultimate users and, therefore, become less effective in representing the concerns of the target users. Some teams work on a rotating basis in which people from the target audience serve as members of the design team for limited periods of time and are then replaced by new target user representatives.

Focus Groups—Focus groups are used to conduct structured interviews with various stakeholders. They allow designers to communicate with diverse users and observe how they interact with each other. These groups provide insight into user opinions and attitudes. Focus groups require an experienced monitor to keep the session on track and see that no one member dominates the discussion.

Questionnaires—Questionnaires and surveys can be used to elicit information from large and geographically dispersed user groups. They can provide insight into user preferences and opinions, but they are more restricted than focus groups. Because there is no contact with the person filling out the questionnaire, it is important that questions are phrased clearly and that intuitive scaling measures are used.

Ethnographic Observations—Ethnographic observations take place at the location where the work is performed. They involve shadowing subjects as they go about their normal routine. The observer take notes based on his or her observations or may also use audio or video recordings. Focus groups, questionnaires, and ethnographic observations are discussed in depth in Chapter 4.

Walkthroughs—A walkthrough is performed by deciding on the user goal or task and then walking through a design proposal to see whether that task can be accomplished. Walkthroughs are meant to uncover any problems that might arise during actual use, and they can be focused on a particular facet of the design or on the design as a whole. Walkthroughs are discussed further in Chapter 5.

Expert Evaluations—Expert evaluations are carried out by usability professionals using heuristics or guidelines from the usability research and human factors literature. This evaluation is approached from the viewpoint of the user who has been documented by the design team. We discuss this further in the section Discount Usability Engineering as well as in the Evaluation section of Chapter 5.

Usability Testing—Usability tests can take many different forms. They can be done in expensive usability laboratories using special mirrors, video cameras, tracking software, and other observational equipment, or they can be done without any technology, simply using a paper prototype, an observer, and a subject.

Usability tests are conducted throughout the design process and focus on different aspects, depending on the phase of development. We discuss usability testing in greater depth in Chapter 8.

3.3. Interaction Design Models

There have been many approaches to interaction design, which have come from diverse domains, including software engineering, HCI, and other design disciplines. There have also been attempts to standardize the process of interaction design, including various life-cycle models, such as the waterfall model, the spiral model (Bohem, 1988), the Dynamic Systems Development Method (DSDM), which originated in the software engineering domain, and the star life-cycle model proposed by Hartson and Hix (1989), which emerged from the HCI domain.

Some of these models are time sensitive, some are more risk sensitive, others put a strong focus on observing users where they work, and still others focus on usability, yet they all share particular aspects. Let's look at some of these models and see what elements they have in common. We will then be able to better understand the structure of a design project and apply that knowledge in a more formalized way.

3.3.1. Waterfall Model

This is a classic model and one of the first ones generally used in the software industry. It emphasizes a linear, sequential approach to software development. It is easy to understand and implement because of its clear-cut phases, each of which must be completed before the next phase can begin. It also seems quite logical: you must first consider the requirements of the system and then have a basic design before you can code and test it.

The waterfall model was introduced but not named in 1970 by Winston Royce. Royce created the model based on his experience with developing software for "spacecraft mission planning, commanding and post-flight analysis"(Royce, 1970). Royce characterized the then-current methodology of software development as comprising two main components: analysis and coding. This, he believed, was sufficient for programs that were not large in scope and were to be used by the programmers who created it, which was a common occurrence at the time for programs created for internal use.

Royce considered that this limited model was "doomed to failure" if applied to larger projects. However, there was an entrenched resistance to implementing additional components that would not directly contribute to the development of the final product and would certainly increase the cost of development. Customers did not want to pay for these additional development phases, and development personnel did not want to implement them. Royce considered the prime function of management was to "sell these concepts" to the client and enforce compliance on the development team.

The waterfall model can be viewed as a progressive step in software development, especially because it places design at the beginning of the process; however, this model is based on the notion that once the requirements have been ascertained, they will not change during the course of development.

Over time this has proven to be an untenable assumption, and in practice there is usually a bit of leeway allowed for making adjustments to the previous stage after reviews are carried out by the design team. Most waterfall models, therefore, include some limited iteration between stages (the dashed lines in Figure 3.2).

The waterfall model is also not a user-centered model in that it does not formally take the user into consideration. The innate rigidity of the waterfall model led designers to look for more flexible solutions to structuring the design process. The waterfall model with its emphasis on early completion of requirements documentation was suitable for software such as compilers and operating systems, but it was not suitable for interactive end-user applications.

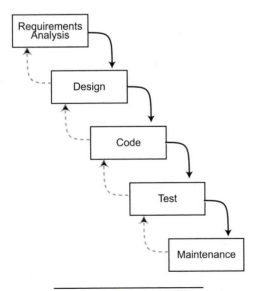

Figure 3.2 Waterfall life-cycle model.

Advantages of the waterfall model include the following:

- Highly disciplined process of documentation
- Easily observable development progress
- Easy to create budget
- Consistent review process

Disadvantages of the waterfall model include the following:

- Document centric; can be difficult for customer to understand
- Not user centered
- Makes assumptions about requirements that are inflexible

3.3.2. Spiral Model

The spiral life-cycle model developed by Barry Boehm in 1988 is a more complex and flexible model and requires a knowledgeable design team. It is centered on risk reduction and breaks up a project into subprojects, each addressing specific risks such as the following:

- Budget and schedule predictability
- System integration problems
- User interface errors
- Requirement instability resulting in code modification at a late stage
- Mission-critical sensitivity to error
- Investment versus productivity gains
- High-level improvements that are incompatible with the client culture
- Mismatches to the user project's needs and priorities

The model was introduced by using a case study covering the development of the TRW Software Productivity System (TRW-SPS). The TRW-SPS was an integrated software engineering environment with the primary objective of significantly increasing software productivity. Boehm reported that the resulting system that was designed with the model increased the productivity of all of the projects that fully used the system by at least 50%.

The model's illustration in Figure 3.3 should be read from two directions. The radial direction around the spiral indicates the accumulation of activities to date, and the angular dimension represents the progress toward completion of each cycle. You may notice that following the spiral "involves a progression the addresses the same sequence of steps, for each portion of the product and for each of its levels of elaboration" (Bohem, 1988, 65).

The spiral model incorporates a prototyping approach and encourages iteration. It starts with a value proposition that usually identifies a particular corporate mission that could be improved by technology. This hypothesis is tested on each

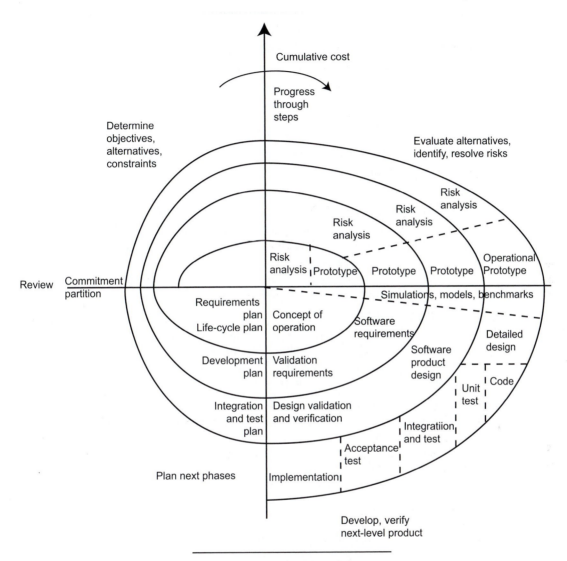

Cumulative cost

Progress
through
steps

Determine
objectives,
alternatives,
constraints

Evaluate alternatives,
identify, resolve risks

Risk
analysis

Risk
analysis

Risk
analysis

Operational
Prototype

Risk
analysis

Prototype Prototype Prototype

Review Commitment
partition

Simulations, models, benchmarks

Requirements
plan

Concept of
operation

Software
requirements

Life-cycle plan

Detailed
design

Development
plan

Validation
requirements

Software
product
design

Code

Unit
test

Integration
and test
plan

Design validation
and verification

Integratiion
and test

Acceptance
test

Plan next phases

Implementation

Develop, verify
next-level product

Figure 3.3 Spiral model of the software process.

pass through the cycle by conducting a risk analysis using prototypes of alternative designs. The risk analysis begins with high-level issues, leaving the elaboration of low-risk software elements to later rounds.

If a risk test fails the spiral, it is terminated; otherwise the process continues to final implementation. A successful hypothesis is tested once again to see whether its implementation satisfies the criteria and to identify any further improvements and maintenance issues.

Advantages of the spiral model include the following:

- Appropriateness for large-scale enterprise systems
- Flexibility in terms of its sensitivity to the dynamic nature of the software industry
- High sensitivity to risk at each stage of development

Disadvantages of the spiral model include the following:

- Complex nature makes it difficult for customers to grasp
- Requires extensive information regarding risk assessment
- Undetected risks can be problematic

3.3.3. Dynamic Systems Development Method

Other approaches to standardizing interaction design include user-centered models, such as the rapid application development (RAD) approach. The most refined RAD approach is the dynamic systems development method (DSDM), which was developed by the DSDM consortium, a not-for-profit group of industry experts concerned about standardization in interaction design (see http://www.dsdm.org).

The DSDM framework is a time-sensitive, business-centered development approach that involves techniques that can be tailored to specific projects. Its main focus is the on-time delivery of high-quality software solutions for current business needs. The framework maintains that 80% of a software solution can be developed in 20% of the time required to complete a total solution.

In DSDM, the project's time frame and allocated resources are fixed, but the functional requirements are flexible and can change with the evolving needs of the company. There are seven components in the framework, which can be grouped into three distinct stages (Figure 3.4). The first stage includes the pre-project, feasibility study, and business study phases, and must be completed in a sequential manner before any other phases can be initiated.

The second stage involves iteration between the functional model iteration, design and build iteration, and implementation phases. How this stage plays out is determined by the particular project team. The final stage is the post-project phase, which may not involve the previous design team. This stage involves maintenance and continuous quality reviews.

The DSDM framework recognizes nine principles:

1. **Active user involvement** is imperative.
2. The **team must be empowered** to make decisions.
3. The focus is on **frequent delivery of products**.
4. **Fitness for business purpose** is the essential criterion for acceptance of deliverables.
5. **Iterative and incremental development** is necessary to converge on an accurate business solution.

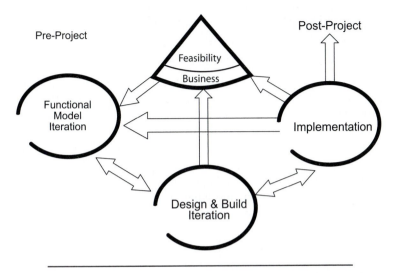

Figure 3.4 Dynamic systems development method (DSDM) framework.

6. All **changes** during development **are reversible**.
7. **Requirements** are baselined at a **high level**.
8. **Testing is integrated** throughout the life cycle.
9. **Collaboration and cooperation** among all stakeholders **is essential**.

The DSDM is user oriented; primary users are called ambassador users. They become part of the design team and provide a communication channel between the business and development communities.

DSDM Core Techniques

A number of core techniques involved in the DSDM framework are applied according to their appropriateness to a particular project; they are not mandated for all projects. These techniques are described as follows:

Facilitated Workshops—Project stakeholders are involved in facilitated workshops that are used to manage the fast pace of the process and engage the business community in the design process. These are designed to foster rapid, quality decision making.

Timeboxing—All projects have fixed completion dates, which are used to create the project's timebox. All design activities are nested within the overall timebox and must be concluded within prescribed time limits. Each timebox generally involves three phases:

- **Investigation**—This is a quick pass that determines whether the team is on target and moving in the right direction.
- **Refinement**—The team uses the results of the investigation to refine the design.

- **Consolidation**—This is the wrap-up phase, during which all loose ends are accounted for and adjusted.

MoSCoW—The requirements of any DSDM project are prioritized using MoSCoW:

Must Haves—Must have for requirements that are fundamental to the system. Without them the system will be unworkable and useless. The Must Haves define the minimum usable subset. A DSDM project guarantees to satisfy all the minimum usable subset.

o

Should Haves—Should have for important requirements for which there is a work around in the short term and which would normally be classed asmandatory in less time-constrained development, but the system will be useful and usable without them.

Could Haves—Could have for requirements that can more easily be left out of the increment under development.

o

Won't Have This Time Around—Want to have but Won't have this time for those valuable requirements that can wait till later development takes place; in otherwords, the Waiting List.

Modeling—Modeling is recommended to ensure that misunderstandings between the business and design communities are kept to a minimum. However, no specific tools are mandated by this framework; these are project dependent and left up to the participants.

Prototyping—DSDM prototypes are designed to evolve over time. Four categories are identified:

1. **Business**—Demonstrate the business processes being automated.
2. **Usability**—Demonstrate how the user interacts with the system.
3. **Performance and Capacity**—Test for system robustness.
4. **Capability/Technique**—Test conceptual designs.

Testing—The DSDM approach to testing is that it takes place throughout the life cycle. Specific testing tools are not prescribed by the framework; however, they must be usable within the timebox.

Configuration Management—There must be a strong and highly organized management structure in place to make sure that the fast pace of development stays on course and that all teams are in sync with the overall project.

The DSDM is an iterative model that is sensitive to changing requirements. It is a time-sensitive and business-oriented approach to systems development. You can find out more about the dynamic systems development method at the DSDM Consortium's Web site, *http://www.dsdm.org/*. At the time of this writing a new version of DSDM is about to be published.

Advantages of the DSDM include the following:

- Provides a technique-independent process
- Flexible in terms of requirement evolution
- Strict time and budget adherence
- Incorporates stakeholders into the development process

Disadvantages of the DSDM include the following:

- Involves progressive development of requirements
- Focus on RAD can lead to decrease in code robustness
- Requires full commitment to DSDM process
- Requires significant user involvement
- Requires a skilled development team in both the business and technical areas

3.3.4. Prototype-Based Models

There are a few, less-structured models that can be used on small-scale projects that have prototypes as the main iteration tool. Prototype-based development allows designers to discuss design issues such as look and feel, scope, information flow from screen to screen, and product concept with customers by showing them how the proposed system would function rather just discuss these issues in the abstract.

Throwaway Prototyping Model

This model can be used when a client is not clear about the scope of the project and cannot accurately describe the project requirements. The prototype is built and used to elicit requirements and then thrown away. The project may then continue with any other design process.

Evolutionary Prototyping Model

This is a trial-and-error method that involves the creation of design proposals in the form of semifunctioning prototypes that evolve over the course of the project, eventually becoming the final product. It is a "proof of concept" model.

Advantages of prototyping include the following:

- Easy for users to give feedback
- Reduced development time and cost
- Involvement of the user in the development process

Disadvantages of prototyping include the following:

- Can be viewed by client as the final product
- May lead to insufficient analysis due to the ease of development
- Difficult for developers to discard and start creating the final product from scratch

3.3.5. **Discount Usability Engineering**

One of the more influential prototype-based development models is the discount usability engineering (DUE) model developed by Jakob Nielsen (1994). DUE was developed to foster the design of more usable interfaces at a time when the industry viewed HCI-based design methods to be expensive, time consuming, and complex, in that they required highly trained usability engineering professionals.

Nielsen argued that the benefits derived from even small amounts of user testing would have a significant impact on the usability of the design. He therefore intended to show the development community that, although more extensive HCI practices would certainly add to the usability of a proposed design, less rigorous methods could also achieve significantly beneficial usability results.

Nielsen argued that these less expensive and more accessible methods were more likely to be adopted by the development community: "the simpler methods stand a much better chance of actually being used in practical design situations and they should therefore be viewed as a way of serving the user community" (Nielsen, 1994). He also noted that the method should follow the basic principle of "early focus on users." DUE is based on the use of the following three techniques:

- Scenarios
- Simplified thinking aloud
- Heuristic evaluation

Scenarios—Nielsen considered scenarios to be a "special type of prototyping." These scenarios were either paper mock-ups or simple RAD prototypes that represented a highly constrained and focused view of the proposed design. By using these minimized versions, designers gain the ability to iterate frequently between testing and designing. This is intended to maximize the opportunities for identifying usability problems.

Simplified Thinking Aloud—Thinking aloud is not a new concept; however, the technique was generally used by psychologists and usability experts only during videotaped interviews with subjects. Nielsen suggested that the technique could be implemented without special equipment or the use of a laboratory, simply by "bringing in some real users, giving them some typical test tasks, and asking them to think out loud while they perform the tasks" (Nielsen, 1994).

One of the tenets of the DUE model is that most usability tests do not require a statistically significant sample, and that "one learns the most from the first few test users" (Nielsen, 1994).

Nielsen showed that the cost–benefit tradeoff curve derived from a number of test trials indicated that testing more than four or five participants provided diminishing returns. Therefore, he argued that even tests that are not statistically significant are worthwhile in that they significantly improve the quality of design decisions.

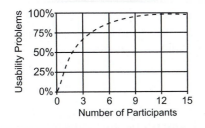

Figure 3.5 Curve of participants and usability problems.

Based on research with Tom Landauer, Nielsen suggested that the number of problems that could be identified from a usability test with n users can be calculated according to the following equation:

$$N[1-(1-L)^n]$$

where:

N = total number of usability problems in a design

L = proportion of usability problems discovered with a single participant

Based on their research, they suggested that a typical value for L is 31%. Figure 3.5 shows the curve for that case. Note that zero problems will be found if one tests zero participants.

Heuristic Evaluation—Nielsen recognized that user interface guidelines were often used successfully by development firms. However, he estimated that the number of guidelines would often run into the thousands, a fact that he considered to be an unreasonable and intimidating barrier to frequent usability testing. He therefore proposed a set of 10 usability heuristics that could be used by designers to investigate and document usability problems. Nielsen's 10 usability heuristics can be found in Chapter 5.

Heuristic evaluation requires some experience and should be performed by someone who has some basic training. However, Nielsen suggested that many usability problems can be identified by most designers by simply applying the heuristics at the early stages of development. Heuristic evaluations should be performed by a few different evaluators to ensure that individual bias does not interfere with the process. This will also give a rough estimation of issue frequency.

3.3.6. Contextual Inquiry

Contextual inquiry (CI), which is based on anthropological and ethnographic methods, involves observing users where they work. The method was developed by Hugh Beyer and Karen Holzblatt and is described in detail in their 1998 book *Contextual Design: Defining Customer-Centered Systems.*

CI involves observing a select group of users in depth and gathering design knowledge through inquiry and interpretation. It is based on four main principles: context, partnership, focus, and interpretation.

Context

CI recognizes the user's context of use from a global perspective. It looks at the larger picture of how and why people use software products. This large view cannot be accomplished simply by testing design solutions in a laboratory.

CI strives to create a rich picture of the user's environment and includes factors that are not directly related to the proposed design. It is felt by practitioners that the context in which the product is used is essential to the design of more usable and useful systems.

Partnership

CI involves partnering with a typical user in a master/apprentice relationship. The observer takes the role of apprentice and tries to understand all of the facets of the work in which the master is involved. This can involve an active dialogue between partners or a purely observational interaction. The objective is to gather as much information as possible about the tasks being performed.

Focus

These observations are focused on collecting information, which can be categorized as follows:

- **Tools**—The various applications people use to perform their tasks.
- **Artifacts**—Nondigital tools required by the work but not part of the design.
- **Terminology**—The labels and terms people use to identify objects and processes.
- **Sequences**—The order in which people perform their tasks.
- **Methods**—Organization techniques used by the workers.
- **Interactions**—How and why people interact with each other.

These categories will be used to create elaborate models of the work, the work flow, and the work context. CI uses affinity diagrams to organize the results of the various observations.

Interpretation

An affinity diagram is a way to sort, organize, and prioritize observations. Observers write specific observations on Post-it notes or file cards. The team then places the notes on a wall based on how they relate to each other, creating groupings of the various observations.

After creating the affinity diagram, the team creates models that document communication flows, information sequences, physical environments, and corporate culture structures. These models provide the basis on which the team begins to construct the conceptual models of the proposed design.

3.4. Overview of Interaction Design Models

All of the models described here have been proven effective in structuring the development of interactive application interfaces, especially for large, enterprise-wide projects. Smaller projects also benefit from a structured approach to design, but they can afford more latitude in the application of the models.

Some of these models are more linear, like the waterfall life-cycle model, whereas some are more user centered, like the RAD models. All of them have definite phases and most incorporate user involvement and some degree of iteration. Particular models also include extensive cost and risk analyses before any user- or task-related data are gathered.

The following is a list of some elements that appear in many of the standard models. Some of the elements are less universal, but they are included to complete the process from cost and risk assessments to maintenance schedules:

- Cost and risk analysis
- Observation
- Task analysis
- Requirements assessment
- Conceptual design
- Physical design

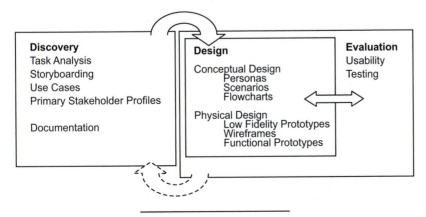

Figure 3.6 The design process model.

- Prototyping
- Evaluation
- Usability testing
- Implementation
- Maintenance

3.4.1. The Design Process Model

For the sake of simplicity, we follow a generic model called the design process model (Figure 3.6), which incorporates many aspects of the models mentioned in the foregoing and follows their basic outlines. Most iterative models can be overlaid on this model, and so it will provide a basis on which other models can be learned and assimilated.

The model involves the following phases, which answer specific design questions:

- **The Discovery Phase**—What are the components of the project, who is involved, what are the current work space and work flow like, and what are the contextual and extraneous factors that affect the work flow?

    ◦ This phase may use participatory and/or observational methods.
    ◦ The results of the discovery phase are articulated in three documents:
        - Mission statement:

            ◦ Project goals
            ◦ Scope
            ◦ Risk

        - Requirements document:

            ◦ Requirements
            ◦ Functional
            ◦ Information
            ◦ Physical

        - Inputs/outputs
        - Constraints
        - Project document:

            ◦ Definition of the tasks involved in the project
            ◦ Evaluation criteria and methods
            ◦ Implementation
            ◦ Training
            ◦ Maintenance
            ◦ Future needs

    ◦ The primary stakeholders are defined using individual user profiles

- **Design**—The design phase has two parts:
  - **Conceptual Design**—What are the possible ways in which the design can address the needs of the problem space, how could the work be structured? This is documented by the various conceptual models created in the process of conceptual design including personas, scenarios, use cases, and so on.
  - **Physical Design**—What are the possible ways that the conceptual design can be realized in the real world? This is documented with the low-fidelity prototypes, wireframes, and functional prototypes. Throwaway and evolutionary prototypes can be used; however, it is recommended that the final product be created from scratch.

- **Evaluation**—How can we determine the relative merits of one design over another, how can we measure the success of a proposed design, how can we get real users to give us feedback about a proposed design, how can we incorporate usability testing at the early stages of the design process? This is documented by the results of formal and informal usability testing.

These phases are not mutually exclusive. We may learn something during a usability test that may cause us to go back to the work place and explore what seemed to be an unrelated process during the initial discovery phase.

Potential users can be involved in every phase of the process: they can view flowcharts, do cognitive walkthroughs, and examine prototypes. The more users are involved, the more the design will be centered on their needs and expectations.

Evaluation is not a discrete phase, it is layered over the entire design phase from beginning to end, and should incorporate as much feedback from real users as possible. Evaluation takes up more of the project's resources as the design nears completion. Formal usability testing on the functional prototype represents the culmination of the development process.

Summary

Interaction design projects can range from small Web sites to enterprise-wide solutions. The interaction design development process does not differ greatly across this spectrum: all projects involve the basic stages of discovery, development, evaluation, and implementation. However, the degree of formalization within the project management structure differs greatly.

It would be a mistake to initiate the development of a small-scale Web site without first gathering some information about the intended purpose of the site and the target user. Ignoring small bits of information at the beginning of the process can cause a great deal of work trying to accommodate additional elements later.

It would also be a mistake not to get the intended user involved in the design process from the very beginning. Most of the development models we have looked at are based on user-centered design philosophies.

Technology serves to help people accomplish tasks, and, therefore, interaction design should be based on the user's abilities, limitations, goals, and environment. A well-structured, user-centered development process will foster the creation of usable and useful interaction designs.

Resources on the Web

www.aw.com/heim

You will find links to websites and journal articles covering the topic of usability and User-Centered Design. You will also find links to information concerning some of the design process models discussed in this chapter.

Suggested Reading

Demarco, T., & Lister, T. (1999). *Peopleware : Productive Projects and Teams,* (2 ed.): Dorset House Publishing Company, Inc.

Larman, D. (2003). *Agile and Iterative Development: A Manager's Guide* (1 ed.): Addison-Wesley Professional.

Mayhew, D. (1999). *The Usability Engineering Lifecycle: A Practitioner's Handbook for User Interface Design* (1 ed.): Morgan Kaufmann.

CHAPTER 4

Discovery

The voyage of discovery is not in seeking new landscapes but in having new eyes.

(Proust, 1982)

The first phase of an interaction design project is the discovery phase. During this phase the design team has to identify and document the existing work flow in rich detail. This is the "collection" part. The team then looks at the information that has been collected and organizes it so that it can be documented. This documentation describes how the work is currently done. It includes all aspects of the work from a global perspective. This is the "interpretation" part, which culminates with a documentation of requirements for the new system.

During the discovery phase, we need to keep an open mind in terms of the impact technology will have on the way people interact with each other as they perform their tasks. We also have to understand the impact the proposed system will have on the way people feel about the work they perform. It is important to view this as a process of true discovery. We should be flexible about what type of system we think is appropriate, as well as how technology fits into the work flow in general.

What we learn at this stage of discovery sets the course of the design process. It is important that we understand the impact technology will have on the work flow and on the people involved in the work. This knowledge will help us to design a system that is appropriate and that does not diminish productivity or the workers' sense of satisfaction with the work they do.

Essentially, during the collection portion, you will formally identify the following elements:

- The people who are involved with the work
- The things they use to do the work
- The processes that are involved in the work
- The information required to do the work
- The constraints imposed on the work
- The inputs required by the work
- The outputs created by the work

You will then interpret the information about the work process by:

- Creating descriptions of the people who do the work
- Describing the different goals involved in the work
- Documenting the work step by step
- Creating different stories about how the various aspects of the work are done
- Creating charts and diagrams of the work flow
- Tracing the different stories identified with the various people through the charts and diagrams

4.1. Discovery Phase Framework

As we saw in the previous chapter, there are many different frameworks and models that have been developed to structure the design process. Some of them are highly scripted and prescribe specific methods; others provide loose frameworks that can incorporate diverse approaches.

What all of these models have in common is that they involve the collection of data about the work domain that must be interpreted and then applied to the design. As in Chapter 3, where we adopted a generic model called the design process model, we will also choose to follow a generic approach in the discovery phase, which can be integrated within more formalized approaches.

This generic framework will be called the discovery phase framework and will incorporate collection activities as well as interpretation activities (Figure 4.1). Once you learn the essential aspects of the discovery phase, you can apply them to any of the formalized methods that may be used by a particular design firm.

MAXIM

The frame of reference must come from the observation and not be imposed on it.

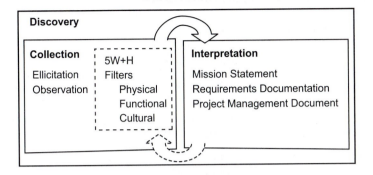

Figure 4.1 Discovery phase framework.

5W+H, who, what, where, why, when and how.

Basically, we must find out what we will need to know about the work that people do. If we don't understand the kind of data required to create the design, we will not be able to create the proper tools for gathering that information.

This does not mean that we should have an agenda or a hypothesis and then try to prove it through observation or testing. It does, however, mean that we should have a framework that will support and guide our activities and assure that we do not miss opportunities to gather important information. This framework should be compatible with the interpretation activities and provide the collected data in an easily accessible format.

4.1.1. Exploring the Work Domain

Interaction design sometimes involves creating an application that will be incorporated into an existing business work flow. This may include inventory tracking, customer orders, and billing. Other projects involve improving an existing application. Still others involve designing new and innovative devices. The design scenario that runs through this book is about the development of a Web site, which is another possible type of interaction design project.

These are all very diverse projects with very diverse requirements and domains. When we think about exploring each work domain we will be thinking about very different types of activities and interactions. It may even seem odd to talk about a Web site visit as a work domain or to think of it in terms of a work flow. However, it is important to understand the underlying concept and the motivating factors involved in this stage of development.

We need to know as much as possible about the people who will be using or in some way affected by the proposed design. That may mean entering data into an application or it may mean finding information on a Web site. These differences are a matter of form not substance. We are interested in the user's behavior in relation to the design, and so that is the focus we will maintain during this phase of development.

It is important to take a systemic approach to the exploration of the existing domain and work flow. We need to know how people actually complete their tasks. Our objective is to add value to that process, and that can only be achieved if the existing process is thoroughly understood and documented.

There are many undocumented processes and a great deal of tacit information involved in most human activities; you must be attentive and have ways to discover and document these hidden aspects. Many of the observation-based approaches to discovery involve the collection of implicit knowledge.

Some of the information you gather during this phase will be used to create the requirement documentation, whereas other information will be used during the design phase. For instance, you may find out that people need to perform particular tasks, and that knowledge may contribute to the requirements documentation. However, you may also find out that people prefer to perform tasks in a certain order, which will be useful when you create the scenarios during the cognitive design part of the design phase.

Stakeholders

Before you can begin to gather information about the work domain, you must first identify the stakeholders involved in the project. Stakeholders are the people that are involved either directly or indirectly in the work flow, such as the people who do the work, the people who manage the people who do the work, the people who are affected by the output of the work, or the people who will benefit in some way from the work.

It is important to identify all of the stakeholders so the proposed design can incorporate their needs early in the design process; otherwise changes may have to be made that might require rethinking the entire design.

Changes that occur late in the process can be expensive and may force the design to be patched together to avoid cost overruns. A patched-together solution will be less robust and probably less efficient because the basic structure of the design was not created to support the additional functionality.

There are four types of stakeholders:

- **Primary**—The person who uses the design directly.
- **Secondary**—The person who either supplies input or receives output from the design.
- **Facilitator**—The person who maintains or develops the design.
- **Indirect**—The person who is affected by the use of the design but has no contact with it, such as the user's superior or coworkers and the client who is paying for the project (the client may or may not also be the primary stakeholder).

The list of indirect stakeholders can be quite long and include second-party vendors, suppliers, stockholders, and many others. Businesses often involve complex interactions among different departments. A software program that is designed to be used by only one department may affect other departments in many ways. For instance, the output result of an application such as a report on inventory may be used by other departments to allocate resources. If the report is produced successfully but is unreadable by the software used in the other department, it will cause unnecessary burdens on that department to convert the report into a readable format.

The primary stakeholders should have the most impact on the eventual design. These are the people who will be using the design, which can mean spending several hours every day in front of the interface. Their productivity and value as employees may be directly affected by the effectiveness and efficiency of the system you design.

> ### MAXIM
> All stakeholders should be considered during design.

It would be a mistake, however, to design without any knowledge of the other people affected by the success of the design. A new system that is not designed to be integrated with the work that other people in the company do may cause needless disruptions and may actually become more of a problem than it is worth.

The Competition

During the initial discovery phase you should also investigate the competition. If you are designing a product, you should find out if other companies have already created a similar product and then learn everything you can about it. If you are creating an internal enterprise-wide system, you should know whether other companies have installed similar systems. If you are designing a Web site, you should examine related Web sites.

In other words, you don't have to reinvent the wheel. If other people have designed a similar object or system, you can learn from their solutions. You can view their design as a prototype and explore the positive and negative effects of particular decisions. This does not mean that you can infringe on other peoples' copyrighted material, but you can learn much from investigating their choices.

Knowing what already exists in the marketplace is also essential for proper risk assessment of a proposed project. Are you competing in a difficult or saturated market? You need fully to understand the market forces involved in the project.

Discovery is an important phase of the design process and should be carried out with care and attention to detail. You must keep an open mind and not judge the relative importance of any piece of information you come across; what may seem inconsequential during an observation session may prove to be important later.

Let's look at some of the information you will need to collect and how best to accomplish the various tasks involved in the discovery phase.

4.1.2. **Organizing the Discovery Process**

There are many different ways to explore a work domain, including interviews and ethnographic observations. These methods have been proven to be effective and robust, and they can capture a great deal of information about the way people work.

It can be difficult, however, to make sense out of the data generated during this process and apply it to the design of an interactive system. Therefore, it is important to understand the process as an integrated whole with many interdependent phases and to implement a structure that will facilitate the transition from data to design.

No matter what methods of data collection or interpretation we use, we will need to have a framework that provides a focus for the collection of information and an organizational structure to process that information once it is collected. This is especially important if the design is for an enterprise-wide solution that involves many people.

In other words, you will likely have to undertake many interviews and observations, and there will be many team members whose activities must be coordinated and collated. Unless there is an effective structure in place, this can become a difficult situation to control.

Collection

The collection framework will be structured on the 5W+H heuristic presented in Chapter 1. This will provide a focus for our data collection activities and a structure that will be easy to use during the interpretation activities.

The collection framework will also incorporate three filters that will be applied to the 5W+H heuristic. These will help us to cross-reference any overlapping information.

Focus—To provide a focus for our data collection activities, we will use the 5W+H heuristic. It is similar to the framework suggested by Goetz and LeCompte (1984) for ethnographic design in educational research and will guide most of our activities during the collection part of the discovery phase.

We will follow the same grouping that was presented in Chapter 1:

What/How—What activities are involved and how are they accomplished? This will include the documentation of the various computer-based and non–computer-based activities and deliverables.

Where/When—We need to understand the impact of physical location on the work flow. Our design may involve changes to the physical location of the people who do the work, so we must be aware of the possible eventual impact on them. We also need to understand the temporal aspects of the work. Are there any prerequisite activities, and, if so, in what order must they be completed?

Who/Why—We must understand who is involved and why they are involved and create detailed profiles of these people so that we understand not only their role in the present work flow, but also how they may respond to any changes implemented. These people are the stakeholders in the project.

Filters (Physical/Cultural/Functional/Informational)—Human activities can be seen from many different perspectives:

Physical—We can describe the physical aspects of the activity.

- Where is it done?
- What objects are involved?

Cultural—We can look at the activity in terms of the relationships among the people involved.

- Are some people in a position to orchestrate and evaluate the performance of other people?

Functional—We can also look at these activities in terms of what actually happens.

- Do some people create things?
- Do other people document procedures and communications?

Informational—We can look at these activities in terms of the information that is involved.

- What information is necessary to perform a task?
- How does the information flow from one person to another?
- How is the information generated?
- How is the information consumed?

All of these perspectives will constitute the filters we will use to categorize the information we collect. We will, therefore, have four different perspectives with which to perceive the way people work:

- Physical
- Cultural
- Functional
- Informational

These filters can help to provide a rich description of a particular activity. We can use them to organize the information we gather about the work flow by applying them to the 5W+H heuristic.

These filters are necessary because much of the information we collect will overlap in the 5W+H heuristic categories. For instance, if we focus on where particular activities are completed, we will also have to discuss what objects are involved. We can notate this information in both categories as related to the physical aspects of the work.

I now give an example of how we might organize our discovery process. The most relevant filters are listed in each category and are also ordered by degree of relevance. This is a suggested listing and not a prescribed format: remember, the frame or reference must come out of the experience of observation and not be imposed upon it:

- What/How

  1. Functional
  2. Physical
  3. Informational

- Where/When

  1. Physical
  2. Functional

- Who/Why

  1. Cultural
  2. Functional
  3. Informational

These heuristic categories and filters do not require any particular methodology of data interpretation and organization. They will, however, guide us in the collection of data and allow us to cross-reference information for the purpose of building models using any of the formalized approaches to interpretation that are used by the various design process models.

Interpretation

> **MAXIM**
>
> Interpretation means going from data to design requirements.

After the data have been collected, they must be interpreted so that they can be applied to the design. This is usually done during brainstorming sessions or team meetings. If the data are collected in an organized manner, they will be easier to work with; if not, one might be faced with an enormous task that consumes too much of the available development resources.

The information gathered during the collection part of the discovery phase must be organized according to criteria that will be useful, and this information must be documented in a format that is easily accessible to the design team.

As with the collection process, there are many effective methods that can be used to distill and codify information, many of which are identified with specific frameworks. We will look at the essential areas that must be described and some of the constructs that can be used to organize this information. This will provide a solid foundation that can be applied to any of the more formalized methods.

The tools we will explore include the following:

- Task analysis
- Storyboarding
- Use cases
- Primary stakeholder profiles

Let's now explore the collection activities in more depth. We will look at the various methods involved in data collection using both observation and elicitation techniques.

4.2. Collection

Early in the design process, you may not know what questions to ask or who to approach for answers. How do interaction designers begin to get a feel for the work flow and needs of the people who will use the new system?

There is really no way to get a complete picture of a human work flow without actually talking with or observing the people involved. These individuals can supply much insight into the work they do and how they think it should be done. They can participate in the design process through interviews and focus groups, they can become members of the design team, or they can be observed in the work place were they actually do the work.

Whether you use participatory or observational methods or some combination of both, it is important that you get potential users to "buy in" to the process. They must feel empowered by the changes that will occur in the work place, not threatened by them.

It is also helpful to provide some remuneration for their time and effort during interviews or focus groups. This might take the form of a fee or just refreshments. Food has a way of putting people at ease; however, you must be prepared for diverse dietary requirements. It would be unfortunate if people were made uncomfortable because they had a particular dietary constraint that prohibited them from eating anything.

Getting people involved in the early stages can foster a cooperative frame of mind, but it may take some convincing to get them to see that their time and energies are being put to good use. You can foster synergy between the design team and the prospective users by making the design process transparent. Updates and project newsletters can be useful for large-scale projects that span months or years and involve large populations within the enterprise.

4.2.1. Methods of Collection

Many methods can be used to collect information about what, how, and why potential users do what they do. Let's take a general look at some common methods that

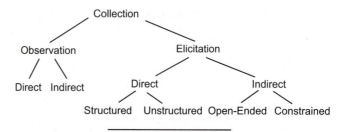

Figure 4.2 Collection processes.

have proven to be effective. There are two basic methods of collecting information about a potential design: observation and elicitation (Figure 4.2).

Observation—Valuable information can be obtained by watching people perform their activities in the context of the work environment. Observations can be made directly during the work day or indirectly using video and auditory recordings.

Elicitation—Elicitation methods also involve direct and indirect methods of investigation, such as interviews, focus groups, and questionnaires.

Optimally, an interaction design team will be able to use multiple methods of discovery to gain insight into the work flow that will be captured in the design. Let's look at these two methods of data collection in more depth.

4.2.2. Observation

People often do not see the ordinary things they do on a daily basis; they simply take them for granted. In addition, we often have difficulty explaining things we do habitually. For instance, try explaining the process of riding a bike: how do you keep your balance, what muscles do you use to steer, and so forth? During the data collection process, you cannot afford to overlook this kind of information because it is often crucial to the work flow.

Because this type of information is also not easily obtained through interviews and questionnaires, you will need to observe the way people do their work in the context of the actual work place. You can do this directly by accompanying people while they perform their work or indirectly using video or audio recordings.

Direct—Direct observation techniques draw on a method derived from anthropology called ethnographic observation. Ethnographic methods involve going to the work site and observing the people that are involved in the work and the infrastructure that supports the work flow.

This is similar to a painter going outside and painting the landscape that he or she sees rather than trying to create one from memory in the studio. The nuances of light and shadow that the painter observes in the real world are so complex and interconnected it would be virtually impossible to conjure them up from imagination.

Indirect—You can use indirect methods of observation by setting up recording devices in the work place. Indirect observation can sometimes pose problems due to its impersonal, "Big Brother" aspect; people do not like to feel that they are being spied on. The use of indirect methods may require a significant degree of transparency and communication between the design team and the people being observed to ensure that they feel comfortable in such a situations.

Recorded observations require release statements and prior approvals before they can take place. Recorded observations also require a great deal of time to review the recordings and document the results. Hence, they are generally reserved for long-term projects with high budgets and large design teams.

Concerns about Ethnographic Observations

One problem with on-site observation is that you actually have to be on-site at the work location, and as a foreign element, your presence will affect normal everyday activities. Your presence can impact a person's behavior both in positive and negative ways. He or she may become self-conscious and nervous as well as engaging and communicative.

As you shadow a worker throughout the course of the day, he or she may tend to perform his or her activities in a way that he or she thinks will garner your approval, or the worker may try to act in a way that makes him or her seem more important or cool. It is therefore necessary to interact with the worker as he or she performs his or her tasks and ask questions such as: Is this the way you normally do this task? Are there other ways to do this? You should take notes or record the interactions, but only if everyone involved is aware of and amenable to the recording.

You must also be careful to not become a nuisance or an obstruction, which would be counterproductive and might alienate the worker. You must also allow the worker his or her personal time to interact with coworkers socially without you hanging around. You might miss some information, but you will help to maintain a good relationship and create a favorable impression if you need to return for a follow-up observation.

Distributed Cognition

During your observations, you should be aware of the phenomenon of distributed cognition. Distributed cognition is the tendency to off-load cognitive tasks to objects in the environment or to distribute them among team members or coworkers.

Distributed cognition may involve memory or calculation tasks. For example, we use daily planners to help us to remember appointments or important dates. We use sticky notes to help us to remember facts and information, and we store phone numbers in our cell phones. We also use calculators to help us to compute equations and solve mathematical problems. These objects are integral parts of our cognitive processing. A photographer's camera and a musician's instrument are integrally related to the outcome of their art in a way that blurs the distinction between artist and artifact.

Cognition can also be shared among team members or coworkers. We often break down complex tasks and divide the work among different people. In complex work environments, some people may monitor one aspect of a process while others keep track of and control other aspects.

You must be aware of this phenomenon in order to most accurately describe the complete process with all of its various distributed tasks.

4.2.3. Elicitation

The aforementioned observation methods are carried out in the work place, allowing people to remember certain aspects of the work they might otherwise not think of or forget. At the same time, however, because they are at the work place, they may not be able to concentrate on their responses without interruptions and other work-related distractions. It is important, therefore, to include elicitation methods of discovery that can be conducted under less disruptive conditions or completed within the workers' time frame.

Tools for eliciting information from the various stakeholders include the following:

- Direct

  - Interviews
  - Focus groups

- Indirect

  - Corporate documentation
  - Logs and notes
  - Questionnaires

Direct Methods of Elicitation

Direct methods of elicitation require communicating face to face with another person who is most likely a stranger and with whom you may have nothing in common. They may be uncomfortable in this setting, and they may feel that it would be inappropriate to say anything negative about the company and the normal work flow. It is your job to make them feel comfortable and open, so that you can collect as much accurate information as possible. You will need to establish a rapport with your subjects.

Aspects of Interpersonal Communication—Two important dimensions of interpersonal communication are the physical and cultural aspects. You should try to be neutral in both of these areas. If there is a dress code, you should try to follow it. You should use appropriate titles when you greet your subjects and then give them the option of using a less formal tone.

Neutral Presentation—Maintain a neutral linguistic approach: do not use slang or sarcasm and avoid puns, idiomatic phrases, and ironic statements. Humor is subjective and culturally sensitive—what may be humorous to one person may be offensive to another. Therefore, it is safest to limit yourself to a formal style of interaction.

Individual Communication Styles—Try to adjust to your subjects' individual communication styles. Some people feel uncomfortable when there is silence; other people take their time and like to think about things before they answer.

In some social environments it is considered impolite to interrupt another person while they are talking, whereas other social environments promote more layered conversations. You should avoid interrupting or preempting a subject's response because you might miss some interesting information.

Tangents—Some people are prone to going off on tangents. You should devise a strategy to gently guide such a person back to the topic at hand. However, keep in mind that some tangents can provide important insights that you did not expect.

> **MAXIM**
>
> Be polite and courteous during interviews.

In other words, be sensitive to the constraints imposed on the interview by various physical, personal, and cultural factors. If you are pleasant, courteous, and polite, most people will respond positively.

People like to be helpful and generally like to share their knowledge. However, unless you establish a connection between what you are trying to do and your subject's personal interests, you will be seen as an annoyance.

Interviews

Interviews can take place away from the work place or they can be done during on-site observations. If they take place in the context of the work flow, people might be reminded of issues and concerns that occur intermittently and might otherwise be forgotten. However, on-site interviews run the risk of being interrupted by work-related matters.

Interviews are generally conducted face to face, although, if this is not possible, telephone interviews or even videoconferencing can be used. Interviews are powerful in that they can capture information that may not be included in other, more scripted methods like surveys and questionnaires.

Interviews can involve both open-ended and closed-ended questions. Open-ended questions allow people to express their opinions in their own words. The have a certain flexibility to discuss related issues that may not be directly addressed in the question. They can be used to explore issues and elicit rich information about complex topics

Closed-ended questions, on the other hand, are less flexible and allow less leeway for the participant to expand on his or her responses. They can generally be answered with a polar yes/no response or a simple description. A sample open-ended question is, "What kind of information would you look for on this site?" A sample closed-ended question is, "Would you look for contact information?"

Unstructured Interviews/Open-Ended Questions—Early in the design process interviews are generally loosely structured. They can help you to get a feel for the kind of activities people do and how they feel about the way in which things are currently done. These interviews generally use open-ended questions.

Structured Interviews/Closed-Ended Questions—As the design process proceeds, interviews can become more structured and focused on specific details and areas of the design. As the design begins to take shape in the form of wireframes and prototypes, you can move toward more highly directed interviews and questionnaires. These generally use more constrained closed-ended questions.

Predefined Scenarios—Even during loosely structured interviews, the interviewer can use predefined scenarios to stimulate conversation and gain insight into the way people view what they do on a daily basis.

For instance, if you were designing a new communication network, you might ask the person what he or she would do if he or she had to arrange a meeting with coworkers at different corporate offices. You might then ask why he or she used those methods as opposed to others. You would then get a sense of how he or she perceives the usefulness of tools like e-mail, instant messaging, and plain old telephony.

Focus of Interview—The information gathered by the interview will have to be processed and understood by the team. It is important that the purpose of the interview is clearly defined.

At the end of the interview it is important that you share your thoughts with the person you interviewed and document the interview as soon as possible. The 5W+H heuristic can supply a framework for the structure and documentation of the interview.

Wrap-Up—People are always curious about what others think, especially if they have been the subject of inquiry. It is important to share your thoughts about the results of the interview. This can lay the groundwork for follow-up interviews.

Sharing your thoughts after the interview can also help to avoid misunderstandings and misinterpretations about what you heard. Because you may want to interview the same person again, it is important that he or she trust you to get the message correct and feels confident that you will not misrepresent his or her opinions.

Advanced Organizers—The concept of advanced organizers can be helpful in setting the frame of the design process for the people you interview. Advance organizers are used to help people understand new concepts in terms of things with which they are already familiar. For instance, you can equate the discovery phase of the design process with going on vacation in a foreign country. This is something with which people probably have some familiarity.

People generally do not go to a foreign country without knowing anything about it; they would probably ask other people who have been there what it is like and what to expect. This idea can be related to the process of asking the people who are involved in the work what you should know about their domain so you can better plan for the new design.

The following are guidelines for interviews:

- Define the purpose of the interview in the context of the project, in terms of how the information will be used and how it helps the design team.
- Make a formal introduction and make it clear when the interview has ended.
- Explain what will happen and how long the process will take.
- Begin with comfortable questions such as the subject's interests and hobbies.
- Keep the questions to a minimum; long interviews can become tedious.
- Keep the questions simple; do not use multifaceted questions because they can be confusing and are hard to interpret afterward.
- Use the terminology with which the subject is familiar.
- Do not ask leading questions; they can bias the answers.

Focus Groups

Focus groups are small discussion groups composed of various stakeholders and a moderator from the design team. Focus groups allow people to share their opinions and concerns with other stakeholders. It can be educational for people to hear the views of others who are involved in different aspects of the work flow.

These groups can be oriented toward a discussion of the existing work flow, as well as of the new system's design. This may lead to new ideas about how to better organize the work flow that can be incorporated into the new design.

Moderator—Focus groups can be loosely structured or more strictly focused, but they always need a moderator to keep the discussion on track and prevent anyone from becoming overly assertive and imposing his or her views on the group.

Some degree of spontaneity should be allowed in the discussion so that new ideas can be explored and so group members feel that they are contributing and are not just engaged in a futile activity with a prescribed outcome.

As with all of these techniques, the facilitator must have clearly defined outcomes in mind before the start of the discussion and a plan for the kinds of discussion that provide the most information about the work flow or a proposed design.

The moderator should provide the group with an overview of the project and its projected benefits to the stakeholders. Giving people an overview of the project will provide them with a context in which to view the work involved in designing the system and may make them more cooperative and forthcoming during the session.

The advantages of focus groups include the following:

- They are relatively inexpensive and easy to set up.
- They can be used early in the design process to help to identify and prioritize features.
- They help you to gain insight into people's attitudes and motivations.

The disadvantages of focus groups include the following:

- They only represent the views of one particular group.
- They are not statistically significant.
- They do not provide information about usability.

Indirect Methods of Elicitation

Although direct methods of elicitation are very useful, there are times when indirect methods are preferable, such as when much useful information has already been documented by a company or there are fact files to which people refer when they do certain tasks.

People are sometimes more comfortable relating information anonymously than face to face. Questionnaires are useful for gathering information that people may be hesitant to communicate out loud. They may also give more honest answers if they are not influenced by an interviewer's facial expressions.

Let's look at some of the indirect ways to collect information from the various stakeholders.

Corporate Documentation—Information can be collected indirectly through corporate documents that reference policies and procedures. This can be an efficient way to gather a large amount of information quickly with relatively little time and expense.

Logs and Notes—Indirect methods can also include user participation; for instance, you can ask people to keep a log of specific activities, or you can collect the notes that they make to remind them of procedures and policies. These may take the form of sticky notes tacked onto a computer or reminders stuck on a corkboard.

Indirect methods can be combined with other, more direct methods. For instance, you might help a subject to fill out a questionnaire or ask him or her to respond verbally while he or she fills it out. You can find out very quickly what they think about your questions, which may help you to create a more effective questionnaire in the future. You should be careful, however, not to influence the subject's responses.

Questionnaires

Questionnaires are familiar to most people. They can include short answers, yes/no responses, multiple-choice questions, short-answer fill-ins, and/or comment areas. Like interviews, they can contain both closed- and open-ended questions.

Questionnaires can include the following:

- Mutually exclusive choices (radio buttons), e.g., yes/no, true/false
- Non–mutually exclusive choices (checkboxes)
- Ranges (overlapping, open-ended)
- Scales (Likert scales, semantic differential scales)
- Short-answer fill-ins
- Comments

Lets see what these elements entail.

Mutually Exclusive Choices—Mutually exclusive choices are "exclusive- or" (XOR) questions. They generally involve binary choices, like true/false and yes/no, or more descriptive choices, like male/female or full time/part time. On electronic forms, they are presented with radio buttons. They can be presented with checkboxes or as fill-ins with specific responses on paper forms.

Non-Mutually Exclusive Choices—Non–mutually exclusive choices involve multiple selections. They might include a list of hobbies, employment responsibilities, or anything that allows more than one option to be selected simultaneously from a group of options. Checkboxes are appropriate for this type of question.

Ranges—Some questions require people to select among a set of value ranges, for example, age groups, income levels, or years of experience. It is important that ranges do not overlap. It would be confusing if age range choices were presented as 20–30, 30–40, and 40–50, If you were exactly 30 or 40 years old, you would be in a quandary.

Ranges can also include some degree of open-endedness. If you need to know, for example, whether a person is older than 21 and younger than 65, you might present three ranges: 20 or younger, 21–64, and 65 or older.

Scales—You may want to find out how people feel about an issue based on a continuum of responses. For instance, you might want to know the level of user satisfaction with a particular interface. To gather this information you can present users with a scale that goes from *very satisfied* to *not satisfied*.

A number of different scales have been verified and tested. Likert scales, which are among the most commonly used, are appropriate for measuring levels of attitude or impressions and can provide effective measures of user satisfaction (Figure 4.3). It is important, however, to identify and define the scale clearly.

1 = Not Helpful, 5 = Very Helpful

How would you describe the Help files?   1   2   3   4   5

Figure 4.3 Likert scale.

The following are guidelines for defining scales:

- Identify the scale and the significance of the units (e.g., 1 = *not important*, 5 = *very important*).
- Use the most intuitive order (1 is less than 5, and therefore it is logical to choose the higher number to represent a greater degree of response).
- You can use positive or negative scales or a combination of the two, but try to make them appropriate to the question and make it clear which is which.
- Use odd numbers when you want to allow neutral responses.
- Use even numbers when you want to force a choice of positive or negative.
- Provide a not applicable (NA) response when appropriate.
- Do not use too many degrees within the scale; seven is considered a general limit.

Questionnaires have the advantage of capturing the thoughts of a large section of target users with relatively little expense. They will return copious data that must be filtered and processed, so it is important that questions be designed appropriately and tested on a small sample before they are sent out.

A simple test of the questionnaire can help to avoid some underlying problems that may not seem obvious to the designer of the questionnaire. For instance, there can be a mismatch between the implied answer to a question and the format supplied by the questionnaire. If you are asking an opinion about something, do not use a polar yes/no format; people may not have strong feelings about the topic and will be annoyed that they are forced to make a polar response. You should also make sure that the answers follow the way the question is phrased and make grammatical sense.

Advantages of questionnaires include the following:

- They do not involve face-to-face contact and can be administered remotely.
- They can be used to supply information for primary stakeholder profiles.
- They can be used to ascertain whether proposed solutions will meet with acceptance as well as to elicit new ideas.
- They can also be used to double-check the feedback obtained from one-on-one interviews.
- They can reach a large audience with relatively little expense.

Disadvantages of questionnaires include the following:

- Vague questions will return ambiguous responses that will serve no useful purpose for the design.

- People do not like to fill out long questionnaires.
- Closed-ended questions can restrict responses.
- Open-ended questions can be hard to quantify.

The following are guidelines for questionnaires:

- Be consistent.
- Phrase instructions clearly.
- Speak the user's language.
- Avoid jargon or technical terms.
- Order the questions beginning with the easy or less controversial ones.
- Use logical grouping.
- Avoid compound questions.
- Use appropriate form elements, for example, radio buttons, checkboxes, and so on.
- Use an appropriate scales for questions with discrete responses.
- Avoid overlapping ranges.
- Include a "None of the above" when appropriate.
- Be sensitive to the balance of positive and negative questions.

We have explored some of the activities and methods involved in data collection. Let's now look at various methods and tools for interpreting the data we have collected.

4.3. Interpretation

We have looked at ways to gather information and gain an understanding of the work flow that will be incorporated into the design. It is now necessary to understand how to organize this information so that it is useful during the design phase.

Interpretation is done during brainstorming sessions and team meetings, using various methods and tools. Different design frameworks involve specific tools; however, some general methods and procedures are common among most approaches.

The tools we will explore include the following:

- Task analysis
- Storyboarding
- Use cases
- Primary stakeholder profiles

4.3.1. Task Analysis

Task analysis is a way of documenting how people perform tasks. We can use task analysis to understand the data collected by observing and interviewing the people who are currently involved in the work flow. This method will help us to understand the processes, functions, objects, and people involved in the work and give us a structure and basis for determining requirements.

A task analysis includes all aspects of the work flow, those that are automated and those that are peripheral to the computerized system. It will help us to understand how the new system fits into the existing work flow and how it will be affected by external processes.

Task analysis at this stage of the design process takes a global view of people's activities and focuses on observable behaviors. It is used to explore the requirements of the proposed system and structure the results of the data collection phase. This is a different approach from the GOMS (goals, operators, methods, and selection rules) task models covered in Chapter 7.

The GOMS models incorporate internal processes, such as deciding between different methods of completing a task, and focus on existing design solutions. GOMS analyses are used toward the end of the design process, whereas task analysis is used at the beginning.

To understand a process, you will have to break it down into its constituent parts. This is similar to creating an algorithm for a computer program, in that it involves defining the steps necessary to go from point A to point B. The algorithms involved in task analysis, however, include factors that influence the flow of the process, such as the purpose of certain actions or the factors that determine when certain activities are done. These are not included in programming algorithms.

There are two ways to approach task analysis: task decomposition and hierarchical task analysis (HTA). These two methods are not mutually exclusive, and they can be used in conjunction to create a rich picture of the task being analyzed. Task decomposition is a bottom-up approach that can be used to create the top-down hierarchical task models.

Task Decomposition

Task decomposition is a linear description of a process that captures the elements involved as well as the prevailing environmental factors. The various processes that need to be modeled will have been identified during the data collection activities. You will have notes on various activities and associated information, such as when, where, why, how, and by whom they are done. This information will be used to complete the task decomposition.

Begin by identifying the process that will be documented. Next, make a list or table that describes the steps involved. You can use many different methods to document the process, but you must include as much information as you can in order to identify the requirements, sequences, and dependences among the individual steps.

Include the following in the task decomposition:

- The reasons for the actions
- The people who perform the actions
- The objects or information required to complete the actions

The important thing is to try to create a picture of the process segmented by the steps involved and to capture the dependences among steps.

Task decompositions should try to capture the following:

- The flow of information
- Use of artifacts
- Sequence of actions and dependences
- Environmental conditions
- Cultural constraints

Let's look at a task decomposition of the processes involved in scheduling a team meeting. Let's assume that we have collected the information we need using the various information collection techniques mentioned earlier. For this example, we will assume that our knowledge of the process is complete.

The task decomposition of the "schedule a meeting" task is as follows:

Goal—This defines the top-level goal for the analysis.

- Schedule a team meeting.

Plans—These describe the order and conditions required to proceed with subtasks.

- Reserve the conference room and audiovisual equipment based on the team members' available dates and times.

Information—This includes all of the information you need to schedule the meeting.

- Team member contact information.
- Conference room schedule.
- Audiovisual equipment use procedures.

Objects—These include all of the physical objects you will use to find the information.

- Conference room calendar.
- Team address book.
- Audiovisual sign-up sheet.

Methods—These are the various ways you can contact the team members.

- E-mail (preferred method).
- Instant messaging.

- Face-to-face communication.
- Phone.
- Notes.

Objectives—These are the subgoals

- Contact team members.
- Confirm responses.
- Coordinate schedules.
- Schedule conference room.
- Schedule audiovisual equipment.
- Confirm team member attendance.

Procedures—These are the triggers that may initiate contingency activities.

- Coordinate team schedules.
- Check conference room schedule.
- Check audiovisual sign-up sheet.

Contingencies—These will describe what you need to do if one of your methods does not work.

- Check e-mail replies.
- Monitor team members' online presence to confirm using instant messaging.
- Speak directly to team members in close proximity.
- Phone members in other locations.
- Leave a note on a team member's desk.

Hierarchical Task Analysis

Once you have a fairly detailed description of the process, you can begin to create a hierarchical flowchart of the various steps involved. HTA provides a top-down, structured approach to documenting processes.

You can create an HTA from scratch, but it will be easier if you have already decomposed the process and listed all of the various elements and factors involved. Because HTAs should be focused on specific tasks, you may end up creating separate charts for subtasks described in the task decomposition.

Start with a specific goal and then add the tasks or subgoals required to achieve that goal. These should be diagrammed using normal flowchart symbols and flow lines indicating a path through the diagram. Add as much detail as necessary to fully capture all of the factors and conditions involved in the process.

Once the diagram is complete, walk through it to check for completeness. You may find that certain steps have been inadvertently omitted; if so, you can add them where they belong.

Separate charts can be linked so that a complete picture of the work flow is available to the design team and can be used to create a complete list of design requirements as well as to check the validity of the requirement list once it has been created.

An HTA is read as follows:

- A box on top of another box describes what we want to do (subgoal).
- The box below another box describes how it is done.
- Plans control the flow between subgoals.

Figure 4.4 shows the first part of an HTA of the "schedule a meeting" task.

Looking at this HTA, we see that the "Contact team members" box describes what we need to do, and the box below it says that we are to accomplish this subgoal by sending a group e-mail.

Contact Team Members—This subgoal involves sending out an e-mail asking each team member to supply a list of available times. The coordinator needs to consult the team address book.

Confirm Responses—This subgoal involves making sure that everyone has responded and supplied a list of available dates. There are a few contingencies available to the coordinator if any team member does not respond to the e-mail.

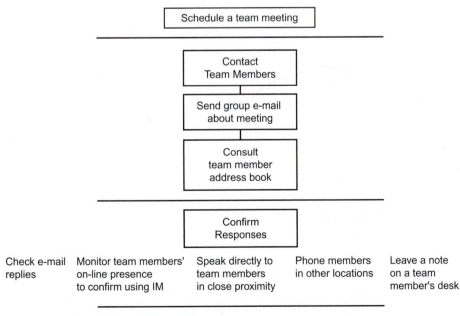

Figure 4.4   First part of the HTA of the "schedule a team meeting" task.

IM, instant messaging.

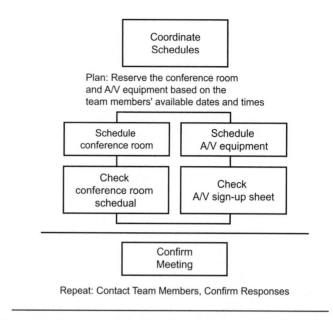

Figure 4.5 Second part of the HTA of the "schedule a team meeting" task.

A/V, audiovisual.

Coordinate Schedules—Once the responses have been coordinated and a list of available dates has been established, the coordinator must reserve the room and equipment (Figure 4.5).

The parallel activities involved in scheduling the conference room and reserving the audiovisual equipment can happen in any order; however, the schedule task logically comes before the check task. The list of team member availability is used to choose appropriate dates.

Once the room and equipment have been reserved, the coordinator must confirm the date with the team, which leads to a repetition of the contact team members and the confirm responses subgoals.

4.3.2. Storyboarding

Another method often used during interpretation is the storyboard technique. Storyboarding involves using a series of pictures that describes a particular process or work flow, similar to the storyboards used to plan a film. Storyboards take the form of a rough scenario that tells a story, and they can be explored at any point to determine the dynamics and objects involved.

Storyboards can be used to study existing work flows or generate requirements. They can facilitate the process of task decomposition and are an effective way to brainstorm alternative ways of completing tasks.

4.3.3. Use Cases

Use cases represent a formal, structured approach to interpreting work flows and processes. They are designed to describe a particular goal and explore the interaction between users and the actual system components. Use cases were proposed by Jacobson et al. in 1992 and have since become incorporated into the Unified Modeling Language (UML) standard.

Use cases have been used in software engineering and enterprise-wide projects. They are also becoming more popular in the interaction design discipline and can be used to clarify the scope of a project as well as to identify the various stakeholders.

Use cases can interpret the data acquired during collection activities as well as to validate proposed designs according to requirements gathered during the discovery phase. Thus, they span the discovery and design phases.

The two main components of use cases are the actors and the use cases that represent their goals and tasks.

Actors—The first step in creating a use case is to identify the actors, which can be anything that has contact with or is affected by the proposed system. Actors are similar to stakeholders, but can also include other systems, networks, or software that interacts with the proposed system.

Use Cases—Each actor has a unique use case, which involves a task or goal the actor is engaged in. Use cases generally do not describe long-term use, but rather discrete goals that are accomplished in a short time period. They must be created for all the identified actors.

The object of a use case is to describe the various ways the system will be used and cover all of the potential functionality being built into the design. Use cases should be clearly defined and documented.

The actors and use cases define the boundaries of the system: the actors define what is outside the system, and the use cases define what is inside the system. You will design everything inside the use case, you will not design the actors.

Let's look at some actor and use case descriptions for the "schedule a meeting" task described earlier.

Schedule-a-meeting actor descriptions:

- **Coordinator**—The person who schedules the meeting.
- **Conference Room**—The room where the meeting will be held.
- **Audiovisual (A/V) Equipment**—The equipment required for the meeting (projector, etc.).
- **Team Members**—The members of the team.

Schedule-a-meeting use case descriptions:

- **Request Room**—The coordinator checks to see whether the room is available and schedules a data and time.

- **Request A/V Equipment**—The coordinator checks to see whether the equipment is available and then reserves the equipment
- **Contact Team Members**—The coordinator informs the team about the time and location of the meeting.

The information in the actor and use case descriptions is then diagrammed as shown in Figure 4.6.

If a use case becomes too complex, it should probably be segmented into separate use cases that define discrete components of the larger use case. These can later be connected using package symbols to represent each individual use case.

Actors and use cases form the basic structure of the design, but they are insufficient to capture all of the dynamic aspects of the process being described. Use cases can include looping and branching activities, as well as conditional structures. You need to document prerequisite conditions for, as well as the outcomes of, the completed use case.

A few statements are also needed to guide the activities that occur during the life of the use case. These may include initiation and termination conditions and can be included along with the use case.

Many possible circumstances may be associated with one use case, including error conditions and alternative activities. There are generally a few different paths

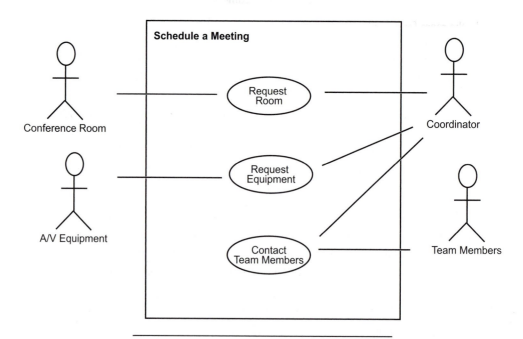

Figure 4.6 Use case diagram of "schedule a meeting" process.

through the use case. We now look at the basic path, the alternate paths, and their scenarios.

Basic Path—The primary path through the use case is the one that is completed without any diversions from error conditions or extenuating circumstances. This is called the main or basic path. It is an error-free path that accomplishes a predetermined goal and does not include any conditional statements.

Alternate Path—Alternate paths capture the various possible branches not captured in the basic path, such as premature termination of a process or the choosing of a different method to accomplishing the same task. These test the exception-handling capabilities of the system. Alternative paths also include possible error conditions, which are used to make sure that the system can recover from such situations.

Scenarios—Each unique path through the use case is called a scenario. Scenarios represent discrete instances that combine to create the complete use case. They are the lowest level of the use case and should cover all conceivable paths and alternatives. It is not possible to arrive at all of the possible scenarios at the beginning of the process, so additional ones may be created as the design evolves.

New scenarios may also require new actors, in which case they should be added to the complete use case. Previous scenarios must then be checked to see whether they are affected by the presence of the new actor.

Let's look at some possible scenarios for the "schedule a meeting" use case:

- The coordinator books the room for a particular date and time, the equipment is available, it is reserved, the team members are informed, and the team members confirm that they can attend by replying to the e-mail.
- The coordinator books the room but the equipment is not available.
- The coordinator reserves the room and the equipment, but team members do not reply to the e-mail.

These different scenarios are then documented in a flow-of-events chart. This is similar to the HTA in that it describes, step by step, the different paths through the use case. Any loops in the process are noted, as well as any pre-conditions, post-conditions, special requirements, and alternative paths.

Flow of events:

1. The coordinator checks the address book and sends a group e-mail.
2. The coordinator checks the e-mail responses.
3. If there is no response, the coordinator uses an alternate method of verification:

   - Monitor team members' online presence to confirm using instant messaging.
   - Speak directly to team members in close proximity.
   - Phone members in other locations.
   - Leave a note on a team member's desk.

4. The coordinator creates a list of available times.

5. The coordinator checks the conference room schedule and reserves the room.

6. The coordinator checks the A/V equipment sign-up sheet and reserves the equipment.

7. If the equipment is not available, the coordinator goes back and alters the room request according to the equipment availability (loop from step 5).

End loop

When we examine this flow of events, we see that the use case descriptions for request room, request equipment, and contact members are broken down into their elements, such as the room schedule, A/V sign-up sheet, and team address book, and that we have arrived at the same level of granularity as the HTA.

It is also clear from the "schedule a meeting" use case that there is an opportunity to make this process easier if we design a solution that combines these descriptions. This may take the form of an online database of team member, conference room, and equipment schedules that could be accessed and queried to determine coinciding dates and times. The design might also have the ability automatically to send e-mail notifications to all team members after the dates are reserved.

At this point, you can begin to see how the conceptual design that begins the design phase is rooted in interpretation activities, and how the artifacts we create during discovery can be used to initiate the conceptual design activities.

Use cases have been incorporated into the UML standard and are often used in interaction design projects. A thorough discussion of the topic is beyond the scope of this book. Readers are encouraged to supplement this brief discussion with other sources that focus specifically on the topic of use cases.

4.3.4. Primary Stakeholder Profiles

User-centered design puts a premium on the user's role in the design process. We have looked at the different types of stakeholders that may be involved in the proposed design. We now explore the primary stakeholder in more depth. This is where our efforts and energies have the most direct impact on the effectiveness and efficiency of the design.

A number of factors influence the way people use computers, and much data can be collected about the primary stakeholder. To apply structure to this process, we will explore these determinants using a "card file"-form framework based on constructs that group related issues, such as social and technical environments or individual skills and experience.

The constructs chosen and the topics included in each are presented as a framework that can be used and modified to better reflect the nature of each individual design project. This is intended as an organizational tool for clarifying the scope and components of a particular design process.

The constructs covered include the following:

- Context of use
- Cognitive ability
- Physical ability
- Individual profile

This process is essentially a way to codify the 5W+H heuristic and apply it to the design process in a structured manner.

Context of Use

Computers are not used in isolation; they are embedded in a context that affects their operation and the way people interact with them. The context-of-use construct covers aspects of where, how, and why computers are used. It places the proposed system within a detailed context that reveals certain requirements essential to the success of the design.

MOTIVATION: Discretionary/Mandatory

One of the things we need to know about context of use is what motivates people to use computers in their work. Are they required to use a particular system or application, or do they use it voluntarily? A user's attitude toward a program and his or her patience with the interface may be affected by whether he or she is required to use a particular program or can choose which one to use.

If a user's job depends on accomplishing a particular task, his or her investment in the outcome of his or her actions will increase. He or she may be more likely to persist at difficult interactions and, therefore, be more likely to become frustrated. Because mandatory users are usually engaged in work-related activities, this frustration may result in a decrease in productivity or efficiency.

Discretionary users are those who do not require the use of a computer but use them either just because they want to or because they see some advantage to them. Discretionary users may avoid annoying interactions by simply not using a particular software package or by purchasing a competitor's package. Discretionary users often judge a system based on effort versus perceived gain.

Users who see some advantage to computers will be more motivated than users who must use them for work-related activities. Highly motivated users will probably spend more time and energy learning complex software applications, whether for work-related activities or entertainment.

Needlessly complex interfaces can reduce a user's motivation and deter him or her from exploring some of the more powerful features of the application.

FREQUENCY OF USE: Nonuser/Infrequent/Frequent

One of the more important factors involved in the mastery of human–computer interaction is the amount of time a person spends using a particular system or application.

Frequent users acquire experience and knowledge about the applications and operating system they use on a daily basis. Much of that knowledge can also be generalized and applied to other applications. This enables the frequent user to manage many tasks that are beyond the ability of less experienced users.

Although some people may use one set of applications frequently, they may only use a fraction of the functionality that the applications have to offer. These users may have large gaps in their knowledge of computers and may not be able to function adequately outside of their normal computing environment.

User Category: Beginner, Intermediate, Expert

The concept of an expert user is debatable. Computer-based interaction is such a vast and complex domain that it is unlikely that anyone can attain mastery over more than a few areas of particular computing environments.

The so-called expert user may be well versed on a particular graphics application but may have no idea how to use a computer-assisted design (CAD) application.

Given the increased level of industry-wide standardization of software practices, the so-called expert user will be able to generalize some aspects of his or her knowledge and climb the learning curve more quickly than less experienced users, but he or she will start at the bottom just like everyone else.

There are a few other terms that are used to identify a user's level of proficiency:

Beginner—Naive

Intermediate—Computer literate

Expert—Power user

These categories are not discrete, nor are they fixed. Users may fall into any category depending on the specific situation and program they are using. They may even have expert knowledge of one area of a program and virtually no knowledge of other areas.

For instance, Adobe PhotoShop®, now the industry standard in graphic manipulation and creation, is used by professional and amateur photographers, Web designers, school children, professional layout designers, and many others. Particular aspects of PhotoShop relate to pre-press issues, for example, and professional Web designers may have no knowledge of this and will therefore not know how to use those features. As another example, many aspects of Microsoft's Office® suite are beyond the knowledge of many information technology professionals.

Given enough time and significant motivation, the so-called expert users will be able to figure out most of a program's features, but until they do, they are still beginners in those areas. Overlapping continuums and relative scales define each user's abilities and knowledge. Users migrate from one level to another depending on the amount of time they spend using a particular software application. An expert user may need to refresh his or her knowledge if he or she stops using an application for a period of time.

Version updates that diverge significantly from previous versions may also cause problems. This is generally true for complete version updates—for example, from version 1 to version 2; smaller-scale updates do not drastically alter the interaction and are given .1 indications, for example, version 1.2 or 1.4.

Updates can drastically alter the interface by rearranging menus and options and placing functionality in different locations. This is generally done to improve the quality of the user's experience; however, this can have an unsettling effect on users who have spent a great deal of time with previous versions and must use the program for work-related activities.

It is frustrating to be made to feel like a beginner when you have already invested time and effort on a particular program. Designers must invest the utmost care in getting it right the first time so that users do not have to relearn an interface later.

TASK NATURE: Mission Critical/Calm

Computers are becoming ubiquitous, permeating many aspects of our daily lives. They can be found in domains as diverse as air traffic control and cell phones. This places a greater emphasis on the need to understand the tasks that the computer will perform.

Mission-critical domains like aviation or medicine are error intolerant. Surgeons must be absolutely sure about the meaning of computer-based interaction because any ambiguities may have life-threatening consequences.

Many different types of errors can occur, such as the following:

- Interpretation errors due to confusing presentation
- Input errors due to ambiguities in labeling
- Output errors due to incorrect input data
- Errors of omission due to incomplete data input

These errors also have consequences for noncritical ("calm") tasks, such as word processing or spreadsheet calculations. If a person must use a difficult interface over long periods of time, or if his or her computer use is job related, these errors can be annoying and detrimental to job performance and may have significant employment ramifications.

INTERACTION MODE: Direct/Indirect, Continuous/Intermittent

Mainframe computing was originally based on an indirect interaction between the user and the system. Many computing tasks were batch processed and did not require any user interaction. Personal computing introduced a drastically different paradigm—direct manipulation.

Although mainframe computing is not currently the dominant computing paradigm, many evolving paradigms use indirect interaction. Ubiquitous computing, transparent computing, and distributed computing are just a few of the emerging computing paradigms that involve indirect interaction.

Some users work in highly focused environments; they have a dedicated space for their system and do not experience interruptions. Other users work in busy environments and may have to interrupt computer use to see to other activities or to interact with colleagues or customers. It is important in these intermittent situations that the user can take up where he or she left off without difficulty while he or she switches back and forth between the computer interface and the surrounding world.

SOCIAL ENVIRONMENT: Public/Personal, Collaborative/Individual, Work/ Entertainment, Synchronous/Asynchronous

As computers become mobile and ubiquitous, research on their impact on social interaction is becoming more significant. There are innumerable situations that involve the use of computers; some are public, such as ticket-dispensing machines, and others are personal, such as PDAs. The social environment in which computers are used imposes constraints on their design.

The "social environment" construct helps to identify many of these constraints and focuses the design on the user's real-life situation. According to the Distributed Systems Online (DSO) group of the Institute of Electrical and Electronics Engineers (IEEE), computer-supported cooperative work (CSCW) is "the discipline that deals with using computers to support groups of people as they cooperate to achieve their goals" (DSO, IEEE). There are many "groupware" packages available for use in CSCW environments. These are basically software packages that are designed to function on a network and support group activities.

Some tasks require synchronous communication and others lend themselves to a less immediate, asynchronous format. For instance, the asynchronous nature of e-mail may be appropriate for scheduling meetings in advance, but it is not appropriate for last minute modifications to a document before an impending deadline.

Many projects and activities involve both synchronous and asynchronous communications at different points in time; the proposed design must account for any information flow requirements and provide the necessary means for that communication.

PHYSICAL ENVIRONMENT: Indoor/Outdoor, Auditory (Noise) Low/High, Visual (Quality) Poor/Good, Haptic (Movement) Constrained/Free

Some computing situations allow for a great deal of control over the physical computing environment. Indoor locations can be adjusted in terms of lighting, noise levels, and physical constraints. Outdoor environments pose greater difficulties related to the variability of the available light, auditory intrusions, and physical obstacles.

Outdoor environments may require special screen specifications and augmentative auditory peripherals, such as earphones or speakers. Environmental conditions such as humidity and wind may have to be factored into the design. Mobile computing poses many challenges that do not affect desktop computing systems.

Intranet	Extranet		Internet
PAN	LAN	MAN	WAN

Figure 4.7 Network scope.

LAN, local area network; MAN, metropolitan area network; PAN, personal area network;
WAN, wide area network.

TECHNICAL ENVIRONMENT: Networked/Isolated, Wired/Wireless, Fixed/Mobile, Peripherals/Contained, Network Scope

The technical environment describes the computing environment from a high-level perspective. It serves as a reference for the final technical specifications that detail the type of hardware to be used (Figure 4.7).

The "technical environment" construct helps to identify high-level concerns, such as security, privacy, maintenance (both hardware and software, available resources, system interoperability, financial impact, range and scope of the system—who can participate in and who is affected by the system), and other areas of concern that need to be included in the design. The "context of use" construct includes (but is not necessarily limited to) the areas of concern shown in Figure 4.8.

A typical "context of use" construct for this description resembles a common office desktop system and can be described as shown in Figure 4.9.

On the other hand, an expert user working in a mission-critical environment under adverse environmental conditions may need a more individualized custom interface and software tools with higher levels of security, accuracy, and privacy controls.

Explanatory Document

Included with the "context of use" construct should be an explanatory document that describes the areas in more detail, explaining the rationale and the ramifications for design. For instance, a design geared toward a mandatory and frequently used system by an intermediate-level user who interacts directly with the system in a non-critical yet work-related capacity may lean toward an "off-the-shelf" solution that is based on a common GUI platform and a suite of commercial productivity tools.

The "context of use" construct can serve to guide the design process in developing an understanding of the scope and characteristics of the proposed design, but it will not adequately substitute for a detailed specification of the final system. Such a specification, however, can use some aspects of the construct, such as the technical environment, as a table of contents.

The construct serves as a "jumping-off point"; the final specifications require many iterative cycles and user testing before any technical considerations can be finalized. This is the heart of the UCD philosophy—design for and from the user.

Context of Use

Motivation
- [ ] Discretionary
- [ ] Mandatory

Frequency of Use
- [ ] Non-User
- [ ] Infrequent
- [ ] Frequent

User Category
- [ ] Beginner
- [ ] Intermediate
- [ ] Expert

Task Nature
- [ ] Mission Critical
- [ ] Calm

Interaction Mode
- [ ] Direct
- [ ] Indirect

- [ ] Continuous
- [ ] Intermittent

Social Environment
- [ ] Public
- [ ] Personal

- [ ] Colaborative
- [ ] Individual

- [ ] Work
- [ ] Entertainment

- [ ] Synchronous
- [ ] Asynchronous

Physical Environment
- [ ] Indoor
- [ ] Outdoor

Auditory (Noise Level)
1 = Low   5 = High
1   2   3   4   5

Visual Quality
1 = Poor   5 = Good
1   2   3   4   5

Haptic
- [ ] Constrained
- [ ] Free

Technical Environment
- [ ] Networked
- [ ] Isolated

- [ ] Wired
- [ ] Wireless

- [ ] Intranet
- [ ] Extranet
- [ ] Internet

- [ ] PAN
- [ ] LAN
- [ ] MAN
- [ ] WAN

- [ ] Fixed
- [ ] Mobile

- [ ] Peripherals
- [ ] Contained

Figure 4.8 "Context of use" profile.

LAN, local area network; MAN, metropolitan area network; PAN, personal area network; WAN, wide area network.

Cognitive Ability

A user's cognitive abilities affect the success of a particular design. There are situations in which the cognitive abilities of the target user are very specific, for instance, educational software geared for a specific grade level and topic such as math or spelling. In other situations, the designer must accommodate a wide spectrum of cognitive abilities, as in Web site design (Figure 4.10).

EDUCATIONAL LEVEL: Preschool to Doctoral Degree (Reading Grade Level)

The user's educational level will be an indicator of his or her reading ability. This may affect an interface's text and help facilities. Educational levels may be addressed on a scale from preschool to doctoral degree, or they may be defined by

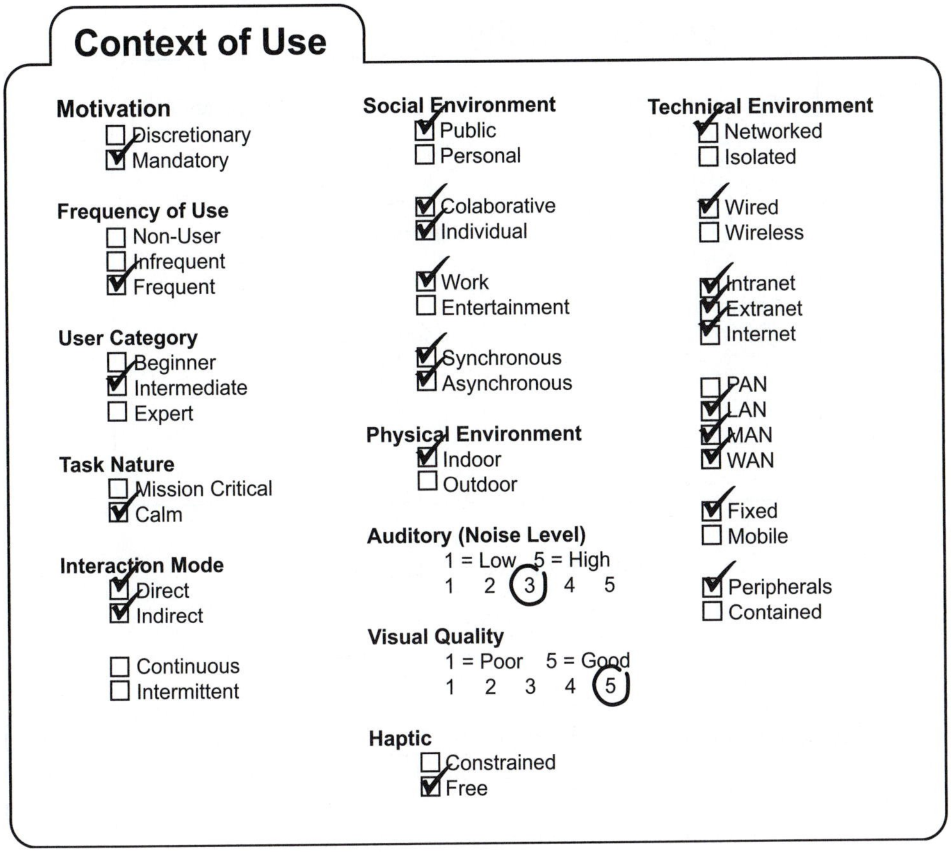

Context of Use

Motivation
- ☐ Discretionary
- ☑ Mandatory

Frequency of Use
- ☐ Non-User
- ☐ Infrequent
- ☑ Frequent

User Category
- ☐ Beginner
- ☑ Intermediate
- ☐ Expert

Task Nature
- ☐ Mission Critical
- ☑ Calm

Interaction Mode
- ☑ Direct
- ☑ Indirect

- ☐ Continuous
- ☐ Intermittent

Social Environment
- ☑ Public
- ☐ Personal

- ☑ Colaborative
- ☑ Individual

- ☑ Work
- ☐ Entertainment

- ☑ Synchronous
- ☑ Asynchronous

Physical Environment
- ☑ Indoor
- ☐ Outdoor

Auditory (Noise Level)
1 = Low   5 = High
1   2   ③   4   5

Visual Quality
1 = Poor   5 = Good
1   2   3   4   ⑤

Haptic
- ☐ Constrained
- ☑ Free

Technical Environment
- ☑ Networked
- ☐ Isolated

- ☑ Wired
- ☐ Wireless

- ☑ Intranet
- ☑ Extranet
- ☑ Internet

- ☐ PAN
- ☑ LAN
- ☑ MAN
- ☑ WAN

- ☑ Fixed
- ☐ Mobile

- ☑ Peripherals
- ☐ Contained

Figure 4.9 **"Context of use" profile: example.**

LAN, local area network; MAN, metropolitan area network; PAN, personal area network;
WAN, wide area network.

reading level, for example, eighth grade. This can be indicated by using precise delineations or with ranges such as 1–6. In the foregoing example educational level is delineated by school level. This is geared toward evaluating a user's intellectual sophistication in terms of his or her being able to comprehend content.

There has recently been an increased focus on users with disabilities, including cognitive disabilities. Section 508 of the Rehabilitation Act specifies the need to consider cognitive disabilities in the design of software-based information applications. This concern can be included in the discussion of the educational level of the targeted user of the proposed design.

Computer Literacy—Computer literacy is often a significant concern for interaction design. One of the more difficult tasks in design is addressing the needs

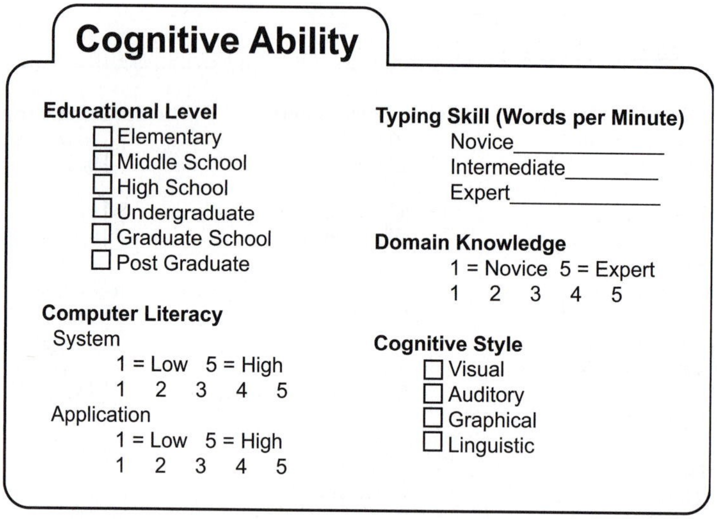

Cognitive Ability

Educational Level
☐ Elementary
☐ Middle School
☐ High School
☐ Undergraduate
☐ Graduate School
☐ Post Graduate

Computer Literacy
System
   1 = Low 5 = High
   1   2   3   4   5
Application
   1 = Low 5 = High
   1   2   3   4   5

Typing Skill (Words per Minute)
Novice_____
Intermediate_____
Expert_____

Domain Knowledge
   1 = Novice 5 = Expert
   1   2   3   4   5

Cognitive Style
☐ Visual
☐ Auditory
☐ Graphical
☐ Linguistic

Figure 4.10 Cognitive ability profile.

of the user who is less computer literate as well as the needs of the user who is an expert. A design will be more successful for both categories of users if the design team has a clear idea of the different levels of computer literacy of the user population.

TYPING SKILL: Novice to Expert (Words per Minute)

Contemporary GUIs may be visually oriented; however, typing is still a common interaction mode. Typing skills may also coincide with task descriptions; for instance, a user who does a great deal of word processing during his or her normal work-related activities will generally have good typing skills.

This cannot be inferred for a casual user who plays digital games or for a professional graphic designer. Although casual users may have advanced typing skills, it is not safe to make this assumption. Typing skills can be empirically ascertained using measurements of words per minute.

Experienced typists may gravitate to keyboard methods, whereas graphics-oriented users may gravitate to mouse methods. Shneiderman and Plaisant (2005) suggest that users involved in typing activities may prefer keyboard methods in order to stay in the linguistic mode, whereas users involved in graphical activities may prefer to use the mouse-oriented aspects of the interface.

For most projects a basic self-reported estimate of typing speed is sufficient. Generally typists can be classified as novice, intermediate, and expert using a range of 40–90 words per minute for the intermediate typist. However, typing accuracy may be a significant issue, and type of typing task may also be relevant to the project, in which case a thorough typing test would be required to determine the skills of the proposed user base.

DOMAIN KNOWLEDGE: Novice to Expert

It is important to understand the level of domain knowledge the target user possesses. Professional users generally use computers to accomplish tasks about which they have extensive knowledge. Measurement criteria for this aspect may vary with domain.

> **MAXIM**
>
> Domain expertise may not correlate with computer literacy.

Such users may not have high levels of computer literacy, but they know their field. Other users of the same software may be just learning about the domain but may have high levels of computer literacy. This is obviously a complex situation that can involve a multitiered solution to the interface design. The design must support the domain expert in terms of functionality and at the same time be easy to use and not draw attention to itself.

If the targeted user definition is restricted to the domain expert, the domain language must reflect this high level of expertise. However, it is important to remember that domain knowledge does not necessarily correlate with computer literacy.

COGNITIVE STYLE: Visual/Auditory, Graphical/Linguistic

Some people prefer to use maps; others prefer written-out directions. Some people can remember a name after hearing it once; others need to see it in writing. Some people have an ability to visualize how a room would look with new furniture or a new color of paint; others cannot. Some people need to see a picture but may still have trouble imagining how the room would look. "Some people are better at verbal thinking, working more effectively with words and equations. Others are better at spatial reasoning—manipulating symbols, and images" (Galitz, 2002, 1).

In short, we all have different ways of dealing with the world. Some of us are visual learners, whereas others gravitate to auditory methods. Self-reporting methods are generally the most economically feasible for many development projects; however, empirical testing can be done to distinguish a user's cognitive style.

The way people think about problems ranges from the analytical to the intuitive. People develop individualized methods of processing information, and it is not always possible to determine how a group of people will react to certain stimuli. It is important, therefore, to use multiple channels of communication, especially if the intended audience is large and diverse.

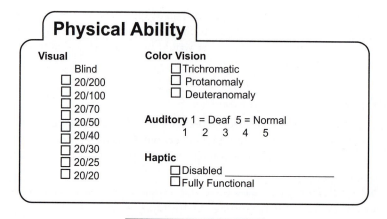

Figure 4.11   Physical ability profile.

Physical Ability

Users' physical abilities may play a large role in interaction design. The human condition includes wide ranges of abilities in all of the senses, of which the visual, auditory, and haptic senses are the most relevant for computer interface design (Figure 4.11).

Guidelines for computer systems related to human physical abilities can be found in Section 508 of the Rehabilitation Act and the Web Content Accessibility Guidelines 1.0 (W3C Recommendation 5 May 1999) published by the W3C's Web Accessibility Initiative (WAI).

VISUAL: Blind to 20/20 Vision

There is a wide spectrum of visual ability, stretching from blindness to 20/20 vision. Strides have been made in the development of screen readers for the visually handicapped; however, there is much work to be done. Interaction designers must be familiar with the state of these tools so that the interfaces they design can be fully accessed with these evolving technologies.

As with other human perceptual systems, human acuity decreases with age and is affected by many factors, from emotional states to environmental conditions. Each project is affected differently by the user's visual abilities; some are more sensitive and thus require more specific information, whereas many projects do not need such specific and detailed reports. Results of normal vision tests (Snellen tests) can be used to measure the user's visual abilities. For many projects the specificity built into the form in Figure 4.11 may not be necessary; a simple Likert scale would probably suffice. There may be times, however, when you need more accurately to calculate issues such as font size and screen distance, so this type of specificity may be necessary.

COLOR VISION: Trichromatic, Protanopic, Deuteranopic

Most people have what is considered trichromatic or normal color vision. However, color perception deficiencies affect about 8% of the male and 4% of the female population in the United States. The most common form is a reduced sensitivity to green, known as deuteranomaly. This condition affects about 5% of male individuals, and accounts for the majority of color deficiencies in female individuals, about 95% (http://www.iamcal.com/toys/colors/).

AUDITORY: Deaf to Normal

Auditory ability declines with age. Table 4.1 shows the generally accepted auditory comfort levels for speech as a function of age.

Hearing tests are documented using various graphic techniques that are very specific and detailed regarding frequencies and decibels; unless the project under development involves extensive auditory feedback, simple self-reporting of hearing ability on a Likert scale is sufficient.

HAPTIC: Disabled, Fully Functional

People with haptic or motion constraints can find many common computer-related activities to be extremely difficult and frustrating. On the other hand, computers can enable severely disabled people to perform tasks that would otherwise be impossible.

Table 4.1   Comfort Level for Speech

Age (years)	→ ←	Sound Level (dB)
15		54
25		57
35		61
45		65
55		69
65	→ ←	74
75		79
85		85

Computer-based augmentative technologies have improved the lives of many disabled people, and this area of research is growing and evolving. However, interaction designers must also consider the user's haptic abilities in the design of general-purpose systems. For instance, typing, touchscreen, and mouse operations assume a certain level of fine motor coordination that may be difficult for very young or older users. Self-reporting of any physical disability will usually be a sufficient measure of physical ability; some additional information regarding the user's difficulty may be required, such as the particular nature of the disability.

Individual Profile

The constructs we have seen so far deal with general issues that affect most users as a group. There are situations, however, in which more personal user information is required for a particular design (Figure 4.12). For instance, some software is targeted to a specific age group and gender, such as action games that are designed for young male users.

Users' occupations may be an important consideration, and their hobbies and interests may have an impact on interface design. Other factors such as country and region may affect some visual aspects.

The user's language can have a significant impact on his or her experience of an interface, especially if directional issues are involved. There may also be times when the user's religion, ethnicity, or socioeconomic circumstances need to be explored in order to avoid offensive visual or textual content.

The way in which you categorize user age may depend on the particular project you are working on. For instance, if you are developing educational software, you may need to specify age by grade level. If you are developing an interactive toy, you may want to specify age in ranges such as 1–4 years or 6–10 years old. The

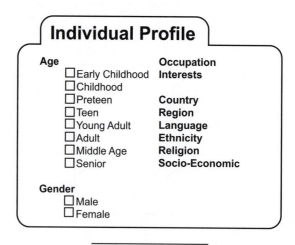

Figure 4.12 Individual profile.

earlier example uses developmental delineations to give general indications that may be suitable for game development; for example, a digital game design may identify a particular user base as young adult, male. Similarly, a fashion-oriented Web site may be oriented toward the female preteen.

4.4. Documentation

We now begin the process of collating the various documents created during the discovery phase and creating the requirements and guideline documentation. This will give us an explicit basis on which to begin our team discussions of possible solutions. This documentation will help to avoid any misunderstandings or misconceptions among team members and will serve as a resource on which to base future discussions and decisions.

During collection and interpretation activities, many documents are created. Working documents to structure interviews and focus groups, documents to capture the results of the observations and interviews, questionnaires, and brainstorming documents are all created. These documents are maintained during the project but are not disseminated. Documents such as the use case diagrams and stakeholder profiles, however, are disseminated for internal team purposes.

The results of the discovery phase are recorded in the following working documents:

- Use case diagrams
- Primary stakeholder profiles

Other documents are created for dissemination to the various stakeholders and clients; these include the formal mission statement, requirements, and project management documents.

The results of the discovery phase are recorded in the following published documents:

- Mission statement
- Requirements document
- Project management document
- Usability guidelines

4.4.4. Mission Statement

The mission statement includes the following:

- Project goals
- Project scope

Project Goals—What is the value proposition? What needs will the new system address, and how will it address them?

The project goals describe the way in which the design will add value to the company. This is the highest level of the design project. The project goals describe how the new system will increase worker effectiveness and/or efficiency. All of the project management decisions are based on the project goals. This helps to prioritize team resources so that the most effort will be spent on the components that directly address the overarching goals of the project.

Project Scope—What does the proposed design include or exclude? What are the external constraints such as time and finances? How will you decide when it satisfies the design proposal?

It is important to clearly define the parameters of the project and make sure that everyone understands what the system will do and what it will not do. There must be clearly defined goals with explicitly defined criteria for goal satisfaction. These goals and criteria must be documented in a way that is explicit and unambiguous.

All too often, projects experience something called "feature creep." This happens when something that was not defined in the early stages is suggested later. There are times when the structure is constructed in such as way that it can incorporate new functionality without affecting the overall design, but there are also times when an additional function creates ambiguities and complications that diminish the design's efficiency.

For instance, Web navigation is often based on a tiered structure with global and local navigational links. Incorporating additional layers or cross-referencing between layers later may create inconsistencies in the navigational design and make it more difficult for the visitor to create a mental model of the information space represented by the Web site.

A clearly defined scope statement or mission statement can help to keep everyone on the same page and avoid potential conflicts with the client. The scope should also include clearly defined criteria for project completion, otherwise it may be difficult to come to an agreement as to what constitutes a completed project.

The scope of the project can be determined through interviews with the client and can be validated with questionnaires, but it should also be informed by on-site observations because people tend to see processes as isolated events rather than systemic components.

4.4.2. Requirements Document

After observing and interviewing the people currently engaged in the work flow, you will need to unambiguously identify the specific functions that the new system will perform.

Previously, we defined the different filters that can be incorporated into the data collection process: physical, functional, informational, and cultural. The cultural filter will help to identify certain aspects of the stakeholder's roles, but the rest relate directly to the description of requirements. Using these filters to "tag" particular information during the collection can help to expedite this aspect of the interpretation process.

The requirements document includes the following:

- Requirements

  - Functional
  - Information
  - Physical

- Inputs/outputs
- Constraints

The requirements are as follows:

Functional—What functions will the design need to incorporate? This is basically the laundry list of system features. It is created by filtering and distilling the information gathered from the interviews and observations.

Information—What information is needed to carry out the various functions? This describes the type of input and the specific formats required by the system. It also describes the various outputs required by the stakeholders.

Physical—What hardware will be required by the design? A thorough review of the existing infrastructure will be required to determine compatibility with the proposed design. Interoperability with legacy systems is a significant issue and can impose constraints on the new system. Hardware specs for the new system involve specifications for memory, processors, I/O devices, networking, and mobile devices if they are needed.

Inputs/Outputs—What are the input requirements and what output should the design create? You will have to determine what inputs the system will require and what outputs will be required of it. Sometimes ancillary systems need to be developed so that the input is created or translated into the proper media and format for the new system. It is also important to understand the uses of the output and to provide the appropriate formats and design the necessary flexibility into the new system.

You must determine whether hard copy should be output, how that output should be formatted, and whether a memory of those settings will be required for later use. It would be unfortunate if the system required the user to reenter commonly used format settings.

Constraints—Are there any constraints on the proposed system? System constraints can involve physical, financial, or time-based issues. They can also involve computational issues such as data storage, networking security, or other constraints. This information is essential and must be collected and updated on a regular basis during the design process. These are nonnegotiable issues that cannot be ignored. Constraints can be identified by studying the existing system, but one should keep in mind that new ones will arise as the design project progresses.

4.4.3. Project Management Document

This document defines the development process and time table as well as the roles and deliverables that the team and stakeholders are to provide. It defines the criteria for evaluation and the process of implementation and maintenance. It also identifies any future needs that may be considered for development at a later date.

The management document includes the following:

- Definition of the tasks involved in the project
- Risk
- Evaluation criteria and methods
- Implementation
- Training
- Maintenance
- Future needs

Definition of the Tasks Involved in the Project—What will need to be accomplished, when, and by whom? This issue generally concerns the allocation of team resources: who does what, and so on. However, some deliverables must be supplied by the client or one of the stakeholders. These components must be described in detail with clearly defined deliverables. The type and format of materials as well as a specific timeline and method of delivery must be made explicit at the outset of the project.

There should also be follow-up contact with the people responsible for the delivery of the materials. These details can get lost in the process, especially in large companies with multiple departmental layers and administrative structures.

Risk—What are the risks involved in the project? Risks may involve finances, personnel, time, security, or safety. It is important carefully to assess the various risks involved in the proposed system, especially if sensitive information like financial reports or personally identifiable customer information is included.

Peripheral costs may have to be calculated, such as installation, maintenance and back-up systems. Extenuating circumstances may also affect the project, such as equipment failures. All projects should begin with a thorough risk analysis and incorporate various risk reviews throughout.

Evaluation Criteria and Methods—How will we evaluate the success of the design and what criteria will we use to judge its value? Language is often ambiguous, and human–human communication is subject to misunderstandings. People sometimes forget details and remember things from a skewed perspective. It is important to create a clear set of objective and quantifiable criteria that will be used to determine the success of the proposed design.

Sometimes this is a clear-cut issue that can be determined by the output of specific data. There are situations, however, in which the success of a system is not clearly defined. How do you judge the effectiveness of a Web site that offers information about a product or service? If the client is not satisfied with the design, what documentation will you have to support your contention that the site does what it is supposed to do?

Evaluation criteria should be developed to check the design throughout the project, and all involved parties should be consulted and required to check off the various components as they are developed. You must strive for as little ambiguity in this process as possible.

Implementation—What will be involved in the implementation of the system? Will the new system be phased in or will it run parallel to the old system before it is switched over? A clearly defined implementation plan should be in place at the outset. This issue should also be factored into the risk analysis.

Training—Will the new system require any training? You should determine how much training will be required by the new system and who will do the training. If you communicate continuously with selected stakeholders, they can be trained as the system is being developed and can train others after it is completed. They will have a close relationship with their colleagues and can help to establish an initial acceptance for the new system.

Maintenance—What is required to maintain the system? Are there any update schedules to consider? What back-up systems are required? These issues can go unnoticed until the implementation phase and can sometimes lead to additional and unexpected expenses.

Future Needs—What issues may arise in the future pertaining to the design? It is very important to look past the completion of the project and make determinations about the maintenance and updating requirements of the system. The people who maintain the system must have the ability to fix problems and do minor alterations that will keep the system up to date.

This may involve effective commenting within the code of a Web page or detailed specification of the hardware components of the system. Once the system is implemented in the work place it should be accessible to the people who may need to alter user settings and adjust the preferences so that you do not need to be called to the location to fix minor problems.

Design Scenario

Circumference Requirements

To illustrate some of the issues and concepts covered in this book, we will follow the development of a Web site created for a poetry journal called *Circumference*. This journal specializes in world poetry translated into English and to date has four published issues.

This project offers some unique opportunities for exploring the use of non-Latin scripts on Web pages, speaking to an international audience using symbols and auditory feedback, and to enabling disabled users to access the cultural richness of world poetry.

Stakeholders

During the discovery phase of the *Circumference* project we identify three significant stakeholders: the site visitor, the journal editors, and the site developers. We consider these the primary, secondary, and facilitator stakeholders, respectively. The requirements for the site development are driven by these stakeholders. As the development proceeds, we will see how the needs and tasks of these stakeholders interact and sometimes conflict with each other.

Collection

The requirements to be presented were developed using many of the methods discussed earlier. For instance, observations of real users with varying degrees of computer experience were conducted using other journal Web sites, especially poetry journal Web sites. Extensive interviews were conducted with the editors of the Web site. The editors were also the direct clients who hired the developers.

In addition, printed and online surveys were distributed to random samples of people who either attended live poetry readings or elected to participate in the survey by responding to notices placed in poetry publications and/or other poetry journals. Finally, focus groups were formed from the people who identified themselves on the surveys as willing to participate in the groups. This also provided a potential source of participants for the usability testing.

Requirements

We now present the requirements that were established during the collection and interpretation activities of the discovery phase. This will allow us to follow the various design and development decisions in the following chapter's design scenarios.

These are typically what requirements look like at this stage of development. It is not possible to capture every requirement, and, as we saw in the discussion of the waterfall model in Chapter 3, requirements usually evolve during the course of the project.

This is a significant issue because requirements that are added later in the project may have an effect on previous design activities such as prototypes, which will affect development schedules and project costs. Therefore, we must strive to be as comprehensive as possible but keep in mind that we will need to make adjustments along the way.

Design Scenario (cont.)

There are some requirements in this phase of documentation that will need to be tested and/or altered and some that will need to be added or developed further. Read through the documentation and see whether you can identify some of the issues that may arise in going forward with this set of requirements.

Requirements Documentation

Functional Requirements

- The site should include the ability to read selected poems in their original languages and English versions. This should be done in such a way as to allow audible browsers access to as much content as possible.
- Printing the pages should be aided by the inclusion of printer-based cascading style sheets (CSS) that send an appropriately formatted version of the page to the printer.
- Online ordering should be available for individual journals and subscriptions.
- Provision should be made for e-mail contact with editors.
- It should be possible to access *Circumference* event videos.

Information Requirements

The site will have the following areas:

About | Submissions | Issues | Contact | Subscriptions | Events | Supporters

About—The following information:

- Journal Mission Statement
- Names of

    - Editors
    - Designers
    - Advisory Board

- Information on tax-exempt status
- Information about printer

Submissions

- Information on submissions to the journal
- Journal mailing address

Issues

- Links to the table of contents for the various issues
- Links on table of contents pages to selected poems
- Selected poem pages with original-language poem and an English translation
- Selected poem pages with poet and translator biographies

Design Scenario (cont.)

Contact

- Contact information for the journal editors
- Journal mailing address

Subscriptions

- Information on the available journals and subscription packages
- Links to purchase journal and packages
- Printable order form (CSS for printing)

Events

- Links to past and future *Circumference* events
- Location and directions for future events
- Possible links on event pages to videos taken at issue launch events

Supporters

- A list of all the institutional and individual supporters of the journal

Hardware Requirements

- The site will require a server, which will be obtained through an Internet service provider.
- The site will be updated periodically when a new issue is published, and, therefore, storage for the Web pages, graphic files, and their templates will be required. These will be kept on the developer's premises.

Inputs/Outputs

Site development and maintenance will require the following inputs:

- Issue cover images
- Sample poem text (original-language and English versions)
- Issue table of contents
- Issue pricing for order forms

Constraints

- The visual presentation should not distract from the poetry reading experience.
- The site must work on all major browsers and platforms; there can be no proprietary technology that is platform or vendor dependent.
- The site must be standards compliant, which will address the previous constraint.
- The site should allow current versions of the most common audible browsers to access as much content as possible.

Design Scenario (cont.)

- Content must be accessible to older visitors.
- Content must be accessible to older technologies.
- Content must be accessible on mobile devices.
- Finances are tight; the project cannot go over budget.
- A reasonable timeframe for development is approximately 6 months.

Assessment of Requirements

One of the most significant issues regarding the requirements as they exist so far can be inferred from one of the hardware requirements, which states that the site will be periodically updated when new issues are published. Here we have a potential conflict of interest between two of the stakeholders; the editors and the developers. How will the site be updated? Who will be responsible for updating the site? These questions highlight a significant risk that is shared by both stakeholders and must be taken into consideration before the development proceeds. A viable solution and plan of action must be developed to address this issue. This is the type of issue the spiral model is designed to identify early in the process.

Summary

All interaction design projects begin with discovery. Even if there is an existing system that is being updated, a large amount of information must be collected. For instance, we need to understand how efficient the current system is in order to locate areas that need improvement. We must also understand the aspects of the current system that worked well and were valued by the people using it. In other words, whatever the context of the project, we must begin by collecting and interpreting data.

Many frameworks have been advocated by various domain experts and used by different design firms. These models have proven to be robust and effective and reflect the various philosophies of the diverse population of interaction design professionals. We have taken an agnostic view of these frameworks and explored the essential phases and tools incorporated within them. These tools can be applied to the existing formalized methods according to the particular model being used for development.

Resources on the Web

www.aw.com/heim

You will find links to Web resources covering some of the collection and interpretation techniques described in this chapter.

Suggested Reading

Cockburn, A. (2000). *Writing Effective Use Cases* (1 ed.): Addison-Wesley Professional.

Courage, C., & Baxter, K. (2004). *Understanding Your Users: A Practical Guide to User Requirements Methods, Tools, and Techniques:* Morgan Kaufmann.

Faulkner, X. (2000). *Usability Engineering* Palgrave Macmillan.

Hackos, J. T., & Redish, J. C. (1998). *User and Task Analysis for Interface Design* (1 ed.): Wiley.

Kuniavsky, M. (2003). *Observing the User Experience: A Practitioner's Guide to User Research:* Morgan Kaufmann.

CHAPTER 5

Design

After sufficient information has been collected, documented, and interpreted in the discovery phase, we begin the design phase of the project. This begins with the conceptual design of the system, which involves organizing the information space of the proposed design. During the conceptual design we test various design ideas to determine whether they meet all of the requirements documented in the discovery phase.

This does not imply that the discovery phase is closed and will never be revisited. According to the iterative method of development, previous activities may be repeated when new information or needs are discovered during the design phase. We may have to go back and observe the work flow, if only to validate a particular aspect of the conceptual or physical design. We can also go back and test an assumption that is exposed during the design phase with the real users in the context of the real work flow. Although discovery activities are significantly curtailed at this point, they are always available if they are needed.

Once the conceptual design is robust and sufficiently complete we begin the physical design. This involves creating prototypes of specific design solutions and evaluating them against a set of criteria. There will be numerous iterations between the physical and conceptual activities.

Essentially, during the conceptual part you will:

- Create stories based on specific goals
- Create diagrams of specific solutions
- Trace the stories against the diagrams to see whether the proposed solution is successful

You will then test your conceptual designs by:

- Creating prototypes of specific design solutions
- Testing the prototypes

5.1. Technology Myopia

Interaction design must be based on a sociotechnical perspective that does not focus myopically on technological solutions, but instead looks at interaction design from a global perspective. This approach must take into consideration the complex nature of human-to-human communication and should explore the implicit knowledge that is involved in most organizational activities.

A system may have aspects that are not technology based but are essential to the quality of the work performed. For instance, substituting human conversations with an electronic communications system may restrict people's ability to learn the tacit aspects of a job or information that is held in the minds of the senior personnel and that evolves during the work flow.

> **MAXIM**
>
> Integrate technology and human activities carefully.

Another issue to consider is that technological solutions may not always be the best for all aspects of the interaction design. For instance, printed output may be more suitable than electronic documentation for meetings in which people need to make annotations and mark up documents for further electronic editing. Therefore, paper documentation may be a significant link between input and output.

We must keep this in mind as we explore potential solutions in the conceptual design phase. We must keep an open mind and allow for the potential of unexpected solutions to arise.

5.2. Conceptual Design

As mentioned previously, the design phase involves the creation of alternative designs. The basic information and knowledge gathered during the discovery phase is used to develop different ideas about how the design will perform and how it will make the various functions available to the user.

We need to impose some structure on the information space, come up with possible solutions, and then determine which design concept to pursue. There are many tools for the interaction designer to use during the conceptual design stage; each one has specific characteristics and often depends on the results obtained with other tools.

The tools we will cover include the following:

- Brainstorming
- Card sort
- Semantic networks
- Personas
- Scenarios
- Flowcharts
- Cognitive walkthroughs
- Use cases

These tools should be used in an iterative way and should not be viewed as mutually exclusive. We will now explore these tools and see how they can be used to create structure and organize the information space on a conceptual level and then help to make determinations about proposed design ideas.

5.2.1. Brainstorming

One of the staples of any design project is the brainstorming session. In this stage the team members get together and work out possible ideas and solutions, which are then pursued in greater depth and brought back to the table for further refinement.

There are many approaches to brainstorming, from loose, stream-of-consciousness interactions to more structured semantic networks. Most of these techniques involve paper and pencil drawings, Post-it notes, blackboards, whiteboards, or any tool that is easy to use and modify during the session.

Storyboarding is useful during brainstorming sessions. Storyboards are easy to create and modify as the session progresses through a particular avenue of conceptualization. Props can also be used along with storyboards. It helps to have on hand actual objects that represent various aspects of the concept under discussion.

Some teams use props to generate ideas and some use role playing to work out alternative solutions. People have a natural tendency to use props and pictures when presenting their ideas. This can be seen in the way children use rocks and sticks when they describe to teammates the way they want a strategy to be carried out during a sports game.

The main goal behind the brainstorming session is to generate as many ideas as possible and be as creative as possible without being critical or imposing restrictions on the process or ideas that are generated. Such sessions generate a great amount of material that must later be filtered and organized.

5.2.2. Card Sort

MAXIM

Card sorting can be used to discover user-centered groupings.

During the design phase you will need to start thinking about organizing the information you collected during the discovery phase. Card sorting is a user-centered method that can help to define information groupings for menus, controls, and Web page content as well as help to generate user-based labels for menus, buttons, and navigation links between pages.

A card sort is done by writing the functionalities identified during the discovery phase on separate index cards, one function per card. The cards are then shuffled and presented to the subject. The subject is asked to sort the cards and create groups of related functionality. He or she is then asked to supply a label for each group.

When this is done, you can examine the results informally by looking for trends. You should focus on general approaches to creating groups of functionality and content. If any cards present problems and your subjects are not able to group them with other cards, you should explore the issue further and try to understand why they are problematic.

The results of the card sort are used to create menus of user-defined groupings with meaningful labels. Card sorts can also be used to define the information space of a Web site by delineating its different sections and creating appropriate hyperlink text for the navigation.

Card Sort Example

Let's look at an example of what a card sort for some aspects of a word processing application might look like. After the various functions have been identified, the designers write them each on a separate card. We consider the following list for this example:

Font size	Copy
Italic	Line spacing
Font face	Cut
Paste	Image insertion
Table creation	Columns
Font color	Spelling
Underline	Word count
Bold	Find/replace
Font style	Page numbers
Grammar	

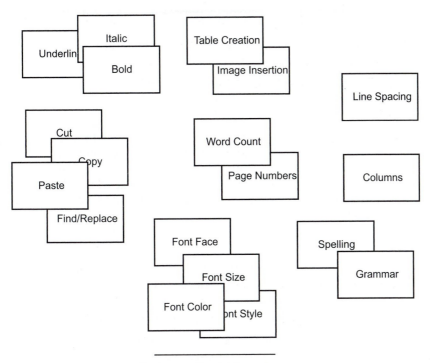

Figure 5.1 Result of a card sort.

The cards are presented to the participant in an unordered pile. The participant is then asked to organize the cards in whatever way seems logical. A typical session might give a result similar to that shown in Figure 5.1.

The participant is then given a set of blank cards and asked to create labels for each pile. As seen in the figure, participants may have trouble grouping all of the cards. This is an important piece of information and should lead to a team discussion concerning the particular labels and/or the functionality itself. You would need to decide whether a simple change in label will fix the problem or whether this functionality really belongs in another part of the application.

These issues may arise with only one of the participants. Other participants may not have the particular problem; if this is the case, you can probably proceed with the results from these other sorts. However, these are the types of problems you should be looking for, and so you should not dismiss them too quickly.

Advantages of card sorting sessions include the following:

- They are quick and easy to perform.
- They can be done before any preliminary designs have been made.
- They will let you know how people organize information.
- They will expose underlying structures.

Disadvantages of card sorting sessions include the following:

- They only involve the elements that you have written on the cards.
- They suggest solutions that imply structures.
- They become difficult to navigate with more categories.

5.2.3. Semantic Networks

A semantic network is a web of concepts that are linked through association. Semantic networks are useful for grouping related items or building menu structures. They are less user centered than card sorting; however, the networks provide a more structured approach and can sometimes be done with stakeholders who may be actively involved in team activities and have been appropriately informed about the method.

Creating a Semantic Network

Consider the concept of text. What associations can be made with this word? Text can be formatted, it can be edited, and it can be checked for spelling and grammatical errors. Let's construct a semantic network based on the concept of text and see what associations we can make and how these associations might be organized.

We put the term "text" at the center of the semantic net. We place our associations around this central term: we can format text, we can edit text, and we can check its spelling. We can also check for grammatical errors, but on closer inspection, we see that the checking of spelling and the checking of grammar seem to be two ways of inspecting text, and so we will use the term "inspect" to include spelling and grammar checking. The specific type of inspection will become a further association of the term "inspect."

Associations may not always be straightforward, and they may require refining, as we saw in the foregoing example. The process of creating associations is also a process of classification: taking a known object and placing it within a structure.

The attributes we identified affect the physical appearance of text on a screen. In this respect they are similar, but they are separated on the basis of function. The formatting commands act on the appearance of the existing text, whereas the inspect commands have the potential to alter the existing text.

Let's continue with the construction of this semantic net and add additional associations. We can further categorize types of formatting: we can modify the text's color, size, font face, line spacing, and column structure.

There seem to be qualitative differences between changing the font's color and size and altering line spacing and column structure. We might account for this difference by saying that text formatting can be done on a character level or a paragraph level. We can now connect the terms "character" and "paragraph" to "format," grouping font color and size with "character" and line spacing and columns with "paragraph." By explicitly articulating the attributes of "format," we were able to identify the categories "character" and "paragraph".

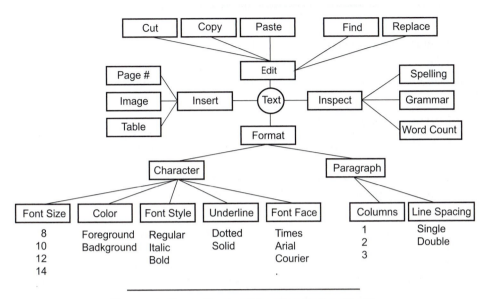

Figure 5.2 Semantic network based on the term "text".

If we continue making associations, we end up with a network of related terms and concepts. This network structure radiates outward from the central term in concentric levels of associations. Consider the network shown in Figure 5.2.

We now have a basic diagram of associations relating to text. In the first ring are Edit, Insert, Format, and Inspect. These four terms are verbs that express what can be done to text and exhibit parallel construction in their terminology. If this is not the case, adjustments should be made to terminology, or a restructuring of associations may be necessary.

Menu construction often requires iteration. Early associations may have to be altered. Parallel construction may alert you to problems in the menu's structure, but it is not a substitute for user testing.

Creating a semantic network of menu options will give you an idea of menu structure and help to clarify terminology, but the actual graphical manifestation will still have to be determined. The choice of menu elements, such as checkboxes, radio buttons, and pull-down menus, will depend on the nature of the menu's functionality. The number of options, the frequency of use, and the computing environment are only a few of the issues that must be considered.

Advantages of semantic networks include the following:

- They allow an easy way to explore the problem space.
- They provide a way to create clusters of related elements.
- They provide a graphical view of the problem space.
- They resonate with the ways in which people process information.

Disadvantages of semantic networks include the following:

- They require knowledge of the problem space.
- They can lead beyond the problem space.
- There is no formal semantics for defining symbol meaning.

5.2.4. Personas

We have looked at the primary stakeholder profiles created during the discovery stage. By this point, they should be well defined and rather detailed, which means that they will be very useful, but they will still be awkward to use during design meetings. These profiles can sound impersonal and create distance between the designer and the target user.

To make the target user feel more real and tangible to the design team, we can use a concept called personas. A persona is basically a user profile with a face, a personality, a history, a skill set, and a back story. The objective behind persona creation is to make the target user more human, which adds nuance to our understanding of the user's abilities and limitations.

Personas are archetypes of actual users, defined by the user's goals and attributes. According to Alan Cooper who has been a major proponent of the technique, "personas are derived from patterns observed during interviews with and observations of users and potential users (and sometimes customers) of a product" (Cooper & Reimann, 2003, 67).

Creating a Persona

A persona is created by identifying the primary stakeholder and creating an identity based on the stakeholder profiles and other collection activities such as interviews and surveys. A persona is a detailed description complete with as many personally identifying attributes as necessary to make it come to life.

The persona is given a name, personality characteristics, and educational and employment histories. The team may also use a photo to represent each persona and tack it up on the wall so they can have a face to go with each description.

User profiles can be seen as "skeletons," whereas personas are the flesh and blood that makes them come alive. All aspects of the persona should be driven by the user profile. When you create a persona, focus on describing the various elements discovered during the collection phase and avoid adding irrelevant details.

For instance, if the profile describes an infrequent user with a beginner level of computer literacy, you would describe the persona by saying that he or she has a basic desktop computer with a common suite of productivity tools, such as Microsoft Office, to write simple word processing documents, uses AOL for e-mail, and plays some of the computer games that come with the system. You might also mention that he or she goes to the neighborhood computer dealer when there are problems with spyware or viruses that come from downloading e-mail attachments.

Details about hair color, weight, height, or other characteristics are useful in making the persona become real to the team; however, they can be inferred from the photo used to represent the persona. Excessive and irrelevant detail diminish the persona's usefulness.

The persona is a tool for creating and running scenarios that judge the design's effectiveness. The design team refers to the persona instead of the user profile when they talk about the target user. Persona use is similar to ethnographic observation, in that both strive to capture the subtle nuances and particulars that make people unique and complex.

Personas should be created for each primary stakeholder. Care must be taken to ensure that each persona represents a unique stakeholder; using too many personas can become problematic and decrease their effectiveness as a design tool.

Personas should be highly differentiated. Some practitioners strive to "push the envelope" and create "extreme personas" to create a broader range of potential users, which can afford a more complete assessment of the viability of a particular design.

Persona Integrity

> **MAXIM**
>
> Personas should be a strict reflection of the information derived from the collection activities.

One of the main issues raised by designers who do not agree with this technique is that designer assumptions that are not based on observation can find their way into a persona's description. A conscious effort must be made to avoid putting anything in the construction of a persona that is extraneous to the results of the collection phase. In other words, if you cannot point to a direct one-to-one relation with an observed user behavior, then that particular persona characteristic is either unnecessary or, more important, erroneous and will lead to incorrect design decisions.

Persona Example

Let's look at a persona definition for the *Circumference* Web site. We will use this example to develop some of the other components in the conceptual design phase that are discussed latter in this chapter. These components will, in turn, serve as the basis for the continuing *Circumference* design scenario at the end of the chapter.

> **Maria**
>
> Maria is a Ph.D. psychologist in her 50s. She emigrated from Italy when she was 11. She loves poetry, especially poetry from around the world. She feels connected to global issues and is politically active in support of peace and humanitarian issues.
>
> Maria is not good with technology, but she uses the computer for some tasks: to schedule clients, create reports, check e-mail, check the weather, book airline tickets, pay bills, and play word games.
>
> Maria uses a dial-up connection with her four-year-old PC. She runs Windows ME and uses AOL for e-mail and web browsing.
>
> Maria heard about the *Circumference* journal at a poetry reading and wants to find out more about it. She lives in the same city as the journal's editors and can easily attend the journal's events. She does not have a journal subscription, but may be inclined to subscribe if she is pleased with what she sees on the journal's Web site.

This description was derived from the profile that was developed from the various observations and interviews carried out in the discovery phase. All of the information presented in the persona can be traced to a specific profile component. For instance, the age, profession, interest in poetry, and ethnic background were derived from the cognitive ability and individual profiles. The information on her computer use stems from the context of use profile.

The last paragraph was derived from interviews with the journal editors. It represents some of the information and activities that the editors are interested in communicating to their user base. These "needs" were then discussed during focus groups with prospective users to see whether these were indeed features in which they were interested.

Advantages of personas include the following:

- They are quick and easy to create.
- They provide a consistent model for all team members.
- They are easy to use with other design methods.
- They make the user real in the mind of the designer.

Disadvantages of personas include the following:

- They can be difficult to create if the target audience is international.
- Having too many personas will make the work difficult.
- There is a risk of incorporating unsupported designer assumptions.

5.2.5. Scenarios, Flowcharts, and Cognitive Walkthroughs

Once personas have been created from the primary stakeholder profiles, a set of goals can be associated with each persona. These goals are used to create scenarios.

Flowcharts then map out the design on screen-by-screen or page-by-page basis. The scenarios are then used to work through the flowcharts by performing a cognitive walkthrough.

Scenarios

The scenario is a description in plain English of a typical task the persona may wish to accomplish with the proposed design. It describes the basic goal, the conditions that exist at the beginning of the task, the activities in which the persona will engage, and the outcomes of those activities.

Scenarios can be used to describe the interaction between a particular persona and the system from the persona's perspective. They are not concerned with the system states that occur during that process or any particular physical implementation. They are only concerned with the available functionality of the design during each step of the scenario and are used to check whether all of the required functionality has been accounted for and is accessible to the user when it is needed.

> **MAXIM**
>
> Scenarios afford a rich picture of the user's tasks.

Scenarios are extremely powerful and flexible tools and should be used often during the design process and should evolve along with the design. They are an important evaluation tool that can also be used in the usability tests covered in Chapter 8.

Scenario Example

Let's look at some scenarios that were derived from the "Maria" persona described earlier. Three scenarios developed from this persona's goal of "Finding out more about the *Circumference* journal" are related to reading samples from the journals and viewing videos of the various poetry events. As a result of these activities, the persona may end up ordering a subscription. We pursue the following scenarios:

1. Read poems from multiple issues.
2. View videos of the last two poetry events.
3. Order a 1-year subscription, issue number 4, and issue number 1.

Flowcharts

Flowcharts have a long history and an established set of symbols and procedures. They are easy to create and modify and can be extremely useful in the conceptual design process.

Flowcharts can be simple network diagrams that identify the pages of a Web site and the navigational links between them, or they can be more sophisticated diagrams that capture conditional junctures and computational processes. Consider the two flowcharts in Figure 5.3.

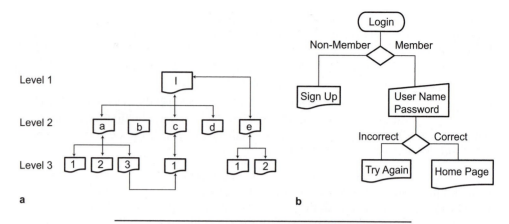

Figure 5.3 (a) Simple network flowchart. (b) Login process flowchart.

The flowchart in Figure 5.3a defines the number of discrete Web pages in a particular section of a site and the possible navigational paths between them. For instance, if you follow the directional arrows on the flow lines you can see that from the top page "I" you can navigate to every page in level 2 and back again.

You can also navigate between all the pages on level 2 except for page "e." We also see that getting from page "a3" to "e2" would require navigating back to page "I" and following the "e" path to "e2," which would require four clicks. However, to get from "a3" to "c1" requires only one click on the "c1" link.

A simple flowchart like this one can be of great help in making sure that a design has no dead ends, and that pages with related information that may be accessed often are not too difficult to navigate between. It is essential to get the flow arrows correct or you will not see an accurate picture of the site navigation. These flowcharts can also be used as the basis for the creation of wireframes later. As we will see, wireframes are basically structural skeletons of screen designs; they show the screen elements but not in detail.

Flowcharts can also be used to capture more complex interactions. Consider the flowchart in Figure 5.3b. It uses some dynamic symbols to describe a typical login procedure.

You can use connector symbols to connect this type of flow chart with a simple one like the one in Figure 5.3a to telescope in and out of complex procedures and still be able to see them in the larger context of the overall site. Outlines can be used along with the flow charts to notate any information that may be needed to clarify any of the symbols, such as page content or additional functionality.

Flowchart Example

Let's now look at some of the flowcharts developed for the *Circumference* Web site. It will help to have an idea of the scope of the Web site. It will have the following major areas:

About | Submissions | Issues | Contact | Subscriptions | Events | Supporters

The most complex areas are Issues, Subscriptions, and Events. We will develop these three areas throughout the book on a chapter-by-chapter basis.

The top level of the site navigation is diagramed in the flowchart in Figure 5.4.

This chart represents the top level of the navigational structure, also called the global navigation. A visitor can access any one of the top-level pages form the home page and can go directly from area to area.

The Issues Area—Read Selected Poems

The requirements document states that the Issues area should include the following:

- There will be links to the table of contents of the various issues.
- The table of contents pages will have links to selected poems.
- Selected poem pages will have the poem in the original language and an English-language translation.
- Selected poem pages will have poet and translator biographies.

The flowchart of the Issues section is diagramed as shown in Figure 5.5.

This chart begins with the Issues link on the global navigation and continues through the next two levels in the navigation structure. A visitor can access any of the existing Issues' table of contents (TOC) pages from the Issues page and can access any of the sample poems from that particular issue.

Cognitive Walkthroughs—During a cognitive walkthrough, the evaluator follows the various scenarios using the flowcharts or the low-fidelity prototypes discussed later. He or she looks for problem areas in the design that may cause difficulties in scenario completion.

The evaluator takes the part of the primary stakeholder and tries to accomplish that stakeholder's various tasks. He or she tries to confirm the completeness of the design and determine the robustness of the system, asking, "Can the

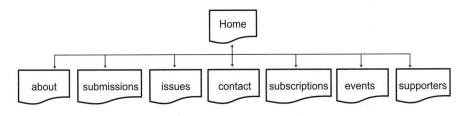

Figure 5.4 The *Circumference* flowchart: Global navigation.

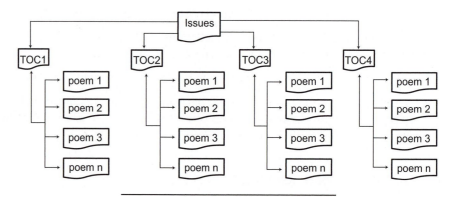

Figure 5.5 The *Circumference* flowchart: Issues area.

persona accomplish the goals set out in the scenario, and can the system recover from deviations from the scenario or user errors?" He or she also tries to uncover any incomplete navigational paths or dead ends built into the proposed design.

During the walkthrough, the evaluator asks questions about the interaction, such as, "What choices are available? Do I know how to proceed? How difficult is it to accomplish the task?" The answers to these questions help to identify any areas that need to be reconsidered.

Cognitive Walkthrough Example

Let's look at an example of a cognitive walkthrough using the Issues flowchart and the scenarios that were developed previously.

SCENARIO 1—Read poems from multiple issues.

The steps required are as follows:

1. From the Home page, click on the "Issues" link.
2. From the Issues page, decide on an issue to look at.
3. Click on the appropriate issue link.
4. Scan the TOC for a poem.
5. Click on the poem's link.
6. Read the poem.
7. Click on the link back to the issue's TOC.
8. Click on the link back to the Issues page.
9. Click on another issue's link.
10. Repeat steps 4–6.

This process takes 12 steps and seven clicks to complete. Another way to accomplish this scenario is to use the global navigation links as follows:

1. From the Home page, click on the "Issues" link.
2. From the Issues page, decide on an issue to look at.
3. Click on the appropriate issue link.
4. Scan the TOC for a poem.
5. Click on the poem's link.
6. Read the poem.
7. Click on the global Issues link.
8. Repeat steps 2–6.

This process also takes 12 steps but only six clicks to complete. This is better, but it is still cumbersome.

We could improve this situation by eliminating the need to either back up along the navigation structure or start again using the global navigation links. We can avoid these steps by linking directly to the other issue TOCs from each issue's TOC page and each selected poem's page. The shortest route through the scenario would then look like this:

1. From the Home page, click on the "issues" link.
2. From the Issues page, decide on an issue to look at.
3. Click on the appropriate issue link.
4. Scan the TOC for a poem.
5. Click on the poem's link.
6. Read the poem.
7. Click on another issue's link.
8. Repeat steps 4–6.

This process takes 10 steps and only five clicks to complete. This is a significant improvement, especially if the visitor wants to read many poems from all of the issues. We should encourage this behavior by making the scenario as easy as possible to perform.

Iteration

By running the scenario, we discovered a weakness in the original navigational structure that was derived from the requirements document. We now need to go back and update the requirements and flowcharts with the information we obtained. This is how the iterative process works at this stage of the project.

If we update the original flowchart with this additional navigational functionality, the chart will begin to resemble a spider web and become less useful. How can we include this important navigation information on the chart without rendering it useless?

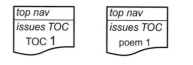

Figure 5.6 Global and local navigation abbreviations.

One way we can include this additional information is by moving in the direction of wireframe creation. A wireframe is a skeleton diagram of an interface screen that includes rough approximations of screen components and context. Although we are not yet thinking about these issues, we are gradually preparing for the transition into the physical design activities.

We can use this concept to add the new navigational information by representing the global links on each page with the label "top nav" and the links to the various issue TOC pages as "issues TOC." This is shown in Figure 5.6.

The "top nav" and "issues TOC" indications should be described somewhere on the flowchart as a key to the diagram so that people can refer to that information when they use the chart for cognitive walkthroughs (Figure 5.7).

Notice also that the flow lines have been simplified to indicate the reciprocal navigation links on the global level (between the Issues page and the TOCs).

Quick Links

Another solution that would make the navigation more efficient would be to include a "quick links" menu on the pages in the Issues area. Such a menu would include links to all of the selections listed by issue and then alphabetically by title. It

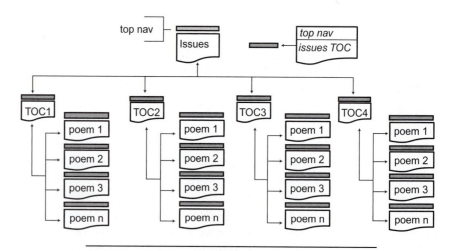

Figure 5.7 Flowchart with global and local navigation abbreviations.

would be an abbreviated menu and would not include the poet's name, the translator's name, the language of the original, or any other information in the TOC listing of the poem. It would be meant for quick access and could not be used in lieu of the full TOC page.

The Events Area—View Videos

Let's continue with this example and look at the Events area of the Web site. The requirements document states that the Events area should include the following:

- Links to past and future *Circumference* events.
- Future events, including location and directions.
- Possibly links on Events pages to videos taken at issue launch events.

We will now look at the flowchart and perform a cognitive walkthrough of scenario 2.

SCENARIO 2—View videos of the last poetry event.

The flowchart for the Events area resembles the one for the Issues area, except that there is a link to an off-site page with photos and a link to a single on-site page that also contains photos (Figure 5.8). The pages that contain videos have the same depth and interrelationships between pages, so the navigation is consistent with the Issues area navigation. This consistency increases the learnability and usability of the site, as we will see in the discussion of design principles in Chapter 6.

A cognitive walkthrough of this navigational structure provides the same results as one of the Issues area.

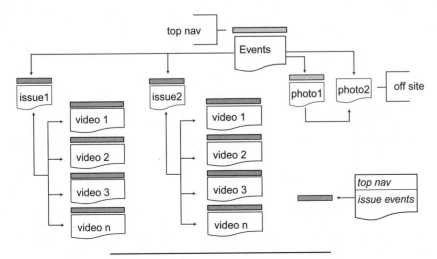

Figure 5.8 The *Circumference* flowchart: Events area.

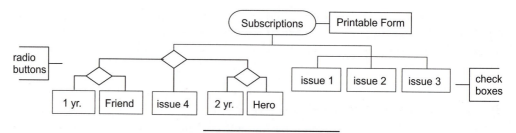

Figure 5.9 Subscription flowchart.

The Subscriptions Area—Order a Subscription

Finally we look at the Subscriptions area. The requirements document states that the subscription area should include the following:

- Information about the available journals and subscription packages.
- Links from which to purchase journal and packages.
- Printable order form.

We now look at the flowchart and perform a cognitive walkthrough of scenario 3.

SCENARIO 3—Order a 1-year subscription, issue number 4, and issue number 1.

The flowchart for the order form describes the functionality of the form and is shown in Figure 5.9.

A cognitive walkthrough verifies that a customer can choose any combination of back issues and can also decided between ordering just issue number 4 or choosing a 1-year or 2-year subscription, each of which includes issue number 4. The customer can also choose between ordering a subscription or ordering a subscription and making a donation: he or she can become a "Hero" with an included 2-year subscription or a "Friend" with an included 1-year subscription.

By treating issue number 4 as mutually exclusive with the subscriptions, we protect the customer from ordering issue number 4 two times (again issue number 4 is included in each subscription). The same concept protects him or her from becoming a Friend or Hero and inadvertently ordering an additional subscription.

5.3. Physical Design

Once the conceptual design has evolved sufficiently we can begin to think about the physical design, envisioning what it will look like, what components it will require, and how the screens will be laid out.

We use the following tools during this phase:

- Low-fidelity prototypes
- Evaluations
- Wireframes
- Functional prototypes

There is no clear-cut distinction between the conceptual design and the physical design phases; there is simply a natural progression that continues to add clarity to the proposed design. This is similar to the way a JPEG file progressively renders on the screen: it starts out blurry, and with each pass the image becomes more clear and focused.

As we have seen, the essence of interaction design is iteration. However, there is also a strong forward movement: a phase starts to occupy less of the team's time and energy, and the activities involved in the next phase move to the forefront. One of the most important considerations is to make sure that the process does not move precipitously into the activities involved in future phases. For instance, when you are working in the discovery phase, you should not let your ideas about what is technically feasible influence the process of data collection and user interviews. This may cause you to miss important opportunities to make the new design more useful.

You must also be careful not to stifle the conceptual design by imposing predetermined ideas about screen layout and interface components. Premature involvement in technical implementation issues will create boundaries that will inhibit your inspiration and creativity.

There will come a point, however, when you will need to show your ideas to other team members. You will also need to get feedback from potential users. You must, therefore, make your ideas explicit. This process was initiated when you created the flowcharts.

You will now follow the logical progression and make these diagrams more focused and explicit by including ideas about actual screen components and layouts. Your diagrams will now take on the appearance of simple prototypes that will be used for evaluation purposes.

5.3.1. Prototypes

Prototypes come in many varieties and levels of detail. They can be global and cover the entire project, or they can be constrained to very specific modules within one particular area of the design. Nielsen distinguishes between two types of prototypes-horizontal and vertical (Nielsen, 1994).

You can create prototypes that represent the breadth of functionality of the proposed design. These are called horizontal prototypes, and they show the design's surface layer without specifying details about subsequent functionality. Vertical prototypes do not show the broad picture; they represent a specific area with a complete drill-down to the lowest levels of functionality in that area (Figure 5.10).

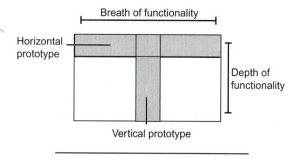

Figure 5.10 Vertical and horizontal prototypes.

5.3.2. Low-Fidelity Prototypes

Prototypes at this stage have one thing in common: they are low-fidelity prototypes. Made by hand, they can be simple pencil drawings or just a set of sticky notes tacked up on a wall. Paper prototypes are more focused on how the design works than on what it will look like (Figure 5.11).

The three main criteria for low-fidelity prototypes are as follows:

- They should be easy and inexpensive to make.
- They should be flexible enough to be constantly changed and rearranged.
- They should be complete enough to yield useful feedback about specific design questions.

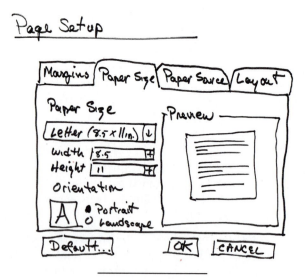

Figure 5.11 Paper prototype.

MAXIM

People are more comfortable criticizing paper prototypes.

Low-fidelity prototypes allow you to get more honest responses and feedback because people feel more inclined to criticize something that does not look as though it required much time and energy. Using these prototypes, you will also be able to do more evaluations and iteration between testing sessions.

You will have to make some decisions before you begin:

- What feedback do you need at this point in the design process?
- How much of the design should you prototype?
- Should you cover all of the areas but without great detail (breadth vs. depth)?
- Should you cover one area in great detail?

These questions will help you to define the scope of the prototype and focus on what you want to accomplish.

To create a low-fidelity prototype, use a sheet of paper for each screen of an application or page of a Web site. Draw boxes and labels that represent the controls and content of each screen. You can also incorporate sticky notes to represent pull-down and pop-up menus. Place these on the sheet of paper and cycle through them as the user follows the scenario.

When the prototype is complete, you can evaluate it using your scenarios and use cases. For instance, you can ask a subject to try to accomplish a particular scenario while you manipulate the paper prototype, changing the various sheets of paper as the subject moves through it. If something comes up during the session, you can create new screens and add controls as needed.

It is generally best to have two team members involved in this process, one to act as a surrogate for the computer, turning the pages of the prototype, and the other to interact with the subject and document the feedback.

Advantages of paper prototypes include the following:

- They can be used early and often.
- They are inexpensive and easy to create.
- They make design ideas visual.
- No special knowledge is required; all team members can create them.

Disadvantage of paper prototypes include the following:

- They are not interactive.
- They cannot be used to calculate response timings.
- They do not deal with interface issues such as color or font size.

5.4. Evaluation

Evaluation is an integral part of the development process and can take the form of an informal walkthrough or a more structured heuristic evaluation. However, it should be done frequently and begun early in the development process.

> **MAXIM**
>
> Begin evaluations early in the design process.

Formal usability testing can begin once a prototype has been developed. Performing evaluations early can help you to avoid some of the problems uncovered in the formal usability tests, providing financial and time-related benefits for the project.

At the early stages of development we are most concerned with completeness. We must make sure that users can actually complete their tasks with the functionality provided by the conceptual design and implemented by the physical design up to this point.

This is a transitional period between the conceptual and physical design phases. We have not begun to determine specific interaction scenarios that include particular interaction styles or screen components; we are still implementation independent.

We will need some way to structure the evaluation process, and must have a clearly defined method of evaluation and clearly defined goals. There are a few different ways to evaluate our designs at this point, ranging from team-based reviews to formal usability tests.

We explore usability testing in more detail in Chapter 8; we recall that there are many different types of usability testing, each with different applications during the various phases of development. Usability testing in the form of evaluations is incorporated into the design process from the start of the project and is performed in an iterative way. More formal testing with target user representatives is also performed throughout the development process. These are triggered by development events such as completion of a prototype or when significant questions arise concerning particular design proposals.

We can perform a cognitive walkthrough to uncover any problematic avenues of design and help to avoid more costly alterations later. Another method employed at this stage of development is the heuristic evaluation. Let's see what this type of evaluation involves.

5.4.1. Heuristic Evaluation

Heuristic evaluations are performed by usability experts using a predetermined set of criteria designed to measure the usability of a proposed design. They can also be performed on existing systems to make comparisons or to identify areas that need to be improved.

The evaluator follows a scenario through the design and tests each step against the heuristic criteria. He or she then makes recommendations to the design team either through a written document or during a team meeting. These recommendations can then be implemented in the next design proposal.

5.4.2. Nielsen's Heuristics

In collaboration with Rolf Molich, Jakob Nielsen developed a set of 10 heuristics for interface design. He called them heuristics because they resemble rules of thumb rather than a set of user interface guidelines. He later revised them based on an analysis of 249 usability problems. The revised set is as follows (http://www.useit.com/papers/heuristic/heuristic_list.html):

Visibility of System Status—The system should always keep users informed about what is going on, through appropriate feedback within reasonable time.

Match between System and the Real World—The system should speak the users' language, with words, phrases, and concepts familiar to the user, rather than system-oriented terms. Follow real-world conventions, making information appear in a natural and logical order.

User Control and Freedom—Users often choose system functions by mistake and need a clearly marked "emergency exit" to leave the unwanted state without having to go through an extended dialogue. Support undo and redo.

Consistency and Standards—Users should not have to wonder whether different words, situations, or actions mean the same thing. Follow platform conventions.

Error Prevention—Even better than good error messages is a careful design that prevents a problem from occurring in the first place. Either eliminate error-prone conditions or check for them and present users with a confirmation option before they commit to the action.

Recognition Rather Than Recall—Minimize the user's memory load by making objects, actions, and options visible. The user should not have to remember information from one part of the dialogue to another. Instructions for use of the system should be visible or easily retrievable whenever appropriate.

Flexibility and Efficiency of Use—Accelerators—unseen by the novice user—can often speed up the interaction for the expert user such that the system can cater to both inexperienced and experienced users. Allow users to tailor frequent actions.

Aesthetic and Minimalist Design—Dialogues should not contain information that is irrelevant or rarely needed. Every extra unit of information in a dialogue competes with the relevant units of information and diminishes their relative visibility.

Help Users to Recognize, Diagnose, and Recover from Errors—Error messages should be expressed in plain language (no codes), precisely indicate the problem, and constructively suggest a solution.

Help and Documentation—Even though it is better if the system can be used without documentation, it may be necessary to provide help and documentation. Any such information should be easy to search, focused on the user's task, list concrete steps to be carried out, and not be too large.

Nielsen's advice on how to conduct a heuristic evaluation includes the following:

- Use multiple evaluators (approximately five) because one person cannot find all of the problems, and different evaluators will uncover different usability problems.
- Evaluators should work separately.
- Evaluations can be done using an evaluator and another person (observer) to record the findings; if you use one observer for all evaluators it will be easier to collate the results later.
- The evaluator should go through the interface several times; the first pass is more general, allowing the evaluator to get a "feel" for the design; subsequent passes are more focused on specific issues.
- The evaluator should compare the interaction against a list of predetermined general heuristics.
- The evaluator may also use heuristics that are more specific to the design that is being evaluated.
- The observer may be enlisted by the evaluator to answer questions about the interface; it is, therefore, a good idea to use an observer who has knowledge of the interface design.
- The evaluation should consist of a list of usability problems and an associated heuristic with an explanation about how the interface violates the heuristic
- After the evaluation the results are collated; using an observer can facilitate this process because he or she will be working from his or her notes and will not have to interpret other peoples' writing.

Heuristic Evaluation Example

Let's look at some typical heuristics that are oriented to the evaluation of a Web site. These heuristics are based on a much larger set of heuristics developed by Deniese Pierotti from the Xerox Corporation for the Usability Toolkit published by the Society for Technical Communication (Pierotti, 1995).

The following heuristics have been adapted and grouped according to some of the most common areas of concern in Web site development. This is only a sample of some of the general heuristic-based questions that might be asked by the evaluator. Each design will have aspects that are unique to that design, which will initiate other questions more specific to the particular design.

Many of these questions concern topics that will be discussed in the following chapters. These heuristics will become clearer after these topics have been fully explored; for now, this list of questions can serve as an example of the types of questions that are considered by an evaluator after some design ideas have been developed using low-fidelity prototypes.

Pages

- Do the pages have navigational indicators to identify the current page?
- Do the pages consist of interrelated content?
- Do all pages have descriptive titles or headers?
- Do all page titles reflect the page contents?
- Are screen components consistently located on all pages?
- Is white space used to give "breathing room" to text areas?
- Do the page elements map easily and naturally to their functions?

Grouping

- Do all page areas have strong visual delimiters such as shading, borders, or color?
- Is white space used to create meaningful groups?
- Do all groups have meaningful titles or labels?

Forms

- Do multipage forms indicate the relationships between individual pages?
- Do multipage forms allow users to navigate back and forth without losing previously entered data?
- Are tasks described using familiar terminology?
- Do the pages of multipage forms have the same title?
- Does the page flow from the upper left corner (upper right in right-to-left language orientations)?
- Are screen messages placed in locations that are likely to be seen by the user?
- Are labels located so that they are visually related to their associated fields?
- Are field labels visually distinct?
- Are field labels descriptive?
- Are optional fields clearly marked?
- Are default selections appropriate?

The types of questions developed for each heuristic evaluation reflect the particular stage of development. They start out as general concerns and gradually evolve into more specific questions. The following are some questions that might be asked after the wireframes and functional prototypes have been developed. They concern issues that arise as the designers become more involved with specific aspects of the design such as icon development and color application.

Icons

- Is icon design stylistically consistent?
- Are the members of an icon family distinct visually and conceptually?
- Do icons use familiar images?
- Do icons match with cultural conventions?
- Do icons have labels?
- Are icons distinct from their backgrounds?
- Has excessive details been eliminated?

Menus

- Does menu terminology reflect the task domain?
- Does the menu structure match the task structure?
- Do menu options begin with the most important word?
- Are menu titles parallel grammatically?
- Is the grammatical style of menu options consistent within and between menus?
- Do menu options follow a logical order?
- Do menu options follow a natural sequence if available?
- Are menu options categorized logically?

Color

- Is color used as a redundant secondary code?
- Is color used prudently?
- Are colors kept to a minimum?
- Are colors easily distinguished?
- Have incompatible color combinations been avoided?
- Is there good color contrast between images and their backgrounds?
- Has the use of blue for small objects and thin lines (such as text characters) been avoided?

Formatting

- Has the used of text rendered in all upper-case letters been avoided?
- Are integers right-justified?
- Are fields and labels left-justified?
- Are typographical parameters used to indicate relative intensities such as importance or quantity?

5.5. Physical Design Continued

Once we have determined that the design is relatively stable and conceptually complete, we can begin to design the actual screens and page layouts. The information we gathered from the discovery and early development phases provides us with information about the actual components of the screens and pages.

5.5.1. Wireframes

During this phase, we create wireframes of the screens and pages. These define basic page layout as well as the screen components. We begin to make decisions about what components to use, what content to include, what labels to use, how to divide the screen, and all of the other decisions factors that will describe the physical interface explicitly and unambiguously.

Wireframes are developed from flowcharts and paper prototypes. They are basically more evolved paper prototypes that include detailed information about the interface elements that exist on the screens and pages.

> **MAXIM**
>
> Wireframes help to create template layouts that can be used to impose a consistent structure throughout the interface.

During wireframe creation, you will begin to think about page layout (Figure 5.12). A few overriding factors will help to guide this process. One is the user's linguistic orientation: does he or she read from left to right or right to left? Given a left-to-right orientation (all other things being equal), the top left corner will be where the user looks first.

Other elements on the screen that have strong intensity will draw the eye; however, the top left is the default starting point. After that, the path of the user's eye depends on his or her tasks and the layout of the screen.

We investigate the principles involved in creating screens in Chapter 6. In that discussion we will see how the application of different design principles can help

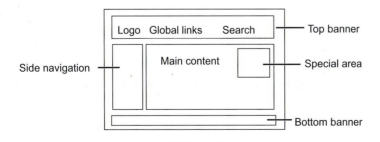

Figure 5.12 Wireframe.

us to direct the user to important components of the screen. You will need to apply those principles during this stage of development and throughout the design process.

Wireframes can be used to perform evaluations in the same way as low-fidelity prototypes. Completed wireframes that have been verified through user testing can also serve as specifications for functional prototypes.

5.5.2. Web Formats

One of the ways you can begin to think about wireframe creation is to study how similar designs have been done. If you are creating a Web site, it will be informative to look at various existing Web sites, especially ones that have a similar domain.

Look at the visual structure of the pages. You can take a screen shot and open the image in a graphics program like Adobe® PhotoShop® or Illustrator® and box out the different areas of the screen. You could even do this by printing the screen shot and marking it up.

If you do this with enough sites, you will begin to see common template structures. For instance, many sites use a template that has a top banner, a side navigation panel, and subareas within the center frame, with a bottom banner that generally contains text links to important site areas. You can see these common elements in the wireframe of Figure 5.12.

> **MAXIM**
>
> Use page layouts that are common to the domain.

Although there are many different ways to design the layout of Web pages, sites with specific domains, such as newspapers, magazines, stores, or museums, tend to use similar layouts.

Notice also where these different kinds of sites place the common elements like logos and tag lines, global links, search functions, quick links, shopping carts, privacy notifications, and the icons for "seal programs" that verify site security such as TRUSTe or VeriSign. You should use these conventional locations whenever possible because they will make your design easier to use.

Flexible Design

> **MAXIM**
>
> Use flexible design for Web pages.

No matter what layout you choose to pursue, you must allow for flexibility in the way the actual page will be seen by different visitors. The web is a wide open environment, and it is unlikely that any two visitors will have exactly the same configuration of platform, operating system, browser and browser version, screen resolution, bit depth, ambient lighting, window dimensions, font and font size, and so on. In short, Web design means flexible design.

With current technologies such as CSS, it is possible to freeze a Web page's layout with pixel precision, and it may be tempting to do so; however, this might cause unacceptable ramifications for people who may need to enlarge the text, stop images from downloading, or have low-resolution monitors and would then have to scroll both vertically and horizontally.

CSS has enabled Web designers to separate information structure from information presentation. It is a powerful, standards-based tool that can be used to create Web site layouts that respond to the user's actual settings and should not be used to create inflexible designs.

5.5.3. Functional Prototypes

After we create wireframes, we can begin to develop the functional prototypes. These are interactive prototypes that represent various degrees of functionality. As with the paper prototypes, they can either be horizontal or vertical.

In other words, they can be broad and cover the entire scope of the design but not be complete with regard to the depth of each area's functionality. They can also be very specific to one area, providing a complete set of functionality for that area and not presenting all other areas of the design. These determinations should be made according to the way the prototype will be used during usability testing.

We explore usability testing in Chapter 8. Let's now look at some of the technologies that you can use to create these functional prototypes.

Development Environments

Rapid application development (RAD) environments have developed to the point at which they offer drag-and-drop simplicity and are easy enough to use that some designers go directly to simple functional prototyping from low-fidelity prototypes. They may even use a RAD environment to create low-fidelity prototypes. This is not uncommon in Web and application development for small-scale projects; however, it does not provide the same flexibility as paper and pencil and is not advised.

Functioning prototypes can be created using RAD environments, such as Microsoft® Visual Studio® or Adobe® Flash®, Dreamweaver®, or Director®. They can also be created as PowerPoint® slide shows or PDF files. Basically, they can be created with any application that provides hypertext linking. In short, the paper prototype is replaced with a computer-based prototype that has some interactive functionality.

Web sites often evolve from the prototype to the final product. This is not the best practice because some of the more time-consuming activities are abbreviated during the design process, such as creating descriptive alt attributes and code comments.

During prototyping of a Web page the presentational aspects of the design are occasionally a conglomeration of markup and CSS, which will contain a great deal of redundancy and be difficult to work with later during the updating and maintenance phases. This is sometimes an unfortunate byproduct of the iterative process. Changes are made to existing prototypes without going back to reorganize the underlying style sheets.

In other words, many short-cuts might be involved in getting a prototype to the point at which it can be used in usability tests. It is better to start from scratch and construct clean code than to get an incomplete and patched-up prototype to evolve into the final product.

5.6. Interface Design Standards

The contemporary GUI environments created for the major operating systems—Windows®, Macintosh®, and UNIX®—have attained a degree of standardization in terms of the types of interface components they incorporate and they way in which these components function. This makes it relatively easy for users to work in a multi-application and even cross-platform environment.

MAXIM

Standards increase efficiency.

The software suites that are marketed by the major software providers generally conform to a set of industry-wide guidelines and norms that allow users to gain and generalize knowledge about functionality and interaction from program to program and even between programs from different manufacturers. Working in a standardized environment increases efficiency and promotes learning (Cooper & Reimann, 2003).

Designing and developing software products is a difficult, expensive, and time-consuming enterprise. To aid in the process, tools have been created that automate some of the low-level programming activities required to develop contemporary GUIs. These tools create a more efficient development environment and allow designers to focus on the user interface without having to spend enormous amounts of time doing repetitive programming tasks. They also promote standards-based designs that have a consistent look and feel.

To understand how these tools work, we briefly examine how application software interacts with I/O devices, such as screens and pointing devices. We build upward from basic screen drawing technologies (graphical libraries) that provide hardware-independent ways to "paint" pixels on the screen to the user interface development tools that enable designers to efficiently create interactive prototypes and applications.

The tools we will explore include the following:

- Graphical libraries
- User interface toolkits
- Visual interface builders
- Web development tools

5.6.1. Graphical Libraries

At a basic level, developers need a hardware-independent, and sometimes cross-platform, application programming interface (API) to "paint" buttons, scrollbars, labels, and other functions to the screen. Graphical libraries provide this functionality. Two of the more common APIs, especially for game environments, are OpenGL® and Direct3D®.

OpenGL

OpenGL® is a specification developed by Silicon Graphics® (SGI) and is currently an open standard. It is maintained by the Architectural Revision Board, a consortium of representatives from some of the major software and hardware manufactures. It contains more than 250 functions that can be used to render 2D and 3D images based on simple primitives.

Hardware manufacturers have created implementations of OpenGL® using the functions and behaviors specified by the standard for all the major platforms—Windows®, Macintosh®, and UNIX®. OpenGL® also uses an implementation written by SGI® that enables hardware acceleration, depending on the computer's graphics card. If this is not possible, slower, software-based acceleration is used.

OpenGL® is a low-level programming technology that can be difficult and time consuming for development purposes. However, the OpenGL Utility Toolkit® (GLUT) can be used for more efficient as well as cross-platform development.

Direct3D

Direct3D® is a Component Object Model (COM)-based proprietary 3D graphics API developed by Microsoft® in 1996. It is a component of the DirectX® collection of multimedia APIs. Direct3D RM® (Retained-Mode) is a higher-level API than OpenGL®, which only functions on Windows® systems.

Scene Graph–Based Libraries

OpenGL® and Direct3D® are both direct draw libraries that require developers to recreate entire screens when simple changes are needed. Scene graph–based libraries reduce this level of complexity by using a screen graph to describe 2D and 3D scenes. The scene graph can take the form of a display list, tree structure, or direct acyclic graph (DAG). When a change is required, the developer simply enters it on the graph; the library takes care of updating the screen.

Java 3D® is a DAG scene graph–based imaging model that was designed for Web development and is, therefore, a cross-platform API. It is well suited for the Web but it is slower than other technologies used for PC-based applications. The OpenGL® scene-graph API makes OpenGL® development easier; however, it still requires knowledge of the low-level OpenGL® calls and interactions, which means that development will remain at a lower level than with Java 3D®.

Graphical libraries offer low-level control that is very flexible but highly complex. They require programming skills beyond those of many interaction designers. Graphical libraries are useful for the newly emerging mobile devices that lack high-level development tools or when unique interaction designs, such as zoomable interfaces, are required. These tools also allow developers to create extremely efficient code for environments that have significant memory and performance restrictions.

5.6.2. User Interface Toolkits

Graphical libraries and window systems constitute a basic layer for putting visual elements on the screen. They are low-level tools that require considerable programming skills and as such do not provide an efficient way to create user interface prototypes that involve quick iteration of design ideas. A higher level of programming abstraction is required so that designers can focus their energies on the complexities of user interaction rather than on writing the complex code required to create a basic command button and its associated behaviors.

This higher level of abstraction can be found in user interface toolkits (UITs), sometimes called GUI toolkits. UITs are available for all of the major platforms and are used with an accompanying programming environment, such as the Microsoft Windows Forms, the Apple Xcode Toolkit®, or the GTK and Qt multiplatform toolkits.

These toolkits supply the designer with the basic tools of interactive application development: widgets. The designer creates the user interface by assembling these widgets into a tree structure. Toolkits are based on object-oriented principles. To construct the interface, the developer creates instances of an interaction object class and defines whatever unique characteristics it must have by assigning values to specific attributes (instance attributes).

Developers with a certain level of programming ability can also use toolkits to create novel interaction objects because many toolkits allow new classes to be developed using either single or multiple inheritance.

Interaction objects have three basic aspects: presentation, behavior, and an application interface. Developers can rely on the basic look and feel embedded within the interaction objects, but they must also control some of the object's attributes to attain the level of functionality required by the emerging interactive application.

Presentation

Toolkits supply developers with a prepackaged look for application widgets that conforms to the style guidelines of the supporting platform in terms of shape and other aspects of the object's visual appearance. This makes it easy for designers to replicate the presentation features of a particular manufacturer's interface.

Toolkits also offer a degree of flexibility in the overall design of the interface. Their programming environments allow developers to position widgets in relation to each other, using a constraint-based format that retains the overall design intent, even when widgets are altered or added or when windows are resized.

Behavior

Widgets are defined by their supported behaviors. Buttons may involve highlighting, pressing, and releasing behaviors. Scrollbars incorporate complex behaviors that involve dragging the thumb as well as the up and down arrow. The basic style guides for each platform concerning widget states (active, inactive), highlighting, and other behavioral concerns are all provided by the toolkit.

Some interaction objects have attributes that can be altered by the programmer, such as multiple and single selection in a list box. These parameterized behaviors must be programmed before the application is run. However, because toolkits supply the basic behaviors for each interaction object, developers do not have to spend time recreating them.

Application Interface

Toolkits define how the interaction objects interact with the rest of the application. User actions can be communicated in three basic ways:

- Call backs
- Active variables
- Listeners

- **Call Backs**—One or more call back functions are registered when a particular instance of a widget is created. These functions are called when the user activates a particular widget. This method splits the logic of the program among many call back functions.
- **Active Variables**—This approach associates an interaction object with an application variable. It uses a controller to update the variable when an event occurs to the associated object. This method can only be used for data-oriented objects such as text fields, and therefore complements, but does not supplant, call back functions.
- **Listeners**—This method associates a "listener" object with one or more interaction objects. The widget registers a user input event with the listener that is set up to "listen" for that particular event. This is more efficient than the "spaghetti of call backs" involved in the call back method (Beaudouin-Lafon & Mackay, 2002, 1024).

Each one of these methods has particular advantages and disadvantages, and they all require considerable programming knowledge. To successfully program the interface the developer must be familiar with the specific methods used by the toolkit. This may be the deciding factor as to which toolkit the design team chooses to use.

Toolkits are limited by the types of presentation, behavior, and application interface methods they use. It is difficult to create novel interaction objects that do not adhere to the specified norm. They also are widget-centric and do not involve component-to-component interactions like those involved in drag-and-drop actions. Style guides for each particular platform must be consulted for interface concepts and procedures that go beyond the aspects of individual interface components.

5.6.3. Visual Interface Builders

Although toolkits afford an efficient, standards-based method for creating interactive applications and prototypes, they do require significant programming abilities. Thus, they do not easily lend themselves to iterative design methods and procedures, and they may also inhibit the exploration of new and evolving design ideas.

To create a more flexible development environment, another level of abstraction is necessary. At this level, instantiation of interaction objects is achieved visually within a graphical editor—visual design is accomplished visually, interaction is created interactively. These graphical environments allow designers to place, size, move, and parameterize widgets using drag-and-drop, menu selection, and text entry methods.

Widgets are chosen from a tool palate and placed on a form where they can be positioned and/or resized. Their attributes can be set using lists, menus, and dialogue boxes, and they can be tested using a test mode view before the application is complied. This creates a flexible and efficient environment for iterative development.

Visual interface builders (VIBs) blend well with iterative design methods. Design ideas and prototypes can quickly be explored and developed, and they can be easily updated and altered according to the results of usability testing. "In these systems, simple things can be done in simple ways" (Mayers, Hudson, & Pausch, 2002, 217). Full-scale interactive applications also can be developed using VIBs such as Visual Basic®, Borland's Jbuilder®, and Microsoft's Visual Studio.NET®.

Benefits of High-Level Software Tools

High-level software development tools have contributed to the development of standardized interface practices and procedures by making sets of consistently designed widgets and window interfaces readily available to programmers and designers. These tools have significantly affected software development efficiency as well as fostered consistent design practice.

Shneiderman and Plaisant (2005, 185) identified the following benefits from the use of high-level software tools

User Interface Independence

- They separate interface design from internals.
- They enable multiple user interface strategies.
- They enable multiple-platform support.
- The establish the role of the user interface architect.
- They enforce standards.

Methodology and Notation

- They facilitate the development of design procedures.
- They help in finding ways to talk about design.
- They create project management.

Rapid Prototyping

- The make it possible to try out ideas very early.
- They make it possible to test, revise, test, revise, ...
- They engage end users—managers and customers.

Software Support

- They increase productivity.
- They offer constraint and consistency checks.
- They facilitate team approaches.
- They ease maintenance.

5.6.4. Web Development Tools

The Web has become an important segment of the Internet. Companies in the retail business have pushed the development of the Web as a tool for increasing their customer base, which, in turn, has influenced the development of software tools that provide a more efficient environment for Web site construction.

There has been increasing emphasis on dynamic Web-based interaction and database connectivity in support of a more powerful and dynamic interaction between companies and their customers. Web sites have become more complex and interactive, and designers are benefiting from the evolution of more sophisticated Web application development tools.

"WYSIWYG" Web Development Environments

Web development applications have evolved to the point at which creating dynamic Web sites can be as easy as drag and drop in a WYSIWYG (what you see is what you get) environment. Programs like Adobe Dreamweaver® and GoLive® allow users to work in different views, including raw HTML, outline (tags are shown in outline form so the nodes of the document tree are more clearly visible), and WYSIWYG. These programs have facilities that enable scripting and CSS development as well as FTP uploads of complete Web sites. These Web development environments make it easy to create Web-based presentations, prototypes, or full-fledged, interactive Web sites.

Flash—Adobe Flash® is a rapid application development environment for the Web. Projects developed with the Flash® application can be exported as Flash® files that include rich graphic environments, interactivity, and Web-based forms or as GIF animations, QuickTime® files, and other dynamic as well as static file formats. Flash® files can include HTML, CSS, and scripts written in the native ActionScript object-oriented scripting language.

The Flash® application development environment includes a drag-and-drop interface for component-based Web applications that require standard components, such as text boxes, list boxes, scrollbars, buttons, checkboxes, radio buttons, combo boxes, and other traditional GUI components. This makes Flash® a suitable tool for prototyping and presentation development.

5.6.5. Emerging Standards

Although there is a consistent flow of evolving technology and interface development, contemporary desktop computing has become, to a large degree, standardized and stable. At the same time, however, there has been tremendous growth in the area of mobile computing and information appliance development. Due to their size, context of use, and many other reasons, these computing paradigms do not readily lend themselves to the desktop environment. Therefore, interface designs for these devices are in a state of flux.

Innovative solutions by talented designers and design firms have appeared, such as the circular navigation interface designed by Apple® for the highly successful iPod® music player. Technological advances in voice and handwriting recognition have enabled new ways of interacting with the new generations of information appliances. Web-based applications and environments are evolving and developing standardized procedures and interaction methodologies.

Existing user interface development tools are designed for the development of traditional graphical interfaces. They foster standardized practices and can be difficult, if not completely unusable, in the development of novel interactive applications. An evolutionary gap between new interaction paradigms and the tools that support their development will always be unavoidable.

Low-level technologies are often required at the early stages of development to explore the design ideas that lead to novel interactive systems. However, the concept of high-level design is well established, and the need for efficient development tools is clear. An active community of researchers is involved in the exploration of high-level abstractions for programming and developing interactive systems. They have a large body of research to draw from; already, there are a number of toolkits such as Jazz and the subsequent Java-based toolkit Piccolo for zoomable interfaces and SATIN for ink-based application development.

Mayers et al. suggest areas of research on interactive systems that will benefit from the creation of novel interactive development environments:

- Ubiquitous computing
- Device prototyping
- Distributed computing
- Recognition-based interfaces
- 3D interfaces
- End-user customization

It is possible to add virtual reality, augmented reality, and the other embodied virtuality environments, such as wearable, ambient, and invisible computing, to this list.

5.7. Designing the Facets of the Interface

At this point you may be thinking that there is something missing from this description of the design process: How do we design the various screens for the prototype? What components should we use? How do we decide on screen layouts? How do we determine the best interaction style? How do we determine the validity of our choices?

To answer these questions we must explore each element in depth. We must understand how to manipulate and apply color, how to create and use icons, how to structure and display text, how to use sound, and how haptic feedback can create dynamic interaction between people and computing devices.

We need to understand what the various interface components do and the specific tasks for which they are suited. We must understand the principles involved in visual design. We must know how people conceptualize their environments and formulate strategies to accomplish tasks.

In the following chapters we explore each of these issues and areas of concern in depth. We begin with the principles of design that can be used throughout the design process and applied to all aspects of interface design. We then look at the various components of the human perceptual systems that are involved—visual, auditory, and haptic.

We explore visual aspects, such as color, icons, and text, and then look at the ways in which sound and touch can be used in human–computer interaction. We then study the various modeling techniques that can capture the process and motivation behind human behavior in relation to computer-based tasks. Finally, we investigate the various approaches to formal and informal usability testing.

Design Scenario

Circumference: Physical Design

We now develop paper prototypes and some general template wireframes based on the results of the conceptual design activities described throughout this chapter. We refer to these and develop them in more detail in the following chapters as we complete the physical design activities.

The activities in this design scenario include the following:

- Low-fidelity prototypes
- Wireframes
- Evaluation—applying design principles

Low-Fidelity Prototypes

Low-fidelity prototypes are generally made using paper and pencil. Figure 5.13 shows a rough draft for the sample poem page, which will be used and modified numerous times. Using it, we will be able to test some ideas and get a sense of the direction we want to take in terms of page layout. The appearance should remain rough, and we should not spend a great deal of time making these prototypes.

Wireframes

The global navigation flowchart developed in the conceptual design phase will be used to create a template wireframe for the entire site (Figure 5.14). This will enforce a consistent layout across all pages.

The wireframe template will be created using a drawing program such as Adobe Illustrator ® and will be based on the paper prototype in Figure 5.13. It will look as shown in Figure 5.15.

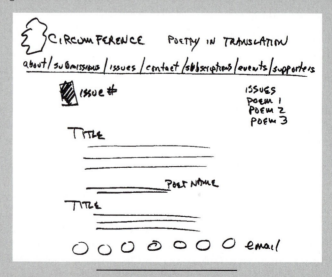

Figure 5.13 Low-fidelity prototype.

Design Scenario (cont.)

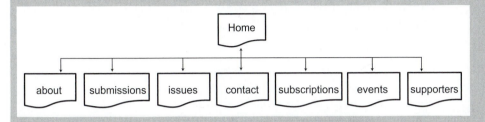

Figure 5.14 The *Circumference* flowchart: Global navigation.

Notice the indication for the fold. This boundary indicates what will be seen in a browser set at 800/600 resolution. The concept of the fold comes from newspapers and relates to the content that can be seen when the paper is folded in half.

Our object is to get the most important information into the area above the fold, to ensure its visibility. This is especially important for Web sites because people do not like to scroll, and if they do not see what they want quickly enough, they navigate to another site.

Feature Creep

Notice that we have included a search function and a bottom navigation strip. Issues like the addition of a search function may come up during different phases. The earlier these issues come up, the better, so that they can be included in the template wireframes.

A quick check with a primary stakeholder will probably be required to verify the usefulness of the additional functionality, but it can be difficult to weigh the additional cost of the implementation against the increased utility. The spiral life cycle approach has risk assessment built into every cycle so that this type of scope creep can be monitored and investigated.

If these issues come up after the physical design phase, it can be difficult and costly to incorporate them into the design. This underscores the importance of the discovery phase and the need to clearly identify the constraints in the requirements document.

Constraints:

• The site should allow current versions of the most common audible browsers to access as much content as possible.

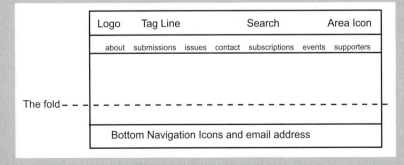

Figure 5.15 Basic *Circumference* wireframe.

Design Scenario (cont.)

- Content must be accessible to older visitors.
- Content must be accessible to older browsers.
- Finances are tight, and the project cannot go over budget.

Notice the last constraint. If the budget does not have any wiggle room, the addition of a search function will probably put the project over budget and will not be an option at this point. The search function issue can be included in the Project Management Document under the Future Needs heading.

The Issues Area—Selected Poems Wireframe

Consider the wireframe for the Issues area shown in Figure 5.16, which includes additional indications about the wireframe's elements. Notice that both versions of the poem are situated on one page; this will require scrolling. We can avoid scrolling by putting each version of the poem on a separate page. How do we decide which format is better? We look at some of the issues related to this design decision in subsequent chapters.

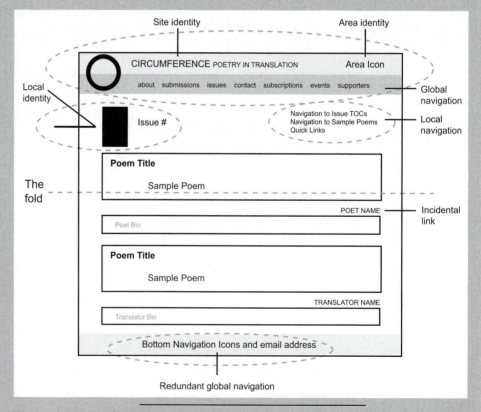

Figure 5.16   Selected poem wireframe: More detailed.

Design Scenario (cont.)

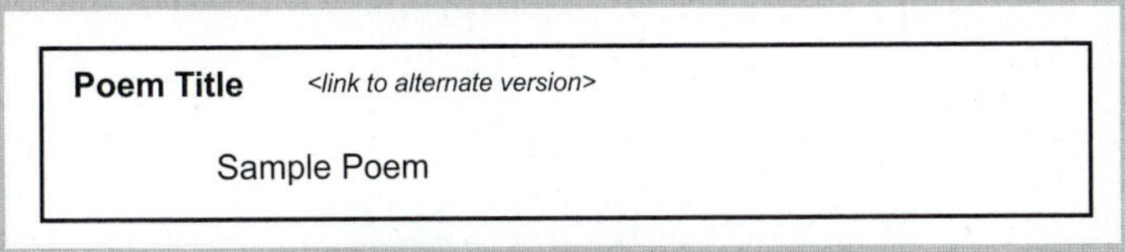

> **Poem Title**   *<link to alternate version>*
>
> Sample Poem

Figure 5.17   Paging link.

We explore the ramifications of scrolling versus paging in Chapter 12, where the issue relates to the comprehension of text; however, we learn more about these formats in Chapter 8, where we use the GOMS model to help us to make a final decision.

The scrolling version of the selected poem page is shown in Figure 5.16. The paging format wireframe looks similar, except that it only has one poem on the page. It also requires a link to the companion poem. We place this link to the right of the poem's title and label the links "English" and "Original" (Figure 5.17; note that in Figure 5.17, <link to alternative version> is used as a placeholder for either label). These are blue and underlined.

Why do we have to decide between different layouts instead of adjusting the layout on a poem-by-poem basis? The answer is that because doing so would decrease the consistent look of the pages and thus decrease predictability. This added complication would call attention to the interface and become a distraction for users.

This distraction would conflict with the requirement that states "The visual presentation should not distract from the poetry reading experience." We should base our

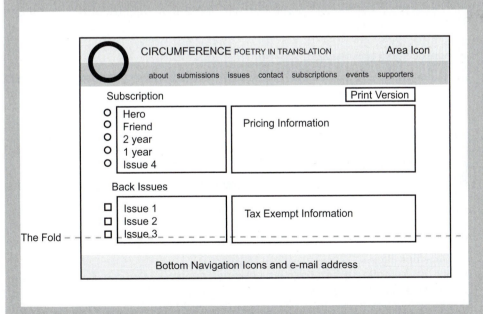

Figure 5.18   Order form wireframe.

Design Scenario (cont.)

design decision on longer poems with long line-lengths so that we do not have to alter the layout on a poem-by-poem basis.

The Subscriptions Area—Order Form Wireframe

The wireframe for the order form will look as shown in Figure 5.18.

The layout of the order form is covered in more detail in the design scenario in Chapter 8.

Summary

The design phase involves both conceptual as well as physical design activities. It is a very iterative phase and involves design, evaluation, and testing activities that culminate in the creation of a functional prototype.

There are many techniques that can be used to explore evolving design ideas such as card sorts and scenarios. These ideas can then be crafted into low-fidelity prototypes that can be evaluated and tested. This process continues until the design becomes relatively stable and robust, at which point formal usability tests are carried out.

The results of these usability tests provide insight into particular design problems and can be used to initiate a new iteration cycle involving some of the conceptual and physical design activities. Testing and iteration are two of the most important aspects of the design phase and are integral to the user-centered design approach to interaction design.

Resources on the Web

www.aw.com/heim

You will find links to Web-based resources that discuss and describe many of the methods, techniques and tools used to design user interfaces that are covered in this chapter.

Suggested Reading

Krug, S. (2005). *Don't Make Me Think: A Common Sense Approach to Web Usability* (2 ed.): New Riders Press.

Nielsen, J. (1999). *Designing Web Usability: The Practice of Simplicity* (1 ed.): Peachpit Press.

Pruitt, J., & Adlin, T. (2006). *The Persona Lifecycle: Keeping People in Mind Throughout Product Design:* Morgan Kaufmann.

Snyder, C. (2003). *Paper Prototyping: The Fast and Easy Way to Design and Refine User Interfaces:* Morgan Kaufmann.

CHAPTER

6

Design Principles

Interaction design is a lengthy process that requires a comprehensive knowledge of computing technologies and a thorough understanding of the psychological complexities of the human mind. It must take into consideration our sense of logic and our sensitivity to aesthetics. In fact, the aesthetic-usability effect says that aesthetically pleasing interface designs are perceived as being easier to use than other, less appealing interfaces, even if that is not actually the case.

How do we create elegant solutions to complex interaction problems?

It can seem daunting to consider all of the technical variables involved in interaction design and come up with something that is useful and usable and, in addition, create a design that is aesthetically pleasing.

How do interaction designers succeed at creating the great designs that are powerful and aesthetically appealing?

Think of the Apple iPod® or the Google™ search engine. These are powerful tools that have enormous appeal and tremendous market success. People like them, and they perform their tasks elegantly and reliably.

To impose structure and order on the design process, interaction designers use principles to guide and inform the many decisions they must make. These principles help designers to make decisions about the way interfaces should look and function. They can assist in the decision-making process when tradeoffs are required, and they can also help to convince other members of the design team on the correctness of certain decisions.

These principles help designers to create more-intuitive designs. They are well established and have a long history in the various design disciplines. Let's look at some of these principles and see how they can be applied to interaction design projects.

6.1. Principles of Interaction Design

MAXIM

Design principles can be used to guide design decisions.

Interaction design, like all design disciplines, is guided by well-established principles. Design principles do not prescribe specific outcomes; they function within the context of a particular design project. They guide the interaction designer and help him or her to make decisions that are based on established criteria.

There are many important principles, and there are many ways to apply them. Their application usually depends on context. We will explore several of these principles and apply them to specific design situations. The principles will be presented in a systematic and structured way using two main categories: effectiveness principles and efficiency principles. Once we begin the design process, however, things will get a lot messier.

Iterative design is a multilayered activity that is subject to many different and often contradictory forces. For instance, we may strive to place screen components in consistent locations, but to prevent the user from inadvertently clicking on a destructive function like Delete, we will break the consistency rule and locate these functions in places that will catch the user's attention.

The way in which we apply design principles depends on the context of the particular design activity in which we are involved. Every decision must be weighed against the whole and determined by the specific circumstances of interaction.

Gulfs of Execution and Evaluation

Design principle can also be used to determine whether there are gulfs of execution or evaluation. Gulfs of execution relate to the effectiveness principles, and gulfs of evaluation relate to the efficiency principles. They can be applied at each of Norman's seven stages (see Chapter 2) based on execution/effectiveness and evaluation/efficiency correlations.

6.1.1. Framework for Design Principles

Design principles are not easily categorized; they are interrelated and may have recursive relationships with other principles. For instance, consider the principles of predictability and memorability. If something has a predictable behavior, such as a button that appears to press in when we click on it, we will be more likely to remember that behavior the next time we encounter a similar button. Therefore, this type of button will have a high degree of memorability. Recursively, the memory of that behavior will increase the predictability of other button components.

To avoid this type of complication, we can take a more structured, although artificial, approach. The following framework serves the purpose of clarifying the discussion; its use does not imply that there are no other ways of viewing the connections and relations among the various design principles. Nor does the method imply a strict hierarchal structure. The framework has the following components:

Usability Goals—There are two main usability goals in the framework—comprehensibility and learnability. These are discussed in more detail later.

Design Principle Categories—As mentioned earlier, the framework also divides the design principles into two main groups—efficiency principles and effectiveness principles. The effectiveness principles can be used to determine required functionality, and the efficiency principles can be applied to the design of the presentation filter (interface). These categories and their related principles are discussed in detail in the following sections of this chapter.

Format for Describing Design Principles—The framework uses the format "serves the principle of ..., which promotes ..." to describe the different principles. For instance, *familiarity* serves the principle of *memorability*, which promotes *usability*. Consider the framework shown in Figure 6.1.

The framework includes two barriers derived from the two main goals: the comprehensibility barrier and the learnability barrier. These barriers can present formidable obstacles for the user and diminish the ultimate usefulness of the design.

For instance, let's look at the principles of customization and flexibility and how they relate to the goal of usefulness. We can say that *customization* serves the principle of *flexibility*, which promotes *usefulness*. However, if the design is difficult to understand, the user may not be able to use the customization features. Therefore,

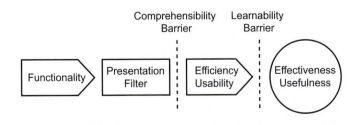

Figure 6.1 Framework for design principles.

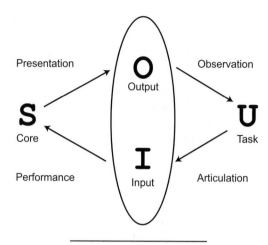

Figure 6.2 Interaction framework.

the comprehensibility barrier will make the design less usable and, consequently, more difficult to learn. This will decrease the ultimate usefulness of the design.

Let's explore this framework and relate it to the interaction framework (Dix, Finlay, Abowd, & Beale, 1998) covered in Chapter 2 (Figure 6.2).

- **Functionality**—The system must have adequate functionality for a particular task. This is expressed in the *core* language of the system *(performance step)* and relates to the user's task.
- **Presentation Filter**—The functionality must be made accessible through the presentation filter (interface). This involves the *presentation*, the *articulation*, and the *observation* steps.
- **Comprehensibility Barrier**— If the presentation is comprehensible, the comprehensibility barrier will be superseded. This depends on the degree of efficiency/usability in the interface design. The user must understand what is required by the *input* language *(articulation step)* and what is being communicated by the *output* language *(observation step)*.
- **Learnability Barrier**—If the interface is comprehensible, it will be learnable; there is a direct relationship.
- **Effectiveness/Usefulness**—If the user can learn the interface, he or she can take advantage of the functionality, and therefore the interface will be useful.

6.2. Comprehensibility

MAXIM

An interface design that is easy to comprehend will be efficient and effective.

The most important consideration in interaction design is comprehensibility. If a user does not understand the interface, he or she will not be able to use it, rendering it useless.

A design's comprehensibility is highly dependent on the way in which the interface communicates its functionality to the user. The functionality that makes a design useful might be present in the design; however, if that functionality is communicated in an incomprehensible way, that functionality becomes essentially invisible.

People are adaptable and generally find ways to accomplish their goals; however, a design that is not easy to understand makes this more difficult and impedes performance. We should, therefore, hold comprehensibility as the highest goal in the design process.

6.3. Learnability

MAXIM

An interface with high usability will be easier to learn.

The learnability of a design is based on comprehensibility: if you can't understand it, you can't learn it. However, even if an interface has high comprehensibility, it might still involve a learning curve. Moreover, learnability and comprehensibility are recursive: we start with comprehensibility, which affects learnability, which in turn increases comprehensibility (Figure 6.3).

This is a powerful feedback loop that can be facilitated by the proper application of design principles. For instance, if we use familiar conventions, the interface will be easier to understand and, therefore, easier to learn. The end result will be a useful design.

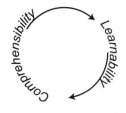

Figure 6.3
Comprehensibility/learnability feedback loop.

Let's now look at each of the principles and see how they can best be applied in the interaction design process. The design principles are organized based on the goal for which they are the most relevant.

- Effectiveness/usefulness

  - Utility
  - Safety
  - Flexibility
  - Stability

- Efficiency/usability

  - Simplicity
  - Memorability
  - Predictability
  - Visibility

6.4. Effectiveness/Usefulness

The effectiveness goal stipulates that a design must fulfill the user's needs by affording the required functionality. This may mean that the design for a drawing program should enumerate all of the tools required to create digital drawings, or it may mean that a Web site has all the information a visitor may need to accomplish his or her goals.

Effectiveness can be measured by the semantic distance (see Chapter 2) between what a user needs to accomplish and the functionality offered by the design. Consider a remote for a VCR that does not contain a button for ejecting a tape. There is a gulf of execution between the need to eject a tape and the functionality afforded by the remote. This design renders the device less useful than it could be.

6.4.1. Utility

Effectiveness can be defined as the utility of the proposed design. The principle of utility relates to what the user can do with the system. A design with good utility can be useful and might prove to be an effective tool for accomplishing particular tasks if that utility is easy to access and use.

Adobe PhotoShop® is arguably one of the most useful applications available commercially. It is used by people from an amazing diversity of domains, from Web site developers to commercial and recreational photographers. PhotoShop® is a good example of an application with high utility and ease of use. Although there is a learning curve for some of its more professional functionality such as commercial pre-press development, the tools are designed with each domain in mind so that professionals can relate to the program's utility in a familiar context.

6.4.2. Safety

Effectiveness also involves the principle of safety. A design that has a high degree of safety is more useful than a design that involves a high degree of risk. Safety issues can involve physical parameters, such as those in mission-critical environments like air traffic control or nuclear facilities. Safety can also mean that people can use the system without the risk of losing or destroying their work. In the *Humane Interface*, Jeff Raskin put forth two rules for interface design that are corollaries to Asimov's laws of robotics (Raskin, 2000). The first one is stated as follows:

A computer shall not harm your work or, through inaction, allow your work to come to harm.

We will discuss the second rule later in the efficiency/usability section. The auto recovery and auto save features available in software applications are good examples of the safety principle being put into effect. The plain truth is that computers crash from time to time, and there is a risk that some work will be lost. These automatic safety features have more than earned their cost of development.

We have already seen some of the risks involved with design flaws in mission-critical environments. The lessons learned from the Apollo 13 space mission and the Three Mile Island disaster stand as monuments to the critical importance of the safety principle in human–computer interaction.

Recovery

Raskin's first rule can be implemented in interaction designs by incorporating appropriate undo functionality and robust error recovery routines. It can also be incorporated in Web design by stipulating the need to retain Web-based form input when users navigate to previous pages in a form fill-in process during Web-based transactions.

6.4.3. Flexibility

An important parameter of effectiveness is flexibility. A tool that is flexible can be used in multiple environments and address diverse needs. This is the "Swiss Army Knife" concept. An effective tool should also have enough flexibility to perform a desired function under many different circumstances.

For instance, a drawing program would have high flexibility, and therefore greater effectiveness, if it could be used to create images for the Web as well as for professional print publishing. It would also be more flexible if it could import directly from a scanner or if it could import and export images in diverse formats.

Customization

Another important consideration in terms of flexibility is the capacity to modify the tool to the individual needs of the user. A tool would have greater flexibility if people were able to customize the interface according to their personal preferences.

For example, users should have the ability to alter settings like default fonts and font parameters. They should be able to modify toolbars and toolbar placement so that they can adjust their working space to be more efficient and memorable. These adjustments should be recorded by the application so the user does not have to adjust them every time he or she uses the program. This is usually accomplished with a Preferences dialogue such as the one shown in Figure 6.4.

6.4.4. Stability

Another important parameter of effectiveness is the stability of the system being designed. A stable system is a robust system. A system that functions consistently well will be more useful than a system that crashes frequently.

The robustness of a Web site design may involve the use of well-established technologies and appropriately tailored content. For instance, content that is not

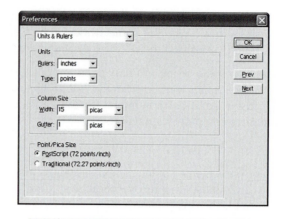

Figure 6.4 Adobe PhotoShop® Preferences dialogue.

Adobe product screen shot reprinted with permission from Adobe Systems Incorporated.

adapted to the connection speeds of the visitor may cause the screen to freeze or the computer to become so slow as to be unusable.

Video is becoming more prevalent on the Web due to the ubiquity of broadband connections. However, a robust design would inform visitors about the size of the video file and afford visitors with slower connections access to a lower-bandwidth version of the video, either through an automated process or manually.

6.5. Efficiency/Usability

MAXIM

Efficiency describes the usability of a design.

The efficiency goal stipulates that a design should enable a user to accomplish tasks in the easiest and quickest way possible without having to do overly complex or extraneous procedures. It is a measure of the usability of the design. Raskin's second rule relates to the efficiency of a design:

A computer shall not waste your time or require you to do more work than is strictly necessary.

There are many factors that affect the usability of an interaction design. They range from the size and placement of a component in a drawing program to the readability of the content of a Web page. These should not be seen as mutually exclusive or isolated components of the design process; they are often interrelated and might also overlap.

These factors may also conflict at times and require tradeoffs. The overriding principle of comprehensibility often can be used to make determinations about the relative importance of competing principles.

6.5.1. Simplicity

Everything should be made as simple as possible, but not simpler.

Albert Einstein

Simplicity is a high-level principle. If things are simple, they will be easy to understand and, therefore, easy to learn and remember. If things are simple, it will be easy to make predictions about their use and functionality. Simplicity can increase the efficiency of an interface and make it more usable. It also can be applied to increase the comprehensibility of an interface design.

Figure 6.5 shows the design of the Google Web search engine. It is an excellent example of a simple yet powerful tool.

One of the hardest things to accomplish is the design of something that is simple yet effective. It is important to understand the difference between simple and simplistic, which refers to something that results from oversimplification. A simplistic design involves "dumbing down" the interface and should be avoided. Simple designs do complex things in simple ways.

Ockham's Razor (The Principle of Simplicity)

The concept of simplicity is eloquently expressed in Ockham's razor, attributed to the medieval English philosopher and Franciscan monk William of Ockham (ca. 1285–1349):

Pluralitas non est ponenda sine necessitate [Pluralities should not be posited without necessity].

Figure 6.5 Google.com.

Screenshot © Google Inc. and is used with permission.

This principle can be understood as follows: given two otherwise equivalent designs, the simplest one is best. This is a widely accepted concept in disciplines as diverse as physics and graphic design. We can also make excellent use of the principle in interaction design.

At the heart of Ockham's razor is the idea that necessity must dictate the components of a design. This is similar to the concept of leveling in icon design, according to which the designer eliminates unnecessary details until only the essential elements are left (see Chapter 11). We must often make decisions about the amount of detail to include in an icon. Through leveling, we reduce the unnecessary detail and isolate the elements that foster comprehension. Similarly, Ockham's razor argues that we should only include those elements that are required to communicate the necessary information.

Ockham's razor can also guide the development of secondary windows (see Chapter 10). Secondary windows such as dialogue boxes that contain occasionally needed functionality should be added if and when they are needed. Unnecessary windows can cause confusion and can involve cumbersome window manipulation tasks.

80/20 Rule

The 80/20 rule was conceived by the economist Vilfredo Pareto, who found that 20% of the Italian population owned 80% of the nation's wealth. This rule has subsequently been used to describe complex systems in various domains and can be used to guide interaction design.

According to the 80/20 rule, 80% of an application's use involves 20% of its functionality. This idea can guide the construction of pull-down menus and toolbars. For instance, the 20% that is an application's most useful functionality should be put into the toolbars, where it can be easily accessed, whereas the other 80% can be put in less accessible pull-down menus. This also relates to the principle of progressive disclosure discussed later.

The 80/20 principle can also be applied to the design process itself. Interaction design often involves updating or modifying a previous design. Given the limited resources that often exist regarding time and personnel, this process might involve making decisions about which aspects of the design should be improved. According to the 80/20 principle, design resources should be allocated to the significant 20% of the interface because working on the other 80% will not be as cost effective.

Satisficing

The 80/20 principle is related to the principle of *satisficing*, which stems from the need to create a balance between satisfying and sufficing.

This principle combines the conflicting needs of finding the optimal solution that satisfies all the requirements and the need to settle on a solution that will be sufficient to proceed with the design. In other words, we must find the 20% that makes the most difference and focus on a solution that will suffice.

Satisficing is born of necessity. In the interaction design domain, resources are often scarce and there is always a deadline. Satisficing can be used when a satisficed solution is better than the previous design or any competing solution. It is a way to deal with resource limitations, especially when a project is complex and contains multiple interacting variables.

Satisficing is not, however, an excuse to pursue the path of least resistance. It is also inappropriate in mission-critical environments. In those situations, less than satisfactory solutions can have devastating results, and satisficing should not be considered.

Progressive Disclosure

With progressive disclosure, the user is shown only what is necessary at any given moment during his or her interaction with the system. This technique can take the form of links like "more info," "view details," or "related topics" on a Web page. It can also take the form of an expandable menu in an application (Figure 6.6) (see Chapter 10). Progressive disclosure serves to simplify available options so the user does not get overwhelmed with irrelevant functionality.

Constraints

The principle of constraints involves limiting the actions that can be performed in a particular design; it therefore controls the design's simplicity. It is applied by constraining the amount of functionality on a screen to only the necessary functions and therefore is related to the principle of progressive disclosure.

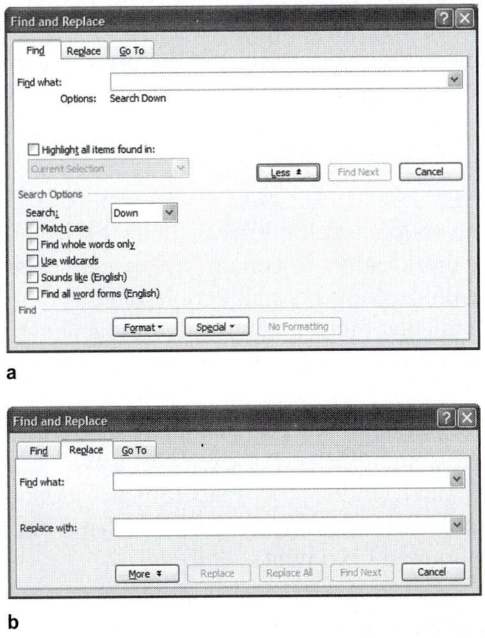

Figure 6.6 Expandable menu: (a) expanded, (b) minimized.

Figure 6.7 Grayed-out functionality.

When it is not appropriate or applicable, functionality can be grayed out, which helps to reduce user errors due to inappropriate commands out of the range of the current system state (Figure 6.7). The appropriate application of constraints can make an interface much easier to learn and use.

Constraints can be categorized as physical or psychological. Physical constraints limit a user's movement by controlling aspects such as direction or distance. Psychological constraints limit a user's actions by influencing the way he or she perceives the interface and its various components.

Physical Constraints

- **Paths**—Physical paths constrain movement to a designated location and direction. Sliders and scrollbars constrain a user's movement to the horizontal or vertical movement allowed by the components track.

- **Axes**—Physical axes constrain the user's movement to rotation around an axis. This can be seen in the way a trackball works. A trackball affords an infinite number of axes on which to rotate the ball and an unlimited length of movement. The user is constrained, however, to the location of the device because translational movement has no effect. For a discussion of rotational and translational movement, see Chapter 14.

- **Barriers**—Barriers provide spatial constraints that can confine the user's movement to the appropriate areas of the interface. The physical barrier provided by the computer screen can be used to help people target buttons and controls that are located in the peripheral areas of the interface. Chapter 7 shows how Fitts' law can be used to support the use of the screen's boundaries to constrain the user's movement and helping him or her to target small interface components.

Psychological

- **Conventions**—Conventions exploit learned behavior to influence a user's actions. For instance, the location of certain screen elements has become standardized and is, therefore, conventional. People tend to look in those locations when they need a particular functionality, and putting all of the conventional elements in the expected location constrains the user's attention to those locations.

- **Mapping**—Mapping can influence the way in which people perceive relationships between controls and effects. For example, a Web page design can take advantage of our natural tendency to map forward motion to the right and backward motion to the left by pointing arrows in those directions (the reverse is true for people who read from right to left).

- **Symbols**—Symbols can influence the way in which we interact with an interface by defining meaning and constraining our possible interpretations of interface elements. Symbols are used mostly for icons and labels. See Chapter 11 for an in-depth discussion of symbols.

6.5.2. Memorability

We can use the principle of memorability to increase the efficiency of designs. Interfaces that have high memorability are easier to learn and use, instilling a sense of control and comfort in the user. It is always comforting to know that the next time you launch a program, you will be able to find the objects and functionality you need without having to search menus or consult a manual.

Many different parameters affect memorability, including the following:

- **Location**—If we place a particular object in a consistent location, it will be easier to remember. The convention of putting the search box in the upper right-hand corner of a Web page makes it easier to find.
- **Logical Grouping**—If we group things logically, they will be easier to remember. For instance, if we put related options together in a menu, their functionality will be easier to remember. Later we explore the issues involved in visual grouping in the section on the Gestalt principles.
- **Conventions**—If we use conventional objects and symbols, they will be easier to remember. The shopping cart symbol is a convention, and therefore its functionality is easy to remember.
- **Redundancy**—If we use multiple perceptual channels to code information, people will be able to focus on the channel they personally rely on the most. There will also be more available associations for long-term memory processing (see Chapter 13 for more information on long-term memory processing).

An interface with high memorability is more comprehensible and efficient because there are fewer things for users to think about. These interfaces allow us to apply previous knowledge to components of the interface.

6.5.3. Predictability

Predictability involves a person's expectations and ability to determine the results of his or her actions ahead of time. Predictable events are obvious, and their results are, to a large degree, foreseeable. Highly predictable events are often considered inevitable.

Predicting the outcome of an action involves memory. We base our judgment on our previous experiences. If our document printed the last time we clicked the printer icon, it will probably print again when we hit it a second time.

If we can predict the outcomes of our actions, we gain a sense of security that allows us to be more productive. This security can also encourage us to explore some of the less familiar aspects of an interface and, therefore, to increase its usefulness.

Consistency and Correctness

Predictability and memorability can be increased by using the principle of consistency. The consistency principle can be applied to every aspect of an interface, from

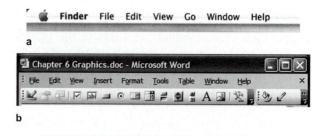

Figure 6.8   (a) Macintosh menu. (b) Microsoft Word menu.

color coding and icon style to button placement and functionality. Consistency reinforces our associations and, therefore, increases our ability to remember and predict outcomes and processes.

Consistency can be seen in the placement and labeling of menus in the common GUIs such as OS X® and Windows®. These interfaces consistently place the File, Edit, and View menus, when they are available, together on the left side of menu bars and the Window and Help menus on the right end (Figure 6.8). The other components of the various windows such as the Close and Minimize buttons are also placed in consistent locations and have a consistent appearance.

We should strive for consistency. Before we enforce consistency, however, we must make sure that we are correct; otherwise we will simply be consistently incorrect. Consistent incorrectness may be preferable to inconsistent incorrectness because people are highly adaptable and pick up patterns easily, so that any amount of consistency is helpful. Consistent incorrectness can mean, however, that the user must consistently do more work than is necessary. It can also mean that the user will simply be consistently confused and have to constantly think about how to use the interface. Neither of these situations is optimal, and they can be avoided with a bit of forethought and testing.

Generalizability

Consistency can help us use the knowledge we gathered from previous experience and apply it to similar situations. This decreases our learning curve and makes us more efficient. For instance, if we know that the Save function is in the File menu and that the File menu is located on the left side of the toolbar in one program, we can predict that the Save function's location will be the same in another program. Searching drop-down menus is time consuming and emphasizes one of their essential disadvantages: they hide things.

Conventions

Conventions are, by their very nature, predictable. They allow us to use our intuitions, which are based on previous experience and logic. Conventions are created through consistency. If something is consistently done in a particular way, that will eventually become the conventional way of doing it.

Consider the shopping cart icon used on most commercial Web sites (Figure 6.9). It was one of the first conventions to appear on the Web and has remained a staple for any site the offers that particular functionality.

Figure 6.9 Shopping cart convention.

Familiarity

Familiarity increases predictability. If we use familiar menu names and options in our designs, users will be able to locate objects and functions more easily. Similarly, if we use familiar images and metaphors, familiar formats and layouts, and familiar ways of doing things, we increase the predictability, efficiency, and comprehensibility of our interface designs.

Location, Location, Location

Location is everything! This bit of wisdom from the real estate domain also has a resonance for interaction design. Not all areas on the screen are created equal. If you understand the conventional use of screen space, you can optimize the predictability of your designs. For instance, Web pages are constructed from a top-left orientation (unless the user orientation is right to left, in which case it is top right), which dictates that the top-left corner is the prime location. This is where the visitor's attention naturally falls unless there are objects with high intensity in other locations drawing his or her attention away. See the later section on stimulus intensity.

The top-left area of the page is typically the place where the logo of the company or institution is placed (Figure 6.10). This is prime screen real estate and is visible no matter what resolution the visitor is using or the size of the browser window. By placing the logo here, we follow the predictability principle and give visitors an immediate indication of the site's identity.

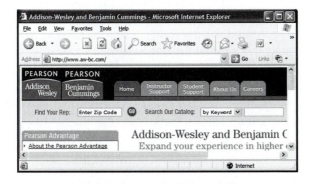

Figure 6.10 Logo of Pearson Education.

Modes

Modes create instability in mental models because they change the way objects function, unfortunately often without warning or any demonstrable indication, decreasing the predictability of the interface.

The simplest example of a mode is the way in which the Shift key affects the characters on the screen by creating an "uppercase mode." This new modality changes things significantly: an "A" can have a very different meaning than an "a."

The fact that we keep our finger on the shift key when using it makes this a toggle, which is easier to deal with than a complete modal transformation because our action constantly reminds us of the alteration in functionality. The Caps Lock key is a bit more problematic because we can forget that the uppercase mode has been turned on.

It can be frustrating to copy a long paragraph and then glance at the screen to see all of the words we just typed with reverse capitalization. This is one of the reasons some word processing applications include a "tOGGLE cASE" in the Change Case formatting menu (Figure 6.11).

Modes can be particularly problematic, especially for anyone who is not a frequent user of a particular application. They are often made more difficult because of the paucity of indications about the system's state while the mode is active, which can create a significant gulf of evaluation.

For instance, in a particular painting program, the text tool can be used to enter text directly onto the canvas at the exact location required. The system automatically enters "text mode" when the text tool is selected, but there is little visual indication that a mode has been entered. The text mode creates a separate layer in which the text remains editable until it is rendered as pixels along with the graphic image.

This is actually a significant improvement over the way text used to be entered in such programs, using a separate dialogue box. The difficulty with the implementation in this case arises when we go to save the file. When the text mode is active, most other functions are inaccessible, including the Save function. Unfortunately, there is no visible indication that the other functions have been disabled until we engage the File menu and see that the options are not available.

The most problematic aspect of this gulf of evaluation occurs if we try to save the file using the Ctrl+S keyboard shortcut. In this case, there is no indication that the Save function is disabled, nor is there any indication that the keyboard shortcut had no effect. We are left to assume, incorrectly, that the file has been saved.

HCI Foundations for Interaction Design

hci fOUNDATIONS FOR iNTERACTION dESIGN

Figure 6.11 Toggle case example.

6.5.4. **Visibility**

Show everything at once, and the result is chaos. Don't show everything, and then stuff gets lost.

(Norman, 1998, 74)

The principle of visibility involves making the user aware of the system's components and processes, including all possible functionality and feedback from user actions. As we saw, this is a significant principle for applications that contain modes.

The principle of visibility dictates that the user must be informed about all of the system's objects and processes. But how is this accomplished? Do we just make everything visible? In a complex application complete visibility could make the interface impossible to use.

Overload

> **MAXIM**
>
> The principles of progressive disclosure and simplicity should be used in conjunction with the principle of visibility.

Following the principle of visibility without also applying progressive disclosure can lead to visual overload. It is easier to make all of a system's functionality visible and let the user be discriminating than it is to meticulously study the temporal aspects of user interaction and craft an interaction space according to the requirements of current tasks, updating the interface as the user completes new tasks.

This is the challenge posed by the principle of visibility. The principle of simplicity can also be used to identify the necessary elements that will define what should be visible and when.

Feedback

Direct manipulation interfaces involve high visibility because they are defined by the immediate visual feedback they provide about user actions. It is the task of the interaction designer to decide what form that feedback takes.

There are conventions concerning feedback, such as the way command buttons behave when they are clicked or cursor hinting, which makes resource-intensive processing visible to the user (see Chapter 10). These conventions should be used in a way that complies with user expectations.

Recognition/Recall

The principle of visibility is based on the fact that people are better at recognition than recall. In other words, recognizing a target option within a set of options is easier than recalling that option from memory. Making things visible when they are relevant helps people to complete complex processes without having to remember all the details involved.

Orientation

People need to be able to orient themselves, especially in complex information spaces. Web site design must be sensitive to the visitor's need to know where he or she is within the context of the site, especially if the site is large and has many different areas. "You are here" orientation is essential for people who navigate the Web using hyperlinks rather than search mechanisms.

The principle of visibility means that a Web site design should supply information for a visitor to know what the site is about, how many areas the site has, and where the visitor is within the site. Page titles, site logos, tabbed interfaces, cookie trails, and color coding are some elements that can help visitors to orient themselves.

We have looked at some of the principles used by designers to help craft more usable and useful interactions. These are high-level principles that can guide decisions about the various tradeoffs required by conflicting requirements. We now look at some of the principles that function on lower levels. These principles are used to make decisions about specific screen controls, menus, and layouts.

6.6. Grouping

> **MAXIM**
>
> Use visual cues to support the logical structure of the interface.

We can increase the comprehension of complex information by creating visual presentations that logically support the intrinsic structure of that information. This involves grouping related things and presenting them in a comprehensible way through the creation of menus with related options or the grouping of related radio buttons on the screen.

It can also mean using borders or backgrounds to group a Web site's navigation links. To help in structuring this process, interaction designers often refer to the principles of perception that were developed by Gestalt psychologists in the early twentieth century.

6.6.1. Gestalt Principles of Perception

Gestalt psychology is based on the concept that we strive to perceive our environment as comprised of whole entities, even if we are not presented with complete information. For instance, emoticons, such as the little smiling face :-) used so frequently to add emotional nuances to e-mails and text messages, are often composed of just three separate text characters, yet we perceive them as complete faces.

At the heart of Gestalt psychology is the idea that we strive to find the simplest solutions to incomplete visual information. Rather than seeing the emoticon as three unique elements that must be considered individually, we gravitate to a simple solution, which interprets them as one integrated object.

Gestalt psychology strives to explain the factors involved in the way we group things. This is of considerable interest to interaction designers, who spend a great deal of time creating menu groupings and arranging content on screens and Web pages. Let's explore some of the principles and concepts of the Gestalt perspective on visual grouping.

Figure-Ground

Gestalt psychology's notion of figure and ground posits that we perceive our environment by differentiating between objects and their backgrounds. Basically, this means that we see some things as being prominent and others as being recessive, or as forming the background of the visual field.

Figure 6.12 The Rubin face/vase illusion.

This concept is often illustrated using the Rubin face/vase illusion shown in Figure 6.12. This image is manipulated in such a way that we must constantly strive to define the figure and the ground; it becomes a dynamic tug-of-war between the faces and the vase.

As another example, consider the Macintosh logo (Figure 6.13). This image creates a tension between its perception as a face in profile and one in frontal view. This is an interesting illusion, which has a potential dynamic effect in icon design; however, would be inappropriate to design an interface that created such visual tension.

Unfortunately, some Web sites use busy backgrounds, which compete with the information on the page. This type of presentation makes it hard to distinguish figures from the ground and diminishes the efficiency of the presentation, sometimes even making essential information invisible to the visitor.

Figure 6.13 Macintosh logo.

If we use these principles correctly, we can create logical groupings of multiple objects that will be perceived as complete entities and become figure components within the visual field of the user. In other words, we can use these principles to impose a logical structure on an interface's visual stimuli. These principles also ensure that the groups are presented in a natural way that is easy to understand.

In summary, according to Gestalt psychology:

- We have a natural inclination to perceive things as whole entities.
- We tend to distinguish foreground objects from background.
- The Gestalt principles of perception define the factors involved in visually grouping items.

A number of Gestalt principles can be useful in guiding the creation of logical groupings and can increase the comprehensibility of the interface. These principles address low-level decisions about the placement and organization of screen elements, such as icons and controls. They can also be used to organize and structure menus.

The Gestalt principles we will explore include the following:

- Proximity
- Similarity

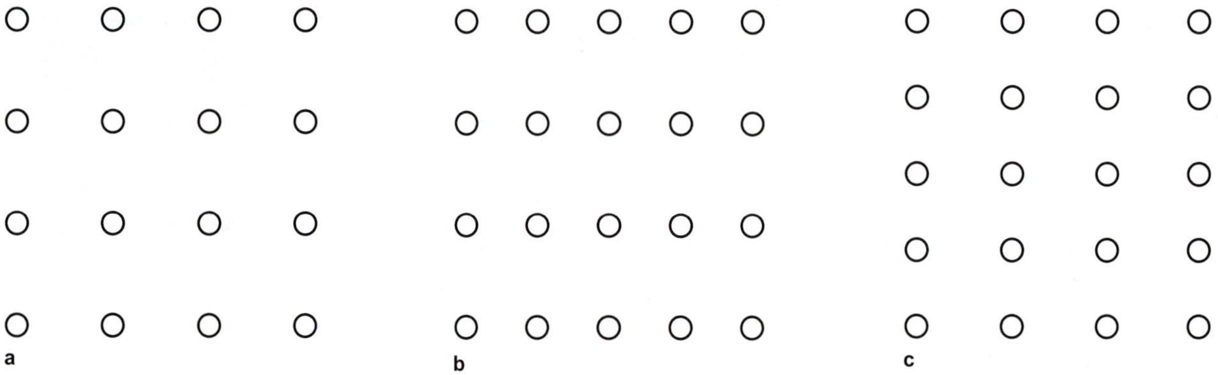

Figure 6.14 (a) Equidistant. (b) Horizontal proximity. (c) Vertical proximity.

- Common fate
- Closure
- Good continuity
- Area
- Symmetry
- Surroundedness
- Prägnanz

Proximity Principle—Objects that are close to each other will be seen as belonging together.

Consider the illustrations in Figure 6.14. We see Figure 6.14a as a group of radio buttons in a table comprised of four columns and four rows without any preference for either orientation. However, if the radio buttons are placed closer horizontally, we tend to see four rows of five buttons, as in Figure 6.14b. When they are positioned closer vertically (Figure 6.14c), we tend to see four columns of five buttons. The principle of proximity causes us to group the buttons that are close to each other.

Let's look at a real-world example. Consider the Preferences dialogue from Adobe PhotoShop® shown in Figure 6.15. The buttons on the far right tend to be seen as two groups rather than as four separate buttons. This is because there is slightly more vertical room between the Reset and Prev buttons, meaning that OK and Reset appear closer and therefore related. The same is true for the Prev and Next buttons. This grouping supports the logical structure of the buttons' functions.

Similarity Principle—Objects that have similar visual characteristics, such as size, shape, or color, will be seen as a group and therefore related.

Consider the illustrations in Figure 6.16. We see Figure 6.16a as rows of radio buttons and checkboxes, whereas in Figure 6.16b we see columns. This is because

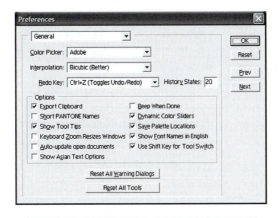

Figure 6.15 Adobe PhotoShop® Preferences dialogue.

Adobe product screen shot reprinted with permission from Adobe Systems Incorporated.

of our tendency to group the similar shapes. We see Figure 6.16c as three checkbox columns and two sets of radio button columns rather than four discrete radio button columns because we group each set of two columns together.

Figure 6.17 shows the Property pane from Adobe's Dreamweaver® application.

This is a complex pane that contains a great deal of functionality. However, if we give it a quick glance, we can see relationships between similar objects. Our eyes pick up all of the text boxes because of the white areas that they have in common.

The drop-down menus appear related because they all have the down-pointing arrow inside a blue square background. The justification icons on the upper right corner are similar in appearance and are therefore grouped.

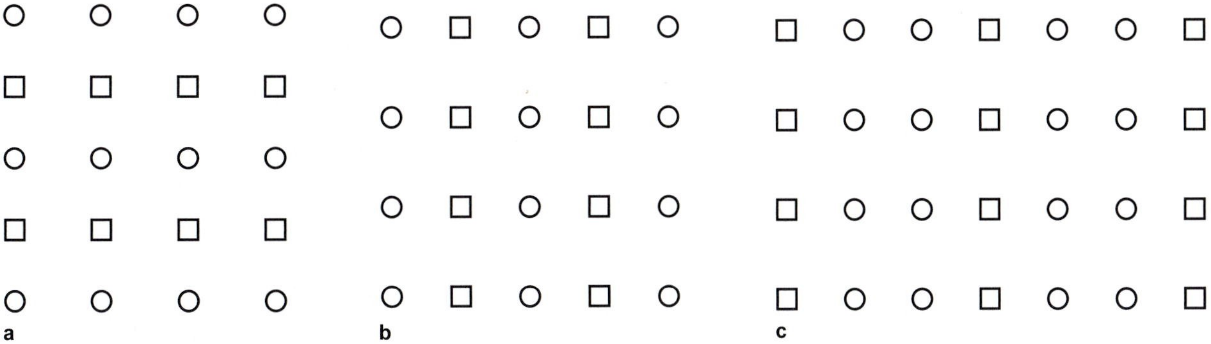

Figure 6.16 (a) Rows of similar objects. (b) Columns of similar objects. (c) Grouped columns.

Figure 6.17   Property pane from Adobe Dreamweaver®.

Adobe product screen shot reprinted with permission from Adobe Systems Incorporated.

The principle of similarity implies the existence of contrast. This is the other side of the coin and can be used visually to separate objects that should not be seen as related. Later we look at this issue more closely in the section on screen complexity.

Common Fate Principle—Objects that move together are seen as related.

This may seem an odd principle for interface design; however, if we understand movement as having a beginning, a direction, and an end, it becomes easier to apply the principle to static elements and it becomes a powerful tool for interface design.

Consider Figure 6.18. The drop-down menus on the left side do not start at the same location and do not end at the same location; hence, they are not visually grouped together and are seen as individual objects. The menus on the right side do start and end together, except for the last one, which just ends with others. These components share a common fate and, therefore, seem related.

A grid structure can be used to control the common fate of screen objects. Consider again the Dreamweaver® Properties pane, which uses alignment extensively to group related functionality. There are also discontinuities that serve to

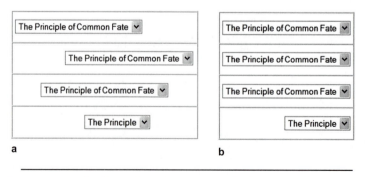

Figure 6.18   (a) Unaligned drop-down menus. (b) Aligned drop-down menus.

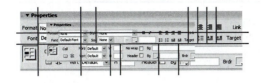

Figure 6.19   Common fate: Adobe Dreamweaver® properties pane.

Adobe product screen shot reprinted with permission from Adobe Systems Incorporated.

separate nonrelated functionality. The underlying grid becomes obvious when we start delineating the visual alignments as in Figure 6.19.

Closure Principle—We tend to see things as complete objects even though there may be gaps in their shape.

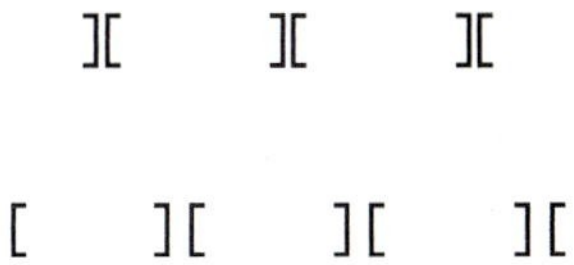

We see the brackets in the first row in Figure 6.20 as three groups of two due to their proximity. If we look at the brackets in the second row beginning at the left, we tend to see three enclosures. If we look at them from the right, however, we again tend to see groups of two brackets.

The closure principle can also be seen in the way the inactive tabs on the Dreamweaver® Results panel in Figure 6.21 are delimited with a line that does not span the entire height of the row of tabs. We tend to see complete boxes in which the links are placed.

Good Continuity Principle—We tend to see things as smooth, continuous representations rather than abrupt changes.

Consider the section of a page from the Apple.com Web site shown in Figure 6.22. Even though the line that delineates the top row is hidden by the image and is not continuous, we perceive one row containing the .mac title and the two round buttons.

][   ][   ][

[   ][   ][   ][

Figure 6.20   Closure principle.

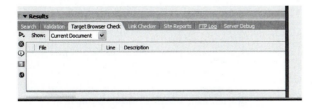

Figure 6.21   Adobe Dreamweaver® Results panel.

Adobe product screen shot reprinted with permission from Adobe Systems Incorporated.

Figure 6.22 Part of an Apple.com Web page.

Consider the page from the Museum of Modern Art (MoMA) Web site shown in Figure 6.23. The principle of good continuity helps us connect the top part of the left column with the part that appears under the dark horizontal strip. The dark strip appears to be placed on top of the white column that extends from the top to the bottom of the page.

The Area Principle—Objects with a small area tend to be seen as the figure, not the ground (also called the smallness principle).

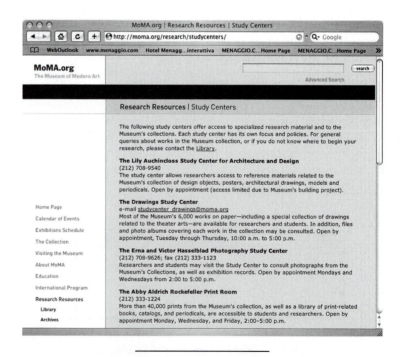

Figure 6.23 MoMA.org Web page.

Courtesy Museum of Modern Art.

a   b

Figure 6.24 (a) Metropolitan Museum of Art Web page (original). (b) Metropolitan Museum of Art Web page (altered) by author.

Consider the page from the Metropolitan Museum of Art Web site shown in Figure 6.24. In Figure 6.24a the large center image creates a ground within which one can see figures. When the same image is reduced in size, it becomes another figure on the page.

Symmetry Principle—Symmetrical areas tend to be seen as complete figures that form around their middle

According to the symmetry principle, we tend to group symmetrical elements into groups defined by a center point. There are a few ways to create symmetry: translation, reflection, and rotation (Figure 6.25).

Consider the page from the XM Satellite Web site shown in Figure 6.26. The center of the page is enclosed within a space created by the two red lines. The bottom line is a 90° rotation of the top line.

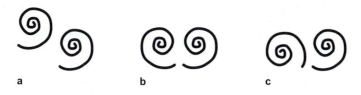

a   b   c

Figure 6.25 (a) Translation. (b) Reflection. (c) Rotation.

Top divider

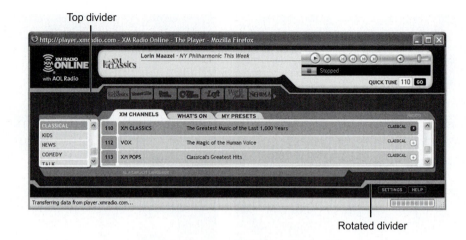

Rotated divider

Figure 6.26   XM Satellite Radio Web-based player.

Surroundedness Principle—An area that is surrounded will be seen as the figure, and the area that surrounds will be seen as the ground.

Consider the page from the Apple Web site shown in Figure 6.27a. Logically, the page seems to consist of top and bottom rows, two side columns, and a center area. If you look at the blurred version in Figure 6.27b, however, the

a

b

Figure 6.27   Surroundedness principle. (a) Original Apple.com page. (b) Blurred Apple.com page.

surrounded center area becomes the figure and the other page areas appear as the ground. This is the visual impression the page has on our perception of its contents.

White Space—The area of a page or screen that contains no content is called white space.

White space is a common design concept (not a Gestalt principle) that is closely related to the surroundedness principle and can be used to distinguish between figure and ground. White space is often used to create breathing room on the page and to set off paragraphs, images, and controls. It can create separations, group related objects, and organize and highlight important components of the screen. Things that are surrounded by white space are seen as related.

White space is discussed in the context of margin width in Chapter 12. Studies have shown that it has an effect on text comprehensibility.

Prägnanz Principle—We tend to perceive things based on the simplest and most stable or complete interpretation.

The overarching Prägnanz principle evolves from the combination and interaction of the other principles. In visual grouping, many Gestalt principles of perception work together, although at times, one principle can work against the influence of another. This can create tension that can be visually interesting but should be avoided in interface design.

For example, the application of a colored background for a set of check boxes and radio buttons should be based on the logical grouping of components and not conflict with that logical structure as it does in Figure 6.28a.

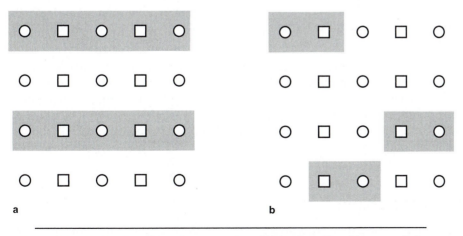

a   b

Figure 6.28 (a) Visual conflict with common fate. (b) Visual conflict with surroundedness.

1	3	**9**	7
4	8	**6**	2
5	7	**1**	3
2	4	**8**	6
7	9	**3**	1
6	2	**8**	4
7	1	**3**	9

Figure 6.29 Stimulus intensity.

The principles we have explored would compel us to group the similarly shaped checkboxes in these images vertically. However, the background color is applied horizontally, creating a surroundedness and similar fate for the components in rows.

The dark background pulls on our perception because it has more intensity than the white background, and we see three horizontal rows surrounded by white. In Figure 6.28b we have the same visual/logical conflict, resulting in the perception of two white rows surrounded by gray.

6.7. Stimulus Intensity

As we have seen, the physical encoding of an object affects our perception of that object according to the Gestalt principles of perception. If we add to this the concept of stimulus intensity, we find that the visual effect can become quite strong.

According to the Model Human Processor developed by Card, Moran, and Newell (see Chapter 7), we respond first to the intensity of a stimulus and only then do we begin to process its meaning. In other words, we perceive the color, shape, or size of an object before we understand what the object is.

In the set of numbers in Figure 6.29, for example, viewers typically perceive the columns of bold numbers before they perceive the rows of odd and even numbers. In this image, the principles of proximity and common fate work together with the intensity of the bold numbers to create the appearance of columns. Only after they process the meaning of the numbers can viewers create logical rows based on odd and even numbers.

6.8. Proportion

Proportion can be used to represent logical hierarchies. The headings element in markup languages uses proportion to visually structure information on a page (Figure 6.30).

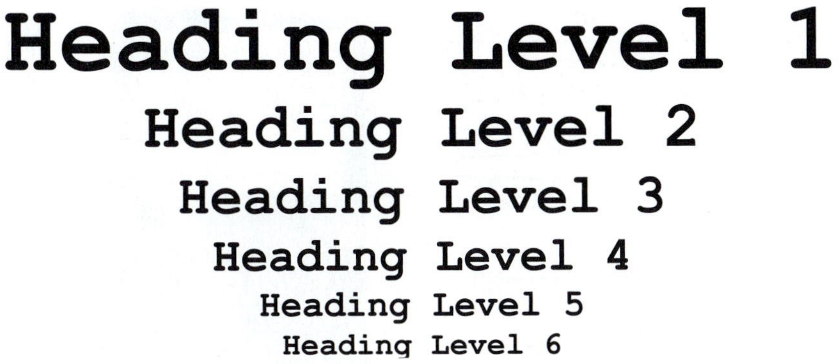

Heading Level 1
Heading Level 2
Heading Level 3
Heading Level 4
Heading Level 5
Heading Level 6

Figure 6.30 **The six levels of heading elements.**

The most important heading on a page should be marked up with a level 1 heading. The browsers render this by using the largest type size and scale down the rest of the levels proportionately.

6.8.1. Golden Ratio

In the so-called golden ratio the relationship between two parameters describing a form such as height and width is expressed through a ratio that is equal to 0.618. For instance, consider the line in Figure 6.31. When the full length $a + b$ is to the longer segment a, as a is to the shorter segment b, the ratio a/b is equal to 0.618.

The golden ratio can be found in nature, for example, in the proportions of the human body such as the ratio between the length of the hand and that of the forearm (Figure 6.32).

The ratio's proportions have an inherently pleasing visual effect and have therefore been used in design throughout history. The height and width of the Parthenon and the façade of Notre Dame Cathedral use the golden ratio.

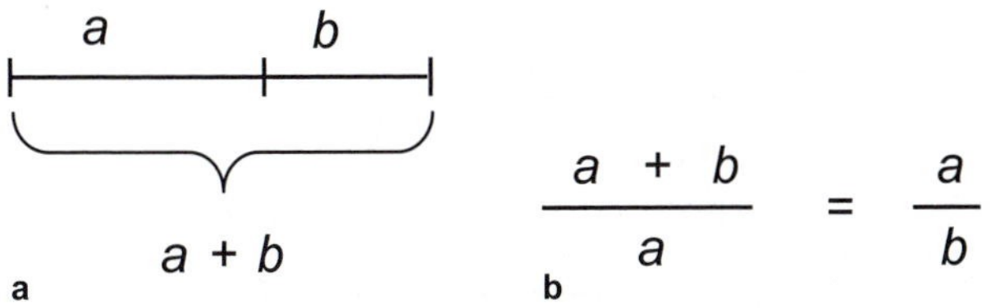

$$\frac{a + b}{a} = \frac{a}{b}$$

Figure 6.31 **(a) Golden ratio. (b) Golden ratio equation.**

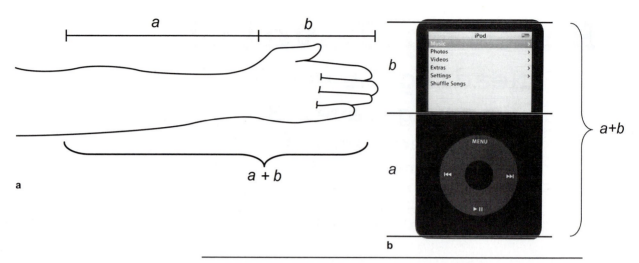

a

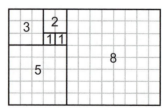

b

Figure 6.32 (a) Golden ratio in human proportions. (b) Golden ratio in the Apple iPod®.

6.8.2. Fibonacci Series

The Fibonacci series is a sequence of numbers in which each number is the sum of the two preceding numbers. The relationship between consecutive numbers in the Fibonacci series is similar to the golden ratio. This similarity increases as the numbers in the series increase:

1, 1, 2, 3, 5, 8, 13, 21, 34, 55, 89, 144, 233, 377, 610, 987, . . .

The sequence is common in nature and is found in the growth patterns of shells and flowers. It has been used in art and can be found in Mozart's sonatas and Beethoven's Fifth Symphony. It was also used by the architect Le Corbusier to create a system of architectural proportions that were in tune with the natural proportions of the human body. We can see the first six elements of the Fibonacci series graphically represented in Figure 6.33.

Both the golden ratio and the Fibonacci sequence can be used to create harmonious proportions for objects and areas on Web pages or application interfaces. They should not, however, be imposed on an information space at the expense of other, more pressing considerations.

Figure 6.33 Fibonacci series.

6.9. Screen Complexity

As computers become more powerful, they offer more functionality, which can make GUIs visually complex and difficult to use. The principles covered in this chapter can be used to guide the design of interfaces, and many of these principles, such as progressive disclosure and simplicity, can help to ensure that the results are not too complex or overwhelming.

The measure of complexity developed by Tullis (1984) can be used to calculate the relative complexity, and therefore the difficulty, of a design. This measure of complexity uses information theory (Shannon & Weaver, 1949) to determine the complexity of typographically designed pages. It is directly related to the Gestalt principle of common fate in that it encourages the use of underlying grid structures to visually simplify complex screens.

The formula for calculating complexity in bits (due to the log base 2) is shown in Figure 6.34.

To calculate the measure of complexity for a particular screen, do the following:

1. Place a rectangle around every screen element.
2. Count the number of elements and the number of columns (vertical alignment points).
3. Count the number of elements and the number of rows (horizontal alignment points).

The original screen used by Tullis, as shown in Figure 6.35, was found to give a mean search time of 8.3 seconds:

22 fields with 6 horizontal (column) alignment points = 41 bits
22 fields with 20 vertical (row) alignment points = 93 bits
Overall complexity = 134 bits

Tullis redesigned the original screen to reduce its complexity, as shown in Figure 6.36.

$$C = -N \sum_{n=1}^{m} p_n \log_2 p_n$$

Figure 6.34 Formula for calculating the measure of complexity.

C, complexity of the system in bits;
N, total number of events (widths or heights);
m, number of event classes (number of unique widths or heights);
p_n, probability of occurrence of the nth event class (based on
    the frequency of events within that class).

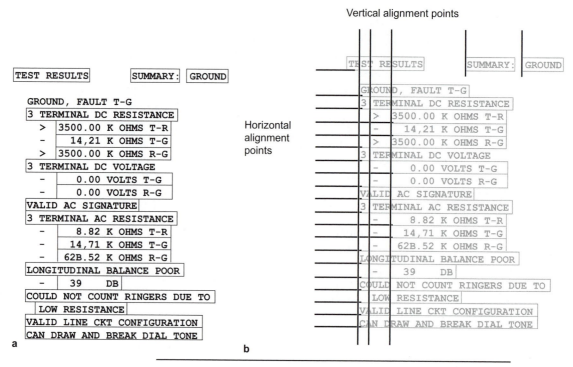

Figure 6.35 **Tullis' original screen, with rectangles. (b) Tullis' original screen, with alignment points.**

The redesigned screen gave a mean search time of 5.0 seconds, and is about 28% less complex than the original screen:

18 fields with 7 horizontal (column) alignment points = 43 bits

18 fields with 8 vertical (row) alignment points = 53 bits

Overall complexity = 96 bits

An easier method for calculating complexity was suggested by Galitz (2002) and consists in counting the following:

- The number of elements on the screen
- The number of horizontal (column) alignment points
- The number of vertical (row) alignment points

The sums for the original and redesigned screens by this measure are as follows:

For Figure 6.29 (original):

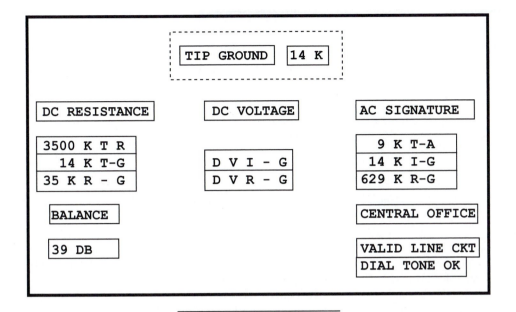

Figure 6.36 Redesign of original screen.

22 elements

6 horizontal (column) alignment points

20 vertical (row) alignment points

48 = complexity.

For Figure 6.30 (redesigned):

18 elements

7 horizontal (column) alignment points

8 vertical (row) alignment points

33 = complexity

This calculation shows that the redesigned screen is about 31% less complex than the original screen. Applied consistently, this formula can be used to perform quick evaluations of two competing designs.

Complexity versus Usability

According to the measurement of complexity, a simple screen should be the least complex and therefore the most usable. However, reducing a screen to its ultimate simplicity might not be the best thing to do. Studies have shown that overly simple screens are less interesting and can actually become less useful, especially if the drive for simplicity causes the screen to contain less functionality and lose some utility.

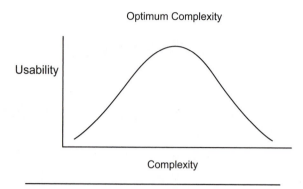

Figure 6.37 Relationship between complexity and usability.

In a study that measured usability in relation to complexity, Comber and Maltby (1997) found that both overly simple and overly complex screens were low in usability. Their results showed a bell curve relationship, with the most usable screens being those with moderate amounts of complexity (Figure 6.37).

Comber and Maltby defined usability in terms of the following three components:

- Effectiveness
- Learnability
- Attitude

They found tradeoffs between usability and complexity:

- As complexity decreased, it became harder to differentiate among screen objects; the screen became artificially regular.
- As complexity decreased, predictability increased.
- Increased complexity meant that there were fewer ways to group objects.
- Excessive complexity made screens look artificially irregular.
- Increased complexity could occur from increased utility.

Research Results

The results of research on screen complexity show that we should strive for logical layouts that contain the necessary functionality, and that we should design them so that the user can visually understand groupings without struggle.

Overly complex screens seem chaotic and unorganized, making it hard for people to make sense of the visual presentation. With overly simple screens, there may not be enough cues to help people group related functionality.

We should strive for a balance and apply all of our principles based on the overriding principle of comprehensibility. If people do not understand what they are looking at, none of the functionality will be useful. People will probably choose not to use the interface unless they absolutely have to, in which case their performance will be diminished and their frustration level increased.

Complexity Guidelines:

- Optimize the number of elements on a screen within the limits of clarity and utility.
- Minimize the alignment points. Use grid structures.

6.10. Resolution/Closure

The principle of resolution, also known as closure, relates to the perceived completion of a user's tasks. (This is different than the Gestalt principle of closure.) When the user's objective is satisfied, he or she will consider the task complete and move on to the next goal. Although this concept may seem trivial, it proved to be significant for the original designs of ATM machines.

A primary reason that we use ATMs is to withdraw money from bank accounts. The original ATM designs required users to insert their cards into the machines. After the transaction was complete and the users had received their money, the card was returned. A problem arose because users considered their task complete when they received money from the machine, and they often left before their card had been ejected. This difficulty was caused because ATM designers had ignored the principle of resolution. It has been rectified by solutions that require users to swipe cards rather then insert them into the machines.

6.11. Usability Goals

As we saw in Chapter 3, user-centered design (UCD) puts the focus on the user's tasks and goals. It also recognizes that interaction designs should facilitate those goals in the most advantageous way possible.

In other words, UCD encourages the development of usability goals that promote more usable interface designs. As we have seen, the generally accepted usability goals state that an interface should be:

- Understandable
- Learnable
- Effective/useful
- Efficient/usable

These usability goals seem logical, and it would be difficult to argue against them; however, it may not be entirely clear how they will affect the design that you are currently developing. How can you promote ease of learning or increase the efficiency of a design? How do these goals affect the many decisions you need to make about color, text, icons, or any other interface element?

To answer these questions, we must first understand how to develop a set of usability guidelines for the project; to do that, we need to understand how to go from general usability goals to more specific design guidelines. Let's see how that can be accomplished.

6.11.1. Goals to Principles

Usability goals provide a foundation not a prescription for design. These goals have been studied by HCI practitioners and designers, and a great deal of research has gone into studying how we can make things easy for people to understand and learn. The result of these efforts is that these goals have been defined according to design principles.

6.11.2. Principles to Guidelines

Design principles can guide us and help us to make informed decisions; however, they must be defined according to each particular project. You must clarify what they mean for your project by defining them in terms of the guidelines that your design must satisfy.

Quantifying usability goals in terms of project guidelines at the beginning of the project provides a basis on which to make design decisions and provides criteria for usability tests later.

These guidelines are documented at the beginning of the project and are referred to when decisions need to be made. They provide a structure for the various evaluations you perform throughout the project.

Even small-scale projects have many guidelines. There is a list of global guidelines affecting every module in the design, as well as sectional guidelines. These guidelines should be listed according to their relationship to the design, making it easier to refer to them during team meetings.

The distillation process from usability goals, to design principles, to project guidelines might resemble the following:

Usability Goal—Easy to use. Most people are interested in completing their tasks and do not enjoy struggling with the tools they need to use. One of the most important goals of user-centered design is to make things easy to use.

Design Principle—Simplicity. Simple things require little effort and can often be accomplished without much thought. If interaction designs are guided by the principle of simplicity, they will be easier to use.

Project Guideline—A project guideline based on the principle of simplicity might require that all dialogue boxes should present only the basic functions that are most often used and that other, less used functions can be accessed using an expandable dialogue with a link for "More Options."

Design Scenario

Circumference: Application of Design Principles

In this design scenario, we apply some of the design principles discussed earlier to the wireframes developed for the *Circumference* Web site in the previous chapter. We will not go into great depth at this point because we will first need to explore the issues of color, text, icons, components, and auditory feedback before we can complete the design phase. These topics are covered in depth in the following chapters. Let's apply our design principle and see what issues still need to be resolved.

Effectiveness/Usefulness

- **Utility**—The functional requirements that were discovered include the following:
  - The site should include the ability for the visitor to read selected poems in their original language and English versions. This should be done in such a way as to allow audible browsers access to as much content as possible.
  - Online ordering of individual journals and subscriptions should be possible.
  - There should be a facility for e-mail contact with the editors.
  - There should be access to *Circumference* event videos.

  All of these requirements, except the one that refers to the audible browsers, can be verified using the wireframes. The Event page wireframes will be similar to the Issues wireframes due to the similarity of the flowcharts for these areas.

- **Safety**—Safety issues involve the collection of personally identifiable information during the order process and the validation of credit card data. This is relevant for both the customer and the provider.

  The wireframes for the subscription area should include an indication of security levels involved in the transaction. This can be in the form of an icon identifying the entity used to verify credit card information.

  Safety was also explored in the discussion of the order form flowchart; see that design scenario for more information.

- **Flexibility**—Using both print and screen-based CSS will allow visitors to either read the poems from the screen or print them. These features are not discernible from the wireframes but are recorded in the requirements document.

  Podcasts can give visitors the additional option of listening to selected poems in both the original language and in English. This issue came up during the evaluation process because the principle of flexibility initiated this discussion.

  Podcasting was not covered in the requirements document and represents another expansion of the project's scope; refer back to the discussion of feature creep in the Mission Statement section of Chapter 4. Adhering to the principle of satisficing can help to keep the reigns on this type of situation.

Design Scenario (cont.)

- **Stability**—No cutting-edge technology will be used because the primary user profiles indicate that visitors will not be technologically sophisticated and may be using outdated versions of browsers and operating systems.

  All pages will be reviewed using all major browsers on all major operating systems and on diverse resolutions and screen types, including cathode ray tubes (CRTs) and liquid crystal displays (LCDs).

Efficiency/Usability

- **Simplicity**—We interact with the principle of simplicity in the overriding importance placed on the sample poems. The text of the poetry must be presented in a clean and readable manner without distracting graphic or auditory elements.
  - **White Space** –White space will be used to frame the poems and clarify navigation.
  - **Progressive Disclosure**—Progressive disclosure will organize and structure the presentation of selected poems from various issues. It will also make the visitor survey more pleasant.
  - **Constraints**—The constraints imposed on the design are covered in the discovery document.
- **Memorability**
  - **Consistency-Correctness**—The site will use consistent terminology that was elicited from real users during interviews and card sorts.
  - **Generalizability**—The colors of the various print issues will also be used as navigational aids.
  - **Conventions**—Memorability will be enhanced by using conventions related to the location of screen elements.
  - **Familiarity**—The site will use familiar labels, images, and hyperlink appearance. The memorability factor will also be enhanced through the use of colors that relate to the published journals.
- **Predictability**—Predictability will be enhanced with templates for screen layout.
- **Visibility**—The principle of visibility will be applied to the functional and content-based elements of the site, including the presentation of selected poems and the journal ordering process.
  - **Overload**—The visual components of the site will be kept to a minimum, and only functional and content-based elements will be used. Colors will be limited to those required for product recognition and navigation.
  - **Feedback**—When an order is completed, a confirmation page will be presented to the customer.
  - **Recognition/Recall**—Sample poems will include the flag of the poet's country of origin and the name of the original language, so visitors will be able to select poems based on their recognition of the flags or language.

Design Scenario (cont.)

- ○ **Orientation**—The global links will indicate the current page by retaining the active look as defined in the CSS.

  We have explored some of the principles covered in this chapter; the rest will be applied to specific page elements discussed in each of the following chapters. Each chapter covers a different aspect of interface design, and the appropriate principles will be discussed in those contexts.

Summary

Interaction design is a complex and difficult process. It involves physical and cognitive abilities and limitations as well as technical intricacies and complications. Combining all of these elements may seem an impossible task at times, and you will often wonder how you will ever achieve a robust and elegant solution that addresses the multiplicity of variables with which you must contend.

As we have seen, many effective and powerful tools are at your disposal. Coming from several diverse disciplines, these can all be put to good use during the development process. Understanding how people will view your design is essential to its success, and an awareness of your target user's mental models will help you gain this knowledge.

During the course of the project you will make hundreds of decisions, both large and small, that will affect the outcome of the project. You will, therefore, need to understand and apply the various design principles repeatedly to every move you make.

Adherence to these principles will provide you with a support system that has been around since humans began designing artifacts to improve their existence. Design principles will guide you through the design process and help you to make the decisions that you will face at every turn.

Resources on the Web

www.aw.com/heim
You will find information relating to user interface design guidelines, principles and links to information on the gestalt principles of perception.

Suggested Reading

Lidwell, W., Holden, K., & Butler, J. (2003). *Universal Principles of Design: 100 Ways to Enhance Usability, Influence Perception, Increase Appeal, Make Better Design Decisions, and Teach Through Design:* Rockport Publishers.

Norman, D. (1999). *The Invisible Computer: Why Good Products Can Fail, the Personal Comptuer is So Complex, and Information Appliances Are the Solution* (Reprint ed.): MIT Press.

Norman, D. (2002). *The Design of Everyday Things* (Reprint ed.): Basic Books.

Williams, R. (2003). *The Non-Designer's Design Book* (2 ed.): Peachpit Press.

CHAPTER 7

Interaction Design Models

Design disciplines use models to develop and test ideas. For instance, architects use models of weight distribution, electronic circuitry, air circulation, fluid dynamics, and lighting systems. They also look at models of traffic flow and space utilization. These models help them to formulate and test ideas about potential designs.

Interaction designers also use models to understand complex systems. Models help them to evaluate design ideas and compare diverse solutions. These range from descriptive analogies and metaphors to predictive mathematical equations, and they give interaction designers an implementation-independent view of the system being designed. They also enable designers to explore designs without the expense of prototype development and actual user testing sessions.

Predictive Models

Predictive models (also called engineering or performance models), such as the Model Human Processor (MHP) and the Keyboard Level Model (KLM), are a priori (pre-experience) models that give approximations of user actions before real users are brought into the testing environment. Many of these models have been validated against empirical data derived from actual user testing and have proven to be highly accurate in their predictive abilities.

Descriptive Models

Descriptive models, such as state networks and the Three-State Model, provide a framework for thinking about user interaction. They can help us to understand how people interact with dynamic systems. A great deal of research and refinement has been conducted with regard to these models, and they have thus increased in their ability to inform and guide interaction design.

It is not possible to cover all of the modeling techniques available to designers. It is the intention of this chapter, however, to explore the use of HCI models in interaction design and to cover some of the representative models that have been demonstrated to be robust and powerful.

First, we look at the Model Human Processor (MHP) developed by Card, Moran, and Newell (1983), which was presented in their seminal work, *The Psychology of Human–Computer Interaction*. This will give us a basis for understanding how human information processing can be modeled and will serve as a foundation from which to explore the related GOMS-based models that follow.

7.1. Model Human Processor

> **MAXIM**
>
> The Model Human Processor can make general predictions about human performance.

The MHP was intended as a way to describe the human information processing system in order to make "predictions of gross human behavior." Card et al. related the MHP to an engineering model that suppressed details in order to more easily envision the system as a whole.

The MHP is a predictive model and is described by a set of memories and processors that function according to a set of principles (principles of operation). It is broken down into three subsystems as follows (Figure 7.1):

- Perceptual system (sensory image stores)

  ○ Sensors (eyes and ears)

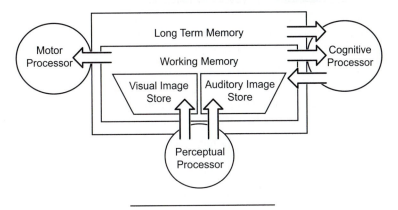

Figure 7.1 Model Human Processor.

- ○ Buffers
    - • Visual image store (VIS)
    - • Auditory image store (AIS)
- • Cognitive system
    - ○ Working memory (WM)—*Short-term memory*
    - ○ Long-term memory (LTM)
- • Motor system (arm-hand-finger system and head-eye system)

The memories and processors are described by the parameters given in Table 7.1.

7.1.1. Working Memory

WM consists of a subset of "activated" elements from LTM. The MHP shows this relationship by placing the WM within the confines of LTM (Figure 7.1). WM is differentiated from the sensory image stores (SISs) in terms of coding mechanisms.

The SISs encode only the nonsymbolic physical parameters of stimuli. For example, the VIS encodes the number "8" as a curving line that creates two stacked

Table 7.1 Parameters of the Model Human Processor

Mu	μ	Storage capacity (items)
Delta	δ	Decay time of item in memory
Kappa	κ	Main code type (physical, acoustic, visual, semantic)
Tau	τ	Processor cycle time (processors can work in a serial manner for some tasks and in parallel manner for others)

circular shapes. SISs are sensitive to the intensity of stimuli, such as the volume of a sound, the brightness of a light, or any other parameter that would cause the stimulus to stand out from its context. These perceptual processors require less time to process stimuli of greater intensity. This is expressed in the variable perceptual processor rate principle:

P1. Variable Perceptual Processor Rate Principle. The perceptual processor cycle time τ_p varies inversely with stimulus intensity.

Shortly after the onset of a stimulus, a symbolic representation is registered in the WM. These representations are encoded by activating elements in LTM. Therefore, the curved line is understood as a numeral representing eight discrete units. This is expressed in the recognize-act cycle of the cognitive processor:

P0. Recognize-Act Cycle of the Cognitive Processor. On each cycle of the cognitive processor, the contents of working memory initiate actions associatively linked to them in long-term memory. These actions in turn modify the contents of working memory.

The SIS can only store a certain amount of information and has a rapid decay rate. Therefore, if the stimuli are complex or voluminous, the WM will not have enough time to encode them, and the perceptual memory trace will fade.

Chunking Information

The activated elements from LTM are called chunks. Chunks can be composed of smaller units like the letters in a word. A chunk might also consist of several words, as in a well-known phrase. The actual contents of a chunk depend on the user and the user's task, as well as on the contents of the user's LTM. For instance, it might be hard to remember the following string, which consists of nine letters:

BCSBMICRA

However, for someone familiar with American corporations, the same letters could be easily remembered if they were grouped into three chunks:

CBSIBMRCA

Chunks can be nested; for instance,

CHUNK-1 = (CHUNK-2 CHUNK-3 CHUNK-4)

where

CHUNK-4 = (CHUNK-5 CHUNK-6)

> **MAXIM**
>
> Chunks in WM can interfere with each other due to LTM associations.

Chunks can be interrelated. For instance, the chunk ROBIN might be related to ROBERT. It might also be related to BIRD, which might be related to WING or FLY.

As this trail of associations progresses, the early associations begin to fade due to the limited resources of the WM. This is called interference and is context dependent. Interaction designers must be aware of the WM's limited resources and the potential for interference between memory chunks.

7.1.2. Long-Term Memory

The cognitive processor can add items to WM but not to LTM (see the arrows in Figure 7.1). The WM must interact with LTM over a significant length of time before an item can be stored in LTM. The longer an item stays in WM, the greater the number of associations that can be created. This increases the number of cues that can be used to retrieve the item later. Items with numerous associations have a greater probability of being retrieved. There is, however, a limit to how long an item can stay in WM, which is calculated as the decay time of WM (δ).

The way an item is encoded will affect its retrieval. This is expressed in the encoding-specificity principle:

> **P2. Encoding-Specificity Principle.** Specific encoding operations performed on what is perceived determine what is stored, and what is stored determines which retrieval cues are effective in providing access to what is stored.

The possibility that other association may interfere with retrieval is expressed in the discrimination principle:

> **P3. Discrimination Principle.** The difficulty of memory retrieval is determined by the candidates that exist in memory and their relation to the retrieval clues.

The number of cycles the cognitive processor must make to accomplish a task is context dependent. However, it is also subject to the variable cognitive processor rate principle:

> **P4. Variable Cognitive Processor Rate Principle.** The cognitive processor cycle time τ_c is shorter when greater effort is induced by increased task demands or information loads; it also diminishes with practice.

7.1.3. Processor Timing

Timings are given as a typical value (Middleman), followed by a bracketed range of potential values (Fastman and Slowman).

Perceptual—The perceptual system captures physical sensations by way of receptor channels, such as the visual and auditory channels. These channels are complex systems with sensitivity ranges that are context dependent and vary from person to person.

- Perceptual coding is physical:

$$\kappa_{VIS} = \text{Physical}$$
$$\kappa_{AIS} = \text{Physical}$$

- Perceptual decay is defined by the half-life index. This is the point at which the probability of retrieval reaches 50%. Perceptual decay is shorter for the visual channel than for the auditory channel:

$$\delta_{VIS} = 200 \ [90 \sim 1000] \ \text{msec}$$
$$\delta_{AIS} = 1500 \ [900 \sim 3500] \ \text{msec}$$

- Perceptual storage capacity is highly variable. Card et al. use

$$\mu_{VIS} = 17 \ [7 \sim 17] \ \text{letters}$$
$$\mu_{AIS} = 5 \ [4.4 \sim 6.2] \ \text{letters}$$

- Perceptual processor cycle time is variable according to the nature of the stimuli:

$$\tau_p = 100 \ [50 \sim 200] \ \text{msec}$$

Cognitive—The cognitive system bridges the perceptual and motor systems. It can function as a simple conduit or it can involve complex processes, such as learning, fact retrieval, and problem solving.

- Cognitive coding in the WM is predominantly visual and auditory:

$$\kappa_{WM} = \text{Visual or auditory}$$

- Cognitive coding in LTM is involved with associations and is considered to be predominantly semantic:

$$\kappa_{LTM} = \text{Semantic}$$

- Cognitive decay time of WM requires a large range:

$$\delta_{WM} = 7 \ [5 \sim 226] \ \text{seconds}$$

- Cognitive decay is highly sensitive to the number of chunks involved in the recalled item:

$$\delta_{WM}(1 \ \text{chunk}) = 73 \ [73 \sim 226] \ \text{seconds}$$
$$\delta_{WM}(3 \ \text{chunks}) = 7 \ [5 \sim 34] \ \text{seconds}$$

- Cognitive decay of LTM is considered infinite:

$$\delta_{LTM} = \infty$$

- Cognitive storage capacity can be measured in terms of pure WM (number of digits recalled from an unexpectedly interrupted string):

$$\mu_{WM} = 3 \ [2.5 \sim 4.1] \ \text{chunks}$$

- Cognitive storage capacity can also be measured in terms of effective capacity* (when working memory works in conjunction with LTM):

$$\mu_{WM}^* = 7\,[5 \sim 9]\text{ chunks}$$

- Cognitive processor cycle time is variable according to the nature of the stimuli:

$$\tau_C = 70\,[25 \sim 170]\text{ msec}$$

Motor—The motor system converts thought into action.

- Motor processor cycle time is calculated in units of discrete micromovements:

$$\tau_M = 70\,[30 \sim 100]\text{ msec}$$

Perceptual/Cognitive/Motor—System integration is calculated as follows:

- The time it takes to complete a task is equal to the combined number of processor cycles:

$$\tau_p + \tau_C + \tau_M = n\text{ msec}$$

Using these timings, one can calculate the relative efficiency of a design based on the complexity of the processing involved. Many examples presented by Card et al. cover tasks that range from simple reaction time to name and class matching. See Card et al. (1983) for an in-depth discussion of the MHP.

7.2. Keyboard Level Model

The MHP provides an engineering approach that can be used to give performance information about human information processing. This model captures human cognition and response timings, but it does not address the actions a user must take on the lowest level of keyboard events. To address this aspect of human–computer interaction Card et al. created the KLM.

> **MAXIM**
>
> The KLM can be used to determine the most efficient method and its suitability for specific contexts.

The KLM is designed to capture and calculate the physical actions that a user will have to carry out to complete specific tasks on a specific interface. Card et al. designed the KLM as a practical design tool. They considered it to be useful when the sequence of actions could be specified in advance and in detail.

The restrictions they put on the model were that it had to be applied to a given task on a given computer system. They documented the restrictions as given in Table 7.2.

Table 7.2 Keyboard Level Model Restrictions

Given:	A task (possibly involving several subtasks)
	The command language of a system
	The motor skill parameter of the user
	The response time parameters of the system
	The method used for the task
Predict:	The time an expert user will take to execute the task using the system, provided that he or she uses the method without error

The conditions require that the task is completed without error and the method of task completion is predetermined. It is therefore designed to predict the time of an error-free execution of a task.

7.2.1. Operators

The KLM is comprised of operators, encoding methods, and heuristics for the placement of mental (**M**) operators. The operators are defined in Table 7.3, (Card, Moran, & Newell, 1983, 264). Which includes descriptions and timings for each operator with averages for various typing facilities.

7.2.2. Encoding Methods

The encoding methods described by Card et al. define how the operators involved in a task are to be written. They describe a "long-hand" version and a "short-hand" version. Consider the DOS "ipconfig" command. It would be encoded in the long-hand version as: (the bracketed items are descriptive)

MK[i] K[p] K[c] K[o] K[n] K[f] K[i] K[g] K[RETURN]

It would be encoded in the short-hand version as

M 8K [ipconfig RETURN]

Either way, this results in a timing of $1.35 + 8 \times 0.20 = 2.95$ seconds for an average skilled typist.

The same function can be carried out in Microsoft XP by using the Network Connection icon and selecting the Repair item in the pop-up menu. This would be encoded as follows:

H [mouse] MP[Network Icon] K[Right Click] P[Prepare] K[Left Click]

This results in a timing of $0.40 + 1.35 + 2P + 2K = 4.35$ seconds.

Both of these timings assume that the user begins at the Command prompt or Network icon. This example makes it clear that the keyboard-based DOS command is more efficient than the menu-based method.

Table 7.3 Keyboard Level Model Operators

Operator	Description and Remarks	Time (sec)
K	Press key or button	
	Pressing the Shift or Control key counts as a separate **K** operation. Time varies with the typing skill of the user; the range of typical values is as follows (wpm, words per minute):	
	Best typists (135 wpm)	0.08
	Good typists (90 wpm)	0.12
	Average skilled typist (55 wpm)	0.20
	Average nonsecretary typist (40 wpm)	0.28
	Typing random letters	0.50
	Typing complex codes	0.75
	Worst typists (unfamiliar with keyboard)	1.20
P	Point with mouse to a target on a display	1.10
	The time to point varies with distance and target size according Fitts' law, ranging from 0.8 to 1.5 sec, with 1.1 sec being an average. This operator does not include the (0.2 sec) button press that often follows. Mouse pointing time is also a good estimate for other efficient analog pointing devices, such as joysticks.	
H	Home hand(s) on keyboard or other device	0.40
$D(n_D/l_D)$	Draw n_D straight-line segments of total length l_D centimeters	$0.9n_D + 0.16l_D$
	This is a very restricted operator; it assumes that drawing is done with the mouse on a system that constrains all lines to fall on a square 0.56-cm grid. Users vary in drawing skill; the time given is an average value.	
M	Mentally prepare	1.35
R(t)	Response by system	t
	Different commands require different response times. The response time is counted only if it causes the user to wait.	

7.2.3. Heuristics for M Operator Placement

The KLM operators can be placed into one of two groups—physical or cognitive. The physical operators are defined by the chosen method of operation, such as clicking an icon or entering a command string.

The cognitive operators are governed by the set of heuristics given in Table 7.4 (Card, Moran, & Newell, 1983, 265).

Table 7.4 Heuristics for M Operator Placement

Begin with a method of encoding that includes all physical operations and response operations. Use Rule 0 to place candidate **M**'s, and then cycle through rules 1–4 for each **M** to see whether it should be deleted.	
Rule 0	Insert **M**'s in front of all **K**'s that are not part of argument strings proper (e.g., text or numbers). Place **M**'s in front of all **P**'s that select commands (not arguments).
Rule 1	If an operator following an **M** is fully anticipated in an operator just previous to **M**, then delete the **M** (e.g., **PMK—PK**).
Rule 2	If a string of **MK**s belongs to a cognitive unit (e.g., the name of a command), then delete all **M**'s but the first.
Rule 3	If a **K** is a redundant terminator (e.g., the terminator of a command immediately following the terminator of its argument), then delete the **M** in front of it.
Rule 4	If a **K** terminates a constant string (e.g., a command name), then delete the **M** in front of it. If the **K** terminates a variable string (e.g., an argument string), then keep the **M** in front of it.

7.2.4. What the Keyboard Level Model Does Not Model

The KLM is a specific tool designed to investigate a highly focused aspect of human–computer interaction. The intention of the KLM as defined by Card et al. was to model the time it takes to perform a routine task. The KLM was not designed to consider the following:

- Errors
- Learning
- Functionality
- Recall
- Concentration
- Fatigue
- Acceptability

With a note of irony Card et al. suggest that, even though the model cannot account for user error, if the method of recovery were known, the model could be used to predict the time it would take to accomplish the recovery task.

Subsequent research on the KLM has enriched the model and improved its value as a design tool by adding perception, memory, and cognition to the original six operators (**K, P, H, M, D,** and **R**). Olson and Olson (1990) summarize the expanded set of operators as shown in Table 7.5. The timings are derived from, and given as, medians of various research results.

Table 7.5   Expanded Set of Keyboard Level Model Operators

Enter keystroke	230 msec
Point with a mouse	1500 msec
Move hands to mouse	360 msec
Perceive	100 msec
Make a saccade	230 msec
Retrieve from memory	1200 msec
Execute a mental step	70 msec
Choose among methods	1250 msec

7.2.5. Application of the Keyboard Level Model

John and Kieras (1996) provide some real-world case studies for the application of the KLM in interaction design. They range from using the KLM as a proxy user for the purpose of comparing performance results in usability testing (Xerox) to using it to determine the most efficient method for searching a database (Bell Laboratories). In all cases, the KLM proved a useful and accurate model for estimating user performance in early stages of interaction design.

Case 1 (Mouse-Driven Text Editor)

During the development of the Xerox Star, a few mouse-based text selection schemes were considered, each requiring a different number of mouse buttons. The designers were concerned about ease of learning and wanted to use as few buttons as possible. However, they also had concerns about affording expert users a mouse with enough functionality.

Because the mouse was then still a novel device, expert users were practically nonexistent. This presented a difficulty for making determinations between design solutions. The solution was to use experimental results based on novice user performance and KLM calculations of the same tasks. The KLMs served as expert proxies. Consequently, tradeoffs could be determined between the learnability of the system for novice users and the functionality it afforded expert users.

Case 2 (Directory Assistance Workstation)

In 1982, the procedures used by the Bell System directory assistance operators (DAOs) were analyzed by members of the human factors group at Bell Laboratories using the KLM to determine relative efficiency. The prevailing wisdom was that the DAOs should type as few keys as possible to bring up an extensive set of results from the database of customer names and phone numbers that could then be searched visually. The concept was known as "key less–see more."

Through the application of a parameterized KLM to a set of benchmark queries arrived at through analysis of the existing database, this theory was found to be faulty. The KLM clarified the tradeoffs between the number of keystrokes entered in the query and the number of returned fields. As a result, the DAOs began to enter longer queries.

7.3. GOMS

The MHP and the KLM cover a great deal of area concerning human–computer interaction. They can determine how long it will take to complete a particular task and the most efficient way to accomplish that task; however, they say nothing about why a person would choose one method over another, and they provide no framework in which to explore diverse methods for achieving those goals.

> **MAXIM**
>
> Goal/task models can be used to explore the methods people use to accomplish their goals.

This requires a model that explores the user's goals and tasks. These are considered goal/task models. They focus on the user's goals and explore the different methods people use to achieve these goals.

Card et al. suggested that user interaction could be described by defining the sequential actions a person undertakes to accomplish a task. The model they developed is called the GOMS model and has four components: goals, operators, methods, and selection rules.

Goals—Tasks are deconstructed as a set of goals and subgoals. To accomplish the top-level goal, such as editing a manuscript, the user must segment higher-level goals into a set of discrete subgoals, such as inserting a punctuation mark. Goals serve as "memory points" that enable the user to evaluate his or her progress.

Operators—Tasks can only be carried out by undertaking specific actions. For instance, printing a document requires issuing a print command, which may involve clicking the printer icon, an operator. This is the lowest level in the model.

Methods—Printing a document can be achieved in different ways. The user can press the printer icon or use an accelerator key combination such as alt + P (Microsoft Windows®). Each of these scenarios represents a specific method of achieving the goal and comprises operators that facilitate its completion.

Selection Rules—The method that the user chooses is determined by selection rules. For instance, if the user is involved in intensive typing, he or she may prefer to use the alt + P method of printing. However, if the user is using a painting program for tasks that are heavily mouse oriented, he or she may choose to click the printer icon with the mouse.

GOMS is a predictive model that gives the timing for a task as the sum of the timings for the individual operators used in the chosen method. It has been refined and expanded by various researchers and designers. There are a few variations that add to the value of the technique, each one with its own advantages and draw-backs.

7.3.1. CMN-GOMS

CMN-GOMS (named after Card, Moran, and Newell) is a detailed expansion of the general GOMS model and includes specific analysis procedures and notation descriptions. A CMN-GOMS analysis can result in a quantitative description of a task and provide an estimate of the timing. It can also provide a qualitative description of the methods that would most likely be used in certain situations.

> **MAXIM**
>
> CMN-GOMS can predict behavior and assess memory requirements.

CMN-GOMS can predict the user's behavior within the confines of the task parameters. The analysis can also judge the memory requirements of a task by looking at the depth of the nested goal structures, thereby providing insight into user performance measures.

GOMS analyses are procedural and describe the steps taken to achieve a goal when the methods for accomplishing the task are already defined. Therefore, the analyst must begin with an already defined set of top-level tasks, which the GOMS model does not provide. GOMS assumes that the solution has become routine and all that is required is to choose among various "known" methods. In other words, GOMS represents skilled behavior.

7.3.2. CMN-GOMS Analysis

A GOMS analysis begins with a global view of the goal hierarchy. Goals are then decomposed into subgoals until the desired granularity of analysis is achieved. A goal involves methods, which, in turn, involve operators.

It is often beneficial to bring the granularity to the level of "primitive operators" (an operator for which further decomposition would have no significance to the analysis), such as keystrokes or mouse clicks.

It is possible that an analysis may consist of one goal and some high-level operators. The analyst must decide on a level of granularity that adequately describes the task being explored. The level of granularity is a determining factor in differentiating between goals and operators.

Consider the following GOMS analysis and its accompanying selection rules. This is an analysis of the cut portion of a cut-and-paste operation:

Example 7.1 GOMS Analysis of a Cut-and-Paste Operation

```
GOAL: Move-Paragraph
.       GOAL: Edit-Unit-Task
. .             GOAL: Locate Paragraph
.       GOAL: Execute-Unit-Task
.       GOAL: Edit-Unit-Task
. .             GOAL: Select-Paragraph
. .                 [select:     Use-Click-Drag
. .     .                        Use-Arrow-Keys
. .     GOAL: Cut-Paragraph
. .                 [select:     Use-Mouse-Popup
. .     .                        Use-Keyboard-Combination
. .     Verify-Unit-Task
```

Selection rules:

- Click and Drag—Use the mouse to perform a click-and-drag operation for text selection when not actively typing.
- Arrow Keys—Use arrow keys (combined with Shift) to select text when actively typing.
- Mouse/Pop-up—Use the right mouse button to invoke a pop-up menu and choose the Cut option when not actively typing.
- Keyboard combination—Use Ctrl + X to cut text when actively typing.

Let's follow the foregoing analysis. The goal is broken down into unit tasks. First the user must visually locate the paragraph to be cut, and then he or she must select the paragraph. The selection operation can be executed using one of two methods—the mouse-based method of click-and-drag or the keyboard-based method that utilizes the arrow keys.

Selection rules govern which method the user will choose. The choice depends on whether he or she is actively typing, in which case it is more efficient to keep the hands on the keyboard. If the user is simply proofreading the document, his or her hands will be free to acquire the mouse.

After the first two unit tasks are accomplished, the user will set the new goal of actually cutting the paragraph. He or she has the option of using the mouse to initiate a pop-up menu that contains the Cut option or of using the Ctrl + X keyboard combination.

The selection rules for choosing between these two methods are the same as for the previous task. After the user chooses between the available methods for cutting the paragraph, he or she must verify that the paragraph has indeed been removed from the document.

7.3.3. Other GOMS Models

Since its creation, there have been a number of variations and developments on the basic GOMS model. We look at some of these GOMS-based models and explore their advantages and disadvantages in terms of their usefulness in interaction design.

NGOMSL

NGOMSL (Natural GOMS Language), developed by Kieras, provides a structured natural-language notation for GOMS analysis and describes the procedures for accomplishing that analysis (Kieras, 1997).

Like CMN-GOMS, NGOMSL can predict user behavior, and it provides a mothod for determining task timing NGOMSL, however, also provides a method for measuring the time it will take to learn specific method of operation and a way to determine the consistency of a design's methods of operation. Kieras has subsequently developed a machine-executable version of NGOMSL called GOMSL which he suggests as an alternative to NGOMSL, see below.

CPM-GOMS

The CPM-GOMS model represents cognitive, perceptual, and motor operators by using Program Evaluation Review Technique (PERT) charts to map task durations using the critical path method (CPM). CPM-GOMS is based directly on the Model Human Processor and assumes that users are able carry out tasks using the perceptual, cognitive, and motor processors in parallel. This makes it unique among the GMOS family, which is predominantly serial.

The PERT chart is set up using the MHP to segregate resource flows—perceptual, cognitive, and motor. Whereas CMN-GOMS defines operators on interface-level actions such as mouse clicks, CPM-GOMS continues to the primitive operators expressed in the MHP. Therefore, a Locate-Paragraph task is expressed as a series of primitive operators, as shown in the PERT chart in Figure 7.2.

The CPM-GOMS model has the ability accurately to represent skilled, expert behavior, which can be characterized as highly parallel in nature. Experts generally know

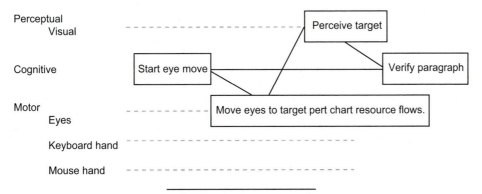

Figure 7.2 Pert Chart Resource Flows.

what their next action will be, so they can perform the cognitive operations required by those tasks while they are still in the process of executing previous motor operations. For example, expert typists habitually read ahead while they are copying manuscripts. CPM-GOMS time estimates are generally faster than those of other GOMS models because they do not allocate as much time for the "prepare for action" operations.

Automating GOMS Analysis

GOMS models have been shown to be beneficial in interaction design for assessing the relative merits of various design prototypes. They also provide a way to test new designs before commencing full usability testing with real subjects, a process that can be expensive and time consuming.

GOMS models, however, have not become integrated into interaction development environments outside of research laboratories to any great degree. It has been suggested that the lack of development tools for automating the calculations may be one reason GOMS has not be widely accepted by the professional design community (Baumeister, John, & Byrne, 2000).

NGOMSL calculations and CPM-GOMS chart creations are tedious, time-consuming, and error-prone activities. However, there have been a few attempts to automate these processes; for example, GOMSL, which was developed by Kieras as a machine-readable language for GLEAN4, a GOMS simulations tool that automates NGOMSL model creation (Kieras, 2004).

There has also been some significant research on automating CPM-GOMS (Freed, Matessa, Remington, & Vera, 2003) One method involves Apex, a software program that uses Procedure Description Language (PDL) for simulating the behavior of intelligent entities such as humans (Vera, Tollinger, Eng, Lewis, & Howes, 2005).

7.4. Modeling Structure

GOMS-based task models are powerful tools that can help us to explore how people choose methods for accomplishing tasks and the relative efficiency with which these methods can be learned and used. At times, however, we must investigate the structural, dynamic, and physical aspects of the design. For such tasks we need different models designed to illuminate these aspects of the design.

Structural models can help us to see the relationship between the conceptual components of a design and the physical components of the system, allowing us to judge the design's relative effectiveness.

Dynamic models allow us to view the design in action. We can follow the process of system use and explore the different states the system enters, giving us a temporal view of the design. Physical models look at the physical aspects of the screen, such as component location and size.

These models can be used to test design ideas, compare solutions, and improve existing designs. Let's look at these models and see how they fit into the design process. We begin with Hick's law, which is used to model menu structures.

7.4.1. Hick's Law

When an application is launched, it opens with a set of default menus. The most common menus do not usually cover all of an application's necessary functionality; some optional menus might also be required. The designer must decide what menus are needed as well as what options are included in each menu.

How do you decide what should be included in a specific menu, and how do you decide when a particular functionality requires the creation of a new menu?

It has been suggested that having more choices at one level (broad structure) is more efficient than having more levels with fewer choices (deep structure). Let's look at the experimental foundations for this guideline and some extenuating conditions that might affect it.

> **MAXIM**
>
> Hick's law can be used to create menu structures.

Hick's law states that the time it takes to choose one item from n alternatives is proportional to the logarithm (base 2) of the number of choices, plus 1. This equation is predicated on all items having an equal probability of being chosen:

$$T = a + b \log_2(n + 1)$$

The coefficients are empirically determined from experimental design; however, Raskin (2000) suggests that $a = 50$ and $b = 150$ are sufficient place holders for "back-of-the-envelope" approximations.

Hick's law is a component of the Model Human Processor's seventh principle of operation, the uncertainty principle.

P7. Uncertainty Principle. Decision time T increases with uncertainty about the judgment or decision to be made:

$$T = I_C H$$

where H is the information-theoretic entropy of the decision and

$$I_C = 150[0 - 157]\text{msec/bit}$$

For n equally probable alternatives (called Hicks' law),

$$H = \log_2(n + 1)$$

For n alternatives with different probabilities p_i of occurrence,

$$H = pi \log_2(1/pi + 1)$$

Table 7.6 Breadth versus Depth

One level of eight items	Two levels of four items each
$a + b \log_2(n + 1)$	$2[a + b \log_2(n + 1)]$
$50 + 150 \log_2(8+1)$	$2[50 + 150 \log_2(4 + 1)]$
$50 + 150 \log_2 9$	$2(50 + 150 \log_2 5)$
$50 + 475.5$	$2(50 + 348.3)$
525.5	$2(398.3)$
	796.6

The probability of choosing any one particular item depends on a number of factors, such as task, user familiarity, and list ordering. Hick's law can give an approximate benchmark by which to judge the relative complexity of a decision. For an in-depth discussion of probability in menu design, see Card et al. (1983, 71). Let's now look at how the Hicks law can be applied to menu design.

Breadth and Depth

Menus are designed to facilitate user tasks. A user must start at the first level of a menu and proceed through a series of options until a task is complete. The time it takes the user to go from the beginning (point A) to the final destination (point Z) can be expressed by the relationship between breadth and depth, where depth is defined as the number of levels that must be traversed and breadth is defined as the number of choices at each level.

Hick's law shows that increasing the number of choices has a logarithmic effect on the time it takes to make a decision. It also shows that menu structures with greater breadth are potentially more efficient than structures with greater depth. In other words, selecting one item from eight is faster than choosing one item from two levels with four items each (Table 7.6).

Numerous other studies have also supported the theory that, given a situation in which all possible menu items are equally probable, menu structures with greater breadth and less depth are the most efficient and the most accurate.

Practical Application

Although having clear guidelines for menu structure would be beneficial, the situation for real users is complex. Consider a situation in which you must choose any word that begins with the letter Y, using word lists accessed from a set of buttons labeled alphabetically from A to Z. You would immediately scan toward the end of the set of buttons and click on the button labeled Y. From the subsequent list, you would select a word. Your probability of choosing a word beginning with Y is high because the alphabetical listing order is logical and relevant to your task.

If, on the other hand, you had to choose any word with four vowels that ended in y, the alphabetic listing would offer you no advantage. All options would have the same probability, and your search would have to be linear and sequential.

MAXIM

Menu listing order must be logical and relevant.

Menus are lists grouped according to some predetermined system. If the rules governing the grouping of menu items are not understood or if they are not relevant to a particular task, their arrangement may seem arbitrary and random, requiring users to search in a linear, sequential manner.

If the system is based on rules that are meaningful, however, the user will be able to use them to facilitate his or her search. These rules might be based on an intrinsic order, as in the months of the year, or they may be numerical or alphabetical. Frequency of use can also structure a list.

Subdivision/Linear Search

The word search example just given allowed for subdivision because users are probably familiar with the alphabetical placement of the letter Y; they would not have to search the buttons sequentially. The second case eliminated the possibility for subdivision by rendering alphabetical order irrelevant: all buttons were potentially suitable, and the list required the user to search each letter group and its words.

The usability and efficiency of organizing structures depends on user tasks; sometimes a structure will aid the user, and sometimes it may not be beneficial at all. We now consider a more complex example to see how a combination of subdivision and linear selection might be presented and used.

Hick's Law Example

Consider a listing of classical music composers and their biographies. One way in which to organize these names is to place them in alphabetical order. The first level of this menu structure would have 26 choices and the second level would present the names beginning with each letter also listed alphabetically (Figure 7.3).

Using Hick's law, we can calculate the time it would take to find a composer's name if all composers had an equal probability of being chosen. This would be the

Classical Composers

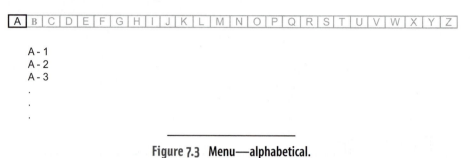

Figure 7.3   **Menu—alphabetical.**

Classical Composers

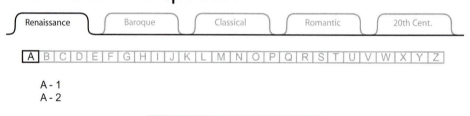

Figure 7.4   **Menu—category/alphabetical.**

case if we knew nothing about classical composers and wanted to find the name of a Renaissance composer.

The first menu contains 26 choices (Table 7.7). For argument's sake, we assume that each letter contains 10 composer's names, 2 from each stylistic period (Table 7.8).

This results in a combined timing of 1332.1 msec.

Table 7.7 Hick's Law—26 Choices
$a + b \log_2(n + 1)$
$50 + 150 \log_2(26 + 1)$
$50 + 150 \log_2 27$
$50 + 713.2$
763.2

Table 7.8   Hick's Law—10 Choices
$a + b \log_2(n + 1)$
$50 + 150 \log_2(10 + 1)$
$50 + 150 \log_2 27$
$50 + 518.9$
568.9

Table 7.9 Hick's Law—Five Choices
$a + b\log_2(n+1)$
$50 + 150\log_2(5+1)$
$50 + 150\log_2 6$
$50 + 387.7$
437.7

Table 7.10 Hick's Law—26 Choices
$a + b\log_2(n+1)$
$50 + 150\log_2(26+1)$
$50 + 150\log_2 27$
$50 + 713.2$
763.2

We could also organize the names by stylistic period: Renaissance, Baroque, Classical, Romantic, and Twentieth Century. This level has five choices, each leading to the next level with an alphabetic menu of 26 choices, which leads to the list of two names beginning with that particular letter, also in alphabetic order (Figure 7.4).

The first level has five choices (Table 7.9).

The next level has 26 choices (Table 7.10).

The last level has two choices (Table 7.11).

The overall timing for a menu choice (1488.6) is longer in this situation because of the addition of the first level, which is only marginally made up for by the shortened last level.

The reality of this example, however, is not as clear-cut as it seems. Because the task was to find the name of any Renaissance composer, the first level of the second menu structure would place all probability on the first category, Renaissance. After that choice, any selection from the alphabetical list would render a sufficient answer.

To find a Renaissance composer in the first menu structure, a user would have to choose a composer and then read his or her biography. This would be an inefficient method of selection. What was previously an organized list now has become a random one that must to be searched in a linear, sequential manner.

Table 7.11   Hick's Law—Two Choices
$a + b\log_2(n+1)$
$50 + 150\log_2(2+1)$
$50 + 150\log_2 3$
$50 + 237.7$
287.7

Other issues also affect the selection of menu items. Some of these have to do with the physical display of screen elements. A carefully constructed menu might suffer from factors such as an overly busy screen, confusing text format, or improper use of color.

Search and Menu Structure

The ultimate goal in designing a menu structure is to make it as easy as possible for users to find the information for which they are looking. This requires knowledge of the user's task and search methodology. It also depends on the nature of the information being searched.

As far as menu structure is concerned, the most important concern is to provide an organizational structure that is meaningful to the user. If there is an innate order to the information listed and if the structure relates to the user's task, the list can be searched in a nonlinear way, by subdividing the items and refining the set of possible targets. This is potentially much faster than a linear search of all possible items in the list.

When all choices are equal, then the basic Hick's law can guide you in determining the most efficient structure for your menus. However, it is more likely that you will need to apply probabilities to the equation in most situations. To determine the probabilities of a particular choice, you must fully understand the user's task.

7.5. Modeling Dynamics

Hick's law can help you to determine the relative efficiency of a design proposal by estimating the time it will take to navigate a menu structure, but it says nothing about the way the system should respond to the user's selections. Structural models do not present the whole picture; we need models that show the dynamic nature of human–computer interaction.

> **MAXIM**
>
> Understanding the temporal aspects of interaction design is essential to the design of usable and useful systems.

Interaction designs involve dynamic feedback loops between the user and the system in the form of a dialogue. User actions alter the state of the system, which in turn influences the user's subsequent actions. Interaction designers, therefore, need tools to explore how a system undergoes transitions from one state to the next.

7.5.1. State Transition Networks

State transition networks (STNs) have been used for many years to describe the dialogue between user and system; they can be used to explore screen elements such

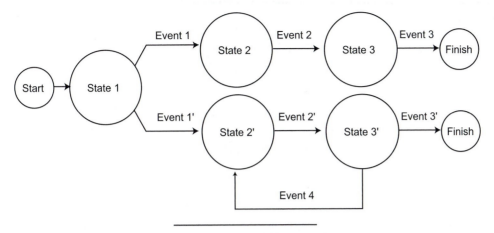

Figure 7.5   State transition network.

as menus, icon, and tools, and they are also appropriate for showing the operation of peripheral devices. They generally take the form of state transition diagrams (STDs). STDs are directed graphs that identify the various states as nodes and the possible transitions between the states as links.

States—States (drawn as circles) are connected to each other by transitions (drawn as lines with directional arrows), which are triggered by events (labeled on top of the transition lines) (Figure 7.5). There are two pseudo states—initial and terminal. They serve to initiate and terminate the chart as well as to connect with other areas of the system.

STNs are appropriate for showing sequential operations that may involve choice on the part of the user, as well as for expressing iteration. For example, in Figure 7.5, the user can go from state 1 to state 2 as a result of event 1, or from state 1 to state 2′ as a result of event 1′.

STNs can also be used to diagram the operation of peripheral devices such as joysticks or mouse pointers. This can help to determine the appropriateness of a particular device, or it can guide the development of a new type of pointing device for a novel interface solution.

7.5.2. Three-State Model

Pointing devices have different states that can be diagramed using a particular STN called the Three-State Model (TSM) (Buxton, 1990). The TSM is capable of describing three different types of pointer movements-tracked, dragged or disengaged movement.

- **Tracked movement**—A mouse device is tracked by the system and represented by the cursor position.
- **Dragged movement**—A mouse also can be used to manipulate screen elements using drag-and-drop operations.

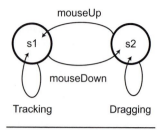

Figure 7.6   Mouse Three-State Model.

- **Disengaged movement**—Some pointing devices can be moved without being tracked by the system, such as light pens or fingers on a touchscreen, and then reengage the system at random screen locations.

> **MAXIM**
>
> The Three-State Model can help designers to determine appropriate I/O devices for specific interaction designs.

The TSM can reveal intrinsic device states and their subsequent transitions. The interaction designer can use these to make determinations about the correlation between task and device. Certain devices can be ruled out early in the design process if they do not possess the appropriate states for the specified task.

Consider how a mouse device operates (Figure 7.6). The user can drag the mouse around, and the system tracks this movement updating the cursor to reflect the position and velocity. This is considered state 1 (s1)—tracking. If the cursor is over a folder icon and the user presses the mouse button (left button on the Windows platform), the folder icon can be dragged around the screen. This is considered state 2 (s2)—dragging. Dragging (s2) is usually followed by releasing the mouse button, which causes the icon to be relocated to the screen position below the cursor. This is considered dropping, which returns the model to s1. This is the definition of a drag-and-drop operation.

Now consider a trackpad (Figure 7.7). If the user's finger is not in contact with the pad, no tracking can take place. This is considered state 0—out of range (OOR). However, when the user touches the screen, the system can begin to track the user's movements. Therefore, a trackpad involves s0—s1 transitions.

The trackpad is not capable of s2 transitions without additional input from another component, such as a button located nearby that the user can activate with another finger or the thumb. The need for this additional component is made explicit by the model.

Now consider a stylus used in conjunction with a graphics tablet or a light pen used with an appropriate screen. The stylus or pen can be moved freely away from

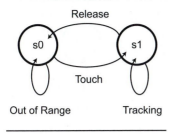

Figure 7.7   Trackpad Three-State Model.

the screen without affecting any screen objects—s0. After the user touches the stylus to the screen, it can be tracked as it is moved—s1. The stylus or pen can also select screen objects and drag them around the screen using various methods, such as pressure-activated tip switches or embedded buttons—s2. These are, therefore, s0/s1/s2 devices.

It is true that the mouse device might be lifted from the mouse pad or table and, therefore, like the trackpad, light pen, and touchscreen, is capable of state 0 transitions. Buxton (1990) argues that the system does not register "mouse lift," which renders this condition undefined. MacKenzie (2003), however, defines s0 in a way that makes the mouse capable of s0 transitions (Figure 7.8).

If, for argument's sake, we agree that mouse devices are capable of s0 transitions like trackpads, light pens, and touchscreens, there still remains a difference in the way these devices behave in s0. With mouse devices and trackpads, the system uses a tracking object (cursor) that remains at the last position when the mouse is lifted or the finger is removed from the pad. When the device reengages with the system, the cursor is reactivated at the same screen location no matter where the user places the mouse or his or her finger; reengagement is location independent.

In the case of a touchscreen or light pen, reengagement occurs at a new location determined by where the user places his or her finger or the pen. In this case, reengagement is location dependent. These are two distinct s0 definitions—location independent s0′ and location-dependent s0.

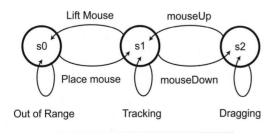

Figure 7.8   Alternate mouse Three-State Model.

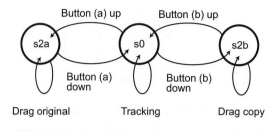

Figure 7.9 Multibutton pointing device Three-State Model.

Another way of looking at this is to say that touchscreens and light pens do not have s0. What would appear to be s0 is actually the tracking s1. The difference is that these devices are inherently tracked by themselves—"the pointing device itself becomes the tracking pointer" (Forlines, Shen, & Buxton, 2005, 1378). This redundancy can be used to facilitate greater functionality, as we will see later when we discuss the Glimpse model.

Contemporary pointing devices are a bit more complex, for instance, pointing devices . . . with multiple buttons can be modeled using state 2 arrays—s2a, 2b, 2c, . . ., 2n (Figure 7.9). Double-clicking can be similarly modeled. In addition, contemporary trackpads are capable of s0—s2 transitions. This is accomplished by tapping, which is interpreted by the system as analogous to a mouse click (Figure 7.10).

The TSM has been used to explore novel uses of pressure input with touchscreens, light pens, and trackpads. MacKenzie and Oniszczak (1997) suggest using pressure to execute a click event in their tactile touchpad (Figure 7.11). Their design also includes spatially placed aural and tactile feedback at the finger tip to afford the same quality of feedback that users are accustomed to with mouse devices.

7.5.3. Glimpse Model

Forlines et al. focus on touchscreens and light pens. They argue that because the pen and finger give clear feedback about their location when they touch the screen and enter state 2, it is redundant for the cursor to track this movement. This redundancy is made explicit in Figure 7.12, which shows that with a non—pressure-sensitive device any contact with the screen results in s0—s2 transitions.

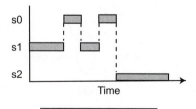

Figure 7.10 Trackpad tapping.

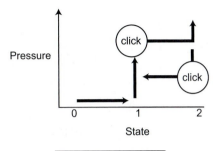

Figure 7.11 Tactile feedback.

Forlines et al. (2005) conclude that pressure-sensitive devices can take advantage of the s1 redundancy and map pressure to other features. Work in this area has shown some interesting possibilities. For instance, Ramos, Boulos, and Balakrishnan (2004) mapped the presence of continuous pressure to various visual properties of screen objects, such as size, rotation, and dispersion. In other words, if the user rests the pen on an object for a prescribed period of time, the object is modified accordingly.

Forlines et al. (2005) suggest that undo commands coupled with a preview function (Glimpse) can be mapped to a pressure-sensitive direct input device as illustrated in Figure 7.13.

They suggest some applications for this type of interaction that could benefit from methods that provide an easy way to preview diverse alterations together with an easy way to return quickly to the previous state:

- Pan and zoom interfaces—Preview different magnification levels
- Navigation in a 3D world—Quick inspection of an object from different perspectives
- Color selection in a paint program—Preview the effects of color manipulation
- Volume control—Preview different volume levels
- Window control—Moving or resizing windows to view occluded objects
- Scrollbar manipulation—Preview other sections of a document

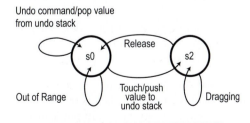

Figure 7.12 Non–pressure-sensitive device.

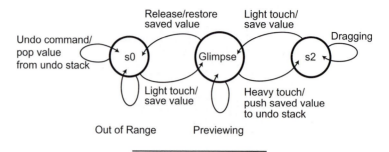

Figure 7.13 Glimpse functionality.

7.6. Physical Models

Some models provide timings for user actions, others show relationships and dynamic transitions between different system states, and still others explore the "how" and "why" of human task completion methods. Now we will use physical models to consider how people interact with the physical components of the interface.

Physical models can predict efficiency based on the physical aspects of a design. They calculate the time it takes to perform actions such as targeting a screen object and clicking on it to execute a command or initiate a drop-down menu. This can help interaction designers to evaluate the efficiency of a design or compare diverse solutions even before any prototypes have been constructed. As our last example, lets look at one of the most widely accepted physical models, the Fitts law.

7.6.1. Fitts' Law

Fitts' law states that the time it takes to hit a target is a function of the size of the target and the distance to that target. This has obvious implications for GUI design, which is heavily dependent on the act of moving a cursor around the screen to activate elements such as buttons, icons, and menus.

> **MAXIM**
>
> Fitts' law can be used to determine the size and location of a screen object.

It can also be used to model drag-and-drop operations, such as dropping a file icon onto a folder icon. Fitts' law is considered "one of the most robust and highly adopted models of human movement" (MacKenzie, 2003, 35).

Fitts published two influential papers in which he extended the use of information theory to the human motor system. Fitts' law is based on Shannon's Theorem 17, which concerns the information capacity of a communication system:

$$C = B \log_2(S/N + 1)$$

where *C* is the effective information capacity (bits), *B* is the channel bandwidth, *S* is the signal power, and *N* is the noise.

Fitts equated electronic signals (*S*) to movement distances or amplitudes (*A*) and noise (*N*) to the tolerance or width (*W*) of the target. Shannon's channel capacity was related to Fitts' index of performance.

There are essentially three parts to Fitts' law:

- **Index of Difficulty (ID)**—This value quantifies the difficulty of a task based on width and distance.
- **Movement Time (MT)**—This value quantifies the time it takes to complete a task based on the difficulty of the task (ID) and two empirically derived coefficients that are sensitive to the specific experimental conditions such as type of input device.
- **Index of Performance (IP)** [also called throughput (TP)]—This value is based on the relationship between the time it takes to perform a task and the relative difficulty of the task.

Fitts' law is concerned with the information capacity of the human motor system. The law is based on the premise that, if the difficulty of a particular task (determined by the Fitts equation as the index of difficulty—ID) is analogous to "information," then the rate at which a human can accomplish that task (TM) is equivalent to the "information capacity" of the human information processing system, which can then be used to calculate throughput (TP) for that action.

In other words, if we know how difficult an action is and we know how fast it can be done, we can calculate a value that represents human performance capacity by dividing the difficulty value by the completion value. We can then use that calculation, which is based on empirical quantifications, to design more efficient interfaces.

In his first paper, Fitts described an experiment called "reciprocal tapping," in which subjects were asked to tap back and forth on two 6-inch-tall plates with width *W* of 2, 1, 0.5, and 0.25 inches (Figure 7.14). During the experiment the plates were placed at four center-to-center distances or amplitudes (A): 2, 3, 8, and 16 inches. Hits were recorded as well as misses. The instructions were to strike the plates alternately and try for accuracy instead of speed.

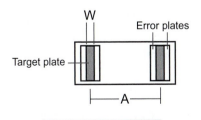

Figure 7.14 Fitts' tapping task.

From the results of his experiments, Fitts proposed that ID, the difficulty of the movement task, could be quantified by the equation

$$ID = \log_2(2A/W)$$

where A is the amplitude (distance to the target) and W is the width of the target.

Fitts equated electronic signals with distance and channel noise with target width. Because the logarithm in the equation uses base 2, the results are considered in "bit" units. The factor 2 was included to ensure an ID of greater than zero.

This equation was later refined by MacKenzie to align more closely with Shannon's law:

$$ID = \log_2(A/W + 1)$$

MacKenzie considered this formulation preferable for the following reasons:

- It provides a slightly better fit with observations.
- It exactly mimics the information theorem underlying Fitts' law.
- It always gives a positive rating for the index of task difficulty.

The average time for the completion of any given movement task can be calculated by the following equation:

$$MT = a + b \log_2(A/W + 1)$$

where MT is the movement time and the constants a and b are arrived at by linear regression (Figure 7.15).

The following issues need to be clarified:

- If MT is calculated in seconds, the unit of measurement for a is seconds and the unit of measurement for b is seconds/bit (ID is measured in bits).
- Both coefficients a (the intercept) and b (the slope) are determined by empirical results and are device dependent.

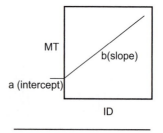

Figure 7.15 Fitts' linear regression.

MT, movement time; ID, index of difficulty.

- "Back of the envelope" calculations can use $a = 50$ and $b = 150$ (units in milliseconds) (Raskin, 2000).
- A and W must use consistent units of distance but need not be prescribed
- For one-dimensional tasks (straight vertical or horizontal movement), width is calculated along the axis of motion (horizontal or vertical).

Information Processing

By calculating the MT and ID, we have the ability to construct a model that can determine the information capacity of the human motor system for a given task. Fitts referred to this as the index of performance, more commonly known as throughput. Throughput is the rate of human information processing, and it has been calculated using ID/MT:

$$TP = ID/MT$$

The reciprocal of the slope has also been used to define TP [see Accot and Zhai (2003) for a detailed discussion]:

$$TP = 1/b$$

If a measure of accuracy is required by an experimental design, then width must be replaced by the "effective target width," which can be calculated as follows:

$$W_e = 4.133 \times SD_x$$

where SD_x is the standard deviation in the selection coordinates computed over a block of trials (MacKenzie, 2003, 39).

This will capture the overall performance of a device, a measure that involves both speed and accuracy, as calculated by the following equation:

$$TP = ID_e/MT$$

where

$$ID_e = \log_2(A/W_e + 1)$$

The International Standards Organization (ISO) 924-9 standard regarding input device performance quality measurements (Ergonomic Requirements for Office Work with Visual Display Terminals—Part 9: Requirements for Non-Keyboard Input Devices) uses this formula for the calculation of TP.

Note, however, that although this measurement provides an accurate determination of a particular device's performance, experiments involving movement time prediction measurements, which are generally used to compare the efficacy of two different devices, should use $MT = a + b \log_2(A/W + 1)$ (MacKenzie, 2003).

Application of Fitts' Law

Card et al. carried out the first application of Fitts' law in HCI research. They compared the MT of a mouse, a rate-controlled isometric joystick, step keys, and text keys for text selection tasks against the MT calculated for the use of a stylus and finger pointing (optimal rate). The mouse was found to be 5% slower than the optimal rate, and the joystick was 83% slower (Card et al., 1983).

They found that the positioning time and error rate of the mouse were superior to those of the other devices and that the mouse offered nearly maximum rates. However, Card et al. put important qualifications on the results of the comparison experiments.

They consider the mapping of hand movement to cursor movement to require less translation with the mouse than with the other devices, which would lower the cognitive load and decrease the error rate. They consider the mouse to be more compatible with the task at hand, a significant factor in interaction design.

An interesting application of Fitts' law, and one that highlights one of its ramifications for interaction design, was published by Jeff Raskin (2000). This application involved a comparison between menus on a computer running the Macintosh operating system (OS) with menus on a computer running the Windows OS.

These two operating systems have evolved since Raskin published his results; however, the significant issue he focused on has persisted through the current versions, Mac OS X and Windows XP. Raskin focused on their menus: those on the Macintosh OS are aligned with the edge of the screen, whereas Windows menus are offset by the title bar.

Because the user cannot move the cursor past the edge of the screen, the outer edge of a menu aligned along the edge of the screen is virtually endless. Therefore, the user does not have to position the cursor very carefully to remain on the menu. Because of their offset, Windows menus, on the other hand, require far more accuracy for the user to remain on the menu.

Raskin found that users tended to stop the mouse about 50 mm from the edge of the display, so he used that measurement for the computed width of the target for the Macintosh OS. He calculated the width of the Windows target to be 5 mm and used 80 mm for the average distance the cursor had to be moved on a 14-inch flat panel screen.

Based on his benchmark coefficients, the results of his Fitts analysis were as follows:

$$ID = 50 + 150 \log_2(80/50 + 1) = 256 \text{ msec for the Macintosh OS}$$
$$ID = 50 + 150 \log_2(80/5 + 1) = 663 \text{ msec for the Windows OS}$$

The advantages of the Macintosh OS design are also supported by Accot and Zhai (2003). We will look at their findings in the later discussion of two-dimensional tasks.

Implications of Fitts' Law

- Large targets and small distances between targets are advantageous.
- Screen elements should occupy as much of the available screen space as possible (given other design constraints such as grouping based on white space).
- The largest Fitts-based pixel is the one under the cursor (pop-up menus activated by the right mouse button on PCs are, therefore, easier than pull-down menus, however, they are limited in terms of visibility).
- Screen elements should take advantage of the screen edge whenever possible (the screen edge extends the width of the element infinitely).
- Large menus like pie menus are easier to uses than other types of menus.

Limitations of Fitts' Law

- There is no consistent way to deal with errors.
- It only models continuous movements.
- It is not suitable for all input devices, for example, isometric joysticks.
- It does not address two-handed operation (some evidence suggests that two-handed operation can increase performance).
- It does not address the difference between flexor and extensor movements (moving toward or away from the body, respectively).
- It does not address cognitive functions such as the mental operators in the KLM model.

Expansions of Fitts' Law

Many Fitts-based analyses involve rectangular targets and cursor trajectories that are perpendicular to the target. In these cases W is computed on the same axis as A (Figure 7.16a).

This also holds true when the target is a circle or a square. When the target is a circle, the diameter is used (Figure 7.16b). It is interesting that two of the tasks in Fitts' original experiments involved circular targets—disk transfer and peg in a hole.

Complications arise when the width and height of the target are not equal and the trajectory is not perpendicular to the target (Figure 7.16c).

In these cases, bivariate data are introduced into the calculation of W. These are two-dimensional tasks, for which width can be calculated by one of the following methods. [See MacKenzie and Buxton (1992) for a detailed discussion.]

- Smaller-Of—The smaller of the width and height measurements:

$$\text{ID}_{\text{min}}(W, H) = \log_2[D/\min(W, H) + 1]$$

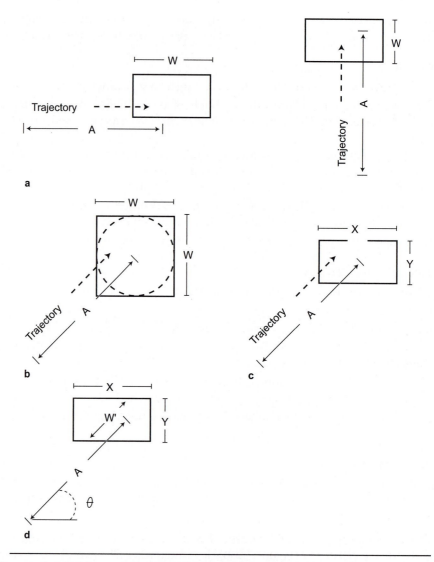

Figure 7.16 **(a) Horizontal and vertical trajectories. (b) Targeting a circular object. (c) Targeting a rectangular object. (d) Apparent width.**

- W—The "apparent width" calculated along the approach vector (Figure 7.16d):

$$\text{ID}_{W'} = \log_2(D/W' + 1)$$

MacKenzie and Buxton also looked at and rejected the following methods for calculating W:

- Status Quo—Horizontal extent only

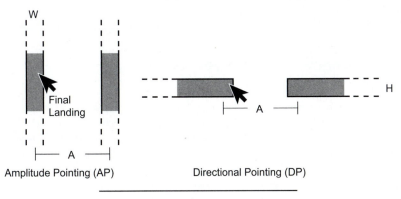

W

Final
Landing

├── A ──┤

Amplitude Pointing (AP)

├── A ──┤

H

Directional Pointing (DP)

Figure 7.17 Amplitude and directional pointing.

- $W + H$—the sum of the target width and height
- $W \times H$— the product of the target width and height

The "smaller-of" and the "W" methods have been used in most of the literature since MacKenzie and Buxton.

In one-dimensional tasks, only the target width (whether horizontal or vertical) is considered; the constraint is based on W, and target height (H) is infinite or equal to W. According to Accot and Zhai, this describes amplitude pointing (AP). If, on the other hand, W is set at infinity, then H becomes significant, which Accot and Zhai consider directional pointing (DP). The constraint is based on H.

These two methods are fundamentally different due to the fact that AP errors are controlled at "the final landing" and DP errors are corrected incrementally during the pointing movement (Accot & Zhai, 2003) (Figure 7.17).

The results of Accot and Zhai's experiments showed that AP and DP function differently, which is plausible due to the different error correction methods they use (incremental and "final landing"). They suggest certain implications for interaction design based on their results:

- Overly elongated objects hold no advantage (W/H ratios of 3 and higher).
- Objects should be elongated along the most common trajectory path (widgets normally approached from the side should use W, those approached from the bottom or top should use H).
- Objects should not be offset from the screen edge (consistent with the Macintosh OS).
- Objects that are defined by English words generally have $W > H$ and should be placed on the sides of the screen. (However, greater amplitude measurements may be significant on the normal "landscape"-oriented screens.)

Design Scenario

Circumference: Scrolling versus Paging

Chapter 5 considered whether to use a scrolling or a paging format for the pages that present the selected poems from the various issues. The print journal places the original and English versions on facing pages; however, this is not an option on the Web site.

We can now explore this issue in greater depth and make an informed decision using the CMN-GOMS model. For the purpose of this comparison, we assume that the user has just clicked the link on the TOC page and has arrived at the selected poem page. We also assume that the entire first appearance of the poem is visible and the user has read it.

Let's first sketch out, in plain English, what is involved in the two formats.

Scrolling—There are three different methods involved with scrolling:

1. A computer without a scrolling mouse: Scroll arrows—The user will have to target the down arrow on the scrollbar and scroll down. He or she will watch the screen to judge when to stop scrolling and then read the poem. Afterward, he or she will have to target the up arrow and scroll back up. This will be repeated as needed.

2. A computer without a scrolling mouse: Thumb—The user will have to target the scrollbar and then click and drag the scrollbar's thumb up and down to compare the two versions of the poem. This is quicker for scrolling long distances. For the sake of simplicity, we consider that using the Page Up and Page Down keys is equivalent to dragging the scrollbar's thumb.

3. A computer with a scrolling mouse—This method does not require targeting the scrollbar at all. The user pushes the scroll wheel forward and backward as needed. This is less efficient for long pages.

Paging—There is one method that can be used with the paging format:

4. The paging format will involve clicking on hyperlinks to go back and forth between the pages.

CMN-GOMS Analysis—Scrolling

Let's create a CMN-GOMS analysis for the first method (scroll arrows). This is intuitively the most complex and least efficient method.

```
GOAL: Compare Poems
    .      GOAL: Edit-Unit-Task
    .   .          GOAL: Read other poem
    .      GOAL: Execute-Unit-Task
    .   . GOAL: Edit-Unit-Task
    .   .   .      GOAL: Locate scrollbar down-arrow
```

Design Scenario (cont.)

```
.   .     GOAL: Execute-Unit-Task
.   .     GOAL: Edit-Unit-Task
.   .   .     GOAL: Move cursor to scrollbar down-arrow
.   .     GOAL: Execute-Unit-Task
.   .     GOAL: Edit-Unit-Task
.   .   .     GOAL: Click -Initiate downward scrolling
.   .     GOAL: Execute-Unit-Task
.   .     GOAL: Edit-Unit-Task
.   .   .     GOAL: Locate other version
.   .     GOAL: Execute-Unit-Task
.   .   .     GOAL: Edit-Unit-Task
.   .   .   .     GOAL: Look at scrolling page
.   .   .     GOAL: Execute-Unit-Task
.   .   Verify-Unit-Task
.   Verify-Unit-Task
```

This process is repeated for each trip back and forth between versions; the only things that will change are the up and down arrow indications, respectively.

The analysis of the second method (thumb) is as follows:

```
GOAL: Compare Poems
.       GOAL: Edit-Unit-Task
.   .         GOAL: Read other poem
.       GOAL: Execute-Unit-Task
.   .       GOAL: Edit-Unit-Task
.   .   .         GOAL: Locate scrollbar thumb
.   .       GOAL: Execute-Unit-Task
.   .       GOAL: Edit-Unit-Task
.   .   .         GOAL: Move cursor to scrollbar thumb
.   .       GOAL: Execute-Unit-Task
.   .       GOAL: Edit-Unit-Task
.   .   .         GOAL: Click/drag - Initiate downward scrolling
.   .       GOAL: Execute-Unit-Task
.   .       GOAL: Edit-Unit-Task
.   .   .         GOAL: Locate other version
.   .       GOAL: Execute-Unit-Task
.   .   .   GOAL: Edit-Unit-Task
.   .   .   .     GOAL: Look at scrolling page
```

Design Scenario (cont.)

```
  .   .    .      GOAL: Execute-Unit-Task
  .   .    Verify-Unit-Task
  .   Verify-Unit-Task
```

So far, there is no real difference between these two methods. However, in the first method, the whole analysis has to be repeated, whereas in the second, only a part has to be repeated as follows:

```
  .   GOAL: Edit-Unit-Task
  .   .      GOAL: Read other poem
  .   GOAL: Execute-Unit-Task
  .   .      GOAL: Edit-Unit-Task
  .   .    .      GOAL: Click/drag - Initiate upward scrolling
  .   .      GOAL: Execute-Unit-Task
  .   .      GOAL: Edit-Unit-Task
  .   .    .      GOAL: Locate other version
  .   .      GOAL: Execute-Unit-Task
  .   .    .      GOAL: Edit-Unit-Task
  .   .    .    .      GOAL: Look at scrolling page
  .   .    .      GOAL: Execute-Unit-Task
  .   .      Verify-Unit-Task
  .   Verify-Unit-Task
```

After a few repeated trips between the poems, the second method requires considerably fewer steps and increases in efficiency with each comparison.

The analysis of the second scenario is as follows:

```
GOAL: Compare Poems
  .      GOAL: Edit-Unit-Task
  .   .        GOAL: Read other poem
  .      GOAL: Execute-Unit-Task
  .   .        GOAL: Edit-Unit-Task
  .   .    .        GOAL: Initiate downward scrolling
  .   .        GOAL: Execute-Unit-Task
  .   .        GOAL: Edit-Unit-Task
  .   .    .        GOAL: Locate other version
  .   .        GOAL: Execute-Unit-Task
  .   Verify-Unit-Task
```

Design Scenario (cont.)

This method is shorter because the user does not have to target the scrollbar and does not have to look back; his or her eyes remain on the page at all times. This is the most efficient method so far.

CMN-GOMS Analysis—Paging

The analysis of the paging format is as follows:

```
GOAL: Compare Poems
.      GOAL: Edit-Unit-Task
.   .         GOAL: Read other poem
.      GOAL: Execute-Unit-Task
.   .       GOAL: Edit-Unit-Task
.   .   .       GOAL: Locate <alternate version> link
.   .     GOAL: Execute-Unit-Task
.   .     GOAL: Edit-Unit-Task
.   .   .       GOAL: Move cursor to <alternate version> link
.   .     GOAL: Execute-Unit-Task
.   .     GOAL: Edit-Unit-Task
.   .   .       GOAL: Click
.   .     GOAL: Execute-Unit-Task
.   .     GOAL: Edit-Unit-Task
.   .   .       GOAL: Locate other version
.   .     GOAL: Execute-Unit-Task
.   .   .     GOAL: Edit-Unit-Task
.   .   .   .       GOAL: Look at new page
.   .   .     GOAL: Execute-Unit-Task
.   .          Verify-Unit-Task
.      Verify-Unit-Task
```

Let's compare this paging format with the different scrolling methods.

- Paging is as efficient as the first method (arrow method).
- Paging is as efficient as the second method (thumb method) the first time; it then becomes less efficient.
- Paging is less efficient than the third method (scrolling mouse method).

The paging format is as efficient as the first method, but is less efficient than the other methods. This supports a decision to use the scrolling format for the page layout.

Design Scenario (cont.)

Fragment Identifier

We might be able to take advantage of the hyperlink-based navigation format by coding it as an intrapage link (fragment identifier) and, therefore, allowing people to navigate between alternate versions on the same page rather than between pages.

This will add some flexibility to the design and allow people to choose their preferred method of clicking versus scrolling. An analysis of this method will be the same as for the paging method, but this version of the hyperlink method can easily be combined with any of the scrolling methods, as we will see in the selection rules.

Selection Rules

The GOMS analysis has so far provided an a priori look at the two formats for the page layout and gives us a solid foundation on which to base our decision that the scrolling format is more efficient. However, it is a rather artificial picture of how real users will behave. In a real-world situation, users might use a combination of scrolling methods, which may include the less efficient options.

We can try to predict user behavior by developing selection rules to determine when people will choose one method over another. Consider the following selection rules:

- Use method 1 on a computer running Mac OS X (the scroll arrows are located in close proximity at the bottom of the scrollbar, which makes it easy to reverse scrolling directions, and the user does not have to move the mouse as in the thumb method).
- Use method 2 if the poem is long and you want to scroll quickly.
- Use method 3 if there is a scrolling mouse.
- Use method 4 (revised to reflect the fragment identifier format) if the mouse is near the link.

Summary

The models covered in this chapter can be used to test design ideas and compare solutions as well as improve existing designs. They allow designers to explore the conceptual aspects of a proposed design, watch it perform dynamically, and make concrete determinations about the physical aspects.

The models can do this in a way that gives the designer important information about the design without requiring him or her to perform time-consuming testing with real subjects. These models are not a substitute for user testing; they can be used, however, to increase the validity of early design decisions and make the initial development activities more efficient and effective. This also increases the effectiveness of the testing activities that involve real users.

The GOMS models have been proven to be effective and powerful tools for interaction design. They can provide the designer with predictions about task timings, preferred methods of task completion, learning timings, and interface consistency.

They can be used to evaluate designs based on performance criteria imposed by the computing tasks and environments. For instance, mission-critical environments often have significant temporal thresholds that must be maintained for the safe operation of the devices involved.

These models can also be used as substitutes for real users for the purpose of evaluating the efficiency of competing design proposals. This has led to significant financial advantages and ramifications in real-world situations.

Resources on the Web

www.aw.com/heim
You will find links to general information on user interface design models as well as information on the various GOMS models.

Suggested Reading

Card, S. K., Moran, T. P., & Newell, A. (1983). *The Psychology of Human–Computer Interaction* (New Ed ed.): Lawrence Erlbaum Associates.

Carroll, J. M. (Ed.). (2003). *HCI Models, Theories, and Frameworks: Toward a Multidisciplinary Science:* Morgan Kaufmann.

Usability Testing

This chapter explores the issues involved in performing a usability test. Previously, we discussed various methods of evaluation, such as heuristic evaluations and cognitive walkthroughs, and we stressed the importance of iterative evaluation for the development of usable interaction designs. However, we have not yet defined the term "usability."

Let's look at a few definitions from some of the influential practitioners and agencies involved in the dissemination of usability information and knowledge.

8.1. What Is Usability?

No one definition of usability is accepted by the diverse communities involved in the design of interactive artifacts; there is, however, a core set of attributes that can be distilled from the various definitions.

> Usability is the measure of the quality of a user's experience when interacting with a product or system. *(Usability.gov, 2006)*

> Usability is a quality attribute that assesses how easy user interfaces are to use. *(Nielsen, 2003)*

Both of these definitions use the term "quality" in reference to the nature of the user's experience, which can be measured in terms of the excellence of that experience. Nielsen refines the term further by referring to the ease of use embedded in the design of the interface.

Both of these definitions are followed by the same list of usability attributes that further refine the definition:

Ease of learning—How fast can a user who has never previously seen the interface learn it sufficiently well to accomplish basic tasks?

Efficiency of use—Once an experienced user has learned to use the system, how fast can he or she accomplish tasks?

Memorability—If a user has used the system before, can he or she remember enough to use it effectively the next time or does he or she have to start from the beginning and relearn everything?

Error frequency and severity—How often do users make errors while using the system, how serious are these errors, and how do users recover from these errors?

Subjective satisfaction—How much does the user *like* using the system?

The ISO standard 9241-11 (1998) Guidance on Usability defines usability as follows:

> The extent to which a product can be used by specified users to achieve specified goals with effectiveness, efficiency and satisfaction in a specified context of use.

Again, the concept of efficiency is mentioned in the definition of usability—it is mentioned in the ISO definition and is one of the elements listed in the definitions just given. Here, we also have the concept of effectiveness. We explored the concepts of learnability, efficiency, memorability, and effectiveness in Chapter 6, but we have not yet addressed the issues of error frequency and user satisfaction.

The frequency of user errors depends on a number of factors, including visibility, comprehensibility, memorability, and consistency. We discussed all of these issues and now have a general understanding of how our interfaces can be designed so that people will make fewer mistakes. We will look at some of the methods that we can use during usability tests to capture that information. This will provide us with important knowledge about our proposed designs.

We can put the knowledge we acquire to good use when we make design decisions and we can test the relative success of our efforts by conducting follow-up usability tests. The concept of user satisfaction, however, is more complex.

User satisfaction is subjective and involves all of the usability goals and design principles we have looked at so far. To promote a sense of satisfaction in users, we must ensure that they can accomplish all of their tasks and do so in a way that is easy and efficient. However, it will be difficult to determine what will *satisfy* people the most unless we explore their attitudes and opinions.

Attitudes and opinions are not quantifiable, and they cannot be tested by timing tasks or calculating errors. These are qualitative attributes whose value can only be ascertained by asking users appropriate and focused questions. This can be done by using a variety of methods, from paper questionnaires to face-to-face interviews, which are among the techniques involved in usability testing that we explore in this chapter.

As we explore the issues and processes involved in usability testing, we will learn how to capture quantitative as well as qualitative data and will see how we can translate that information into recommendations that can be used to improve our designs.

8.2. What Is a Usability Test?

A usability test is a structured process used to explore the interaction between an objective participant and a proposed design. The test is usually focused on a specific aspect of the design in order to identify and understand any problematic areas or components.

Usability tests can evaluate a design based on specific, predetermined usability criteria, or they can explore a design and uncover new and previously unconsidered problems.

Usability tests can involve elaborate laboratories, sophisticated equipment, and large testing teams. However, there also are budget usability testing methods that can be employed frequently with little investment of time or money, such as the methods employed by Nielsen's discount usability engineering model discussed in Chapter 3. These budget methods can provide significant knowledge about the usability of a design.

Dumas and Redish (1999) identify a list of attributes common to most usability tests:

- The goal is to improve a product.
- Participants are real users.
- The participants do real tasks.

- Participants are formally observed.
- The data are analyzed.
- Recommendations for improvement are made.

A usability test has three basic components: the participant, the design, and the tester.

Participants—The participants are representatives of the target users that are enlisted and screened by the test facilitator. They are not members of the design team; they are actual users who are asked to perform realistic and representative tasks using a proposed design.

Design—The proposed design that is used in the test may be a fully functioning prototype or it may be a simple, limited, paper prototype; this depends on when in the design process the test is given.

Tester—There might be only one tester or there might be a testing team. Tests that are conducted by one tester will be limited in scope and will involve few participants, whereas tests conducted by test teams can be rather extensive and involve hundreds of participants.

Testers can take different roles: administrator, moderator, data logger, technician, prototype expert, or passive observer. These roles can be carried out by different team members or can be shared among the team. We explore these roles later in the section Who: Select Participants, Testers, and Observers.

Constraints on Usability Testing

A number of constraints might be imposed on the usability tests that you perform. The degree to which these affect the tests depends on the specific project's resources.

- **Time**—Usability tests generally require about an hour to an hour and a half to perform. Most projects require four or five tests to uncover most problems. The time it takes to design, prepare, administer, and analyze the results must also be taken into consideration.
- **Finance**—Many costs are associated with usability tests, including equipment and software, laboratory time, recording media, participant compensation, and refreshments.
- **Personnel**—Formal usability tests require a team of at least four people. They must be available and knowledgeable about their areas of responsibility.
- **Laboratory**—You can perform a usability test without a dedicated laboratory. You can even conduct a test without any technological equipment. However, to perform a formal usability test, a dedicated laboratory is required.

Human Subject Protocols

Whenever you use human subjects in an experimental design you must be aware of the potential for negative consequences stemming from the testing situation. Many governmental bodies have strict regulations that govern the way institutions carry out experiments using human subjects, and these must be strictly followed. The safety and well being of the subjects must be the highest priority in any experimental design.

If you are using real subjects you must be fully aware of the regulations imposed by the various institutions and regulatory bodies that pertain to your experimental design. Your subjects must also be aware of these regulations and should be given an informed consent form that must be maintained by the concerned institutions.

There are many resources for information on the federal regulations regarding human subject protocols as well as some template forms that can be modified for your specific situation. The U.S. Department of Health and Human Services has a Web site, *http://www.hhs.gov/ohrp/,* developed by the Office for Human Research Protections (OHRP), that contains a great deal of valuable information and resources regarding this critical topic.

Advantages and Limitations of Usability Testing

Rubin (1994) identifies some of the benefits that can derive from usability testing as well as some of its limitations:

Advantages

- **Minimize help desk calls**—Identifying usability problems before a product is released can help to minimize calls to the help desk from customers; this has the potential to save money and improve profitability.
- **Increase product loyalty**—Products that perform well for real users will create a positive association and increase the potential to retain or even gain new customers.
- **Provide benchmarks for future products**—Conducting usability tests can provide documented benchmarks that can be used for future upgrades to the product.

Limitations

- **Artificial context**—Usability tests are conducted in an artificial setting without the distractions and interruptions common in most work places.
- **Not definitive of product acceptance**—Usability tests can be rigorous and exhaustive and can be used to explore complex and extensive applications, but they will not be able to guarantee product acceptance by the public.
- **Skewed sample of users**—Usability tests can only provide feedback from the participants you test. It is possible that your screening process did not identify the most appropriate set of participants, and, therefore, your results will be skewed to a particular population.
- **Not always efficient**—Usability tests can be expensive and time consuming; they are not always the best way to evaluate a proposed design.

8.2.1. **Phases of a Usability Test**

Usability tests are invaluable to a design project, especially if the new system is large and complex and involves many users. Usability tests, however, require resources in the form of time, money, and personnel. Usability testing for large projects is often done by an outside testing firm, which further increases the drain on a project's financial resources. Given these factors, it is essential that the testing process be well thought out and planned in advance.

Even if you use one of the budget methods and conduct the tests yourself, you must still dedicate time and energy to planning, recruiting, testing, and analyzing the results. Usability testing can provide important feedback about your design, and you will understandably want to put in the most effort in order to get the most "bang for your buck."

To maximize your investment, you must integrate the testing process into the structure of the project as a whole. At this point, it can be confusing as to how this should be done, but once you understand the different types of testing methods and procedures, you will have a better understanding of the kinds of information you can gain from the different testing situations. You will then be able to see how you can best integrate the testing process with the rest of the development activities.

Usability testing has four phases: designing the test, preparing for the test, performing the test and, finally, analyzing and documenting the test results The 5W+H heuristic can help you to structure some aspects of the process as follows.

Design the Test

Why are you testing?

- Define the purpose

What are you testing?

- Define your concerns and goals
- Define the tasks
- Create the scenarios
- Define the measurements

How will you test?

- Define the test method

Where will you test?

- Determine the location of the tests

Who will be involved?

- Select participants, testers, and observers

Prepare for the Test

When will you test?

- Create a test schedule

Writing scripts

- Introduction and instructions
- Testing interaction
- Debriefing

Running a pilot test

Perform the Test

Preliminaries

Test phases

- Pre-test
- During the test
- Post-test

Process the Data

Activities performed during testing

- Collect
- Summarize
- Organize

Follow-up activities

- Categorize
- Analyze
- Document

Each one of these four phases must be documented in the form of a usability testing program. This will provide an opportunity for the team members to critique the plan and provide any additional information that might be useful. It will also clarify any misconceptions that team members might have about the purpose of the tests and the effect they will have on the future development of the design.

Let's look more deeply into each of these phases and see what they involve and what issues may arise.

8.3. Design the Test

The two principal facets of the test design process are the "why" and the "what." If you are not clear about the reason you are conducting the test, you will not be able to maximize its benefits. All of the other facets are derived from this one.

Once you know why you need to perform a test—for instance, if you want to see whether your navigational scheme is usable—you can identify what you need to test. In this case, you might need to test the link labels, the locations of the links, the link colors, the specifics of the link targets, and any other issue involved in the navigation of the design.

Once these questions are explored and made explicit, you will be able to determine the testing method and location, identify the participants, and schedule the tests. Let's look at each of these facets in more depth.

8.3.1. Why: Define the Purpose

You will define the purpose in a purpose statement that describes the high-level reasons for conducting the test. This defines the value the test will provide to the project. For instance, the purpose of a test might be to find out whether people are comfortable using an automated communication system instead of using the phone or interoffice mail. Another purpose might be to see what effect a design will have on the amount of help desk calls users need to make.

The purpose statement should also clarify the effect that the test results will have on the project. It describes the thresholds that will trigger iterations or initiate subsequent phases of design. For instance, you might determine that a certain level of success in terms of time or error rate will allow the project to proceed toward the development of a functional prototype or that additional clarification will be included in the documentation.

Making the purpose of the test explicit will also help to clarify any misconceptions about the test on the part of the client or any team members who are not familiar with the process. It is important that the stakeholders with a financial interest understand the importance of the test and are comfortable with the possibility that the results may initiate an iteration cycle.

Questions that the purpose statement should answer include the following:

- What do you expect to gain from the test?
- What affect will the results have on the project?
- How much of the design can be changed?
- Are there differences of opinion within the team?

8.3.2. What: Define Your Concerns and Goals

You must now refine your purpose by identifying your concerns about the design. For instance, you might be concerned that users may not understand the icons, or you might be concerned about a specific menu's options.

Concerns are more specific than the overarching purpose we just explored. They will be generated from the various task analyses and evaluations you have performed during the design phase of the project. Your concerns will also evolve over time, relating to the specific development activities in which you are involved. This will have an effect on the kinds of tests you perform.

How do you generate concerns?

- Task analysis
- Evaluations
- Constraints—personnel, time, and finances

After you identify your concerns about the design, you will refine them into a set of goals. Dumas and Redish (1999) describe concerns as questions you may have about the design and describe goals as statements that are derived from those questions. Your concern about the menu structure, for example, will be described by a set of goals:

- The user will be able to choose the correct menu on the first try.
- The user will be able to navigate to the correct third menu level in less than 5 seconds.

As we have seen, a purpose statement is a high-level description of a usability test. The purpose is then defined by a set of concerns, each of which has a few associated goals. By defining this level of granularity you will be able to make determinations about the rest of the facets of the test design.

If you know what your goals are, you will also know who you need to test, how you will test them, what measures you will need, what tasks you must define, and many other elements involved in the usability test. In other words, the design of the test begins with a set of well-defined goals. Without these, your test will have no focus, and it will be difficult to derive any benefit from your investment.

Selecting Features

Another way in which to approach this aspect of test design is to focus on the features you want to test. The 80/20 rule says that 80% of the work will be done by 20% of the features. Therefore, testing that 20% will be more productive than testing the rest of the features.

This method can be used to streamline the testing process, especially when project resources have been depleted. The trick with this method is to correctly identify the critical 20%. This can be accomplished through questionnaires or interviews if the questions are geared to the capture of this kind of information.

You can also use the results of previous tests to determine the important features of the design: the ones that are used most often or the ones that cause the majority of the problems.

When you are trying to determine what features to test, you should consider new features or alterations to existing features. Destructive features, such as delete functions, should also be tested.

8.3.3. What: Define the Tasks

You now have to define the tasks that you will use during the test. You should choose tasks that involve the features or aspects of the design that relate to the goals you have defined.

The following is a list of some of the issues that you might consider when you are developing the tasks for the test:

- **Critical**—Tasks that involve potentially destructive actions.
- **New**—Tasks that involve new functions or aspects of the design.
- **Problematic**—Tasks that have been identified as causing problems for the user.
- **Frequent**—Tasks that are performed often.
- **Typical**—Tasks that are commonly performed by most users.

You do not want to create tasks limited to the functionality you are testing. This would artificially focus the user's attention on that specific feature. Instead, you should try to choose tasks that will cause the user to utilize the various areas of the design in which you are interested.

For instance, if you are interested in the usability of your search function, you could ask the participant to use the search function to find product X. Although this may seem like a logical way to test the search function, the user would be highly and unusually focused on that particular aspect of the design.

A better approach would be to ask the participant to find product X and compare it with product Y. In this way, he or she will make the decision to use the search function and naturally use it more than once during the task without giving it undue focus. This will create a more natural context for the participant. You will be able to observe whether the participant looks for and can easily find the search box or if he or she first scans the page for links to the product information.

You must craft the tasks carefully so that you can obtain clean data that relate specifically to the issues you are exploring. You might need to clarify certain actions by asking the person questions while he or she is involved in the task activities. The following is a list of task attributes that can be used to craft successful tasks.

- **Reasonable and Doable**—The tasks you choose should involve sensible actions. Do not ask your participants to do anything that is not likely to happen in the real world. For instance, using a word processing program to do complex spreadsheet calculations would be suspect even though the potential for that activity may be present.
- **Derived from Real User Goals**—The tasks should involve the completion of real user goals. If the participant understands the motivation for the task, he or she will be more likely to give you accurate feedback about the process. Otherwise the task is an abstract action with no real-world context.

- **Specific and Focused**—You should create tasks that are explicit and unambiguous. This will help to maintain consistency among testers and participants and allow you more easily to compare results.

Arrange the Tasks

After you have created the tasks, they should be arranged in some logical way. This may be based on a typical work flow or it may be ordered according to difficulty. It would be discouraging for a participant to fail at the first task. Failure can create a negative frame of mind. If you get a few of the easier tasks out of the way, the participant will feel as though he or she has accomplished something and may be further motivated to attempt the more difficult tasks.

Some tasks will require actions on the part of the participant; other tasks will involve impressions and opinions. The initial tasks can be based more on the participant's observations and impressions about color or page layout. These tasks involve exploration. The later tasks can be more action oriented, and the participant will be asked to accomplish things.

Quantity of Tasks

The number of tasks you can test depends on how much time is allotted, and you should therefore try to estimate the length of time each task will take. You can base these estimates on trial runs performed with other team members. Remember to pad the estimates because your teammates are familiar with the design and will not behave like an objective participant. You will, however, get a base limit with which to calculate.

Task Resources

Some of the tasks that you create will require specific resources. These may be hardware, software, or information related. Some tasks may require specific I/O devices or a database.

Other tasks may require specific external information. For instance, if you are testing a flight reservation interface, you will give the participant an itinerary so that he or she does not have to come up with one out of the blue. Such a requirement would take time away from the test and might make the participant nervous if he or she were not able to come up with something on the spot.

8.3.4. What: Create the Scenarios

After you define the tasks, you need a way to present them to the participants. You do not want to simply give participants the task list because you might want to observe how and why they choose the methods they use.

Scenarios can be used to present tasks without telling participants how to accomplish them. Scenarios are short, one-paragraph stories that set up a task or tasks. Be careful not to involve more than two discrete tasks in one scenario; it may become hard to analyze the results later.

A scenario tells a story that revolves around a goal, such as sending a group e-mail or printing out a product description. A scenario makes the task real and gives the participant motivation for his or her performance. Scenarios are like personas in that they put a face on the task and turn it into something to which the participant can relate.

A scenario is a description of a goal; it is not set of step-by-step directions. Try not to create an algorithm for participants to follow. Instead, present them with a story they can understand and use to formulate strategies and methods to achieve their goals. Try not to bias their decisions by referring to interface components by location, label, or title.

The following is a list of scenario attributes:

- **Short**—Scenarios should be brief, perhaps one paragraph.
- **Complete**—Scenarios should contain all the information needed to perform the task.
- **Unambiguous**—Scenarios should be clearly worded and should not include confusing terminology or information.
- **Familiar**—Scenarios should involve situations with which the participant is familiar.

Scenarios and Tasks

There is a natural recursive relationship between tasks and scenarios. You may often discover new tasks as you prepare your scenarios; in fact, some developers use scenarios to drive task creation. If you consider this part of the test development process to be iterative; you will be able to develop more representative tasks and richer scenarios.

8.3.5. What: Define the Measurements

After you decide on the tasks you want to use, you need to determine how to measure the results that you observe. There are two basic types of measurements: quantitative and qualitative.

The measures you use will depend on the tasks you choose. For instance, if you want to determine whether your menu groupings are appropriate, you can calculate the number of errors the participant makes or you can calculate the time it takes him or her to make a selection; these are quantitative measures.

These quantitative measures are important, but they do not tell the whole story. If you want to know why the user had problems with the menu, you will need some qualitative data. This type of data can be gathered by using the think-out-loud technique or some "during-test" questions.

If you want to determine which page layout is preferable, you can use a post-test questionnaire or you can ask the participant to think out loud as he or she performs particular tasks. This will provide a qualitative measure of user satisfaction.

Quantitative—Objective performance measures can tell you that something is wrong. This type of test is based on quantifiable data, such as time to complete a task, number of errors, number of repeated errors, or time to recover from an error. If you use quantitative measures, you might need a significant sample to get adequate data. These are generally more formal types of tests.

Qualitative—Subjective, opinion-based measures can tell you what is wrong. You will need fewer subjects for this type of test, and the test methods can be more informal.

When you define the measures you will use to evaluate a task, you will also be defining your usability goals. It is one thing to say that the menu structure should be comprehensible. If you define a measurement for a task that involves the menu, however, you will have a way to test for that usability goal. That measurement might take the form of a time range or it might be defined by the number of errors.

Regardless of your measurement scheme, you will now have a testable indication of your usability goal. This forces you to define what you actually *mean* by usability goals like "ease of use" or "ease of learning."

The types of measurements we use affect the types of analyses we perform after the test. The analyses we perform affect the kinds of recommendations we make. We will look at the issues involved in analyzing the results of a usability test later in the section Process the Data.

8.3.6. How: Define the Test Method

Once you know what your testing goals are and how you will measure the results, you can determine what type of testing method will best satisfy your needs. There are three basic types of usability tests: diagnostic, comparative, and validation tests.

The goals you pursue and the type of testing method you choose will depend on the particular phase of development you are in. Diagnostic tests are designed to investigate usability issues and problems in conceptual and physical design solutions and are generally performed in the early stages of development.

Comparison tests are used to decide between competing solutions that arise during development. Validation tests are generally used toward the end of the development process to check the usability of functional prototypes.

Some of these tests are conducted informally to get rough estimates before more rigorous testing takes place. Diagnostic and comparative tests can be performed using simple drawings and paper prototypes without any computer-based interaction.

Results can be notated by an observer as the test is conducted. Validation tests are usually more formal and involve sophisticated laboratories with video and sound recording, key tracking, and other computer-based testing apparatus.

Let's look at the different types of test and see how they apply to the goals that we would like to explore and the types of measurements those goals require. Rubin (1994) identifies four types of usability tests: exploration, assessment, comparison, and validation. We will use these categories, but we will include the exploration and assessment tests in a larger category of diagnosis tests.

Diagnosis—Diagnosis tests are designed to investigate and evaluate proposed design solutions. There are two types of diagnostic test: exploration and assessment.

- Exploration—Exploratory tests are used to make determinations about conceptual design solutions. You might want to determine the completeness of a design: does it have the proper functionality?
- Assessment—Assessment tests are used to investigate physical designs, such as paper prototypes and wireframes. These tests can be used to explore the functionality of pull-down menus or radio buttons.

Comparison—Comparison tests are used to explore alternative designs and make determinations about competing solutions. These are more complex because they measure each solution and compare the results. There are two basic types of comparison tests:

- Independent—group design—The simplest form of a comparison test involves using a different set of participants for each task or set of related tasks. This is called an independent-group design and requires many participants.

  To make sure that this type of experimental design is robust, provides an accurate measure of usability and has a significant statistical result, you must use an adequate number of participants.
- Within—subjects design—If it is not possible to get enough participants, you can use a within-subjects design, in which you use one group for all tasks. One of the concerns with this type of design is that people may be able to transfer what they learn from one task to another task. To avoid this transfer of learning, you need to balance the test by randomizing the order in which the tasks are presented.

Validation—These tests are used to verify that the design adheres to a predetermined set of usability criteria. These are generally performed late in the design process and can measure both performance and user preferences.

Validation tests are often used to see how the design works as an integrated whole. Parts or modules that are developed by different teams are brought together to see how the pieces fit and if they perform as well as they should in conjunction.

8.3.7. **Where: Determine the Location of the Tests**

Usability tests can be done in a fixed usability lab that is equipped with the hardware and software required for formal testing. They can also be done in the field using a portable usability lab.

A typical fixed usability lab has a good deal of fairly expensive equipment, including a few computers, video equipment, and special one-way mirrors. This type of testing environment may not be financially feasible or even appropriate for your testing needs.

Recent developments in portable usability lab technology have achieved a significant level of functionality. It is now possible to conduct sophisticated usability tests at the client's location. These tests are performed using portable usability labs that fit inside a medium-sized shipping case.

If the budget is tight or if you do not have access to a formal usability lab, it is still possible to perform a successful test using just a video camera and a computer.

There are also times when you may need to perform a usability test without any equipment, just a pencil and paper. There is no reason why a usability test cannot be accomplished under such situations. Let's look at the various types of usability labs and see what kind of equipment is involved.

A typical fixed laboratory (Figure 8.1) includes the following equipment:

Computer Stations—There are a number of computer stations. One is dedicated to the testing component and includes screen capture and key-logging software as well as the prototype software.

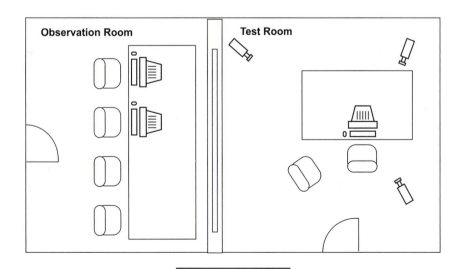

Figure 8.1 Fixed usability lab.

There are also a number of other networked computer stations to monitor the participant's computer and the video and audio feeds. Some of the monitor stations can take control of the testing station and video devices remotely.

Video Equipment—There are a few video cameras. Some might be free standing, others might be mounted on the walls or ceiling. Some might even have motion detection so that they can track the participant's movements. They are set up to capture the participant's facial expressions, hand movements, posture, and head movements. Some might be set up to capture the participant's interaction with the test monitor.

Audio Equipment—Audio equipment is used to capture any conversations between the participant and the test monitor or any of the think-out-loud feedback.

Mixers—Mixers, either hardware or software, are used to process the various video and audio feeds. These control line levels and settings, such as tone, brightness, focus, and other parameters.

The mixers are also used to combine the various signals into a split-screen or picture-in-picture version of the test observations. The audio might also be fed into a mixer and monitored by observers in another room. The results of the video and audio recordings are then recorded to a final tape.

Monitors and Speakers—There are a number of extra video monitors and speakers to display the various raw or processed video feeds.

Rooms—There are at least two separate rooms—one for the test and one for observation. There is also a one-way mirror so observers can see directly into the test room.

Portable labs have the basic equipment to capture the participant's screen as well as the video and audio feeds. These labs use smaller screens, and all of the equipment is hard wired and mounted in the shipping case. This allows the testers quickly to set up the equipment and begin testing.

Benefits of a Fixed Lab

- One can invite more observers (it is often an eye-opening experience for the client).
- It is easier to perform a formal test and observation.
- Setup time is less.

Benefits of a Portable Lab

- It is less expensive.
- It allows for a more flexible schedule.
- The test is performed in a more natural setting.

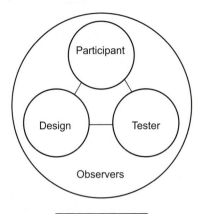

Figure 8.2 Usability test.

8.3.8. Who: Select Participants, Testers, and Observers

A usability test requires two people: a participant and a tester. As we have seen, evaluations can be done by experts using guidelines or heuristics. However, if a real user is not involved, it is not a usability test. There may be some controversy over the specific terminology used to distinguish between usability evaluations that do not involve real participants and usability tests that do use actual user representatives; for the sake of clarity, however, this book will use the terms usability evaluation and usability testing to distinguish between these two types of activities.

Because the presence of a real user is fundamental to usability testing, it is important to select participants carefully; they are the core of the test, and the results emanate from them. However, if the person who performs the test is not properly prepared or does not have enough experience in conducting usability tests, the results will suffer.

A usability test is a dynamic interaction among the participant, the tester, and the design (Figure 8.2). You must be careful to create a situation that will foster a successful dynamic between these three, allow the information to flow between the nodes and the necessary data to be collected.

Let's look at the process of choosing the people who will be involved in the testing and the kinds of qualities and attributes they should possess.

Select Participants

During the discovery phase we identified and documented the project stakeholders. We then created detailed profiles of the primary stakeholder, or the person who will be using the design. Such individuals are also referred to as target users.

MAXIM

Participants should be real users.

We now need to identify real people who fit the primary stakeholder description and recruit them as participants in the usability tests. If we are designing a system for a company's internal use, we look at the people currently involved in the work flow. If we are designing a product for commercial purposes or a Web site for a public audience, we look at the public for stakeholder representatives.

One of the questions you should ask is: what users am I most interested in? You cannot test everyone, so you will have to narrow your scope to those users who represent the target audience for your design.

How Many Participants?

The next question is: how many people do you need to test? We looked at Nielsen's DUE model in Chapter 3. He described the diminishing returns involved in testing more than four or five representative users. This has become a benchmark for most usability testing designs.

> **MAXIM**
> You do not always need to test a great many users.

The DUE model is based on the premise that some testing is better than no testing. The model recognizes that you will not capture every usability problem with this limited sample; however, the expense involved in testing more subjects will soon outweigh the benefits of finding more usability problems. Both the principle of satisficing and the 80/20 rule support this type of discount usability testing.

If you are doing research that requires statistically significant results, you will need to test additional users. You might consider, however, that the cost benefit derived from using fewer participants will help to support more iterations of the testing process and will be far more important in the long run.

Screeners

We are looking for participants who are "most representative" of the stakeholder profiles, and, therefore, we have to screen the people we recruit for our usability tests based on those criteria. This can be done over the phone, through e-mail, or with paper questionnaires.

The questions used to screen for potential participants are generated by the stakeholder profiles. Because we are looking for a match, we will do best to stick with questions that relate specifically to the characteristics described in these profiles.

The people you recruit should have the following basic characteristics:

- Availability
- Responsiveness
- Objectivity

Availability—Once you have screened potential participants, how do you know which participants to recruit? This is not an easy question to answer; there are many factors to consider.

You must schedule the test in an appropriate timeframe so that your participants have time availabilities that match the team members' availabilities. You also need to synchronize their availability with that of the usability lab.

Responsiveness—You are interested in people who will give you honest and informed feedback, so you should be looking for people who have recently been involved with a similar product or Web site and are articulate in describing their experiences.

Objectivity—You should also be aware of any interests potential participants might have in the product you are testing. People who are chosen from the company that makes a product will have a vested interest in its success, and they may also be less inclined to criticize it objectively.

Each project has many possible conflicts of interest. You should be aware that there is a potential for this type of conflict, and try to include questions that might reveal some of these conditions.

The following steps will help you to develop a questionnaire to use for screening:

- List the significant characteristics in the primary stakeholder profiles.
- Create questions that will test whether the person fits the profile.
- Create a logical order for the questions; start with the easy, noninvasive questions.
- Test the questionnaire on a team member.

Select Testers

Usability testing is a complex process that requires a group of well-informed and experienced testers. There are many different kinds of usability test teams. Some tests are performed by professional usability firms that have well-developed methods and procedures.

Each member of the test team will have an area of expertise. These professionals might perform diverse tasks during a test and will generally be responsible for very specific tasks, such as data logging or video production.

Smaller design teams can also perform usability tests, but they must understand the required roles and have some experience with their tasks. If the test team is small (there should be at least two members—one to interact with the participant and one to record the observation), each member will have to perform multiple roles.

Instead of describing individual responsibilities, we will look at the various tasks required for the performance of a usability test. These will be defined by the kinds of activities each role involves.

The roles include the following:

- Administrator
- Moderator
- Data logger
- Technician
- Prototype expert

Administrator—This is the person who is responsible for the test—the test project manager.

The administrator's duties involve the following:

- Coordinating team member activities such as screening participants, writing the scripts, setting up the room, documenting the results, and overseeing every aspect of the test.
- Scheduling test time and place and notifying the team. This also involves managing the participants.
- Overseeing the preparations, for example, checking that the cameras been set, the microphones positioned, and so on.
- Collating the results of the observation and managing the documentation.

Moderator—This is the person who interacts with the participant during the test. He or she might simply make the introduction, explain the test, and then do a wrap-up debriefing, or he or she might actively engage the participant in conversation during the test in order to elicit subjective feedback.

Data Logger—This person is responsible for the data-logging activities. He or she must be experienced with the software used to capture the participant's actions and be able to process the results.

Technician—This is a catch-all role that involves the setup, maintenance, and operation of the A/V equipment. This role might also involve some timing aspects of the test. The technician might also be in charge of the networking software and hardware.

Prototype Expert—This role involves knowing how the prototype functions in case it crashes during the test. For a simple prototype this is not a significant issue; if the test is performed late in the project, however, the prototype may be quite sophisticated and getting it back online may require knowledge of the programming code.

Select Observers

If you are using a fixed lab, there will be at least two rooms. The only people who should be in the test room are the participant and the moderator. Because the participant cannot see into the observation room, you can invite other people to observe the test.

Potential observers include the following:

- Other design team members not involved in the test
- Clients
- Programmers responsible for the final product

These additional people might include other design team members who are not involved in any aspect of the test. Their participation will allow them to gain a better understanding when they study the results.

You may also want to invite a representative of the client or the clients themselves. This will help them to gain an appreciation for the objectivity of the results and help them to understand the importance of the tests and might prepare the way for future testing if necessary.

Another potential audience for these tests is the production department, which could include the programmers who will be creating the final product. Programming is a demanding task and it is hard to gain a user-centered perspective once you are writing thousands of lines of loops and functions. If the programmers can see how difficult some tasks are for target users, they might gain a greater understanding and appreciation of the testing process.

8.4. Prepare for the Test

We have explored the various issues involved in designing a usability test. We now need to understand what is involved in preparing for the test.

Test preparation involves the following:

- Creating a test schedule.
- Writing scripts to follow during the test.
- Setting up a pilot test.

8.4.1. When: Create a Test Schedule

To schedule the test, you have to coordinate the participants' schedules, the team members' schedules, and the availability of the laboratory. This takes time and requires organization. The screening process alone is complex and time consuming; if you are not organized, the process can become overwhelming. Let's see what is involved in creating a test schedule.

There are a few different levels of scheduling that you must consider:

- Project level
- Test preparation level
- Test execution level
- Task execution level

Project Level

The project level involves the development process as a whole. Usability testing, whether formal or informal, takes time, but it is an essential part of every phase of development. One of the fundamental tenants of user-centered design is iteration, which includes iterative usability testing. Therefore, you must determine the test schedule at the beginning of the project.

You might not be able to determine precisely when you will be testing alternate solutions; however, you can estimate that during the conceptual and physical development phases you will have some questions about different approaches to the design. Often, these decisions can only be made by testing the solutions.

You will need to allocate a certain amount of time for these activities. If you do not allow time for testing at the beginning of the project, it will be very difficult to squeeze tests in later. In the worst case, you will have to forgo testing just to stay on schedule and within budget.

Test Preparation Level

After you do the initial project-level scheduling, you will need to make some estimates of how long the testing process will take from inception to results documentation and presentation. Many steps are involved in a usability test, and many of them require advanced notice.

Because most people lead busy lives, you cannot expect participants to show up the next day; they will need at least a week or two to arrange their schedules. You might also encounter obstacles in terms of vacations and work schedules that you will have to work around.

You need to calculate the time it will take to screen the potential participants, confirm the test date, prepare the test materials and scripts, reserve the lab, perform the tests, analyze the results, and prepare the documentation to present to the team.

These activities might involve a few weeks. Careful planning and contingency plans will help you to avoid holding up the project because of unexpected obstacles.

Test and Task Execution Levels

You now need to calculate the length of each test so that you can create a schedule for each day allocated for testing. This involves many factors, which can include the following:

- Test and task length
- Fatigue
- Organization and preparation
- Extenuating circumstances

Test and Task Length—You need to know how long the test will take before you can create the daily schedule and send out the confirmations to the participants. To calculate the length of each test, you need to calculate how long it will take to perform each individual task within the test.

Fatigue—Your test design may involve a number of tasks. Depending on the nature of the tasks, their accumulation can become tedious and may cause fatigue. You might need to plan for a few breaks during the test. You can always use these breaks as an opportunity to interact with the participant and establish a rapport.

Organization and Preparation—You might also need to catalog and organize the results of the test before the nest participant begins. Some tests will also require some time to reset the equipment and the prototype. In general, a half-hour buffer between tests will be sufficient. After you perform a pilot test you will have a better idea about your scheduling requirements.

Extenuating Circumstances—Things never go exactly as planned, and there are many opportunities for extenuating circumstances; you should allow for some flexibility in the schedule. You can schedule as many tests as you think you can practically carry out, but you should allow for late arrivals, problematic software, equipment complications, and other conditions that might arise the day of the test.

8.4.2. Writing Scripts

To avoid any bias in the test as a result of variable moderator–participant interactions, you need to create a script for each moderator to follow. This will help the moderator to maintain a consistent rapport with each participant and avoid any alterations in instructions due to memory failures or distractions.

The scripts should cover every aspect of moderator–participant interaction and should also cover any contingencies such as participant frustration or prototype errors. Let's look at some of the basic issues to cover in the scripts. We present some suggested conversational topics and representative dialogue; however, you must create scripts that are tailored to your specific requirements.

No matter what kind of test you are conducting, you will need to establish a rapport with the participant. Most people are not used to the testing environment, so you should spend some time letting them get acquainted and making them comfortable.

Greeting the Participant

- Basic greeting
  - How are you?
  - I'm glad you could come today.
  - Did you have any trouble finding the room?
- Introduce other people in the room
  - This is _____. He will be taking down some notes during the test.
- Set the stage
  - Thank you for helping us.

- ◦ We are designing an interface for _____.
- ◦ It is supposed to help people perform the following tasks _____.
- ◦ We are very interested in what you think of the design so far.
- ◦ We are testing the prototype, not you.
- ◦ We will record the test for analysis purposes only.
- ◦ We have other observers on the other side of the one-way mirror.
- ◦ The test will take _____ long to complete.
- ◦ We expect to make changes in the design.
- ◦ Please do not hesitate to tell us anything you see or think about the design.
- ◦ I will be giving you directions in a moment.
- ◦ You will then take the test.
  - • I would like you to think out loud and describe why you do things and how you feel about the way they are done.
  - • You can ask me questions, but I may not be able to answer them directly; I will try to answer them after the test.
  - • Remember, there are no right or wrong answers.
- ◦ We will have a chance to discuss the test after it is finished.
- • Have the subject practice thinking out loud
  - ◦ When you look at the screen what are your first impressions?

You then perform a short interview to gather some basic information and get the participant thinking about things related to the tasks he or she will perform.

Preliminary Interview

- • Warm-up questions
  - ◦ We would like to find out a little bit about you before we start.
  - ◦ Ask questions about the participant that relate to the design.

You then tell the participant about the tasks he or she will be performing. Depending on the specifics of the test, you might give him or her verbal or written directions. Some tests involve a great deal of moderator–participant interaction, so you will be able to explain the tasks when it is time to carry them out.

Other tests might only allow interaction at the beginning and end. In this case, the participants have to remember what they are supposed to do. In these cases you should prepare some contingency plans if the participant gets hopelessly stuck and cannot continue.

Providing Instructions

- • Provide the directions for the tasks (they may be repeated as the test proceeds).
- • Orient the participant to the screen objects and test elements.

- Provide an opportunity to clarify the instructions:

  ◦ Are the directions clear?

  ◦ Do you have any questions?

The kind of script that you use during the test depends on the type of test you are conducting. If the test requires a great deal of interaction, you need to create a step-by-step script that covers the duration of the test. If the test does not call for much interaction, you should prepare a few remarks to deal with any unforeseen complications.

Monitoring the Test

- Elicit and record observations

  ◦ Why did you choose that method?

  ◦ Do you normally do it that way?

  ◦ Yes, that seems difficult. Thank you for pointing it out.

  ◦ That's an interesting question; let's talk about it at the end of the test.

- Capture participant's impressions

  ◦ We would like you to think out loud as you perform the tasks.

  ◦ Make comments designed to encourage thinking out loud.

Debriefing the Participant

After the test is over you might need to go through the formalities of thanking the participant and giving him or her the opportunity to ask you any questions, or you might want to engage the participant in a brief interview so that you can capture any subjective information that you could not capture during the test.

These debriefing interviews generally take the form of a few leading questions that are designed to elicit the participant's opinions and attitudes about the design. They might also involve a post-test questionnaire. You might also get the participant's impressions in a short verbal interview after he or she has completed the questionnaire.

Although each test has different criteria, the following is a list of some of the questions you might ask during a basic post-test interview to explore the participant's impressions:

- Was there anything that seemed unnecessarily difficult?
- Did anything seem confusing?
- Have you used other software like this?
- If so, how would you compare this software with that other software?

8.4.3. Running a Pilot Test

Before you implement the usability test, you need to run a pilot test to check for problems and see whether the tasks are doable. To run the pilot, you prepare everything just as you would for the actual test.

If it is possible, you should use an objective participant; however, a team member will suffice. The pilot test should be performed in a timely manner so that you will have enough time to correct any problems or make any required adjustments before the day of the actual tests.

> **MAXIM**
>
> Be organized!

On the day of the test there will be much to think about and manage. Your main objective is to focus on the test and the participants; you do not want to be worried about technical issues or misunderstandings among team members. It is, therefore, important to be organized.

Because you will be performing the same activities numerous times with different people, it is natural to tend to abbreviate or even dispense with some of the more tedious tasks. Be careful; this kind of abbreviation will create inconsistencies that may affect the outcome of the test.

To avoid introducing any bias into the test design, you should have everything organized ahead of time so that everyone follows a consistent plan. You should plan the day thoroughly and document the activities. You should also document the time schedules for the day's tests so that the people involved can manage their activities efficiently.

The following lists describe some of the things that you can do to create a successful testing environment:

- **Be Organized**—This cannot be emphasized strongly enough. There are too many details for you to remember, especially when you are performing under a certain level of stress.
  - Create folders for each participant (use a numbering system to identify each participant). These will be used to collect the following:
    - Informed consent form
    - Personal information forms
    - Test results
  - Create folders for the schedules, scripts, and questionnaires
  - Create check lists for:
    - Equipment (notate settings and media type)
    - Team responsibilities
  - Have backups available, including:
    - Equipment
    - Recording media
- **Be Presentable**—On the day of the test you will be meeting strangers who will identify you with the test and the prototype. Strive to make a positive and professional impression so that they approach the experience with a serious attitude.

8.5. Perform the Test

The administration of the test can be a hectic and stressful experience. As mentioned earlier, it is important to have a documented plan of action that can be followed by everyone involved in conducting the test. This should include all of the roles and responsibilities of the team members and the schedule of the tests that will be performed that day.

Arrive early so that you can review the day's schedule and go over the check lists. Make sure that the equipment is warmed up and working and that the settings are correct.

8.5.1. Test Phases

Let's look at what a typical test day schedule might involve.

Pre-Test

- Greet the participant.
- Have the participant sign the informed consent form.
- Have the participant fill out any pre-test questionnaire.
- Proceed with scripts.

During the Test

- Maintain a log or observation check list for each task.
- Create a problem list to capture anything that is not covered by the check list. You will not be able to remember everything that happens, especially if you are conducting multiple tests. Have a prepared sheet, with the participant's identification, on which to take notes during the test.
- Notate problems and jot down any hypotheses that occur to you about the problems. These hypotheses can also be written after the test if you need to concentrate on the test.

Post-Test

- Debrief the participant. This may take the form of a post-test questionnaire or a verbal interview.
- Thank the participant and provide compensation.
- Collect, summarize, and organize test data.
- Reset the room for the next participant.

8.6. Process the Data

We have explored usability testing from an organizational perspective, and we have looked at the processes involved in designing, preparing, and performing a usability test. We now focus on the data that are collected during a usability test.

The type of data we collect and the way we analyze that data depend on our reasons for performing the test in the first place. We have looked at the different types of measurements that we can use when we design usability tests—qualitative and quantitative measurements.

We have also looked at some of the different types of usability tests (diagnostic, comparative, and validation) that can be used to collect the different types of data. We now look at the issues involved in processing the data. There are two phases of data processing activities—activities performed during the test and follow-up activities.

8.6.1. Activities Performed on the Day of the Test

The day of the test will be very busy; you need to plan your activities in advance so that you can maximize your effectiveness. These activities include the following:

- Collecting data
- Summarizing data
- Organizing the materials

Collecting Data—You will most likely be collecting data during the test. This might include specific points, such as number of and reason for errors, or it might be feedback from thinking out loud.

Collection activities performed during the tests might include the following:

- Filling out an observation check list of possible problem areas prepared before the test.
- Creating handwritten notes of your impressions and participant responses.
- Creating a list of the problems that participants have with specific tasks.

Summarizing Data—You will need to summarize the data you collect as well as your impressions and hypotheses about any problems that might have occurred. It might be difficult to do this during the test, and you might want to wait until after the test; however, many experienced usability experts find it helpful to document their impressions during the test.

Summarizing activities might include the following:

- Documenting your impressions of specific events that happened during the test.
- Creating a list of the problems the participant has.
- Hypothesizing about the issues written on the problem list.
- Creating audio recordings of your thoughts (only after the test).
- Creating a formal problem list and adding new problems or occurrences of the same problem as happened with other participants.

Organizing the Materials—After the test is completed, you need to organize the materials collected before and during the test. These materials include questionnaires filled out before the test and recordings of the test.

Organizing activities performed after the tests include the following:

- Transferring task timings and error rates onto a spreadsheet
- Organizing questionnaires

- Creating a formal problem list that aggregates all of the problem lists
- Collating all information and observation documents
- Backing up video tapes
- Transcribing audio tapes

You should get as much of the summarization and organization work done as soon after the test as possible because your impressions will be fresh at that point and you will need to free your mind before you begin another test. You do not want to influence the next participant with your impressions from the previous test, so you should try to document as you go.

Benefits of summarizing and organizing directly after the test include the following:

- Increased effectiveness—Your impressions will be fresh in your mind and, therefore, easier to remember.
- Verification that you are capturing what you want—You will be able to see whether you are capturing the kind of information you need and adjust accordingly if you are not.
- Assurance that all testers are consistent—You can check and verify that all moderators are collecting the same kind of information in a consistent way.

8.6.2. Follow-Up Activities

After the tests are completed, you need to analyze the results and document your recommendations. Follow-up activities include the following:

- Categorizing
- Analyzing
- Documenting

Categorizing

Most usability tests provide copious data that must be processed. Before you can make sense out of the data you need to categorize them in a way that coincides with the reasons you performed the tests in the first place.

In other words, you must now find a way to categorize the information based on the usability issues you identified before the test. There are two basic approaches to this process: top-down and bottom-up (Barnum, 2002).

Top-Down—A top-down approach begins before the test. This approach involves establishing categories of usability issues and then creating tasks that are designed to address the issues in those categories. This is similar to the heuristic approach that uses a predetermined set of measures.

The top-down approach provides common ground for everyone involved in the testing process, from the testers to the team members who analyze the data afterward. It also makes logging the observations easier during the test because you can have a list of categories with which to notate your observations.

This approach does have the disadvantage of directing people to look at the test from a more structured viewpoint, which might blind them to some of the more unexpected results.

Bottom-Up—The bottom-up approach is more time consuming because the results of the tests must be aggregated from a multiplicity of sources without any connecting thread or framework.

Affinity diagrams (see Chapter 3) can be used with this method, allowing all members of the testing team to participate actively in the categorization process. These sessions provide an opportunity for team members actively to engage each other and probe for underlying impressions and opinions about the results.

Analyzing

Depending on the kind of test you perform, you may have quantitative or qualitative data. In other words, you will have task timing and error rate data or attitudinal and user preference data. Generally, you will have a mixture of both.

You need to analyze the data so that you can see significant trends. There are two types of data that will have been collected:

- Quantitative—data that represent timings and error rates.
- Qualitative—data that represent user attitudes and opinions.

QUANTITATIVE DATA

Quantitative data can be analyzed using statistical methods, such as the calculation of medians or ranges of the task timings or error rates. This is generally done using simple mathematical equations and involves the following types of data:

- Execution data
- Accuracy data

Execution Data Calculations—Most of the quantitative data that you collect will be derived from the following:

- Task timings
- Error rates

These data can be useful in measuring the comprehensibility and efficiency of a design. There are various measures that you can apply to this type of data:

- Mean
- Range
- Median
- Standard deviation

Each of these measures provides specific insights into the performance of the participants as a whole and a way to create benchmarks and thresholds that can determine the relative success of specific design elements.

- **Mean**—This is a measure of the average time it takes for all participants to complete a task. This will tell you how difficult it is to perform the task or how long it takes people to figure out how to complete the task. It is calculated as follows:

$$\text{Mean} = \frac{\text{sum of all completion times}}{\text{number of participants}}$$

- **Range**—This represents the highest and lowest scores. This gives a measure of the outside thresholds for a particular task. You can use this information to determine whether the design is appropriate for a wide audience or whether you need to design features that will accommodate the users that fall on the extreme ranges.
- **Median**—This is the actual score that is midway between two extreme ranges. It is the most typical score and can be used as a benchmark for normal performance.
- **Standard Deviation (SD)**—This is a measure of how close the scores are to each other and the mean time. It tells you about the score distribution. A higher SD means that the scores are distributed over a larger time frame. A lower SD means that most of the scores are similar in terms of the time of task completion. A wide distribution might indicate important differences between participants and might therefore warrant further investigation to determine the cause of the variation. SD is given by

$$SD = \frac{\sqrt{\Sigma x^2 - \dfrac{(\Sigma x)^2}{n}}}{n-1}$$

Where:

Σx^2 = the sum of the squares of each of the scores

Σx = the sum of all scores

n = the total number of scores

Accuracy Data Calculations—You may need to determine what percentage of the participants performed the tasks successfully or what percentage completed the task within an acceptable time limit. You can also calculate the percentage that performed error-free or the percentage that required assistance.

You can use the same data that you used to calculate execution and error rates and calculate these percentages according to your needs.

QUALITATIVE DATA

As mentioned previously, quantitative data can tell you what is wrong, but unless you also gather qualitative data, you will not understand why there is a particular problem. You need to understand what people are thinking when they make certain errors. The data derived from the think-out-loud technique can provide invaluable information about the proposed design. You need to analyze this information carefully and relate it to the quantitative data.

You also need to calculate the data that pertain to people's likes and dislikes regarding specific aspects of the design. This might involve impressions of the color scheme or whether they prefer to use the search function or to navigate using hyperlinks.

You can collate the reactions to these questions and sum the different responses according to positive and negative categories. You can do this with simple yes/no questions and with the data obtained with Likert scales.

Free-form questions can also be grouped into categories, and the responses can then be calculated in terms of positive and negative impressions.

Document

At this point you have categorized the data in terms of the goals developed for the tests. You have also analyzed the data and have obtained a statistical perspective of the results. You now need to try to understand what the results say about the design and document your recommendations for improvements. In other words, you need to translate the results into recommendations that will improve the usability of the design.

This process involves the following activities:

- Identify problems
- Prioritize problems
- Theorize reasons
- Theorize solutions
- Identify successes
- Identify areas of uncertainty

Identify Problems—During this process you will identify the results that indicate problems in usability. One of the most common methods of identifying problems is to document errors. You need to document the severity of the errors (could the participant proceed, or did he or she hit a dead end?) as well as the frequency of the error across participants:

- Severity
- Frequency

You also need to categorize the errors in terms of the type of error: did the participant miss functionality or did he or she perform the wrong action?

- Errors of omission
- Errors of commission

Prioritize Problems—You then prioritize these problems in terms of their critical importance: how serious was the error, and how likely is it to occur during normal interaction?

Theorize Reasons—This is the bridge point at which you identify the aspect of the design that caused the error. Some reasons are obvious and solutions are readily apparent, but others are not so obvious. This is where the design of the test tasks becomes crucial.

If your tasks are complex and involve multiple aspects of the design, you will have difficulty in trying to isolate the problematic element. Many errors are often the result of a combination of factors, each contributing to the situation in subtle ways.

These types of errors are usually best addressed by a more strict application of design principles or heuristics to that particular facet. For instance, if the participant has trouble with a task that involves navigating to a particular area of the site, you may need to address the principle of consistency by rethinking the terminology or location of your hyperlinks.

Theorize Solutions—After you have a prioritized list of problems and have hypothesized the reasons why they occurred, you need to propose solutions in the form of formal recommendations. This step cannot be done without first identifying reasons as described in the previous steps.

This is perhaps the most tentative of all the steps. Some solutions are obvious because the reasons are obvious; however, many will require you to make an educated guess.

Remember, the decisions that you make here will affect the next round of usability tests. Therefore, if you have documented your results and organized your hypotheses well, you will have a better chance of locating the cause of the problem.

Do not jump to conclusions. You must be careful to take all of the errors committed during the test into consideration. Most human–computer interactions are complex and involve a multiplicity of factors; wait until all of the errors have been identified and prioritized before you attempt to propose solutions. An alteration in one aspect of the design usually has an effect on other aspects of interaction.

Identify Successes—It may seem logical to focus on the usability problem uncovered during the tests; after all, this is why you conducted the tests in the first place. However, it would be a mistake to ignore the successes identified.

It is important to document what went right so that these facets of the design do not inadvertently get changed when you start dealing with potential solutions to problems uncovered. You can also use the successes as a source of potential solutions. If something worked well in one part of the design, you might try to duplicate that success by using the same approach to other, more problematic areas of the design.

Identify Areas of Uncertainty—You will not be able to answer all of your questions, and by answering one question, you might create other questions. This is one of the benefits of usability testing: you learn things about your design of which you were not previously aware.

You should view this as an opportunity and a source of concerns and goals for the next round of tests. This is part of the iterative process that pushes the knowledge path forward.

Design Scenario

Circumference: Defining and Refining Usability Goals

We have looked at the processes involved in usability testing and we have acquired a general idea of the overall scope and structure of these tests. Using the *Circumference* design, we now explore the process of defining and refining the usability goals we will use in our usability tests. First, it will be beneficial to identify the basic qualities of a usability goal.

Qualities of a Usability Goal

Unambiguous—Usability goals must be clearly understood by the design team. They must be defined and stated in terms that are specific and informative.

Measurable—Usability goals must be measurable with either quantitative measurements or quantitative measurements.

Relevant—Usability goals must be relevant to the identified stakeholders that are being tested.

You can check how well your usability goals satisfy these qualities by asking the following questions. We will apply these questions to one of the usability goals developed for the *Circumference* Web site.

Usability Goal: Visitors must be able to locate the appropriate menus and options for their tasks without difficulty.

Did you state the objective of the usability goal?

It is important to state the objective of the usability goal clearly so that everyone understands why they are using it in the testing process. The objective of this goal is to analyze the structure of the various menus and the wording of their labels and options to see whether they cause any usability problems.

Did you identify the stakeholders affected by the usability goal?

The stakeholder that is most affected by this usability goal is the site visitor. It directly affects the quality of his or her experience. If the design is difficult to predict, it will become something that visitors have to think about, which will take their attention away from their goals.

Other stakeholders, such as the journal editors, will also be affected (although less directly) by the visitor's experience on the Web site. An unpleasant experience will cause the visitor to leave the site and not return, which would diminish the possibility that he or she will order a subscription.

Is the goal relevant to that stakeholder?

You must make sure that you are testing something that is relevant. For instance, we do not need to determine whether the Circumference *visitor can see the journal's*

Design Scenario (cont.)

address when he or she is filling out the order form. This is not something a visitor needs to do. However, predicting the location of the sample poems is a relevant goal.

Is your usability goal relevant to an identified design principle?

The usability goal we are considering is directly related to the general principle of understandability. It reflects the efficiency of the design and more specifically the predictability of the menu and option labels. Therefore we can structure our testing to determine whether our participants can predict whether a specific menu will lead them to the information they require.

Did you identify the conditions under which the goal is defined?

This goal relates to behavior that will occur often during a site visit. Visitors will generally navigate the site using the menus, so this is a goal that must be addressed during most site visit conditions, for instance, looking for contact info, reading poems, or other activities.

Did you determine the criteria for measuring success?

When you test a usability goal it is crucial that you determine the criteria you will use to measure the results. These metrics will be used to develop the testing scenarios as well as the methods of analysis used to understand the results. As we have seen, we can use qualitative and quantitative measures to get a full picture of a usability problem. This involves absolute, discrete measures as well as relative measures that reflect relationships. We also need to determine the performance levels and their meaning.

The usability goal we are considering can be measured by tracking the errors a participant makes in menu selection—a quantitative, discrete measure. We also need to understand why these errors were made; was it the particular label that was not predictable? This involves a qualitative measure that can be obtained by questions posed to the participant during the test.

We must then determine what performance levels we are looking for. Are four errors significant? Are two? We might need to also look at how these performance levels affect other goals such as memorability. In other words, do participants who make more than five errors the first time make none the next time they use the interface? How does that affect acceptable error levels in the first usability goal?

Did you set a priority level for the goal?

You will be getting a great deal of information from your tests. You will need to determine how important your goals are so that you can prioritize the results and spend

Design Scenario (cont.)

your time on the most significant problems. The usability goal we are considering must be considered a high-priority goal because it is so pervasive and important to the visitor's interaction with the interface.

Did you identify the user goals, tasks, and scenarios that relate to the usability goal?

This is where you define how you will test the usability goal. The case we are considering involves creating some scenarios that will test how easy it is for the participant to choose the correct menu.

In one of the scenarios we will ask participants to find the address of the journal after they have read a few sample poems. We are trying to see whether the location of this information is predictable, given the various menu labels.

One of the results from this particular usability goal is that participants tried to find the address by clicking on the About label. In Chapter 4, the information requirements for the About page were stated as follows:

About—this area includes the following:

- Journal Mission Statement
- Names of

  - Editors
  - Designers
  - Advisory Board

- Information on tax-exempt status
- Information about printer

As you can see, the participant who chooses the About option incurs an error because that information was not included on this page.

Did you state the rationale for the goal? How does it affect the usability of the design?

The goal of locating the correct menus and options is important because we do not want the visitor to be confused by the various menus and options. This would make it harder to use the site and more difficult to learn and remember where information can be found.

We now have a clearly defined usability goal and a great deal of information about how the testing scenarios and tasks need to be set up. Again, we must understand that this is an iterative process. We can revisit our usability goal documentation as we learn more about a particular usability test design.

Summary

Usability tests represent significant nodes on the knowledge path from discovery to implementation (Figure 8.3). Once thought to be a way to validate an existing product, much like quality assurance testing, they are now understood by many people in the software industry to be an integral facet of an iterative design process.

Usability tests can take many forms, from informal verbal interviews using questionnaires and paper prototypes to formal laboratory-based testing with functional prototypes.

As the project evolves, the type of tests you perform will change accordingly. The results will most likely initiate an iteration cycle, which, at the early stages, may even involve supplemental discovery activities, but it will always involve a reassessment of certain design decisions.

There has been a gradual acceptance in the software industry of the need for usability testing; however, there are still many constraints in terms of time and money that will pose obstacles to implementing an exhaustive program of usability testing.

You must make sure that everyone involved in the project understands that it is more cost effective to invest in one usability test and find one usability problem than to address 100 calls to tech support.

Resources on the Web

www.aw.com/heim

You will find links to information on general usability topics, usability standards, heuristic evaluation and usability testing.

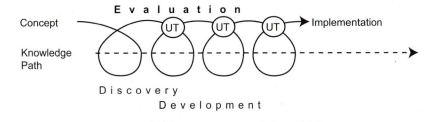

Figure 8.3 Usability tests on the knowledge path.

Suggested Reading

Brinck, T., Gergle, D., & Wood, S. D. (2001). *Usability for the Web: Designing Web Sites that Work* (1 ed.): Morgan Kaufmann.

Patton, R. (2005). (2 ed.): Sams.

Russell, M. C. (2006). *Investigating Contributions of Eye-tracking to Website Usability Testing* ProQuest.

Shaffer, E. (2004). *Institutionalization of Usability: A Step-by-Step Guide:* Addison-Wesley Professional.

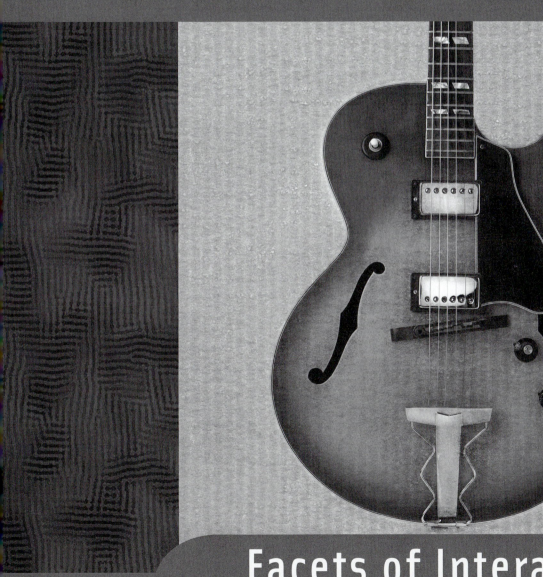

SECTION III

Facets of Interaction

This section discusses various facets of interaction. This includes an in-depth look at the elements that make up contemporary user interfaces, such as, among others, color, text, and icons. It approaches human–computer interaction from the viewpoint of the human visual, auditory, and haptic perceptual channels. The knowledge gained from this discussion is then applied to specific aspects of interaction design. This furthers our understanding of the relationship between human perception and interaction design. It also provides a foundation for better understanding the elements that comprise emerging interactive environments such as virtual reality and ubiquitous computing.

CHAPTER

9

Color

Color has a strong impact on people. Artists throughout history have used color to evoke emotion, add realism, and define the structure and composition of a painting or illustration. Color has also become an important part of GUI design. Interaction designers use color to help people find icons or buttons. They use color to make the interaction more pleasant. They can also use color to organize information and group objects on the screen.

Color can be a useful tool in interaction design; however, it depends on human perception, and human color perception is a complex issue. In general our visual receptors have specific characteristics and limitations that are common to most people. However, we have personal strengths and weaknesses as well as preferences and expectations.

Color can make human–computer interaction more productive and pleasant, but if it is not applied properly and in accordance with our perceptual abilities and limitations, color can confuse and annoy or cause us to make critical mistakes.

9.1. The Human Perceptual System

To understand how best to use color in interaction design, many questions and issues need to be explored. We need to understand how people see color and what characteristics of human color perception can affect interaction design. In this chapter first we explore human color perception, then we see how color can be applied to interaction design, and finally we look at some of the technical issues involved in computer-based color manipulation.

9.1.1. Color Perception

Consider the nature of color perception. First, we need to understand the nature of light waves. Light waves are electromagnetic waves, like radio waves or microwaves, which together form the electromagnetic spectrum. Visible light occupies a small range of this spectrum.

Human color perception depends on the way in which light waves interact with objects in the environment. Some things look transparent, some translucent, and others opaque. The reason that we can see through glass and not through cement is that glass allows for the passage of most light waves—it is transparent.

Not all the light passes through a glass object, however, and so it is visible to us; an object that allowed all light to pass through would be invisible. Cement does not allow any light to pass through, and therefore it is opaque. Some materials fall midway between transparency and opaqueness: they allow enough light to pass through to appear translucent, such as a thin piece of paper held up to a light.

Furthermore, when light hits an object some of the waves that are not allowed to pass through are absorbed and some of them are reflected. The frequencies of the reflected waves determine the color of the object. If all frequencies are absorbed, the object appears black. If all frequencies are reflected, the object appears white.

The color we see relates to the relative strength of the reflected frequencies. For instance, if the reflected frequencies in the blue range are stronger than the other frequencies (they have more energy), then the object appears blue. The degree of "blueness" of the object depends on the relative strengths of the other frequencies. As the red frequencies get stronger, the color shifts toward purple.

Light Source

The color of an object depends on the light source and the nature of the light it emits. Sunlight is very different from the light from an incandescent bulb or a fluorescent tube.

> **MAXIM**
>
> The perceived color of an object can change drastically under different lighting situations.

If we compare the light from two different sources, we might find that some frequencies from one source are either not available from the other or have different degrees of energy. When these different light sources illuminate an object, the available frequencies might not be the same. Because the object can only reflect the frequencies that are available, that particular combination of reflected colors will give the object the appearance of color unique to that particular light source.

If the light source is altered and more frequencies become available, the object will have the potential to reflect these additional frequencies. If this occurs, the object's color will appear to have changed. This phenomenon is known as metamerism.

Human Visual System

After light strikes an object (some is absorbed, some is allowed to pass through, and the rest is reflected), it is picked up by our visual system (Figure 9.1). The eye has receptors called cones and rods, which respond to the spectrum of frequencies that comprise a color and code each in specific ways.

The cones are sensitive to color and are more prevalent in the central part of the retina—a layer of cells at the back of the eye that are photosensitive. The rods are situated mostly in the periphery of the retina and are sensitive to motion and low-light environments.

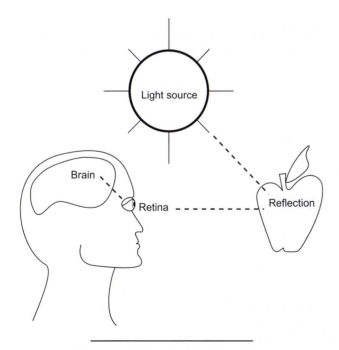

Figure 9.1 Light reflecting off an object.

We have three types of cones, each sensitive to different frequencies, corresponding to the red, blue, and green portions of the spectrum. When these receptors are activated by spectral stimuli, messages are sent to the brain along the optic nerve.

Our response to these visual stimuli is determined by many factors, such as culture, age, fatigue, emotions, and other incidental aspects of our daily lives. They all play a part in how we react to the stimuli we receive.

Visual Limitations

To make proper color choices, interface designers must understand the strengths and limitations of human visual receptors.

> **MAXIM**
>
> Avoid using blue for text and small screen elements.

Our eyes are the most sensitive to the middle frequencies (green and yellow). Furthermore, our sensitivity to blue is weak; we just do not have that many receptors attuned to that frequency. Jackob Nielsen suggests that if we were to reinvent the World Wide Web we would not choose blue as the default link color; it is not a good choice due to the way our eyes are constructed.

> **MAXIM**
>
> Our ability to distinguish color is directly related to the size of an object.

We also have difficulty in determining the color of small objects. The smaller an object is, the less we perceive its color. This causes dark colors to appear black, whereas lighter colors lose their vibrancy.

Given that we cannot easily distinguish the color of small objects, combined with the fact that we have fewer receptors for blue frequencies, it is understandable why so many experts suggest that blue is a poor choice for text of any sort.

> **MAXIM**
>
> Color perception is weak in our peripheral vision.

Most of our color receptors are located in the center of our visual field (foveal vision) and decrease toward the periphery (peripheral vision). Our peripheral vision is not good at perceiving color in general, but it is particularly weak at distinguishing red and green hues. We are a little better with the blue and yellow frequencies, however, which suggests that yellows and blues may be better choices for color coding objects that are situated within our peripheral vision. Saturated reds and greens should be avoided.

MAXIM

Movement in our peripheral vision is distracting.

Our peripheral vision has a greater sensitivity to movement. The rods, which are sensitive to motion, are more numerous at the perimeter of the eye. Sit in front of a CRT monitor, look straight at the screen, and turn your head slightly. You will gradually become aware of a slight flicker in the screen. This is due to the movement of electrons as the screen refreshes.

The amount of flicker depends on your computer's refresh rate. Most screens refresh at a rate of approximately 60 Hz, fast enough to appear to be steady in our central vision. LCD screens use a different technology and are not subject to flicker.

Movement in our peripheral vision can be a significant consideration in designing for industrial or mission-critical environments. Consistent movement in our peripheral vision can be highly distracting because our attention is naturally directed to these stimuli. It would be potentially dangerous to distract users during sensitive activities such as surgery or working in hazardous environments.

You should not place blinking text or lights in a person's peripheral vision unless you want to grab the person's attention and send him or her a warning or danger signal.

MAXIM

Do not rely only on color to delineate shape.

We understand shapes by looking at their edges. If there is a great deal of contrast between an object and its background, we see a clearly defined shape. It is, therefore, advisable to use a delineating line between objects as opposed to simply using color.

The eye can be fooled, however, into perceiving greater contrast by manipulating the color of the object. Certain colors appear darker than others do; this is known as the "perceived weight" of the color. We explore this phenomenon later in this chapter. It is also important to remember the issues involved in contrast sensitivity discussed in Appendix A because they are directly related to color contrast perception.

9.1.2. Color Deficiencies

Color is a subjective issue; photoreceptors vary greatly from person to person. Most people fall within the normative range of color perception and can relate to the prevailing consensus about color. Others differ to a greater extent and cannot reconcile their experience with the norm. These people are said to have some degree of color blindness.

As mentioned earlier, we perceive color as a result of light waves hitting cones in the retina. People with photoreceptors that do not respond to certain frequencies do not perceive those colors in the same way that other people do. In rare situations the receptors for a particular color may be absent altogether. Therefore, color blindness can range from a weakness in perceiving a particular color to the inability to perceive a specific color at all.

There are three types of cones, each sensitive to a specific wavelength (colors are generally specified in relation to wavelength, which is defined as the frequency of a wave divided by c, the speed of light in a vacuum). Some cones are attuned to red, which has a wavelength of greater than 630 nm (spectral wavelengths are measured in nanometers, or millionths of a meter). Some receptors are tuned to the frequency of green—between 480 and 560 nm. Blue is one of the shortest visible wavelengths, and lies below 480 nm. Trichromatic vision is considered to be the normative state, in which all three types of cones are present and tuned to the "proper" wavelengths.

Color perception deficiencies affect about 8% of male individuals and about 0.4% of female individuals in the United States. The most common form is a reduced sensitivity to green, known as deuteranomaly. This condition affects about 5% of male individuals and accounts for the majority of color deficiencies in female individuals, about 95%.

Types of Color Blindness

There are three types of anomalous trichromatic vision—vision that results when all cones are present but some are misaligned:

Protanomaly:	Diminished sensitivity to red
Deuteranomaly:	Diminished sensitivity to green
Tritanomaly:	Diminished sensitivity to blue

Dichromatic vision anomalies occur when one of the cone types is missing:

Protanopia:	No ability to perceive red
Deuteranopia:	No ability to perceive green
Tritanopia:	No ability to perceive blue

Figure 9.2 shows examples of the way in which people with particular color deficiencies perceive the color wheel. This can be compared with the trichromatic or normal color vision example. It is also interesting to note that in the grayscale versions certain colors appear darker than others. This is known as the perceived weight of a color and is covered in detail later in the chapter.

Problems Related to Color Blindness

MAXIM

Color must be used as one factor among many in interface design.

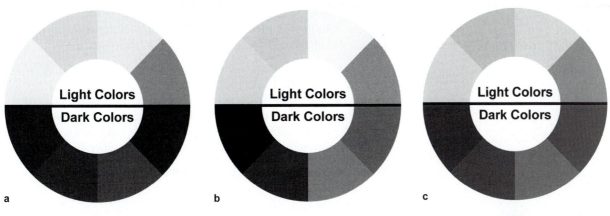

Figure 9.2 **(a) Protanopic color vision. (b) Normal trichromatic color vision. (c) Deuteranopic color vision.**

The tool used here to convert the color version to the color blind versions is available at http://www.vischeck.com/downloads/. It is a PhotoShop plug-in, but an online version is available free on the Web site http://www.vischeck.com/vischeck/vischeckImage.php.

Color can be a crucial element in mission-critical environments such as aerospace, medicine, and heavy industry. For instance, if an interface depends exclusively on color for warnings and other crucial information, users with any degree of color blindness will have difficulties. An interface that relies only on color to convey warning signals will eventually cause error or injury.

The most common color deficiency is red/green, which Western cultures associate with diametrically opposed system states: green for on, go, and normal operation, and red for off, stop, and error conditions. Notice Figure 9.3 how difficult it would be for a person with red/green color blindness to understand the information coming from an interface if it depended only on color.

Imagine a system that has only one light. The light flashes green under normal operating conditions, but if there is a system failure, the light flashes red. How would a color blind operator tell the difference? Let's assume the operator is not color blind, but has to focus his or her attention on the controls placed just a few feet from the warning light. What kind of problems might arise? The low sensitivity to color in our peripheral vision reduces the likelihood that the operator will see the

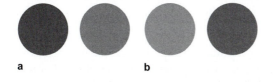

Figure 9.3 **(a) Normal color vision. (b) Deuteranopic color vision.**

change in color. Furthermore, habituation to the steady blinking will cause the operator to filter out the stimulus, rendering the warning light completely useless. An interface that relies only on color can cause problems for everyone.

Other Factors Affecting Color Vision

It is obvious that people with color deficiencies will experience interface designs differently than people with normal trichromatic vision. What might not be so obvious is that two people with normal color vision may not perceive color in the same way. Many factors affect perception, making color vision a very subjective experience.

Factors affecting color perception include the following:

- Culture
- Age
- Fatigue
- Emotions
- Ambient light
- Light sources
- Blood oxygen levels

> **MAXIM**
>
> Color deficiency and human subjectivity must be considered important factors in interaction design.

Because color perception is, to a large degree, subjective and affected by culture and various human factors, it is imperative that color use be treated as carefully and systematically as possible. The specifications of an interface color scheme must be clear and unambiguous to the person using the interface. The end user must be clearly identified by the design team, and the issues of color deficiency and human subjectivity must be taken into consideration from the beginning of the design process.

9.1.3. Individual and Cultural Issues

Each of us is a product of our experiences; it is hard to divorce ourselves from our preconceived ideas about the world. We also have very individualized ideas about color. We have certain expectations and associations related to specific colors. For instance, ask a person to name his or her favorite color and what it reminds him or her of; if you then ask another person about the same color, you will probably get a completely different response.

Some colors carry natural associations that are universally consistent. We should stick to these common associations when we find them. For instance, the sky is blue and the sun is yellow. Ultimately, it is up to the interaction designer to understand how a potential user might respond to certain color choices and applications.

Figure 9.4 Inappropriate colors.

Preferences and Expectations

> **MAXIM**
> It is important to understand the target user's color associations and expectations.

Error messages are, unfortunately, not uncommon to computer users. These ominous warnings often appear in red on the screen. Although expectations regarding the use of red for danger and high-risk conditions might be subject to a user's geographic location, they are quite strong in countries that use red, yellow, and green traffic signals to indicate stop, caution, and go, respectively.

These are by no means the only associations people have with these particular colors, but they are strong ones. Ignoring this fact increases the risk of confusing the user. It would not be appropriate to use red lights for a Walk signal and green lights for a Don't Walk signal (Figure 9.4). Likewise, using green for error messages would be inconsistent with the expectations of most people.

Emotional Response

Color can increase the aesthetic appeal of an interface design. It can also make it more realistic and believable. We can achieve very subtle effects with color that are beneficial to a user. On the other hand, we can also create extremely garish affects that are annoying to look at. Color can affect people on many levels.

> **MAXIM**
> Color can evoke emotional responses.

For centuries artists have explored color as a means of expression. The Fauvist movement in the early twentieth century, which included artists like Henri Matisse, Albert Marquet, Andre Derain, and Maurice de Vlaminck, celebrated color over all other aspects of form and design.

The artist Vaslav Kandinsky gives us a glimpse into his emotional associations with color: "Light warm red has a certain similarity to medium yellow, alike in texture and appeal, and gives a feeling of strength, vigour, determination, triumph. In music, it is a sound of trumpets, strong, harsh, and ringing" (Kandinsky, 1977, 40).

a

b

Figure 9.5   (a) Mexico |#282. (b) Mexico| #268.

With permission www.jimnilsen.com.

Color has an unmistakable appeal. Most people prefer color displays, and they report an improvement in performance and confidence (Horton, 1994). Color can also affect our emotions, and this can have a powerful effect on the user. Shneiderman and Plaisant state that color can "Evoke strong emotional reactions of joy, excitement, fear, or anger" (Shneiderman & Plaisant, 2005, 510). Consider the work of the contemporary photographer Jim Nilsen shown above (Figure 9.5). Nilsen's photography exhibits a strong sense of color which communicates on formal as well as emotional levels. "Color is the most important element of my compositions. It provides me with the emotional stimulus to take the photo." (Nilsen, 2006).

Globalization—Localization

When color is used to imply meaning we say it has a connotation, implication, or association. The connotations that people have about certain colors can vary greatly among different cultures as well as between people within a culture. There are regional as well as national influences, local issues and issues relating to specific professions and disciplines. For instance, some interfaces are designed for internal corporate use, perhaps on a company's intranet. Other designs are used remotely by clients and business associates. Still others are oriented toward the general public.

Coporate designs must be sensitive to the local corporate culture, including corporate branding, as well as industry practices. Along with elements such as type face, slogans, and taglines, companies use logos and identifying graphics that usually incorporate a color scheme to reinforce the corporate identity and product branding.

A company also belongs to a community of industry professionals. Certain colors may have specific industry-wide connotations. Furthermore, many companies are multinational with branch offices all over the world. In this case, issues related to cultural diversity play a significant role in interaction design.

Designs that are destined for the Internet or products with global distribution outlets have the potential to reach a vast audience with a multiplicity of expectations and opinions. Let's look at some of the factors that need to be considered:

- **Emotions:** The emotional impact of color varies from culture to culture. Associations with yellow range from grace and nobility in Japan, to cowardice and caution in the United States, to happiness and prosperity in Egypt (Russo & Boor, 1993).

- **Age:** People of different generations have observable and often contrasting preferences in color. Toys are manufactured and packaged in bright primary colors—red, blue, and yellow—due to the attraction these have for young children.

- **Gender:** In most cultures gender can greatly influence color decisions. One need only scan the display shelves in the doll section of a department store to pick up more than a hint of pink, whereas blue is usually associated with male-oriented items.

- **Physical appearance:** There may be conventions about the standard physical appearance of objects. For instance, mailboxes have distinctly different colors in different countries. In the United States they are blue, in England they are bright red, and in Greece they are bright yellow.

- **Industrial or professional community:** Many industries and academic disciplines have specific color connotations. University graduation ceremonies are resplendent with colored robes and hoods delineating different academic areas.

- **Corporate identity and product recognition:** Familiarity is strengthened through the use of color in product branding. The Coca-Cola logo is red; American Express is associated with blue, and the United Parcel Service of America, Inc. (UPS) has begun to call itself simply "Brown."

9.2. Using Color in Interaction Design

Color can be used to make information more accessible. If we use it properly, it can help people to find information and accomplish difficult decision-making tasks. We must keep in mind, however, that not all tasks are aided by the addition of color. In addition, when color does prove beneficial, it is important that the colors are chosen properly. Therefore we need to know which tasks are enhanced by the addition of color, which colors are appropriate, and, as we have seen, any potentially problematic factors related to human color perception and cognition.

Aaron Marcus suggests six ways in which color can be integrated into an interface to support the user experience (Marcus, 1995):

Clarification, Relation, and Differentiation

- Identify subsystems or structures
- Add coding dimensions

Searching

- Emphasize important information

Comprehension, Retention, and Recall

- Increase comprehensibility
- Reduce errors of interpretation

Emotional Response

- Increase believability and appeal

9.2.1. Clarification, Relation, and Differentiation

Color can be used to create structures and subsystems. We can use color to group objects and to make connections between them. A consistent and understandable color code can make it easier to see underlying relationships that would be difficult to see otherwise.

> **MAXIM**
>
> Color can be used to clarify differences and similarities and communicate relationships.

Color codes can be used to support a logical information structure. The important word here is "support." There are other factors to consider, such as number of screen elements and element shape, size, and location. We examine these factors in Chapter 11 when we look at the use of icons in interaction design.

We are surrounded by a vast amount of data in our daily lives. To make sense of these data, we have to filter them and impose structures, which can transform them into useful information and then into knowledge. With the appropriate application of color we have the ability to enhance the meaning and the structure of this information.

Consider the wires in an Ethernet or telephone cable (Figure 9.6a). Different strands are coded with specific colors; color-coded schematics enable technicians to determine proper wire selection. Public transportation systems also use color to communicate information. For instance, riders of the underground train systems in large metropolitan cities can quickly identify a particular route by glancing at a color-coded map. Different routes are often identified by their color, such as the Boston subway system's Red Line, Green Line, Orange Line, and Blue Line (Figure 9.6b).

Color can be used to show data that involve multiple variables. For instance, color coding a histogram or bar chart can facilitate the presentation of additional information when the use of more than two variables is critical. This enables a decision maker to come to an informed judgment more quickly.

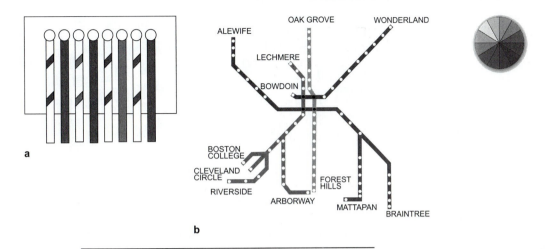

Figure 9.6 (a) Ethernet wires. (b) Map of the Boston subway system.

A multivariate display such as the parallel coordinate plot in Figure 9.7 is much easier to understand if the different variables are color coded.

9.2.2. Searching

Color can be used to help people search for things. Consider a situation in which you have to find a blue circle among many equally sized blue squares (Figure 9.8a). Now consider the same situation but with the circle red and the squares still blue (Figure 9.8b). It is obviously easier to find the red circle than the blue one. Color can be a strong factor in helping people to find one object out of many.

> **MAXIM**
> Color can be used to catch the attention of the user.

Color can be used to emphasize important information by increasing the impact of a screen element. A bright color or a large shape will catch the viewer's attention.

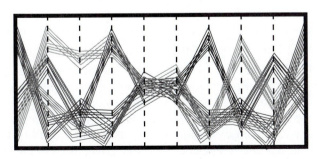

Figure 9.7 Parallel coordinate plot.

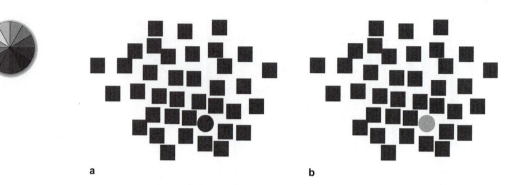

a   b

Figure 9.8   (a) Blue squares and a blue circle. (b) Blue squares and a red circle.

The viewer will respond to the intensity of this stimulus before he or she understands what the stimulus is. We can use this concept to help people to search.

Consider a search mechanism that color codes all the keywords it finds in the searched document. These color-coded words stand out from the rest of the text, which makes it easier to find them. We can also make the search mechanism show proximal relationships with other occurrences of the search word or words. If the search turns up five occurrences of the search word in one paragraph, they might be colored with one color, but if they show up on two different pages, they might be colored a different color.

Some searches are specifically based on the proximity of two keywords; for instance, you might be looking for antique dolls. Your search could turn up "antique dolls," or it might turn up "antique furniture for doll houses." Given this situation, a system of color coding could be used to show degrees of proximity. The visible spectrum (red, orange, yellow, green, blue, indigo, and violet) could be used to show the different degrees of proximity.

The spectrum has been shown to be an intuitive means of presentation. A red, orange, yellow scale seems naturally to lend itself to descending values as in the example in Figure 9.9 of an alert system.

In the case of our search example, word pairs that are within a small interval of words might be coded red; pairs that are farther apart might be coded yellow; and the furthest pairs might end up coded by colors at the far end of the spectrum.

Many WYSIWYG (what you see is what you get) or graphical programming environments use color to differentiate types of code strings. For instance, a Web page editor might color all the HTML tags red and all the comments blue, leaving only the text shown in the browser as black. This would enable a developer to locate tags and correct mistakes more quickly and easily. As a matter of fact, when Netscape Navigator 7.1® displays the source code of a Web page, it colors the element names purple, the attribute names black, the attribute values blue, the comments green, and character entities orange (Figure 9.10).

Figure 9.9   Color code alert system.

9.2.3. Comprehension, Retention, and Recall

Color can be used to increase comprehensibility. If it is used properly (according to the parameters of the human visual and cognitive systems), it can communicate information unambiguously. This can reduce comprehension errors and avoid misinterpretations. However, it must not be used in isolation but rather in conjunction with other variables such as size and location.

```
<!-- This is the content area of the page  -->
<table cellpadding="2" cellspacing="2" border="1"
style="text-align:left; width: 100%;">
<tbody>
<tr>
<td style="vertical-align:top; text-align:center;">

  When Netscape Navigator 7.1 displays the
source code of a web page, it colors the element
names purple, the attribute names black, the
attribute values blue, the comments green and
character entities orange.

</td>
</tr>
</tbody>
</table>
```

Figure 9.10   Color-coded markup.

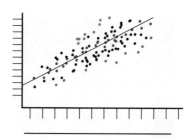

Figure 9.11 Color-coded scatter plot.

MAXIM

Color can enable us to comprehend patterns in complex data structures.

Our ability to make comparisons based on color can enable us to comprehend patterns in complex data structures. For instance, the scatter plot in Figure 9.11 reveals information about the different color-coded variables that would otherwise be difficult to determine.

By making patterns, relationships, and differences obvious, color can help people to learn and gain insight into complex subjects.

MAXIM

Color can aid in remembering and recalling information.

Color can be used to help people recall information, especially if the person has an association with a particular color and that is consistent with how the system functions. By taking advantage of this connection, you can facilitate the recognition required by the system.

For instance, given a number of new gauges to monitor, a technician can easily understand acceptable levels if the dials are coded red for the potentially dangerous levels (Figure 9.12). Safe levels will then be self-evident, allowing the technician to use recognition (the technician can see when the dial is in the red), which is an easier cognitive task than recall (the technician would have to remember the specific threshold numbers for each control) (Krugman, 1986).

Figure 9.12 Color-coded dials.

9.2.4. Tasks and Performance

Research shows that the effect color has on performance cannot be separated from the specific nature of the task at hand. Hoadley conducted experiments in which subjects were shown information using different presentation methods (pie charts, line graphs, bar graphs, etc.) that were both multicolor coded and monocolor (Hoadley, 1990). They were then asked to answer questions pertaining to the information in the presentations.

Hoadley's experiments showed that in some situations color facilitates a user's task, based on measurements of accuracy and time. However, the specific nature of the graphical presentation (pie charts, line graphs, etc.) influenced the results in both positive and negative ways. These results are consistent with other studies that explored the effect of color on specific tasks.

Hoadley summarizes some tasks that are enhanced by the application of color. Color improves performance in the following tasks:

- Recall task
- Search-and-locate task
- Retention task
- Decision judgment task

9.2.5. Redundant Coding

Color can enhance human–computer interaction, but it can also create confusion. One way to avoid potential color-related problems is to use redundant coding.

> **MAXIM**
>
> A clear structure and presentation must already be present before color is introduced.

If an interface relies solely on color for information structure, there is a risk of confusion or worse: the structure may be invisible to some users. A clear structure and presentation must already be present before color is introduced. Begin by creating a noncolored version of a design and test its effectiveness. If all goes well, color can then be added to reinforce the relationships. In this way, color is used to introduce another dimension to the existing structure.

Color must be used in conjunction with other organizational methods and not in isolation. Studies have shown that people are better at search tasks when the targets of the search are coded using more than one parameter, for instance, color and shape (Thorell & Smith, 1990). You will create a more robust system if you use multiple sensory cues.

9.3. Color Concerns for Interaction Design

There are obviously concerns regarding the use of color in interaction design. Many studies have shown that poor application of color will at best add no benefit, but has the potential to degrade user performance. If we apply color improperly, we can make it difficult for people to perform efficiently because they are distracted, or, confused by the color code we have created. It is important, therefore, to remember that the uncritical addition of color to an interface may not be beneficial.

9.3.1 Indistinguishable Differences

It is true that color can aid recognition and recall, but there is a limit to how many colors we can remember. Our ability to distinguish between similar colors is also an area of concern.

> **MAXIM**
>
> Our ability to perceive subtle changes varies from color to color.

The human eye has limitations to its ability to detect subtle variations in a color's properties. Our ability to perceive subtle changes also varies from color to color. For example, it is more difficult to detect small changes in reds and purples than small changes in other colors.

> **MAXIM**
>
> Target objects must use highly diverse colors from those in their surroundings.

If we are going to ask people to recognize colors in isolation, we must make sure that the colors they are looking at are very different from each other. For example, if we expect a user to be able to associate an object on one screen as belonging to a group on another screen, the color code we use must be very distinctive.

We are much better at making comparisons if we can see two colors side by side, but that is also a matter of degree. The colors we are comparing must be different enough for our color receptors to be able to detect the difference. The two colors in Figure 9.13 are not the same, but they are very similar; it is debatable whether we could make a judgment call if they were separated and surrounded by other colored objects.

Figure 9.13 Similar colors in close proximity.

Even if two colors are presented simultaneously, the more similar the colors are, the more time it takes to compare them and make the necessary determination.

It is true that our visual receptors are very sensitive, and we have the ability to perceive millions of different colors, but our ability to identify individual colors is much lower; we can only identify about 10 (Dix, Finlay, Aboud, & Beale, 1998). This limitation becomes a problem if we intend to color code multiple variables. As the number of color-coded objects increases, the number of required colors also increases, making it more difficult to use clearly differentiated colors. If we increase the number of possible targeted objects, we increase the time it takes to search. We must not make the situation more difficult by using colors that are difficult to differentiate.

9.3.2. Optimal Colors

It has been found that the colors red, blue, green, and yellow are the most beneficial in learning environments.(Thorell & Smith, 1990). They are highly differentiated and can be easily identified. Let's see how we might use them to clarify relationships.

Consider an interface with four main categories of information, each having three subcategories. We color code the main categories red, blue, green, and yellow. We code the subcategories of each main category by variations on the main color (Figure 9.14). Given our visual grouping, viewers will only have to choose elements from the subgroup.

By using a color code we limit the number of possible choices, but we must also indicate relation by other parameters such as shape or size. In this way, color becomes a secondary delineating factor, one that enhances the existing cohesion between the visually related subgroups. If the colors chosen for the main groups are distinct, subgroups from different main groups will be distinguishable from each other.

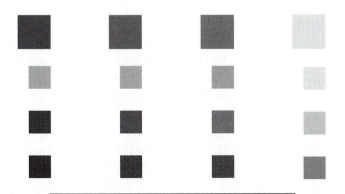

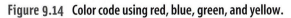

Figure 9.14   Color code using red, blue, green, and yellow.

9.3.3. **Number of Colors**

The number of colors used for coding information should be limited. Thorell and Smith (1990) recommend five to nine if memory tasks are required, but for simple differentiation they suggest that any number is acceptable, provided there is sufficient contrast.

In other words, if we expect viewers to remember a color and then recognize it later, we should use only a few distinct colors, but if we only want viewers to be able to tell the difference between two adjacent color-coded objects, we can use more colors, we just have to make sure they are not too similar.

> **MAXIM**
>
> Interface colors should never distract the user or compete with content.

We have seen that color can help people to accomplish search and other types of tasks; we must keep in mind, however, that an overly colorful display can actually hinder the user and cause confusion. Because color has the potential to overwhelm, a structured approach to color choice is essential. Shneiderman (1998) suggests that we should stay within a limit of four colors on a single screen and within a limit of seven colors for an entire interface. In other words, use discretion, and do not create a kaleidoscope of color; viewers will become overwhelmed or they will simply avoid your interface.

9.3.4. **Incompatible Differences**

Certain color combinations cause jarring effects. They can be difficult to look at or just annoying; in any event, they cause problems and should be avoided. For instance, combining saturated blue and saturated red can create focusing difficulties because of the extreme disparity of their wavelengths. The red appears to come forward and the blue recedes. The eye must shift its focus from the front to the rear, which creates additional strain on the user.

Some specific color combinations cause unique problems:

- Colors at opposing ends of the spectrum such as red and blue require the eye to use two different focal lengths, which, over time, may cause fatigue.
- Positive contrast (white text on a black background) makes characters appear to glow. This gives them a more blurry look than characters on a printed page. This effect is known as halation.

Table 9.1 shows some problematic color combinations. They are taken from the user interface guidelines created for the Goddard Space Flight Center.

Some of these combinations lack contrast, such as saturated yellow on green, yellow on white, blue on black, or green on white. Some combinations create

Table 9.1 Color Combinations to Avoid: Problematic Color Combinations

Saturated yellow and green
Yellow on white
Blue on black
Green on white
Saturated red on blue
Saturated red on green
Magenta on green
Saturated blue on green
Yellow on purple
Red on black
Magenta on black

difficulties in focusing, such as saturated red on blue. Other combinations create optical effects that are distracting, such as saturated red on green, or magenta on green. Other combinations simply make it hard to read the text.

9.3.5. Color Backgrounds

MAXIM

The perceived color of an object is affected by the color of its background.

Color perception is affected by context. Background colors can shift the perceived text color; for example a surrounding blue will shift other colors toward yellow. Consider the color backgrounds in Figure 9.15. The purple, boxes in the top left side of the figure are the same color purple, but they appear different because of the change in background color. The same is true for the other examples; the small boxes are the same color in each pair, but they do not appear that way.

The effect that a background color can have on an object is often subtle; however, it will become more pronounced if highly saturated colors are used as in Figure 9.15.

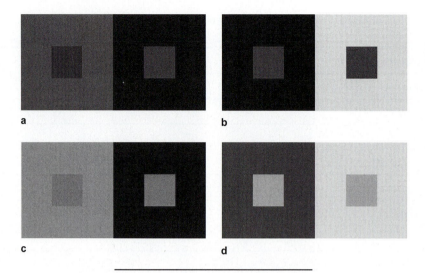

Figure 9.15 Foreground and background colors.

9.4. Technical Issues Concerning Color

Now that we understand how people see color and how some of the characteristics and limitations of our visual system affect interaction design, we must look at how color is created on the computer screen. We must understand some of the technical aspects and learn some of the skills required to apply what we know about color and interaction design to interfaces prototypes and interactive systems.

9.4.1. Color Displays

Computer screens create color by mixing red, green, and blue (RGB) light. This is called the RGB color model. Any perceivable color can be obtained by mixing varying levels of the RGB light beams (Figure 9.16). The RGB model is an additive process, as opposed to the mixing of paint, which is a subtractive process.

Figure 9.16 Additive color process.

Additive color systems involve a source that emits light waves. As shown in Figure 9.16, the secondary colors are created by combining the light waves of two of the primary colors, usually red, green, and blue. Magenta is created by mixing red and blue; yellow is created by mixing red and green; and cyan is created by mixing green and blue. White is created by combining light waves of all of the primary colors.

Subtractive color systems involve reflection. Pigments and dyes absorb some color frequencies and reflect others. When they are mixed, the frequencies that are reflected determine the color of the object. The primary colors are red, yellow, and blue. This is the color model with which most people are familiar, and so it takes some adjusting to work with the computer-based additive process. Yellow is probably the least intuitive of the additive secondary colors.

Color manipulation is a complex task. It becomes even more difficult when one has to convert what one sees on the screen to what is printed out on paper. Many industries spend enormous amounts of time and money tackling these conversion issues.

Most commercial printing processes are based on CMYK values—combinations of cyan, magenta, yellow, and black that are used to produce the primary colors. In this so-called CMYK model, magenta and yellow are mixed to produce red; magenta and cyan are mixed to produce blue; and cyan and yellow are mixed to produce green.

Color matching between the RGB model and the CMYK model is complex and requires specially calibrated equipment. The accuracy of the conversion from additive light to subtractive pigment is of the utmost importance to the printing industry.

Color experts work in controlled environments with specially calibrated monitors to match and control color properly. However, according to Fraser, "despite the best efforts of the prepress industry, the single most common reason dissatisfied users cite when they return clothing purchased from a mail-order catalog is that the color wasn't what they expected" (Fraser, 1996, 45). The industry can control the production environment but not the environment in which the customer views the catalog.

Computer screens are not all created equal, nor are people. We must work within the limitations of the human perceptual system and within the limitations of computer screen technology. We must also understand the nature of the tasks people will be doing because it can alter the way color is perceived. There is one more factor that we need to consider—the environment in which people use computers. The use of color in interaction design involves the following four components:

Human perception + Display technology + User tasks + Computing environment

9.4.2. Computing Environment

MAXIM

Monitors vary widely in the colors they display.

Not all monitors are calibrated equally, and, therefore, the colors they display differ by varying degrees. The problem of consistency across displays is exacerbated by the fact that different manufactures vary in the standards they use. In addition, users may change the manufacturer's setting on their monitors. Add to this situation the light from an overhead light source as well as the sunlight filtering into a room, and you begin to get a sense of the complexities involved.

Ambient Light

MAXIM

High levels of ambient light cause colors to lose their vibrancy.

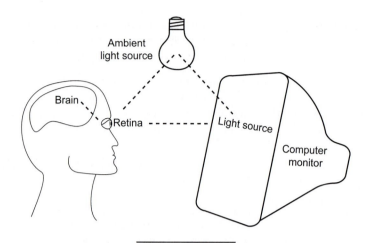

Figure 9.17 Ambient light.

A typical work space has a few sources of light. There might be overhead flo-rescent lights, desktop incandescent or halogen lamps, and windows that allow sun-light into the room. All of these light sources create what is called the ambient light in the room (Figure 9.17).

Ambient light can affect how we see colors on a computer screen. The greater the ambient light, the more colors lose their vibrancy and appear washed out. Another factor to consider is screen glare; this happens when light reflects off the glass and prevents us from seeing the screen clearly. Screen glare reduces our abil-ity to distinguish color variations.

CRT screens have been traditionally more vibrant than the liquid crystal diode (LCD) screens used on laptop computers, although with current technology, the dif-ferences in image quality are diminishing. In addition, LCD screens have advantages over CRT displays; they are flicker-free and are far less subject to glare.

It is important to know where your interface will be used. Will it be used on a desktop in an office, or will it be used in a public kiosk in an outdoor setting? There are many factors to consider:

- Ambient light
- Screen type
- Screen glare
- Screen calibration
- Printed output

MAXIM

Designs should be tested in as many different environments as possible.

It may not always be possible to test your interface in all potential environments, especially for Internet-based interfaces, but at the very least you should view it on a few different monitors and system platforms and in a few different locations with diverse ambient lighting (indoors and out).

9.4.3. Color Systems

There have been numerous attempts to systematize color manipulation, and many of them share similar concepts and rules. Isaac Newton contributed much of what is considered to be the basis of the modern understanding of color phenomena. It was originally thought that white light contained no color, and that prisms somehow added color to a light beam. With a simple experiment Newton showed this to be false. He passed white light through a prism, which dispersed the colors of the spectrum. He then chose a frequency to isolate—blue, for example— by passing that ray through a small hole. He then passed this ray through another prism.

When the blue ray passed through the second prism, the color did not change; there was no further dispersion. The white light had contained all the colors, and Newton had been able to isolate the frequencies.

From this foundation, Albert Munsell developed a system of color that has become the de facto standard. Munsell divided color into three basic elements: hue, value, and chroma:

- The difference in our perception of the colors red, green, and blue is determined by changes in *hue*.
- Shades of color can be defined as the result of changes in *value*, such as the difference between light blue and dark blue.
- The pureness of a color is determined by *chroma*. Changes in chroma can make a color change from a vibrant color to a muted or muddy color.

Other terms are sometimes used to express these properties:

- Hue
- Value/luminance/brightness*
- Chroma/saturation

This text uses the terms hue, saturation, and brightness. These are the terms used in Adobe PhotoShop, which has become the industry standard for working with computer graphics.

---

*Brightness and luminance are not strictly synonymous. Brightness is considered a measure of human perception that describes the strength of a light wave. Brightness is perceptual not empirical, whereas luminance has a quantifiable value.

Table 9.2 Changing Hue

Name	RGB levels (in decimals)	Swatch
Dark sea green	143, 188, 143	
Teal	62, 189, 144	

Light Blue   Dark Blue

———

Figure 9.18

Green   Dark Sea Green

———

Figure 9.19

Hue, Brightness, and Saturation

We can talk about a color as the combined effects of hue, saturation, and brightness. The interplay among these elements affects how we perceive color, and a change in any one of these elements affects the color's RGB values and therefore its overall appearance.

If we change the proportions of the colors we mix together, we affect the hue. For instance, we might change the levels of red, green, and blue in the color "dark sea green" and end up with a color more like teal (Table 9.2).

Changes in hue can also affect the color's saturation and brightness levels. To better understand the complex nature of hue, we will first explore how brightness and saturation affect our color perception and then add hue to the mix. (Pun intended.)

Brightness refers to the amount of white or black that is present in a color. Differences in brightness cause us to say that a color is either, for example, light blue or dark blue (Figure 9.18). We can create this affect by altering the brightness of the color.

Saturation describes the "gray-to-hue" ratio of a color. When we add gray to a color, it gives it the appearance of becoming muted or even muddy. The effect is a more subtle color without the vibrant quality of the pure hue: for example, green (saturation 87%) as opposed to a "dark sea green" (saturation 23%) (Figure 9.19).

Brightness

It can be difficult to understand how changes in one of the parameters affect how we see a color. The relationship between the three parameters can be complex, so we will change one at a time and keep the other two constant. Let's start by looking at brightness and keep saturation and hue from changing.

The easiest way to do this is to use a grayscale chart because gray, by definition, has 0% saturation, which means there is no hue. Our grayscale chart contains varying levels of gray. The lower limit is black and the upper limit is white. As long as we do not reach these levels, we will be within our grayscale range. Because the "gray-to-hue" ratio is shifted to all gray, the swatches have no saturation.

Table 9.3 Grayscale Chart

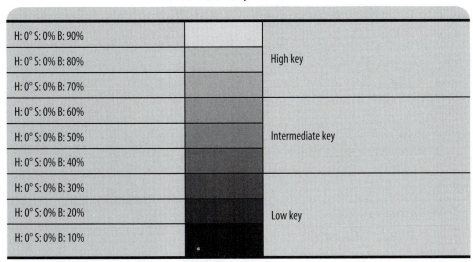

H: 0° S: 0% B: 90%		High key
H: 0° S: 0% B: 80%		
H: 0° S: 0% B: 70%		
H: 0° S: 0% B: 60%		Intermediate key
H: 0° S: 0% B: 50%		
H: 0° S: 0% B: 40%		
H: 0° S: 0% B: 30%		Low key
H: 0° S: 0% B: 20%		
H: 0° S: 0% B: 10%		

H, hue; S, saturation; B, brightness.

People can perceive 256 gradations of gray, which is how black and white photographs and illustrations are created. It quickly would become difficult to work with this many levels, so we adopt a method used by Wong (1997). We take nine values of gray and group them into three levels—high key, intermediate key, and low key, from light to dark, respectively. Each step in the scale is separated by 10% brightness (Table 9.3).

Now let's choose a color or hue of green (H:120°), saturate it 100%, and alter the brightness in the same way that we did for the grayscale chart (Table 9.4).

MAXIM

Altering brightness makes the color appear lighter or darker.

According to the chart, our color still has the same hue of 120° with full saturation at 100%, yet it changes from lime green to dark green, passing through forest green.

Saturation

Now let's apply changes in saturation to a green hue of 50% brightness (this will give us a benchmark), and see the effect this has on our perception of the color. The hue will remain constant and the brightness will stay at 50%; we will merely

Table 9.4   **Brightness Levels**

H: 120°	S: 100%	B: 90%
H: 120°	S: 100%	B: 80%
H: 120°	S: 100%	B: 70%
H: 120°	S: 100%	B: 60%
H: 120°	S: 100%	B: 50%
H: 120°	S: 100%	B: 40%
H: 120°	S: 100%	B: 30%
H: 120°	S: 100%	B: 20%
H: 120°	S: 100%	B: 10%

H, hue; S, saturation; B, brightness.

add 10% more gray at each interval, thereby altering the saturation of the color (Table 9.5). The green colors toward the top are more saturated; they have less gray.

> **MAXIM**
>
> Decreasing saturation by adding a greater percentage of gray makes colors muted.

It is interesting to view the chart in Table 9.5 in grayscale (the column on the Right is 0% saturation and 50% brightness). In the grayscale version there is no indication of hue, so it is difficult to distinguish between the different swatches. Because the green swatches maintain the same hue and brightness, the differences we perceive in colour must only be based on saturation.

Let's review the discussion. Color can be broken down into three components—hue, saturation, and brightness:

- To alter a color's brightness, we change the amount of white or black present. We refer to these as light and dark colors.
- To alter only the saturation, we add and subtract percentages of gray. We refer to this as muting the color and making it more subtle.
- If we push the brightness to 100% and saturation to 0%, we get white; if we keep saturation at 0% and lower brightness to 0%, we pass through various

Table 9.5   Saturation Levels

H: 120° S: 90% B: 50%		
H: 120° S: 80% B: 50%		
H: 120° S: 70% B: 50%		
H: 120° S: 60% B: 50%		
H: 120° S: 50% B: 50%		
H: 120° S: 40% B: 50%		
H: 120° S: 30% B: 50%		
H: 120° S: 20% B: 50%		
H: 120° S: 10% B: 50%		

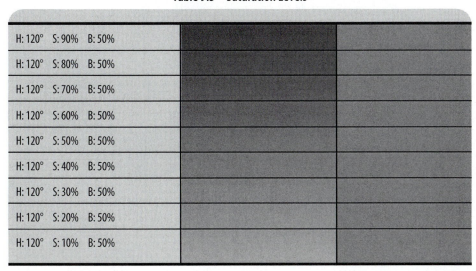

H, hue; S, saturation; B, brightness.

shades of gray until we finally arrive at black. If the saturation level remains high enough to show a hint of hue, then subtle changes in these two parameters can create numerous colors within that same hue.

Hue

> **MAXIM**
>
> Colors with the same brightness levels can appear lighter or darker than each other.

Our perception of hue is a bit more complex than that of saturation or brightness. Colors that technically have the same brightness level might appear to be lighter or darker than one another. For instance, look at the color wheel in Figure 9.20a. It is based only on hue; each of the colors has 100% saturation and 100% brightness. The colors in the top half of the wheel appear to be lighter than the colors on the bottom half. We say that the colors on the bottom have more perceived weight even though they have the same brightness levels.

This phenomenon is made more obvious when we look at the grayscale version of the color wheel (Figure 9.20b). We can use grayscale conversions to help us control for the effect that perceived weight has on viewers. If we stick to just the numbers, we are not considering the limitations of the human perceptual system.

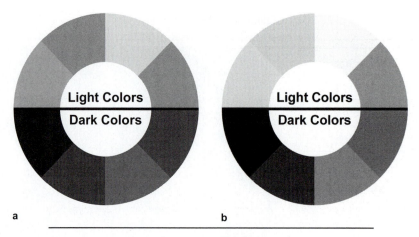

Figure 9.20 (a) Light and dark colors. (b) Light and dark colors—grayscale.

People see some hues as being darker than others. This might mean that we need to decrease the brightness levels of the top colors if we want them to appear similar in terms of brightness.

In the section of their Web site entitled Designing for People with Partial Sight and Color Deficiencies, Lighthouse International, the leading resource worldwide on vision impairment and vision rehabilitation, states that designers should pick dark colors from the bottom half of the wheel and contrast them with light colors from the top half of the color wheel (http://www.lighthouse.org/color_contrast. htm). They also suggest that designers should avoid contrasting dark colors from the top half with light colors from the bottom half. Although this might not always be possible, it is a good tip to keep in mind.

9.4.4. Color Contrast

The highest possible contrast is between black and white. As you read this book, you are experiencing negative contrast—black print on a white background. This is the most legible format for the display of text and the most universal format across culture, age, and individual differences. Negative contrast has been used for centuries and is embedded in our expectations. Positive contrast (white type on a black background) is not as user-friendly; there is a tendency to see a halo effect called halation around positive-contrast text.

MAXIM

Positive contrast becomes tedious and annoying after extended periods of use.

It is of interest that Lighthouse International suggests that people with limited vision find positive contrast a bit more legible. This knowledge can be exploited for different effects; however, when designing an application-type interface it is not well suited for long-term use.

> **MAXIM**
>
> Color contrast is affected by the perceived weight of the colors involved.

It is not uncommon to have a design that involves colored backgrounds. If you introduce color into a design, you must be careful about the degree of contrast between foreground colors and background colors. If you use colored backgrounds, you should view the design in grayscale to make sure that the contrast between colors holds up across a wide spectrum of human color vision abilities. In the early stages of development you should refer often to the grayscale versions of the design.

Complementary Color Scheme

The colors we choose for backgrounds or for text must be considered in the context of the other colors used on the screen. There are a few ways to approach the issue of an overall color scheme.

Let's look at the color wheel again. Notice that some colors are opposite others. For instance, yellow is opposite purple, and blue is opposite orange: these pairs are referred to as complementary colors (Figure 9.21a, b). To create a dynamic effect, you can create palettes that use complementary relationships.

Analogous Color Scheme

We can create more subtle effects if we chose colors that are adjacent on the color wheel. This color scheme is referred to as analogous because it uses colors that are contiguous on the color wheel (Figure 9.21c, d).

Split Complementary Color Scheme

We can also consider a scheme based on colors that are adjacent to the complementary color. This creates a split complementary color scheme (Figure 9.21e, f).

Monochromatic Color Scheme

Color schemes can be created by using only one hue and varying the saturation and brightness settings. This is called a monochromatic color scheme, and it produces more subtle effects.

As you can see, many diverse effects can be achieved through the intelligent application of color to an interface. If we choose analogous hues, we get a more subtle palette. Complimentary colors tend to create a more dynamic effect. With a controlled manipulation of saturation and brightness, we can achieve almost limitless variation and impact.

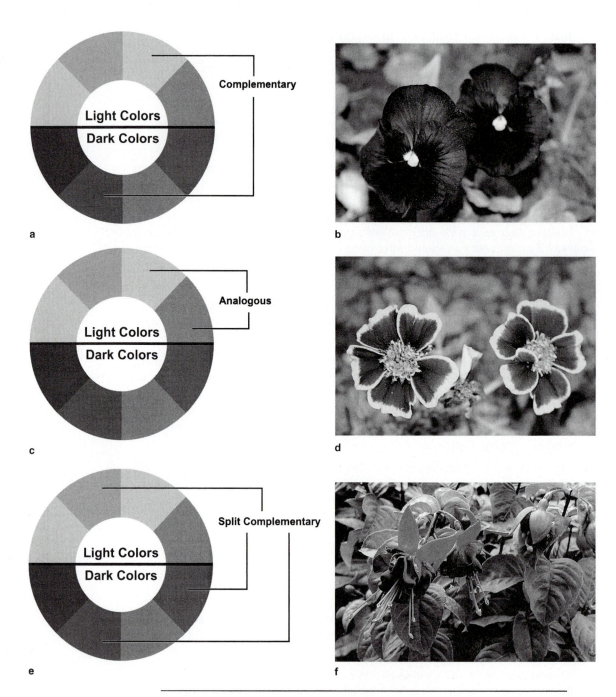

Figure 9.21   (a) Complementary colors. (b) An example from nature of complementary colors. (c) Analogous colors. (d) An example from nature of analogous colors. (e) Split complementary colors. (f) An example from nature of split complementary colors.

It cannot be stated often enough that intelligent, subtle use of color can enhance an interface and make the experience more pleasant and productive. An undisciplined use of color can degrade the usefulness of an interface. Decisions about color coding must be based on clear and logical reasoning.

9.4.5. Color Space

Computer monitors use the additive RGB color model, and printers use the subtractive CMYK color model; the actual values for the colors are not specified by the model, however; they are specified by the color space that is associated with the model.

The hue, saturation, and brightness (HSB) color space, which is also referred to as the hue, saturation, and value (HSV) color space, is only one of many possible RGB color spaces. There are others, such as sRGB (standard RGB), Adobe RGB, RGBA (RGB with an alpha channel for transparencies), and Adobe Wide Gamut RGB.

RGB color spaces map color on three axes, one for each component, and create a three-dimensional space; it is often easier, however, to consider color spaces on a two-dimensional plane as in the HSV color wheel shown in Figure 9.22. The wheel represents hue variations, and the triangular shape in the middle defines the saturation from top to bottom and the value from left to right.

Contemporary color spaces are based on the CIE L*a*b* color space created in 1976 by the International Commission on Illumination (CIE). The CIE-based spaces

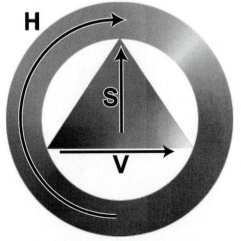

Figure 9.22 The hue, saturation, and value (HSV) color space.

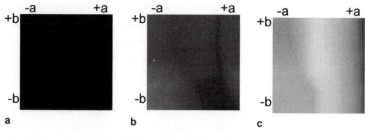

Figure 9.23   The International Commission on Illumination (CIE) L*a*b* color space.

are based on luminance (L) and variations between green and red (a) plotted against variations between blue and green (b) (Figure 9.23).

The CIE L*a*b* space is the most complete mathematical representation of the entire spectrum of colors that are visible to the human eye. It is too complex for most practical purposes, but it serves as a reference for all other commonly used color spaces. These derivative color spaces are more manageable but offer a narrower range of colors.

Most of the devices that people work with, such as computers, printers, scanners, and digital cameras, use different color spaces. This makes it difficult for them to share graphic files and images in a consistent, standardized way. You have probably noticed that images do not always print out in the way that they look on the screen.

The International Color Consortium (ICC) was created to develop a standard for color information interchange. Its founding members include Adobe Systems Inc., Agfa-Gevaert N.V., Apple Computer, Inc., Eastman Kodak Company, FOGRA (Honorary), Microsoft Corporation, Inc., Sun Microsystems, Inc., Taligent, Inc., and Silicon Graphics.

The ICC created a format that provides an across-platform device profile. The profile can be used to translate color information between devices that use diverse color spaces. The color space information is embedded within the graphic file as an ICC profile that contains the color space information of the device that created the file. Other devices can read the profile and translate it into their own color space. This process ensures that all devices that read the profile will display the color information correctly.

9.4.6.   Web-Based Color

XHTML, the current incarnation of the markup language used to create Web pages, uses hexadecimal coding to specify the RGB values of a color. For example, the hex value for saturated red is #ff0000; this is the equivalent of R = 255,

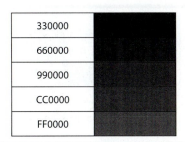

330000	
660000	
990000	
CC0000	
FF0000	

Figure 9.24 Shades of red that are browser safe—manipulating only the red light.

G = 0, and B = 0. Saturated green is coded as #00ff00, and saturated blue is coded as #0000ff.

The first two characters represent the level of red light, the second two characters represent the level of green light, and the last two characters represent the level of blue light. To get yellow, we mix red and green, #ffff00, and to get magenta, we mix red and blue, #ff00ff. All possible values between 0 and 255 are available for ff [note that hex goes from 0 to 15 (0 to f), and then carries to the next column (the 16's column)], but there is a limit to the colors that we can safely use in all situations.

MAXIM

An 8-bit monitor requires a browser-safe palate.

A computer with a monitor set to 8-bit color (256 colors) only allows for 216 colors to be shown in a Web browser because the operating system restricts 40 of the possible 256 colors for its own use. When the monitor is set to 8-bit color, the system uses a look-up table for each individual color, and there is one table that is used by all browsers. For this reason, we talk about the browser-safe pallet.

A browser-safe pallet is a chart based on colors that are confined to the hex values of 00, 33, 66, 99, CC, and FF. Notice, also, that characters controlling each color of light must work in pairs. Therefore, levels of red light are restricted to the colors in Figure 9.24.

Other shades of red are made possible by adding equal levels of blue and green light. For instance, a light pink is coded FFCCCC (Figure 9.25.)

FFCCCC	

Figure 9.25 Increasing levels of blue and green.

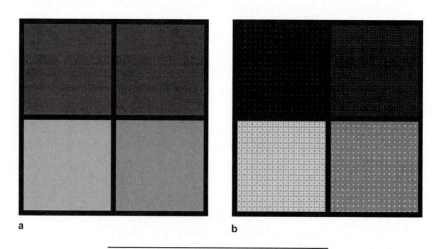

0	1	2
3	4	5
6	7	8

Figure 9.26   Color look-up table.

This pallet of colors is also referred to as a color look-up table (CLUT). Colors are referenced according to their position in the table. For example, if a color table had blue in the top left corner, as in Figure 9.26, a graphic that needed that color would reference it as 0, it would reference yellow as 6, white as 8, and so on.

If the CLUT were substituted with another that had yellow at 0, the graphic would still use the color that was referenced at the 0 location, and it would therefore have an unexpected appearance.

If a graphic contains colors that are not in the CLUT, the system will try to create the colors by interpolating between two similar colors. This will cause an image to have a polka-dotted appearance known as dithering, as shown in Figure 9.27b.

If a Web page has a background color that is not browser safe, the system will substitute the closest matching color in the browser-safe palette or CLUT. This can cause unwanted effects.

The background colors of images on a Web page must often match the background color of the page itself. In this situation, the shift in the background color of

a   b

Figure 9.27   (a) Normal version. (b) Dithered version.

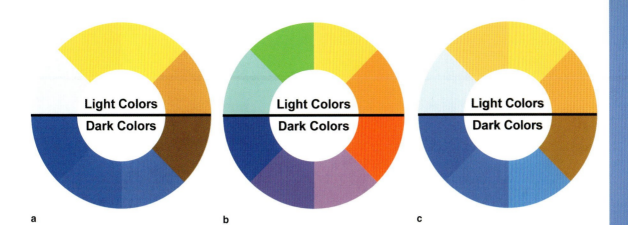

a   b   c

Figure 9.2   (a) Protanopic color vision. (b) Normal trichromatic color vision. (c) Deuteranopic color vision.

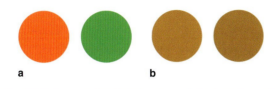

a   b

Figure 9.3   (a) Normal color vision. (b) Deuteranopic color vision.

Figure 9.4   Inappropriate colors.

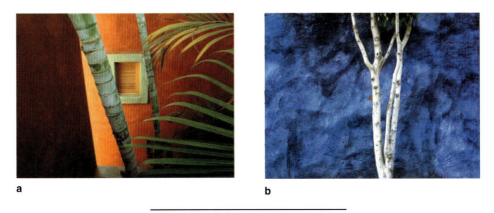

a   b

Figure 9.5   (a) Mexico | #282. (b) Mexico | #268.

With permission www.jimnilsen.com.

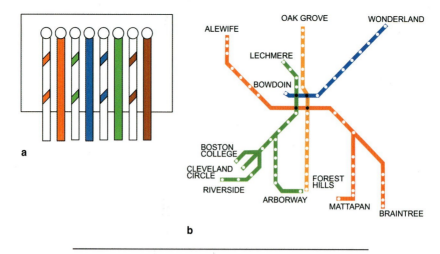

a

b

Figure 9.6 (a) Ethernet wires. (b) Map of the Boston subway system.

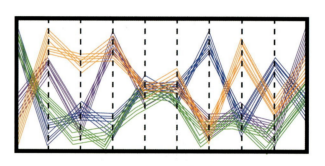

Figure 9.7 Parallel coordinate plot.

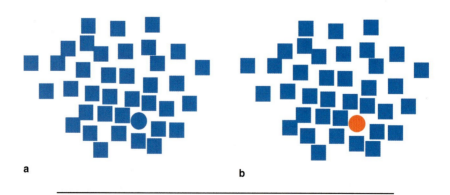

a   b

Figure 9.8 (a) Blue squares and a blue circle. (b) Blue squares and a red circle.

Figure 9.9 Color code alert system.

```
<!-- This is the content area of the page  -->
<table cellpadding="2" cellspacing="2" border="1"
style="text-align:left; width: 100%;">
<tbody>
<tr>
<td style="vertical-align:top; text-align:center;">

  When Netscape Navigator 7.1 displays the
source code of a web page, it colors the element
names purple, the attribute names black, the
attribute values blue, the comments green and
character entities orange.

</td>
</tr>
</tbody>
</table>
```

Figure 9.10 Color-coded markup.

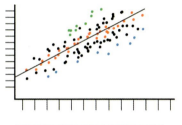

Figure 9.11 Color-coded scatter plot.

Figure 9.14 Color code using red, blue, green, and yellow.

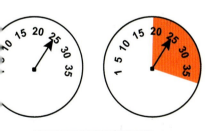

Figure 9.12 Color-coded dials.

ure 9.13 Similar colors in close proximity.

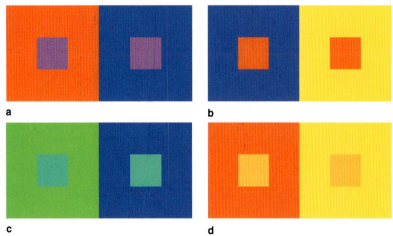

Figure 9.15 Foreground and background colors.

Table 9.1 Color Combinations to Avoid: Problematic Color Combinations

Saturated yellow and green	Saturated yellow on green
Yellow on white	Yellow on white
Blue on black	Blue on black
Green on white	Green on white
Saturated red on blue	Saturated red on blue
Saturated red on green	Saturated red on green
Magenta on green	Magenta on green
Saturated blue on green	Saturated blue on green
Yellow on purple	Yellow on purple
Red on black	Red on black
Magenta on black	Magenta on black

Figure 9.16 Additive color process.

Light Blue   Dark Blue

——

Figure 9.18

Green   Dark Sea Green

——

Figure 9.19

Table 9.2 Changing Hue

Name	RGB levels (in decimals)	Swatch
Dark sea green	143, 188, 143	
Teal	62, 189, 144	

Table 9.3 Grayscale Chart

H: 0° S: 0% B: 90%		
H: 0° S: 0% B: 80%		High key
H: 0° S: 0% B: 70%		
H: 0° S: 0% B: 60%		
H: 0° S: 0% B: 50%		Intermediate key
H: 0° S: 0% B: 40%		
H: 0° S: 0% B: 30%		
H: 0° S: 0% B: 20%		Low key
H: 0° S: 0% B: 10%		

H, hue; S, saturation; B, brightness.

Table 9.4 Brightness Levels

H: 120°	S: 100%	B: 90%	
H: 120°	S: 100%	B: 80%	
H: 120°	S: 100%	B: 70%	
H: 120°	S: 100%	B: 60%	
H: 120°	S: 100%	B: 50%	
H: 120°	S: 100%	B: 40%	
H: 120°	S: 100%	B: 30%	
H: 120°	S: 100%	B: 20%	
H: 120°	S: 100%	B: 10%	

H, hue; S, saturation; B, brightness.

Table 9.5   Saturation Levels

H: 120° S: 90% B: 50%		
H: 120° S: 80% B: 50%		
H: 120° S: 70% B: 50%		
H: 120° S: 60% B: 50%		
H: 120° S: 50% B: 50%		
H: 120° S: 40% B: 50%		
H: 120° S: 30% B: 50%		
H: 120° S: 20% B: 50%		
H: 120° S: 10% B: 50%		

H, hue; S, saturation; B, brightness.

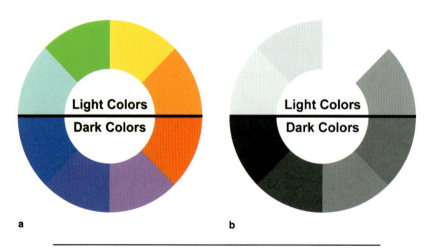

Figure 9.20   (a) Light and dark colors. (b) Light and dark colors—grayscale.

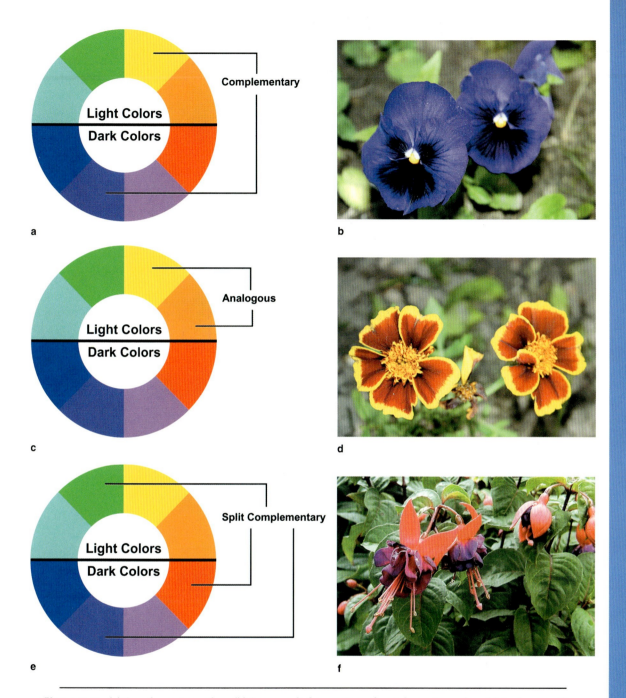

Figure 9.21 (a) Complementary colors. (b) An example from nature of complementary colors. (c) Analogous colors. (d) An example from nature of analogous colors. (e) Split complementary colors. (f) An example from nature of split complementary colors.

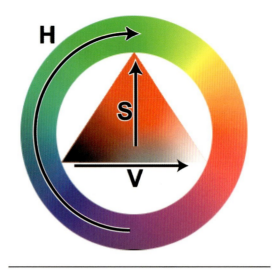

Figure 9.22   The hue, saturation, and value (HSV) color space.

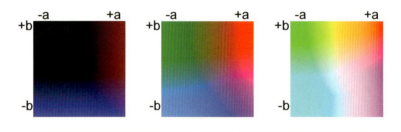

Figure 9.23   The International Commission on Illumination (CIE) L*a*b* color space.

330000	
660000	
990000	
CC0000	
FF0000	

Figure 9.24   Shades of red that are browser safe—manipulating only the red light.

FFCCCC	

Figure 9.25   Increasing levels of blue and green.

0	1	2
3	4	5
6	7	8

Figure 9.26   Color look-up table.

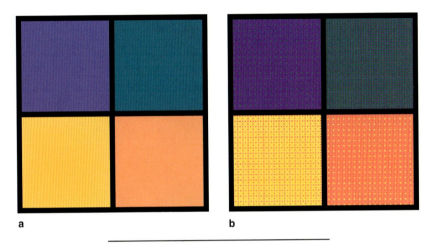

a   b

Figure 9.27   (a) Normal version. (b) Dithered version.

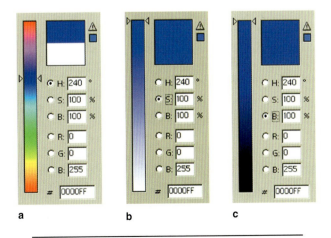

a   b   c

Figure 9.28   Color picker. (a) Hue, (b) saturation, (c) brightness.

Table 9.6   Issue Cover Color Swatches

	R: 250	H: 1°		R: 168	H: 215°
	G: 37	S: 86%		G: 183	S: 19%
	B: 35	B: 98%		B: 205	B: 80%
	Hex: fa2523			Hex: a7b7cd	
	R: 6	H: 162°		R: 208	H: 42°
	G: 148	S: 99%		G: 188	S: 89%
	B: 92	B: 62%		B: 23	B: 99%
	Hex: 019d6d			Hex: febc1d	

Figure 9.30   Published issues of the journal.

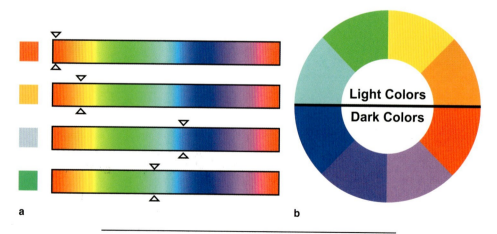

a

b

Figure 9.31   (a) Color Picker showing all cover colors. (b) Color wheel.

Table 9.7

	R: 250	**H:** 1°			**R:** 133	**H:** 1°
	G: 37	**S:** 86%			**G:** 72	**S:** 60%
	B: 35	**B:** 98%			**B:** 70	**B:** 52%
	fa2523				853735	
Issue 1 cover			Altered version of Issue 1 cover			
	R: 254	**H:** 42°			**R:** 252	**H:** 42°
	G: 188	**S:** 89%			**G:** 234	**S:** 24%
	B: 29	**B:** 99%			**B:** 192	**B:** 99%
	febc1d				fceac0	
Issue 4 cover			Altered version of Issue 4 cover			

Table 9.8

	R: 168	**H:** 215°			**R:** 0	**H:** 213°
	G: 183	**S:** 19%			**G:** 31	**S:** 100%
	B: 205	**B:** 80%			**B:** 68	**B:** 27%
	a7b7cd				001f44	
Issue 3 cover			Altered version of Issue 3 cover			
	R: 6	**H:** 162°			**R:** 57	**H:** 152°
	G: 148	**S:** 99%			**G:** 96	**S:** 41%
	B: 92	**B:** 62%			**B:** 78	**B:** 38%
	019d6d				39604E	
Issue 2 cover			Altered version of Issue 2 cover			

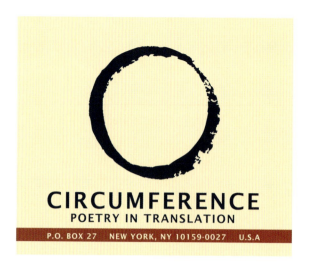

Figure 9.32 *Circumference* logo for the splash screen.

Figure 9.33 Top banner with logo and tag line.

Table 9.9

Issue Covers	Original Colors	Darker Colors
	①	①
	②	②
	③	③
	④	④

Figure 9.34   Deuteranopic color icons.

Figure 9.35   Deuteranopic versions of the issue covers.

a   b   c

Figure 11.40   (a) Subscription icon. (b) Contact icon. (c) About icon.

Figure 11.41   Supporters icon.

a   b   c

Figure 11.42   (a) Issues icon. (b) Events icon. (c) Submissions icon.

a   b

Figure 11.43   (a) Video icon.
(b) Photo icon.

Chapter 11   Flags.

Figure 12.11   Hypertext links at Useit.com.

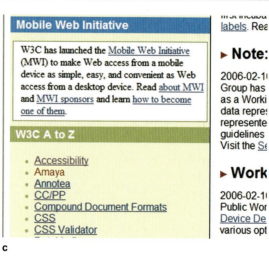

Figure 12.12   (a) Hypertext links at the W3.org Web site. (b) Nonfunctional hyperlink. (c) Visited link.

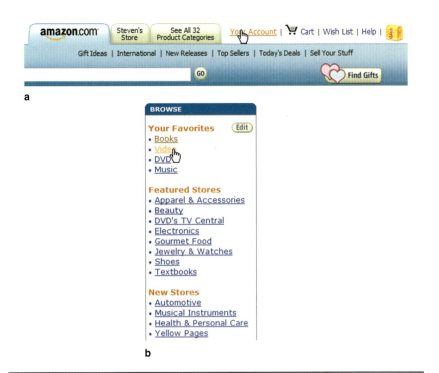

a

b

Figure 12.13 (a) Hover and active links on the Amazon.com Web site. (b) Side navigation links.

Figure 12.17 (a) Page with images turned off. (b) Page with images turned on.

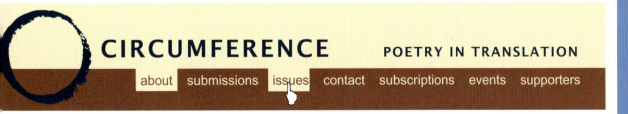

Figure 12.18 Global hover state.

CIRCUMFERENCE POETRY IN TRANSLATION

about submissions issues contact subscriptions events supporters

Issue 4
Sample Poems
Names with asterisks link to bios.

① ② ③ ④

The Sky
Ask Socrates Marilyn Said
Danse Macabre
"Life is ... to remember"

"Even though the wind envelops"

"Anche se il vento copre"

Anche se il vento copre
la primavera, il popolo
canta alla notte.

L'ascolto io dal mio letto. Lascio

« La vita di Gesù ». Ardo a quel canto.

written 1927–1938
*SANDRO PENNA

Sandro Penna (1906-1977) was born in Perugia. At the age of 23, he moved to Rome, where he lived for the majority of his life. Penna never had a solid career and often bordered on poverty. As a young man, he developed a friendship with the poet Umberto Saba, who helped Penna publish his poems, leading to his first book, Poesie (Poems), in 1939. Several collections

followed. Penna was awarded the Premio Viareggio award in 1957.

Figure 12.19   Example poem from Issue 4—complete page.

Issue 4
(2006)
Table of Contents and
sample poems

Issue 3
(Sping/Summer 2005)
Table of Contents and
sample poems

Figure 13.6   Links to issue tables of contents.

the page will not match the interpolated background in the image. Although it is possible to use the alpha channel in the GIF and PING image formats to create transparent backgrounds, this will not help if some parts of the background blend into other image colors.

Because the current target monitor for Web development safely can be assumed to be in at least 16-bit color, the issue of browser-safe color is not as significant as it once was. However, browser-safe color should not be considered totally irrelevant, and every effort should be made to try to accommodate this limited target mode if there is a significant number of people who will access the site with 8-bit monitors.

9.4.7. The Color Picker

Adobe PhotoShop has become the industry standard for digital graphic manipulation and creation. People from many different domains, such as professional photographers and Web site developers, use PhotoShop. It is a powerful and easy-to-use application that offers precise control over color manipulation. Let's see how some of the tools work.

Clicking on either the "Set foreground color" chip or the "Set background color" chip on the main toolbar brings you to the Color Picker (Figure 9.28). Looking at the controls, you see values for hue, saturation, and brightness. Click on the H, S, or B radio button, respectively, to toggle the slider on the left between hue, saturation, and brightness. The #0000FF on the bottom shows the hex code for saturated red.

There are also controls for CMYK and L*a*b* color spaces; however, most of our work will be done for screen purposes, and so the RGB, HSB, and hex controls will suffice. We will use the color picker in the following design scenario.

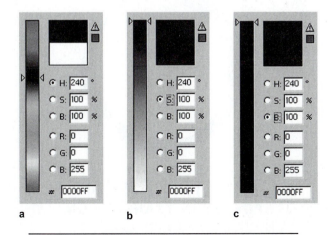

Figure 9.28   Color picker. (a) Hue, (b) saturation, (c) brightness.

Design Scenario

Circumference: Color Scheme

In this design scenario we explore the application of color to the *Circumference* Web site design.

The activities in this design scenario include the following:

- Color analysis and documentation
- Color scheme creation
- Color alteration using brightness and saturation
- Color contrast
- Color blindness
- Redundant coding

The elements that we have from the print journal are a circular black and white logo that resembles a coffee stain, created by the journal's designer Dan Visel (Figure 9.29). The journal also uses a particular font for its name and tag line.

Neither of these elements contains color; however, the journal has published four issues, and each issue's cover uses a single, solid and strong color as shown in Figure 9.30.

We can create a color scheme for the site by using these colors as a starting point. We might also wish to use images of the covers on the site, so it would be a good idea to use a color scheme that can accommodate these strong colors.

Figure 9.29 *Circumference* Logo.

Design Scenario (cont.)

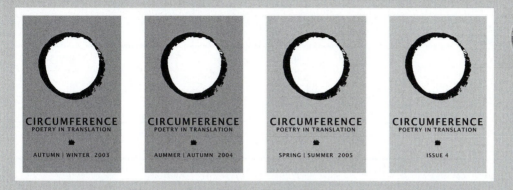

Figure 9.30 Published issues of the journal.

Design Principles: Familiarity, Simplicity, Recall, Memorability. Readers will identify the journal with these colors, so we can support the product's identity as well as create a simple color environment for the site. We can use the colors to indicate areas that relate to specific issues and tap into the visitors' recall to help them navigate the site. This will also help them to remember the site navigation.

Color Analysis and Documentation

First we need to scan the covers, calculate the colors used, and create color swatches that we can use to construct some mock-ups of the Web pages. We might also be able to get this information from the designer of the covers. However we collect this information, we need to view the color swatches that we create on a few different screens so that we can judge the general look the color will have on the Web page.

In an optimal world everyone who visits the Web site would use a calibrated monitor; however, that will probably never be the case, and so it is important to see what the color swatch looks like on many different monitors—LCD, CRT, calibrated, default from factory, Macs, PCs, and so on.

Now that we see how the color will appear to different people we can begin to explore different color schemes. We will document the various parameters so that we will have them available when we need them (Table 9.6).

Color Scheme Creation

Let's look at the Color Picker and see where our colors are located in relation to each other (Figure 9.31a). Issues 1 and 4 are in close proximity. The yellowish color H: 42° is very close to the red H: 1° and sits within an orange area of the spectrum. They are also both very saturated and bright colors. The blue and green colors are also close to

Design Scenario (cont.)

Table 9.6   Issue Cover Color Swatches

R: 250	H: 1°		R: 168	H: 215°
G: 37	S: 86%		G: 183	S: 19%
B: 35	B: 98%		B: 205	B: 80%
Hex: fa2523			Hex: a7b7cd	
R: 6	H: 162°		R: 208	H: 42°
G: 148	S: 99%		G: 188	S: 89%
B: 92	B: 62%		B: 23	B: 99%
Hex: 019d6d			Hex: febc1d	

each other on the spectrum, but the blue has a very low saturation and high brightness, whereas the green is highly saturated and has a midrange brightness setting.

A glance at the color wheel (Figure 9.31b) shows that the red and orange colors are adjacent to the blue and green colors. We will use this to develop an overall complementary color scheme for the site.

At this point we make a global decision to reserve the blue colors for hyperlinked text and images or icons. This decision is based on the convention of using blue for hyperlinks, which is well established on the Web. Therefore we will use the red and orange to create the color environment for the site's screen areas and backgrounds.

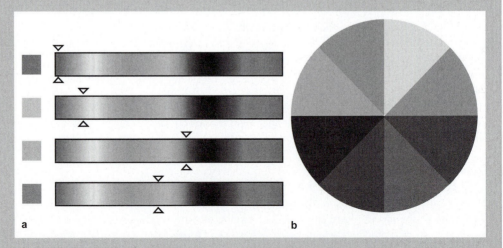

Figure 9.31 (a) Color Picker showing all cover colors. (b) Color wheel.

Design Scenario (cont.)

Table 9.7

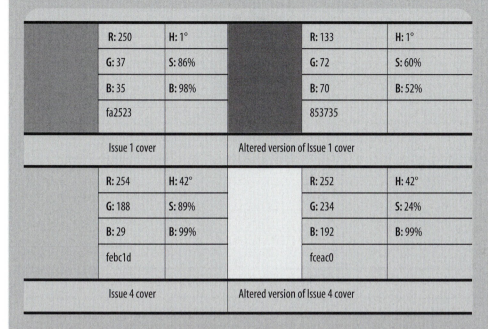

R: 250	H: 1°			R: 133	H: 1°
G: 37	S: 86%			G: 72	S: 60%
B: 35	B: 98%			B: 70	B: 52%
fa2523				853735	
Issue 1 cover		Altered version of Issue 1 cover			
R: 254	H: 42°			R: 252	H: 42°
G: 188	S: 89%			G: 234	S: 24%
B: 29	B: 99%			B: 192	B: 99%
febc1d				fceac0	
Issue 4 cover		Altered version of Issue 4 cover			

Color Alteration Using Brightness and Saturation

We begin by developing some dark colors and some light colors. The orange color has less perceived weight than the red, and so we push the orange lighter and the red darker. This is also consistent with the recommendation by Lighthouse to combine light colors from the top of the color wheel with dark colors from the bottom of the color wheel.

The colors we create have to provide an environment for all the colors we use, including full-saturation images of the journal's covers, and so we desaturate and reduce the brightness level of the red and desaturate the orange, which is already at 99% brightness (Table 9.7).

We now need to develop some colors to use for the logo and journal name from the blue and green issue covers (Table 9.8).

Color Contrast

The blue color creates a more striking look against the light background and will be related to elements that are hyperlinked; this color decision has a significant impact on the rest of the color decisions that we make as we develop the rest of the page elements. The dark red color is used as a background for the address, which uses the light color. We now have a splash screen logo for the site (Figure 9.32).

Table 9.8

R: 168	**H:** 215°			**R:** 0	**H:** 213°
G: 183	**S:** 19%			**G:** 31	**S:** 100%
B: 205	**B:** 80%			**B:** 68	**B:** 27%
a7b7cd				001f44	
Issue 3 cover			Altered version of Issue 3 cover		
R: 6	**H:** 162°			**R:** 57	**H:** 152°
G: 148	**S:** 99%			**G:** 96	**S:** 41%
B: 92	**B:** 62%			**B:** 78	**B:** 38%
019d6d				39604E	
Issue 2 cover			Altered version of Issue 2 cover		

After entering the site we continue this color scheme for the banner on each page (Figure 9.33). This creates continuity with the splash page and reinforces the product's identity.

Let's address one more color adjustment before we leave the development of a color scheme. We need to create icons for the different issues, and the circle logo can

Figure 9.32 *Circumference* logo for the splash screen.

Design Scenario (cont.)

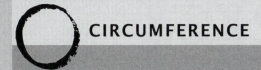

Figure 9.33 **Top banner with logo and tag line.**

be used with a number to represent each issue. This is a common way to present numbers that we address in the chapter on icons; now we just need to develop usable versions of the four colors.

We know that the human eye does not pick up the color of small objects very well and that it has a lower sensitivity to the blue frequencies. You can see how these factors affect our perception of the icons in the second column in Table 9.9. These icons use the original colors from the journal covers.

The third column uses the same saturation levels and hues as the second column but decreased brightness levels. These versions are more legible but retain the connection with the hue of the issue covers. You will have to use your eye to judge the perceived weight of the colors when you adjust the brightness levels.

Color Blindness

A check to see whether the colors are distinguishable for people with deuteranopia shows that there is enough difference for people to tell them apart (Figure 9.34).

Table 9.9

Issue Covers	Original Colors	Darker Colors
⬤	①	①
⬤	②	②
⬤	③	③
⬤	④	④

Design Scenario (cont.)

Figure 9.34 Deuteranopic color icons.

Redundant Coding

The same will be true for the images of the covers that use the original colors. Notice how much difference the black and white logo circles make; this helps to create redundant coding in the images (Figure 9.35).

CIRCUMFERENCE
POETRY IN TRANSLATION

AUTUMN | WINTER 2003

CIRCUMFERENCE
POETRY IN TRANSLATION

AUMMER | AUTUMN 2004

CIRCUMFERENCE
POETRY IN TRANSLATION

SPRING | SUMMER 2005

CIRCUMFERENCE
POETRY IN TRANSLATION

ISSUE 4

Figure 9.35 Deuteranopic versions of the issue covers.

Summary

Determining color specifications can be complex; many factors must be taken into consideration:

- Is performance aided or degraded by the application of color?
- Can the colors be differentiated?
- Does the design rely solely on color?
- Is the color scheme obvious?
- Can the color scheme be remembered?

We have investigated the importance of color and some of the issues it poses in interface design. In an industrial or mission-critical environment, proper treatment of color can mean the difference between an interface that is consistent and predictable and an interface that fosters human error. The importance of light sources and ambient light cannot be ignored.

Guidelines for the use of color are clear and are based on the strengths and weaknesses of human visual receptors. Certain conventions should be followed, and cultural associations must be taken into consideration. A professional graphic designer can achieve amazing results by manipulating limited pallets and tightly controlled color schemes. When working with color, the axiom "less is more" applies!

Performance enhancement depends on the relationship between color and task. However, it would be impossible to identify every situation that would benefit from the application of color. Each task must be evaluated individually, and concerns about user expectations must always be considered. We can, however, be mindful of some basic heuristics to avoid possible degradation of user performance:

- Use color sparingly.
- Use color as a secondary element.
- Avoid perceptually difficult combinations.
- Understand user expectations and limitations.
- Test, test, and test again.

Resources on the Web

www.aw.com/heim
There are links to information on color guidelines, color blindness and Web-based color manipulation tools.

Suggested Reading

Fraser, B., Murphy, C., & Bunting, F. (2004). *Real World Color Management* (2 ed.): Peachpit Press.

Sharma, A. (2003). *Understanding Color Management* (1 ed.): Thomson Delmar Learning.

Weinman, L. (2002). *Designing Web Graphics.4* (4 ed.): New Riders Press.

Interface Components

GUIs comprise various components, sometimes collectively called widgets. These are the atoms with which an interface is constructed. Each of these components is designed to carry out certain tasks, and each has a role to play in the interface. We must understand what they do best so that we can apply the appropriate components to specific tasks.

People who have even just a basic level of computer literacy have developed some expectations as to what the various components do and how to use them. The task of the interaction designer is to pair the most appropriate component with the task and do it in such a way that the user understands the relationship and can draw on existing knowledge. Let's look at the various components that are available to interaction designers and how best to apply them to interface designs.

10.1. The WIMP Interface

Contemporary GUIs are sometimes called "WIMP" interfaces because they comprise windows, icons, menus, and pointers. There are other types of components, such as buttons and checkboxes, but the WIMP components are the backbone of the interface, and we will explore them first.

10.1.1. Windows

GUIs are windowing interfaces: they use rectangular boxes called windows to present the components of an application or the contents of a folder. Windowing was first demonstrated by the Xerox Alto and later incorporated into the Apple operating system and Microsoft Windows.

Windowing, like the desktop metaphor, has become so entrenched in our minds that it is hard to conceive of any other way to organize a GUI. The success of the major windowing system manufacturers is testimony to the degree of public acceptance of this type of interaction. However, windowing interfaces can pose difficulties for users, especially beginners, and must be designed correctly to avoid user frustration and diminished productivity.

> **MAXIM**
>
> Multiple windows can pose management difficulties.

There are two types of window managers: the operating system software that manages the appearance and behavior of the windows, and the user who must minimize, maximize, resize, access, and organize windows. Studies have shown that the advantages offered by windowing systems can be negated by excess window manipulation requirements.

Window management is going to be part of user interaction for the foreseeable future, so it is important to understand how windows function and how best to maximize their benefits.

Window States

Once an instance of a window is created, it has three possible states:

- Maximized—The window occupies the whole screen.
- Minimized—The window is reduced to a button or icon.
- Restored—The window returns to the previous dimensions. The window also becomes resizable and can overlap other windows.

Restored Windows—In the restored or resizable state, windows have three possible presentation styles. They can be made to tile the whole screen, they can cascade, or they can be placed randomly, overlapping one another.

Tiled windows collectively occupy the entire screen and resize themselves to allow all running programs to be visible. The system window manager allocates the

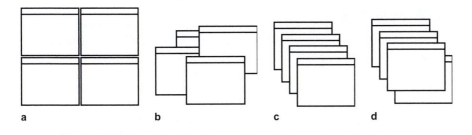

Figure 10.1 (a) Tiled windows. (b) Overlapping windows. (c) Cascading windows. (d) Interrupted cascade.

size and position of the windows on the screen. In this presentation style, all windows are visible to the user; however, each window retains its title and tool bars. This method can use up a great deal of screen real estate. The windows might also become too small, severely restricting the visible content.

> **MAXIM**
>
> Tiled windows afford drag-and-drop methods.

Tiled windows allow users to drag and drop objects between windows (Figure 10.1a). This is a more direct method than copying to the clipboard, accessing the target window, and pasting into the new document.

Overlapping windows can be positioned and sized by the user, and each window will maintain its size and location until further altered by the user (Figure 10.1b). This presentation style allows the user to see some of the window's contents, unless the window is completely obscured by another window. The active window overlaps all other windows. Any window becomes active when it is clicked on.

> **MAXIM**
>
> Overlapping windows use screen real estate efficiently, but they can become overwhelming.

This presentation style also allows drag-and-drop operations and uses screen real estate more efficiently than tiled windows. However, it is also more complex and has the potential to become overwhelming if too many windows are open at the same time. This style may involve much window manipulation and, therefore, create unnecessary work.

Cascading is a special type of overlapping presentation style. Windows are placed by the system window manager so that they overlap each other in diagonally offset columns (Figure 10.1c). Like the overlapping style, cascading makes efficient use of screen real estate; however, it takes positioning and sizing control away from the user, and it can be disconcerting when the cascade is created.

> **MAXIM**
>
> Cascading windows use screen real estate efficiently and can be used to create visual organization.

Cascading files can be organized by file name, activation sequence, size, file type, or other characteristics. Therefore, this is an efficient way to organize the screen work space. Cascaded windows are activated when they are clicked on, bringing them to the top. However, after a user accesses various different windows, random overlapping can occur. This may cause some windows to become partially covered or entirely obscured by other windows (Figure 10.1d).

Minimized Windows—Windows that are not needed immediately but will be required later can be minimized. Minimized windows are reduced to small buttons or icons and placed in a special location on the desktop. They appear on the Task Bar in Microsoft Windows and the Dock in Mac OS X. For simplicity we will use the PC terms "task bar" and button. To bring these windows back, the user must click on the button, returning the window to its previous state, whether maximized or resizable.

Maximized Windows—Maximized windows occupy the entire screen, and each open application has a corresponding button in the task bar. This presentation style allows the user to see all of the window's content that fits within the screen, which depends on the screen resolution. The maximized presentation style is the easiest format in which to work, but drag-and-drop operations are not possible between programs.

Because a user cannot click on another program's window to make it the active window (it is completely covered by the active application's window), a method is needed to switch between programs. This is generally done by clicking the new application's button in the task bar. Other methods, such as the Alt/Tab method in Microsoft Windows, are not usually documented and generally have no visible indication of the functionality. They are, therefore, useless to the users who need them the most—beginners.

> **MAXIM**
>
> Maximized windows are visually less complex, but they require easy navigation methods to get from window to window.

The maximized presentation is the preferred format because it is visually less complex, it optimizes screen real estate, and users can switch between programs using the task bar. In addition, copy and paste operations between programs are relatively easy.

Window Components

Most windowing systems use standardized windows that look similar and behave consistently. Windows are generally populated with standard components that are located in prescribed locations. Although there are slight differences among systems, current windowing systems are very similar. Consistency of terminology, look, and placement is also standard within each particular system (Figure 10.2).

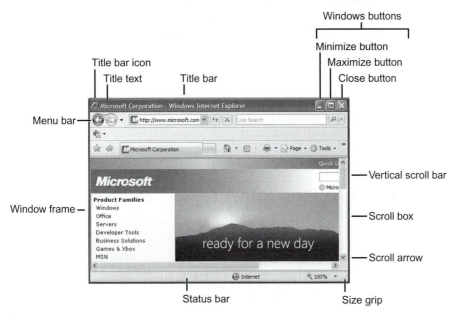

Windows buttons
Minimize button
Maximize button
Close button

Title bar icon
Title text   Title bar

Menu bar

Vertical scroll bar

Window frame

Scroll box

Scroll arrow

Status bar   Size grip

a

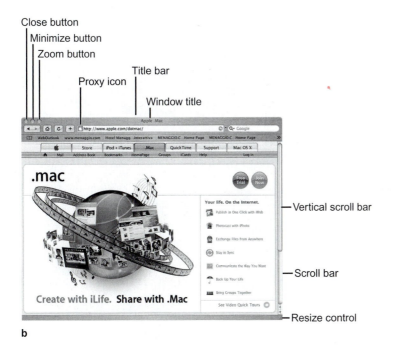

Close button
Minimize button
Zoom button
Proxy icon
Title bar
Window title

Vertical scroll bar

Scroll bar

Resize control

b

Figure 10.2 Typical windows. (a) Microsoft Windows XP. (b) Mac OS X.

Numerous possible components appear on windows depending on system states and window type. Figure 10.2a shows some of the more common window components found in the Microsoft Windows XP® and Mac OS X® operating systems.

Window Interfaces

When an application is launched, it opens a primary window. This window generally contains the basic window components mentioned previously, as well as other components, depending on the type of application. We discuss these other components in the sections on menus and components; now we explore a more fundamental issue. The application designer must decide whether the program will be application- or document-centric. This will determine which type of window interface will be used—multiple document, single document, controlled single document, tabbed, or detachable tabbed.

Multiple Document Interface

The multiple document interface (MDI) is application-centric. An MDI application launches a primary window that serves as the work space for all open documents. This interface has only one primary window, which can contain multiple instances of application documents each residing in a child window (Figure 10.3).

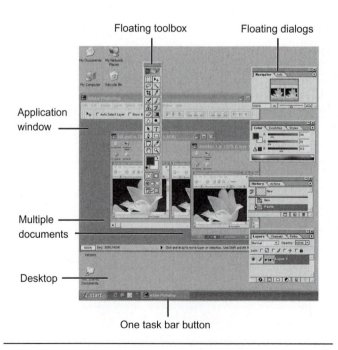

Figure 10.3   Multiple document interface—Adobe PhotoShop® application.

Adobe® product screen shot reprinted with permission from Adobe Systems Incorporated.

The child windows reside within the confines of the primary window and are visually constrained (clipped) by it. Other objects, such as dialogue boxes, are free floating and are not constrained by the primary window. The menus and toolbars are located on the primary window and pertain to all instances of application documents.

Window managers generally put one button on the task bar that represents the application no matter how many document windows are open. Therefore, switching between documents can only be done in the primary window by means of the window pull-down menu if the child windows are maximized. When the primary window is closed, all document instances close as well.

This type of interface conserves system resources because only one instance of the application runs at a time. This method was created to address the user's need to work on more than one document simultaneously at a time when computers had limited memory and processing resources.

Many existing applications use the MDI format. However, with the increases in computing power available to most users, its benefits in terms of system resource efficiency are outweighed by its deficits in usability. Novice and infrequent users can become confused if they have several applications open and each of those programs contains a few open documents. This can be especially confusing if the primary window allows resized child windows that can tile, overlap, or cascade.

Free-floating dialogue boxes that are not clipped by the primary window can add to the screen's visual complexity, especially if the primary window is resized and overlaps other windows. These dialogue boxes conflict with the concept of a coherent work space and might be mistakenly associated with other application's windows.

The following are some of the advantages of MDIs:

- They conserve system resources—there is only one instance of an application.
- They create minimal visual clutter—only one menu or toolbar is required for all documents.
- They provide a coordinated work space—all documents maximize, minimize, resize, and close simultaneously. (The system should remember window size and location when the application is closed.)
- They allow multiple documents to be simultaneously visible—Documents within the primary window can be minimized, maximized, tiled, cascaded, or overlapped.

The following are some of the disadvantages associated with MDIs:

- Menus change according to the state of the active document—This can be visually confusing and creates menu and tool bar inconsistencies. This can increase the learning curve, intensify the cognitive load, work against human memory limitations, and quickly become annoying.

- Document windows must remain within the MDI primary window—This eliminates the advantages of using multiple displays.
- Child windows can be minimized within the parent window—This increases the visual complexity of the screen, which may have other open parent windows.

Many of the operational benefits of the MDI are also available in the single document interface, which offers a less confusing visual environment. For this reason, the industry is migrating in that direction, a trend that Microsoft® (the moving force behind MDI) supports.

Single Document Interface

Single document interfaces (SDIs) are document-centric; they open new primary windows for each instance of an application document (Figure 10.4). This relates more to the user's point of view. A user is interested in the document that represents his or her work, not the application that is the tool that he or she uses to do the work.

Each primary window contains all of the program's menus and toolbars and is represented by a new button on the task bar. Each instance of the application can have only one instance of a document window. When an application instance is closed, only its child document window is closed; other instances of the application and their child document windows remain open.

Multiple primary windows

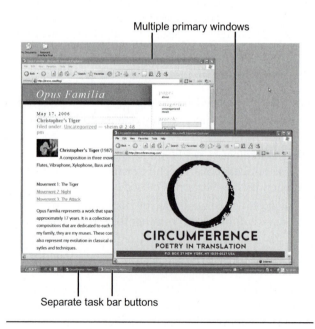

Separate task bar buttons

Figure 10.4   Single document interface—Microsoft Internet Explorer®.

This format is a more consistent than the MDI format because the tools and menus that pertain to a specific document remain the same for that document and do not change if the user works on another document. This creates consistency in menu and toolbar settings and a stronger connection between document and application.

The following are advantages of SDIs:

- They are document-centric—The menus and toolbars refer only to the one child document window; this reflects the user's point of view.
- They are less visually complex—The primary window and the document window are connected; they open, close, maximize, minimize, and resize together.

The following are some of the disadvantages of SDIs:

- They do not provide a way to group diverse but related document windows—Window managers generally group task bar entities by application.
- Related documents cannot be separated from other documents of the same file type—Task bar entities are arranged by the order in which they were created.
- The task bar can become full when too many documents are open—Window managers might group multiple document instances by application into a single pop-up entity that must be activated to see the available document instances.
- Cycling between windows can become difficult—This is an inherent problem in all windowing systems. Researchers are exploring novel ways to overcome this difficulty such as by using 3D and virtual reality interfaces.

The differences between MDIs and SDIs are becoming blurred. Some SDI applications now allow users to switch between documents using the task bar but also include a window menu that contains a list of all open documents. Some MDI applications create multiple task bar entities for each document instance.

In addition, the controlled single document interface (CSDI) is used for applications that manage multiple document windows that do not have menus or toolbars. CSDIs, like MDIs, have only one primary window. Unlike MDIs, the CSDI child windows do not reside within the primary window, and they have their own separate task bar buttons.

Tabbed Document Interface (Workbook)

MDI applications generally use a window menu that contains a list of open windows. This is used to switch between documents (as mentioned earlier, some also add a task bar entity for each document). A version of the MDI called the tabbed document interface (TDI) or workbook incorporates the use of tabs to switch between documents (Figure 10.5).

There a few different variation on the TDI format. Some TDIs fix all document windows in a maximized state, and, therefore, no tiling or overlapping is possible. Others allow documents to be resized and minimized, which removes the tabs and

Three open documents

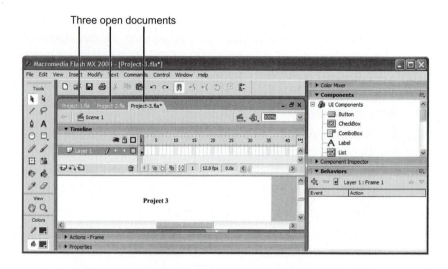

Figure 10.5 Tabbed document interface—Adobe Flash® application.

Adobe® product screen shot reprinted with permission from Adobe® Systems Incorporated.

makes the TDI behave exactly like an MDI. When any window is maximized, the tabs reappear for all the child windows.

Some TDIs allow the user to detach a tab and view it in a separate window. These are called detachable tabbed document interfaces (DTDIs), and they incorporate the best of the SDI and MDI formats. If the user wishes to group some documents, he or she can leave them in the parent window; he or she can detach others and move them to the side.

MAXIM

Tabs let users see which windows are open.

Tabs allow the user to always see which documents are open and to easily cycle through them without accessing the window menu. Tabs tend to reduce visual clutter, but they prohibit the user from seeing two documents side by side.

Dialogue Boxes (Dialogues)

MAXIM

Dialogue boxes provide a container for related, secondary functionality.

Dialogue boxes are a type of secondary window. They are used to support less common tasks and provide sets of related functionality in a well-defined

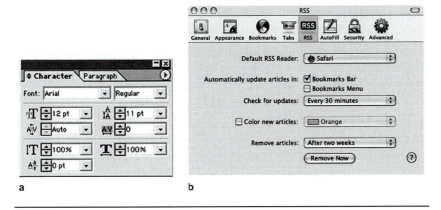

a   b

Figure 10.6 **(a) Text formatting dialogue—Windows XP. (b) Preferences dialogue—Mac OS X.**

container. Dialogue boxes range from simple alert boxes with a title, message, and OK button to more elaborate tabbed property boxes containing all the functionality relating to a specific task, such as text formatting and preferences dialogues (Figure 10.6).

Dialogue boxes can also be used to separate destructive, confusing, or infrequently used actions from tools that are used in the main work flow. Sometimes they are put up by the system to inform the user about a critical error or a potential problem. They can be removed by the user, or they can be removed automatically by the system after a certain amount of time.

Dialogues usually have title bars and close buttons, but they do not have title bar icons, status bars, or sizing buttons. They also do not have resize handles, and they cannot be resized by dragging the sides. There are no standards that govern the appearance of dialogues, only the components that may appear on them.

Modal/Modeless

Dialogues can be modal or modeless. Modal dialogues freeze the application to which they belong and prohibit the user from doing anything until he or she addresses the issues raised by the dialogue. This might simply mean clicking OK, or it might entail entering specific data the program needs to continue.

When these dialogues appear, the user can switch to another program, but if he or she tries to access other functionality within the same program, it will respond with a beep. Modal dialogues cause the user to stop his or her work and can cause a significant interruption in the normal work flow.

Modeless dialogues are not as common as modal dialogues. They are constructed much like modal dialogues, but the user can access all program functionality when the dialogue is visible. Although the sudden appearance of the dialogue may still be distracting, users are not frozen in their tracks; they can continue working. Users can even switch the particular object that will receive the parameter alterations made within the dialogue. This makes them behave more like floating tool pallets.

The dialogue is a powerful tool, especially if the user needs access to all the property controls that relate to a specific object. However, because dialogues float over the main window, they may obscure the information that is requested by the dialogue. If the dialogue is modal, the user might not be able to access this information.

All dialogues should be movable so that users can manipulate them to see what lies beneath. Recent versions of Mac OS have incorporated transparent dialogues, a development that alleviates this obfuscation problem to some degree.

Dialogues can be used for many different purposes, including the following:

- Setting and altering the properties of an object, such as table formatting in a word processing application.
- Executing a function such as Save (the Save dialogue will also contain some property components such as file name and type).
- Carrying out a process such as Copy (the dialogue gives the user an option of canceling the process; it shows the amount of time the process will take and exactly what process is taking place).
- Confirming actions.
- Alerting the user about errors and so on.

Expanding Dialogues

Some dialogues afford experienced users access to advanced functionality by clicking a button that expands the size of the dialogue and exposes other options. The button is generally labeled More and switches to Less when the dialogue is expanded (Figure 10.7).

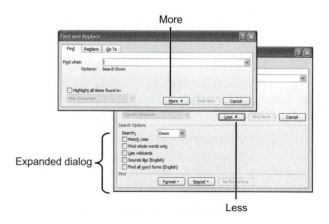

Figure 10.7 Expanding dialogue.

Concerns

Unlike modal dialogues, modeless dialogues do not have standard components or standard layouts. They often use different terminology either to dismiss the dialogue or to carry out actions. For example, they may use either Insert or Copy, both appropriate terms, although using both of them in a program will create inconsistencies and cause the user to spend time interpreting the label's meaning. Cooper and Reimann (2003) suggest that the traditional OK of modal dialogues should be used here as well, for the sake of consistency.

Even though modal dialogues behave differently than modeless dialogues, there is no real visual distinction between them. This can be confusing and annoying for users, who will have to test the dialogues to determine whether they are modal.

Panes, Frames, and Tabs

Complex applications use frames or panes to create areas of functionality within the primary window. This is most often found in MDIs and TDIs, though many SDIs use them for search, help, or other functionality. SDIs generally hide the panes until the user calls for them. MDIs usually open the primary window with a few of the most common panes visible by default.

> **MAXIM**
>
> Panes provide visual grouping for related functionality.

Panes are an efficient way to provide functionality required by other aspects of an application without forcing the user to leave the document window and navigate menus. Panes can be used to group related functionality, thereby providing a memory aid for the user (Figure 10.8).

Frames can be resized by dragging the splitters at their edges. They can also be minimized by double-clicking on their title bar. Frames are sometimes used in Web pages to create separate navigation areas for sites that are more application based, such as Microsoft Web Outlook®.

Although frames are supported by most contemporary browsers, their use is not recommended by many Web experts because they may cause problems with bookmarking, search engine indexing, and other navigational functions.

Another way to separate the components of a window is to use tabs. TDIs use tabs to keep track of different windows, whereas dialogues, especially those containing many elements, use tabs to group functions.

In a sense, tabs increase the size of the dialogue by stacking layers on top of each other and allow more elements to be accessed from one dialogue. Stacked tabs might cause problems because they move around to accommodate the different levels, and they destroy any location consistency on which the user might depend.

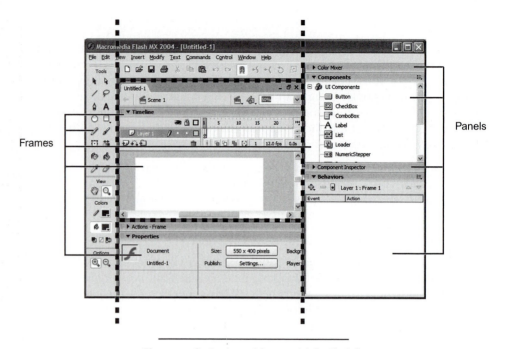

Figure 10.8 Panes and frames, Adobe Flash®.

Adobe® product screen shot reprinted with permission from Adobe® Systems Incorporated.

This becomes a problem when there is more than one row of tabs. When a tab in the back row is clicked, the entire row moves to the front, and the active tab presents its contents. The row that was previously in front now moves back. This shuffling can be visually disconcerting and decreases the dialogue's predictability and consistency (Figure 10.9).

Window Rationale

Windows can be understood as containers. For example, a document window contains the contents of the file. These might be text or graphic elements (dynamic or static) or any combination of the two. The primary application window might contain any number of these document windows as well as other components, such as panes, menus, or toolbars. The desktop can be thought of as a unique type of window that contains folder and application windows.

Windows hold content and can sometimes have nested containers. In this way, they are similar to Russian nesting dolls: the largest doll contains a smaller doll, which contains an even smaller doll, and so on.

This container nesting can be confusing to inexperienced users, especially when they have many applications running simultaneously, each with multiple open documents. Add to these applications a browser displaying a few linked Web

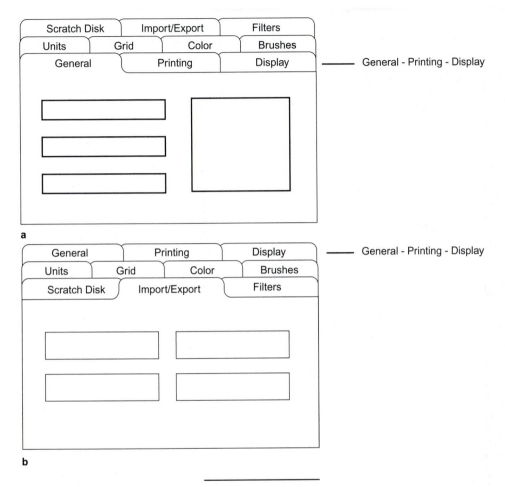

Figure 10.9 Tabbed dialogue.

pages with no obvious link trail, and the situation can quickly become difficult to overwhelming.

Windows are used to contain things, but what things and how many of these things should each window contain? Designers need to decide which type of interface to use (MDI, SDI, or TDI). They need to make sure that the window components are sufficiently related, and they must find the proper balance between having too many windows (each with only a few components and functions) and too few windows (each with an overwhelming amount of components and functions). This is often a question of depth versus breadth. We discuss this issue further in the Menus section. That discussion will apply to windows as well.

Some situations might require secondary windows that contain occasionally needed functionality. However, primary windows should contain all the functionality that is normally needed for work that is done within that window. For instance, basic text formatting tools are used frequently and should be available when a user is working in a text document window. More global functions such as kerning and leading, however, are used less frequently and can be allocated to a secondary window.

> **MAXIM**
>
> Secondary windows must address a discernible need.

Necessity is the mother of invention, and it can serve as a litmus test for the creation of a secondary window. We should only add a window if and when there is a need. Unnecessary windows can cause confusion and can add cumbersome window manipulation tasks (see the discussion on Ockham's razor in Chapter 6 for a supporting principle of design). However, crowded windows can also be confusing and time consuming for users who must stop and search through too many elements. This means that designers must weigh carefully the need for each element in a window and test the designs with objective subjects.

The following issues should be considered when designing secondary windows:

- Avoid window clutter.
- Windows should be created because of a need that cannot otherwise be filled.
- Window components must be related.
- Too many components in one window can be inefficient and confusing.
- Too many windows with little functionality can create needless window manipulation tasks.
- Tabs and/or panes can be used to organize window functionality.
- Frequently used components must be readily available.
- Less frequently used components can be placed in a secondary window.
- Windows must visually indicate activation state.

10.1.2. Icons

Icons are signs and represent a significant degree of cognitive complexity. They play an important role in direct manipulation interfaces, and if they are designed properly, they can enhance the user's experience. They can also run the risk of being obscure and ambiguous, creating confusion and frustration. See Chapter 11 for a detailed discussion of icons.

10.1.3. Menus

Menus are basically lists of options.

Menus afford access to system functionality; this functionality may execute immediately, or the selected menu option may lead to a dialogue containing groups of related functionality. Menus have titles that are always visible. These titles aid long-term memory. Once a menu is activated, its list of options provides further information as to what a user can access at that time.

The following list covers some of the issues involved in menu design:

- Menu option lists can consist of any type of data such as images or symbols, but text usually works best.
- Options are generally indented in relation to the title.
- Frequently used items should be placed at the top.
- These lists can be ordered or unordered.
- Ordered lists can have a separate section at the top for frequently used items that might normally appear near the bottom.

Menus afford easy access to system functionality; however, they require the user to shift focus away from the window in which he or she is working and move his or her hand from the keyboard to access a pointing device. This interruption in the work flow can be mitigated, to some degree, by the inclusion of keyboard shortcuts and keyboard accelerators. However, this depends on prior knowledge that may not be available to novices. Menu options are also smaller than icons or buttons and are more ̲ ̲ ̲ ̲ ̲ with a pointing device.

Standards

MAXIM

Designers s ̲ ̲ ̲ ̲ ̲ xpect.

Menus hav ̲ ̲ ̲ ̲ ̲ g environments. Their behavior, labeling ̲ ̲ ̲ ̲ ̲ andardized as well. People have become ̲ ̲ ̲ ̲ ̲ xpect to encounter them. Designers sho ̲ ̲ ̲ ̲ ̲ at will allow them easily to find the tools ̲ ̲ ̲ ̲ ̲

Although ̲ ̲ ̲ ̲ ̲ of an interface design with reference to t ̲ ̲ ̲ ̲ ̲ r experience, standard practices must als ̲ ̲ ̲ ̲ ̲ , a brief survey of standard menu practic ̲ ̲ ̲ ̲ ̲ of menu types.

Structure

- Menus s ̲ ̲ ̲ ̲ ̲ ise they should be combined with an ̲ ̲ ̲ ̲ ̲
- Menu o ̲ ̲ ̲ ̲ ̲ rs such as lines or backgrounds.
  - Op ̲ ̲ ̲ ̲ ̲ be isolated from other options.

Presentation

- Consistency in placement, order, wording, highlighting, and all other aspects should be maintained.
- Titles and options must be unambiguous.

- ○ Apple suggests using the standard menu titles and options because they are visually familiar and are used like icons.
- Options should be listed in Title Case.
- Options should visually include indications of function keys and keyboard accelerators. This is an opportunity for the designer to educate beginners about these more advanced features, and it can serve as a memory aid to others. Whenever possible, mnemonics should be used. Avoid conflicts with common system shortcuts.

Behavior

- Options should be highlighted when the pointer passes over them.
- Activated options should have a visual indication such as a check mark.
- If an option is not available, it should be made inaccessible and visually "grayed out."
  - ○ Inaccessible (grayed out) options should remain on the menu in their usual location. This promotes consistency and fosters a strong mental model.

Secondary Menus

- Menus can incorporate secondary, cascading menus to group related options. This simplifies decisions by limiting possible choices.
  - ○ However, secondary menus reduce option visibility. The user must search primary lists and sometimes use trial and error to find secondary menu options.
- Options that lead to secondary menus should have visual indicators.
  - ○ Options that lead to secondary menus should have a visual indication such as an arrow.
  - ○ Options that lead to secondary windows should use an ellipsis (three trailing dots).
- Menus can be detached and free floating or docked on the sides or bottom of the window.

  The following is a list of some of the standard menus used in contemporary GUIs:

- File
- Edit
- Window
- Help

  Some of the optional menus include the following:

- View
- Insert
- Format
- Tools

The File menu is usually located in the upper left-hand corner of an application, followed from left to right by the Edit, Window, and Help menus. If optional menus are used, they usually appear between the Edit and the Window menus. The File menu is used to group functions that relate to the document on which the user is working. Although the name "File" is very system oriented, it has become an industry standard, and many guidelines suggest using it because of its recognizable word shape.

The Edit menu groups the functions that work within the document, like cut and paste or find and replace. It can be argued that many formatting functions are similar to cut and paste operations and should be kept together under the Edit menu. Although an argument can be made for this decision, there may be numerous options that come under the heading of "format," which would argue for a separate Format menu so that they can be kept together. We will look at the issues involved in menu structure in the section on breadth and depth.

The Window menu is generally used to group functions that pertain to the application window. This menu might have options for window tiling or cascading, and might allow users to navigate between various documents that are open in different windows.

The Help menu is all too often a source of confusing and obtuse references to system functions and procedures. Its function is to allow users access to Help files and Help functionalities, such as the What's This? feature, which contains short explanations of interface elements such as buttons and icons.

Menu Titles

> **MAXIM**
>
> Menu titles must convey all the necessary information needed for a user to select one menu over another.

Menus have two essential elements—titles and options. These are both examples of instrumental text (see Chapter 12 for an in-depth discussion of interface text). Choosing an appropriate menu title is extremely important. The title must convey all the information needed to choose one menu over another.

The two most important characteristics of menu titles and options are as follows:

* Descriptiveness
* Consistency

Menu titles tell people what to expect when they access the menu; they teach the user about application functionality. The way in which we group functions into discrete menus communicates essential information about what specific functions do and at what level they operate. The user gets to see what other options are related and therefore gets a sense of the application's potential.

> **MAXIM**
>
> Menus are geared to novice users.

As an interaction style, menus are geared toward novice users. More experienced users gravitate to more efficient interaction styles, such as accelerator keys and keyboard shortcuts. They also make more use of the toolbars when they are available.

> **MAXIM**
>
> Menu titles should be unambiguously descriptive of the task.

Menus contain a great deal of information for the novice user. It is therefore essential that menu titles and options are clear and informative and that they do not use system terminology, but instead use terminology that is familiar to novice users and reflects their tasks.

These titles should be consistent across the various menu levels as well as across the diverse menus within a program. Consistency allows users to generalize concepts and phrase structures.

> **MAXIM**
>
> Use standard menu titles; they are recognized as icons, not words.

When we navigate with hyperlinks or choose a menu option, we relate to the words as visual elements rather than as text. This supports the Apple guideline that standard menu titles must be used because their word shapes function more like recognized icons than words.

Parallel Construction

> **MAXIM**
>
> Parallel construction can reduce cognitive load.

Parallel construction is a tool that should be used, whenever possible, to choose the wording for menu options and titles. If people can apply a preconceived structure to the wording of a menu option, it will save them time in understanding the option's implied functionality. They will also not have to spend energy and time reformulating the proper grammatical syntax for each item in the list.

For instance, a formatting menu might contain font styles such as bold and italic. When we read the menu we might think "make the selection bold" or "make the selection italic." If the menu options were worded "bold" and "italicize," we would have to mentally rephrase the command for each option by thinking "make the selection bold" and then "italicize the selection." We might opt instead to mentally reword the options to conform to a standard syntax. Either way, we expend more cognitive energy and our attention is momentarily shifted from our work to the interface itself, a situation that should be avoided whenever possible.

Menu Accelerators

Menu accelerators allow menu items to be accessed from the keyboard. This function is essential for visually impaired users and is highly suggested for experienced users.

Galitz (2002) suggests guidelines for menu accelerators:

- Supply a mnemonic for all menu items.
- Use the first character of the menu item's description.
  - In case of duplication use the first succeeding consonant.
- Underline the character in the menu.
- Use industry standards when available.

Mnemonics, or meaningful keyboard equivalents, will be easy for users to remember, which is why many guidelines suggest using the first character of the menu option as the menu accelerator. However, this may not always be advisable. Keyboard designs are not universal—many countries use different key configurations, and therefore many function keys, as well as some character keys, are located in different places on different keyboards.

This situation is further complicated by the need for keyboards to accommodate many different languages. The creation of a localized version of a program will likely require altering all of the keyboard accelerators to conform to the local language.

> **MAXIM**
>
> Use industry standards, when available, for keyboard accelerators.

To facilitate interface internationalization, del Galdo and Nielsen (1996) suggest that keyboard mnemonics be placed at fixed locations on the keyboard. That is, they should be consistently placed on the same physical keys regardless of the keyboard's language. These fixed locations would make it easier to create international user manuals for programs; mnemonics could be indicated by simply pointing to the keyboard keys.

For this reason, the cut, copy, and paste mnemonics are Control X, C, and V, respectively. The mnemonic for "copy" uses the first letter of the English-language word, but there is no such direct English-language reference in the commands for "cut" or "paste." These keys are also located in close proximity for ease of use (del Galdo & Nielsen, 1996).

Menu Bars

The menu bar, like the title bar and the Close and Minimize buttons, is a basic component that all windows must have. It is basically a menu of pull-down menu titles.

The menu bar is a menu of pull-down menus.

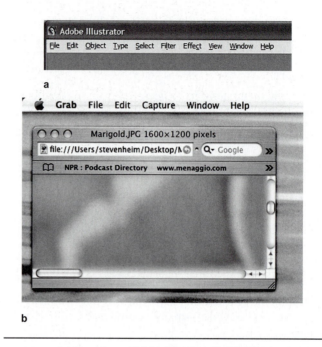

a

b

Figure 10.10   (a) Menu bar—Adobe Illustrator®. (b) Menu bar—Mac OS X.

Each heading in a menu bar represents a unique pull-down menu. It stretches across the top of the window just below the title bar (Microsoft Windows®).

Menu bars are used for common and frequently used functionality. The pull-down options generally do not execute functions; instead, they allow access to other components such as pop-up windows and property sheets.

Option labels, positions, groupings, and other aspects of menu bars have become standardized. Depending on the type of application, menu bars should have the following standard options, starting from left to right: File, Edit, View, and Window (Figure 10.10a). Mac menu bars are placed at the top of the desktop, as shown in Figure 10.10b.

They should also have a Help option, usually at the far right side of the window. Other options are added according to the requirements of the individual application, but they should not supplant these expected, standard options.

Pull-Downs

> Pull-downs are used for long lists of options.

Pull-down (drop-down) menus open a list of options when the user clicks on the title. They are an efficient way to provided lists of options and can be placed wherever they are needed. If they are used repeatedly, their position should be standardized.

Alternating options, such as redo and undo, can be used if their relationship is obvious and the list is very long (Figure 10.11). Otherwise, listing both options and

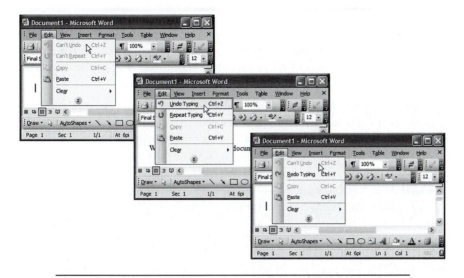

Figure 10.11 Pull-down menu with alternating options: Can't Undo/Undo Typing.

graying out the irrelevant one is preferable because it creates less confusion about the option's function and maintains consistency in list content. It also serves as a constant reminder of possible functionality.

Cascading Menus—Cascading menus are a type of pull-down menu (Figure 10.12). They can be difficult for beginners to operate because they require greater control of the pointer.

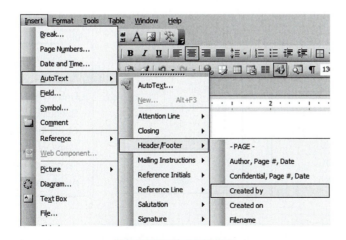

Figure 10.12 Cascading menu.

The more cascaded menus there are, the more difficult it becomes to remember where the secondary menus are located; there are no visual clues, only the abstract concept of functionality groups. These menus are efficient and can accommodate a large number of functions in a relatively small space, but due to their complexity and dexterity requirements, they should be left as a last resort.

Expanding Menus—A more recent development in menu structure is the expanding menu. The expanding menu reflects the most frequently used options; all other options are hidden. These hidden options can be accessed by hovering over, or clicking on, an arrow at the bottom of the menu.

> **MAXIM**
>
> Expanding menus make some information invisible.

Although they were meant to make the menu more user-friendly, this kind of menu decreases the visibility of the functionality, which is not good for novice users, who may not be aware of the functionality. They also provide an ever-changing list of menu items.

Each time a new option is chosen from the hidden options, it becomes visible the next time the menu is activated. This changes the list of visible items and alters their order within the menu because each option shifts to make room for the new option (Figure 10.13).

A better way to implement this type of interaction is to put the more frequently used functions in the toolbars, where they are always visible and can be easily accessed.

Menu-based interfaces are suited to novice users because they show all the functionality the application contains; expandable menus simply make some of that information invisible and are inconsistent.

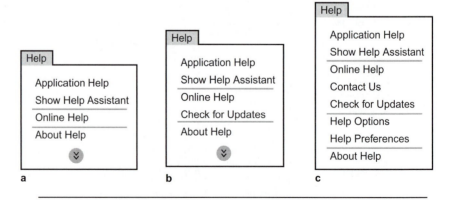

Figure 10.13 (a) Default condensed menu. (b) Menu after Check for Updates was selected (it appears in the second grouping). (c) Full menu.

Pop-ups

Pop-up menus are similar to pull-down menus, but they are not always visible. They offer context-sensitive options and are located within the work space. They are activated when the pointer is over a "hot spot" and sometimes require a specific mouse click, such as a right-click, to become active. They remain visible until the user either makes a selection or "clicks away" from the menu.

Pop-ups are used for context-sensitive lists.

Radio Buttons

Radio buttons are similar to list boxes (see the Other Components section later) that allow only single choices; however, all possible choices are always visible. Radio buttons toggle on, and are made active by, clicking directly on them. They toggle off when the user clicks on another button in the set. The set can have a default choice already selected or can be entirely nonactive (Figure 10.14).

Radio buttons represent implicit choices: if one button is pressed, it becomes active and the other buttons in the group either become, or remain, inactive. Through trial and error, the user can deduce which buttons belong to which group; however, the groupings of the radio buttons must be made explicit so the user can understand the scope of each group without having to waste time experimenting.

Radio buttons offer a set of mutually exclusive choices.

Figure 10.14 Radio buttons.

Checkboxes

Like radio buttons, checkboxes can have a default choice already selected or can be blank (Figure 10.15). They toggle on and off by clicking on them. They have no implicit function that can be observed by the user because they are designed to allow multiple choices. Therefore, it is imperative that some sort of explicit visual grouping be provided.

Checkboxes offer a limited set of non–mutuality exclusive choices that are always visible.

Menu Concerns

Menu bars are visually constrained by the width of the screen. This can become a problem for small devices, where screen real estate is at a premium. If many titles are needed, a second row can be added, but this is not recommended. Activating a

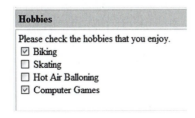

Figure 10.15 Checkboxes.

title in the top row will open a list that may obscure some of the titles in the second row. Pull-down menus also require a certain degree of fine motor coordination and can become difficult to navigate if they involve more than two cascading secondary levels.

There is no visual indication as to the presence of a pop-up menu; the user must be aware of its existence. This requires previous experience and adds to memory load. Therefore, pop-up menus must be used as a redundant feature. Advanced interface components and their functionality must be accessible by more visually obvious means or some users will never be aware of the functionality. Because they are located within the work space, they can also obscure other screen elements when they are activated.

Radio buttons and checkboxes should be horizontally and vertically aligned. They require explicit visual groupings like borders or backgrounds. They should have short, single-line labels or titles that are placed to the right of the component; however, this must be reversed for languages that read from right to left. There should be enough room between each component and label pair so that the label can be easily associated with the correct component.

10.1.4. Pointers

Pointers instigate actions and provide context-sensitive information about processes.

The pointer (cursor) is the visual manifestation of the mouse or pointing device and, as such, acts as the user's proxy in the virtual GUI environment. The pointer can be used to instigate actions, such as clicking buttons or making selections, but it can also visually communicate important information, such as system states, to the user.

> **MAXIM**
>
> Cursor hinting can help to inform the user about system states and functionality.

The pointer can change its appearance to indicate the presence of screen elements, such as a hyperlink or a section of editable text. Cooper and Reimann (2003) call this "cursor hinting" (Figure 10.16).

Most operating systems include multiple pointer images that can be used to convey specific information. These include the insertion bar, which indicates text insertion; the pointing finger image, which indicates a hyperlink; and a circle with a diagonal slash, which indicates an illegal operation. Pointer images are also used to

Figure 10.16 Cursor hinting.

give visual feedback about selection, resizing, progress, zooming, panning, the presence of context-sensitive help, and drag-and-drop and move operations.

> **MAXIM**
> The cursor will often fall within the user's foveal vision.

The pointer acts as the user's proxy and will therefore remain close to, if not be the focus of, the user's attention, and it generally falls within the user's foveal vision (the user's central area of visual focus). This is an optimal location for dynamic, context-sensitive information. It is, therefore, essential not to confuse the user with obtuse, nonstandard pointer images.

Pointer Concerns

One of the problems with cursor hinting is that the cursor manifests the state of the currently active program. For instance, in Windows XP, when a program is processing large amounts of data, the rotating hourglass cursor image appears. This informs the user about the progress of the operation. However, when the cursor is moved to another program that is not processing data, the cursor reverts to the image relevant for the new active program. This means that the user is no longer receiving information about the progress of the previous operation.

10.2. Other Components

Windows, icons, menus, and pointers are the main elements of a GUI; however, there are other components, and each has specific attributes that make it suitable for particular functions. The remaining components can be placed into one of five categories—lists, controls, display components, text entry components, and tool containers.

10.2.1. Lists

Some components offer an array of options, values, or properties from which the user can make a selection. Some are suitable for a small number of choices that are always visible. Others can hold more choices but hide some of them until the user interacts with the component.

Although these list components can be considered menus, they are more limited and do not represent functionality or dialogues. They can be found within dialogues and are used to choose from a set of values or properties that will be applied to a selected object when the user presses a related button control within the dialogue. Some applications include a preview control so the user can immediately see the result of his or her choice.

Listbox

Listboxes always have some options visible. The number of visible options depends on the vertical size of the box and is determined by the designer. They can contain

> A listbox is a single-level drop-down menu with a list of choices that never lead to further options.

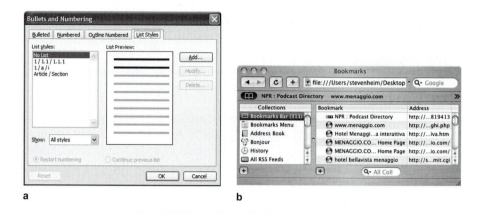

a   b

Figure 10.17   Listbox: (a) Windows XP, (b) Mac OS X.

mutually exclusive options, in which case they are similar to a group of radio buttons, or they can have options that are not mutually exclusive (multiple selection) and therefore resemble a list of checkboxes. Listboxes are more compact than either radio buttons or checkboxes and thus are advantageous for small screens (Figure 10.17).

Combobox

> Comboboxes are useful for long lists that may be cumbersome for scrolling.

A combobox is like a listbox that also includes a text box for search criteria (Figure 10.18). The user can select an option from the list or can enter text in the text box. As the user types into the text box, the list responds by automatically choosing the first option that matches the text being typed. Comboboxes can also contain spinners (see next paragraph).

Spinner

> The spinner contains a limited list of values that can be incremented or decremented using two arrows.

A spinner is a text box with two arrows, one pointing upward and one pointing downward (Figure 10.19). Users may also enter values directly into the text box. A default value is displayed until the user activates the spinner. These are appropriate for short lists of predetermined, discrete choices.

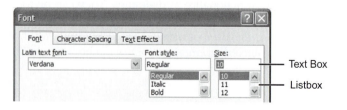

Figure 10.18   Combobox.

Figure 10.19 Spinner.

Slider

A slider is manipulated by moving an arm on a track either back and forth or upward and downward (Figure 10.20). A box might be included on the calibration scale to indicate the currently selected value. The box might also allow the text input of values that reposition the arm along the track accordingly.

A slider might also include a spinner that can either match the calibrated tics or have more finely calibrated values. The slider track might be filled as the user moves the arm to indicate the proportion of the scale that is being indicated.

A slider is a calibrated tool, such as a thermometer, that displays a continuum of values.

List Concerns

Lists and comboboxes make their first option visual by default or display the option that has previously been selected. Because some of these options might not help the user understand the list's function, lists must have descriptive labels associated

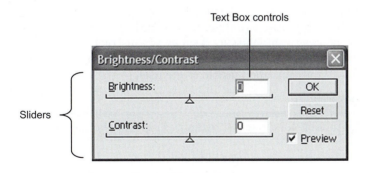

Figure 10.20 Slider.

with them. These labels are not inherently a part of the control and must be added by the designer.

> **MAXIM**
>
> Use listboxes and comboboxes for multiple options that do not fit on the screen.

Listboxes and comboboxes should be used instead of checkboxes or radio buttons when the number of choices is too large to fit efficiently on the screen. However, they hide some options, which the user must actively search the list to locate.

The spinner also hides some of the list items, and, because it is generally used to present a list of calibrated values, users may not be aware of the ordering system or the incremental values until it is activated. Sliders alleviate this problem by visually showing the entire range of values as well as the increment units if they are not positioned too close together.

The slider, however, can only be used with a continuum of minimal range because the entire continuum must fit on the screen. The range of a spinner is not restricted, but it should not be too large; otherwise the user may lose orientation.

> **MAXIM**
>
> Calibration values used in lists should be alterable.

List components contain a fixed set of options that cannot be changed by the user and are therefore not very flexible. However, users might need to change the entire set so that it conforms to a different standard; for example, the user may want to shift from degrees Fahrenheit to degrees Celsius or from miles to kilometers. Therefore, the calibrated values should be alterable. This may require additional controls to make the translation visible to the user.

> **MAXIM**
>
> Lists are suitable for groups with a limited number of options.

List components expose all possible choices; however, they also require significant amounts of screen real estate. This makes them suitable only for groups with a limited number of options.

10.2.2. Controls

Control components execute functions immediately.

The most common control component is the button. Buttons are generally rectilinear objects that are rendered with a 3D look and appear to become depressed when the user clicks on them. This is accomplished through shading and a subtle shifting of the button label.

The light source is assumed to be coming from over the user's left shoulder. This is a standard and should not be altered or some users may become confused and make incorrect assumptions about the state of the interface.

Figure 10.21
Command buttons.

Command Buttons

A command button is a common type of button control that incorporates a short text label on the face of a button such as the Submit and Reset buttons illustrated in Figure 10.21.

Command buttons can be placed in many different locations and can be used for multiple functions The OK and Cancel buttons found at standard locations in dialogues and message boxes are common examples of command buttons.

> Command buttons have short labels and a 3D appearance.

Toolbar Buttons

Toolbar buttons are found on toolbars and can be visually grouped by line separators or backgrounds. Recent versions of toolbars contain what Cooper refers to as butcons. These are icons that act like buttons. In their normal state, they look like icons; when the user passes the cursor over the icon, however, it is highlighted and assumes a square, outlined appearance. When the user clicks, it appears to press in and down like a command button.

> Toolbar buttons function like command buttons, but they have icons instead of labels and often do not have a 3D appearance.

A toolbar button might also have an associated drop-down toolbar that contains variations on the tool being represented. For instance, a painting program might have a paintbrush toolbar button with an associated drop-down that includes other brush shapes or brush types. Once the user selects one of the alternate choices, that icon is displayed and the drop-down disappears (Figure 10.22).

The presence of the drop-down is indicated by a small arrow on the side or bottom-right corner of the toolbar button. The drop-down might appear below or to the right of the button. It is fixed in place until the user makes a selection, and then it disappears. These drop-downs allow users to make immediate changes to the tools in the toolbar without having to leave the toolbar to access and manipulate other menus or dialogues.

Hyperlinks

Hyperlinks are considered control components because they perform actions immediately, but they do not visually resemble anything in the real world. The original manifestation of a hyperlink was a string of blue underlined text. That is changing with the adoption of cascading style sheets, which give Web designers more control over the look of hyperlinks.

> Hyperlinks are used to navigate between and within documents (usually Web pages).

Control Concerns

Toolbar buttons use icons instead of text labels and are subject to all of the issues involved in the comprehension of visual imagery and signs. Once the images are

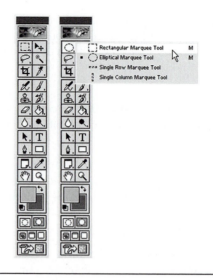

Figure 10.22   Toolbar buttons—Adobe PhotoShop®.

Adobe® product screen shot reprinted with permission from Adobe Systems Incorporated.

learned, they can be used and generally communicate efficiently. However, they can easily be misunderstood or even incomprehensible. (See Chapter 11 for a discussion of icons.)

The drop-down menus associated with toolbar buttons are hidden, and their existence must therefore be known and remembered. They also require fine motor coordination and can be difficult to manipulate with a pointing device. They are not suitable for beginners or users with certain types of disabilities.

Web design experts often discourage the alteration of hyperlink appearance because the blue underlined text is a familiar standard and clearly indicates the presence of a link. However, altered links are becoming common, and designers are becoming adept at creating easily identifiable alternative visual indications. It is extremely important to be consistent with custom styles so that users do not have to guess about the existence of a link and are not fooled by text that is simply formatted differently. (See Chapter 12 for a discussion of hypertext.)

10.2.3. Display Components

Some components are used to alter screen configurations so that more information can be made accessible. They might be commonly used components, such as the scrollbar, or more obscure components, such as the window splitter. Other components, such as the Maximize and Close buttons, also affect the appearance of the screen, but these function like other buttons and therefore belong in the controls category. The components we look at here are more idiosyncratic and do not function like other components.

Scrollbars

Scrollbars are an unfortunate necessity in windowing environments. Windows can be too small to show all of the necessary content, especially in word processing files that contain multiple pages. There are ways to view the contents of long documents besides scrolling, such as using the Home and End buttons or arrow keys; these are generally coarser in their actions, however, moving through large sections of the text at each press. They do not allow for fine-scale manipulation of the file such as moving line by line.

Scrollbars are used to move within long documents (by line, page, section, and so on).

The scrollbar was designed for, and is uniquely suited to, fine-scale navigation of long text documents or large graphic files. It is also an integral part of list components that have multiple list options.

The scrollbar comprises a track that houses a thumb that can be dragged back and forth or upward and downward with the cursor. It also has two arrow keys that can control the thumb's position. The user can also click any location within the track and the thumb will move to that position.

The position of the thumb within the track indicates the user's relative location within the document. The size of the thumb in relation to the track reflects the length of the document. When the user clicks the thumb, a pop-up can be used to specify the exact page number, which can be updated as the user scrolls through the document.

Scrollbars are usually positioned on the right side or bottom of a window, away from the actual screen content. When a scrollbar is placed on the bottom, it is usually located above the status bar and sometimes above some toolbars. Side scrollbars may have a few "dead" pixels on the very edge of the screen that do not respond to click events.

Splitters

Splitters are not often visible; the user must know that they exist, and so they are not appropriate for beginners (Figure 10.23). They use cursor hinting to make their functionality visible.

Splitters are used to segment widows into separate panes.

Display Component Concerns

Scrollbars are manipulated by the cursor; therefore, to use them, users must lift one hand off the keyboard to access a pointing device. This causes an interruption in the work flow, which is especially detrimental for keyboard-intensive tasks. Scrollbar manipulation also requires a degree of fine motor coordination.

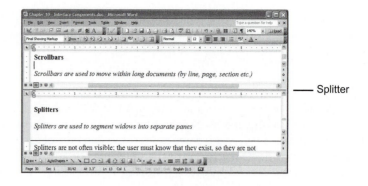

— Splitter

Figure 10.23   Splitter.

To manipulate a scrollbar, the user must access the thumb or arrows, which can be small at high screen resolutions. Scrolling quickly becomes an exercise in arrow targeting or thumb sliding, which can become tedious. One solution to this difficulty is the scrollable mouse (a mouse with a scroll wheel between the mouse buttons). The document scrolls as the user rotates this wheel. This is appropriate for accurate short-distance scrolling but can become tedious for long documents. Grabbing the thumb with the cursor and dragging it is still the fastest way to scroll to distant locations within a document.

Windows are sometimes too small to show the entire horizontal contents of the document. In this case, the window manager places horizontal scrollbars at the bottom of the window. Horizontal scrollbars are inefficient because the user must constantly scroll back and forth to read consecutive lines.

10.2.4. Text Entry Components

Users often need to enter alphanumeric data. They might need to fill in information on a Web form, such as their name and address, or they might need to set the value of a property in an application, such as the number of columns in a table. The main component for text entry is the text box. It can be used alone, or it can be part of a complex component such as a combobox or slider.

Text Boxes

A text box should be used when there is a need to gather small, discrete amounts of information.

A text box is a single-line box of designer-determined length that can accept a considerable number of characters (Figure 10.24). If the number of characters is greater than the width of the box, the extra characters will be hidden, but can be accessed with the arrow keys or by dragging the cursor to the right.

To use a text box, the user must first select it by clicking on it it, at which point the text box displays a flashing insertion bar. It is highly recommended that tab indices be included for the components of a Web form so that users can easily tab from one input component to the next. Most users also appreciate having the focus on the first input component.

Figure 10.24 Text box and text field.

Text Field

Text fields behave similarly to text boxes when text is entered, but when the end of the visible line is reached, the text wraps to the next line. If there are more lines than the height of the field will accommodate, a vertical scroll bar appears on the right side.

> Text fields are multiline text boxes and are used to collect paragraph-length text.

Text Entry Concerns

Text boxes do not have built-in indications of their purpose or allowable input. Therefore, labels or captions are required. Hinting can also be used to instruct users about acceptable formatting, for example, with date or currency notations.

Bounded/Unbounded and Validation

Some text boxes allow the user to type anything (unbounded); others restrict the user to a predetermined set of data (bounded). If a control requires data from a restricted set—such as font names, zoom percentages, or RGB values—there is a potential for the user to make an invalid entry. Invalid data can cause significant problems, especially in mission-critical situations.

In an ideal world, all users would be aware of the required data type and the restrictions on possible values, if any. In the real world, this will not always be the case, so the designer must try to educate the user about the required input. Clearly articulated labels and captions that are visually connected to a particular entry box can be used, as well as examples of the kind of input or format required.

Text entry boxes that require a specific number of characters, such as a Zip or postal code, can be set to accept only the maximum number of characters; further typing will have no effect. However, even if text entry components have clear labels and captions explaining their requirements, the user can easily ignore them or not read them carefully enough.

Figure 10.25   Toolbar.

It is never beneficial to allow the user to enter invalid data. Data entry should be carefully validated at the point of entry, where it can most easily be altered and corrected. If there are any validation issues, the form should be returned to the user with indications of the invalid fields. These indications can be red exclamation marks with a brief description of the problem and an example of what a valid entry might look like. It is important in this situation to maintain the valid information that the user has already entered so that he or she does not have to enter it again.

> Toolbars contain buttons or icons for an application's common functions and are generally found at the top or bottom of the primary window.

10.2.5. Tool Containers

Tool containers float above the primary window. They do not have explicit controls, however, such as "open" or "maximize" buttons. They are used to group a set of tools together. Many are reconfigurable, allowing the user to add and remove tools. Some tool containers can be docked on the side of the primary window or can be "torn off" and allowed to float.

> Tool palettes also contain tools for the most common application functions.

Toolbars

There are generally a few default toolbars that appear when an application is launched; these can be turned off, and other toolbars can be added by the user. This is usually done using the View menu.

Toolbars are normally found in a docked state. That is, they attach to the sides, top, or bottom of the primary window and form a single line of icons bordering the window (Figure 10.25). They can sometimes be torn away from the border and made to float over the primary window. In this state they can be resized to form a rectilinear shape with multiple rows and columns of tools.

Figure 10.26   Tool palette.

Tool Palettes

Tool palettes differ from toolbars in that they generally float over the primary window (Figure 10.26). Some tool palettes are dockable, although when they attach to the sides of the window they do not lose their shape. With the appearance of resizable, tear-off toolbars, there is little difference between toolbars and tool palettes, except their default state and the way in which toolbars conform to horizontal rows or vertical columns when they are docked.

Design Scenario

Circumference: Web Form

We will now create a form for the *Circumference* Web site so that people can subscribe to the journal and a survey form to find out more about the site's visitors.
   The activities in this design scenario include the following:

- Creating Usability Guidelines for forms

- Determining the contents of a form

- Organizing the contents

- Choosing the proper components

    ◦ Radio buttons

    ◦ Checkboxes

    ◦ Text boxes

    ◦ Text areas

    ◦ Command buttons

    ◦ Drop-down menus

    ◦ List box (multiple-selection drop-down)

- Reviewing Design principles

- Ensuring accessibility

- The visitor will be shown how many pages are involved and where he or she is in the process.

Usability Guidelines

- The tab index attribute will be used to make sure that people easily can tab from component to component efficiently.

- Components will be horizontally and vertically aligned.

- Components will be clearly labeled.

- Components will be grouped logically.

Determining the Contents

First we need to list and categorize the products we have to offer:

- One-year or two-year subscriptions
- Individual issue purchases
- Donations (this is a not-for-profit organization)

    ◦ Hero level

    ◦ Friend level

Design Scenario (cont.)

Organizing the Contents

Next we need to list and categorize the information required to order a subscription:

- Shopping cart information
    - Purchase item/s
    - Purchase quantities
    - Price

- Customer information
    - Name
    - Address (mailing address)
    - Telephone number
    - E-mail address

- Shipping information
    - New
    - Same as purchase information

- Payment information
    - Credit card information
    - Currency

- Donation information
    - Tax-exemption and sponsorship information

- Miscellaneous information
    - Additional information that the subscriber might want to send to the journal.

Choosing the Proper Components

Before we choose the components we must understand the nature of the objects represented by the form components and the relationships between these objects. Let's begin by analyzing the products on the Subscription page and then identify the appropriate from components.

Subscription Page—The subscription page is where visitors go to select the products they wish to purchase. When the visitor selects a product, it is placed in the shopping cart.

- One- and two-year subscriptions (two and four issues, respectively) are mutually exclusive choices.

- The latest issue is part of either subscription package, and so it is mutually exclusive with either subscription; however, there is also the possibility of just ordering

Design Scenario (cont.)

the latest issue. This can lead to confusion, and the situation must be clearly communicated to the user. We address this issue later.

- Individual back issues are not mutually exclusive.
- Donations include subscriptions, which makes them mutually exclusive with the subscriptions; this must be clearly indicated.

  ◦ Hero level ($100 and up) gets a two-year subscription with a $90 tax deduction.
  ◦ Friend level ($40 to $99) gets a one-year subscription with a $30 tax deduction.

The following products form a group of mutually exclusive choices and should be listed with radio buttons:

- Hero (four issues including Issue 4) plus tax deduction
- Friend (two issues including Issue 4) plus tax deduction
- Two-year subscription (four issues including Issue 4)
- One-year subscription (two issues including Issue 4)
- Issue 4

The back orders are the only non–mutually exclusive products, and, therefore, they should be kept separate from the other choices and listed with checkboxes.

The flowchart for the order form is shown in Figure 10.27. Using the wireframe developed in Chapter 5 and shown here in Figure 10.28, we end up with the form in Figure 10.29.

Reviewing Design Principles

There are many design principles involved in the design of the Circumference forms. Let's look at some of them. We begin with the "Subscribe" form:

Design Principles: Logical Grouping, Similarity, Proximity—There are two logical groupings that are created by the visual aspects of this screen—Subscriptions and Back Issues. The mutually exclusive radio buttons are grouped by similarity and proximity, as are the multiple-choice checkboxes.

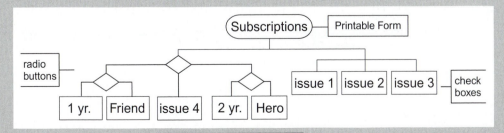

Figure 10.27 Subscription flowchart.

Design Scenario (cont.)

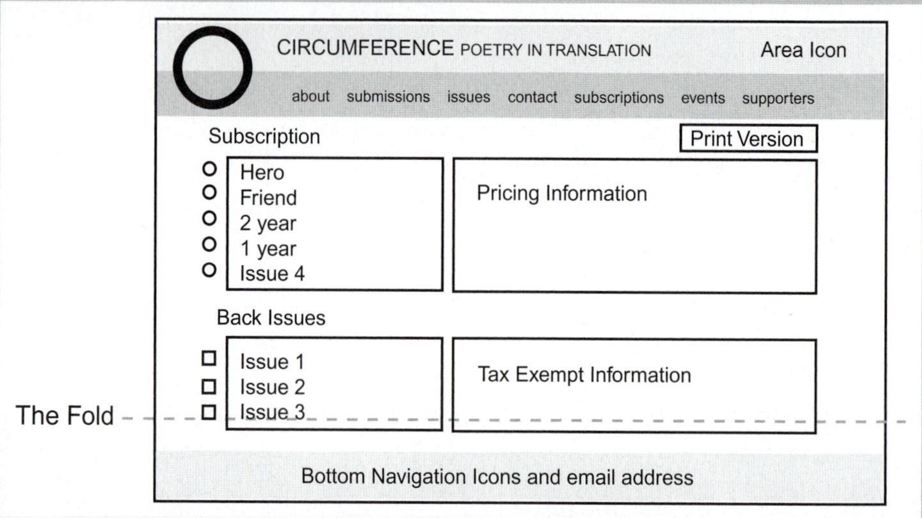

Figure 10.28   Order form wireframe.

Design Principles: Surroundedness, Area—The background colors are manipulated to make the white area that contains the labels for the radio buttons and checkboxes form logical groups. The smallness of the white area causes it to become the figure; the darker color becomes the ground. Therefore the eye is drawn to the more important information.

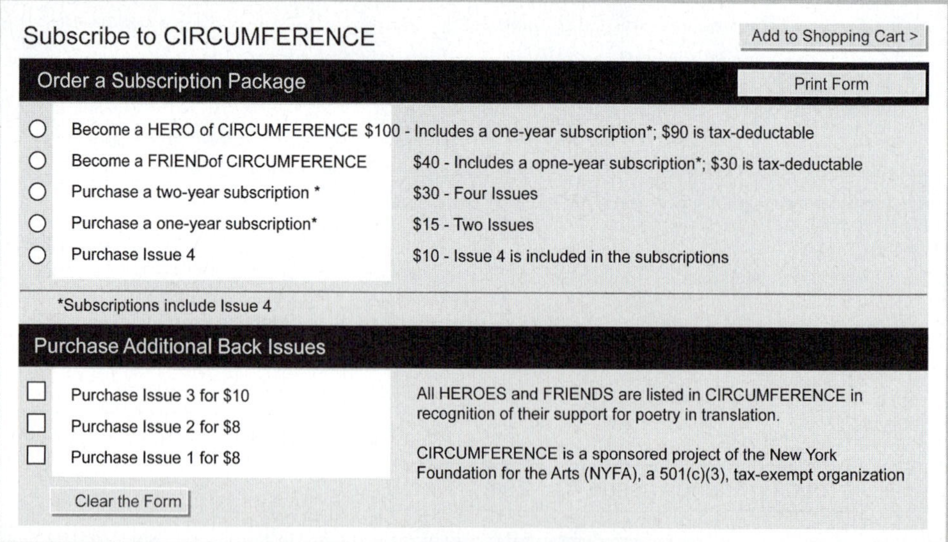

Figure 10.29   *Circumference* subscription form.

Design Scenario (cont.)

Design Principles: Common Fate, Screen Complexity—The form elements are placed on the left of each element's label and lined up vertically. The dollar values are also vertically aligned and right-justified. The use of a grid for the screen layout decreases the visual complexity of the screen.

Design Principle: Visibility—The different sections of the form are labeled and clearly delineated. The fact that Issue 4 is included in the subscriptions is clearly presented. This is important for people who are interested in the subscriptions as well as for people who are interested only in Issue 4.

Design Principle: Safety—There are two command buttons on the form that will either clear the form or add the selected items to the shopping cart. They are separated on the form. This will help to avoid any mistaken destructive actions by the user.

Design Principles: Feedback, Resolution, Recognition—After the products are place in the shopping cart the visitor should see a summary of his or her purchase and be given the option of returning to the site, altering the purchase, or proceeding with the checkout. This summary of supplies important feedback to the customer informing him or her that the order was registered successfully and provides resolution to that activity. It also shows the customer the details of the order so that he or she will not have to remember what was ordered in case he or she wants to make additional purchases.

Design Principle: Flexibility—The visitor is offered a few options after the order is placed in the shopping cart that increases the flexibility of the site.

If the visitor decides to proceed with the checkout, the rest of the information must be gathered. Let's now look at the check out forms.

Design Principles: Screen Complexity, Progressive Disclosure—The checkout process can be completed on one page that would require scrolling or on a few pages. We choose the paging format for this example. This choice limits the number of elements on each page and presents a less complex screen. It also avoids the possibility of overwhelming the customer with many questions all at once. The scrolling format would contain the same form elements and labels but not the navigation between the pages of the form.

The check out process is divided into three pages:

- We collect:

    ◦ The visitor's name, address, and contact information.
    ◦ The shipping information.
    ◦ The payment information.

- We then ask whether the visitor wants to make a donation or send any miscellaneous information to the editors.

Design Scenario (cont.)

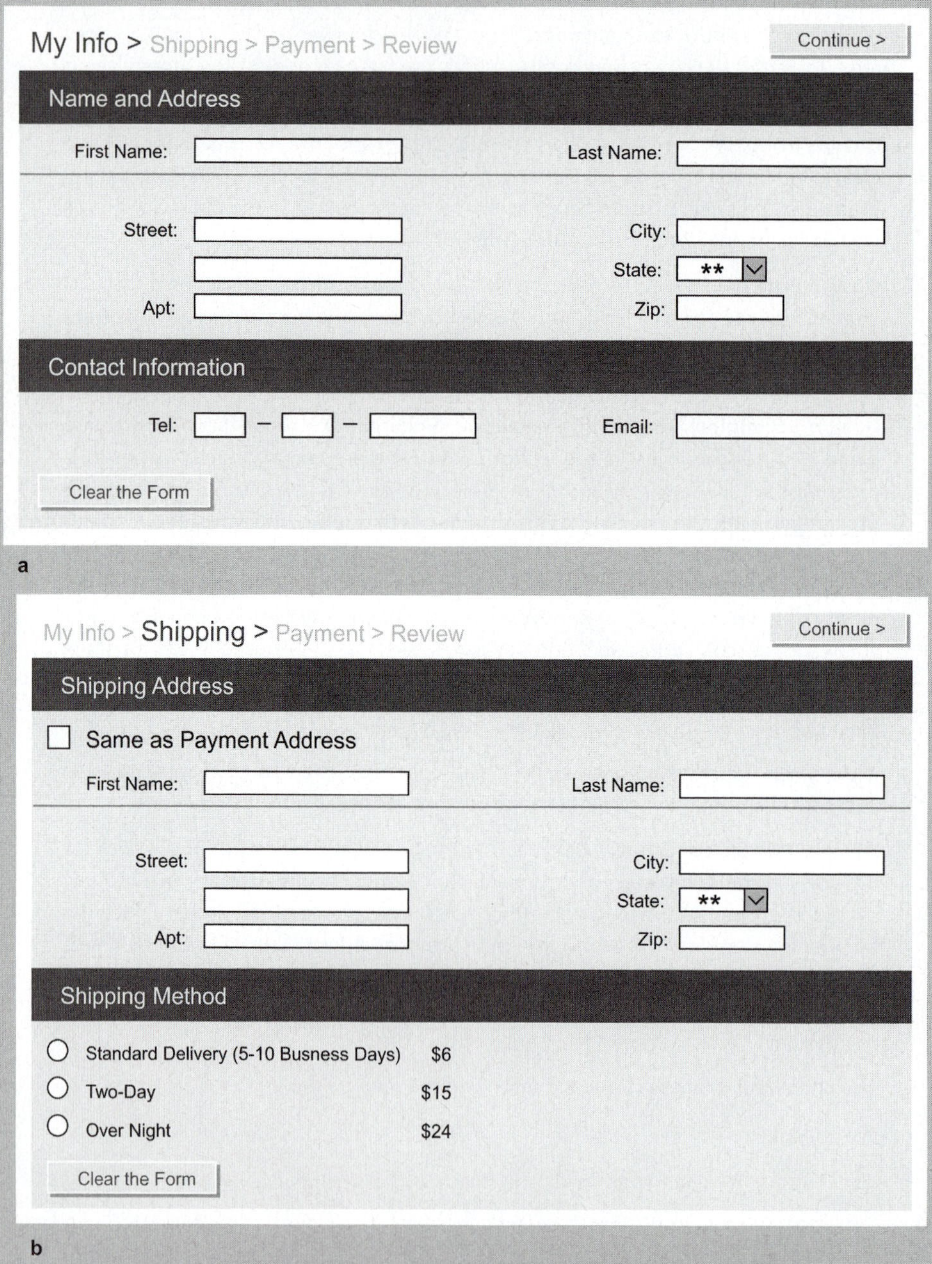

a

b

Figure 10.30   *Circumference* order form: (a) page 1 and (b) page 2.

Design Scenario (cont.)

- We then present all the information to the visitor and allows him or her to either change some information or submit the order.

The My Info page captures the name, address, and contact information (Figure 10.30).

Design Principle: Affordance—The State information is a long list of state names that a drop-down menu can handle easily, which is a conventional way to collect these data.

Design Principle: Safety—The Zip code input box is sized and restricted to five characters. The telephone number is divided into three sections that restrict the number of characters to three, three, and four, respectively.

Design Principle: Consistency—The shipping information form is similar to the payment form (this makes the form visually consistent and, therefore, more efficient) with the additional option of a Same as Payment Address checkbox, the omission of the contact information, and the addition of the Shipping Method radio buttons.

Design Principles: Orientation, Visibility, Feedback—Notice the "bread crumb" trail at the top of the form that lets the customer know how many pages there are and where he or she is in the process.

To complete the process there will be a payment page and a review page. The payment page offers mutually exclusive options for various types of credit cards (small icons of the cards aid the user) and some text boxes for the person's name and the credit card number. The credit card text boxes can be divided into groups of numbers with restrictions on the number of input characters, similar to the phone number input boxes.

The final page shows all of the options and information input by the visitor as well as buttons that allow alteration on the order and a text area for additional information the visitor might want to send to the editors of the journal.

A page is then sent to the browser confirming the receipt of the offer and telling the visitor that a confirmation e-mail will be sent. A nice feature would be a link to a printer-friendly version of the confirmation screen.

Design Principle: Flexibility—This can be accomplished by creating another page, linking to a PDF version of the form, or alternatively the CSS for the confirmation page can use the media attribute to identify an appropriate style sheet for printing.

We will want to gather some information about the visitors to the site so that we can gain a better understanding of their needs and preferences. This will be accomplished using a user survey page. Let's now look at how that survey is constructed.

The survey form has two parts (Figure 10.31). The first part asks how the visitor heard about *Circumference*. This helps us to determine the success of the various publicity outlets in which the journal has invested. There are currently three possible

Design Scenario (cont.)

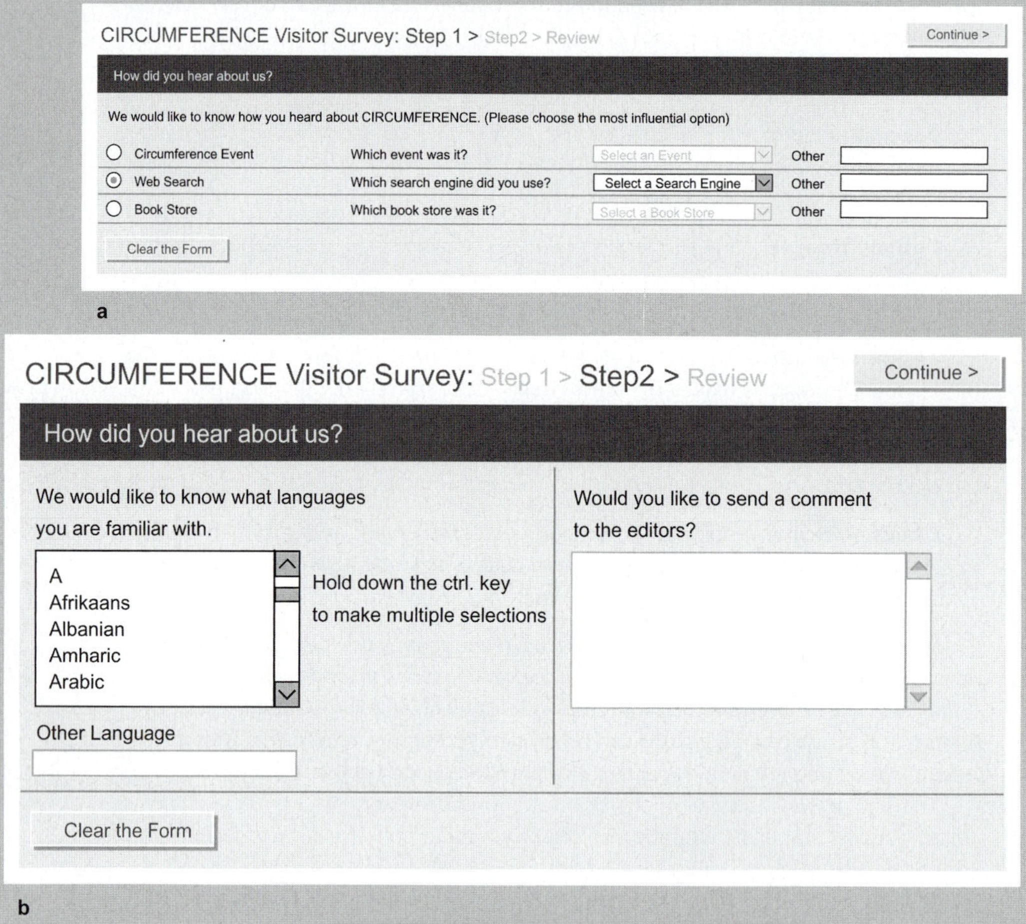

CIRCUMFERENCE Visitor Survey: Step 1 > Step2 > Review   Continue >

How did you hear about us?

We would like to know how you heard about CIRCUMFERENCE. (Please choose the most influential option)

○ Circumference Event	Which event was it?	Select an Event ▾	Other [ ]
◉ Web Search	Which search engine did you use?	Select a Search Engine ▾	Other [ ]
○ Book Store	Which book store was it?	Select a Book Store ▾	Other [ ]

Clear the Form

a

CIRCUMFERENCE Visitor Survey: Step 1 > **Step2** > Review   Continue >

How did you hear about us?

We would like to know what languages you are familiar with.

| A |
| Afrikaans |
| Albanian |
| Amharic |
| Arabic |

Hold down the ctrl. key to make multiple selections

Would you like to send a comment to the editors?

Other Language
[ ]

Clear the Form

b

Figure 10.31   Visual survey form. (a) Part 1, (b) part 2.

choices—*Circumference* events, Web searches, and book stores. These may or may not be mutually exclusive choices; a visitor might have heard about *Circumference* in a number of ways, so we ask for the most influential option, and therefore the choices are mutually exclusive and should be rendered with radio buttons.

We also need to know which event, search engine, or book store. These choices are presented with a drop-down so the visitor can just select one of the options that are of significance to the journal. Notice the extra instructions in the drop-downs (Select a Search Engine, and so on). We might also want to give the visitor the chance to enter an option that was not included in the drop-downs; this requires a text box.

Data integrity is an important concern; we do not want to get invalid information. For example, the visitor may choose Web Search and then a book store from the

Design Scenario (cont.)

Book Store drop-down. This can happen for a number of different reasons, and it will be problematic when we assess the results.

Design Principles: Safety, Feedback, Progressive Disclosure—To keep the data clean, we disable the drop-down menus until the visitor chooses the associated radio button; this can be seen in the grayed-out look of the Event and Book Store drop-downs in Figure 10.31a.

Part 2 of the survey collects information about the visitor. Due to the multilingual aspect of the site, we would like to determine the languages with which our visitors are familiar. This can be collected by letting the visitor write in the languages they know, but that may involve typos and other anomalies.

A list box is appropriate, but they are not available, as such, in the markup language. We can cause a drop-down menu to act like a list box, however, with the following code:

```
<select size = "5" multiple>
```

Design Principles: Affordance, Visibility, Customizability—The "multiple" attribute allows people to make multiple selections using the ctrl key combination. The "size" attribute holds the drop-down open, exposing the specified number of options. In case we have missed any languages, we have also included a text box for additional entries.

Ensuring Accessibility

One final concern for the forms is making them accessible to an audible browser like IBM's Home Page Reader®. Let's look at some of the guidelines for accessible Web forms:

- Text prompts for select menus, text areas, or text fields must be placed to the left of or above the component within the same table cell, or, if that is not possible, the prompt should be placed in the cell to the left of the component.
- Text prompts for radio buttons or checkboxes should be placed to the right of the component within the same table cell or in the next cell to the right.
- Home Page Reader will read the value attribute of a button or, if that is absent, it will read the type attribute's value
- Use the "label" element with the "for" attribute to explicitly associate a text prompt with a form component.

Home Page Reader will have a problem with the phone number text boxes in the checkout form. There is no obvious way to explicitly associate all three boxes with the text prompt. The current version of Home Page Reader reads the title attribute of an input element; it is highly recommended to include it in all the input components.

Summary

Much of the work that interaction designers do involves GUI design. It is the most common interaction style, and there are many tools that facilitate rapid GUI development. GUIs already have an extensive set of standardized screen components, including menus, buttons, and windows, to name a few. Each component is suited for specific tasks and should be used accordingly.

Improper use of screen components can make it harder for people to accomplish their tasks. People have expectations and base many of their actions on logical assumptions. You must study the user's tasks and make sure that the interface supplies the proper controls at the proper time.

Standardization has made it easier to construct complex interaction designs in a short amount of time, and that has lead to the development of more usable interfaces; however, this has also created the impression that the current face of most interaction designs, the GUI, is the only possible one.

You must learn the standard practices and become familiar enough with them to apply them instinctively. However, if Bush, Engelbart, and Sutherland had not pursued alternate ways of doing things, we would not be where we are today. Innovation is at the heart of interaction design and it should not be stifled by standardized practices.

Resources on the Web

www.aw.com/heim
You will find links to the various user interface guidelines for some of the more popular user interfaces such as Microsoft Windows and Apple's OS X as well as some of the less common and some experimental user interfaces.

Suggested Reading

Abascal, J., & Nicolle, C. (Eds.). (2001). *Inclusive Design Guidelines for HCI* (1 ed.): CRC.

Cooper, A., & Reimann, R. M. (2003). *About Face 2.0: The Essentials of User Interface Design* (1 ed.): John Wiley & Sons.

Galitz, W. O. (2002). *The Essential Guide to User Interface Design* (2 ed.): Wiley.

Norman, K. (1991). *The Psychology of Menu Selection: Designing Cognitive Control at the Human/Computer Interface*: Ablex Publishing Corporation.

CHAPTER

11

Icons

As noted in chapter 10, a graphical user interface (GUI) is also called a WIMP interface because it is made up of windows, icons, menus, and pointers. One of the most important components of a GUI is the icon. Icons are small images that are used to represent objects, such as files and folders, or functionality, such as printing or copy/paste operations. They can represent object attributes such as colors or gradient fills, as in paint programs. Icons can also be used to convey critical system warnings and errors.

Screen technology has advanced to the point at which high-quality visual displays are not only possible, they are also inexpensive enough to be used in common digital appliances such as cell phones and portable game players. In the process the icon has become a de facto staple of computing environments.

11.1. Human Issues Concerning Icons

Many questions and issues need to be explored to understand how people interact with computers through the use of icons. In this chapter we discuss these issues by looking at the research literature and applying the various findings to design questions regarding the use of icons.

11.1.1. Novice User

Icons, even if they have labels or tool tips, do not tell the user how to accomplish tasks. There is nothing to prompt the user about what to do or how to proceed. The user must already be aware of certain required actions; all information must be inferred from the images and related to previous knowledge.

To use an icon for the first time, the user must discover what is depicted on the icon and then link that representation to the corresponding command. This assumes that the user is familiar with the application's functionality and procedures. For instance, in a word processing application, the ability to copy and paste must be known. The procedure of selecting text and then choosing a function must also be known.

This all requires an understanding of the clip board, the insertion bar, the cursor, the highlight effect, as well as the copy icon and the paste icon. In a GUI there are no prompts or sets of instructions; the user must have prior knowledge of the interaction style. This may not be knowledge to which a novice user has access.

Icon-based systems do not necessarily afford novice users a self-explanatory interface. They must learn how to use the icons to accomplish their tasks. Tool tips can facilitate this process; however, they require active participation by the user.

Icons belong to a language that is understood by the interface designers and people who have learned to use a particular application. Icons can be ambiguous to users worldwide. It is only after their functionality is learned and understood that they offer a benefit to anyone, even experienced computer users.

11.1.2. The Dual Nature of Icons

People learn how to use icons in time, and they become quite efficient at it; they can also generalize what they learn to other icons. One interesting phenomenon that occurs when people interact with icons is that, on one hand, they relate to icons as the representations of objects, and, on the other hand, they perceive the icons as the objects themselves.

When we place a file icon into a folder we might think of it as the actual document, but when we change the file name or change the image we think of the icon as a picture that represents the document. It is important that the symbols and metaphors we create do not prevent people from moving between these two perspectives. It is a natural tendency, and we do not want to set obstacles that might distract the user and draw attention to the interface. People want to get their work done; they do not want to sit and ponder a small image on their computer screen.

Using images that people can associate with the underlying object or process helps to avoid this problem.

MAXIM

Icons should not be created in isolation.

A GUI is a visual world full of images and graphical components that coexist in a small space, and when we design we must consider the entire interface as a global entity, a visual ecosystem. We should be careful, therefore, not to design icons in isolation; they must fit in with all the other components and metaphors in the interface. We must create a plausible and integrated work environment.

11.1.3. Real-World Expectations

GUIs use metaphorical relationships to real-world objects like files and folders because it is generally assumed that these connections to the real world will help us to use our increasingly complex computers. We must remember, however, that people have associations that are connected to the appearance and functionality of these real-world objects.

The associations that people have create expectations that affect their perception of an icon's physical properties. When we design icons we must be aware of these expectations and make sure that we do not do anything to conflict with them. In other words, an icon of a trash can should look and behave like a trash can; it should not represent functionality that is not associated with a real trash can.

One of the more famous interface mistakes was the way the original Macintosh trashcan functioned. Not only was it used to delete files, it was also used to eject floppy disks. You can imagine the panic this caused to new users who had just learned to delete files by dragging them to the trash and then saw their floppy disks treated in such a way.

11.1.4. Recall/Recognition

People have a natural tendency to communicate using images. But do people relate to pictures differently than to written explanations? If they do, which mode is more advantageous in interaction design?

MAXIM

Icons have an advantage over text in terms of recognition and recall.

Research on symbols reveals that pictures have certain advantages over text. Our ability to recall images is superior to that for text. Users can also distinguish one image from another more easily than they can distinguish one word from another, especially if the words are capitalized. This can help us to make decisions more efficiently. It has also been shown that the accuracy with which people recognize previously viewed images is almost perfect.

- Recall of images is superior to that of text.
- Images are more easily distinguished than text.
- People have almost perfect image recall.

Interface designers can take advantage of this increased speed and accuracy by choosing images that foster this process. However, the benefits to recognition and recall should not always be assumed: it has been shown that improper use of images can hurt performance. The images must be chosen carefully, and they must be rigorously tested.

To choose the best possible images, we must understand the process that occurs when people view an image and try to understand its meaning. Let's see what is involved in that process.

11.1.5. Icon Analysis Chart

We begin by exploring what happens when we look at an image and document the process using the Icon Analysis Chart. When we look at an image, we first respond to our physical impressions and gradually make associations until we arrive at the object it represents. We document this articulatory distance (see Chapter 2) between the image and the understanding of its meaning by creating a separation trail. Each distinct element on this trail is a degree of separation, which we will notate at the end of the process.

For example, the deconstruction of the envelope symbol used for e-mail involves two processes: one takes place on the perceptual level (the observation of a rectangular shape with lines and a square in the upper right-hand corner) and the second on the cognitive level (the association of that object with a postal envelope, which triggers an association with e-mail). The image's shape resembles a postal letter, which leads to an association with e-mail, the desired functionality.

Consider the Icon Analysis Chart. In the fourth column we identify each of the levels, both perceptual and cognitive, and specify the particular elements involved in the separation trail—the trail that documents the articulatory distance. The final column shows the degree of separation between the symbol and its associated task. The chart is organized to show both perceptual and cognitive degrees.

The first four icons follow similar paths, resulting in one degree of perceptual and two degrees of cognitive separation. They are all shapes that are recognizable abstractions of real-world objects. The file folder, on the other hand, relates to the file hierarchy of the operating system, and might be a problematic association for new users. However, once it is learned, it has the same number of degrees of separation as the other three symbols and can therefore attain the same level of understandability. The home page icon is similar to the folder icon in that the concept of a home page does not reflect a real-world object.

The next three icons, the formatting commands, are different than the previous icons because they use two perceptual coding devices. These icons are letters, and

Chart 11.1   Icon Analysis Chart

Icon	Name	Distance		Separation Trail	Degrees
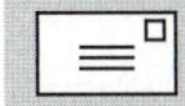	Mail	Perceptual		Shape/	1/2
		Cognitive		Letter/e-mail	
	Home	Perceptual		Shape/	1/2
		Cognitive		Home/home page	
	Folder	Perceptual		Shape/	1/2
		Cognitive		Folder/directory hierarchy	
	Shopping cart	Perceptual		Shape/	1/2
		Cognitive		Shopping cart/purchases	
B	Bold	Perceptual		Letter/ bold/	2/2
		Cognitive		Letter 'B'/bold command	
I	Italic	Perceptual		Letter/ italic/	2/2
		Cognitive		Letter 'I'/italic command	
U	Underline	Perceptual		Letter/ underlined/	2/2
		Cognitive		Letter 'U'/underline command	
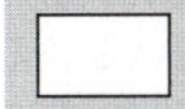	Rectangle tool	Perceptual		Shape/	1/1
		Cognitive		Rectangle	
	Ellipse tool	Perceptual		Shape/	1/1
		Cognitive		Ellipse	
	Elliptical marquee	Perceptual		Shape/dashed/	2/1
		Cognitive		Ellipse marquee	
	Rectangular marquee	Perceptual		Shape/dashed/	2/1
		Cognitive		Rectangle marquee	

they are also visually formatted according to the functions they provide. The cognitive coding here involves identifying the letter and then relating it to the command. This process requires two degrees of perceptual coding and two degrees of cognitive coding.

The third set of icons are a bit simpler because each image is a physical replica of its interface element. The rectangle tool, when applied to the application's canvas, looks just like the icon, so its perceptual coding is straightforward. Perceptual coding is processed rapidly, so each of these icons is quickly recognized for what it represents.

Application of the Icon Analysis Chart

The Icon Analysis Chart can be helpful in determining the complexity of a particular icon. Obviously, the simpler the relationship between the image and its function, the less processing is involved and therefore the smaller is the articulatory distance. Once learned, however, even complex visual relationships can become second nature, but they require practice and experience.

Some icons have apparently little relationship to their function, and it may be difficult for a user to solve the visual riddle they present. With a careful and structured approach to icon design, many such problems can be avoided. If you use the Icon Analysis Chart, you will be able to identify and avoid ambiguous and personal associations and create stronger symbols with less articulatory distance between image and meaning.

Icons that combine multiple images can communicate dynamic relationships or processes. They also require a bit more processing. In this case, each individual image must be decoded and then related to the other images. You can track each image individually until they merge and represent one process or state. One of the more familiar multiple image icons is the hyperlink icon . It uses an image of the world and an image of chain links.

If you arrive at a point at which no meaning can be inferred from an image, you must consider the symbol to be arbitrary and that it will require explanation. If people must spend time decoding images and pondering their meanings, needless delays will be added to the process, and errors will become more likely.

Successful icon creation is difficult and should always incorporate user testing in its earliest stages. The Icon Analysis Chart can serve as a useful tool for investigating the nature and usability of icons before the testing phase. Its use will help to structure the thought processes involved in icon design, but it will not guarantee that all your designs will be understood.

You must also analyze your icons using objective subjects. Comparing your results with the experience of actual users will provide you with useful insights into your own biases and associations. With time, the process of making your personal associations explicit will increase your abilities as an icon designer.

11.2. Using Icons in Interaction Design

We have looked at some of the ways in which people interact with icons and images. We now explore how they can be used in interaction designs. We will see how they affect the way in which we search for things and how they can be used to aid these types of tasks.

We also look at how images can be used to maximize the limited screen real estate of small portable devices. We must be aware of the different conventions that have evolved and use them in predictable ways. We then consider some of the principles involved in icon creation.

11.2.1. Search

> **MAXIM**
>
> Humans respond first to the physical qualities of icons and then to their semantic associations.

People process visual stimuli first by their physical qualities and then by their meaning. (Card, Moran, & Newell, 1983). In other words, an icon will stand out if one or more of its physical attributes are emphasized. Real-life situations, however, are far more complex, and we do not fully understand the extent to which icon attributes affect search activities in actual user environments. There is significant evidence, however, to suggest that the intensity of an icon's physical characteristics is an important factor.

Studies show that people perform better with icon targets than with text targets (Repokari, Saarela, & Kurkela, 2002). The benefit of using icons also increases when there are many items to search; text is usually not as variable in appearance as images tend to be. Icons tend to have a stronger immediate impact. The icons, however, must be sufficiently differentiated or they lose their advantage.

When people search for an icon (target) they must distinguish one symbol from many others (distractors). The intensity of an icon's physical characteristics must be manipulated to avoid confusion. The question is, does the use of icons to represent screen objects help people to find the things they are looking for? Research indicates that they do; however, an icon's attributes must be fully understood and manipulated appropriately for people to benefit from their application.

In this context, the designer should ask the following questions:

- Do all possible targets have the same shape, color, or size?
- Do they have the same amount of detail?
- Is the expected functionality available and appropriately grouped and placed on the screen?

These questions only cover some of the physical attributes and are by no means definitive. However, they suggest the complexity involved in icon design and selection. Let's look at some of the physical attributes that can affect the way we perceive icons and how they can be used to aid search activities. We look at the following attributes:

- Detail
- Color
- Size
- Shape
- Location

Detail

> **MAXIM**
>
> There is a range of acceptable detail that will benefit icon search.

Whereas some research indicates that greater detail helps people to recognize icons because it provides more information (Biederman, 1987), other research shows that users recognize simple cartoon-like images more quickly (Ryan & Schwartz, 1956). Byrne (1993) found positive results in search tests with simple as opposed to complex icons, suggesting that icons with a high level of detail are inferior to simple ones.

From these results we can conclude that there is a range of acceptable detail that will benefit icon search, provided there is no interference with other informational aspects of the icon. This implies that extraneous detail should be removed. Rubens and Krull (1988) call this process leveling. Leveling can be applied in two ways—by removing details from an existing design or by incorporating it at the early conceptual stages of design. Both procedures are appropriate and are usually used iteratively between initial conception and usability testing.

Color

> **MAXIM**
>
> Varying the color, size, or shape of an icon will make it easier to locate.

Color can be used to help people distinguish between icons; however, you must use discretion. The number of visually distinct colors is limited by the human perceptual system, and distinguishing color targets becomes more difficult if the distractors are similar to the target in color.

Murch (1987) suggests that it is best to use approximately six easily discriminated colors. Marcus (1995) recommends a maximum 5 ± 2 colors if we want people to remember their meaning. Galitz (2002) suggests using a maximum of four colors at a time on any one screen.

Although it might be confusing to be presented with so many varying opinions, the essence of the advice is to use color economically. Each of these guidelines may have validity in particular situations, but they all stress that color should be limited to the minimum amount required for the successful completion of the user's task.

> **MAXIM**
>
> When applying color, start with fewer colors; additional ones can be added later.

Interface designs that conform to a strict use of color can be expanded later to use one or two more, if absolutely necessary, but it is far more difficult to eliminate extraneous colors later in the design process.

Size

Most contemporary systems use standardized icon sizes, but there is no standard requirement for the size of the images on the icons. This freedom in image size allows us to vary the perceived size of the icon, and an appropriate use of image size can aid the user during icon search.

For instance, for the File icon, one can take advantage of this situation by making its vertical dimension greater than its horizontal dimension. This is more in keeping with the dimensions of a real-world document. To meet the required area size, the horizontal dimension of the image must be reduced, leaving the vertical size equal to the icon's 16- or 32-pixel requirement. We still use the square area for the icon, but the image contained in it is re-proportioned and uses less of the allotted canvas (Figure 11.1).

Figure 11.1 File icon.

Galitz recommends an image of 24 by 24 or 26 by 26 for a 32-pixel-square icon. This size is adequate for detail recognition on the image while leaving room for a border or perceived space between icons that have to be placed in close proximity.

Shape

> **MAXIM**
>
> Icon images should have distinctive shapes.

As we just saw, icon shape is standardized: icons are square, but the image on the icon does not have to be. Remember, the image will likely be smaller than the icon to allow for borders and space, so we can use irregular shapes and maintain some white space between icons.

Image shape should differ from icon to icon. Varying the shapes of the images will increase the distinctiveness of the icons and make them easier to locate on a busy screen.

Location

> **MAXIM**
>
> Icons may facilitate search if their location is properly designed.

Research has shown that there is a relationship between an icon's shape and its location. This relationship is influenced by the user's familiarity with the icon's shape. Familiar shapes mean more to people than location, but people will use location if the shapes are not familiar (Moyes, 1994). Research has shown that ease of learning is an overriding factor. People tend to rely on the attribute that is most easily learned and overlook other characteristics.

11.2.2. Screen Real Estate

> **MAXIM**
>
> Icons can save screen real estate.

Computing devices are getting smaller and more powerful. These smaller devices have smaller screens, but they often have increased functionality. Given the need to conserve screen space, it would seem natural to use icons because they are more compact than text.

Often, what can be communicated with a small icon would otherwise require a lengthy textual explanation. For this reason, icons have been traditionally used on maps where space is at a premium. We have to be careful, however, because if an icon is not understood or if its relationship to the underlying functionality is not discernible, it does not matter how much space is saved, because the interface becomes unusable.

One way to help people to learn the meaning of icons is to use tool tips. These are short labels that pop up when the cursor hovers over an image. The tool tip may make it hard to see the screen behind it, but the user can still see most of the screen and can still click the icon. This momentary overlapping is an economical way to use space and maximize information in a small screen environment.

Images are processed more quickly than text, and icons take advantage of this by affording experienced users a more efficient working environment. A domain expert, such as a graphic designer using a drawing program, would probably understand the word "rectangle" to represent the "draw a rectangle on the canvas" functionality, but a simple image of a rectangle, □, would take up less space and be easier to find among many other commands.

In design, practical necessity is always an important issue. The size and legibility of the display as well as other user issues, such as the user's level of computer literacy, play a large role in deciding whether to use icons or text or some combination of the two. As always, the parameters involved, such as color, shape, number of choices, and so on, require frequent usability testing.

11.2.3. Conventions

If something is usually done in a certain way, it becomes common practice or a convention, and people expect it to be done in that way. For example, writing from left to right is a convention for many languages, and writing from right to left is a convention for others.

> **MAXIM**
>
> Icon conventions should be used whenever they are appropriate.

There are many conventions, and we generally do not think about them until we are presented with a design that does not adhere to them. This usually makes the user stop and ponder the situation. This obviously represents a decrease in efficiency and can also become very annoying. Conventions should be used whenever they are appropriate.

Let's look at some symbols that have become conventions. The Web is an interesting place to start because it is still evolving, and at a rapid pace, so we get to see conventions evolve in a shortened time span.

The World Wide Web has been nurtured in large part by commerce. The business world seized on the Web's potential for publicizing merchandise and transacting business. In the process, a language of symbols evolved that enabled the easy transfer of information and facilitated the interactions involved in buying and selling.

One of the first symbols to evolve was the shopping cart, an abstraction of a common object that has become synonymous with the act of collecting products to purchase. There are slight variations in the implementation of the shopping cart function among sites, but for the most part, people can predict the behavior and meaning of this icon whenever they come across it (Figure 11.2).

🛒 Shopping **Cart**

Figure 11.2 Amazon.com shopping cart.

Another convention often seen on the Web is the use of tabs to indicate site structure or areas of related activity. Tabs are used by many large Internet businesses such as Amazon.com, Apple.com, and Sun.com (Figures 11.3 and 11.4).

Figure 11.3 Amazon.com tabs.

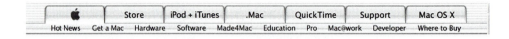

Figure 11.4 Apple.com tabs.

Figure 11.5 Audio icon—speaker.

Figure 11.6 Audio icon—notes.

Figure 11.7 Home icon.

Sites that sell music use the symbols shown in Figures 11.5 and 11.6 to indicate that an aural sample of a song or musical composition is available.

Where would we be if we couldn't find our way home (Figure 11.7)?

Locks are common indicators of secure connections (Figure 11.8).

Many sites use arrows or hand images to indicate "previous" and "next." By convention, the right-pointing arrow ⇨; or hand ☞ indicates the next page, and the left-pointing arrow or hand indicates the previous page. This convention is based on the left-to-right convention of Western text presentation, and would not be intuitive for cultures that read from right to left or top to bottom.

Most sites with search functions use a version of the icons ⊙ ⊃ to initiate the beginning of a search (Figure 11.9). Again, the implication of the first symbol is that the user understands English, which is a risky bet on the Web. The second icon signifies "proceed with the search," but it also functions in a left-to-right linguistic world.

The figure of a globe has become a common symbol for the World Wide Web, and a magnifying glass combined with the globe indicates a search of the entire Web (Figure 11.10).

The Web search icon brings up issues of localization. People in other parts of the world may not accept your view of the globe; they might live in a different hemisphere. When representing the globe, it is a good idea to avoid portraying any particular hemisphere.

On the other hand, you might want to take advantage of localized symbols to indicate a particular geographical area. The use of national flags is a convenient way to indicate nationality or global location.

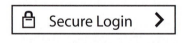

Figure 11.8 Secure Connection icon.

Figure 11.9 Amazon.com Search.

Figure 11.10 Web Search icon.

Be careful when using stereotypical symbols to represent different cultures; you run the risk of alienating the very people you hope to reach. Before proceeding with a design, it is a good idea to consult native residents for their impression of the symbols you plan to use.

11.2.4. Context

Icons do not exist in a vacuum; they appear on screens populated by other elements, such as scrollbars, pull-down menus, text, graphics, and other icons. We perceive icons in relation to all these other screen elements, that is, in relation to their context. Context supplies a frame of reference.

The power of context can be demonstrated by considering the effect of yelling "Fire" in a crowded movie theater as opposed to yelling "Fire" on an artillery range. The exclamation is identical, yet the meaning and effects of the word are quite different.

> **MAXIM**
>
> Icons have no meaning without context.

Without context, icons are meaningless. Horton (1994) offers the following statement to summarize this concept:

$$\text{Icon}_i + \text{context}_j + \text{viewer}_k \Rightarrow \text{meaning}_{ijk}$$

Consider the formatting icons **B**, *I*, and <u>U</u>. The only time we associate formatting functions with these symbols is when we see them in the Format toolbar. Otherwise, they are simply letters with particular formatting styles applied to them.

The Justify text icon ☰ and the Columns icon ☰☰ in Microsoft Word are identical to the first and second hexagrams, respectively, used in the ancient Chinese oracle the I Ching (Figure 11.11).

If we were working in Microsoft Word, we would not misconstrue these icons for I Ching symbols. However, taken out of context and seen in isolation, there is no way to differentiate between the two meanings. These symbols are given meaning through the context in which they are viewed.

Context can be affected by the color, shape, size, or number of elements on a screen and by the qualities of contrast and distinctiveness. During a search, users

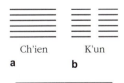

Ch'ien   K'un
a   **b**

Figure 11.11 I Ching hexagrams.

first examine the visual features of icons to locate a set of possible targets, and then they examine the labels and names to narrow down the possibilities (Byrne, 1993).

If one attribute of an icon, such as its size, differs greatly from that of all the others, it becomes more distinct, and therefore is easier to locate. If an icon is not contextually distinct—if it does not contrast greatly with the other screen elements—it becomes more difficult to locate. Finding a yellow icon among blue icons would not be difficult. Finding a five-sided yellow icon among six-sided yellow icons would require more time.

Icons can be seen in many different contexts:

- Physical
- Cognitive
- Metaphorical
- Temporal

Physical Context

Physical context can be affected by factors such as location, juxtaposition, contrast, and density.

- **Location**—The way in which an icon is perceived is affected by its location on the screen. People become accustomed to finding particular icons in specific locations, and they might not look in unusual places. Conventions have evolved on standard locations for certain screen elements. Consider the placement of toolbars at the top left-hand corner of most windows and the order of pull-down menus: File, Edit, and Help. People relate to these common labels as if they were shapes (icons). Consistent icon placement aids users in their searches.

- **Contrast**—Differences in color, size, and shape between icons can affect the user's perception of them. The degree of differentiation between screen elements can be used to convey meaning, such as similarity or nonrelatedness. It can also be used to communicate unavailable functionality. For instance, an icon that is grayed out as opposed to colored in informs the user that the underlying functionality is not available.

- **Juxtaposition**—The placement of icons next to each other may imply related functionality, or it may make an icon difficult to find. Icons that represent related functionality should be placed in close proximity. However, certain icons should not be placed near each other to avoid critical user errors. For instance, the Save and Delete icons should be placed a safe distance away from each other to avoid having a user click on the wrong one in error.

- **Density**—The density of the screen (the number of elements in a defined space) affects how icons on that screen are perceived. If an image is surrounded by many other stimuli, it will be perceived differently than if it were presented in isolation. It has been suggested that only a small number of icons should be present on any one screen to increase their effectiveness (Haramundanis, 1996).

Cognitive Context

The cognitive context of an icon is determined by factors related to the user's personal knowledge, including level of experience as well as emotional state and expectations. People are also affected by the difficulty of their tasks. If someone is intently focused on one aspect of task completion, he or she might not even see other elements that make up the screen context. The nature of the task environment can also affect icon perception. Shneiderman and Plaisant suggest that "while you are working on visually oriented tasks, it is helpful to 'stay visual' by using icons, whereas, while you are working on a text document, it is helpful to 'stay textual' by using textual menus" (Shneiderman & Plaisant, 2005).

Metaphorical Context

As we have seen, an icon's capacity to communicate can be augmented by its placement within a collective metaphor. The most common collective metaphor in contemporary GUIs—the desktop—is based on the real-world office model. This model is the essence of the Microsoft Windows and Mac OS X interfaces.

The desktop concept was originally popularized by the Apple Lisa, which was based on work done at Xerox's Palo Alto research facility on the Xerox Star. This metaphor is characterized by file and folder images that are arranged on a desktop complete with a recycle bin or trash can. These icons are pared-down images, stripped of all detail, and are not meant to be realistic. Yet the collective metaphor of the office environment ties them together and creates a cohesive environment that is familiar.

Temporal Context

Marcus (1998) defines context as "The arrangement of signs in space and time." When we work with applications the various objects on the screen change to reflect the different system states that result from our actions. We then respond to this altered visual context. This dynamic interchange progresses over time, until a task is complete.

During this dialogue between the user and the system, the context in which icons are viewed evolves. Sometimes icons are grayed out (when the associated functionality is not available), and sometimes entire toolbars with new sets of icons appear, to facilitate particular task goals. We must design icons with these shifts of context in mind; otherwise unfortunate visual combinations may occur as users interact with the system.

11.2.5. Globalization–Localization

Images are often considered to be superior to labels because they do not depend on a particular language. They are considered to be "language agnostic" and therefore to have greater potential for the global community. This is why images

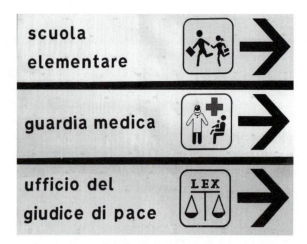

Figure 11.12 Italian street signs.

are used for international road signs and other public signage, such as public toilets and no-smoking signs. Consider the images in Figure 11.12 indicating the locations of an elementary school, a medical facility, and an office of a justice of the peace.

For these international symbols to work, there has to be some consensus about their meaning. This consensus can be surprisingly lacking at times. For instance, throughout the European Union (EU) traffic signage is consistent. Native drivers are familiar with most of the signs and assume that everyone else is (Figure 11.13). Many of these signs are, however, quite different than the signage used in the other parts of the world and without knowledge of their meaning foreign drivers risk getting traffic tickets or getting into accidents.

Signs can also be localized and reflect very specific conditions that do not exist in other locations, as shown in Figure 11.14.

Culturally dependent symbols, such as a hand being held up to signify stop (✋), may be powerful signs within the originating culture, but they can have unfortunate implications within others. Horton (1994) observes that "There is almost no arrangement of the human hand that is not an obscene, rude, or impolite gesture somewhere

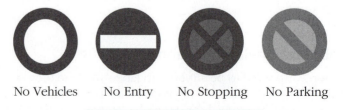

Figure 11.13 European Union traffic signs.

a   b

Figure 11.14   (a) Cow warning sign. (b) Deer warning sign.

in this world." He suggests that if you use the image of a hand, it should be presented holding or pressing something.

Universally accepted international signs can be used in icon design, but there still may be variations to consider. A red cross is often associated with the International Red Cross and might conceivably be used to indicate first aid for a system problem; however, in Arabic-speaking countries the institution is referred to as the Red Crescent.

It is a good idea to generalize an image as much as possible while retaining its overall impression. For instance, a globe used to indicate the World Wide Web should not reflect a particular hemispheric location, but rather an abstracted version of the land masses (Figure 11.15).

Figure 11.15   Globe icon.

It is true that certain conditions are universal and experienced by all people. Natural events such as rain, sunrise, and sunset and physical items such as land topology and bodies of water are consistent in nature and may be considered universal references. It is possible to use these more universal elements in the design of global icons. An understanding of their cultural meanings, however, remains essential. A raindrop in a rain forest has a very different significance than a raindrop in a desert.

Sometimes words are used in conjunction with graphic symbols, for example, in "stop" signs. These words often become well known and are viewed as an image more than a word. Using text within icons can be problematic, however, because the text may have to be translated for specific users. This alteration might necessitate a new version of the icon and perhaps a redesign of the entire icon to incorporate the larger or smaller text areas required by other languages. This can be become expensive.

11.3. Technical Issues Concerning Icons

We have looked at the way in which people interact with images and icons. We have also considered how icons can be used in interaction design. We now consider the technical aspects of creating icons. To do this, we need to understand the basic components of images and how to manipulate them.

Before we begin we need to clarify the terminology used to describe how different symbols function. This will help us to attain an understanding of how certain images function as icons so that we can apply a more structured approach to icon creation.

11.3.1. Icon Terminology

The terminology used to describe icons is often inconsistent and cryptic. Different people use some terms to mean diverse things or several terms to mean the same thing. Let's look at some of the terms used.

Phonogram

An alphabetic character represents a speech sound, and thus it falls under the definition of a "phonogram," which is a sign or symbol representing a word, syllable, or speech sound. Phonographic systems are based on the physical shapes of their members. If the shapes of the letters of the alphabet are altered too much, the connection to the sound is lost. It is important to consider the ramifications of relying on phonograms for a global audience because they depend on this specific knowledge of a particular alphabet.

Pictogram

A pictogram is a picture that resembles what it signifies such as the envelop icon used to represent email.

Abstract Shapes

Abstract shapes can also be used as symbols. Disciplines such as mathematics, logic, science, and music have sophisticated notational systems whose symbols are recognized internationally (see, for example, Chart 11.2).

Punctuation marks are essentially abstract shapes that refer to concepts: the question mark (?) relates to a query, and the exclamation mark (!) conveys emphasis. They are not as universally understood as mathematical symbols; however, it is reasonably safe to use them. For example, the exclamation mark is often used to indicate caution on traffic signs (Figure 11.16).

It is possible to create an abstract shape that has no symbolic connotation. This would be considered an arbitrary shape. Although designers are free to use these

Chart 11.2   Mathematical Symbols

+	=	−	×	÷
Plus	Equals	Minus	Multiplication	Division

Figure 11.16 Exclamation mark indicating caution.

nonsymbolic or arbitrary abstract shapes to represent system or application functionality, it would be more difficult for users to make a connection to the underlying functionality, so there must be a compelling reason to choose such shapes.

Ideogram

Ideograms are symbols that stand for ideas or concepts; for example, the letter "I" can mean "help" or "information available." Many applications use the image of a floppy disk to represent the concept of saving a file, not only to a floppy disk but also to the desktop or folder. This is an ideographic reference because it relates to the general idea of saving a file, not to the specific object—a floppy disk.

Logogram (Logograph)

A logogram is a symbol that represents a word, such as the image of a human eye to represent the word "I," the picture of a heart to represent the word "love," and the letter "U" to represent the word "you" (Figure 11.17).

Logograms can also be symbols that do not indicate pronunciation, such as the symbol "4," which represents the word "four" in English and the word "quatro" in Italian.

Figure 11.17 Logogram phrase.

MAXIM
Icons function on many levels of meaning simultaneously.

Icons are often difficult to characterize as purely logographic, ideographic, phonographic, or pictographic. For example, is the "I" icon used as a logogram to represent the word "information" but not as an ideogram used to represent the idea that "Information is available here"? Does the fact that this symbol is a letter (phonogram) mean that it is not also a pictogram? After all, it no longer behaves like the "I" phonogram that represents the first sound in the word "Information."

Images often fall into multiple categories depending on the user's background, experience, and task. There is no clear-cut boundary between categories, and multiple levels of meaning can occur simultaneously.

Semiotic Terms

Semiotics is the study of signs. It is a philosophical discipline that explores the ways in which signs achieve meaning and how this meaning is conveyed. Icons are signs; they are designed to communicate information about system functionality to users. We are often confused, however, about the meaning of certain icons, we do not always intuitively understand their meaning. We can gain a deeper understanding of icons and improve icon design by assimilating some of the core concepts of semiotics.

The American semiotician Charles Sanders Peirce developed a system of classifying signs based on the relationship between the signifier and the signified—the sign and the thing it represents (sometimes referred to as the referent). Three of his classifications of signs are of particular interest to us (Peirce, 1991; Williamson & Barry, 2001):

- Iconic
- Indexical
- Symbolic

Iconic—Signs that represent objects through resemblance to these objects are considered "iconic." The folder icon 🗁, for example, visually resembles a physical folder and is therefore iconic. A file icon is also a graphic depiction of the entity it represents, a document. These signs are pictographic. They do not represent words or concepts; they represent actual objects through resemblance. In this sense its iconic classification remains on the perceptual level of the Icon Analysis Chart.

Icons should be intuitive or obvious. They should take advantage of the user's knowledge. If a user is familiar with an application domain—a graphic designer using a drawing program, for example—the tools that are represented by iconic signs should be familiar and thus aid the user in understanding and remembering their function. It has been found that "Familiarity and domain expertise increased the association of an icon to its referent" (Kurniawan, 2000).

To add a rectangular or oval shape to a digital canvas area, a graphic designer chooses the rectangle or oval tool by clicking on the rectangle or oval shape in the tool box. In this case, the signs and the resulting shapes are visually equivalent. Justification icons are also visually equivalent to justified text. Thus, abstract shapes can become signs that make a direct connection between icons and commands and "have the potential to be understood with minimal training of the user" (Williamson & Barry, 2001). Horton (1994) believes that iconic icons are the most direct, and are therefore the best ones to use.

Indexical—The indexical sign category leads to some interesting possibilities. Indexical signs have a direct causal relationship with the object to which they refer, as indicated by the phrase, "where there's smoke, there's fire." Smoke is considered the index to fire. An indication of causation is the essence of this classification. A progress bar shows the amount of progress for an ongoing process. A volume slider shows the output level of a sound source.

Signs that are indexical imply a dynamic link between the referent (signifier) and the signified. For instance, the image of a printer on the print icon is an index to the process of printing; it does not refer to the printer or its attributes. The printer is the cause of the printing.

When the cursor changes from an arrow to a hand as it passes over a hyperlink, it becomes an indexical sign, indicating the presence of a link. The change in the cursor's shape is an indexical sign that an underline means the presence of hypertext functionality.

Symbolic—Peirce's concept of symbolic signs does not differ from the definition presented previously; the meaning of a symbolic sign is derived through convention. However, he suggests that a symbol also involves indexical and iconic characteristics. To clarify this, consider the hyperlink icon . This icon uses two logographic images, one of a few chain links and the other of a globe. The hyperlink symbol is created by the relationship between these indices—link and world—and is the result of the iconic representation of a hyperlink. Understanding this triad of index, symbol, and icon will enable us to examine the way in which icons function in further detail.

Abstraction

According to Dreyfuss (1972), symbols fall into three categories: abstract, representational, and arbitrary. In his schema, representational symbols are equivalent to the pictographic symbols discussed previously. His abstract and arbitrary categories, however, can clarify our discussion.

- "Abstract symbols reduce essential elements of a message to graphic terms."
- "Arbitrary symbols are those that are invented, and accordingly must also be learned."

Dreyfuss cites zodiac signs, with their origins as depictions of gods or animals, as examples of abstract symbols. The symbols for Aries (Υ) and Taurus (Ω) are the most recognizable because of the animals they represent, and they provide insight into the process of abstraction through which they evolved.

Arbitrary symbols are invented, and they generally have little to do visually with what they represent. Mathematical symbols are perhaps the best-known examples of this category. They are meaningful only if you have learned their significance. Once learned, however, the symbols can be generalized to express relationships outside their specific discipline. For instance, the plus sign ($+$) can be used to combine any recognizable entity (Figure 11.18).

The equation in Figure 11.18 may or may not be universally true, but it conveys meaning through the use of symbols—some arbitrary (the plus and equals signs)

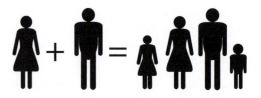

Figure 11.18　Arbitrary and iconic symbols.

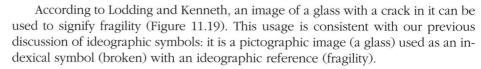

Figure 11.19　Broken glass icon.

and some representational (the human silhouettes). The symbols for radioactive substances (☢) and bio-waste (☣) are also arbitrary, but they are strong images that, once learned, communicate effectively.

Lodding and Kenneth (1990) use the same three categories as Dreyfuss, but they define abstract symbols according to the way they are used and not by how they evolved visually. They state that abstract icons "attempt to present a concept to a viewer that is apart from the concrete image."

According to Lodding and Kenneth, an image of a glass with a crack in it can be used to signify fragility (Figure 11.19). This usage is consistent with our previous discussion of ideographic symbols: it is a pictographic image (a glass) used as an indexical symbol (broken) with an ideographic reference (fragility).

Lodding and Kenneth caution that we can only define a symbol's category with regard to its context, explaining that symbols can "migrate across the class boundaries" and "simultaneously occupy different categories." The symbol in Chart 11.3 can operate in three different categories and have three different meanings, depending on its context.

11.3.2.　Principles for Icon Creation

Now that we have a clearer understanding of icon terminology, we turn to the elements that make up icons.

We begin by exploring the organization of the visual elements within an icon, such as points, lines, and areas (Horton, 1994), and their subsequent relationships.

Chart 11.3　Symbol with Multiple Meanings

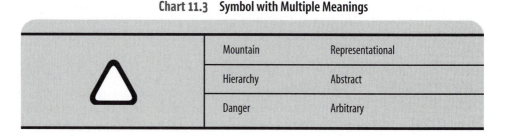

	Mountain	Representational
	Hierarchy	Abstract
	Danger	Arbitrary

We call this the internal syntax of the icon, where syntax is defined as "orderly or systematic arrangement"; thus, we study the principles that govern the arrangement of the icon's elements or features.

We use the following principles to explore the internal syntax of an icon:

- Simplicity/complexity
- Cohesiveness
- Distinctiveness
- Familiarity

Simplicity/Complexity

As we have seen, the level of detail used in an icon's image affects user performance, but there is disagreement on whether it does so positively or negatively. According to the recognition-by-components (RBC) theory, increased detail should aid recognition (Biederman, 1987). Recognition of an image does require a certain amount of detail; however, excessive detail can lead to a degradation of recognition performance (Ryan & Schwartz, 1956).

Research shows that the use of simple icons makes the process of finding files easier (Byrne, 1993). However, it has also been found that users prefer high levels of detail and, in contrast to previous findings, detail reduces search time in some experiments (Helbing, Jenkins, Kim, & Miller, 1993).

Signal to Noise Ratio

The research on complexity is conflicting; what does it mean? Although the experimental results on icon complexity are conflicting, it is clear that the level of detail affects performance in some way. The questions are, how much, under what conditions, and to what extent? If we borrow the concept of the signal to noise ratio from electroacoustics, we will be able to better understand the underlying issues.

The two components in this ratio are "signal" and "noise." The signal is the information we are seeking, and the noise is the interference, or potential distractions:

Signal/Noise   Information/Interference

The information we want from an icon is anything that will help us to understand the meaning of the image. The noise is anything that inhibits that understanding. A successful icon has a high signal to noise ratio—a greater signal size in comparison to noise.

In electroacoustics, the signal is often easy to define; in icon design, however, it is not. There are occasions when a detail that makes up part of the image to one person might be considered noise by another. There is no system of universal metrics to determine how much detail makes up the signal and how much is noise.

With each particular icon, many factors are involved. Horton (1994) suggests that we include only the necessary details for the icon be understood and avoid excessive detail. This is the process of leveling, which can be used iteratively. We must then test the icon to see whether we have correctly identified those elements that successfully convey meaning.

Cohesiveness

Icons that perform related functions should be created as a family and should share some visual characteristics. The process of creating an icon family begins with the selection of an icon type, such as a pictograph or an abstract shape and continues through each phase of the iterative process. Icons within a family should be consistent, but icon families should be distinguishable from other icon families.

Distinctiveness

Just as icon families must be clearly differentiated, the icons within each family must communicate their unique identity. People will learn to distinguish between icon families as well as siblings within a family. They will gain an understanding of the features that represent similarity and differentiation, and the designer can support this understanding by adhering to a logical system.

Familiarity

Icons should be familiar to the user; for example, if we use a mail box image for an e-mail icon, it is important to choose a version of a mailbox that will be familiar to the user. Apple's interface guidelines give four examples of mail boxes from different European Union countries (Apple Computer Inc., 1992). Although some of these images might be decipherable across cultures, others seem quite singular (Figure 11.20).

Ideally, we would be able to use the appropriate image for each country. This might not always be practical, however, and the substitution of a more universal image might be required.

It is not enough just to use familiar images. There must also be a true relationship between the real objects and the system objects. A familiar image used for functionality that is only remotely connected with that object will cause users to question the relationship and make it harder for them to learn and remember the meaning of the image.

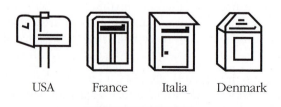

| USA | France | Italia | Denmark |

Figure 11.20 Mailbox icons.

The designer should also use images of objects that are familiar in the relevant domain. A paintbrush is not a common tool for spreadsheet tasks and should not be used to represent background color attributes in a spreadsheet program. Although a paintbrush is a familiar object, it is not relevant to disciplines that use spreadsheet functionality. A paint program, on the other hand, would seem strange without a paintbrush tool.

Certain abstract symbols—shapes or designs that have no representational qualities—have attained universal acceptance and comprehension and can be considered familiar to the majority of users. Arrows that represent "previous" and "next" or "back to top" are generally understood, as are a great many mathematical signs.

We must remember, however, that familiarity, like beauty, is in the eye of the beholder. A quick glance the diverse domains in Table 11.1 shows the different meanings for some common shapes (Dreyfuss, 1972).

Table 11.1   Common Shapes and Meanings by Discipline

	Chemistry	Astronomy	Biology	Botany	Architecture	Electronics	Landscaping
+	Positive charge		Longer than	Spores with male nuclei		Crossed conductors	
–	Negative charge		Shorter than	Spores with female nuclei		Direct current (DC)	
⊙		Sun	Sex-linked inheritance	Annual			
◉					Flush floor Sign outlet		Existing trees
○	Atomic's orbital	Full moon			Lighting outlet, Ceiling		Use
△	Apply heat		Head	Evergreen	Transformer	3-Phase 3-Wire (Delta)	Behavior

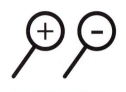

Figure 11.21 Zoom icons.

11.3.3. Icon Grammar

The principles that govern the internal structure of icons form a grammar. This grammar is constructed on rules and procedures that serve to facilitate the logical organization that helps people to understand the meaning of icons and their relationships to each other.

Zoom icons traditionally use a magnifying glass with a plus or minus sign (Figure 11.21). The plus sign signifies zooming in to see greater detail, and the minus sign signifies zooming out to see the overall view. These icons represent related functionality and are visually similar. The difference between the two is confined to the changing of the sign, which establishes a grammatical rule in the mind of the user.

This type of grammatical system is also found in icons used in drawing programs. The act of drawing in a drawing program involves placing "Bezier points" on the electronic canvas with the pen tool. There are a few possible options; the user can place a new point, add a point to a line, or subtract a point. The tools for all of these actions are represented by pen images. The "add a point tool" includes a plus sign, and the "subtract a point" tool has a minus sign (Figure 11.22).

Paint programs have a selection tool called the lasso tool, whose icon image is a representation of a lasso. This tool has two possible variations: the polygonal lasso tool and the magnetic lasso tool. The lasso image is consistent between these two variations, but there is a slight difference to show how the tool will attach the "selection marquee" to the image on the canvas.

Grammatical logic requires that the polygonal tool show the points of attachment, hence the variation in the contour of the lasso. This is consistent in the magnetic lasso, which adds a small magnet to the image. In this sequence of icons, the family resemblance is clear, as are the grammatical variations among siblings (Figure 11.23).

> **MAXIM**
>
> The grammatical rules must be observable, logical, predictable, and consistent.

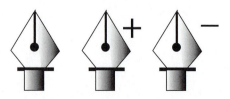

Figure 11.22 Pen icons.

Figure 11.23 Lasso selection icons.

We must make significant and observable changes to the icon siblings; however, there is a limit to how subtle these alterations can be and still be noticed by the user. This requires the establishment of rules to guide the development process. These rules form the grammar of the iconic language.

Horton (1994) suggests that a graphical grammar should specify the following:

- Which elements are required and which are optional.
- How elements can be graphically combined, for example, by antithesis, addition, and intersection (see the section on aggregate symbols).
- How elements are arranged left to right, top to bottom, and front to back.
- How each element is represented, for example, as a border, as an object within the border, as an attachment, or as a modification of a standard element.
- Which elements are the same for all icons in the series and which vary from icon to icon within the series.
- How many elements can be combined before the resulting symbol is too complex.

11.3.4. Universal Systems

> If a system of symbols could be compiled that would be equally recognizable in Lagos and Lapland, perhaps the dream of a universal basic means of communication could be realized. *(Dreyfuss 1972, 18)*

With the worldwide reach of modern software products and the exponential growth of the World Wide Web, globalization has become a topic of great interest to interface designers.

It has been suggested that icons allow for easy internationalization of interface design. However, the assumption that icons are universally understood could not be farther from the truth. This does not mean that we should forget about trying to make our designs as easy to understand as possible. There have been attempts to create universal symbolic languages, and we can gain some insights from their structure. Let's see how they are constructed.

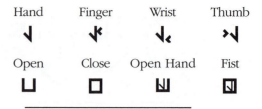

Figure 11.24 Blissymbols with grammar.

Semantography

With the goal of universal communication in mind, Charles K. Bliss created what he considered a "simple system of pictorial symbols" called Semantography (Bliss, 1965). His system was based on symbols called Blissymbols that incorporated a symbolic logic and semantics.

Bliss's work can be a source of inspiration and guidance when designing icons and icon families (Marcus, 1996). The simplicity of his symbols and the clarity of his grammar are powerful features that can be used to great effect in icon design (Rubens & Krull, 1988).

Let's take a look at some Blissymbols and their grammatical structures. Notice the grammar involved in the symbols in Figure 11.24. In the first row, the small > and < marks point to locations on the abbreviated hand symbol, (◀) refining the sign's meaning. In the second row, the hand is combined with the signs for "open" and "closed" to signify open hand and closed hand (fist), respectively.

Consider the symbols in Figure 11.25 and their innate logic. Simple combinatorial processes can communicate sophisticated concepts.

Bliss used these seemingly simple elements and concepts to create an expressive symbolic language that can be easily learned and has the ability to communicate sophisticated and complex linguistic structures. He reported that, within an hour, children could learn to write whole sentences and read new combinations easily.

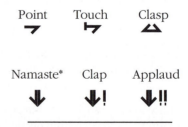

Figure 11.25 Blissymbols combined.

The gesture (or mudra) of namaste is a simple act made by bringing together both palms of the hands before the heart and lightly bowing the head (*http://www.exoticindiaart.com/ article/namaste*).

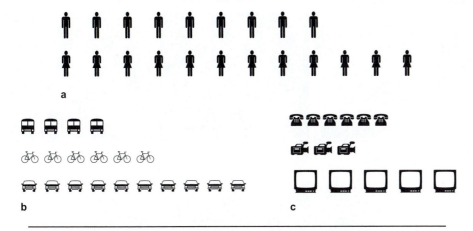

Figure 11.26 (a) Male and female population 65 years and older. (b) Modes of transportation in millions. (c) Retail appliances in percentage per capita.

ISOTYPE

Otto Neurath created the **I**nternational **S**ystem **O**f **TY**pographic **P**icture **E**ducation (ISOTYPE) in an attempt to make information accessible to a universal audience (Neurath, 1972). ISOTYPE was never implemented as the educational tool he intended, but it has influenced the way in which we visualize statistical information in charts, reports, and journals. It has also laid the foundation for modern traffic signs and public utility symbols.

ISOTYPE's potential for visualizing statistics like population density is quite powerful. This system relies on representational symbols resembling actual objects, or pictographs, to convey meaning (Figure 11.26).

Public Signs

It is a worthwhile exercise to explore the symbols that you encounter each day, from traffic signs, to airport signs, to the icons used on automobile dashboards. When you do this ask yourself some questions:

- Do you know what the images represent?
- Do you understand the symbols intuitively?
- What gives them meaning?
- Can you remember their meaning when you see them again?
- A universal system must be understood by everyone. What are the chances that everyone will understand all of the symbols that you encounter each day?

Consider the road signs shown in Figure 11.27. Do they make sense? Can you determine what they mean?

Figure 11.27

Figure 11.27a cautions drivers to be aware of crumbling pavement. Figure 11.27b cautions about falling rocks. Figure 11.27c shows road work ahead, and Figures 11.27d and 11.27e show no honking and pedestrian crossing, respectively. Now consider the two aggregate traffic signs in Figure 11.28. Can you decipher their meanings?

The set of signs in Figure 11.28a shows a car with skid marks followed by snow flakes and then a rain cloud. Together with the 2-km indication these signs warn drivers of slippery conditions for the next 2 km when there is precipitation.

The set of signs in Figure 11.28b uses the European No Parking (large circle with a diagonal line through it) and Parking Allowed (the letter "P") signs together with an image of a man pushing a loaded cart. This indicates that parking is prohibited except for loading and unloading.

11.3.5. Deconstructing Icons

The current generation of computers are generally equipped with powerful graphics cards and are capable of displaying rich color images and photorealistic graphics. Icons can use these capabilities to great effect. With color, they can show system states or imitate a realistic 3D look.

Before exploring the use of color in icon design, we first look at the simple shapes and forms that are the basic building blocks of complex symbols. We then see

a   b

Figure 11.28

how we can enrich the semantic information they communicate by manipulating indicators, using different styles, determining the best view, and combining symbols.

- Basic shapes
- Indicators
- Styles
- Canonical view
- Aggregate symbols

Basic Shapes

MAXIM

Complex shapes can be created from a few basic elements.

According to Horton (1994), all graphics can be decomposed into points, lines, and areas. We begin with two fundamental elements—lines and points. Simple combinations
of these basic elements allow us quickly to generate complicated symbols (Figure
11.29a). We can create areas by connecting the lines into basic geometric shapes
(Figure 11.29b), and further combinations can add to our vocabulary (Figure 11.29c).

Using these basic elements, we can also create symbols that resemble real-life objects. These symbols are abstractions of their real-world counterparts (Figure 11.29d).

Figure 11.29 (a) Basic elements. (b) Basic shapes. (c) Basic combinations. (d) Real-life symbols.
(e) Enter/Exit symbols.

These representations convey information easily, but they are best suited to depicting objects, not actions. A dynamic vocabulary of actions and processes, however, can be achieved through the use of additional indicators.

Semantography addresses the need for a vocabulary of action through the use of a simple but powerful grammar. The Blissymbols in Figure 11.29e represent the actions of entering and exiting.

As seen from these images, many kinds of meaning can be conveyed using a few basic lines and shapes. Now let's see what conventions we can use to enhance our icons and communicate dynamic information.

Indicators

Lines that emanate from an image, such as in depictions of light rays (⊏▤≶) or sound waves (◁))), can be used to suggest the presence of light (which is sometimes used to indicate search functionality) or sound (often used for volume control or to indicate a sound file).

These two types of symbols fall under the heading of iconic type. Remember, however, that as obvious and universal as these indicators may seem, they do rely on cultural consensus.

Horton (1994) uses the term "graphical dynamics" to include speed lines (▱▤▱), shake lines (⚡), and ghost images (▱). These can all be added to images to indicate motion or a change of state. Notice the slant, or "posture of action" (Horton, 1994), in the first and second images—this tactic further suggests the motion of the objects.

Bliss (1995) used indicators to create a grammatical system that allowed images of nouns, such as ear and eye, to become related action verbs, such as listen and look, respectively (∂! ⊙!).

Arrows can be added to images to show direction, transformation, relation, or movement (Dreyfuss, 1972). This kind of directional arrow is also common in traffic signs and other location indicators. This sign, however, highlights a potential problem for directional symbols; the people seem to be walking in the wrong Direction (Figure 11.30). This sign, however, highlights a potential problem for directional symbols; the people seem to be walking in the wrong direction.

The arrow in the following image is used to indicate the action "save to folder": ▣▱

Figure 11.30 Arrow used to show direction.

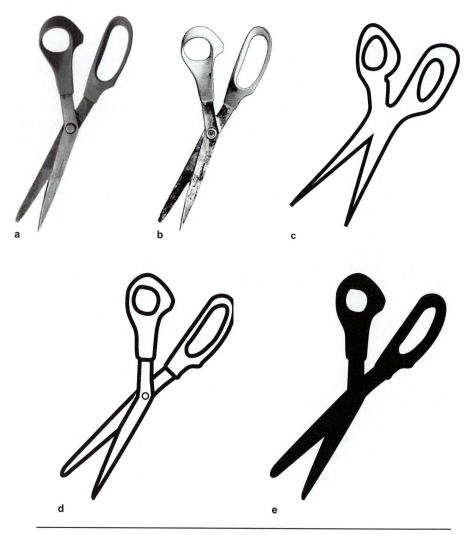

Figure 11.31   Icon styles. (a) Photograph. (b) Drawing. (c) Caricature. (d) Outline. (e) Silhouette.

Style

Horton identifies five basic styles of icon design, as shown in Figure 11.31. When you are designing an interface, choose one of these styles and stick with it. Mixing styles can give the interface a haphazard and cluttered appearance. It can also be effective, however, to use one style for one family of icons and another, closely related style for a different family. This technique increases the contrast between the two families without creating too much visual confusion on the page.

If you try this method, remember that the caricature, outline, and silhouette styles are more closely related to each other than the others are. They will blend more easily with each other than with the photograph and drawing styles. A more jarring effect would be created if you combined, for example, a group of caricature images with a group of photographs.

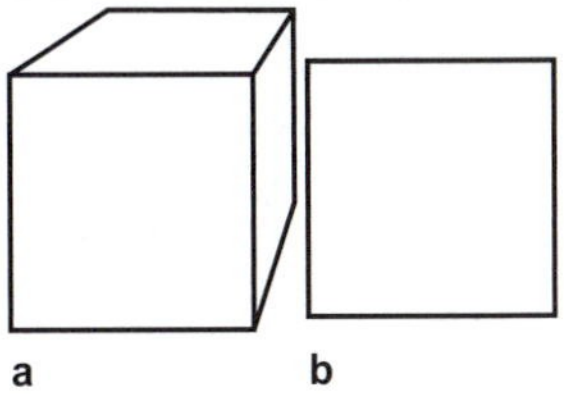

Canonical View

You can use a 3D perspective to help users to recognize an image. Three-dimensional rendering is encouraged by both the current Apple and Microsoft specifications. A three-quarter perspective or linear perspective can help users to recognize an object if it is common for the object to be seen in that way.

The most common view of an object, that is, the view that typifies the object and is most easily recognized, is called the object's canonical view. For instance, a box is more recognizable in a 3D rendering than in a 2D one (Figure 11.32).

A 3D image of a file icon, however, would probably not help because text documents are more often seen from a flat perspective. In this case, a 3D view would not be the object's canonical view.

Figure 11.32 (a) Canonical view. (b) 2D view.

Aggregate Symbols

> **MAXIM**
>
> Symbols can be combined to communicate complex information.

You can combine images to create a sense of action. Consider the search symbol in Figure 11.33a, which is a combination of the file symbol—representing the thing we wish to search—and the magnify symbol—which has an indexical relation to the idea of searching for something.

We can also combine arbitrary or phonographic symbols with representational symbols. For instance, It has become standard practice to use the arbitrary sign of a

Figure 11.33 (a) Aggregate search symbol. (b) Aggregate "No Smoking" sign. (c) Aggregate information symbol.

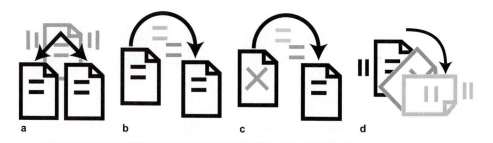

Figure 11.34   Action symbols. (a) Make a copy. (b) Copy and paste. (c) Cut and paste. (d) Delete.

circle with a slash through it to signify a prohibition of an action, as in the "No Smoking" sign in Figure 11.33b. You can Iso show file information functionality by using the letter 'i' as a logogram combined with an iconic file image as in Figure 11.33c.

You can create a rich vocabulary of actions and procedures by combining symbols and indicators, as shown in Figure 11.34.

Horton identifies four methods for combining images to create meaning:

- Overlap
- Addition
- Antithesis
- Specification

Overlap—You can use an overlapping technique to put related images on the same icon. With overlapping you can convey a more inclusive or generalized message than you could with the use of only one of the images. Tools, for example, are often combined to signify system tools or utilities (Figure 11.35a). A more specific message, such as cut, would be communicated if only one of the tools were used (Figure 11.35b).

Addition—The addition technique is more complex. It uses images that, when combined, create a unique message. For example, in the search icon in Figure 11.36, the individual icons have an indexical relation to the concept being communicated.

Antithesis—Antithesis involves the combination of opposite or contrasting images, as in the icon shown in Figure 11.37 for the Inverse Image command.

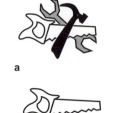

a

b

Figure 11.35   (a) Tools icon.
(b) Cut icon.

Figure 11.36   Search icon.

Figure 11.37   Inverse Image
icon.

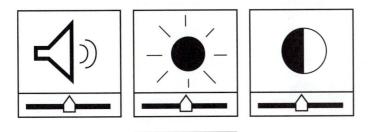

Figure 11.38 Specification.

Specification—Specification is used to distinguish between related objects or functions. A unifying image is used, and various details are added to indicate differences. Icons for data types and icons for volume, contrast, and brightness controls make effective use of specification (Figure 11.38).

11.3.6. Icon Size

MAXIM

Icons are always square and standardized at fixed dimensions.

The Microsoft user interface guidelines identify three preferred sizes and two color depths for icons:

> Supply icons for your application in 16-color and 256-color versions and in three sizes: 16 × 16 pixels, 32 × 32 pixels, and 48 × 48 pixels.

> The system automatically maps colors in your icon design for monochrome configurations. However, you should convert to grayscale to check your icon design. If the result is not satisfactory modify the design and include monochrome icons as well. *(Microsoft Co., 2006)*

The Apple user interface guidelines present a similar set of specifications. You need to provide at least the following files:

> A 128 × 128 image (for Finder icons)
> A mask that defines the image's edges so that operating system can determine which regions are clickable . . .
> For the best-looking icons at all sizes, you should also provide custom image files ("hints") at two other sizes: 32 × 32, and 16 × 16 . . . (Apple, 2007)

As you can see, with icon design, we are dealing with an art of the miniature. It requires a great deal of skill and experience to create a convincing image on a canvas of 16 × 16 pixels. In most cases, a team's graphic designer will develop the final image, but input should come from all members.

The process will go more smoothly if everyone on the team understands the icon's necessary dimensions and the limitations that must be obeyed. A more informed team discussion will occur if the miniature scale of icon specifications is thoroughly understood by everyone involved.

11.3.7. Transparency and Background

MAXIM

To make areas of an icon transparent, include a mask.

Some icons use backgrounds that are transparent so they can blend in with the desktop or folder background. An icon with a mask can take advantage of the system's transparency effect. A mask is a grayscale shadow of an icon's image shape that is included in a special channel called the alpha channel. It tells the system where the image's transparent and opaque areas are.

A mask may be applied to application icons that appear on the desktop, but with one consideration: there is no way to predetermine what the background color will be because users have the ability to change background colors and desktop images. The color of the background can significantly alter the appearance of colors in the icon, making it seem darker or lighter.

It is also possible that a change in background color can make parts of your design invisible. Consider the common arrow cursor—it is a white arrow. When the cursor passes over a black background it is very visible. What happens when it passes over a white background? It does not disappear because it has a black border. This makes the image very useful in just about any situation. Icons are generally more visually complex than a cursor image, but the concept is the same—it must be visible on diverse backgrounds.

You can use an icon's entire allotted square area and not take advantage of its transparency potential, but that would be limiting, and it does not require much effort for you to check your icon design on various colored backgrounds with different brightness settings. The potential benefits are worth the effort.

GIF Transparency

Transparency is also an important consideration in icon development for Web pages. The GIF and PING file formats include a parameter that causes one color to be rendered transparent. This is a common situation on the Web that is often required by the graphic design of the site. In this situation, the edges of an icon's opaque areas and its background color will be juxtaposed, which can cause some unwanted color contrast effects.

Remember, the black border of an opaque shape will disappear on a black background, so test your images to make sure that they will work in as many situations as possible. Anti-aliasing can also cause unwanted results by creating a fuzzy glow around images placed on darker backgrounds (Figure 11.39).

There are many adequate applications for icon creation, such as IconForge® by Cursor Arts *(http://www.cursorarts.com/index.html)*. These applications supply all

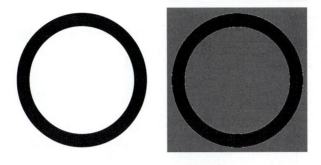

Figure 11.39 Transparency.

the tools that you will require and afford easy access to the palettes and settings for all icon variations. These applications create the proper file formats and masks, allowing you to spend your energy on design. As always, these applications will not create the designs for you. That is work that only you can do.

11.3.8. Current Practices

MAXIM

Higher graphic quality does not always imply greater intelligibility.

The latest operating systems released by Microsoft and Apple have greatly advanced the graphic quality of icons. Larger sizes are possible, as well as greater bit depths, allowing for more color variations. The possibility for photorealist icon design is at hand. This is, however, a mixed blessing. Adding details that do not help a user to recognize an image might interfere with the important details. This confuses people and slows them down.

People generally like higher-quality images. However, as we gain the ability to use more colors and larger sizes for the design of icons, the temptation to rely on graphic images as symbols also becomes greater. Just because we can use photorealistic images as icons does not mean they will be any more useful or effective than their more illustration-like predecessors.

It is possible for a user to confuse these rich graphics with other images that do not represent functionality. This can diminish the predictability of the interface and cause general confusion.

Detailed information on the development of icons for the Apple OS X is available at *http://developer.apple.com/documentation/UserExperience/Conceptual/ OSXHIGuidelines/*. Information on Windows XP icon development can be obtained at: *http://msdn2.microsoft.com/en-us/library/ms997621.aspx.*

Design Scenario

Circumference: Icons

We now revisit the *Circumference* Web site and apply what we learned in this chapter to the development of icons for the site.

This site offers poetry in many different languages and translations of those poems into English. This is an excellent opportunity for the development of icons because of the global and multilingual nature of the site.

It is assumed that people will come to the site that speak English and want an exposure to poetry from other countries. It is also assumed that people from the countries represented in the journal will come to the site to read poetry in their native language. In other words, English is not assumed as the language of all the site visitors. The site has a global scope and can therefore benefit from the use of images and icons that are language agnostic.

The concept covered in this design scenario include the following:

- Icon type
- Icon color
- Conventions
- Aggregate symbols
- Localization
- Search

The global navigation covers the seven major areas of the site:

About | Submissions | Issues | Contact | Subscriptions | Events | Supporters

We cover these major areas first, and then look at some of the other opportunities to use images to help visitors understand and navigate the site.

Icon Type

The first consideration is to decide what style of icon to use. Because we want to create images with the widest global understanding, we will stay with the style used for the international signage found in airports and on traffic signs. They are generally pictographs that have iconic or indexical associations with the underlying functionality.

This type of sign often resembles ISOTYPE symbols, but we will also include some of the grammatical concepts we saw in Blissymbols.

> **Design Principles:** Familiarity, Simplicity—We will use a style that is based on the one used for international public signage; it will be a look that people are familiar with. These signs use basic outlines that create strong, simple images.

This kind of image is best suited for the GIF or PING file format. They are illustrations that use solid blocks of color and thus benefit from the lossless compression offered by these formats. A lossless compression algorithm does not reduce the information in the image file so the quality of the image does not diminish when the compression occurs. These images can best be created using a drawing program like Adobe Illustrator®.

We will also use photos on the Web site from the various events sponsored by the journal. These are better suited for the JPEG format because they involve subtle gradients of color. This type of image is best developed using a painting program like Adobe PhotoShop®. These formats use a lossy compression algorithm that actually reduces some of the information in the image, which eventually leads to a diminished image quality. The image begins to appear grainy or blurry as the amount of compression is increased.

The basic rule for deciding on graphic file formats is that illustrations, diagrams, and any image that uses solid fields of color should be rendered in the GIF or PING format and any photorealist, painted, or other images that use color gradients or complex textures should use the lossy JPEG format.

The JPEG compression format introduces artifacts (a discernible graininess or distortion) into the solid fields of color used in illustration-type images. These artifacts are also introduced into photorealist images, but they are not as noticeable due to the more complex color combinations involved in the gradients and textures.

Icon Color

The icons will be used to navigate the site so they will become hyperlinked images. According to the color scheme developed in the previous chapter's design scenario, we conform to convention by using blue to indicate hyperlinks; therefore, we use a dark version of the blue color derived from the color of Issue 3 (R: 0 G: 31 B: 68 or Hex: #001F44). We also bring in the dark version of the green color (R: 6 G: 114 B: 68 or Hex: #067244) to add contrast to the images and bring out some of the details.

> **Design Principle:** Conventions—There are conventions that already exist on the Web, and we should strive to use them so that our visitors can use their knowledge, which will make the site more intuitive.

Conventions

There are two obvious areas that can use existing conventions—contact and subscriptions. The contact icon will use the convention of an envelope, and the subscription icon will use the shopping cart convention.

Another convention is to use the logogram "i" to indicate information. We will use this symbol to link to the About page where visitors can find information about the journal. We now have the three icons shown in Figure 11.40.

Notice the use of leveling in the shopping cart image; much of the unnecessary detail has been eliminated. Also notice the use of action lines in the contact image; this gives it an indication of action—sending e-mail. The About icon uses a circle, which is a conventional way to present phonograms, but also reflects the

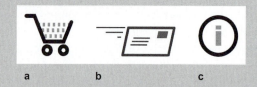

Figure 11.40   (a) Subscription icon. (b) Contact icon. (c) About icon.

Figure 11.41   Supporters icon.

Circumference logo and is mirrored in the issue icons we used to explore color manipulation in Chapter 9.

We can also draw on another convention derived from ISOTYPE symbols to represent the supporters of the journal. These are the people who contribute to the journal, and this can be represented by outlines of people as shown in Figure 11.41.

Aggregate Symbols

We now have three icons left to develop—submissions, issues and events. For the issues icon we simply use a highly leveled image of some journals (Figure 11.42a). We can then use this image and combine it with the image of a person to create an aggregate image that will indicate poetry readings (Figure 11.42b). Notice the action lines that indicate speech. Finally, we use the indexical image of a pencil with an open journal to indicate submission to the journal (Figure 11.42c).

Localization

The journal has examples of poetry on the site that are presented in both the original language and the English translation. These examples are linked from a table of contents (TOC) page for each issue. This is a good opportunity to use the flags of the counties of origin to indicate the presence of an example of poetry.

> **Design Principles:** Familiarity, Recognition—People are familiar with many of the flags associated with the poets' country of origin, which affords them the use of recognition.

Consider the following section of the TOC from Issue 4 of the journal. We can easily understand the country of origin from the use of the flag. This requires knowledge of the individual flags, but it will be an additional aid to people who do not speak English and wish to read poetry in their native language. They will be familiar with the flag of their own country.

Figure 11.42   (a) Issues icon. (b) Events icon. (c) Submissions icon.

Design Scenario (cont.)

Example 11.1 Excerpt from the Table of Contents of Issue 4

One interesting issue to consider is the miniature nature of these icons. They do not support a high level of detail, which can be problematic for some of the images. Notice the first flag for the Greek poem. There are a number of small white strips and a small white cross. This image is still clear at this small size but the blue color is not that strong.

Consider the image in Figure 11.42. This is an alternate version of the official flag that was used during a brief period in the mid twentieth century. It is simpler than the current official flag and is not uncommon. This affords a degree of automatic leveling for the image that may be beneficial at very small sizes. If a situation like this presents itself, it may be necessary to take advantage of it, but unsupported alterations will decrease the value of the image.

Figure 11.43 Alternate Greek flag.

Search

Notice how the colors of the flags cause them to pop out. This helps people to locate the links to the poetry examples. The other entries have no images and, therefore, blend in with each other. This helps people to locate the poem titles that have accompanying text. It is important to get the colors and proportions of the flags correct; otherwise people will become confused. There are many resources on the

Design Scenario (cont.)

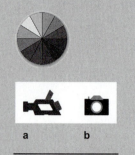

**Figure 11.44 (a) Video icon.
(b) Photo icon.**

Web for information about country flags, such as the Flags of the World Web site (*http://www.fotw.net*).

> **Design Principle:** Stimulus Intensity—The poem titles with flag icons will stand out from the other titles because the color, shape, and size of the icons have greater intensity and are more quickly perceived.

The *Circumference* site also has photos and video clips from the different launch readings. These can be found in the Events area. The videos include some of the poems that are listed in the various TOCs for each issue.

We use an icon to help people to locate these videos. The most likely candidate is to use a conventional symbol of a video camera for the videos and a regular camera for the photos. The images we will use are very basic and will not include much detail—just enough to recognize the image (Figure 11.44).

> **Design Principle:** Simplicity—Leveling has been used to eliminate all extraneous noise from the images. What are left are the most recognizable features of the actual objects.

The following is an excerpt from the events page showing how these icons are used to indicate the presence of videos and photos.

Example 11.2 Excerpt from Events Page

VIDEO FOOTAGE

> 📹 *Issue I - Launch Reading, November 20, 2003
> Teachers & Writers Collaborative, New York City*
> 📹 *Issue II - Launch Reading, August 24, 2004
> Swiss Institute—Contemporary Art, New York City*

PHOTO GALLERY

> 📷 Mary Ann Caws, Farnoosh Fathi, Eliot Weinberger, and Liz Werner.
> May 17, 2004 - Pete's Candy Store, Brooklyn, NY
>
> 📷 Jen Hofer, Christine Hume, Pierre Joris, and Matthew Zapruder.
> March 26th, 2004 - Delilah's, Chicago, IL

We now have a number of icons that we can use to support the navigation of the site. We also have icons that can help people to find things of interest such as poetry in their native language, videos, and photos of *Circumference* events.

Summary

Graphical user interfaces are quite common. Most digital appliances, such as cell phones and PDAs, take advantage of this approach and incorporate icons in their interfaces. These small graphic signs have advantages and disadvantages for interaction design. We have seen how they allow for recognition rather than recall and tap into our ability to remember graphic details over an extended period of time. We have also looked at some of the problems involved in decoding the meaning of an image, from cultural implications to ambiguous designs.

With the movement toward the use of smaller devices, it has become clear that icons may be better suited than text for limited display areas. These tiny images may require text explanations at first, in the form of tool tips, but once learned, they convey a great deal of information in a limited space.

We have explored the effect of images on searches, and how the attributes of detail, color, size, shape, and location affect user performance regarding icons. These are complex issues requiring the simultaneous manipulation of multiple factors.

Identifying the principles involved in icon design adds more structure to this complex task. Such structure enables us to establish a foundation on which to base the aesthetics of design.

Understanding the context of an image is essential to successful icon design. Icons do not exist in a vacuum; our perception of their attributes is affected by the context in which we see them. With the evolution of the World Wide Web this contextual environment is reaching global proportions.

Icon design is a complex process that involves an aesthetic approach. A careful study of the available research can establish a solid foundation for this creative work and contribute to the successful design of icons.

Resources on the Web

www.aw.com/heim
You will find links to information concerning icon creation, tools and guidelines.

Suggested Reading

Hora, M. (2005). *Official Signs & Icons 2:* Ultimate Symbol Inc.

Horton, W. (1994). *The Icon Book: Visual Symbols for Computer Systems and Documentation* (1 ed.): John Wiley & Sons.

Liungmand, C. G. (1994). *Dictionary of Symbols*: W. W. Norton & Company.

CHAPTER 12

Text

Text is an important element in interaction design. Computer screens are often filled with textual information related to tasks and goals. Interface controls have labels to inform users of their function. Icons have tool tips (small text boxes that pop up when a user hovers over the image). Menus have titles and options. Contextual help facilities are available to explain control functions and processes. Much of the work that takes place in the contemporary office environment involves computer-generated and/or computer-manipulated text.

It is important to understand how people relate to text on the screen. What are the issues involved in this interaction, and how can they best be applied to interface design? In this chapter we look at the factors involved in reading. We consider the different types of text used in computer interfaces and we explore how the physical characteristics of text affect people's perception and comprehension.

12.1. Human Issues Concerning Text

First we consider the issues involving interface text from the human perspective. We explore how and why people read. We then look at the issues involved when people read from a computer screen instead of paper. We need to understand these basic issues before we can design usable interfaces that involve text, which is just about every user interface with which we will be involved.

12.1.1. The Reading Process

We begin by looking at the reading process. It is important to understand how people read so that we can create designs that tap into their strengths and avoid their weaknesses. We need to understand the physical aspects of reading so we can make proper determinations about text presentation. We want to make it as easy as possible for people to read the text we put on the screen. Text is one of the most efficient means of communicating information; we do not want to diminish its usefulness by designing screens that are hard to read.

Saccades–Fixations

Eye movement during reading can be broken down into two basic components—quick, jerky movements called saccades and intermittent pauses on areas of interest called fixations. Saccades move the eye in a forward direction, about 8 to 10 letters at a time. At the end of a line, a saccade in the opposite direction drops our eyes to the next line of the text. This is basically a line-feed, carriage return operation.

Visual and cognitive processing occurs during fixation but not during saccades. If text is difficult to comprehend, if it includes long or unfamiliar words, fixations increase in duration. A backward saccade, called a regression, might also occur, allowing the reader to revisit the section in question.

Regressions of approximately 10 letters are generally related to comprehension or readability, whereas regressions involving fewer letters are related to poor legibility. We explore these issues in the Legibility/Readability section.

We can determine how legible a section of text is by calculating how long it takes to read the passage. When text is of poor quality, the eye must scan forward as well as backward to acquire enough information to decode the letters, requiring numerous saccades and regressions, which slows down the reading process. Periods of fixation also increase in duration while the reader strives to process the visual cues. Poor legibility can also cause visual fatigue, which reduces reading speed even more.

Word Shapes

MAXIM

Experienced readers recognize word shapes.

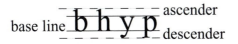

Figure 12.1 Lowercase letters.

Reading is a two-step process. First we distinguish letter or word shapes, and then we associate meaning. Experienced readers immediately recognize word shapes; they seldom decode words letter by letter as they did when they were learning to read. Studies show that we can recognize words as quickly as we recognize single letters. Therefore, it is apparent that we decode the word as a unit instead of processing each individual letter (Mills & Weldon, 1987).

MAXIM

We read extended text passages more quickly in lowercase than uppercase.

Studies have shown that we are able to identify letters or words more easily and from a greater distance if they are in uppercase. Nonreading tasks, such as entering single letters on a computer, have also shown an advantage for uppercase letters.

However, it is easier to read continuous text if it is in lowercase or lowercase with initial caps. Lowercase presentation is more common, so our experience becomes an advantage. With lowercase letters, words also have more distinctive shapes, which make them easier to differentiate.

The descending lines that cross the baseline in letters like "y" and "p" and the ascending lines in letters like "b" and "h" give lowercase words unique shapes that can be recognized quickly and accurately (Figure 12.1).

Uppercase words present less differentiated shapes due to the uniformity of letter height and shape. As shown in Figure 12.2, the words "word" and "shape" are more distinct in lowercase than their uppercase counterparts "WORD" and "SHAPE." Optimal reading performance depends on our ability quickly to interpret these shapes and suffers if they are not easily recognized.

The shapes of the first and last letters might be more significant than the shapes of the internal letters. It has been shown that people can read words with the letters

Figure 12.2 Word shapes—uppercase and lowercase.

out of order if the first and last letters are correct. Consider the following modification of this paragraph:

> The shpaes of the fsrit and lsat lrettes might be mroe sginifinact than the shpaes of the itenranl letetrs. It has been shwon that popele can raed wodrs wtih the ltetres out of odrer if the fisrt and lsat leetres are crorect.

Notice, however, that alterations of the smaller letters are less problematic because they do not alter the overall shape as much.

12.1.2. The Reading Purpose

Reading is not a singular task; it involves many different types of activity. Reading a novel, for example, is a continuous process—we immerse ourselves in the flow of the text. At other times we just scan for words or letters of interest in a disjointed way. We also do not read from computer screens in the same way that we read from paper documents.

Reading involves many different kinds of tasks. How does this affect interaction design? How can we support these different kinds of reading tasks through our interface designs? We consider these issues in the next section on interaction.

12.1.3. Paper versus Screens

The benefits of digital documentation are just beginning to be understood. Searching for keywords and editing on electronic documents are much easier than on paper. The storage of paper documents presents an archival issue; they require a huge amount of physical space. Electronic media have practically no physical storage requirements. The dissemination of digital documents is easier than that of paper documents. With the advent of the Internet, digital documentation is available instantaneously worldwide.

> **MAXIM**
>
> Paper is more flexible than electronic media.

There are, however, advantages that paper has over screens. Paper can be used more easily than computer screens in certain situations. Paper documents are more portable and do not require electricity. Notebook computers have enabled computers to be used in a more flexible way, but they are still much heavier than paper documents and require appropriate environments with adequate space and surface characteristics. Laptop computers can operate on battery power, but batteries do not last forever.

Figure 12.3   Place holders.

Paper documents afford the use of place holders and allow us to make determinations of text length and location within the text (Figure 12.3).

MAXIM

We often rely on our spatial memory when we search for information.

We also rely on spatial cues to help us comprehend what we read, and we use page location to help us remember related facts. For example, we might find a passage we are seeking by recalling that it is before an illustration or toward the end of a chapter. This enables us to use our spatial memory to retrieve information, and helps us to understand the document's structure.

Using spatial cues works quite well and efficiently with paper documents and books because we are able to tap into our tactile relationship with the physical properties of paper, such as its thickness or weight.

We cannot, however, apply the same spatial memory tactics to electronic documents that we use with paper. Screens have a limited amount of information visible at any given time. To view more information, you must often scroll through a document. The parts of a document we do not see reside in a space beyond our perception. The application interface acts as a flexible viewport into the document, and our understanding of location is inhibited because we no longer have fixed spatial cues.

What exists beyond the window is only hinted at by an electronic document's interface. The location and size of the scrollbar slider, for example, are often proportional to the length of the document and show us our approximate location, but we would have to check the number of pages in the document to fully understand its implications.

Word processing applications allow for a "page view" format that mimics the dimensions of paper documents, but these often do not afford us a view of the entire page, and they provide no tactile sense of where we are in the document. The shear thickness of the remaining pages in a book gives us valuable information not available in electronic documents.

Flexibility

Paper documents are easy to manipulate physically. They can be spread out across a desk, for example, exposing multiple documents concurrently. Screens are not as flexible; desktop computers with large screens are usually fixed in place, and are not easily given to the simultaneous display of multiple documents.

Although some of the beneficial properties of paper are also found in electronic documents such as highlighting and bookmarking, they remain more difficult to use and are often inconvenient. Norman suggests that some of the functionality possible with electronic documents is actually rendered useless because it is not visible to the user or requires knowledge and skills the user does not possess. Our machines are now so complex that the days when a GUI made system functionality visible are over (Norman, 1998).

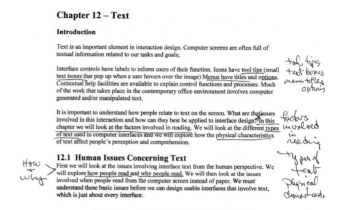

Figure 12.4   Annotated paper document.

Annotation

> **MAXIM**
>
> The ability to annotate aids comprehension.

One of the most significant features of paper is the ability it affords us to annotate text with comments, to highlight, and to underline (Figure 12.4). It has been shown that by annotating the information we read— a process called active reading—we can increase our ability to learn and deepen our understanding (Adler & van Doren, 1972; O'Hara, Sellen, & Bentley, 1999).

This is a significant concern in the design of interactive devices. How can we create interfaces that allow people to actively annotate and mark up text? Does this mean that drawing and handwriting functionality should be incorporated into the textual display?

There is already software that allows the use of a stylus on a tablet PC to create this type of annotation. Some of the latest interactive white boards also allow the entering of annotations that can be saved with the text file. We are at the beginning of this area of development, and research has shown some positive directions for the future (Wolfe, 2000).

12.2. Using Text in Interaction Design

Many different kinds of text are found in computer interfaces, ranging from menu titles, to hyperlinks, to tool tips. They each serve a different purpose and must be treated accordingly. For instance, there are important usability considerations regarding text used for menu titles and icon labels that are different than those concerning hypertext. We will differentiate between text that informs as opposed to text that does work—commentary text and instrumental text, respectively.

Commentary Text

Commentary text makes system states or system functionality visible. For example, tool tips inform the user about the underlying functionality of icons, system messages convey information about system states and error conditions, and a form may have instructions as to how to fill in its entry boxes.

There are many different types of online documentation, and the most common is online help. No matter what kind of interface you are building, some sort of help facility will be required. Help resources range from tool tips and balloon help to online tutorials. Help text is commentary in nature.

Microsoft uses the following categories to differentiate help methods: contextual, procedural, referential, and conceptual. Each different type of help resource has a specific format for what should be included and how this text should be written. The formats range from short phrases, as in tool tips, to lengthy explanations, as in conceptual help resources.

Microsoft defines these categories as follows:

- **Contextual help** provides immediate assistance to users without requiring them to leave the context in which they are working, such as pop-up menus.
- **Procedural help** provides the steps necessary for carrying out a task.
- **Reference help** serves as an online reference book.
- **Conceptual help** provides background information, feature overviews, or processes.

Instrumental Text

Instrumental text refers to underlying system functionality. It is "text that does work" (Ramey, 1989). For example, links and menu options perform actions and alter the state of an interface either immediately or eventually. When a link is clicked, new information is displayed. When a menu option is selected, a command is carried out. By choosing the Bold command, the user reformats the selected text. Instrumental text represents functionality and relates directly to user actions.

Controls—Instrumental text is most often related to the controls found on the screen such as buttons, checkboxes, radio buttons, and icons. These controls often require labels to clarify their function and operation. While this may seem like commentary text, the control's function and its label are viewed as one entity.

A group of these controls can be considered a menu, offering the user a set of choices. Because they share many characteristics with other menus, the choice of their labels should reflect the same advice given earlier for menus: the labels should be descriptive, consistent, and use parallel construction.

Hypertext—It is significant that two of the protocols that define the World Wide Web are the Hypertext Transfer Protocol (HTTP) and the Hypertext Markup Language (HTML). At the core of the Web is the ability to link to other resources. This is usually done by way of hypertext links, although other linking mechanisms are possible, such as linked images or image maps.

> **MAXIM**
>
> Hypertext links must give unambiguous indications of the target destination.

Hyperlinks, like menu titles and options, must supply enough information to users so that there is no question about where the link will take them. The wording of the link text is the strongest indicator of the link's destination. In this situation, context is a significant factor that can help to clarify ambiguities; however, a clear, descriptive phrase remains essential to avoiding confusion and delay in the navigation of a Web site.

In his book *Don't Make Me Think* Krug (2006) suggests that what is important is not so much the number of links that a visitor must click but rather the quality of the links—how obvious the links are. In other words, an interface that requires two clicks to reach a destination may be harder to use than an interface that requires four clicks to reach the same destination. It all depends on how easy it is to decide which links to click on. If the link labels in the interface that requires two clicks are ambiguous, it will take longer and the visitor will be more prone to error than it will to make the four clicks in an interface with clear and easy-to-understand hyperlink labels.

Hyperlinks are found in the body of Web page text as well as in navigation menus. The form that body text links take varies according to the context; however, it is important that navigation menus always contain descriptive and consistently worded links. We look more closely at the visual aspects of hyperlinks in the section on Web text.

12.2.1. Legibility

No matter what kind of text we are designing, our primary concern is legibility. To read a word, we have to be able to distinguish the characters or word shapes. The characters must be clear, distinct, and large enough to see and contain enough contrast so that they can be distinguished from the background.

Environmental conditions must also be adequate: there must be enough light, minimal glare or reflection from the screen, and no obstructions. All other issues are irrelevant if the text is illegible.

> **MAXIM**
>
> Legibility is an essential first step in the reading process.

We use the term legibility to describe the process of distinguishing the physical aspects of reading. Legibility is an essential first step in the reading process. As legibility decreases, so do reading comprehension, speed, and accuracy. It is only when legibility is not an obstacle that can we begin to understand what we are reading.

> **MAXIM**
>
> Design for the least favorable conditions.

Computer displays are found in all sorts of environmental conditions. Indoor computing environments can range from well-lit offices to obscure industrial warehouses and dimly lit factories. Open-air environments have tremendous ranges of lighting and climatic conditions.

We must take these environmental conditions into consideration when we are making determinations about font size and foreground/background contrast. It is best to design for the most problematic conditions first. If the text is legible under the worst conditions, it will most likely be legible under more favorable conditions as well.

> **MAXIM**
>
> Our capacity to perceive details decreases with age.

When we tink about legibility we must also consider age and possible vision impairments. Visual acuity, the capacity to perceive details, decreases with age and varies from person to person. Common conditions such as near-sightedness can significantly affect decisions about screen distance in relation to the user.

12.2.2. Readability

After we process the physical aspects of text we begin to the process of understanding what we are reading. Comprehension is affected by many variables, such as line length, line spacing, formatting, margin width, and scrolling. It is also affected by grammatical issues, such as semantics and syntax. We use the term readability to describe the comprehensibility of a passage of text. Let's look at some of the issues that affect the readability of text.

User's Language

We should strive to use language the user will understand. We sometimes use words that refer metaphorically or symbolically to actions in the real world. We "launch programs" and put the screen "to sleep." These are examples of domain jargon, which must be learned. New users will not intuitively understand the meaning of these expressions. You should avoid this type of terminology in Help text.

Jargon often becomes part of our lexicon. Program names are sometimes used as verbs; for example, we can "zip files," which refers to the Winzip® compression application, or say "Google that for me," referring to the use of the Google search engine. This type of usage is not always understood by users and can quickly become outdated.

MAXIM

Use the terms people will see in the interface.

Whenever possible, use the terminology that the user will see in the interface. If the interface uses the term "exit," use it in your help and instructional text; do not use other, similar terms such as "close" instead.

MAXIM

Technical terminology should be avoided.

You should avoid technical terminology unless the target user is a domain expert and requires specific technical indications or directions.

MAXIM

Word-for-word translations can create confusion.

To accomplish tasks, computers often require behavior that has no counterpart in real life, for instance, the scrolling and clicking of interface objects. Because these terms do not have translations into many languages, the English terms are often used. Attempting to translate these terms into local languages can have humorous, although potentially confusing outcomes. For instance, the English term for the mouse input device would not normally be translated into the equivalent of a small furry rodent.

Ambiguous Text

Users must be able to understand what is required by the interface for them to complete their tasks. Since this often relates to the readability of interface text the designer needs to consider the following questions:

- Is the text clear and unambiguous?
- Is the text contradictory in any way?

Ramey cautions against the possibility of what she calls "Escher effects" (Ramey, 1989). This term relates to the graphic illustrator M. C. Escher, who used perceptual ambiguities in 2D depictions of 3D scenes to create physically impossible objects, such as the impossible trident in Figure 12.5.

When we encounter an impossible object we are forced to contemplate its nature. We cannot conceptualize the object because its parts conflict with each other. We are forced constantly to refer to the object's individual parts without the advantage of a unifying mental image.

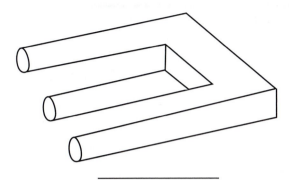

Figure 12.5 Impossible trident.

Language may also create similarly "impossible objects." Sometimes, a particular sentence structure can imply multiple meanings. We use punctuation marks to eliminate many of these ambiguities. For instance, the phrase "that that is is" makes no apparent sense. However, by applying punctuation to the sentence, it becomes a statement of fact: "that, that is, is."

Linguistic "Escher effects" can also be created by context. Consider the phrase "input mode." If we anticipated a command request by the system, we would most likely interpret the word "input" as a verb and try to tell the computer which mode we wanted. If, on the other hand, we expected that the computer was indicating a system mode, we would probably interpret "input" as a noun and determine that this was the "input mode" as opposed to the "output mode." Similarly, the phrase "search results" can refer to the results of a search, or it can indicate the possibility of searching the results of a previous search.

MAXIM

Avoid noun stacks; they are ambiguous.

Due to the need for economy in many interface designs, text phrases are often reduced to the bare minimum. Although it is important to be concise, it should not be at the expense of clarity. In informal language, we sometimes string together groups of nouns, dropping intervening propositions. This is known as a "noun stack" and can create needless confusion for users. For instance, consider the phrase "display device bridge number." What are the possible interpretations of this phrase? Is there a bridge number for the display device, or is there a number for the display device bridge?

Linguistic Escher effects draw our attention to the individual words in a sentence and cause us to ponder the conflicting possible meanings. In this situation, we are forced to deal with the text as text rather than as content, struggling with semantics and syntax before we can proceed to meaning.

12.2.3. Physical Factors

Reading is a complex process of interdependent variables. No single factor can be manipulated to increase reading performance. To create the most efficient screens, we need to understand the various factors that affect reading performance.

The factors we explore include the following:

- Font size
- Line length
- Margin width
- Vertical line spacing
- Alignment
- Contrast
- Scrolling versus paging

Font Size

The ISO 9241-3, 1992 standard suggests that fonts should have a visual angle of 20 to 22 minutes of arc with an 18-inch distance from the screen for normal text reading. This is the average size of newspaper print, and the angle is larger than the visual angle that defines normal 20/20 vision (5 minutes of arc). That measurement is meant to test vision; it is not a comfortable size for extended reading periods.

There are a number of factors that affect decisions about text size. In some situations, it may be necessary to decrease font size to maximize the amount of text that is visible on the screen. This might minimize scrolling or paging and increase the user's reading speed. Larger font sizes would also increase the size of the text area. This would require more time to read equal amounts of information.

Kiosks and other computer displays may be positioned farther from the viewer than a normal PC screen, necessitating a larger font size. Calculations can be done with the visual acuity formula to determine appropriate font sizes for different viewing distances:

$$X/2 = d \tan(\theta/2)$$

where θ(theta) is the viewing angle, d is distance, and X is the character height. See Appendix A for a more detailed discussion on this topic.

Dix et al. (1998) suggest that text sized between 9 and 12 points is equally readable. This is a common benchmark found in the research literature. However, not all experimental conditions are comparable; variables such as display type and user experience can affect the desired font size.

Horton (1994) identifies some factors that affect font size:

- **Reading Distance**—Greater distances require larger text.
- **Screen Resolution**—Smaller text requires greater resolution to keep the characters clear and legible.

- **Text/Background Contrast**—Negative contrast is optimal (black type on a white background).
- **Visual Acuity of User**—Not all users have 20/20 vision.
- **Type of Reading**—Text can be scanned, read word by word, or read character by character.

Horton also provides an example of the appropriate font size, given near-perfect conditions:

Distance = 20 inches

Visual angle = 0.35 degrees (21 minutes of arc)

Character size = approximately 0.12 inch

Screen resolution = 75 dpi

According to Horton's calculation, characters will be 9 pixels high.

The complete formula for a general benchmark for font size, given normal vision and optimal conditions, is

Font Size = $2d(\tan(\theta/2)) \times$ DPI

Although this can provide a benchmark for default font size settings, actual font size might be altered due to some of the previously mentioned factors.

Another significant consideration is that users may need to change the font size to satisfy their needs. In most situations it is important that you allow this kind of control; you cannot design for all possible circumstances equally, so allowing users to customize their interaction is usually a good idea.

There are times, however, when user control of certain interface settings is not advisable. For instance, a public device such as an ATM machine must be used by a wide spectrum of the population. It would be unwise to allow people to alter font size in this setting because they might make it difficult for the next person to use the interface.

Line Length

MAXIM

Line length affects reading performance but not comprehension.

Studies have shown that the length of a line makes no difference in reading comprehension (Duchnicky & Kolers, 1983; Dyson & Haselgrove, 2001). However, line length has been shown to be a factor in reading performance in terms of speed and accuracy. It is not clear from the research, however, what the optimal line length might be. Studies show conflicting results concerning the most efficient line length, but very short lines—25 characters per line (CPL) and less—have generally been shown to adversely affect performance.

> **MAXIM**
>
> Lines of greater length are read more quickly.

Duchnicky and Kolers found that lines that extend to the full screen (7.4 inches) are easier to read than lines one-third of the length of the screen (2.4 inches). In general, the literature shows that the optimal length for reading speed seems to fall in the range of 75 to 100 characters per line (CPL).

> **MAXIM**
>
> People prefer medium line lengths.

People sometimes indicate a preference for line lengths that are not the most efficient. Results have indicated that users prefer a moderate line length, in the area of 4 inches, or 55 CPL (Dyson & Kipping, 1998; Youngman & Scharff, 1998)

Dyson and Kipping also found that users preferred a three-column format over the faster one-column format. Bernard, Fernandez, & Hull, (2002) found that the preferred length for adults was between 65 and 75 CPL, and that children preferred lengths of 45 CPL. These findings led them to suggest that shorter line lengths are better.

Research Results on Line Length

It is difficult to make comparisons among many of the studies just cited because the experimental conditions vary from one experimental design to another; however, some general conclusions can be made. Bailey's review of the literature concludes that line lengths of 7.4 to 9.6 inches are optimal for increasing reading speed, but that users prefer lengths of around 4 inches. Lines of less than 2.4 inches were found to be the most difficult to read (Bailey, 2002).

Margin Width

Line length might not be the only factor involved in reading performance. Youngman and Scharff (1998) found that there is a significant relationship between line length and margin width. They found that the use of shorter lines—4 inches—with large margins increased reading performance, suggesting that the larger margins facilitated reading by making the text stand out more. This can be considered the basis for guidelines that suggest maximal use of white space.

Vertical Line Spacing

The spacing between lines of text (single spacing, double spacing, etc.) is called leading. The term is derived from the strips of lead that were used to separate lines of type in manual printing processes. Double spacing has been shown to improve reading speed (Kolers, Duchnicky, & Ferguson, 1981). Because double spacing reduces the number of lines that can be viewed on a screen, however, it might necessitate a smaller font size to increase the amount of visible information per screen. Research shows that screens with more information are read faster. Therefore, a careful balance must be maintained among font size, line length, margin width, and vertical spacing.

Reading performance and comprehension are affected by a dynamic interaction among the following factors:

Font Size + Line Length + Margin Width + Vertical Spacing

Alignment

There are four ways in which to align the margins of text blocks, as shown in Table 12.1. The default alignment in most programs is left. This alignment is based on languages that read from left to right and is the most common and readable format for those languages.

> **MAXIM**
>
> For optimal reading of lengthy texts, right and center alignments should be avoided.

Readers processes word groups along a line using forward saccades and fixations. At the end of a line, a large backward saccade is made as the reader continues reading the next line down.

Alignment of the left margin helps the reader's eyes return to the proper location at the beginning of each line. When text is aligned to the right, the reader's eye has to search for the beginning of the next line, which slows reading performance. This searching also occurs with centered text. For these reasons, right and center alignments should be avoided for optimal reading of lengthy texts.

Justified text adds extra spaces between words to achieve the exact line length it requires. While this can be used for most languages it can be problematic for languages like Thai because spaces are used to delimit sentences, not words. In Thai, the addition spaces to achieve justified text would automatically create an artificial sentence structure and potential confusion for the reader.

> **MAXIM**
>
> Text should also be considered a graphical component of a page.

Table 12.1 Text Alignment

Left aligned—The text is aligned to the left margin leaving the right margin ragged.	**Right aligned**—The text is aligned to the right margin leaving the left margin ragged
Justified—Both the left and right margins are aligned, leaving no ragged margins	**Centered**—Text is aligned to a center point, leaving both the right and left margins ragged

Text alignment for short interface elements, such as captions, labels, or headings, must be considered a graphical element of the page layout. When aligning graphical elements, you must take the overall shape of the page into consideration.

Contrast

Interaction designers must make sure that the text contrasts sufficiently with its background. Sensitivity to contrast decreases significantly with age, so text/background contrast must be maintained at the highest possible level for older users. If colors are required by an interface design, user testing is imperative, preferably with grayscale versions first.

The most readable format for text presentation is negative contrast: black type on a white background. This is the standard for most textual information. It offers the highest degree of contrast between the characters and the background. If one of these values is altered, for example, if the text becomes lighter the contrast degreases and legibility suffers.

Three basic trends can occur: (1) The background remains white and the characters are lightened until they also become white (Figure 12.6a), (2) the text remains black and the background becomes darker until it becomes black (Figure 12.6b), and (3) the characters are lightened as the background becomes darker (Figure 12.6c). As you can see there are some problematic combinations that should be avoided.

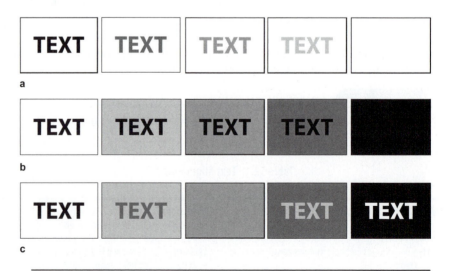

Figure 12.6 (a) Foreground shades. (b) Background shades. (c) Foreground and background shades.

Color Contrast

It has been found that in terms of legibility, green text on a white background is a close second to black text on a white background (Mills & Weldon, 1987). Because black and white have the highest contrast, however, the addition of any color will reduce the contrast.

There is no clear cutoff point or universal threshold for contrast. However, a conversion to grayscale will give a quick indication of legibility. If you want to maintain legibility when color is added to text, you can increase the width of the lines, either by increasing the size of the font or by using bold text.

> **MAXIM**
>
> Luminance contrast is more significant than color contrast.

Color contrast is a significant issue; most of the literature suggests, however, that specific color combinations do not affect legibility as much as luminance or brightness contrasts do. These concerns, therefore, should have the highest priority (Bouma, 1980; Bruce & Foster, 1982; Ohlsson, Nilsson, & Ronnberg, 1981; Radl, 1980; Thorell & Smith, 1990).

Scrolling versus Paging

Electronic documents—Web pages in particular—can be much longer than the browser window, and therefore they might require scrolling to access the entire document. Word processing documents might also require scrolling, but many word processing applications allow for a "page view" format that simulates the pages of a paper document. This format allows users to employ spatial indicators to locate things on the page and orient themselves.

Web pages, on the other hand, are not structured in a page-oriented way; they are single-document screens of undetermined length. Web page designers create their own page dividers using the horizontal rule element or some other graphic device if this effect is required. These page dividers can help users to orient themselves as they scroll through a long page.

When Paging Is Appropriate

There are two alternative ways to move through a Web page. We can use the "page up" and "page down" keys to jump to different locations approximately one page (browser window) away. The designer can also group the text in smaller chunks and then disperse the chunks on separate pages (Figure 12.7). We would then use hyperlinks to access the different pages of the document. This process is known as paging.

Studies have shown that people prefer paging over scrolling. It has also been shown that paging is superior to scrolling for reading and revising text (Kolers, Duchnicky, & Ferguson, 1981; Schwarz, Beldie, & Pastoor, 1983). One of the reasons for this may be that scrolling makes it difficult for users to grasp the structure of the document; reading stops while they are scrolling, and they can only approximate how far to scroll. Scrolling has also been shown to be slower than paging because it

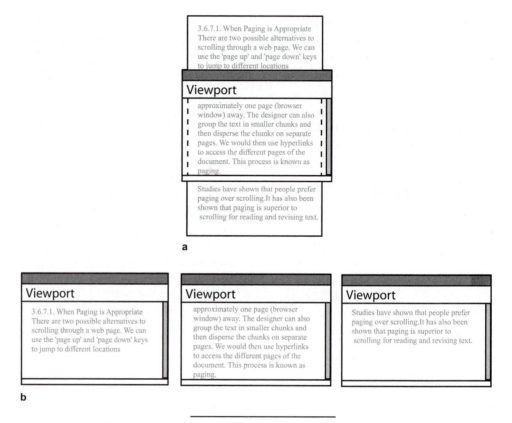

Figure 12.7 (a) Scrolling. (b) Paging.

requires extra time to locate the pointing device and place the pointer on the scrolling controls.

Users often skim Web pages for the information they need and prefer not to read long text passages. A paging format allows users to employ their spatial memories to visually associate information with the page it is on. This is something we are quite efficient at with paper documents. It also enforces the grouping of related information.

If the hyperlink navigation bar is appropriately and consistently placed on all pages, users do not have to move the pointing device, allowing them to concentrate on reading the text. The links for "previous" and "next" in Figure 12.8 are placed at the top of the page and, therefore, remain in a constant location regardless of the amount of content on the page. Redundant links can also be placed at the bottom of a long page.

If the links in Figure 12.8 were placed only below the images, they would bounce around according to the vertical dimension of the particular image on the page. The user would then have to relocate the link to navigate to the next or previous page.

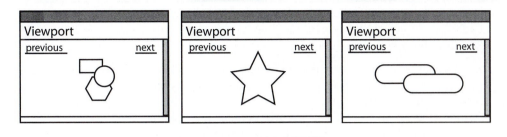

Figure 12.8 Consistent link location.

When Scrolling Is Appropriate

> **MAXIM**
>
> Scrolling facilitates maintenance and printing.

Even though users prefer paging to scrolling, there are times when scrolling is more appropriate. Paging imposes space requirements on page content: all related information must fit in a predetermined amount of screen real estate. Because not all viewers will be using the same software to access the page, you cannot be 100% certain what they will see.

Many Web pages are updated regularly. New information becomes available, and the content of the pages must be altered. This might involve adding pages to the site, which would also mean changes to the navigation. This can be a time-consuming process even for sites that are dynamically created.

People often print out Web pages so they can read them from paper rather than from the screen. They might also want to keep a record of the information or show it to someone without having to use a computer. A site that was page based would be more tedious to print; every page would have to be accessed and printed separately. In this case it would be adviseable to make a print version available that would put all the pages together on a long, scrolling page.

Research Results on Scrolling versus Paging

Before we consider the issue of scrolling versus paging to be closed, we must consider some conflicting research results. A study by Baker (2003) required users to read passages from three different layouts. The first condition presented the passage on four separate pages (Paging), the second condition used two pages with no scrolling (Full), and the third condition placed all of the text on one long page that required scrolling (Scrolling).

Baker found that the paging condition was considerably slower than the scrolling condition, and that subjects preferred the scrolling format over the paging format, which they considered to be "too broken up." These results are surprising in light of previous studies, but they might be attributed to the fact that the subjects said they were more familiar with the scrolled Web page format than the paged one. Familiarity grows over time, and the Web has been around long enough to have influenced the way a generation of computer users reads.

The results also suggest that the length of a scrolled page can affect reading performance as well as user preference. These findings emphasize the importance of user goals and experience and the ways in which these factors affect their performance and preferences. This led Weinschenk and Schaffer (2003) to suggest that, despite research to the contrary, moderate amounts of scrolling may be more suitable than paging in certain situations.

> **MAXIM**
>
> The choice of paging versus scrolling depends on task and layout.

Before a decision can be made about the specific layout of text pages, it is beneficial carefully to study the user's tasks, abilities, experience, and preferences. Design requires tradeoffs among conflicting factors. In some studies, subjects found that clicking back and forth between pages to compare information was cumbersome and slow; they were able to work more efficiently using the scrolling layout, by which they could more easily maneuver around the document.

Other studies found that subjects were able to use their spatial memory to locate information in a paging layout more accurately than in a scrolling layout (O'Hara, Sellen, & Bentley, 1999). Task and layout are inevitably connected. Very long scrolled pages become cumbersome and confusing, whereas multiple pages containing minimal information can require excess work and time to get from page to page, especially if the system is slow to respond.

12.3. Technical Issues Concerning Text

We looked at the human issues involved in reading and how we can use text in interface design; we now consider the technical issues involved in computer-based text.

The Web has enabled a form of global communication that involves many different languages and their respective scripts. Some interaction design projects require the use of these various scripts, but all designs have textual elements in one form or another.

To process and manipulate computer-based text, we must understand the basic components of digital fonts and screen characters. We now explore some of the issues involved in rendering text on computer screens.

12.3.1. Components of Digital Text

A character is basically a concept. The first letter of the English alphabet is represented by the character "A." This is only one form the character can take; it can also be represented by "a" or "*a*" or "*A*" or any number of variations on this basic shape. These variations, however, are not random or limitless. The character "a" has various required features, and at a certain point, the image will no longer be recognized as the letter it is meant to represent.

Sometimes there are only small differences in shape between characters, as for the letters O and Q or the letter I and the number 1. Sometimes the differences are quite large, as in the letters I and W. The further away a character is from its standard shape, the harder it is to recognize or distinguish from other characters. However, font designers sometimes exhibit a great deal of creativity in their designs and retain enough indicators to make the shapes easily recognizable.

A glyph is the physical representation of a character. However, there may not always be a one-to-one relationship between characters and glyphs; sometimes it takes more than one glyph to represent a character. For instance, the æ ligature is a combination of the "a" and "e" glyphs. The "1/2" character combines the "1," "/," and "2" glyphs.

All written languages use specific scripts that contain all the glyphs necessary to create the required characters. This is known as the character repertoire. Some languages, such as English, Italian, and many other European languages, use the same script, which is based on the Latin alphabet, although many of the languages do not use every single character in the repertoire. Some languages require more than one script. Japanese, for example, requires the *hiragana* and *katakana* syllabaries and the Chinese *kanji* ideographs.

Character Sets

Simply put, screen text comprises graphical patterns (glyphs) created by groups of pixels. Each of these patterns is related to a number, and these groups of numbers form a character code. The character code values are encoded onto bit groups. The encoding method is referred to as the character encoding scheme. Usually, groups of 8 bits (bytes, sometimes referred to as octets) are used, but other encoding schemes are possible.

A character set refers to the character repertoire, the character codes, and the encoding scheme (Figure 12.9):

Character Set = Character Repertoire + Character Codes + Encoding Scheme

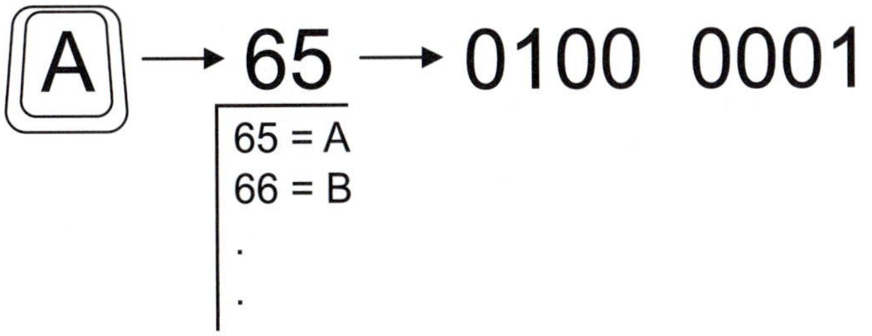

Figure 12.9   Character set.

On a keyboard, keys are mapped to a particular character set. To change from one script to another, from English to Arabic for example, the keyboard mapping must be altered. After the setting is changed, each key will map to a different character code, which then relates to a different character repertoire.

ASCII

Character sets are basically bit-mapping routines for character codes and character repertoires. Each set contains the characters required by a particular script. Some languages share characters and can therefore use the same set. Character sets are finite, however, and can only represent a certain number of characters. Different codes must be created for different scripts.

The most common character code is the American Standard Code for Information Interchange (ASCII). It was proposed by the American National Standards Institute (ANSI) in 1963 and came to fruition in the ANSI Standard X3.4 in 1968. This standard was created to afford interoperability among diverse computing systems. Other competing standards were developed, such as IBM's Extended Binary-Coded-Decimal Interchange Code (EBCDIC), but ASCII achieved industry dominance.

Basic ASCII uses 7-bit encoding, which allows it to represent 128 characters. These characters include alphanumeric as well as nonprinting characters such as Backspace and End of Transmission. Because the 7-bit format is fairly limited, ASCII was extended to 8 bits, allowing for 256 characters. Some of these extra positions were used for national variants, including some specific letters and symbols.

These extended ACSII versions, however, were still insufficient to handle many Asian languages. Not based on the Latin script, these languages often require more than 256 characters. Therefore, an effort was started to create a universal character set.

Unicode

The Unicode project was established with a mandate to promote the development of resources that would enable computer representation of worldwide scripts:

> The Unicode Consortium is a non-profit organization originally founded to develop, extend and promote use of the Unicode Standard, which specifies the representation of text in modern software products and standards.
>
> The Unicode Standard is a character coding system designed to support the worldwide interchange, processing, and display of the written texts of the diverse languages and technical disciplines of the modern world. In addition, it supports classical and historical texts of many written languages. (Unicode Consortium)

The Unicode standard is a work in progress. It includes 8-bit, 16-bit, and 32-bit encoding schemes, and as the standard expands, new characters are added to include all known character repertoires.

Figure 12.10   (a) Serif character. (b) Sans serif character. (c) Cursive character.

Most current browsers support the Unicode standard, ISO/IEC 10646. The XHTML meta tag for Unicode is as follows:

```
<meta http-equiv="Content-Type" content="text/html;charset=utf-8" />
```

To develop Web pages that involve languages with non-ASCII characters, it is necessary to use a Unicode-enabled text editor such as BabelPad.exe on a PC. Unicode Checker is a useful tool for Mac users. That is, of course, unless you wish to translate the text into character references as in the following example:

Ρώτησέ το ο Σωκράτης είπε η Μαίρυλιν

```
&Rho;&#974;&tau;&eta;&sigma;&#941; &tau;&omicron; &omicron;
&Sigma;&omega;&kappa;&rho;&#940;&tau;&eta;&zeta;
&epsilon;&#943;&pi;&epsilon; &eta;
&Mu;&alpha;&#943;&rho;&upsilon;&lambda;&iota;&nu;
```

Fonts

Different fonts—also called typefaces because of their origins in printing—can be considered variations on a theme. Font designers take basic character shapes and create different versions. There are font categories, which share common characteristics. Some of the most common categories are:

- Serif
- Sans serif
- Cursive

Serif fonts have small tags on their strokes called serifs (Figure 12.10a). These fonts are well suited for extended reading. Sans serif fonts do not have the extra strokes, or serifs (Figure 12.10b). These are more often used for headlines and titles. Cursive fonts imitate natural handwriting, with delicate, flowing strokes (Figure 12.10c).

The widest letter in most Latin-based scripts is the capital "M." The letter with the smallest width is "I." A font either can allow just enough width for every individual character or it can assign the same amount of space for each character—logically, this would be the width required for the widest letter.

Fonts that use one standard width for all characters are called fixed-width fonts or monospaced fonts, as opposed to the variable-width fonts, which are also called proportional-width font (Table 12.2).

Table 12.2 Variable- and Fixed-Width Fonts

Variable-width font	ioioioioio
Fixed-width font	`ioioioioio`

Texts that use fixed-width fonts, such as Courier, resemble text that was typed on a typewriter. These are often used to display computer code. Fixed-width fonts take up more screen space than their counterparts:

```
Courier
This is an example of a fixed-width, serif font.
```

Times New Roman
This is an example of a variable-width, serif font.

Arial
This is an example of a variable-width, sans serif font.

Cursive Scripts

Some languages, such as Arabic, only use cursive scripts; their characters do not have print versions. Cursive characters are connected to surrounding characters, creating four possible situations. A character:

- Can be connected to other characters on both sides
- Can be connected to another character on the left side only
- Can be connected to another character on the right side only
- Can stand alone

Therefore, for a printed Arabic text to be acceptable to native readers, the character set must accommodate all of these possible manifestations for each and every letter, thus greatly increasing the number of required patterns for the set (Amara & Portaneri, 1996).

MAXIM

Cursive text requires high-resolution screens.

Cursive text uses graphically more complex symbols that require complex and delicate shapes. Low-resolution screens can destroy some of the subtle shapes required to make the characters recognizable. It is, therefore, important to avoid cursive text when low-resolution screens will be used.

12.3.2. Web Text

Web pages are basically information repositories, and most of the information is presented in text format. It is important, therefore, to understand what is involved in putting text on a Web page. It is beyond the scope of this book to present a complete tutorial on markup languages; however, we will cover the basics and provide an overview of what is involved.

Structure

The title of the page will be used in the title bar of the browser window and by search engines to determine whether the content of the page matches the search criteria. Titles should be descriptive and clearly reflect the content of the page. They can support the navigational scheme, and they can be used to support product recognition:

```
<head>
<title>Company Name—Area of Site—Specific Page</title>
```

Web pages generally have a global reach and may involve multiple languages. It is important to identify the main language of the page and any subsequent language shifts so the software used by visually impaired people can pronounce the words using their native pronunciation:

```
<html xmlns="http://www.w3.org/1999/xhtml" xml:lang="en" lang="en">
<!-- The main language is English -->
    .

    .

<span lang="Fr">Sandra Moussempés</span>
<span lang="En">was born in Paris in 1965. She is the author of three books of poetry,
<span lang="Fr">Exercices d'incendie(Fourbis,</span>
<span lang="En"> 1994),</span>
    .

    .

</div>
```

In some cases it may be necessary to also specify the direction of the language, for example, dir="ltr" or dir="rtl".

We use the "headings" elements to clarify the structure of the page. There are six levels that can be used to structure the hierarchy of the page content; level 1 is the most important:

```
<h1> Topic #1</h1>
<h2>Sub-topic #1</h2>
<h2>Sub-topic #2</h2>
    <h3>Sub/Sub-topic #1</h3>

<h1>Topic #2</h1>
    <h2>Sub-topic #1</h2>
    <h2>Sub-topic #2</h2>
```

We use the semantic markup tags to clarify the purpose and meaning of the various text elements of the page; for example,

```
<abbr title="Social Security Number">SS#</abbr>
```

```
<acronym title="Cascading Style Sheets">CSS</acronym>
<address>Any Town USA</address>
<blockquote>"There is nothing either good or bad, but thinking
makes it so."</blockquote>
<caption>Illustration of the solar system<caption>
<cite>(Adler & van Doren, 1972; O'Hara, Sellen, & Bentley, 1999)</cite>
```

There are markup elements that can be used to add structure:

- Emphasis <em> and <strong>
- Labels <label>
- Table headings <th>
- Legends <legend>
- Menu options <option>

There are markup elements that affect the function of the text:

- Subscript <Sub>
- Superscript <Sup>
- Stricken text <Strike>

Markup can be used to structure the information on the page and create structures such as paragraphs, tables, lists, and forms. It is important to use markup properly so that screen readers and search engines can access the information correctly.

Presentation

After the structure of the page has been created we must focus on the presentation. People don't read markup, they look at how that markup is rendered by the browser. Presentation should be defined by Cascading Style Sheets (CSS) and kept separate from structure; however, remember that they are both derived from the content of the page. They are two sides of the same coin—one addresses the needs of the automated agents, and the other addresses the needs of the user.

CSS was developed by the World Wide Web Consortium (W3C) as a way of separating the presentational and structural aspects of a Web page. It is used to define the visual aspects of a page and provide the Web developer a powerful way of presenting Web-based information. We will look at some of the ways in which Web developers can use CSS in designing the presentational aspects of a Web page.

When we create visual styles for the structural elements of the page there are some important issues to take into consideration:

- Some markup elements have inherent presentational qualities.
- Styles must be appropriate for the markup elements to which they are assigned.
- Styles must be derived from and serve to clarify the content.
- Styles should not compete with the content.
- Styles should not conflict with user's expectations.

Heading elements make the text bold and alter its size. These presentational effects are inherent in the way browsers render the various heading elements. However, they may conflict with the design and layout of the page. CSS can be used to alter these presentational qualities; we just need to know the equivalent CSS properties and then alter them to suit our needs.

Bold is defined in CSS as font-weight and can be delineated as numerical values or relational equivalents:

100|200|300|400|500|600|700|800|900|normal|bold|bolder|lighter

Size is defined as font-size and can be delineated as

- Absolute-size —xx-small, x-small, small, medium, large, x-large, xx-large
- Relative-size,—larger, smaller
- Percentage—120%
- Length; Relative and Absolute
    - Relative
        - em: the width of the character "M"
        - ex: the height of the character "x"
        - px: pixels (depending on screen resolution)
    - Absolute
        - in: inches (1 inch = 2.54 cm)
        - cm: centimeters
        - mm: millimeters
        - pt: points (1/72nd of an inch)
        - pc: picas (1 pica = 12 points)

There are many ways in which to control font properties with CSS, such as font-style, font-variant, font-weight, font-size, and font-family. Text can also be altered using controls such as text-decoration (underline, overline, line-through, blink) and text-transform (capitalize, uppercase, lowercase).

These effects can be used to clarify and communicate the structure of the information. For example, titles can be set off by using a sans serif font, whereas body text can be set in a serif font. We look at how to communicate information through text formatting in the Design Scenario later in the chapter.

Web Fonts

Web pages are increasingly being accessed by mobile devices with very small displays, and text clarity decreases when fewer pixels are available to render the font's characters. We can use the CSS font-family property to control which font the browser will use to render the text, but there are a few issues to consider before we can choose the proper fonts.

CSS allows us to specify specific fonts for Web pages; if the font is not already on the user's computer, however, it cannot be used by the browser. If the font is not resident on the user's machine, the system will substitute the browser's default font. This may have significant and unwanted presentational consequences for the page design.

Operating systems and browsers come with their own set of fonts. These fonts can be used as back-ups in case the font you prefer is not available. It is a good idea to pick at least one font from these "safe font" lists. There are innumerable resources on the Web related to this issue, and a simple search on "safe fonts" will turn up a wealth of information.

Some fonts require more pixels for legibility and are, therefore, less suitable for the Web. Decorative and cursive fonts generally suffer the most at low pixel sizes. This is the most critical for body text and captions, which are necessarily smaller than page headings.

Serif fonts like Times New Roman and sans serif fonts like Arial are the most prevalent on the Internet due to their large installed user base. At large font sizes, Times New Roman and Arial are equally legible.

However, it has been shown that at low point sizes, serif fonts suffer reductions in legibility more than their sans serif counterparts. At smaller sizes, the serifs, which aid reading speed at larger sizes, become visual noise and therefore an impediment to legibility. Some of the newer fonts, such as Georgia, Verdana, and Trebuchet, maintain legibility at small sizes and have been designed to facilitate reading on the Web.

The CSS font-family property can take a comma-delimited string of possible font names. Because the font must reside on the user's machine, it is a good idea to list a few possibilities starting with the preferred font and ending with a generic family; for example,

```
body { font-family: Gill, Helvetica, sans-serif }
```

We have only scratched the surface in terms of the power CSS has to control the presentational aspects of text. CSS can drastically alter the look of a Web page while retaining the underlying structure. To get an idea of how powerful CSS is, go to *http://www.csszengarden.com/*. It is a Web site devoted to CSS and has many illustrations of what CSS can do with some simple markup.

Hypertext

XHTML has three settings for hyperlink states—link, visited, and active. The classic formatting for these states is underlined for all, blue for a link, red for an active link, and purple for a visited link (Figure 12.11). This formatting can be seen on a number of Web sites and is highly recommended by Jakob Nielsen (2003) because it is a convention and therefore there is no question of whether a string of text is a link or not.

The CSS specification offers four link states—link (link), active (alink), visited (vlink), and hover, and gives the following example:

```
a:link    { color: red }    /* unvisited links */
a:visited { color: blue }   /* visited links   */
a:hover   { color: yellow } /* user hovers      */
a:active  { color: lime }   /* active links     */
```

useit.com: usable information technology

useit.com: Jakob Nielsen's Website

Permanent Content

Alertbox
Jakob's column on Web usability

Users Interleave Sites and Genres (February 6)
When working on business problems, users flitter among sites,
alternating visits to different service genres. No single website defines
the user experience on its own.

Year's Best Intranets (January 23)
Search Engines (January 9)
Internet Growth (December 19)

All Alertbox columns from 1995 to 2006

News

Usability Week
- New York, Mai
- London, May 2
- San Francisco,
- Sydney, July 1

In-depth trainin
- 3-day Intensiv
- 3-day Immers

New research o
- Eyetracking
- B2B websites

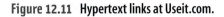

Figure 12.11   Hypertext links at Useit.com.

These styles would effectively alter the expected link colors and make unvisited links look like active links (red) and visited links look like unvisited links (blue). This would be confusing, and this type of alteration should be avoided. However, the W3C does use CSS to style the links on their Web site, as follows.

Figure 12.12a shows that the unvisited links are blue and underlined and that Technical Reports is a visited link and New Visitors is an active link (it has the same appearance in the hover state). The tool tip is a function of the title attribute of the link element and is essential for visually impaired users who use screen readers; it is also an excellent way to supply users with more information about the link, and is highly recommended.

The Technical Report link takes the user to the Technical Reports and Publications page, where the Technical Reports link is not a functional link (because the user is already on the page; this practice is highly recommended) and has a different font and background color (Figure 12.12b).

The W3C Web site also uses a more traditional link style for some of the secondary and incidental links on the site, as shown in Figure 12.12c. Here Amaya is shown as a visited link (the active state has the same appearance), and the Accessibility link was visited before the Amaya link.

Another style of hyperlink can be found on Amazon.com®. Figure 12.13a shows the hover and active states of the Your Account link. The set of links that it belongs to are not underlined in their unvisited or visited states. The underline appears in the active and hover states, which also change the color from blue to orange. The set of links on the next line below also add the underline in the active and hover states, but they do not change color.

Amazon.com has another hyperlink style for their side navigation menu. As shown in Figure 12.13b, all links are underlined, Books shows a visited link, and Video shows an active link.

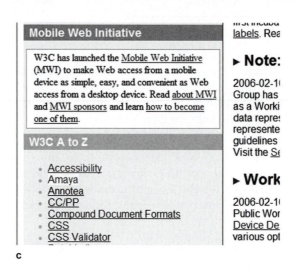

Figure 12.12   (a) Hypertext links at the W3.org Web site. (b)Nonfunctional hyperlink. (c) Visited link.

Hyperlinks are evolving away from the traditional blue underlined style. There are many alternatives on the Web; some are successful, and some are just confusing. CSS gives us a great deal of power to alter the presentational aspects of a Web page, but we must be careful to base the presentation on the structure and not confuse the user with gratuitous visual bells and whistles.

MAXIM

Hyperlinks must be obvious.

One of the most important issues to keep in mind is that users must be able to identify the links on the page without hesitation. A clear, obvious, and consistent approach to hyperlink styles is crucial. We explore this issue further in the Design Scenario at the end of the chapter.

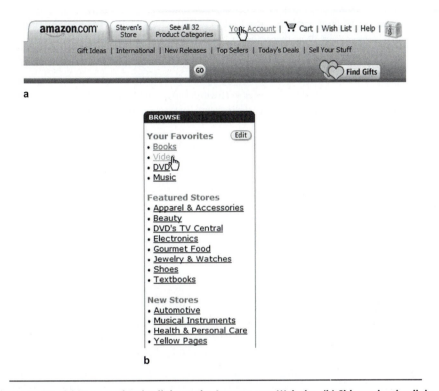

Figure 12.13 **(a) Hover and active links on the Amazon.com Web site. (b) Side navigation links.**

Downloadable Fonts

At the time of this writing, CSS is in its second version (CSS 2.0). The next version of CSS will incorporate scalable vector graphics (SVGs), which will enable Web designers to embed specific fonts within the page, in the same way that PDFs embed fonts in their files. CSS 3 is a few years away, but in the meantime, Microsoft has offered a solution to the resident font problem by creating an application called WEFT® (Web Embedding Fonts Tool®). WEFT does not embed fonts, but it allows designers to specify a font that users can then download.

WEFT creates an embedded open type (EOT) font object that is linked to the page. Once the link is coded on the page and the EOT font is uploaded to the Web server, users have the ability to download the font, which has been compressed to a manageable file size.

Not all fonts are in the public domain, and some must be purchased from the manufacturer. However, there are a great many fonts available free of charge on the Internet, which you can specify for downloading. There may even be fonts already resident on your machine that can be made available to Web site visitors.

There is, however, one significant caveat to the WEFT scenario: it requires users to view the page using Microsoft Internet Explorer (IE) because other browsers will not recognize the EOT font. This means that HTML and CSS must be written properly to maintain an acceptable Web experience for users who do not use IE.

12.3.3. Globalization/Localization

There are many structural differences among languages, including different alphabets, reading directions, and word delimiters. Let's examine some of these issues:

- Direction
- Alignment
- Space
- Collating sequences
- Delimiters
- Diacriticals

Direction

Sukaviriya and Moran (1990) identify three orientations for world languages:

- Top-to-bottom (T-T-B) character sequence and right-to-left (R-T-L) line sequence (Korean, Japanese, and Chinese; these languages now use Western style as well).
- R-T-L character sequence and T-T-B line sequence (Semitic languages: Arabic and Hebrew).
- Left-to-right (L-T-R) character sequence and T-T-B line sequence (Western style; these include languages from Europe, America, India, and Southeast Asia).

> **MAXIM**
>
> Directionality is an issue not only for text presentation, but also for the design of the entire interface.

Users with a right-to-left language orientation approach application interfaces from right to left, and begin to read the screen from the top right-hand corner. This affects pull-down menus, text box labels, and many other interface elements.

Language directionality is an essential factor in screen design and must be identified early in the design process. The W3C maintains information on language directionality at *http://www.w3.org/International/questions/qa-scripts.html*.

Space

> **MAXIM**
>
> A translation will not use the same amount of space as the original text.

When a section of text is translated into another language, it will not occupy the same amount of space as the original. The Print Preview command, for example, when translated into Italian becomes La Stampa Vede in Anteprima. In this case, 13 characters become 27—more than double. In interface design, in which screen real estate is at a premium and alignment can be a crucial factor, this change in the amount of text can become a significant issue and may require rewording.

Delimiters

Tokenization and segmentation are the first steps in natural language processing (Chen & Jin, 1996). Tokenization relates to the delineation of words, and segmentation defines sentence structure. Tokenization facilitates features such as double-clicking to select words. If word tokenization is unambiguous (the delimiters are easily identified), sentence segmentation can be easily accomplished.

This is not difficult when a language uses features such as white space, slashes, or hyphens to separate words (tokenization). However, not all languages identify word boundaries; Chinese and Japanese texts, for example, do not separate words and sentences. Words and sentences can be separated in multiple ways, each one radically altering meaning.

Diacriticals

Many alphabets use diacritical marks—marks that are added to letters, altering their pronunciation—such as accents, umlauts, and tildes. Sometimes, the addition or subtraction of diacriticals can drastically change the meaning of a word. In Italian, for example, "Papà" means "Daddy," but the "Papa" is the Pope.

Local customs also affect the use of diacriticals. It is not uncommon in France for native speakers and writers to drop accent marks when words are capitalized. However, if you do not speak a language fluently, do not alter the accent marks; unfortunate situations can arise:

BISCUITS SALÉS—Salty biscuits
BISCUITS SALES—Dirty biscuits

Collating Sequences

We are often in situations in which we must work with lists of numbers or words. These lists can be sorted alphabetically or numerically in ascending or descending order. The character code values assigned to each character in a set are used to create order. For instance, ACSII assigns the letter "A" a value 65 and the letter "B" a value 66; therefore, alphabetic listing is accomplished by greater than–less than numerical comparisons. Languages that use the same character set, such as English and Italian, should not pose significant problems for collation sequencing. However, we must still consider various localization issues.

Many European languages use diacriticals and double letters that are treated as separate characters. For instance, the Spanish alphabet contains 29 letters: all 26 letters of the English alphabet plus the letters ch, ll, and ñ. They are sometimes listed as distinct letters and sometimes integrated into the section including their first letter.

The Italian alphabet contains 21 letters with the addition of the following letters for foreign words: j, k, w, x, and y. These foreign letters are sometimes listed separately and sometimes integrated within the alphabet.

Both German and Swedish use Ä and Ö, but list them differently. The German alphabetizes first A, then Ä, and O, then Ö. Swedish alphabetize all characters that have diacritical marks, such as Ä and Ö, at the end, after Z. The German Ü is included in the Swedish alphabet to accommodate German names, but it is listed with Y due to their similar pronunciation.

Other Linguistic Concerns

There are semantic and syntactic differences among languages. Even within a particular language there are complex semantic situations in which one word can have many different meanings depending on the context. The designer must be careful to address these issues early in the design process, especially if the project has a global scope.

Puns

MAXIM

Avoid puns; they do not translate well.

Words often have more than one meaning, and they sometimes acquire new meanings in technological situations, as in the phrases "boot the system" or "crash the system." Puns that take advantage of ambiguities and double-entendres can often be quite humorous. They do not, however, work particularly well or consistently across linguistic boundaries. An icon presenting a noose or guillotine, for example, as a symbol for "execute" would not translate well.

Abbreviations and Acronyms

MAXIM

Abbreviations and acronyms must be used carefully.

Abbreviations and acronyms do not translate particularly well and should be avoided. Some acronyms, however, are so well known in other languages that they become part of common lexicon and need not be translated. Even if cognates like disk and disco are used, the syntax may be different. DOS (Disk Operating System), for example, would become SOD in Italian (Sistema di Operazion del Disco), making it unrecognizable. These acronyms and abbreviations should appear in their native languages, and their unabbreviated version should appear somewhere in the interface to diminish the possibility of misunderstanding.

Formats

The way in which people format numbers and dates differs from country to country. This may have a significant effect on the design and placement of text boxes and other form elements. The following is a list of some areas of concern:

- Numerics
- Currency

- Units of measurement
- Date
- Time
- Phone number
- Address

Numerics

The use of the period as a decimal point is not universal; some countries use a period, whereas others use a comma. The delimiter used for orders of magnitude is also variable. For instance, the number "two thousand, three hundred, twenty four, and four tenths" is written as 2,324.4 in the United States and England but as 2.300,4 in most European countries.

Currency

With the introduction of the Euro, the issue of multiple European currency signs and exchanges has become less complex. The € symbol has been added to many character sets and covers the currencies of all nations that belong to the European Union (EU) except England, Denmark, and Sweden. There are, however, many European countries that do not belong to the EU and therefore retain national currencies. A global interface must still accommodate a multiplicity of currency terminologies and symbols.

Units of Measurement

Although the metric system is fast becoming a global standard, it is still not used in all countries. Many countries are in the process of adopting the metric standard, but it will be some time before different national systems are eliminated. Therefore, for the time being, global interfaces must either have conversion capacities or use both the metric and national systems.

The scientific community often requires specialized forms of measurement, such as the Kelvin scale for temperature. In cases in which accuracy and usability are degraded through the adoption of dual or general measurement presentations, localized and specific systems should be used.

Date

There are many possible permutations for notating date information, and most of these can likely be found in use somewhere in the world at any given time. Some notation possibilities are:

2/4/10

4.2.10

April 2, 2010

2-APR-1910

The potential for misinterpretation is evident. Is the first date in this list (2/4/10) meant to be read as month, day, and year or as day, month, and year? In other words, does it represent the fourth of February or the second of April?

Because both interpretations can be correct, people must make an educated guess based on the country and language system in which the date was written. In the first two formats in the list the century is also ambiguous. Depending on the context, this date can refer to 1910 or 2010. Although it is unlikely, confusion with other centuries is possible, and using a four-digit year is always advisable. The Y2K problem (sometimes erroneously referred to as the "millennium bug") is a perfect case for the use of unambiguous date formats.

The international standard (ISO 8601 or European standard EN 28601) for date notation is YYYY-MM-DD. There are many advantages to this format:

- Computers easily manipulate numbers
- The format is independent of language
- It is unambiguous
- It offers a logical presentation of high to low ordering
- It is of consistent length
- It is similar to the format used by many countries
- The year is given in four-digit form

This format is not meant to replace month names, but rather to standardize numeric date information. The *Chicago Manual of Style* (CMS) acknowledges the benefits for automation with the numeric date format. It also encourages the use of month names or abbreviations for formal writing, however, due to "practical as well as aesthetic reasons" (CMS, 2003).

If dates are in tabular form, the CMS suggest using the dd month yyyy format with possible abbreviations for month names. Microsoft also recommends the use of month names to avoid numeric ambiguities and suggests the following format: month dd, yyyy. (MMoS)

The least ambiguous way to present date information is to use month names or abbreviations. Table 12.3 shows three possible formats.

If you are collecting date information as well as displaying it, you should use a consistent format. Unless you use three input elements to separate the day, month, and year, users will enter date information in the format that is most familiar to

Table 12.3 Date Information

5 Oct 2003	For multiple-entry presentation; no period for the abbreviation
Oct. 5, 2003,	For American formal writing; when this is used in a sentence, the year is followed by a comma
2003 October 5	Abbreviations allowed

them. If you allow unstructured date input, you must also allow for different kinds of delimiters, such as hyphens, commas, periods, spaces, or backslashes or no delimiter at all. Month names and abbreviations will also vary in length.

You should make every attempt to guide the user toward the format you require. You can provide an example or model of the format, such as dd mm yyyy for a numeric entry or dd month yyyy for an alphanumeric entry. These can be placed inside, above, or next to the input boxes. Be aware that these models are language dependent. In Italian, for example, corresponding models are gg mm aaaa or gg mese aaaa, which correspond with giorno (day), mese (month), and anno (year).

Time Format

The ISO 8601 format for time of day is hh:mm:ss. It is based on a 24-hour cycle sometimes referred to as military time. Both 00 and 24 represent midnight, to clarify the ambiguity implicit in the notation 00:00:00 to 00:00:00. A 24-hour period would begin at 00 and end at 24. Minutes range from 00 to 59, and seconds range from 00 to 60. Occasionally, a second is added to the scale to allow for the synchronization of atomic clocks with the rotation of Earth. A 24-hour period would be notated as

00:00:00 to 24:00:00

Time Measurement

The International Bureau of Weights and Measures maintains a number of clocks around the world that are based on the atomic properties of the element cesium. This duration is the standard of measurement used for Coordinated Universal Time (UTC), previously referred to as Greenwich Mean Time (GMT). The name GMT should be avoided, and UTC should be used instead. To indicate UTC time, a "Z" (zero meridian) is appended: for example, 12:25Z.

Most countries use the 24-hour time format as opposed to the 12-hour format, which requires AM and PM qualifiers. To globalize an interface, Microsoft suggests using the 24-hour format and avoiding AM and PM notation.

Time Zones

International time zones are indicated by their distance or difference from UTC. For instance, 13:00 in Vatican City is 1 hour later than UTC, so the indication is 13:00 (UTC +1) or 1300+01. The time in Greenwich, England, is equal to UTC, and so it is notated 1200Z.

Formats for time ahead of UTC:

+hh:mm, +hhmm, or +hh

Formats for time behind UTC:

–hh:mm, –hhmm, or –hh

People who work in technical and scientific environments are often more aware of global standards than the general population, but in more informal settings, local formats are generally required. The degree to which you globalize or localize an interface should be determined on a case-by-case basis.

Table 12.4 Phone Numbers

	Country Code	City Code	Local Number
United Kingdom	(+44)	(71)	0000 000 0000
Japan	(+81)	(3)	0000-0000
United States	(+1)	(212)	000-0000

Phone Number

International phone numbers require country codes, city codes, and the line number. These can add up to many digits, so you must make sure that your input and output areas for telephone number fields can handle the entire phone number. In this case, delimiters are not standardized and are often dropped. However, country codes, city codes, and American area codes are often delimited by parentheses. Local numbers should follow local conventions (Table 12.4).

Address

You may have to collect address information to process orders or to communicate with clients. Web sites often have forms that users fill out and submit to remote servers that serve this purpose. It is important that you gather appropriate data and make the process of providing the information as easy as possible.

No one likes to fill out long forms, especially if they must do it more than once because of an input error. The only way people know what information to enter in each field is by the associated label. If they do not understand what information is required, they might not be able to successfully complete the form.

There are two issues involved in this situation: does the user understand the terminology you are using, and do the input fields make sense? If the form asks for or requires irrelevant information, the user may become confused or annoyed.

Although address formats are more or less similar worldwide, they are not identical. Normally, addresses contain addressee, house/building, street, city, state or province, postal code, and country information, but there is no universal standard.

12.3.4. Dynamic Text Presentation

Electronic documents afford a degree of flexibility not possible with print media. With electronic documents, many character parameters, such as size, color, type face, and format, can be customized by individual users.

Delivery formats are also flexible: electronic documents can be published on the Internet or on corporate intranets; they can be transferred on various media such as floppy disks, CD ROMs, DVDs, portable hard drives; and they can also be attached to e-mail messages.

MAXIM

Dynamic text might be suitable for small displays.

The dynamic nature of the contemporary computing environment also allows for animated text presentation formats. These formats can range from Times Square Scrolling (TSS) to Rapid Serial Visual Presentation (RSVP). There has been increased interest in this area due to its spatial efficiency and, therefore, its potential use in cell phones and PDAs.

In general, users dislike this type of presentation, but recent research has explored various ways it can be enhanced and has shown some positive results, which suggest a potential for future development.

Some issues involved in dynamic text presentation include the following:

- Presentation units
  - Pixels
  - Characters
  - Words
  - Phrases

- Amount of information presented simultaneously
  - Number units
- Rate of presentation
  - Automatic
  - User defined

- Pauses
  - Location
  - Duration

- Scrolling format
  - Direction—horizontal/vertical
  - Smooth and gradual or chunked presentation

Rapid Serial Visual Presentation

In RSVP, words are presented at a fixed screen location. The rate of presentation is usually fixed, but it can range from individual words to groups of words. Consider in Table 12.5 the quote from Hamlet "There is nothing either good or bad, but thinking makes it so," as it would be presented in RSVP.

Studies have investigated the effects of using the following:

- Variable rate presentation
- User control of presentation speed

Table 12.5 Rapid Serial Visual Presentation

Frame 1	"There is nothing
Frame 2	either good or bad,
Frame 3	but thinking
Frame 4	makes it so."

- Pause length between word groups
- Diverse word group lengths

RSVP has been shown to be as fast as page format and results in comparable understanding (Juola, Ward, & McNamara, 1982; Masson, 1983).

Times Square Scrolling

TSS derives its name from the large public displays in Times Square, New York City. In TSS, words scroll from right to left at a continuous fixed rate (Table 12.6).

Variations on TSS include presentation modes that can be pixel by pixel, character by character, or word by word and presentation rates in which speed and user control can vary. TSS has been found to be slower than page format but with relatively similar comprehension (Sekey & Tietz, 1982).

TSS versus RSVP

Kang and Muter (1989) compared RSVP with two versions of the TSS, one with pixel increments (PTSS) and one with character increments (CTSS). They found that

Table 12.6 Times Square Scrolling

Frame 1	"There is
Frame 2	"There is nothing
Frame 3	"There is nothing either
Frame 4	"There is nothing either good or
Frame 5	nothing either good or bad, but
Frame 6	either good or bad, but thinking
Frame 7	good or bad, but thinking makes
Frame 8	bad, but thinking makes it so."

the modes were comparable, and both were preferred to RSVP. They did suggest, however, that RSVP may be more appropriate for very small displays that do not allow for successful fixation during scrolling, in which words simply leave the screen before they can be processed.

It has also been suggested that RSVP is better than TSS for scanning lists or text for specific information because in this format, it is more likely that every word will be read (Potter, Kroll, & Harris, 1980). Potter et al. further suggest that RSVP has a potential role in the training of young or visually impaired readers.

Castelhano and Muter (2001) suggest ways to enhance the effectiveness of RSVP. In their study, they added six features to the standard RSVP format:

- Punctuation pauses
- Sentence-oriented processing
- Interruption pauses
- Completion meter
- Proposition integration
- Common word duration

They found that people preferred some of these enhancements, especially after an initial period of adjustment to the experimental conditions. People responded favorably to the punctuation pauses, which added time to the presentation of words that included punctuation, especially at sentence boundaries. This tactic has been shown to allow for postprocessing and information integration.

Kang and Muter (1989) increased subject preference further by adding interruption pauses to the previously enhanced RSVP. Interruption pauses allow the reader to pause the presentation in mid sentence. Users have more control: they can pause for unfamiliar words or to correct a misunderstanding of the text. When sentence presentation was used, they often used these pauses to return to the beginning of the sentence.

Subjects also preferred using the completion meter, which showed the whole passage and changed as each sentence was read. This tool gave subjects a sense of how much they had read and how much was left to read.

Readers generally spend more time processing words like "although" and "because." These words help us to understand the meaning and structure of the entire sentence. Propositional integration allows for extra time when these words are presented, helping readers to identify the clause boundaries of sentences and delineate syntactical structures. The common word duration modification increased the speed of familiar and common word durations.

Although dynamic text presentation may not be the preferred method of reading, there are situations in which the size of the display area might require some sort of condensed format. This is an area of ongoing research that indicates some useful applications.

Design Scenario

Circumference: Text Formatting

In this Design Scenario we use CSS to set up the text formatting for the **Circumference** Web site. The page we work on is a sample of poetry from one of the issues. This is the most complex type of page in the site in terms of text because of the multiple character sets that are involved. All of the design decisions we make in regard to this page will be generalized across the entire site.

The activities in this design scenario include the following:

- Designing legibility
- General font formatting
- Visualizing the information hierarchy
- Link styles

The page will include commentary text:

- Global information
  - Site branding—logo, journal name
- Local information
  - Particular issue
- Content
  - Poem title
  - Poetry—native language, English
  - Poet's/translator's name
  - Poet's/translator's bio

The page will also include instrumental text:

- Structural navigation—this includes links that navigate to different sections of the site
  - Global: other site locations—About, Subscriptions, and so on
  - Local—links to other issue's TOCs and other poem titles, which create a second TOC of excerpts from the issue
- Incidental navigation—this includes links that target locations within the page, cause drop-downs to fire, or create pop-up windows; they do not navigate away from the page
  - Indigenous: biographical information about the authors and translators

The flowchart in Figure 12.14 shows how the pages are linked to each other.

The wire-frame in Figure 12.15 shows the page layout and the locations of the various text elements.

Design Scenario (cont.)

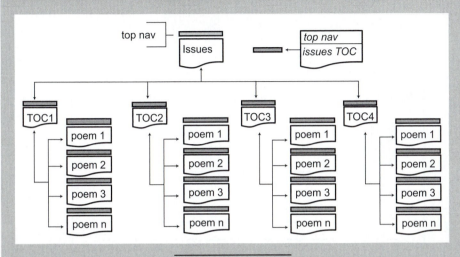

Figure 12.14   Issues flowchart.

Legibility

The people who come to this site will be interested in reading the poetry, so legibility will be a high priority. Therefore, the poetry text will be presented in negative contrast. This dictates a white background and black text.

> **Design Principle:** Flexibility—We use a flexible font size so that visitors can adjust the text to their requirements. We also use a comfortable default size that will be legible without adjustments.

The journal uses a unique uppercase, small cap, sans serif font for its name and tag line. The site will use this font for the journal's name and the tag line that appears on every page (Figure 12.16).

The font we choose might not be available on a visitor's computer. If we want to use an uncommon font, the only solution currently available is to create an image of the text. This should be considered a last resort because it makes the text unavailable to people with screen readers or search engines and people who have images turned off.

> **Requirement:** Constraints—The site should allow current versions of the most common audible browsers to access as much content as possible.

Therefore, it is important to use a descriptive alt attribute with the image element in the markup code so users will be able to read the alt text when images are turned off or hear it read by an audible browser (Figure 12.17). Search engines will also be able to read the alt text.

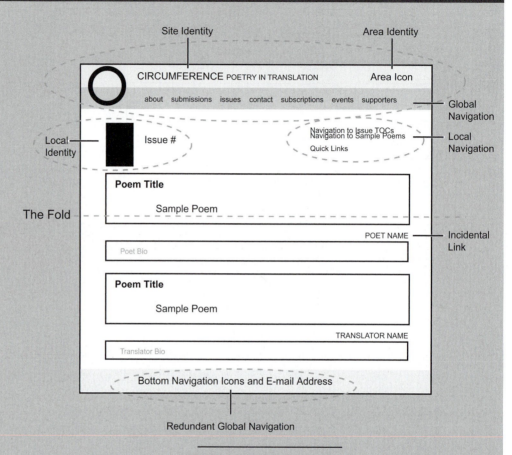

Figure 12.15   Poem page wireframe.

Because we are required to use graphic text, it is important to test the legibility of the image because small text is sensitive to anti-aliasing. Anti-aliasing smoothes out the jagged lines and tends to make shapes and lines look better on computer screens, but it also tends to blur text. This can make small text unreadable. For small

CIRCUMFERENCE

POETRY IN TRANSLATION

Figure 12.16   Logo and Tag Line.

Design Scenario (cont.)

 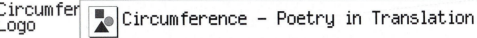

a

CIRCUMFERENCE   POETRY IN TRANSLATION

about submissions issues contact subscriptions events supporters

b

Figure 12.17 (a) Page with images turned off. (b) Page with images turned on.

graphic text an aliased rendering of a sans serif font should be used. Legibility must be maintained, or readability becomes a mute point.

General Font Formatting

The journal name and tag line will be maintained throughout the site, which means any font decisions will have to take this into consideration. This is a bold font with a strong look, and we do not want to use any other styles that will either conflict or compete with it. This would create a complex-looking screen that might distract people and take away from their poetry reading experience. However, we can use the uppercase, sans serif, and bold aspects to create other text styles that will blend comfortably on the same page.

> **Design Principle:** Simplicity—Using a limited amount of related font styles helps to enforce simplicity within the design.

Font Size

As mentioned earlier, font sizes will not be hard coded in fixed units. Users may want to enlarge the text so that it is easier to read. Furthermore, a portion of the site's visitors will probably be older, and they will require larger text. If we hard code fixed pixel values, people who use Internet Explorer will not be able to use the browser's text size controls to change the size of the text, so we will avoid using pixel units and use the percent units instead.

Design Scenario (cont.)

The percent unit will be defined by the user's browser setting and will resize accordingly. A size of 100% will be the same as the browser's default setting. Our minimum size will be set at 70%; any smaller would go below the threshold that is normally suggested in the research on Web-based font sizes.

Font sizes can also be prescribed in the following units, as listed in the W3C CSS 2.1 Specification *(http://www.w3.org/TR/CSS21/)*:

Absolute size: xx-small, x-small, small, medium, large, x-large, xx-large
Relative size: larger, smaller
Length:

Relative units

- em: the "font-size" of the relevant font
- ex: the "x-height" of the relevant font
- px: pixels, relative to the viewing device

Absolute units

- in: inches
- cm: centimeters
- mm: millimeters
- pt: points—1 poiny is equal to 1/72 inch
- pc: picas—1 pica is equal to 12 points

Font Face

The fonts used on the site will be either serif or sans serif, and will be chosen from common font families; this will ensure the existence of a similar font residing on the visitor's computer. The results of computer-based substitutions can be less than optimal.

Cursive fonts are very distinctive and more fragile than serif or sans serif fonts. They have very thin lines and complex flourishes that do not render well on the Web. Furthermore, they are not commonly available, which would require graphical versions that inherit all the ramifications of graphical text.

The research on which fonts are best for Web pages shows that there is no significant difference between serif and sans serif fonts in terms of legibility or user preference. However, serif fonts suffer more at the smallest sizes, so we will use sans serif fonts for the text that is set to 70%.

Visualizing the Information Hierarchy—Sample Poem Pages

We use various formatting styles to structure the page visually. We do this by creating a hierarchy for the various text elements and assigning the formatting accordingly. The

Design Scenario (cont.)

sample poem page has the most varied text formatting, so we delineate the styles for the hierarchy on those pages:

1. Commentary text
    a. Journal branding
    b. Issue
    c. Poem title
        i. Poem
    d. Poet/translator name (hyperlink)
        i. Poet/translator bio

This hierarchy will help us to develop a structured approach to text formatting that is based on the relative importance and the structural nature of the text elements.

Design Principle: Comprehensibility—We use the visual presentation to support the underlying logical structure of the content.

We use the intensity of the visual effects that the various formatting styles create to clarify the hierarchical structure.

Design Principle: Stimulus Intensity—Bold text has more intensity as a visual stimulus, and so we use it for the most important text elements.

Large text also has more intensity, and so we apply font sizes according to the levels of importance. Font color can also be used to prioritize text elements. There are other properties that can help us to create a visual hierarchy for the page. We need to define CSS rules for the following properties:

- Font-weight
- Font-size
- Color
- Font-variant
- Text-decoration
- Font-family

The first element on the hierarchy is the journal branding; this is already decided, and it will maintain the look of the printed journal. The next element is the particular issue. We use the issue color and a sans serif font. Because this text sits at the top of the page, it will automatically seem more important, and so there is no need to increase the font size.

The title of the poem is the main identifier for the page, and so we make it distinct by using a large, bold font with a strong color (the dark red used in the top banner) (Example 12.1).

Design Scenario (cont.)

Example 12.1

CSS Rules for Poem Titles	Poem Title and Text

```.poemTitle {```
 ```color:#853735;```
 ```font-size:150%;```
 ```font-weight:900;}```
	Irla Igandea da hondartzan asmo oneko jendearentzat. Hango harrabots urruna entzuten da irlatik.

Link Styles

We want to make sure that the navigational text is clearly differentiated from the commentary text. Because there are existing conventions regarding the formatting of hypertext links, we will start there and, in the process, restrict certain formatting styles just to hyperlink text.

> **Design Principle:** Constraints—We constrain the use of blue to indicate hypertext.

> Our hierarchy for navigational text looks as follows:

> 1. Instrumental text
>   a. Structural
>   i. Local (right-side navigation rail)
>   ii. Global (top navigation strip)
>   b. Incidental
>   i. Poet/translator name to open bio (the name itself)

Blue underlined text is the traditional approach to hyperlinks; however, Nielsen (2004) suggests that links do not have to be underlined if they are obvious due to color or because the page design clearly indicates the presence of navigational links, such as a side navigation rail with a background color or other navigation menus.

Global Navigation

On the **Circumference** site we have three types of links—global, local and incidental. The global links fall easily into the category suggested by Nielsen (2004); they are navigational menus that are isolated from the rest of the text on the page by their location, grouping, and background. We eliminate the underline by setting the text-decoration property of all states for these links (link, active, visited, and hover) to "none."

Design Scenario (cont.)

CIRCUMFERENCE   POETRY IN TRANSLATION

about   submissions   issues   contact   subscriptions   events   supporters

Figure 12.18   Global hover state.

The hover state will reverse the text and background colors. We use similar formatting for the nonlinked version of the text on the target page. This indicates to visitors that they are currently on that page. Figure 12.18 shows that we are currently on the About page and the cursor is hovering over the Issues link.

Local Navigation

The local navigation links that go to the different poems in the issue also fall into Nielsen's category of obvious navigation. They are grouped together on the right side of the page but have no background color. To support the indication of hypertext, we maintain the underline and color the different states according to the CSS style definitions in Table 12.7.

Table 12.7   CSS Styles for Global and Local Links

Global Link Styles	Local Link Styles

`a:link.top {`
`color: #fcfdc1;`
`text-decoration: none;}`
	`a:visited {`
	`color: #001f44;}`

`a:active.top{`
`color: #c00;`
`text-decoration: none;}`
	`a:active {`
	`color: #c00;}`

`a:visited.top {`
`color: #fcfdc1;`
`text-decoration: none;}`
	`a:link{`
	`color: #546FA3;`

`a:hover.top {`
`color:#853735;`
`background-color:#fceac0;}`
	`a:link{`
	`color:#546FA3;}`

`.locationNoLink {`
`color:#853735;`
`background-color:#fceac0;}`	

Design Scenario (cont.)

Example 12.2 shows "The Sky" as a visited link and "Ask Socrates Marilyn Said" as the current page title without a link.

Example 12.2 Local Navigation

```
                              The Sky
            Ask Socrates Marilyn Said
                      Danse Macabre
            "Life is ... to remember"
      "Even though the wind envelops"
```

Incidental Links

There are incidental links that open a drop-down area with the poet/translator bios located just below the poem. It is important to clarify the functionality of this text in the context of the rest of the page.

Underlining is a strong indication of hypertext, and so we have not underlined any of the commentary text. We can use the underline for the incidental links within the page such as the poet/translator names. This will give a visual indication of link functionality.

We also pick up on the uppercase aspect of the journal's name for these links. The actual bio text will be smaller (75%) and lighter so it does not compete with the poetry on the page if the drop-down is left open (Example 12.3).

Example 12.3

CSS Rules for Poet Name	Poet Bio Link and Drop-Down Text

<pre>.poetName {
font-variant:smallcaps;
font-size:75%;
font-weight:900;
font-family: Georgia, "Book
Antigua",serif;
}</pre>
	*KIRM
	
	Kirmen Uribe is the author of Bitartean heldu eskutik (Meanwhile Hold Hands), which won Spain's 2001 Premio de la Crítica, and whose Spanish translation will be published this fall. His 2001 multimedia collaboration with the musician Mikel Urdangarin was made into Bar Puerto, a CD-book. Uribe lives in Vitoria-Gasteiz (Euskadi, Spain)

Design Scenario (cont.)

Readability

As we have seen, reading performance and comprehension are affected by a dynamic interaction among the following factors:

Font Size + Line Length + Margin Width + Vertical Spacing

We looked at the issue of font size and decided that the poetry text should be set at a comfortable size for each visitor, which means that a unit of 100% will present the text at the default size set on the visitor's browser. By not using fixed units, we also allowed for the visitor to alter the size.

The issue of line length is dictated by the poetry. We must make sure, therefore, that the proper line breaks are entered with the forced line break element <br> and that resizing the browser window does not affect the wrapping of the text. We accomplish this by setting the poems within a block container such as a paragraph or div element that does not have a fixed unit width, and then set the CSS white-space property to nowrap.

The vertical spacing can be manipulated by the CSS line-height property, which can be set to reflect the poet's visual intentions on a poem-by-poem basis. The margin width issue can be manipulated by the CSS margin property as well as by using the block markup elements such as the paragraph or div elements.

> **Design Principles:** White Space, Surroundedness—We use white space to surround the poem text and take advantage of the effect that margin width has on readability

It is not recommended to use the blockquote element for text that is not an actual quote; this will diminish the semantic structure of the page and cause problems for automated indexing and search engines.

Paging versus Scrolling

When a visitor navigates to a sample poem from the journal he or she will expect to see the native-language version of the poem as well as the English translation. The printed journal has the two versions on facing pages so the reader can see both versions without turning pages. This makes it easy to compare the original version of the poem with the English translation.

This format, however, will not always be possible on the Web site due to the long line length of some of the poetry. Poems with long line lengths require a horizontal scrollbar. If a poem is longer than the viewport, it also requires a vertical scrollbar. This becomes cumbersome after awhile and should be avoided.

The design problem we must consider is whether to put both versions on the same page, which would require a bit of scrolling, or put each version on a separate page and require the visitor to navigate back and forth between pages.

This issue came up in Chapter 5 when we were creating the wireframes for the site's pages. We did not make a definitive decision at that point because we wanted

Design Scenario (cont.)

to explore this issue in terms of reading comprehension; we can now address the issue from this perspective.

As we have seen, the issue of scrolling versus paging depends on the user's task and the fact that previous experience also affects people's preferences. Let's explore the kind of reading in which the **_Circumference_** visitors will be engaged and some of the issues that arise from research on the scrolling versus paging issue.

- **Speed**—Reading poetry is not like reading a novel. People spend time on each line and often just on a single word; that is the art of poetry—crafting words to form images and present ideas. Reading speed is not an issue that will affect our decision.
- **Skimming**—Reading poetry is very different from reading Web pages; people do not skim poetry in the way they skim Web pages.
- **Spatial Orientation—**The formatting of the poetry in terms of paragraphs and placement on the page will be determined by the poetry itself and will define the spatial cues that affect the way we perceive the text.
- **Printing**—Viewers may wish to print the text, and so the scrolling format will be easier for this task.
- **Broken-Up Text**—Some of the studies on scrolling versus paging show that people may feel that the paging format is too broken up, and navigating back and forth can become cumbersome.

Reading poetry involves a particular reading style that is deliberate and time intensive, it is very different from reading for information or reading extensive prose. The process of reading poetry on the Web is also different from reading Web pages in general.

The issues that will most affect the design of the sample poem pages are related to the aesthetic quality of the layout and the diverse scripts used by the different languages, the ease of use that the design affords, and the efficiency it allows.

Figure 12.19 shows an example of the page layout so far with all the text formatting and with the drop-down poet bio activated.

CIRCUMFERENCE POETRY IN TRANSLATION

about submissions issues contact subscriptions events supporters

CIRCUMFERENCE
POETRY IN TRANSLATION
▶
ISSUE 4

Issue 4
Sample Poems
Names with asterisks link to bios.

①②③④

The Sky
Ask Socrates Marilyn Said
Danse Macabre
"Life is ... to remember"

"Even though the wind envelops"

"Anche se il vento copre"

Anche se il vento copre
la primavera, il popolo
canta alla notte.

L'ascolto io dal mio letto. Lascio

« La vita di Gesù ». Ardo a quel canto.

written 1927–1938
***Sandro Penna**

Sandro Penna (1906-1977) was born in Perugia At the age of 23, he moved to Rome, where he lived for the majority of his life. Penna never had a solid career and often bordered on poverty. As a young man, he developed a friendship with the poet Umberto Saba, who helped Penna publish his poems, leading to his first book, Poesie (Poems), in 1939. Several collections followed. Penna was awarded the Premio Viareggio award in 1957.

Figure 12.19 Example poem from Issue 4—complete page.

Summary

Text is the graphical manifestation of language, and language is one of the most important modes of human communication. The importance of text in human—computer interaction cannot be overemphasized. Designers must be aware of the limitations of the human visual system and how our perception is affected by the physical aspects of screen text.

The role that text plays in a GUI is very different from the role it plays in the command-line systems and menu-driven interfaces, but it is nonetheless important for system manipulation and the successful completion of user tasks.

The proper application of text can contribute to a graphical user interface's ease of use. Text is often essential to the usability of a graphical interface.

This puts a strong emphasis on getting the text right. You must choose the proper labels and titles, supply understandable directions, and make the screen text both legible and readable.

Resources on the Web

www.aw.com/heim

You will find links to general information concerning typography. There also are links to information concerning writing for the Web and links to some of the guidelines for interface text developed by Apple Co. and Microsoft.

Suggested Reading

Lupton, E. (2004). *Thinking with Type: A Critical Guide for Designers, Writers, Editors, & Students* (1 ed.): Princeton Architectural Press.

Microsoft (Ed.). (2003). *Microsoft Manual of Style for Technical Publications* (3 ed.): Microsoft Press.

Peck, W. (2003). *Great Web Typography*: Wiley.

Speech and Hearing

Sound exists in time and over space, vision exists in space and over time.
(Gaver, 1989)

Hearing is our most important sense after vision, and verbal communication is perhaps the most common form of human auditory interaction. It has been suggested that we have an innate capacity for speech, or that we are wired for speech.

We live in a world that is also rich in nonspeech auditory stimuli. We are surrounded by the sounds of everyday life, from the traffic on the street to the sounds of nature. We are constantly receiving auditory information from our physical environment. We have also learned to use sound to create works of art that entertain, inform, and inspire. Music is an important part of our cultures.

Given that the auditory channel plays such a large role in human-to-human interaction, why do computer interfaces not offer these same interaction capabilities? We will now explore the elements of human auditory perception and how the auditory channel can be used to enrich human-computer interaction as well as some of the obstacles this type of interaction entails.

13.1. The Human Perceptual System

Contemporary GUIs are becoming visually complex, demanding more and more from our visual channel. It is possible that we might become overloaded with visual stimuli and miss important information. Alternatively we can use auditory stimuli to code information and design interfaces that are multimodal. The subsequent reduction in the visual load can help to make interfaces easier and more efficient to use.

We are quite good at using our auditory and visual channels simultaneously in real-life situations. These modes of interaction are interdependent and create a synergy that allows us to interact efficiently with our environment. The combination allows us to choose the more efficient mode.

Ambiguities in one mode can be clarified by the other. In addition, the multiple stimuli assigned to an element (redundant coding) can help us to remember things. Let's now look at some of the issues involved in auditory interaction and investigate how sound might be put to better use in human–computer interaction.

13.1.1. Hearing

To see something, we must look at it, but we can pick up audio signals that are all around us without focusing our attention on the source of the sound. In other words, sound works in the dark and around corners.

MAXIM

Our ears tell our eyes where to look.

Our sense of hearing allows us to monitor aspects of our environment that are out of our range of sight. If we hear a sound coming from behind us, we can turn to see what it is. Essentially, "our ears tell our eyes where to look" (Brewster, 2003, 222).

We are constantly monitoring our environments for signs of danger and to gain information. We tend to select sounds out of the vast ocean of auditory stimuli that we encounter every day. In a crowded room, we can detect the mention of our names in a remote conversation by separating one stream or "auditory object" from the rest, a phenomenon generally known as the "cocktail party effect." This effect was first explored by Colin Cherry, who coined the term "cocktail party problem" (Cherry, 1953).

MAXIM

People become habituated to continuous sounds.

Sometimes, we tune out an entire auditory scene. For example, we become habituated to continuous sounds, such as a humming refrigerator, and only become aware of the sound when it stops. This has significant implications for sound-based human–computer interaction. If users do not hear the sound, they might not be aware of that particular aspect of the interface. This can have significant consequences. We should avoid using continuous sounds for significant interactions— people might become habituated and then ignore them.

Locating Sounds

Research shows that we can respond to audio input more quickly than we can to visual stimuli. We also have the ability quickly to locate the source of a sound. There is a slight delay between the moment a sound reaches one ear and the moment it reaches the other ear. Our brains use this delay to calculate the sound's direction. This delay varies from person to person and is known as the interaural time difference (ITD).

The density of the head also affects our perception of sound. The intensity of the sound received by the ear that is farther away from the sound source is diminished by the "shadow" of the head. This is known as the interaural intensive difference (IID). Together the ITD and the IID enable us to calculate the relative position of sounds.

Auditory Presence

It has been suggested that sound plays a vital role in our sense of connectivity to our environment. Subjects who participated in experiments that eliminated auditory input in normal daily activities reported that they felt like they were "floating" or that they were "out of things," like a "zombie" or an "observer rather than a participant" (Murray, Arnold, & Thornton, 2000, 610). Auditory input helps us to establish a sense of presence and connection to our surroundings.

This finding has led researchers to conclude that an increase in the quality and intensity of a user's sense of presence can lead to the creation of more realistic virtual environments with greater user engagement: "The experience in an auditory virtual environment can be extremely compelling, in a way that is rarely, if ever, achieved in a visual virtual environment" (Gilkey, Simpson, & Weisenberger, 2001, 609).

Localization

Some criticisms of virtual auditory environments concern the low quality of sounds and the impression that the virtual auditory environment is something the user is listening to as opposed to being an immersive, realistic environment.

By calculating ITDs and IIDs, we can spatially situate sounds in the virtual environment so as to make them appear to come from inside the subject's head rather than from the external environment.

To create a more realistic virtual auditory environment, measurements must also be taken of the auditory signals close to the user's eardrum. These measurements are then used to create mathematical functions that, when applied to the virtual sounds, alter them in a way that closely replicates the actual acoustical environment and the individual user's physiognomy. These are called head-related transfer functions (HRTFs).

Sounds that are filtered with the appropriate HRTFs can be presented with headphones and retain the quality of being localized outside of the user's head. The ability to localize the source of an auditory stimulus is considered by some to be the most important factor in creating a convincing auditory display.

Increasing the quality of an interface has been shown to be beneficial to task performance and, as we have seen, can also increase the sense of presence. This might involve quality/expense tradeoffs in the development of the interface. The determining factor is the system's ultimate use.

If the ultimate goal is to supplement a visual display with an auditory layer, a low-fidelity representation might suffice. However, if the goal is to create a convincing auditory display, for example, one that can be used to assist visually impaired persons to function in mission-critical environments, then the fidelity of the system should be considered the highest priority and more care and effort should be put into crafting an accurate representation of the actual 3D auditory space.

13.1.2. Speech

Speech is a significant part of our interaction with the world. Not only do we interact verbally with other people, we can also interact verbally with machines. Technology allows us to issue simple commands to "smart devices" that respond to a set of predetermined words. We can navigate telephone menus by stating our selection chosen from a set of menu items, or we can dial our home phone numbers on our cell phones by saying "Home."

These examples are hardly equivalent to human-to-human speech, but some experts see them as an improvement over other forms of human–machine communication, such as command-line or menu-driven interfaces, because they implement a more natural form of communication.

Advantages of Speech

Speech has the following advantages over text-based communication:

- People gravitate to verbal modes of communication.
- It is easier to speak than to write.

People gravitate to verbal modes of communication; in fact, our impulse to speak is so strong that we often do so to inanimate objects, even though we fully understand the futility of this. For example, while rushing to copy a document, we might verbally encourage a copy machine to warm up more quickly. If the phone rings repeatedly before we can pick it up, we might exclaim in exasperation, "I'm coming, I'm coming."

It is even easier to understand why we speak to computers, which appear to have human-like intelligence. Norman (1997) calls this tendency "false anthropomorphizing." If something appears to be intelligent, we tend to want to communicate with it verbally.

> **MAXIM**
>
> We can speak faster than we can write.

Verbal communication has the potential to be more efficient than text-based interaction styles because, among other factors, we generally speak faster than we write. Speech can also be used in conjunction with other human activities such as moving a mouse or visually searching a screen.

Disadvantages of Speech

Speech has the following disadvantages:

- It requires the knowledge of a language.
- It is more efficient to read than to listen.

Speech-based interaction requires knowledge of a particular language. Languages have steep learning curves, especially for older people. Language can pose a significant barrier for interaction. Imagine facing an ATM machine that is set to a foreign language; it would probably take only a few seconds before you frantically searched for the exit button.

> **MAXIM**
>
> We can read faster than we can listen.

There is another side to this coin, however—we can read faster than we can listen. Listening to speech is a linear task; we must follow the auditory stream to its completion at the speed of delivery. Reading, on the other hand, can proceed at any pace and can involve scanning and skimming to facilitate comprehension. This also has ramifications for interaction designs.

The most efficient method of communication depends on the context. If we wish to communicate information efficiently to the user, then reading is superior to speech. The user can read the text at his or her preferred speed or simply skim it. If we want to help the user to communicate information efficiently to the computer, then speech is superior to writing. It is faster and easier simply to speak to the computer than to type in commands.

Interaction designers must also consider technological context. The ability of a system to process and transfer auditory information has a considerable impact on the type of communication medium that is suitable for specific situations. For instance, in some Web-based applications the bandwidth available might not be sufficient for anything other than text-based communication.

13.1.3. **Nonspeech**

We depend on our auditory input channel for a great deal of essential information, much of which is not speech based. From the alarm that wakes us in the morning, to the sound of the car engine as (we hope) it starts, to the ambulance siren warning of an approaching emergency vehicle, we monitor our nonspeech auditory environment habitually and, to some degree, unconsciously.

Advantages of Nonspeech Sound

Nonspeech sound has the following advantages:

- It informs us about the success of our actions.
- It can be processed more quickly than speech.
- It does not depend on the knowledge of a language.

> **MAXIM**
>
> We often judge the success of an action by auditory feedback.

We often judge the success of our actions through the auditory feedback we get from mechanical and electronic devices. It is not difficult to manufacture a telephone the does not beep when the keys are pressed or a computer keyboard that functions silently, but these would not supply the kind of feedback we require to ascertain the successful completion of our actions.

Nonspeech sounds are more succinct than speech and can be processed more quickly. Speech is sequential and, therefore, requires a certain amount of time before meaning can be extracted. Nonspeech sounds can be associated with events or processes and can deliver a message in much less time. They are also more universal and do not depend on the knowledge of a particular language.

Disadvantages of Nonspeech Sound

Nonspeech sound has the following disadvantages:

- It can be ambiguous.
- It must be learned.
- It must be familiar.
- It does not have high discrimination.
- It is transitory.
- It can become annoying.

It has been suggested that visual analogies would equate speech with screen text and nonspeech audio with graphic images. According to this analogy, nonspeech auditory stimuli would suffer from same type of ambiguity affecting icons. Sound can be used to convey information that does not have to be monitored visually, such as the completion of a printing task; however, the significance of the sound must be learned in advance.

Sounds do not intrinsically convey information unless their significance is familiar to the user, such as if they are the same as sounds encountered in the real-life environment or if they are standard interface sounds used by many applications and operating systems. An interface filled with unfamiliar sounds would be difficult to use and potentially overwhelming.

Our auditory perception is not as refined as our visual perception. We cannot distinguish easily between subtle changes in auditory parameters such as volume, location, and pitch. We are also likely to experience a change in one parameter as affecting other parameters as well. For example, we might perceive a change in pitch as a simultaneous change in volume, even though no change in the volume parameter has occurred. This would limit the perceivable resolution of auditory output.

> **MAXIM**
> Auditory stimuli are transitory.

As with any auditory stimulus, nonspeech audio is transitory. Unless there is some mechanism to replay the sound, we can not benefit from a "second glance." Without a replay mechanism the user would have to remember the sound, which would put an added load on the user's memory and might interfere with other interface tasks that require memory functions. This limits the use of audio to information that is temporary in nature.

> **MAXIM**
> Sound can be annoying or inappropriate.

Depending on the type of sound and the way it is used, there is a potential for it to be annoying. Sounds are not easily ignored—we don't have "ear-lids"—and they can be inappropriate in certain environments, such as libraries and classrooms. If a user finds a sound to be particularly offensive or grating, he or she might turn down the volume or shut off the computer's sound. This would have a drastic effect on any interface that uses sound exclusively to convey particular information.

13.2. Using Sound in Interaction Design

If sound is used properly, it can be a natural reflection of our real-world experiences. However, excessive auditory feedback can become tiring and distracting. How do you decide when to use sound and how much auditory stimulation is too much?

As with all design decisions, the user's task must be considered the deciding factor. We use the following heuristics to determine when auditory feedback should be used:

- If auditory feedback does not aid the user in the efficient completion of his task, it should be considered unnecessary.
- If auditory feedback represents an unnecessary annoyance, it should be prohibited.
- If auditory feedback adds to the user experience either in terms of efficiency or user satisfaction, it should be considered.

13.2.1. Redundant Coding

Contemporary GUIs make limited use of audio output:

- Graphical buttons might click.
- Windows might swish when they open.
- Dialogues might initiate synthetic speech.
- Alerts might indicate the completion of a process.

Systems can also be configured to emit additional user-defined sounds that accompany actions and system events. Commercially available GUIs such as Microsoft's Windows® or Mac OS X® use sound to make interfaces feel more realistic and responsive. These are basically auditory display layers that serve as redundant coding for basic events and processes.

Research shows that redundant coding has certain benefits:

- It aids memory by adding additional associations.
- It increases efficiency by allowing the most efficient mode for a particular task to be chosen.
- It allows users with perceptual deficits to take advantage of their strengths in other channels.

Because audio can support user tasks through redundant coding, it is logical to suggest that it should be applied to interfaces in a more aggressive and robust way. However, we must seriously consider the inclusion of auditory stimuli and not just add gratuitous sounds that do not enhance the user's experience in significant ways. One of the issues we need to consider is whether to use sound as negative feedback or positive feedback.

13.2.2. Positive/Negative Feedback

In our everyday life, we experience a great deal of positive auditory feedback. When we leave a room we might hear the door close behind us. If we do not hear the door, we might look back to see whether it did not shut properly. When we pick up the phone we listen for a dial tone, which signifies that the line is available. If there is no dial tone, we might think that the line is dead. We depend on positive audio feedback to let us know that a task has been successfully completed and that everything is functioning properly; we often interpret silence as a negative response.

Contrary to the real-world auditory experiences just mentioned, one of the most common uses of sound in interfaces is as an error signal. A system might beep if an illegal action is requested or if we attempt to access unavailable functionality.

Often, systems allow us to configure our own auditory pronouncement of user error by letting us choose our own "beep of admonishment." Cooper and Reimann (2003) call these examples "negative audio feedback," and suggest that they are an unfortunate use of an interface's auditory potential.

As a general rule, people do not enjoy being told about their mistakes, especially in a way that is evident to everyone within ear-shot. Taking this fact together with our real-life experience of auditory feedback as a signal of success or completion, it might be advisable to rethink using sound to signal errors. The concept of positive auditory feedback suggests that successful events and processes should be accompanied by sound and errors should be conveyed through silence.

This argument has a practical logic; however, there are issues to consider. As mentioned earlier, most GUIs use redundant auditory feedback to convey successful button clicks and processes such as copying files and, therefore, already incorporate a degree of positive feedback.

It is also true that we rely on negative auditory feedback to inform us of problems in the real world. For instance, a squeaky door communicates the need for oil; a car with a manual transmission will quickly inform us if we do not shift the gears properly. There are innumerable auditory cues that communicate negative feedback in real-life situations. Many of these are essential for our survival.

How we use auditory feedback in interaction design must be determined by the user's task. Redundant auditory alarms might be crucial to the safe operation of computer-operated machinery in mission-critical environments. However, general computing interfaces that announce every mistake the user makes should be seriously reconsidered.

13.2.3. Speech Applications

For some time, researchers have been interested in the idea of making human–computer interaction more like human–human interaction. Because speech plays such an essential role in human communication, it is natural to explore the ways in which speech can play a role in human–computer interaction. Karat, Vergo, and Nahamoo (2002) identify four conversational tasks and suggest ways in which these tasks can be supported by technology:

- Composition
- Transcription
- Transaction
- Collaboration

Composition

Creating and editing text documents has been a staple computing activity for business, scientific research, and education, among many other fields. Composing a formal document is a complex iterative process. Numerous drafts need to be created before the final document is ready for publication or distribution.

Digitized speech can be used to facilitate and augment the process of composing documents. Digital recordings can substitute for other analog methods in the initial creation of the document, or they can be used further along in the process as a means to communicate changes that need to be made.

For example, it would be possible to accompany a text file with digitally recorded annotations, or to transform a printed document into a sound file that is read to a remote participant over a cell phone or other mobile device.

Digitized speech can be used:

- As a source from which a document is created
- As a means of annotating for editing purposes
- As a means of dispersal both during document creation and after completion

Transcription

A searchable record of the spontaneous conversations that occur in business meetings could prove advantageous for future perusal and discussion, especially if speakers were identified. The identification of speakers would add another searchable parameter to the data. For instance, if a participant made a statement that needed to be quoted later, the minutes of the meeting could be digitally searched, going through each statement by the person in question until the quote was located.

Multimedia is another application for computer-based transcription. Audio/video (A/V) documents are becoming more and more common, and they bring with them new challenges and opportunities for indexing and searching the data. Lai and Srinivasan (2001) discuss these issues in terms of multimedia indexing applications. They suggest that transcriptions of A/V documents with time offsets that synchronize the text with related images would enable easy indexing and afford users the possibility of keyword searches of the document.

They suggest that searching a document's textual representation would be quicker and more efficient than searching its A/V manifestation. Searching an A/V document would require sequential playback, a rather time-consuming activity, whereas text can be scanned for required information in a nonlinear way (Lai & Srinivasan, 2001).

A/V documents also present a potential benefit to disabled and visually impaired employees, who could use these documents to gain greater access to the creative and informational processes involved in decision making. An audio record is easily created from a transcription and can include any subsequent annotations appended to the file.

Transaction

Computers are often used to carry out tasks that are initiated by a user; this is a form of transaction. These interchanges usually involve the user pointing and clicking or inputting text. Pointing is not the most efficient form of communication in real-life transactions, and it would be awkward for us to use text for the numerous interchanges we participate in on a daily basis. Speech is far more efficient. Similarly, it can be advantageous to use speech as a method of human–computer transaction rather than text or the pointing and clicking required in graphic direct manipulation interfaces.

Home networking continues to evolve, and new wireless technologies, such as Bluetooth and WiFi (ISO 802.11*x*), have brought us closer to the vision of an intelligent household infrastructure. The potential of verbal transactional interfaces at home, as well as in the office or classroom, is great, and we might soon begin to see climate and lighting control systems based on spoken commands.

These evolving home networks and their subsequent interfaces require users to navigate complex menu structures. Finding a musical recording among many hundreds or even thousands of other recordings, for example, can be a difficult and time-consuming process. Verbal navigation of this and other systems would allow for more efficient and successful operation.

Collaboration

Collaborative tasks involve human–human conversations; they are facilitated by vocal discourse between people. The classic example of computer-assisted collaboration is the contemporary telephone system. Telephone conversations begin as analog voice signals, which are converted to digital signals at the central phone office and subsequently become photon pulses in fiber optic cables.

Other examples of computer-assisted collaborative tasks include audible IM sessions and the sound track of a video conference. These collaborative environments involve two basic areas of speech—speech recognition and speech generation. We will explore these issues later on in the chapter.

13.2.4. Nonspeech Applications

In general terms, we can classify nonspeech sound as being either concrete or abstract. Concrete sounds are those that exist in nature. Abstract sounds are those created by humans, such as musical sounds.

We can use these two distinct categories to explore the application of non-speech sounds to human-computer interaction.

- Concrete (auditory icons)
  - Ecological listening (natural sounds)
    - Distal stimulus (sound source)
- Abstract (earcons)
  - Musical listening (synthetic sounds)
    - Proximal stimulus (physical sound properties)

Concrete or everyday sounds include the rustle of paper, scraping noises, or the sound of a door closing. These sounds are referential in that they refer to events in the real world. The use of concrete sound is exemplified in Gaver's auditory icons, which are discussed next.

Abstract sounds, on the other hand, have no reference to real-world events; they are abstract and structured much like musical sounds, on the basis of pitch, volume, and tone. They are the basis of the earcons developed by Blattner and are discussed later.

Auditory Icons

> **MAXIM**
>
> People generally attend to the source of a sound rather than the acoustic properties of the sound wave.

Gaver (1989) suggests that people listen to sounds in an ecological way. That is, they do not attend to the "physics of the sound waves" (the proximal stimulus), but they listen for the sound source (the distal stimulus).

When people interpret everyday sounds they consider the material properties of the sound source—for example, was the object that created the sound made of metal or wood? They also listen for signs of the object's size—low-pitched sounds indicate large size, and high-pitched sounds indicate small size. We gain valuable information about the nature of real-life objects by the sounds those objects make.

During ecological listening, people also respond to the resonating qualities of the environment in which the sound is created. Clicking your fingers in a small, heavily carpeted room will create a very different sound then clicking them in a large, cavernous hall with marble walls.

Gaver applied the concept of ecological listening to the computer interface. Using recordings of everyday sounds, he created auditory icons that exploited analogies with real-world objects and events. File types were related to different materials, such as wood and metal. A file's size might also be related to other parameters, such as volume and pitch. When a user selected a file, its sound informed the user of its type and size.

The resonating properties of the acoustic space related to the amount of system processing going on, and the clarity of the sound indicated whether the event occurred in the active window or another, hidden window.

SonicFinder

In 1989 Gaver created the SonicFinder®, an auditory layer that ran on top of the Apple® Finder. The finder's interface icons and actions were assigned auditory icons that referenced their real-life equivalents. For instance, selecting a file caused a tapping sound, dragging it caused a scraping sound, and dropping it in the trash created a crashing sound.

This coupling of visual and auditory elements was based on intuitive connections with real-world information and thereby resulted in a multimodal experience that did not require training or prior knowledge beyond everyday experiences.

As with visual metaphors, there are times when no corollary for particular system objects exists in the real world. In these situations, the interface elements become idioms rather than metaphors. Consider the scrollbar or status indicator; these have no real-life counterparts or metaphorical relationships. In these situations, Gaver suggested using sound effects with metaphorical qualities to represent these actions, as in the case of the pouring sound used to represent the file copy operation. These sound effects are more like abstractions than representations.

The SonicFinder was a redundant layer that reinforced essential feedback about tasks and allowed users to attend to certain tasks visually while using audio feedback to monitor others. It also afforded users a stronger sense of engagement with the interface. Many subjects reported that returning to the standard silent Finder was like wearing earplugs.

Synthesized Auditory Icons

Using recorded samples of concrete sounds to create auditory icons can be difficult and complicated. Concrete sounds are by their nature embedded in noisy acoustic environments that make clean (high signal-to-noise ratio) recording difficult. High-quality recording equipment is expensive, and even if the sound-producing objects can be extracted from their natural environments, adequate recording studios are not always available and can be costly to rent.

Even good samples retain the problem of needing to be modified according to interface events. For instance, the playback of a pouring sound to represent a file copy operation would have to be timed precisely to the length of the process.

These different lengths could drastically alter the sound of the file, eventually making it unrecognizable. If the sounds cannot be altered in real time, there must be numerous samples to account for various dynamic situations, quickly and drastically increasing the sound's storage requirements.

For these and other reasons, researchers have been interested in creating algorithms for synthesizing auditory icons. Synthesized auditory icons would allow for complete real-time control of high-level parameters. Playback could easily be connected to particular events and manipulated according to random user actions. Finally, storage requirements could be significantly minimized.

Progress Bar Sounds

It has been suggested that continuous processes could be represented by wave or wind sounds (Conversy, 1998). They are familiar sounds with an intuitive connection to long-term processes. Because these sounds evolve slowly, it would be inappropriate to use them for rapid processes.

These auditory icons easily could be related to the ongoing status of a progress bar. The individual wave sounds or gusts of wind could be used as a heartbeat informing the user that a process is continuing. To avoid habituation, the sound would diminish during the middle of the process and get louder toward completion.

It would be difficult to use actual sounds for these processes, however, Beaudouin-Lafon and Conversy (1996) suggested that Sheppard-Risset tones could be used to provide feedback about the progress of long system operations. These are tones that seem to go up or down indefinitely while actually remaining on the same pitch. This auditory illusion is similar to M. C. Escher's endless staircase in his etching "Ascending and Descending" (Figure 13.1).

The illusion is created by shifting the partials (or overtones—sympathetic vibrations that accompany a sound; see Section 13.3.1) either upward or downward. These altered partials eventually decrease in volume, and new ones appear in the lower frequencies. This gives the impression that the pitch is rising even though it remains fixed.

The shift in partials can be sped up or slowed down to reflect different aspects of a continuous process. For example, as a process draws to completion, the shifting of partials can increase in speed, giving the impression that the tone is ascending

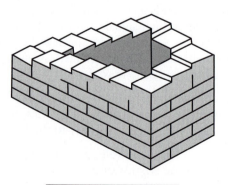

Figure 13.1   M. C. Escher staircase.

more rapidly. This would give the user an indication of how much longer the process will take.

The initial speed could be used to indicate the scope of the process. If a process is going to take a long time, the shifting can begin slowly and increase until completed. If the process is relatively brief, the shifting can begin more rapidly.

The sound might also be used intermittently with a rhythmic motive so that it does not become annoying. The rhythmic pattern could also communicate information about the duration of the process.

Benefits of Auditory Icons

Due to the increasing complexity of GUIs, designers must address the potential for users to become visually overwhelmed. Users who work in visually complex environments or who must monitor simultaneous processes can benefit from the addition of auditory feedback that disperses some of the cognitive processing over multiple channels.

Gaver (1989) suggests that auditory icons can be used as enhancements to a visual interface, as well as to extend interfaces, allowing users to interact simultaneously with screen objects and with objects beyond the view of the screen.

Gaver also demonstrates the advantages of auditory icons in collaborative computing environments. In his ARKola project, he showed that although it might not be possible for all collaborating team members to attend to a computer screen at the same time, auditory feedback was continuously accessible to all members, and tasks could be distributed immediately on arrival of the auditory output.

Concerns

One of Gaver's concerns about the use of auditory icons is the learnability of the mapping between the icon and the object represented. He discusses this concern in terms of the articulatory directness of the mapping.

Hutchins, Hollan, and Norman (1986) point out that onomatopoetic sounds such as "oink" and "bow wow" have high articulatory directness and, therefore, are easy to learn. A swishing sound accompanying a paintbrush tool also has high articulatory directness. A system beep however, carries no information about the error it represents and, therefore, would require learning. Nevertheless, familiarity and experience, have been found to be more important than the nature of the relationship between the sound and the object.

Guidelines

Although there are only a few formal guidelines for the creation of auditory icons, Mynatt (1994) puts forward some issues that must considered in their creation:

Identifiability—The user must be able to recognize the sound's source. Familiar sounds will be more easily recognized and remembered.

Conceptual Mapping—How well does the sound map to the aspect of the user interface represented by the auditory icon?

Physical Parameters—The physical parameters of the sound, such as length, intensity, sound quality, and frequency range, can affect its usability. No one parameter should be allowed to dominate; the user may infer significance.

User Preference—How the user responds emotionally to the auditory icon is also important. Is the sound harsh or too cute?

Cohesion—The auditory icons used in an interface must also be evaluated as a cohesive set. For example, each auditory icon must be relatively unique. They should not sound too similar to each other.

Mynatt also suggests the following procedural guidelines for auditory icon creation:

1. Use sounds that are:

   a. Short

   b. Of wide frequency range

   c. Equal in length, intensity, and sound quality

2. Use free-form questions to determine how easy it is to identify the sounds
3. If it is not easy to identify the sounds, evaluate how easy it is to learn them
4. Evaluate sets of icons to determine whether they conflict with each other

   a. Do they mask each other?

   b. Do the mappings conflict?

   c. Are they easy to tell apart?

5. Conduct usability tests

Earcons

In 1989, Blattner, Sumikawa, and Greenberg suggested that sounds could be used in the same way that visual images are used for icons. They called these groupings earcons and defined them as "nonverbal audio messages used in the user–computer interface to provide information to the user about some computer object, operation, or interaction" (Blattner et al., 1989, p. 12).

Earcons are short musical phrases used to represent system objects or processes. Earcons involve musical listening and are based on the concept of the musical motive (a short set of notes with a particular rhythm). Motives also involve recognizable instrumental sounds. One motive might sound like a piano and another might sound like a flute.

Musical Parameters of Earcons

Before we discuss earcons, we clarify some of the terminology used to define the musical properties of sound. Table 13.1 gives the definitions of the different aspects of musical sound.

Table 13.1   Musical Parameters

Pitch	**Melody**—this is the effect of notes presented successively
	Harmony—this is the effect of notes presented at the same time (chords)
	Register—this refers to the grouping of notes according to highness or lowness
	Vibrato—this is a quick, slight alteration of pitch to enhance a note; for example, this can be produced by a quick shaking of the hand on a violin string as the note is being played.
Timbre	**Instrument**—this refers to the quality of sound that differentiates, say, a trumpet from a flute
Dynamics	**Accent**—this is the effect of one note of a group played louder than the others
	Foreground/background—softer sounds recede into the background and give the impression that the source is far away, whereas loud sounds seem to be closer
	Crescendo/decrescendo—the volume of the sound increases or decreases as the note is played
	Contrast—one note may be softer or louder than another; an echo is softer than the originating sound
	Tremolo—in this effect, there is a quick fluctuation of volume between loud and soft while a note is being played
Duration	**Rhythm**—this is the pattern created by the combination of long and short notes
	Articulation—notes can be played according to the length of a time slot but may not sound for the entire duration of that time slot (staccato); notes can be stretched so that they take the full duration of their time slot (legato)

The sounds used by earcons are abstract, whereas those used in audio icons are everyday concrete sounds. Because earcons use musical motives, they can take advantage of the structural properties of music. These structural properties are based on relationships that can be associated with related interface elements such as menu options.

Sounds with similar attributes are perceived as related. For example, all sounds with a flute-like timbre will sound related. High-pitched notes will sound similar to the listener and, therefore, also sound related. Hierarchical structures can be created using these relationships.

Using just timbre and pitch, we can create a structure with two categories and three levels (Table 13.2). We can create more complex structures by manipulating other parameters. These musical relationships can be superimposed on interface elements such as menus and commands. For example, timbre can be used to differentiate between different menus, rhythm can be used to distinguish between the different levels, and pitch can be used to delineate the options at a particular level.

Table 13.2   Pitch Levels and Timbre

	Violin	Flute
High	High violin notes	High flute notes
Middle	Middle violin notes	Middle flute notes
Low	Low violin notes	Low flute notes

Earcons can exploit these and other innate musical structures to create an auditory layer that supplements and reinforces the visual cues built into icons and icon families. They can also support menu structures and navigational structures.

Earcons can be used to:

- Reinforce icon family relationships
- Support menu hierarchies
- Support navigational structures

As with visual icons, earcons can be used to represent system objects as well as system processes. Simple motives, however, are limited with regard to what they can communicate, so researchers have explored ways to combine earcons.

Compound Earcons

When you combine two earcons, you create a compound earcon. For instance, an earcon for a file might consist of three short high notes, and an earcon for delete might consist of one long, low note that starts soft and gets louder (crescendo). To represent the "delete file" event, we would play the delete earcon followed by the file earcon. The user would hear the low note get gradually louder followed immediately by the three short higher notes. Together these sounds would be considered a compound earcon.

Compound earcons can also represent the nodes in a hierarchical menu structure. Each node could inherit the motive from the level above and append its own unique motive, creating a compound earcon.

Consider Figure 13.2. The main level is represented by a bass drum note, which is inherited by each subsequent node. The second level is represented by medium length notes of different timbres and the third level by short notes. Therefore, the third option in the third level of either path is represented by a bass drum note followed by a medium-length note (flute or violin), followed by three short notes (xylophone or vibraphone).

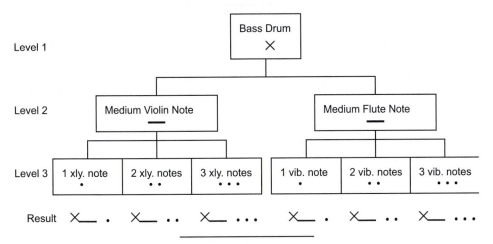

Figure 13.2 Menu differentiation.

xyl., xylophone; vib., vibraphone.

Hierarchical Earcons

Compound earcons have the disadvantage of eventually becoming too long, and therefore they are only practical for simple events or menu structures. This has led to the development of hierarchical earcons.

The hierarchical earcons suggested by Brewster (2003) use five parameters: rhythm, pitch, timbre, register, and dynamics. These parameters are used to create earcons that reflect the levels in a hierarchical menu structure.

According to this method, each node in a hierarchy inherits the attributes of the previous level. The parameter qualities inform the user about the menu's hierarchical structure. For example, one level is represented by a timbre and another by a rhythm.

These two parameters—rhythm and timbre—are not mutually exclusive. They can be combined to create a unique instance of a motive that reflects a unique node. This motive instance will have the parameter qualities of the present level combined with the inherited parameter qualities of the previous level. By the use of this method, earcons can convey a great deal of information in a compact and efficient way.

Brewster created a family of hierarchical earcons for error events (Figure 13.3). His hierarchy has three levels. The first level is represented by a rhythmic pattern of one medium-length note followed by two short notes half the length of the first note. These notes have no pitch information and are represented as clicks. This pattern is inherited by all subsequent nodes.

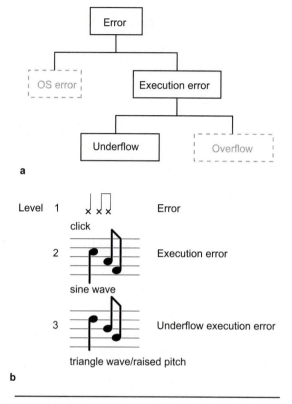

Figure 13.3   (a) Hierarchical structure. (b) Hierarchical earcons.

The next level introduces pitch. The motive for this level consists of the previous rhythmic pattern using different pitches. The notes are played with the neutral timber of a sine wave. A sine wave sounds something like a soft flute tone.

The next level uses the rhythmic and pitch patterns of the previous levels but raises the pitches to make them sound higher. This level also changes the timbre to a triangle wave, which has a coarser, raspy quality. Once the user arrives at the third level, he or she hears only the result of the inherited qualities, that is, only one motive using the original rhythmic pattern but at a higher pitch and with the altered timbre.

The research on hierarchical earcons has shown that subjects can identify hierarchical earcons with 80% to 85% accuracy using approximately 25 node structures.

Parallel Earcons

Another way to shorten the length of earcons that represent complex hierarchical structures is to present various complete motives concurrently. This combined sound is called a parallel earcon. Let's look at the earcons created by Brewster for a File object and the Create action.

Create Earcon—The Create earcon consists of a long note that starts softly and gradually gets louder. This dynamic quality is called a crescendo.

File Earcon—The earcon for File consists of two notes each of a different pitch, the first higher than the second, and each half the length of the Create earcon.

The File and Create earcons are presented simultaneously. They begin at the same time and, because the two notes in the File earcon are both half the length of the Create earcon, they end simultaneously, achieving a 50% reduction in the length of time required to present the earcon.

Earcons have been shown to be an effective way to use auditory stimuli in interface design:

- They can be used as an auditory layer in hierarchical menu structures.
- They can represent objects as well as actions.
- They can also represent the act of applying an action to an object, as in the "create file" event just mentioned.

Application

It has been suggested that earcons, like other auditory interaction concepts, may increase the usability of complex electronic devices, especially those that lack the screen space required by contemporary GUI designs. Brewster's work with earcons has shown potential for an increased usability in wearable and mobile computing devices.

He has been able to demonstrate the practical application of earcons in a prototype Nokia mobile phone and suggests that "[d]evelopers can now use nonspeech sounds to aid in navigation through their interfaces knowing that these can make significant improvements to usability" (Brewster, 2000, 5).

Concerns

Because earcons use musical sounds as well as the inherent concepts and structures of these sounds, it has been necessary for researchers to determine whether musical training affected users' ability to use and understand earcons. Most experimental designs used to explore the effectiveness of earcons involved groups of people with musical training versus people with no musical training. Results showed that musical training afforded no significant advantage for the recognition of both compound and hierarchical earcons.

Studies have shown that discrimination between earcons requires a high degree of differentiation in design; that is, large differences in pitch range and timbre are necessary for people to be able to discriminate between simple earcons as well as for hierarchical and compound earcons.

Because earcons depend on pitch recognition to distinguish between different motives, interaction designers must consider the possibility that users may have auditory pitch recognition deficiencies or amusia, commonly referred to as tone deafness. This is a condition that affects people's ability to distinguish between different pitches. Amusia can be caused by many factors, including brain damage as well as congenital disorders.

There has been increased interest in research into the types of music agnosia that are due to brain damage. The results of this research may help us to better understand how people process musical sounds. However, the topic of tone deafness is only superficially understood. Brain damage, congenital defects, and insufficient musical training can all play a role in a user's inability to differentiate pitch; we must be clear that, whatever the reason, some users will not be able to differentiate between earcon motives based on pitch.

Guidelines

The following is a set of experimentally derived design guidelines for earcon creation taken from the literature.

Timbre

Timbre is the most important grouping factor and the most easily recognizable parameter.

Use sounds with multiple harmonics.

Pitch and Register

Do not use only pitch and register as a cue if absolute judgment is required.

All pitches in a motive should span only one octave.

Use major and minor scales for pitches within a motive.

Use two- or three-octave differences between earcons when using register only.

Use pitches within the 125 Hz to 5 kHz range.

Rhythm, Duration, and Tempo

Rhythm is the most prominent characteristic of a motive.

Make rhythms as different as possible.

Use different numbers of notes.

Do not use notes shorter than 0.03 second.

Use different tempos to differentiate earcons.

A motive should be long enough to convey meaning but no longer.

Intensity/Dynamics

Use intensity and dynamics sparingly due to the potential annoyance factor.

Threshold limits are from a maximum of 20 dB to a minimum of 10 dB.

Spatial Location

Use stereo or full three-dimensional spatialization to differentiate families and parallel earcons.

Earcons versus Auditory Icons

Earcons and auditory icons need not be mutually exclusive. Both categories often serve the same purpose, and each has its advantages and disadvantages. A combination is recommended if the applications are appropriate. It is even possible to merge the two into a richer medium for communicating information.

The everyday sounds used for auditory icons can be incorporated into the musical structures of earcons and used in much the same way as timbre. For example, we can alter the pitch of the sound made by a drop of water. Each drop of differing pitch can then be assigned to a specific node in a hierarchical menu. It is interesting to note that Blattner et al. state that "an earcon is any audio message and need not be a motive" (Blattner et al., 1989, 23).

A group of auditory icons can be related as a family through the manipulation of properties such as pitch, duration, and dynamics. For example, the icon for a spreadsheet application might use a metallic auditory icon consisting of two long sounds. The icons for the spreadsheet files could then be higher-pitched metallic sounds using four short notes.

By blurring the distinction between auditory icons and earcons, we gain the ability to combine them within the same interface, benefiting from the positive characteristics of each category and maintaining a consistent sound ecology. By manipulating musical properties, we can create auditory icon families that relate to corresponding visual icon families.

It is important to consider the entire structure of an interface, and design its auditory layer with a consistent sound ecology.

Globalization—Localization

Auditory icons involve ecological listening, which highlights concerns about location and environment. The sounds with which we are familiar may not be common in other cultures. Because auditory icons derive a great deal of their functionality from their relationships with real-world sounds, they are to a large extent predicated on specific cultures and geographic locations.

> **MAXIM**
>
> Musical sounds are culturally biased.

Earcons may have a greater degree of global relevance than auditory icons due to their abstract nature. However, timbre is highly dependent on instruments, which are by nature cultural artifacts. The strong impact that Western European music has had on the world stage makes it easy to overlook the fact that not all cultures use Western instruments.

Many world music systems do not even use the same basic intervallic structures that are the basis of Western music. Some systems use much smaller note divisions than does Western music, which divides the octave into 12 atomic intervals. These structures are based on microtonal divisions, whose usage greatly affects a listener's perception of pitch.

The basic elements of pitch, rhythm, dynamics, and timbre can be approached from many different perspectives. It would be a considerable mistake to assume that listeners worldwide have the same sensibilities and understanding of the structures and characteristics of music.

13.3. Technical Issues Concerning Sound

We looked at the human issues concerning speech and hearing. We also considered the ways in which sound can be used to enhance human–computer interaction. We now look at some of the technical issues involved in computer-based sound.

13.3.1. Sound Waves

Sound, like light, is made up of waves and therefore can be described in terms of frequency and amplitude. A sound wave is transmitted through the air and cannot exist in a vacuum. Like most wave structures, it can be graphically represented on rectangular coordinates (x and y axes).

As a general model, we can think of a wave as starting at a neutral point or midline, rising to a crest, returning to the midline, and passing through a low point or trough before it finally returns to the midline, thus completing a cycle. The number of cycles a sound wave completes during the interval of 1 second determines its frequency, which is measured in Hertz. The human ear can perceive sound in the range of 20 to 20,000 Hz (20 kHz).

The distance of the crest and trough from the midline is called the wave's amplitude and is perceived as the loudness or softness of the sound. Amplitude is measured in decibels and relates to the dynamics or intensity of the sound.

We use the wave's shape to differentiate between one sound source and another. This is why we can tell one instrument from another even if they are playing the same pitch (frequency) at the same dynamic (amplitude). The sound waves we encounter in our daily lives are complex and have irregular wave shapes.

Geometrically perfect wave shapes do not exist in nature and can only be created synthetically. Electronic instruments, such as synthesizers, can produce geometrically regular waves. Figure 13.4 shows the four basic synthetic wave shapes.

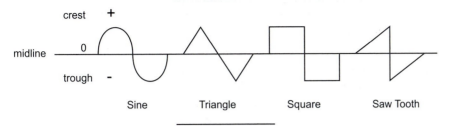

Figure 13.4 Sound waves.

These wave shapes range in timbre from the flute-like sine wave to the raspy-sounding square wave. Each wave shape creates its own unique timbre and can be combined with other waves to achieve additional timbres. The phenomenon of timbre is complex and involves many factors, such as how the sound is initiated, the acoustic environment in which it is created, and the overtones—sometimes called harmonics or partials—that each wave produces.

Overtones are sympathetic vibrations that accompany a sound. The relationship between the fundamental pitch, the sound on which we focus, and the additional frequencies affects the way in which we perceive the sound. Waves that produce overtones that are proportionally related or harmonic have a more "pure" quality, such as those produced by the musical instruments that play melodies.

Waves with irregular overtones (inharmonic) may sound more "noisy," like the sounds produced by a pair of cymbals or a drum. Our ears are quite sensitive to these overtones, and this phenomenon allows us to distinguish between different sounds of equal pitch and dynamics.

13.3.2. Computer-Generated Sound

To use auditory stimuli in an interface the computer must be able to create the required sounds. There are two basic ways in which computers generate sound: they can use preexisting recorded sounds called samples that are stored on chips, or they can create the sounds from scratch.

Synthesis

To synthesize sounds from scratch, a computer must be able to generate a signal or sound wave. This can be done either internally or by using external hardware. Digital signal generators use software to create sound waves. Once the basic wave is generated, it can be processed in many ways to produce an almost unlimited range of sounds.

An early form of sound synthesis, called frequency modulation (FM) synthesis, was developed by John Chowning at Stanford University in the early 1970s. FM synthesis uses the frequency of one sound wave (the modulator) to affect the parameters of a second wave (the carrier). For instance, the frequency of the modulator might be set to control the amplitude of the carrier, causing the volume of the carrier to rise and fall with the modulator's cycles.

After the parameters are set, the resulting signal can be further processed by applying filters. Some filters limit the output to a certain range of the spectrum. For example, a band pass filter might be set to block some of the upper partials of a sound, which would have the effect of reducing its treble portion, causing it to seem muffled or to have more bass.

One of the problems with FM synthesis is that it is difficult convincingly to imitate acoustic instruments. Synthesized sounds often have a mechanical quality, which can be less than satisfying if a more realistic sound is required. One of the advantages of synthesized sounds, however, is that they do not require storage space because they are generated dynamically as needed.

Sampling

The artificial quality of FM synthesis can be appropriate for certain applications—it was commonly used in gaming applications—but as we have seen, more realistic sounds can enhance the user's sense of "being there," increasing his or her engagement with the simulation.

Higher-fidelity sounds can be obtained by using digital samples of actual instruments. A sample is basically a snapshot of a sound wave at a certain point in time that captures its amplitude information.

According to the Nyquist-Shannon sampling theorem, for the digital version of a sound wave to be acceptable, the wave must be sampled at twice the rate of its highest frequency; otherwise noise will be introduced into the sample. This effect is referred to as aliasing. Commercial music CDs are sampled at a rate of 44.1 kHz, which is slightly greater than twice the human threshold of 20 kHz.

The amount of information captured by each sound sample depends on the number of bits used to encode the information. Each sample captures amplitude information and encodes it into a bit stream. Sound waves are analog in nature and, therefore, are capable of an infinite number of amplitude levels.

Samples are digital and must convert the analog wave into discrete value levels. Values that fall between these discrete levels must be averaged or quantized to the next closest value. There is a predefined limit to the number of quantization levels that can be captured; an 8-bit sample, for example, is capable of storing 256 discrete quantities. Higher-quality samples can be obtained by using more bits; this affords additional quantization levels, thus creating a digital signal with higher resolution.

Wavetable synthesizers store digital sound samples and access them according to a look-up table. To accommodate an appropriate range of sounds, these synthesizers generally must contain hundreds of samples, which can become problematic with regard to the storage capacity of the hardware.

To address this problem, the sound sample is broken down into three parts: the initial attack, the sustained sound, and the trailing off at the end of the note. Wavetable synthesizers store the complete attack and decay sections of the sound but only a small segment of the sustain section. This sustain section is then looped to create a note of any required duration.

The timbre of certain instruments is highly dependent on the initial attack. For example, if the attack section of a note played on a piano is removed from the sample, a listener will hear something similar to a flute sound, depending on the register of the note played.

Wavetable synthesizers are capable of creating convincing synthesized musical instruments because they begin with the actual instrument sound. They require a great deal of storage space, however, especially if the sampling rates are of high quality. It takes about 10 MB to store 1 minute of CD-quality sound.

MIDI

Whether we synthesize sounds from scratch or use digital samples of real instruments, we must have some way to control their pitch, duration, and intensity. One of the most popular methods is the Musical Instrument Digital Interface (MIDI) standard, which prescribes a hardware and software solution.

The classic way of understanding MIDI is to think of it as analogous to the piano roll on a player piano. A player piano is an actual instrument that creates sound in the same way a normal piano does: the keys activate hammers that hit strings, which then vibrate and create sound waves. The only difference is that the piano roll takes the place of the piano player and determines which keys are pressed and for how long. In other words, a MIDI file contains information about pitch, duration, and intensity but nothing about timbre; it therefore does not contain the actual sound wave. For this reason MIDI files are extremely small compared to sound samples.

Because MIDI files contain no timbre information, they can be used to control both FM and wavetable synthesizers. MIDI files send messages to the synthesizer about which sound or patch should be used, and it is then up to the synthesizer to actually generate the sound wave. If a different set of sounds is required, one can either swap the bank of sounds in the synthesizer or make a simple change in the patch number sent by the MIDI file. MIDI controls the properties of pitch, duration, and dynamics, but the synthesizer maintains information about the ecological property of timbre.

Speech Generation

Computers can also be used to generate synthetic speech. This can be a significant benefit to people with visual handicaps, besides being the only alternative to visual displays for blind people. Applications that convert text to verbal output are called "text to speech" (TTS) systems.

TTS systems have been used for:

- Information access systems that facilitate remote access to databases
- Transactional systems that process customer orders
- Global positioning system–based mobile navigation systems that output driving directions
- Augmentative systems that aid disabled users

There are two basic phases involved in TTS systems. First, text must be prepared (normalized) for input, and then verbal output must be generated.

There are two systems for speech generation:

- Concatenated synthesis
- Formant synthesis

Concatenated synthesis uses sampled voice sounds that are spliced together according to the text's requirements. A human must be involved in the creation of these samples. Formant synthesis is based on the artificial generation of vocal sounds according to algorithms that mimic human vocal processes. This system does not involve people; the sounds it uses are synthesized sound waves.

Terms

Artificial speech generation, whether concatenated or formant, is based on the structure of human speech. Linguists have identified and labeled the basic elements involved. The smallest unit of language is called a phoneme. English has between 40 and 45 phonemes, depending on the dialect of the speaker and the system used by the linguist.

A phoneme may occur at the beginning, the middle, or the end of a word and has a slightly different pronunciation according to where it is placed. These subtly different sounds are called allophones and constitute the members of the phoneme group. Consider the phoneme /l/. When used in the words "lip," "clay," and "tool," the /l/ has a slightly different sound. These sounds represent three of the allophones in the /l/ phoneme. The transition between allophones is called a diphone, and it changes according to each particular allophone pairing.

A speech generation system that simply presented strings of allophones would be intelligible, but it would have a very artificial sound. People do not rely on these basic sound units alone to communicate; they use other parameters, such as volume, pitch, and duration to convey meaning. In human speech, emphasis is often achieved by increasing the volume of a particular word or by raising the pitch of the voice. We can also achieve emphasis by pausing or elongating a word.

A system that does not address these issues will be less than satisfactory for long-term use. Prosodic elements—such as inflection for questions and intonation for emotional significance—must be incorporated into a text generation system for it to provide a convincing substitute for human speech.

Concatenated Synthesis

A speech generation system based on concatenated synthesis relies on a database of diphones and demisyllables. Demisyllables are samples taken from the beginning of a syllable to its midpoint and from its midpoint to its end. The system concatenates or strings together these units into morphemes, which are the smallest unit of a language that convey meaning.

For example, the word "unstoppable" has three morphemes: "un," "stop," and "able." Each of these morphemes conveys meaning; when concatenated, they help to create a word that conveys the collective meaning. Words are strung together to create phrases and sentences. This output must be further processed to account for the various prosodic aspects essential to human speech.

The complexity of human speech is problematic for speech generation systems. They need to have a great many samples stored on disk, and the processing involved in real-time applications can be taxing on the system. High-end systems that use gigabytes of samples and hours of stored sound can rival human speech, but they are generally prohibitively expensive.

Some systems use larger units, such as whole words, to cut down the processing and storage costs, but even though they use actual human voice samples, their output can often sound unnatural and be difficult to understand.

Formant Synthesis

Formant synthesis is based on artificially generated waveforms, and its output generally sounds robotic and artificial. The generation of speech from formant synthesis will never be confused with a real human voice, as is sometimes the case with the results of very sophisticated concatenation systems. However, formant systems can be advantageous in situations that require less processing and data storage.

A convincing synthesis of human speech is not always necessary for speech generation systems, and the prohibitive cost, processing, and storage overhead of concatenation systems might far outweigh the advantages of its high-quality output.

As discussed before, a violin sounds different from a trumpet and is said to have a different timbre. This difference in timbre can be identified by the different peaks in an instrument's waveform called formants. Instruments that create waveforms with similar formants sound similar. That is why we can identify any two violins, or any two trumpets, as being different but similar instruments.

The position of the formants in a wave form depends on the resonating physical structure that produces the sound. Human speech is created by the manipulation of the vocal tract and nasal cavities. As we perform these actions, we alter the placement of the formants, thus creating diverse vowel sounds.

By imitating this process with an artificially generated waveform, we can simulate vocal sounds. Although this does not cover the creation of consonant sounds, which requires processes other than formant placement, it does constitute the basis of formant synthesis systems.

Formant-based systems have total control over output and, therefore, can incorporate a great many prosodic qualities. These flexible systems allow for the output of questions and statements as well as various tones of voice, intonations, and emotions.

Text Normalization

Before a speech generation system can begin to generate auditory output, the input text must be normalized. Abbreviations must be converted into full words and acronyms must be considered. Numbers must be classified as to their common uses and pronunciation.

For example, the Zip code 11123 should not be read "eleven thousand, one hundred twenty three"; it should be read "one, one, one, two, three." Similarly, phone numbers and addresses with numerical building numbers or street names should be read in specific ways. Rules for number pronunciation are also affected by regional factors.

Punctuation marks, such as hyphens, must also be considered contextually. A hyphen can be read as "dash," "minus," or "hyphen" or not verbalized at all, as in compound words such as "real-time." Periods also have different uses and must be read accordingly. A period at the end of a sentence signals a pause and a slight change in pitch. A period used as a decimal point in a monetary indication requires different treatment. Lists of items that have no final punctuation must be understood by the normalization software and treated accordingly.

Differences and variances in pronunciation pose all sorts of difficulties for text generation interfaces. Consider the phrase "it was during her bow that her bow fell." The English language is full of homonyms (words that are spelled differently but pronounced identically, such as "pair" and "pear") and homographs (words that are spelled the same but pronounced differently, as with "bow" and "bow" in the phrase just given).

After thousands of years of migration, local populations often include people from diverse ethnic and linguistic backgrounds. The pronunciation of people's names can be confusing due to the different linguistic rules governing their pronunciation.

Many languages also incorporate foreign words into their vocabularies. In their new context, these words are subject to different rules of pronunciation. Although understanding context can help us to clarify some of these issues, the normalization of text for verbal output is a complex process.

Many human conditions affect speech output, including age, gender, accent, and social class. A voice generation system might need to address some of these issues to operate effectively. Consider a TTS system that is used to read the script of a play. Characters are clearly identified in the script and could be assigned different voices according to their gender or age.

An augmentative system that enables a mute person to communicate over a phone system should take the gender of the user into consideration. These systems require that voice be character dependent, whereas other systems can be character independent and allow users to choose voices they prefer. Character-independent applications might be used for public address systems that require lower processing and storage costs.

Contemporary screen readers and audible browsers often allow users to assign different voices to different functions. For example, text might be read by one voice, whereas hyperlinks are assigned to a different voice. This is a good use of currently available software's capabilities and a step in the right direction for such software in general. However, there is still much work to be done before we can afford users the ability to communicate using their own voices and unrestricted vocabularies in TTS applications.

13.3.3. Speech Recognition

Speech recognition software has two distinct applications: transcription and transaction. Automatic speech recognition (ASR) systems allow users to speak continuously into a microphone attached to the computer; this input is converted into text that is displayed on the screen in real time. Two of the more popular applications are Dragon Systems' NaturallySpeaking® and IBM's Via Voice®.

Contemporary ASR applications have relatively low error rates and require only brief periods of orientation for the user to establish a profile. These orientations enable the software to recognize regional accents and personal speech idiosyncrasies. Generally, a selection of text comprising a few paragraphs is read by the user during the initial setup.

User profiles can be updated periodically, adding particularly problematic words, but in general, the software provides adequate results after the basic orientation. It is possible to use the software without going through the setup process, but results are not as accurate.

Commercially available applications have eliminated, for the most part, the two most problematic aspects of speech recognition: speaker independence and continuous speech processing. These applications have large, unrestricted vocabularies that are adequate for general use and allow users to enter domain-specific terminology to increase accuracy in specific applications.

Editing Commands

Although contemporary ASR applications are adequate for general use, problems arise when editing is required. This brings up the other aspect of speech recognition:

transaction. As a user dictates to the ASR, he or she can see the results of his or her speech printed to the screen.

In this process, two types of errors can occur. First, the user might misspeak a word or add extraneous utterances such as "um." These are errors of intent, which can usually be detected early in the process because the user is directly involved. Second, errors occur when the system misinterprets the input and prints an erroneous word to the screen. If the user is not attentive, these misrecognition mistakes might not be detected until later if at all.

If an error occurs and the user is aware of it, he or she can stop dictating and verbally instruct the program to delete the error, or he or she can choose from a menu of possible word alternatives and continue with the dictation. These programs have an almost seamless transition between transcription modes and transaction modes.

Unfortunately, users do not find the verbal correction of errors to be easy or intuitive—research has shown that this kind of editing takes longer than traditional keyboard and mouse methods—and this is the area in which the efficiency of most ASR systems is reduced.

A difficulty with verbal editing arises due to the fact that if the computer did not understand a word the first time, chances are good that it will not do much better on a second verbal attempt; this creates the possibility for compounded errors. Novice users tend to use the system's verbal editing functionality and edit while they dictate, whereas experienced users get better results dictating whole paragraphs and using the keyboard and mouse for editing afterward.

Concerns for Speech Recognition

These ASR systems are adequate for general computing environments but not for mission-critical situations, in which the acceptable margin of error is extremely low. Accuracy can be improved to acceptable levels, however, if recognition is limited to restricted vocabularies consisting only of domain-specific terminology. Further accuracy can be achieved if these systems remain speaker dependent and train for specific pronunciations and accents.

It has been shown that these highly specialized systems are usable in military environments in which ambient noise is high and the user is under significant levels of cognitive stress. Specialized ASR interfaces have been studied in tank and helicopter control systems and show promise for future application (Hass, 2001; Williamson & Barry, 2001).

MAXIM

Speech can interfere with problem-solving activities.

When designing speech recognition interfaces, we must keep in mind that it is difficult for people to speak and solve problems at the same time. These activities use the brain in similar ways and therefore interfere with each other. Physical motor activity, on the other hand, is controlled by a different part of the brain, which is why people find it easier to type and think than to speak and think.

In experiments that required users to calculate an equation while navigating an interface, subjects that could physically scroll with the mouse were more efficient than subjects that used verbal scrolling commands. The verbal processing interfered with the memory task and required subjects continuously to refer back to the previous information.

Social and Physical Issues

There are social and physical issues to consider with regard to ASR interfaces. To increase accuracy in ASR systems, users must place a microphone very close to their mouths; the best results are obtained with head-mounted microphones. These inhibit users' movement by essentially wiring them to their computers. Wireless technology can alleviate this constraint to some degree, but this continues to be subject to the kind of electronic interference that can decrease a system's accuracy. Wireless or not, these microphones can also be uncomfortable for extended wear.

> **MAXIM**
>
> Verbal input can be inappropriate in certain situations.

Verbal input can be inappropriate in certain situations, such as when confidential financial and personally identifiable information is required by an interface. A system that requires the verbal input of a password is not only unwise, it also probably will never be used. Imagine a public ATM machine that asked you to speak your account number, user ID, and password! Context of use must be considered a high priority when designing for speech recognition. User acceptance and trust are crucial to the success of these systems.

Similar issues arise with TTS systems that, because of the constraints of location or the confidential nature of the text being dealt with, require additional gear, such as headphones. The extra work needed properly to maintain peripheral devices such as microphones, headphones, keyboards, and mouse input tools can often make then impractical for public use.

Figure 13.5 is a diagram of the speech-related issues covered in this chapter.

Searching Speech

One of the reasons we archive documents is so that we will be able to access the information they contain at a later date. Often, we are only interested in some of a document's content and must locate that information to use it. With text documents, archiving can be done based on diverse criteria. Titles and headers can be used to create categories for easy subsequent retrieval. Keyword searches are also very effective in locating specific information in the content of the document.

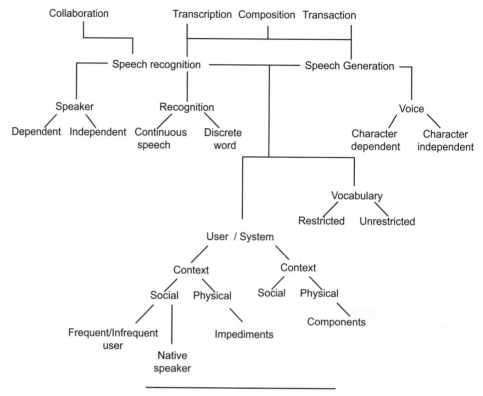

Figure 13.5   Diagram of speech-related issues.

Speech files, however, do not afford easy opportunities for such indexing and searching. It is difficult to extract semantic meaning from verbal data, and it is even more difficult to then equate these data with those contained in other, similar documents—the process by which we create groups and categories of related documents and ideas.

Speech files are also not easily searched for content. Because speech is inherently linear, to access the information contained in a document the user must listen to the file until the appropriate reference is located, which is a tedious and time-consuming process.

Text, on the other hand, can be scanned quickly and efficiently, taking advantage of visual reference points such as headings, titles, paragraphs, and other typographical indicators such as underlining, bolding, and italicizing.

Transcribed Speech

ASR systems can be used to transcribe speech files and create transcripts that can be searched like any other text file. This process can also be applied to the sound track of videos that contain dialogue. In this case, a text file of the video's speech track is created, with links to the video's time code. In this way, the video's dialogue can be scanned and searched using typical textual methods.

Nontranscribed Speech

Arguments can be made for the ability to search raw speech files without transcribing them first. These arguments are similar to those in favor of auditory displays over visual displays. There are times when the visual display of data is either not appropriate or simply not possible.

A nonvisual interface that allows us to search speech documents is obviously advantageous to disabled users. Such an interface also would be advantageous in an automobile when a driver might need to search for street directions for a specific reference, and in other locations where visual displays are inappropriate or dangerous.

Searching audio content requires linear searching, which can be very time consuming. Researchers have explored ways of compressing speech data so that they take less time to parse. The easiest of these methods is to speed up the sound file, which is limitless in terms of speeds that can be achieved and the subsequent gain in time.

As the speed of an audio recording increases, however, the pitch of the speaker's voice rises, eventually making him or her sound comical or silly. There may not be a technical limit to the speed a sound file can achieve, but there is a limit to our ability to comprehend accelerated speech.

Other time compression methods have been successfully applied to speech files. One of the more common approaches is called sampling, which involves the removal of redundant information from the signal. The various methods that accomplish sampling all function by removing small segments of sound waves and smoothing over the resultant transitions.

Another method for sound file compression is to shorten or remove the small pauses between words. Significant compression rates can be obtained in this way; subjects often find the resulting sound files draining to listen to, however, as if speakers never paused to catch their breath.

Furthermore, not all pauses carry the same meaning. whereas some pauses are unintentional and contribute nothing to the meaning of speech, other pauses convey essential information about content and allow listeners to digest the information they have just heard. The removal of pauses drastically reduces intelligibility.

Applications

The SpeechSkimmer interface developed by Arons (1997) uses diverse compression techniques that combine different types of sampling with pause shortening and removal. SpeechSkimmer also incorporates techniques for scanning speech to find specific information. The concept is to develop a "fish ear" view of the information analogous to a "fish eye" view of a visual scene.

Users of the SpeechSkimmer interface scan speech based on pitch, pauses, energy, speaker identification, word spotting, or various combinations of these parameters and then preview a short segment of the speech at that particular location (Arons, 1997). These scanning techniques approximate the kinds of activities involved in text scanning, and subject response has been favorable.

Other researchers have explored possibilities for the simultaneous auditory presentation of localized voice streams. The AudioStreamer project (Schmandt & Mullins, 1995) simultaneously presented subjects with multiple spatially located auditory newscasts that were positioned in front of the user at 60 degrees apart.

The user's chair was equipped with a sensor that tracked the direction of the user's gaze and increased the volume of the sound stream toward which his or her gaze was pointed. When this occurred, the other streams faded into the background, and very little information bled through from the other channels. When a story boundary was reached, the voice stream emitted an audible signal, at which point the user could turn to that newscast, increasing its volume and decreasing the volume of the other streams.

Nontranscribed speech searches are purely at the experimental stage, but they show great potential for situations in which visual displays might be inappropriate or not feasible.

Multimedia Indexing

With the advent of digital multimedia, the general public, as well as the professional user, has become increasingly involved in the creation and archiving of sound and video files. Large collections of multimedia documents are being created in domains as diverse as medicine, entertainment, and education. The process of digitization offers the potential to manipulate speech as we do other data sources, such as text or images.

The idea of using speech as data, however, also creates a unique set of problems. Archiving speech according to content can be difficult: the system must not only recognize the meaning of spoken language, it also must create relationships according to content. Many speech documents do not have formal structures such as titles or paragraphs. Often these documents are recordings of informal meetings or conversations.

Multimedia has become a common element in contemporary computing environments, however, we have only begun to understand how to take advantage of its potential. It is an area of interest to people in diverse domains such as education, politics as well as HCI.

Design Scenario

Circumference: Auditory Display

GUIs can pose significant problems for people with visual impairments. However, screen readers like Freedom Scientific's Jaws for Windows® and Window-Eyes® by GW Micro and audible browsers like IBM's Home Page Reader® (HPR) have contributed significantly to the accessibility of online content for visually impaired users.

Screen readers can read Web pages as well as any content rendered on the screen; audible browsers can only read Web pages. Both types of applications create a linearized version of the document object model (DOM) of the Web page. They do not actually read the screen. The reader essentially creates a one-dimensional text string of the Web page and then feeds it to a speech synthesizer for output to the user.

Audible browsers only read Web pages, and, therefore, they have much simpler interfaces and more accessible commands. They are less expensive than the screen readers and are very useful tools for accessible Web page development. For simplification purposes, we focus this design scenario on HPR, which is the most popular audible browser.

Information on HPR can be found on the IBM Web site http://www-3.ibm.com/able/solution_offerings/hpr.html

Because HPR reads the markup of the page, it is important to write the code properly so that each auditory component can be understood in the context of all the elements on the page. Let's see how we can make the *Circumference* Web site accessible to people who are listening to the pages rather than looking at them.

The activities in this design scenario include the following:

- Creating page titles
- Creating accessible

    - Links
    - Images
    - Active images
    - Skip links
    - Page content

Heuristic for Audible Feedback

We base our decisions about auditory feedback on the previously stated heuristics:

- If auditory feedback does not aid the user in the efficient completion of his or her task, it should be considered unnecessary.
- If auditory feedback represents an unnecessary annoyance, it should be prohibited.
- If auditory feedback adds to the user experience either in terms of efficiency or user satisfaction, it should be considered.

Simply put, if something is irrelevant, we make sure that HPR does not render it in audible feedback. If something is redundant (repetitions can become annoying),

Design Scenario (cont.)

we make sure that the visitor has an option to skip the feedback. If something enhances a visitor's understanding of the page, we make sure that HPR makes it explicit to the user.

When we create auditory feedback for visually impaired visitors we must add one more heuristic:

- Auditory feedback must supply equivalent information.

We must make sure that the information offered to the visually impaired visitor is equivalent to the information presented to the sighted visitor.

Page Title

The first thing that we must do is make sure that the page titles are descriptive of the page's content. Page titles are rendered on the browser's title bar, they are used by search engines, and they are the first thing HPR reads aloud when it gets to a new page:

- Page titles must be descriptive of the page's content.

Here are a few examples of page titles we will use:

- About *Circumference*
- Submissions to *Circumference*
- Previous and Current Issues
    - Issue 4 Table of Contents
        - Issue 4 Poem Title [*poem title*]

Links

The default setting for hypertext in HPR is to read the text of the link in a female voice. This is how the user knows that there is a link and what the link is for. It is important to tell any visitor, sighted or blind, where a link will take them. Sighted people can also see the tool tip created by the title attribute, which can supply more information about the link; however the hypertext itself should be unambiguous as to its target:

- Clearly identify the target of a link in the hypertext itself.

Images

Next we must use the proper coding for the images on the page. Images are problematic for visually impaired users; however, HPR reads the text that is assigned to the alt attribute of an image:

- Alt attributes must be descriptive of the image's purpose.

There are three basic types of images used on Web pages: active images, informational images, and noninformational images. We look at active images later.

Design Scenario (cont.)

Noninformational Images

Transparent GIFs are often used to space content; these images and other decorative images convey no information, and therefore should use a null alt attribute (alt=""):

- Images that do not supply information should use a null alt attribute.

Informational Images

There are many types of informational images. *Circumference* uses a few, such as graphic text for the journal name and tag line and photos of various events:

- Graphic text—These images should simply use the text that is rendered on the graphic.
- Photos—These images require more explanation. This can be done with longer alt text, descriptive image captions, or links to a page that has a fully written out description of the subject of the photo or image.

Active Images

Hyperlinked images such as icons, and in this case the journal logo, must also indicate the link target. This can be done through the alt attribute of the image. These must be descriptive and provide equivalent information about the images as well as the hyperlink.

Sometimes hyperlinked images are grouped with a text link to the same target. In Figure 13.6 the image of the issue's cover is linked to the same page as the hypertext that follows.

If we use a descriptive alt attribute for the image, the visitor will hear that information twice—once when the image's alt attribute is read, and again when the hypertext is read. This conflicts with the heuristics that caution against inefficient and annoying feedback.

 Issue 4
(2006)
Table of Contents and
sample poems

 Issue 3
(Sping/Summer 2005)
Table of Contents and
sample poems

Figure 13.6   Links to issue tables of contents.

Design Scenario (cont.)

If we do not include an alt attribute, HPR will read each letter of the file path and name, which can also be annoying and inefficient:

```
Issue4/Issue4.html
```

If we give the active image a null attribute, HPR will ignore the image. This would be acceptable in most cases; however, some audible browsers may list the link in a separate dialogue and not indicate its target, which would be confusing. The best solution is to include both the image and the text in the same anchor element and include a null attribute for the image. HPR will then simply read the hypertext.

There is one problem with this solution. Figure 13.6 shows that the image is in a different table cell from the hypertext. Because you cannot wrap two table cells in the same anchor element, this solution would require a restructuring of the page layout.

Restructuring the page by putting the image in the same cell as the hyperlink and then wrapping them both in the same anchor element creates much better auditory feedback for the visually impaired visitor, and it is worth the effort.

With this solution HPR reads the modified table structure with the female voice to indicate the presence of hypertext as follows:

```
Issue 4

2006

Table of Contents and sample poems

Issue 3


Spring/Summer 2005

Table of Contents and sample poems
```

This gives unambiguous and efficient feedback to the user.

Navigating within the Page

Consider the completed page from the previous chapter's design scenario as shown in Figure 13.7.

The top banner contains the site's logo, name, and tag line followed by an image representing the area of the site, in this case the Issues area. The dark strip contains the global links. By the time a visually impaired visitor arrives at this page he or she will have loaded three pages with almost the exact same top banner and will have heard it read in its entirety each time.

People with intact vision can simple ignore the top banner and look directly at the page content. People with audible browsers have to sit through the auditory feedback in a linear manner and wait for the new content to be read out loud. As mentioned earlier, people do not have "earlids," and so they cannot tune out this feedback. Even if they could, they would still need to know when to attend to the information or they will miss important feedback.

Design Scenario (cont.)

 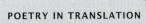

CIRCUMFERENCE   POETRY IN TRANSLATION

about   submissions   issues   contact   subscriptions   events   supporters

Issue 4
Sample Poems
Names with asterisks link to bios.

① ② ③ ④
The Sky
Ask Socrates Marilyn Said
Danse Macabre
"Life is ... to remember"
"Even though the wind envelops"

"Anche se il vento copre"

Anche se il vento copre
la primavera, il popolo
canta alla notte.

L'ascolto io dal mio letto. Lascio
« La vita di Gesù ». Ardo a quel canto.

written 1927–1938
*SANDRO PENNA

Sandro Penna (1906-1977) was born in Perugia. At the age of 23, he moved to Rome, where he lived for the majority of his life. Penna never had a solid career and often bordered on poverty. As a young man, he developed a friendship with the poet Umberto Saba, who helped Penna publish his poems, leading to his first book, Poesie (Poems), in 1939. Several collections followed. Penna was awarded the Premio Viareggio award in 1957.

Figure 13.7   Example poem from Issue 4—complete page.

We need to filter the auditory feedback to make sure that only the information deemed necessary by the user is read out loud. An important issue to remember, however, is the information required by search engines; we do not want to negatively affect automated indexing. We can create a more efficient experience by using the following guideline:

- Include an intrapage link (fragment identifier) to allow people to skip to the section of the page in which they are interested.

The first thing we need to do is analyze the informational structure of the page. We need to determine the different places a visitor might want to go on the page. Looking at Figure 13.7, we can identify three main jumps a visitor might want to make:

- Jump to the Table of Contents
- Jump to the native-language version of the poem
- Jump to the English-language version of the poem (this is below the fold and not shown in the figure)

Design Scenario (cont.)

We need to create "skip" or "jump" links to these three sections of the page, and we need to do this in a way that is accessible to the visually impaired visitor but does not conflict with the visual presentation of the information. One way in which to do this is to make the jump links invisible to sighted visitors. This can be accomplished in a number of ways, such as the following:

- Use a linked transparent GIF with a descriptive alt attribute and small dimensions.
- Make the hypertext the same color as the background, use a small font size, and locate it in an unobtrusive place on the page. We choose this method; the CSS and markup are as follows:

```
<div style="position:absolute; top:200px; color:#fff;
left:0px; font-size:0px; text-decoration:none;">
<a href="#table of contents" style="color:#fff;">
Jump to table of contents</a>
</div>

<div style="position:absolute; top:200px; color:#fff;
left:0px; font-size:0px; text-decoration:none;">
<a href="#native language version" style="color:#fff;"> Jump to
native language version</a>
</div>

<div style="position:absolute; top:200px; color:#fff;
left:0px; font-size:0px; text-decoration:none;">
<a href="#English version" style="color:#fff;"> Jump to
English version</a>
</div>
```

We simply need the corresponding targets placed in the proper place on the page:

```
<a name="table of contents" />
<a name="native language version" />
<a name="English version" />
```

Page Content

We now look at the content of the pages and see how it should be coded to assure appropriate auditory feedback. Tables are often used for page layout; they hold the content of the page and control how it is structured visually. HPR reads tables in their entirety and then moves on to the rest of the page. It also reads each table cell entirely before it reads the next cell in the row. When the row is finished it moves to the leftmost cell in the next row. This determines the order in which the page's content is read, and the layout tables should be coded accordingly:

Design Scenario (cont.)

- Tables are read in their entirety.
- Table cells are read entirely before the next cell in the row.

HPR does not render logical elements such as the "emphasize" (<em>) or "strong" (<strong>) elements any differently from regular text, and so these cannot be used to alter the auditory feedback. It does, however, recognize the lang attribute, which is a significant issue for the *Circumference* Web site.

Language Attribute

HPR can detect language shifts; however, it is not that reliable. Therefore, we need to use the lang attribute frequently. HPR 3.0 recognizes the following languages:

1. American English
2. British English
3. Spanish
4. French
5. German
6. Italian
7. Brazilian Portuguese
8. Finnish

A Japanese version of HPR is also available.

An excerpt from one of the poet bios shows how the lang attribute should be used:

```
<span lang="Fr">Sandra Moussempès</span>
<span lang="En">was born in Paris in 1965. She is the author of
three books of poetry,
<span lang="Fr">Exercices d'incendie(Fourbis,</span>
<span lang="En"> 1994),</span>
<span lang="Fr">Vestiges de fillette (Flammarion,</span>
<span lang="En">1997), and </span>
<span lang="Fr">Hors champs (CRL Franchecont,</span>
<span lang="En"> 2001),</span>
<span lang="En">in which the poem in this issue appeared.
Her next book, Captures,is forthcoming from</span>
<span lang="Fr">Flammarion.</span>
```

If the lang attribute is not used, the auditory feedback can become completely nonsensical in any language. Consider the following phrase: "A police sale." In English this has one meaning, but in Italian it means "to thumb salt." Let's say that this is the title of an Italian poem (poems sometimes have unusual titles); if a bilingual visitor

Design Scenario (cont.)

was listening to some English text that referred to this title and it was not coded as Italian text, the listener would never know because the English pronunciation would not sound like gibberish, it might just seem like a strange title for a poem.

Other Auditory Components

HPR uses a synthesized voice that can sound artificial, especially when it reads poetry. One solution to this problem is to make audio recordings of a human reading the poetry available. This is similar to the way Web sites that sell CDs include short samples of the songs on the CDs.

There is usually an icon, such as, ◁⑼, ♫, or 𝄞, to indicate the presence of an audio sample. We use the 𝄞 symbol because the other two are more appropriate for music samples. The sound recordings can be made available in a number of different formats, such as MP3, WAV, or AIFF.

People, sighted or blind, might also appreciate a link to a podcast of the journal, which can include video and text as well as audio and enhanced audio that incorporates both audio and JPEG files. We discussed podcasting in Chapter 6, and because it represents a conflict with the financial and timeframe constraints, it should be put under the category of "future needs." Because of its increasing popularity, it probably should be placed on the top of that list.*

*Apple has extensive information about podcasting at http://www.apple.com/itunes/podcasts/techspecs.html.

Summary

There are many different ways in which sound can be integrated into human–computer interaction. Some are complex and pose formidable challenges, as with natural language interaction. However, on the whole, auditory displays have been shown to enhance the user experience and increase efficiency.

Auditory displays can play an important role in making human–computer interaction accessible to users with disabilities. The proper application of auditory stimuli can also play a crucial role for users whose visual channels are overwhelmed or otherwise occupied, especially in mission-critical environments.

Humans have a facility for manipulating sound. We can comprehend complex musical structures comprising multiple, simultaneously presented melodies, rhythms, and timbres. Research has shown that musical structures can be applied successfully to interface design and can significantly improve human efficiency and accuracy in task completion.

There is still much to learn about the way in which humans interact with their auditory environments, and the research has only begun to scratch the surface in the development of auditory displays. Work has begun, and some goals have already been met, and there is great potential for future development.

Resources on the Web

www.aw.com/heim
Here you will find general information on computer generated sound as well as auditory interaction, auditory displays, sonification/audification and MIDI.

Suggested Reading

Follansbee, J. (2004). *Get Streaming!: Quick Steps to Delivering Audio and Video Online*: Focal Press.

Kramer, G. (Ed.). (1994). *Auditory Display: Sonification, Audification, and Auditory Interfaces*: Addison-Wesley Publishing Company.

Miranda, E. (2002). *Computer Sound Design: Synthesis Techniques and Programming* (2 ed.): Focal Press.

Peres, S. C. (2006). *Dimensions of Sound in Auditory Displays: The Effects of Redundant Dimensions*: ProQuest/UMI.

Touch and Movement

Our sense of touch is connected with our ability physically to move our bodies; together touch and movement make up our haptic system. Haptic interaction with our environment is constant and essential to our daily routines. The acts of pushing, pulling, and lifting are all facilitated by our haptic system.

Although we depend a great deal on our haptic system when we interact in the real world, we use it in a minimal way in human–computer interaction. In the standard computing environment, haptic stimuli play no part in our interaction with data and interface objects. Our haptic interaction with computers is basically limited to physical contact with keyboards and pointing devices.

Common input devices such as track pads, joysticks, and touchscreens also require physical contact to receive input from our physical movements. However, in most general computing environments, the computer outputs information visually with limited amounts of auditory feedback. In other words, user input is mainly achieved through touch and movement, and computer output is basically visual.

Haptic-based human–computer interaction can tap into our natural understanding of the world around us and create a more intuitive and realistic computing environment. To develop haptic interaction technologies that involve both the input and output channels of the computer and the user, a thorough understanding of the human haptic system is required. Let's look at the various elements and concepts involved.

14.1. The Human Perceptual System

Much like our visual system, our haptic system is well suited for the acquisition of knowledge about the physical and spatial aspects of our environment. It is often redundant with our visual system and is therefore an extremely important sense for the visually impaired.

It is more restricted, however, than our visual system because it depends on contact with the environment. Proximity is a critical issue in haptic interaction, a dependence that is also one of its core strengths. It is mainly through physical contact that we proactively affect and alter our environments.

14.1.1. Physical Aspects of Perception

The physical aspects of the human haptic system can be broken down into two main categories: touch (tactile/cutaneous) and movement (kinesthetic/proprioceptive). These components are highly integrated and ultimately must be understood as a cohesive whole. An independent exploration of each part, however, will enhance our understanding of the global systemic dynamics.

We then integrate these physical properties and structures with the psychological aspects of the haptic system to gain a greater understanding of the design requirements for haptic human–computer interaction

Tactile/Cutaneous

Our sense of touch, which is located in the skin, enables us to feel texture, heat, and pain. There are three types of receptors involved in tactile sensing: thermoreceptors, which respond to temperature; nocioreceptors, which respond to pain; and mechanoreceptors, which respond to mechanical stimuli that create skin deformations, such as force or vibration. These Mechanoreceptors are the most important receptors in haptic interfaces.

Mechanoreceptor Types and Characteristics

There are five major types of mechanoreceptors, each corresponding to a specific kind of mechanical deformation of the skin. These receptors respond to differences in stimulus intensity, duration, and location and have different rates of response and adaptation. They are also affected by the way in which we explore tactile stimuli, whether we move around the object or the object is moved over our skin.

Mechanoreceptors respond to changes in the skin. Some are sensitive to skin deformations, some are sensitive to stretching, and others are sensitive to vibrations. The following list identifies the different mechanoreceptors, what they respond to, and how that sensation is perceived:

Pacinian corpuscles respond to vibration, which is interpreted as:

- Acceleration
- Roughness (for example, the vibration of an electric shaver)

Ruffini endings respond to skin stretch, which is interpreted as:

- Lateral force
- Motion detection
- Static force

Meissner corpuscles respond to velocity or flutter, which is interpreted as:

- Slip
- Grip control
- Movement at the skin surface (for example, a glass slipping through the fingers)

Merkel disks respond to skin curvature, which is interpreted as:

- Spatial shape
- Texture (for example, Braille letters)

Sensation of Pressure

Force is measured in newtons, named after Isaac Newton. One newton (N) is defined as the force required to give 1 kilogram (kg) of mass an acceleration of 1 meter per second squared (m/sec^2). A force must be greater than 0.06 to 0.2 N/cm^2 for the cutaneous receptors to register it as a stimulus.

Large forces have a tendency to degrade tactile receptivity, which means that haptic interfaces must be calibrated according to the relative receptivity of the skin. Pressure limits, however, are not the same for everyone, nor are they uniform throughout the body; they depend on factors such as age, body location, and gender. To give an idea of the range, "just-noticeable values range from 5 milligrams on a woman's face to 355 mg on a man's big toe" (Hale & Stanney, 2004).

Let's look at some of the factors involved in haptic sensation and see how they affect our sense of touch.

Sensorial Adaptation—Sensorial adaptation is measured by the rate at which a receptor adapts to a stimulus.

- Rapid adaptation receptors (RARs) stop firing shortly after the initial stimulus. We experience this sensation when, for example, we forget that we are wearing a pair of eyeglasses—we no longer feel them after awhile. RARs must be continually stimulated by movement or vibration to maintain the sensation.
- Slow adaptation receptors (SARs) maintain a sense of contact with a stimulus, providing us with a sense of continuity with our environment.

Pressure Detection—Studies have been conducted to determine the smallest perceivable pressure (absolute threshold) and the smallest detectable difference in pressure (just-noticeable difference [JND]).

- **Absolute Threshold**—The absolute threshold is a value that is determined by averaging a range of stimuli representing a statistically significant perception of pressure.

- Absolute thresholds are highly variable, and depend on factors such as age, gender, location, type of stimulation (vibration, pressure, etc.), and size of contact field.

- The size of the contact area alters the number of receptors that are affected by a particular stimulus, which, in turn, affects the perceived intensity of the sensation.

- **Just-Noticeable Difference**—The JND is the smallest degree of change in pressure that can be perceived.

  - Studies have shown that the pressure JND decreases with an increase in the area of stimulation. In other words, people feel smaller differences in pressure when the area of stimulation is increased.

  - Studies have shown that the JND increases with an increase in stimulus intensity. In other words, when the stimulus intensity increases, a greater difference in pressure is required for us to perceive a change.

Subjective Magnitude—Our perception of stimulus intensity is subjective and is affected by size of contact area, stimulus frequency, and temporal factors.

Apparent Location—When two stimuli are applied at the same time we have a tendency to feel the stimulation at a point somewhere between them. This phenomenon is known as "apparent location." The apparent location depends on the relative intensity of the two stimuli. If one stimulus has a greater intensity than the other, the location of the perceived stimulation drifts toward the stronger location.

Masking—In this condition the presence of one stimulus interferes with the detection of another. This affects the location of haptic stimulators (actuators) and the rate at which haptic information can be communicated to the user.

Spatial Resolution—Our ability to know how many stimuli are being applied to the skin is affected by the location of contact. Our sensitivity to single-point stimuli is greatest in the nose and mouth, followed by the fingertips. Our ability to make two-point discriminations (limens), which is defined as the ability to know whether there is more than one stimulus, however, is greatest in the fingertips, followed by the nose and mouth.

- **Spatial Masking**—Spatial masking occurs when multiple stimuli are perceived as a single point of contact. To avoid spatial masking, different frequencies can be used for each stimulus. It has been suggested that using a frequency below 80 Hz for one stimulus and a frequency above 100 Hz for the other stimulus promotes the perception of two distinct stimuli.

Temporal Resolution—The timing of stimuli can also affect our perception. Two stimuli presented within a short interval might be interpreted as one stimulus. The threshold for temporal presentation is known as the "successiveness limen," which has been determined to be 5 msec. For order discrimination (understanding which stimulus came first), the limen increases to 20 msec.

- **Temporal Masking**—If two stimuli are presented too close in time, temporal masking occurs and the user's perception is of one stimulus. It has been found that the target stimulus is masked by the distractor stimulus if the two are presented within the range of 100 to 1200 msec of one another.

Active and Passive Exploration—There are significant differences in the perception of haptic stimuli when the stimuli can be explored actively as opposed to passively. In passive exploration, the stimulus is presented to the skin while the finger or hand remains still. Active touch involves movement on the part of the person who is haptically exploring, such as feeling for a lost coin under a piece of furniture.

Adaptation—If stimuli of the same frequency continue for a certain period of time, our perception of their magnitude decreases and the absolute threshold increases. Adaptation is a gradual process; it can take up to 25 minutes. Recovery takes about half the time. Switching between frequencies reduces the effects of adaptation.

Significance for Haptic Devices

The nature of the human haptic system directly affects the design of haptic interfaces. To communicate information, haptic signals must be perceived by the user; therefore a haptic interface must be tuned to human sensitivity thresholds and limitations. We can deduce from the issues mentioned above that successful haptic communication depends on the following factors:

- Rapid adaptation receptors must be continually stimulated to maintain a sense of touch.
- Absolute thresholds are variable and must be determined according to specific situational factors.
- The smallest perceivable difference in pressure is affected by the amount of pressure being applied.
- Our ability to determine the number of pressure stimuli is related to their distance from each other; this distance changes depending on the location of stimulation.
- The amount of time between stimuli can affect our perception of the number of stimuli.
- Some haptic stimuli can mask other stimuli, depending on spatial and temporal factors.
- We can gather more haptic information if we are allowed actively to explore a stimulus.

Portable Haptic Devices

Dosher, Lee, and Hannaford (2001) considered the potential for using haptic effects in small portable devices, such as PDAs and cell phones. This requires extreme efficiency in the design of the haptic mechanisms in terms of space and energy consumption. Because this efficiency requirement allows for only small haptic effects, they considered it important to determine the weakest effects that can be effectively detected and used.

This concept is different from the absolute detection thresholds. It is oriented more to the practical application of haptic effects. Dosher et al. intended their investigation to complement the psychophysical perceptive limits of the human haptic system "by aiming to find the point at which a human can perceive meaningful information from a realistic haptic device" (Dosher, Lee, & Hannaford, 2001).

In their experiments, subjects were asked to determine whether a haptic target (icon) had a force applied to it. In an interesting observation, the authors found that when the intensity of the stimulation was decreased, the subjects became aware of the pulse in their fingertips, which masked the stimulus.

From their experiments, Dosher et al. identified a few factors that can affect detection thresholds:

- The nature of the haptic device.
- The shape of the applied force—triangle, sinusoid, rectangle, trapezoid, or Gaussian.
- The size of the icon.

They also stressed that even though it is probably necessary to find detection thresholds, they may not be sufficient benchmarks for an effect to be useful; higher levels of stimulation are probably required.

Proprioception/Kinesthesia

Close your eyes, hold out your hands with outstretched arms, bring each hand around one at a time, and touch your nose. This is one of the standard field sobriety tests (SFSTs) used by police officers to determine the sobriety of a driver.

To successfully complete this exercise, you must be able to determine the location of your hands, the location of your nose in relation to your hands, and how far your hands must travel to reach your nose. To accomplish this task, your sense of proprioception must be intact. In other words, you need to be able to understand the location of your body and its appendages as well as the direction and speed of your movements.

We use the angles of our joints to determine the position of our limbs, and we determine movement by the rate of change in the position of those joints. This motion detection is affected by a sense of force in the muscles and tendons. We consider this issue in the Rotational Dynamics section.

Let's look at the kinds of receptors involved in our ability to move our bodies and to sense where our limbs are.

Proprioceptic/Kinesthetic Receptors

Proprioceptors are found in the muscles, tendons (tissues that connect muscles to bones), ligaments, and capsules (tissues that connect bones to each other). These receptors can all be classified as stretch receptors: they fire according to the various extensions and contractions executed by the muscles, tendons, and ligaments (Figure 14.1).

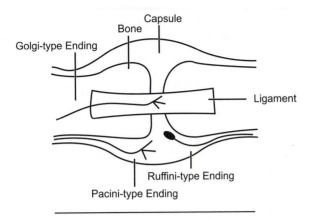

Figure 14.1 Proprioceptic/kinesthetic receptors.

The proprioceptors located in the muscles respond to the rate of muscle change and sustained muscle stretch. They are the most numerous in fine motor movement muscles. The proprioceptors located in the joints respond to twisting force, direction, velocity, pressure, angle, and muscle contraction. They are sensitive to a small range of joint angles (within 15° of a possible 180°).

Bidirectionality

> **MAXIM**
>
> The haptic system senses external forces coming from the environment as well as exerts force on the environment.

To understand the physical properties of an object, we must interact with it. We touch, push, brush, lift, pull, roll, and otherwise put energy into the environment. We receive energy from the objects we touch in the form of varying degrees of resistance and tactile information. We interpret this information based on previous haptic experiences as well as input from our other senses.

When an object in the environment exerts a force on our body or a resistance to our movement, we experience this as the properties of movement, fixedness, and hardness inherent in the object. An object that is heavy offers a particular amount of resistance to our movement, and this force is registered by our proprioceptors.

Similarly, if an object is hard, its surface resists our probing, whereas if an object is soft, we feel some "give" as we apply pressure. We sense the amount of resistance or force feedback offered by the object and use this information to make determinations of its pliability.

By lifting an object we determine its weight (perception, input) and alter its position (action, output) simultaneously. This is an example of the bidirectionality of the haptic system.

Just as we use the angle of our joints to determine where our limbs are, it has been suggested that we also use the movements of our joints to calculate the forces that are exerted by the objects in our environment. We explore this issue as well in the Rotational Dynamics section; for now let's look at the various types of movement of which our bodies are capable and how those movements are described.

Joint Movement

To describe joint movement, the body's starting point, or point of reference, must be understood. This point is known as the "anatomical reference position," and it can be described as follows:

- Erect standing position
- Feet flat, separated slightly
- Arms relaxed and at the sides
- Palms facing forward

Different movements are considered and labeled in relation to this resting position. Table 14.1 defines the possible body movements in relation to the anatomical reference position.

Planes and Axes

Human joints are considered to move "on a plane" and "about an axis." The body is divided into three planes—the frontal, sagittal, and transversal planes (Figure 14.2):

- The frontal plane runs parallel with the shoulders and dissects the body vertically at its midpoint, creating anterior and posterior segmentation. Orientation on the frontal plane is determined by X and Y coordinates.
- The sagittal plane runs perpendicular to the shoulders and dissects the body vertically at its midpoint, creating left and right segmentation. Orientation on the sagittal plane is determined by Y and Z coordinates.
- The transversal plane runs parallel to the waist and dissects the body horizontally at its midpoint. This creates cranial and caudal (top and bottom) segmentation. Orientation on the transversal plane is determined by X and Z coordinates.

Table 14.1   Body Movements in Relation to the Anatomical Reference Position: Direction of Joint Movement

Distal—farther from torso	**Proximal**—closer to torso
Medial—closer to midline	**Lateral**—away from midline
Anterior—toward front (ventral)	**Posterior**—toward back (dorsal)
Caudal—away from head (inferior)	**Cranial**—approaching head (superior)

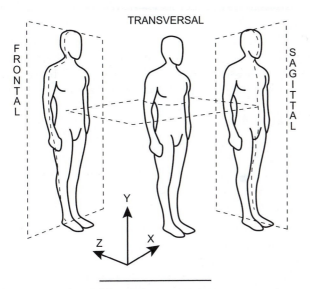

Figure 14.2 Planes and axes.

Axes are drawn perpendicular to a plane. The anterior/posterior (AP, sagittal) axis runs perpendicular to the frontal plane and will be referred to as the Z axis. The medial/lateral (ML, frontal) axis runs perpendicular to the sagittal plane and will be referred to as the X axis. Transversal plane rotations occur around the longitudinal axis, which will be referred to as the Y axis. Transversal plane rotations occur around the Y axis, sagittal plane rotations occur around the X axis, and frontal plane rotations occur around the Z axis.

Degrees of Freedom

Movement on a plane is called translation and is determined using an X, Y, Z coordinate system (Figure 14.3). Movement around an axis is called rotation and is defined as pitch, roll, and yaw, corresponding to rotations around the frontal, sagittal,

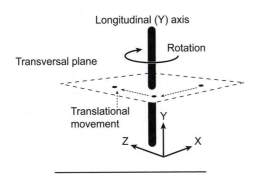

Figure 14.3 Rotation and translation.

and longitudinal axes, respectively. Rotation is determined on a fixed point of orientation.

Each of the movements just described is called a degree of freedom (DOF). Therefore, there are six possible degrees of freedom for each joint—the translational X, Y, and Z degrees and the fixed-point rotational pitch, roll, and yaw degrees.

Rotational Movement

Consider the ways in which the human head can move. Starting from the anatomical reference position, the head can nod up and down, keeping the eyes parallel with the line of the shoulders, but altering their distance from them. In many cultures this motion signifies a positive response or "yes." As the head nods, it rotates on the X axis, an example of pitch (Figure 14.4a).

The head can also rotate from side to side, as it does when we look over one shoulder and then over the other, again maintaining a constant distance from the

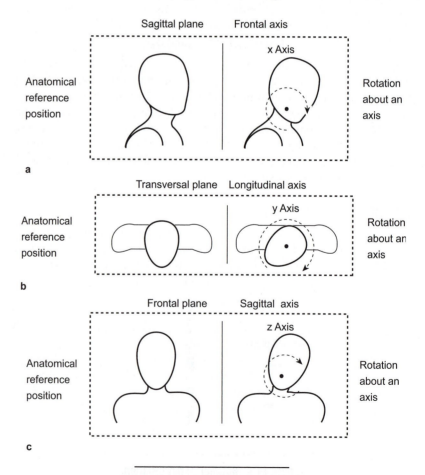

Figure 14.4   (a) Pitch. (b) Yaw. (c) Roll.

shoulders, but moving in a perpendicular relationship. This movement often signals a negative response or "no." In this case the head rotates on the Y axis, an example of yaw (Figure 14.4b).

Finally, looking forward, we can use the neck to tilt the top of the head toward one shoulder, creating what could be considered a quizzical posture. Here, the head moves into a diagonal relation with the shoulders. In this case, the head rotates on the Z axis, an example of roll (Figure 14.4c).

Translational Movement

Translational movement of the head is more restricted than rotational movement. However, the neck does have a limited ability to move the head to a different location along the Z axis, as, for example, when we crane our neck by pushing our chin forward (Figure 14.5a).

The neck's ability to move the head to a different location along the X axis is even more limited. This type of movement is not uncommon in some Southeast Asian dancers: the eyes remain parallel with the shoulders as the head moves from side to side (Figure 14.5b).

It is quite difficult, even impossible, for the head to move up and down along the Y axis while the rest of the body remains immobile. This movement is perhaps only the province of space creatures such as E.T. from the film *E.T. the Extra-Terrestrial*.

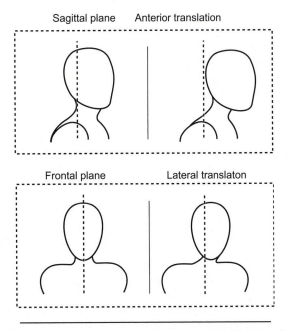

Figure 14.5 Possible translational movements of the head.

As we have seen translational movement of the head is limited, however, the body can move forward or back, carrying the head to different posterior and anterior positions along the Z axis. Similarly, the body can carry the head laterally along the X axis. The body can also move up or down, carrying the head to different locations along the Y axis.

Tactile/Kinesthetic Integration

There is a high degree of integration between our cutaneous receptors and our proprioceptors. We tend to use them as a unified system of perception. For example, our sense of touch helps us to determine how much pressure to exert when grasping an object.

To judge the surface properties of an object, we might slide our fingertips over it. As our fingers pass over the surface, any large deformation is detected by our proprioceptors due to the movement of our fingers at the joints. The small textural characteristics, in turn, cause deformations of our skin that will be registered by our cutaneous receptors. These then inform us about the surface properties of the object.

It would be difficult to take advantage of our sense of touch without the ability to place our hands on an object. Our extensive system of limb joints allows us to position our hands to achieve the most tactile information possible from an object of interest.

Our fingers can explore the geometric aspects of the object, but we will not have an accurate conceptualization of the object if our sense of touch is removed. If we are wearing gloves, for example, we will miss a great deal of information about the object.

Studies have shown that subjects who have been given local anesthesia on their fingertips exhibit deterioration in grasping control. This is because the sensory-motor control loop forms a link between perception and action that is much stronger in the haptic system than in any of the other sensory systems.

Haptic Spectrum

Haptic vibrations are waves, and, like any waves, have frequency and amplitude. If a vibration increases in amplitude, we perceive it as increasing in strength. If it increases in frequency, we might perceive it as changing from a pulsation to a buzzing.

These sensations and perceptions are the result of changes in the wave's temporal qualities and can be induced electronically in a variety of ways, as we will see. However, we can also use the wave model to express spatial haptic qualities, such as shape and texture.

Place a small coin on a table and lay your finger on top of it; you can perceive that it is a low, round object. Now place your finger on a piece of sandpaper; it feels rough. The coin sensation was one of shape, which has a low spatial frequency. The rough texture of the sandpaper, on the other hand, has a high spatial frequency.

The difference between touching a small coin and grasping a large object like a book is an increase in spatial amplitude with a relative consistency in spatial frequency. If you press harder against the sandpaper, you increase the spatial amplitude of that high-spatial-frequency sensation.

There is a point, or more likely a range, of sensation at which our perception of a stimulus changes from a feeling of texture to a feeling of shape. This creates a range of ambiguity in object recognition that is highly subjective.

14.1.2. Psychological Aspects of Perception

Now that we have a basic understanding of the underlying physical structures involved in our sense of touch and movement, we must investigate how this information is interpreted and understood. In other words, how do we haptically perceive our environment?

Kinetic Space Perception

> **MAXIM**
>
> The haptic system involves action–perception coupling.

Our haptic system is based on a perceiving–acting cycle. We move our bodies and appendages to gain information about our physical space. For example, to determine the texture of an object's surface, we must place our hands on the object. To climb a ladder, we must coordinate our arms and legs, gripping the rungs as we ascend.

To complete these actions successfully, we must have a sense of where our bodies and limbs are and we must be able to direct them in the proper direction with appropriate force. This process is called active or dynamic touch.

Rotational Dynamics

The proprioceptors in our tendons, ligaments, and muscles are sensitive to the angle of our joints and monitor the energy required for achieving and maintaining body postures or limb extensions. Our limbs move in rotations that are centered on the axes of our joints. This movement can be described by rotational dynamics, which involves the angular acceleration, the force applied (torque), and the center of mass (CM) of the limb that is being rotated. Carello and Turvey (2000) suggest that rotational dynamics is fundamental to haptic perception.

Through a series of experiments, Carello and Turvey show that a person will generally have an accurate idea of how far his or her reach extends (our sense of peripersonal space), even if the person cannot see his or her arms. However, if a weight is placed on the person's wrist, thereby altering the CM, he or she will incorrectly estimate his or her reach to be longer than it actually is. These studies present a significant finding for haptic device design. If a haptic device alters the CM of a user's appendage, then the user's sense of peripersonal space will be altered.

Much of Carello and Turvey's work centers on activities that require subjects to estimate the length of a welded rod. They use different lengths, shapes, materials, and gripping positions along the rod. Subjects generally overestimate rod length when the CM is shifted further away from the axis of rotation. By using rotational dynamics, Carello and Turvey accurately determined the results of these seemingly haptic illusions.

Parallelity

> ### MAXIM
> Haptic space perception does not correlate accurately with physical space

Although we might respond predictably (according to rotational dynamics) to changes in our haptic environment, proprioception does not create an entirely accurate representation of our physical space. Studies have shown that our haptic perception of the parallelity of objects in our environment is not exact. In fact, some subjects have even reported that objects arranged in a perpendicular layout were parallel when they perceived them haptically (Gentaz & Hatwell, 2003; Kappers, 1999).

The studies in question explored various factors that might influence our perception of haptic information. The basic experimental design for much of this research is simple. The experiments involve a reference rod that is not visible to the subject but can be explored haptically through dynamic touch. The subject is instructed to alter the orientation of a test rod so that it becomes parallel to the reference rod (Figure 14.6).

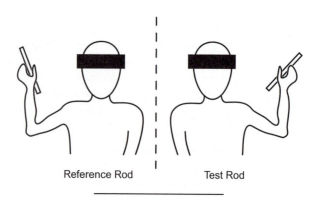

Reference Rod   Test Rod

Figure 14.6   Bimanual condition.

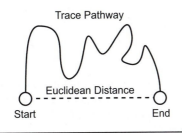

Figure 14.7 Non-Euclidean space experiment.

These experimental designs used stimuli located on the sagittal, frontal, and transversal planes. They explored unimanual and bimanual conditions and presentations as well as the effects of different angles of presentation.

The results of these studies show that performance varies according to some experimental conditions. For instance, errors were more pronounced in oblique presentations. Even though results varied with experimental variables, subjects were consistently inaccurate in determining parallelity.

Non-Euclidean Space

This distortion of haptic perception has led some to suggest that haptic space is non-Euclidean, in other words, not compliant with empirical measurements. They also suggest that because our haptic perception does not provide an accurate account of what is real, it must be based on a different set of criteria—perhaps an internal sense of haptic space.

Faineteau, Gentaz and Vivani (2003) conducted experiments in which subjects were asked to trace a line (the "trace pathway") with their finger. These lines departed from straight paths and took many detours, as shown in Figure 14.7. The subjects were then asked to determine the Euclidean distance (actual distance of a straight line between the starting and ending points.)

They found that people consistently overestimated the real distance, and that they made greater errors as the length of the trace pathway increased.

Research Results

The results of the research on kinetic space perception indicate that we cannot depend on our haptic sense alone; we must also receive information from other channels, especially our visual channel, to accurately interact with our physical environment.

This has significant ramifications for haptic interaction. Haptic stimuli must be used as a secondary feedback mechanism that supports other kinds of feedback. Haptic feedback is closely aligned with visual feedback in our normal interactions with our environment. It can enrich our perceptions of the world around us, but it cannot provide accurate information about actual spatial conditions.

We have looked at the way in which we perceive our kinetic space; let's now explore the way in which we perceive our tactile sensations.

Tactile Perception

The sensing of texture is an integral part of our haptic perception; it allows us to distinguish a piece of sandpaper from a sheet of note paper. Many blind people rely on their ability to perceive small skin deformations when they read the slightly raised dots of Braille displays.

Perhaps texture can be used in a similar way to color for the differentiation of data on a graph or chart. It might also be possible to use it in commercial Web-based applications, by allowing, for example, customers to "feel" the material before they purchase an article of clothing.

It will be helpful at this point to look at the various ways in which we use our sense of touch to interact with our environment.

Object Recognition

Studies have shown that we are quite good at recognizing objects from their haptic qualities alone. How do we accomplish this recognition, and what are the factors involved?

One possible answer to this question is that edge detection, a method used in visual shape recognition, might play a role in haptic shape recognition as well. Studies have shown, however, that shape recognition through edge detection is slow and inaccurate, whether subjects explore three-dimensional objects, two-dimensional fingertip-sized objects, or larger two-dimensional objects.

If edge detection is not as important to haptic shape recognition as it is to visual recognition, what other factors are more significant? Klatzky et al. (1985) suggest that the material of which an object is made plays a roll in our ability to identify it.

> **MAXIM**
>
> Cutaneous information can aid in object identification.

At times, touch might be more significant to the identification of objects than kinetic information. There is compelling evidence that, in certain situations, object recognition can be based on the material properties of an object alone and, therefore, be accomplished through cutaneous perception.

Familiar View—Object recognition is generally more accurate if a familiar view of an object is used. For our visual sense, the front view of an object is the most familiar; however, haptic recognition tends to be more accurate when it is based on the back view of an object. This might be related to the orientation of our fingertips to objects when we hold them.

The haptic familiarity of the backs of objects might also be an aspect of its complementary nature to our visual system, which is oriented to the front of objects. Taken together, these two orientations give us a richer representation of an object.

Multiple Points of Contact—Recognition is also enhanced when multiple points of contact with an object are possible, as is the case when we use multiple fingers or the whole hand to explore an object. Experiments that limit subjects to a single point of contact show a degradation of performance and an increase in error compared to experiments using a multipoint dynamic touch.

Coding Tactile Information

Tactile stimulation can be used to code information by using various parameters of haptic stimulation such as location, temporal patterns, frequency, and intensity. People are sensitive enough that complex information can be coded by manipulating these parameters; however, there are limitations on our ability to perceive these signals. Let's look at some of the issues involved.

Location—Body location can be used to code information; for example, a tap on the left shoulder might mean turn or look to the left. A tap in the middle of the back might mean move forward. If we want to communicate more complex information, we must be aware of the spatial resolution of the particular body location. There are large discrepancies in our ability to detect different stimuli depending on where they are located on the body. The hands and face have high spatial resolution, whereas the back and legs do not.

Temporal Pattern—The temporal sensitivity of the skin is quite high. We can discriminate between signals 10 msec apart. We can also detect signals of as little as 10 msec duration. This of course depends on the location of stimulation. However, we are capable of detecting subtle differences in temporal patterns. These can be considered tactile motives that involve rhythm and frequency much like earcons.

Frequency—Vibrotactile displays can use frequency to code information. However, there are limits on the resolution of haptic stimuli. Van Erp and Spapé suggest that having nine levels of frequency is a viable limit for human differentiation, and that the frequencies should be diversified by at least 20% (van Erp & Spapé, 2003).

Frequency discrimination is affected by range. Goff (1967) concluded that frequency difference thresholds were greater at the 250-Hz level. According to Cohen and Kirman (1986), frequency discrimination is also affected by duration. Van Erp and Spapé point out that "For a 100 Hz standard, the difference threshold was between 16 Hz (duration larger than 50 ms) and 26 Hz (duration 30 ms)" (van Erp & Spapé, 2003) (p.112)

Research by Sherrick and Craig (1982) suggests that users can differentiate 3 to 5 levels of frequency and 3 levels of amplitude, but that when both parameters are involved simultaneously, they can distinguish 10 different categories of frequency.

Intensity—Haptic stimulus intensity or amplitude also can be used to code information. However, amplitude discrimination thresholds are small, and van Erp (2002) suggests that a maximum of four different levels should be used.

A high potential for annoyance, or even pain, is inherent in the application of increasing stimulus intensity. This does not, however, entirely rule out the use of intensity in coding information because we can still use the ambiguities inherent in the human perceptual systems to create the illusion of increasing intensity. This is known as "subjective magnitude."

There are a few ways to increase subjective magnitude:

- Size of stimulated area—Enlarging the area that is stimulated increases the perception of the stimulus magnitude.
- Frequency of stimulation—Subjective magnitude can also be affected by frequency.
- Temporal enhancement—If two stimuli have the same frequency and are separated by a range of 100 to 500 msec, the second stimulus will be enhanced.

Frequency/Intensity—Vibrotactile stimulation can be used to great effect and can convey diverse levels of emotional meaning. This was demonstrated by van Erp and Spapé (2003) with so-called "tactile melodies." Tactile melodies are defined as complex stimuli of modulating frequency and amplitude. We can think of them as sensations that get stronger and weaker and change from pulsing to buzzing.

Their study showed that these melodies could expand the information rates of tactile displays by eliciting feelings in the user based on the characteristics of intrusiveness (characterized as being in a range from soft and polished to loud and aggressive) and tempo (which ranged from cheerful and melodious to shrill and fast).

The tactile melodies created by van Erp and Spapé are quite sophisticated in terms of the complexity of tactile stimulation involved. Thus, it is difficult to understand them in terms of the interaction of their different tactile parameters. Nonetheless, it remains clear that frequency and intensity can be used to code information haptically.

Research Results

What can we conclude from this research? First, it is clear that people respond to differences in tactile frequencies, and so this can be used to code information. However, there is a limit to the number of different frequencies we can discriminate.

MAXIM

To code haptic information, we must use multiple parameters and significant differences.

Our perception is also affected by the frequency range (how high or low the frequency of the vibration is), intensity, and duration of stimulation. Therefore, if we want to communicate complex information haptically, we must use multiple parameters and use significant differences.

Considerations for Haptic Interfaces

The following factors should be taken into consideration in the design of a haptic interface:

- The weight of a wearable haptic device can affect our perception of our bodies.
- Perception of haptic space is not accurate.
- Tactile and kinetic perceptions are connected and should not be separated in haptic interfaces.
- We can recognize objects by their tactile aspects.
- Object recognition depends on familiarity with the view and the number of contact points.
- Information can be coded by using various tactile parameters such as location, temporal patterns, frequency, and intensity or by using combinations of these parameters.

14.2. Using Haptics in Interaction Design

Haptic technologies have evolved to the point at which they offer significant benefits to a wide range of users. There are diverse applications for haptic displays, ranging from aerospace to digital sculpture. Advances in haptic technologies have also led to improvements in the quality of life for disabled persons and show great potential for future developments in education, medical procedures, and rehabilitation therapies.

Haptic feedback has been used to:

- Provide critical alerts
- Support hand–eye coordination
- Increase a sense of presence
- Assist the disabled community
- Create more realistic training simulations
- Augment human capabilities
- Afford a more natural working environment
- Decrease visual load
- Substitute for vision in limited display environments or when vision is otherwise occupied
- Substitute for audio when sound would be distracting or not audible

14.2.1. Teleoperation

The teleoperation of remote robotic devices has been shown to be beneficial in hazardous environments. Through the use of teleoperation technologies, the manipulation of dangerous materials or the performance of tasks in polluted or life-threatening environments can be accomplished with minimal risk.

Remote control of mechanical devices is generally considered a one-way interaction. The operator moves a controller, and the device responds in a predetermined manner. However, teleoperation of a remote-controlled robotic tool can also involve force feedback. For example, when a remote device encounters resistance to its movement, an equivalent force can be communicated back to the operator via the controller.

The teleoperation of remote vehicles is difficult. Maneuvers that would be commonplace in a regular vehicle become far more complicated. When we operate a vehicle, we depend a great deal on haptic cues to inform us about the vehicle's status. We determine the effects of inertia, momentum, and speed on the stability of the vehicle and make appropriate adjustments.

Without this haptic information, we would make errors that could be significant and costly. The addition of haptic feedback to teleoperation can provide additional, and at times crucial, information and afford greater control of remote devices.

System Latency

Haptic simulation of remote interaction can be computationally demanding and financially prohibitive. High refresh rates and data throughput are required to maintain a sense of presence and allow the user the kind of control necessary to successfully maneuver in difficult environments and hostile terrains.

Because these entire systems are based on remote interaction, network quality is extremely significant. Because of the bidirectional nature of our haptic system, latency can have a detrimental effect on the user's perception of the remote environment, which is a significant issue considering the mission-critical nature of some teleoperations.

14.2.2. Medical Uses

It is not uncommon for medical students to train on safe and reusable plastic or rubber models. However, these models lack realism and do not offer students some important physical feedback. Cadavers are useful for surgical training but are problematic in terms of availability and reusability. The tissue quality of cadavers is also different from that of live tissue.

Virtual reality simulations have the potential to address some of these issues and are being given serious consideration for medical training and assessment. Significant developments in this area have been made by companies such as Immersion Medical, Surgical Science, Mentice, and Reachin Technologies.

The use of haptic simulations has also been explored for dental training. Dental students traditionally train on artificial teeth and jaws, which are not appropriate for tooth extraction and do not provide realistic replication of bleeding or tissue lesions. VR simulations can be used instead, but they lack the tactile experience required for students to learn proper force application, not an insignificant skill for a dental practitioner. The addition of haptic feedback to these simulations can have a significant positive effect on the quality of medical training experiences.

ImmersiveTouch™, designed by Luciano et al. (2004) at the University of Illinois at Chicago, is a haptically augmented virtual reality (VR) system that can be used for medical or dental multisensorial simulations and training applications (Figure 14.8). ImmersiveTouch combines force feedback with head and hand tracking and uses a high-resolution, high-pixel-density stereoscopic display to provide stereo visualizations of 3D data in real time. This is combined with 3D audio to provide an immersive VR environment.

Palpation and Instrument/Tissue Interaction

Doctors physically interact with patients in two basic ways: they either use their hands to explore tissues and organs (palpation), or they use instruments such as stethoscopes and surgical tools. Both of these methods involve acute haptic sensing, but they have different sensitivities and abilities.

During palpation, the doctor can feel directly the volumetric and textural qualities of a patient's tissue or organs. In procedures that require the use of implements or apparatus, the doctor must learn to interpret the haptic effects of tissue/instrument interactions.

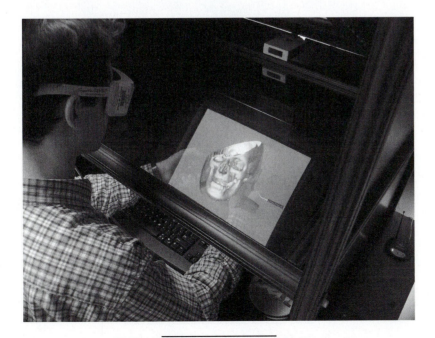

Figure 14.8 ImmersiveTouch.

Virtual simulations used in conjunction with exoskeletal haptic devices worn on the hands, such as the Rutgers Master II, can simulate the tissue deformations felt by doctors during palpation examinations. Simulations can also be combined with point devices, such as SensAble's PHANTOM®, to simulate instrument/tissue interaction.

Minimally Invasive Surgery

The advent of minimally invasive surgery (MIS) is a significant development for surgical procedures. MIS uses tiny cameras, a video display, and special surgical tools that are inserted into the body and manipulated remotely.

Surgeons must rely on haptic feedback that is one step removed from the actual tissue/instrument interaction. Therefore, the training required for MIS is very different from that required for classical surgical procedures. This type of training lends itself to haptically enhanced virtual reality simulations that can offer flexible and time-intensive training.

The Laparoscopic Impulse Engine® is a five-DOF device designed by Immersion Corporation (Figure 14.9). Used in conjunction with the Karlsruhe Endoscopic Surgery Trainer®, it is capable of producing highly realistic simulations of a number of surgical instruments and endoscopic cameras.

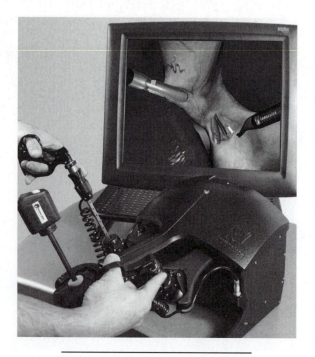

Figure 14.9 The Laparoscopic Impulse Engine.

The system was first installed for MIS training at the University Hospital in Tübingen, Germany, in 1996. More recently, the Immersion Corporation developed the Laparoscopic Surgical Workstation® to work with the Reachin Laparoscopic Trainer® by Reachin Technologies. This system records the movements of the instruments and their interaction with the patient's tissue for later analysis and study.

Rehabilitation Therapy

Haptic technologies are also being used to enhance and improve rehabilitation and therapeutic procedures. These technologies offer flexible therapeutic environments that can be easily adjusted to each patient's body and physical condition. They also offer accurate and detailed information about the patient's progress so that the therapy can achieve maximum efficacy.

Multimodal feedback can be used to encourage patients and foster in them a sense of progress. For example, virtual reality displays that use visio-haptic feedback, such as flight simulators, can be adapted to therapeutic situations that enable patients to monitor their activities and provide motivational feedback for them to achieve goals while they exercise affected limbs or joints.

14.2.3. Users with Disabilities

There is a great deal of interest in developing haptic technologies for the blind and visually impaired. The situation is complicated, however, by the proximal nature of the haptic system. Whereas sighted people can use their vision to calculate the relative dangers of an environment from a safe distance, the haptic system requires physical contact and, therefore, is less adaptive in dynamic environments in which physical objects move around and can occupy any location in three-dimensional space.

Electronic Travel Aids/Human Navigation Systems

> ### MAXIM
> Haptic stimulation can aid with navigation in real-world as well as virtual environments.

Researchers have attempted to use haptic technologies to either augment or supplant the traditional white canes that blind people have historically used to navigate physical spaces. These devices are called electronic travel aids (ETAs) or human navigation systems (HNSs) and are generally equipped with sonar tracking instruments to locate obstacles.

GuideCane—An interesting version of this approach is the GuideCane created by Ulrich and Borenstein (2001). It houses 10 ultrasonic sensors and rolls on wheels that determine its relative motion (Figure 14.10). When it detects an obstacle, a servo (an electromagnetic device that controls the performance of a machine) directs the wheels so that it suggests an alternate path to the user, avoiding the obstacle.

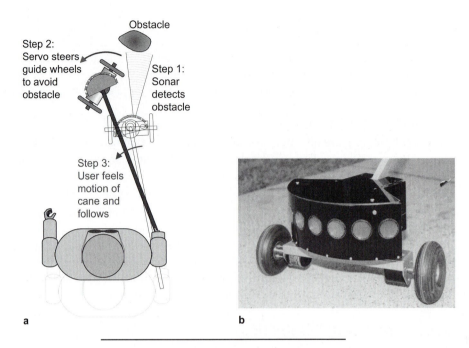

Obstacle

Step 2:
Servo steers
guide wheels
to avoid
obstacle

Step 1:
Sonar
detects
obstacle

Step 3:
User feels
motion of
cane and
follows

a   b

Figure 14.10   The GuideCane. (a) Top view. (b) Front view.
©1997 IEEE.

Intelligent Glasses—Velázquez, Maingreaud, and Pissaloux (2003) explored the development of "intelligent glasses" that create a haptic rendering of physical space (Figure 14.11). This system uses a "stereo vision non-calibrated camera configuration" that captures a scene and then transmits it to a "scene analyzer module," which calculates the location of obstacles in relation to the user.

This information is then communicated to the user through a tactile interface. This system can sense obstacles that are at ground level, obstacles that protrude from above, such as tree branches, and environmental hazards that are below ground level, such as holes or ditches.

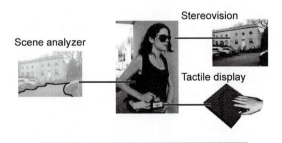

Stereovision

Scene analyzer

Tactile display

Figure 14.11   Intelligent glasses. System diagram.

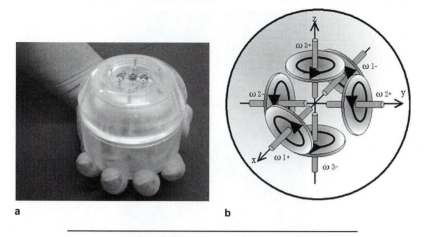

a   b

Figure 14.12 **(a) The GyroCubeWireless. (a) Outside. (b) Gyroscopes.**

GyroCubeWireless—The GyroCubeWireless is a palm-sized portable sphere that uses gyroscopes set up as "three pairs of twin motors" to deliver torque feedback (Figure 14.12). Designed to work with the HapticNavi system, it is described by its developers as "an ungrounded and portable torque display, which is put on the palm and wirelessly controlled with infrared rays" (Nakamura & Fukui, 2003). The system delivers directional information by pulling the user's hand toward a specific location.

ActiveBelt—The ActiveBelt, developed by Tsukada and Yasumrua (2004), is a wearable haptic device that uses the location of a tactile stimulus to convey directional information (Figure 14.13). They incorporated this belt into a human navigational system called FeelNavi. The belt has eight vibrators that signal directional information to the user, who walks in the direction of the vibration.

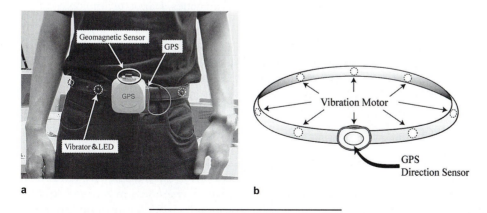

a   b

Figure 14.13 **Device architecture of ActiveBelt.**

GPS, global positioning system; LED, light-emitting diode.

Figure 14.14   HAL-5 (Hybrid Assistive Limb), CYBERDYNE Inc.

www.cyberdyne.jp

Motor Disabilities

People with physical motor disabilities can find it difficult to perform simple functions such as pushing a button or opening a door. This difficulty can affect their ability to function and engage in work-related activities. Haptic technologies can be used to enhance human performance and enable people with handicaps more fully to participate in vocational activities.

There are a number of projects worldwide involved in the development of exoskeleton devices to aid people with motor disabilities and enhance the abilities of people who work in physically demanding environments. For example, the HAL-5 (Hybrid Assistive Limb) developed at the University of Tsukuba and built by Cyberdyne Inc. is shown in Figure 14.14.

14.2.4. Aerospace

Vibrotactile stimulation was incorporated into a tactile torso display by van Erp and van Veen to help NASA astronauts with orientation awareness in zero-gravity situations (van Erp & van Veen, 2003). This stimulation conveys information through localized vibrations. These tactile stimuli are mapped directly to body coordinates and present spatial information in an intuitive way. Van Erp and van Veen show how haptic stimulation applied to the torso can lead to a sense of external direction, which they call the "tap on the shoulder" principle.

14.2.5. Scientific Visualizations

Haptic technology has been applied to scientific visualizations such as the rendering of molecular conformations and atomic models. Complex data sets, such as 3D force fields and tetrahedralized volume data sets of the human head, have also been rendered through the use of a PHANTOM device that sends force feedback to the hand of the user.

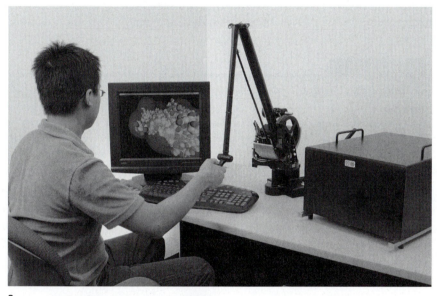

a

b

Figure 14.15 **(a) PHANTOM Premium 3.0/6DOF haptic device. (b) PHANTOM Omni™.**

Part a, © SensAble Technologies, Inc.®. Used with permission. The SenSitus molecular docking software package shown is courtesy of Stefan Birmanns, Ph.D., of the Laboratory for Structural Bioinformatics, University of Texas Health Science Center at Houston.

14.2.6. **Modeling**

Computing technology has evolved sufficiently to enable affordable, real-time, 3D digital modeling. Digital modeling applications have also matured to the point at which they have become integrated into the industrial design process.

Three-dimensional software packages offer industrial designers the ability quickly to try out new ideas as well as update and modify existing designs at relatively little expense. This facilitates the dissemination of an initial idea to a wide variety of interested parties early in the design process. The benefits of this type of "virtual prototyping" can be extended to a wide range of design activities, including product visualization, fit analysis, dynamic simulation, and maintenance analysis.

> **MAXIM**
>
> Haptic stimulation can enhance the sense of realism in virtual environments.

A drawback of these applications is that the designer is one step removed from the physical aspects and materials involved in the design. However, with the inclusion of haptic technologies, a sense of realism can be achieved that would otherwise be lacking.

A problem encountered by these devices is the lack of precision offered at later stages of design. It is difficult to control a haptic interface to the degree necessary to achieve smooth surfaces on cutout forms and varying surface textures. Designers generally switch to the more accurate calibrations of computer-assisted design (CAD) programs when their designs are ready for the final stages of development.

14.2.7. **Art**

Another area of research is the application of haptic interaction to the applied arts. This involves craftspeople and designers who work with their hands and whose creativity is intrinsically connected to the materials with which they work.

Unfortunately, there is a perceived disconnect between this domain and computer science. The Tacitus project, involving the Edinburgh College of Art and the Edinburgh Virtual Environment Centre, is concerned with bridging these two seemingly disparate worlds. The project's mission is to explore the development of multisensory computer applications and 3D haptic interfaces that can be used for artistic creation and design.

Haptic technologies can enrich the experience and process of digital artistic creation. Applications for haptic displays have been developed in artistic domains such as sculpture, painting, engraving, and carving, as well as for texture painting in 3D modeling applications.

a

Type	Examples	Model	Structure	Surface	Example Strokes
Round					
Flat/ Bright					
Filbert					

b

Figure 14.16   (a) DAB Haptic Painting System. (b) Paint brushes, virtual equivalents (skeletal structure and surface mesh) and example strokes.

Digital graphic environments generally lack the tactile qualities that are essential to artists as they work with different mediums. The addition of tactile feedback can increase an artist's sense of immersion and afford him or her a more realistic environment.

Haptic painting applications such as DAB (Figure 14.16) (Baxter et al, 2001) allow the user to manipulate the stylus of a PHANTOM device as if it were a paintbrush. The DAB systems uses haptic feedback to simulate brush/canvas friction in a way that realistically approximates the feeling of painting with various types of brushes.

Haptic displays can also help museums to offer their visitors the ability to touch virtual 3D objects without the risk of destroying the real, precious objects. These objects can also be made available for inspection from remote locations.

McLaughlin, Hespanha, and Sukhatmeare (2002) are working on a project at the Annenberg School for Communication that involves the creation of a haptic museum. Haptic technologies can make displays more interactive while still preserving valuable artifacts: "In short, haptics can be used to allow museum visitors to explore objects in ways that cannot be permitted in physical museums due to concerns about breakage and deterioration of the object surface" (McLaughlin, Hespanha, & Sukhatme, 2002).

At the Integrated Media Systems Center of the University of Southern California, researchers have developed a PHANTOM-accessible kiosk presentation of digitized daguerreotype cases for the Seaver Center for Western Culture at the Natural History Museum of Los Angeles County. The Museum of Pure Form at the Museo dell'Opera del Duomo in Pisa, Italy, has also presented numerous exhibitions involving haptic displays.

14.2.8. Collaboration

> **MAXIM**
>
> Haptic stimulation can increase a sense of presence.

Haptics can play an important role in collaborative environments in which more than one person is working in a virtual domain. Through the use of haptic stimuli, collaborative partners can have a more intuitive and immersive environment in which to work.

Collaborative environments have incorporated haptic feedback not only to offer users a greater sense of presence, but also to help them more easily locate others in the environment. Handing over virtual objects between users in virtual environments can also be facilitated through haptic feedback.

The "tele-handshake" system developed by Alhalabi and Horiguchi (2001) allows two users from remote locations to meet over the Internet in a virtual room. The users, represented by virtual arms that are controlled by a PHANTOM device, are able to shake hands and instantaneously feel the force exerted by the contact among other interactions.

Gentry, Wall, Oakley, and Murray-Smith (2003) created a "haptic lead and follow dance" application that allows a user to either follow a computerized leader or engage in a dance with a remote live partner. It is implemented with a

PHANTOM device and uses haptic cues with an auditory sound track but no visual display.

14.2.9. Data Representations—Graphs

MAXIM

Haptic stimuli can be used to represent data.

Line graphs are an efficient and powerful way to communicate mathematical, statistical, and scientific information. Because of their visual nature, however, line graphs present significant obstacles for the visually impaired. Consequently, there has been increasing interest in the exploration of other modalities for the dissemination of this type of information. Positive results have been obtained from multi-modal graphic presentation.

The experimental designs in this area generally present a line graph rendered haptically on a background field. This creates a path that can be tracked by a haptic feedback device, such as SensAble's PHANTOM force feedback device. In studies carried out by Yu, Ramloll, Brewster, and Riedel, 2001), a virtually carved out channel is used instead of a ridge so that the haptic device can more easily track the line.

After exploring the haptic graphical presentations, the subjects of these experiments were asked to accomplish tasks including:

- Counting the number of lines
- Identifying the smoothness of a line
- Counting the number of bends on a line
- Counting the number of intersections, if any

Yu et al. based these tasks on the assumption that line graphs tend to present data trends and provide difference comparisons. They found significant positive results—in the range of 89.95% and 86.83% correct answers.

14.2.10. Gaming

Contemporary digital gamming systems use haptic feedback to create a more realistic and engaging experience for the players. Haptic feedback has been incorporated into controller devices such as joysticks, gamepads, and wheel-based controllers. It is mapped to game events through the software and generally uses the sound card to generate the haptic effects.

Haptic feedback can allow game players to sense the physical constraints of the environment. For example, force feedback can tell players when they hit a wall or when they are hit from behind. It can allow them to feel the weigh of objects they pick up or to feel objects in the dark. It can also be used to make firing a weapon feel more realistic. Full force feedback can represent turbulence, recoil, and G-forces.

Tactile feedback can allow players to feel the texture of objects or sense the rumbling from a moving vehicle such as a train or car. It can also be used to simulate the surface of a road or landing strip. Together with force feedback, tactile information can be used to represent the friction of the surface on which a player is driving so that he or she can feel slippery surfaces, which may indicate a skid or an out-of-control car.

The Immersion Corporation has created a suite of application program interfaces (APIs) and applications based on their TouchSense technology. The designer can use these technologies to create haptic feedback for games or Web pages. These effects can be picked up by many touch-enabled devices such as joysticks and game controllers.

There are tools and toolkits for applications such as Authorware®, Director®, Dreamweaver®, Flash®, and Visual Basic. There are also ActiveX controls and plug-ins for Internet Explorer and some Netscape browsers.

Developers use Immersion Studio® to design haptic effects, which are exported in an Immersion Force Resource (IRF) file. This file contains methods that can be called by scripting languages such as JavaScript, Visual Basic, and the Lingo script use by Director.

The following list shows some of the haptic effects that can be created using the Immersion Studio for Gaming:

Position-Based Effects

- **Wall Effect**s—these effects create the sensation of a wall that is horizontal, vertical, or placed at an angle
- **Enclosure Effects**—these effects create the sensation that the cursor is constrained either inside or outside of an enclosure
- **Inertia Effect**—this effect gives the sensation of pushing something that has wheels
- **Slope Effect**—this gives the effect of rolling a ball up or down a hill
- **Texture Effect**—this creates the impressions of a series of bumps

Resistance Effects

- These effects create the sensation of viscosity; they can simulate friction (damper, friction, inertia)

Time-Based Effects

- These effects change over time and can create sensations of vibration, sway, pulsing, ramp, or vector force

14.3. Technical Issues Concerning Haptics

We looked at the basic elements that comprise the human haptic system, and we saw some of the applications for haptic human–computer interaction. We now explore some of the technical issues involved in computer-based haptic interaction.

14.3.1. Haptic Displays

A haptic display provides force feedback and/or tactile output and is responsive to the position of and forces exerted by a user through the use of a haptic-enabled device. Numerous attempts have been made to create haptic displays. Some have been realized and used in experimental research; others have remained at the design stage.

Some devices are commercially available, such as the PHANTOM and the CyberForce systems (see Figure 14.19), which are used in medical training, commercial design, and research-related activities. There are also a number of haptic controllers for digital game environments.

The available devices are varied and, for the most part, address highly specialized applications. Some are oriented to our kinetic sense, whereas others are oriented to our tactile sense. Some engage both senses but are restricted to specific body parts, such as the hand, fingers, or arm. Let's now look at the different types of haptic displays, the information they transmit, and how they transmit it.

14.3.2. Tactile Displays

Ideally, a tactile display should be able to capture and communicate a virtual object's surface information to the user and respond to pressure information supplied by him or her. For example, in medical training simulations it would be advantageous to allow the user to feel the temperature or roughness of an organ.

It would also be advantageous if the virtual tissue could deform in accordance with the pressure applied to it by the virtual hand during palpation examinations. This might give the user important information about the resiliency or elasticity of the tissue.

The abilities to detect pressure exerted by, and to produce skin deformations on, the users are essential for the creation of realistic simulations. Therefore, a tactile display should be able to sense the pressure applied by the user (sensors) as well as communicate the tactile properties of a virtual object to the user (actuators). We will now look at the various technologies involved in these two processes.

Tactile Sensors

Tactile sensors translate mechanical input into electrical output that is digitized and read by a computer. This tactile information can then be used by a virtual reality, robotic, or any other type of application. There are numerous tactile-sensing technologies, which involve diverse mechanical, electrical, ultrasonic, and optical designs.

Each technology offers advantages to specific applications that range from industrial machinery, to aerospace robotics, to virtual reality simulations. Each application also brings with it specific criteria, such as portability, ruggedness, size, and cost, that are addressed differently by the various sensor technologies. The choice of sensor technology depends on the application for which the device is designed. Let's look at some of the different types of sensors that have been used in haptic devices.

Force-Sensitive Resistors

These sensors use a thick polymer sheet that changes resistance when pressure is applied. The electrical resistance decreases in proportion to the increase in pressure. This change in resistance is predictable and, therefore, can be used to calculate the pressure applied to the sensor.

Ultrasonic Force Sensors

These sensors use a deformable pad and an array of ultrasonic transmitters and receivers. They measure pressure by calculating the thickness of the pad. The process uses a high-frequency pulse that is transmitted through the pad, and the time it takes for the pulse to be reflected back to the sensing element is calculated to determine the amount of pressure applied to the pad.

Piezoelectric Stress Rate Sensors

Piezoelectric materials produce an electric field or voltage when they are stressed by a mechanical force, a phenomenon called the piezoelectric effect. A device that uses piezoelectric sensors uses the voltage generated to calculate the amount of force applied to the material.

Tactile Actuators

Tactile actuators apply stimulation to the cutaneous receptors. This stimulation can be in the form of vibration, pressure, electronic charge, temperature changes, or skin stretch. As in the case of sensor technologies, the choice of actuator type is application dependent. Actuators are subject to the same criteria as sensors—portability, ruggedness, size, and cost.

Vibrotactile Systems

As the name implies, vibrotactile systems use vibrations to stimulate the cutaneous receptors. One of the most common uses of vibrotactile stimulation is in cell phones. You can set your phone to vibrate in situations in which an audible ring tone would be distracting or offensive, such as a library or a theater. You can also set specific frequencies and wave shapes to represent voice calls as opposed to text messaging or to identify a particular caller.

This is a very rudimentary use of vibrotactile stimulation, which is capable of much more sophisticated applications. For example, it can be used for object identification by simulating the shape contours and surface textures of virtual objects. To be convincing, this vibrotactile feedback must be calibrated to conform to the location and intensity of the contact forces in the virtual environment.

Vibrotactile feedback can be created in diverse ways:

> **Voice Coils**—Vibrotactile stimulation can be produced by voice coils—lightweight vibrating disks that are small enough to fit on the end of a finger. These coils vibrate at a set frequency and at varying amplitudes to provide different sensations of touch.

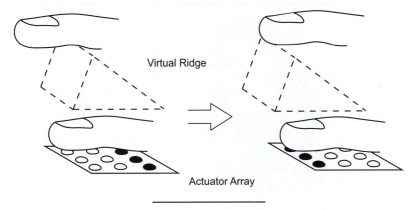

Figure 14.17 Micro-pin array.

Loudspeakers—Vibrotactile stimulation can be produced by miniature loudspeakers hooked up to a haptic device in such a way that the vibrations from the speakers are felt by the user as he or she grips the device.

Micro-Pin Arrays—Another way to produce vibrotactile stimulation is to use micro-pin actuators that apply tactile stimuli to the skin. Micro-pin actuators are small pins (tactors) that are usually set up in arrangements that vibrate in accordance with the haptic properties or texture of a virtual object. As the user passes his or her finger over an object in the virtual environment, specific tactors aligned with the coordinates of the virtual object stimulate specific cutaneous receptors on the user's skin. This creates the sensation that the user is actually touching the virtual object (Figure 14.17).

Electrotactile Systems

Another way in which to produce tactile stimulation is to use electrodes that send very small electrical charges to the tactile receptors on the skin. Electrotactile technologies have a few advantages over vibrotactile methods because they are generally lighter and more energy efficient and involve fewer moving parts.

Although these characteristics are advantageous for portable applications, these electrotactile technologies also involve higher risks of skin irritation due to the electrical currents that are applied directly to the skin, a fact that might decrease their effective range.

Thermotactile Systems

Although the use of thermotactile stimulation is relatively new to the arena of tactile displays, studies have already shown potential for its application. Many thermotactile devices use Peltier thermoelectric heater/coolers, also known as thermoelectric modules. These are small (a few millimeters thick) solid-state devices that act as heat pumps.

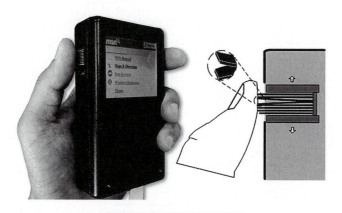

Figure 14.18 STReSS tactile display.

Lateral Skin Stretch

Without friction, we would not be able to function in the real world: walking would be more like ice skating, and common objects such as books and telephones would feel as if they were dipped in motor oil. Without friction, we would not be able to grasp anything; objects would simply slip out of our hands. Friction, however, also causes heat and wear, which is why we need to maintain an appropriate level of oil in an automobile engine.

We perceive friction by the way in which it causes our skin to stretch. If the surface texture of an object is very smooth, it slips from our hands. This causes a lateral deformation of the skin, or stretching. We often respond to this sensation by tightening our grip on the object. Without our sensitivity to skin stretch, we would have to rely on visual cues to tell us whether an object was sliding out of our hands. Skin stretch is an important aspect of grip control and an essential factor for the modeling of surface friction in virtual environments.

Pasquero and Hayward (2003) developed a device called STReSS that uses actuators to cause lateral skin stretch. The STReSS device is capable of producing so-called "tactile movies," which they describe as sequences of tactile images that are presented in rapid succession. The display uses an array of 100 laterally moving skin contactors (Figure 14.18).

14.3.3. Force Feedback Displays

Force feedback devices provide resistance to a user's movement. This enables the user to feel the weight or stiffness of a virtual object. The feedback might involve a finger or an arm movement, or, with the larger exoskeleton devices, it might respond to full-body movements.

Devices that offer force feedback come in a variety of configurations. They can be full-body exoskeletons, manipulator arms, dexterous gloves, or stylus-like, single-point interaction devices. All of these devices are designed to transmit low-spatial-frequency information, such as contour, shape, and collision; they do not have the resolution required for cutaneous feedback.

- **Exoskeletons**—These are large, full-body devices such as the HAL-5, which can be used to aid people with physical disabilities by augmenting their physical capabilities. Much of the research has involved military applications that augment a soldier's capacity to run and traverse hostile terrain.

- **Manipulator Arms**—These devices sense the location and position of the user's arm and translate that information to remote robotic devices or virtual representations of the user's arm. They also use force feedback to communicate a virtual object's properties such as weight and stiffness.

  The Grips Force Feedback Manipulator® is a seven-function, hydraulic manipulator developed by Kraft TeleRobotics (Figure 14.19). The Grips system uses electric actuators located on the individual joints of the master to sense the forces acting on the manipulator arm. These forces are then feed back to the operator.

  Grips manipulator systems have been used for deep-ocean, nuclear, aerospace, electric utility, and military applications. According to Kraft TeleRobotics, "Force feedback dramatically improves operator awareness and allows the operator to perform tasks more quickly and perform tasks of much grater complexity" (Kraft TeleRobotics brochure, personal communication, 2006).

- **Manipulator Gloves**—These devices are used like manipulator arms, but they afford a greater degree of flexibility by tracking the movement and position of the hand as well as each finger rather then the whole arm.

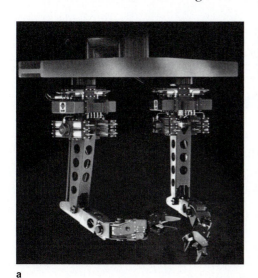

a   b

Figure 14.19 (a) The Grips remote manipulator arm. (b) The Grips operator controls.

a

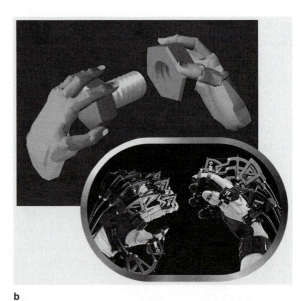

b

c

Figure 14.20   (a) CyberGlove II. (b) CyberGrasp. (c) CyberForce.

The Immersion Corporation makes a complete haptic system based on their CyberGlove® (Figure 14.20a), which uses a proprietary technology to output real-time digital joint-angle data based on the user's finger movements. There is also a mounting option that interacts with wrist sensors to detect forearm movement for X, Y, Z and pitch, roll, and yaw orientation information.

The CyberGlove fits into an exoskeleton device called the CyberGrasp™ (Figure 14.20b), which adds force feedback to each finger for use with the virtual reality computer interface. The system also provides a backpack the makes the actuator module portable and greatly extends its work space.

The system can be extended to include the entire arm with the CyberForce® force feedback armature (Figure 14.20c), which provides six-DOF positional tracking of translation and rotational movements of the hand.

The CyberGlove also comes with a vibrotactile feedback option called CyberTouch™, which uses six small, individually programmable vibrotactile stimulators, one on each finger and one on the palm of the CyberGlove. The CyberTouch component of the CyberForce system adds a high-spatial-frequency tactile display component to the interaction.

14.3.4. Desktop Devices

Haptic desktop devices generally offer single-point force feedback interaction by way of a stylus or thimble; multiple-point interaction is also possible, however, with devices such as the Space Interface Device for Artificial Reality (SPIDAR) (Sato, 2002). They can be used to sense the spatial properties of virtual objects such as stiffness, shape, and certain resolutions of surface texture. They can also be used in modeling and painting applications to create a more realistic environment for the user.

SensAble PHANTOM haptic devices—The most popular force feedback device is the PHANTOM device from SensAble technologies. Different models in the PHANTOM product line meet varying needs (Figure 14.21). The PHANTOM Premium models are high-precision instruments and, of the PHANTOM product line, provide the largest work spaces and highest forces; some offer six-DOF output capabilities. The PHANTOM® Desktop™ device and PHANTOM Omni® device offer affordable desktop solutions.

Stringed Force Feedback—Stringed force feedback interfaces are web-like devices that use steel wires attached to a cubic structure. The wires stretch from the

a   b

Figure 14.21 **(a) PHANTOM Premium 1.5 & 1.5 high-force haptic device. (b) PHANTOM Premium 1.0 haptic device.**

© SensAble Technologies, Inc.®. Used with permission.

a   b

Figure 14.22   (a) SPIDAR-8. Rubik's Cube. (b) Finger attachments.

frame of the supporting structure to an attachment for the fingertip. The location of the fingertip is calculated by the wire tension, which means that the strings can only be used to pull, not to push.

Stringed devices have the advantage of being lightweight and offering an ample amount of work space. Their work space mainly comprises thin strings, so they create no significant viewing obstructions. One of the more popular stringed force feedback devices is the SPIDAR (Figure 14.22).

Although a great deal of progress has been made recently, the task of creating a fully functional haptic display is still a daunting one. Our haptic system is involved in a multitude of activities, such as shape detection, texture discrimination, motion and position sensing, collision detection, and force resistance, to name only some.

Each of these activities is spatially complex and temporally dynamic and involves active and/or passive interaction. Current haptic technologies can only address a limited range of haptic interaction. Further research is necessary to better understand the requirements of haptic devices. We also need to understand how people respond to these devices during both short- and long-term use.

14.3.5. Haptic System Concerns

Some of the issues and concerns identified in the current literature on haptic devices involve the use of the system:

How is it used by a human operator?

How might the user be negatively affected?

Some concerns address the integrity of the system itself:

How quickly must it respond?

What is the possible range of values?

Let's look at some of these issues and see how they affect the design of haptic systems.

System Use

The following list of issues involved in haptic system use is not all-inclusive, but it presents the main topics of concern in haptic display design:

- **Perceptual Thresholds**—It is important that the user can perceive the haptic feedback generated by the haptic display. To ensure that the user has the optimal experience, all human perceptual thresholds and JNDs must be taken into consideration. Spatial, temporal, and magnitude resolutions must be clearly defined early in the design process.

- **Size/Weight**—Size is an issue on two levels. Sometimes the size of the apparatus is just too unwieldy, as in the case of full-body exoskeletons. With increased size comes increased weight. Therefore, novel, lightweight materials with strong and rigid properties are required for the creation of practical and usable devices.

- **User Fatigue**—Many haptic displays are attached to appendages, such as arms or hands, some are worn like a vest and others like a belt, some are carried, and others require the user to hold a posture for long periods of time. In all of these situations, there exists the possibility that the user will become fatigued by the use of the device. All efforts should be made to ensure that the user is comfortable and that extended use does not cause unnecessary fatigue.

- **Pain**—As with all human perceptual systems, there is the possibility of exceeding comfort levels and causing actual pain to the user. It is possible to cause pain from force feedback that exceeds safe levels or vibrations that are too intense. Cutaneous stimulation can also become painful if human pain thresholds are not calculated correctly.

- **Annoyance**—It is easy to create situations that are simply annoying to the user. Excessive, inappropriate, or distracting feedback can cause frustration or even render a device unusable.

- **Cost**—The current cost of most haptic devices is beyond the realm of the general population. For the most part, this technology is relegated to institutional research programs. Judging by recent trends in computing technologies, however, in time, the cost will drop and more general applications for haptic interaction will arise. There are some "affordable" haptic technologies available for the disabled community, such as Braille displays for visually disabled users (these displays still cost thousands of dollars) and some haptic controllers for computer gaming environments.

- **Portability**—Haptic devices are generally tethered to the computing station. Some are even fixed in place, either bolted to the ceiling or attached to the desktop. Most current devices are restricted to a finite work space; even haptic glove designs (with the exception of Immersion Corporation's CyberGlove back pack option) are limited to a predetermined operational area. To benefit truly from haptic interaction, portability must be seriously explored. The full benefits of exoskeleton technology require independent movement in large spatial ranges.

- **Computing Environment**—The physical location of the user and/or the haptic display might interfere with the proper functioning of the device.

  This might be due to the presence of uncontrollable parameters such as:

  ○ Extraneous vibrations from the external environment or the device
  ○ Unintentional skin contact that can be misconstrued as part of the haptic display
  ○ Unexpected user body movements that can cause "haptic noise"
  ○ Changing frames of reference that are caused by disruptions in the environment
  ○ Altered equilibrium due to environmental undulation or rocking

System Integrity

There are a few basic concerns regarding the integrity of a haptic device. They affect the ability of the device to communicate haptic information efficiently to the user and can determine the success or failure of the device in creating a believable haptic experience. Some of the concerns are as follows:

- **Backdriveability**—Optimally, a haptic device acts as a proxy for part of the user—the arm, hand, finger, or whole body. Therefore, one should strive to have the device be invisible to the user so that the illusion of haptic interaction is not disrupted by contact with it.

  This extraneous "haptic noise" would have to be filtered out by the user, increasing his or her cognitive load. The ability to move without interference from the device is called backdriveability and is an important issue in device design. This is especially important when users are navigating empty space; there should be no haptic sensation at all.

- **Latency**—To maintain the illusion of contact, a haptic system must be responsive to a level below the threshold of the human haptic system, otherwise cause and effect relationships will be diluted and eventually become uncoupled. System latency must therefore be considered, especially in teleoperation applications that require significant network involvement.

- **Stability**—Haptic systems deal with forces that can sometimes affect the functioning of the system itself. Unwanted system vibrations can cause interference, especially with vibrotactile displays. A buildup of system forces can cause instability and, in extreme situations, create significant safety concerns for the user. Noise from motors can also cause distractions that interfere with the functioning of the system.

Design Scenario

Coding Information for a Haptic Navigation Device

Augmentative technology is one area that can benefit from the application of haptic stimulation. Because the visual system and the haptic system overlap in the acquisition of spatial information, haptic displays can be used to compensate for lack of vision. Let's explore the issues involved in creating haptically coded information for a human navigation system (HNS).

The issues involved in this illustration are as follows:

- Haptic display application
- Choosing feedback type
- Haptic perception
- Coding information haptically

We need to decide on the kind of information that a user needs.

A user needs to know the following:

- The direction in which to walk
- Deviations in the terrain
- The presence of any obstacles
- How close he or she is to an obstacle (proximity)
- About urgent critical situations

We need to decide how best to communicate this information.

This information can be communicated in the following ways:

- Body location can be used to code directional information.
- Temporal/location patterns can be used to indicate terrain deviations.
- Location, frequency, and temporal patterns can be used to indicate obstacles.
- Temporal coding can be used to indicate proximity.
- Intensity can be used to give critical alarms.

We also need to decide what haptic stimulation to use.

The possible feedback options are as follows:

- Force feedback is not appropriate because the device will not be stationary like a PHANTOM device, and an exoskeleton would be cost prohibitive and awkward to use.
- Electrotactile feedback could become irritating due to the long duration of use, perhaps an entire day.
- Vibrotactile feedback is the most suitable method of signal delivery; it can be used in a portable device and at multiple body locations.

Design Scenario (cont.)

Now we must decide where the device should be worn.

Current HNSs are designed to be worn as vests or belts. Others can be carried in the hand or are modeled on the traditional white cane. An HNS also might be worn on the arm, like a sleeve, or around the neck, like a necklace. We should also consider the possibility of glove-type devices that give feedback to different parts of the hand and fingers.

It might also be possible to integrate these different formats into one cohesive device that relays various types of information. We use the integrated option and communicate different information through the various devices.

The devices include the following:

- Belt
- Vest
- Sensors embedded in a pair of glasses
- Global positioning system
- Mapping software

The mapping software will be used to enter the target location and create a route. The GPS will monitor the user's progress toward the target.

We now must decide how to code and deliver the information.

Direction—We use body location to indicate direction; given the need for a 360-degree resolution, the belt option is the most suitable for this type of information. Different actuators can be placed around the belt to indicate direction. The activators give constant indications of the required direction by vibrating with a measured pulse. The spatial acuity of the specific location must be taken into consideration when determining how far apart the actuators must be.

Terrain—Users must be informed about any deviation in the terrain such as curbs, pot holes, and stairs. We use the vest to indicate these deviations, on the chest area. A row of actuators across the chest will fire, followed by another row below, to indicate a step down such as a curb, and will be followed by another row above to indicate a step up. The signal will increase in speed as the user approaches the deviation and continue for the duration such as during the climbing of a flight of stairs. It is suggested that the gaps between signals be at least 10 msec and that the signals be at least 10 msec long. This is a benchmark that will be affected by location and type of stimulation.

This information will only be supplied if the user needs to continue in the direction of the terrain deviation. The device can ignore that information if the user is turning away from the deviation.

Obstacles—Location can be used to indicate the presence of an obstacle. The vest is the most suitable device for this information because it covers the most area and, therefore, can communicate information about high- and low-lying obstacles.

Design Scenario (cont.)

If there is a low-lying branch in front of a walking user, an actuator placed in the highest location might signal an alert. If there is an obstacle jutting out from the side, an actuator on that side might be activated.

Proximity—Simply coding the presence of an obstacle, however, is not sufficient. A user must know how close he or she is to the obstacle. The intervals between directional pulses can get shorter as the user nears his or her destination—10-msec pulses and 10-msec gaps are appropriate for temporally coded information.

Degree of Urgency—The most urgent events require an alarm system that can communicate relevant information, such as the degree of danger, as well as information about the nature of the event, such as the direction from which it is coming. This can be accomplished by increasing the intensity of the stimuli from the vest to indicate the degree of urgency. It is suggested that no more than four levels of magnitude be used to code haptic information.

We now have a number of body locations being used to indicate diverse information. It is essential that this information be communicated unambiguously. We need to code this information so that the signal is clearly articulated to the user.

Finally, we need to code the information.

We use rhythmic patterns to differentiate the meaning of the different signals.

Pattern Recognition—We have coded the information on terrain and obstacles using the vest actuators. We must now differentiate this information as well as the degree of urgency and obstacle location information.

The directional information communicated through the belt must remain steady, but obstacle and degree of urgency information is by nature variable. Normal obstacles such as low tree branches will appear in the course of the user's progress and can be dealt with progressively. A sudden intrusion by a foreign object, however, would require the user to stop his or her forward progress immediately.

We need to code all of this information in an unambiguous way so that the user is not confused about the meaning of the haptic signals. We use location on the belt to indicate direction, and location on the vest to indicate the presence of obstacles. We use location together with temporal coding on the vest to indicate terrain deviations. We use intensity and temporal coding to indicate degree of urgency related to obstacle proximity. We must now make sure that one signal does not mask another signal.

If the directional information pulses are in sync with the location of obstacle information, the user might be momentarily confused and interpret them as one signal. To differentiate the directional information from the obstacle information, we use two different patterns of haptic stimulation.

People have a unique ability for pattern recognition, and this facility can be used to code complex information. For example, because the belt uses a steady pulse, the vest can use a pattern to indicate the presence of an obstacle—perhaps a three-pulse

Design Scenario (cont.)

pattern (short, short, long) that increases in speed to indicate the proximity of the obstacle.

Critical situations must be communicated quickly and clearly. The vest covers the largest body area and is, therefore, the most suitable for communicating this type of information. All of the actuators would fire using an alarm pattern such as three short, strong, and very quick pulses.

Overstimulation—The haptic system, like all human perceptual systems, can be overloaded. Sensory overload is not uncommon. Too many signals in too short a span of time can confuse and overwhelm people, causing them to misunderstand, ignore, or even fail to register the presence of the stimulation.

After a critical alarm the system should be quiet for a period, thereby causing the user to pause until the situation changes and it is clear to proceed. In the same vein, the directional information can be suspended when, for example, the user is either ascending or descending a flight of stairs. If there is a landing, the directional signal can resume until the user nears the next set of steps and the vest reactivates.

By suspending some of the more continuous signals when a deviation or obstacle appears, we reduce the risk of overwhelming or overstimulating the user, which would decrease the usefulness of the device.

Summary

Haptic interaction implies input as well as output on the part of both participants in the dialogue. A haptic display should allow us to gather information about display objects through our haptic system. We should be able to feel the spatial, textural, and volumetric qualities of interface objects just as we do in the real world.

It should also allow us to input haptic information, such as the position of our hands and the force exerted when we grip an object. In other words, haptic displays have two basic functions:

- To measure the positions of, and the forces that are exerted by, our hands, fingers, arms, or other body parts
- To display the positions and forces of our bodies in relation to the virtual objects they encounter and return the appropriate tactile and/or force feedback

Haptic human–computer interaction has the potential to aid disabled users, provide realistic simulations for medical procedures, and allow people to perform high-risk operations accurately and safely. Haptic technologies are evolving and have already become available to the general public in devices such as game controllers. The future holds much potential for even greater development.

Resources on the Web

www.aw.com/heim
You will find information on industry resources as well as research activities regarding haptic interaction.

Suggested Reading

Burdea, G. C. (1996). *Force and Touch Feedback for Virtual Reality* (1 ed.): Wiley-Interscience.

Hatwell, Y., Streri, A., & Gentaz, E. (Eds.). (2003). *Touching for Knowing: Cognitive Psychology of Haptic Manual Perception:* John Benjamins Publishing Co.

McLaughlin, M. L., Hespanha, J. P., & Sukhatme, G. S. (2001). *Touch in Virtual Environments: Haptics and the Design of Interactive Systems* (1 ed.): Pearson Education.

APPENDIX A

Vision

Of all of our senses, vision is the most important. We interpret our environment and make decisions based predominately on visual cues. The physical characteristics and limitations of our visual system affect our perception of interface elements such as color schemes, icon shape and size, screen location, and page layout. It is, therefore, a significant factor in interaction design.

The process of seeing can be divided into two parts: the physical input of light waves and the cognitive interpretation of those signals. We process the physical input first, responding to the intensity of the stimuli. A bright color or a large shape will catch our attention, which might then stimulate the cognitive process of understanding what we see.

Vision is our most highly developed sense, and currently is the most common channel of communication between humans and computers. The effect of visual stimuli is both immediate and of long duration. Graphic elements can increase the understandability of an interface by allowing people to create associations with real-world objects.

The proper visual environment can aid in learning and facilitate work flow. A confusing and incoherent visual environment can have quite the opposite effect. Before we begin to explore the visual aspects of human–computer interaction we need a basic understanding of the human visual perception system. Let's see how vision works.

Foveal–Peripheral

Human vision can be divided into two types—foveal and peripheral. Foveal vision results from stimulation of the central area of the retina, which is called the foveal region. It is used for focusing on areas of interest, detecting color, and perceiving small details. Peripheral vision, which results from stimulation at the edges of the retina, is sensitive to movement, and it functions well in low-light environments. It informs us about the area surrounding our foveal vision but has very little sensitivity to detail.

These systems work in conjunction with each other, but they also compete for our attention. A slight movement in our peripheral vision can catch our attention and shift the foveal vision to another location. While we focus on the center of fixation the peripheral stimuli will not be attended to, that is, until the next significant distraction. Our peripheral vision directs the focus of our foveal vision. Even during fixation the eye remains in constant motion.

Visual Acuity

Visual acuity is a measure of how clearly we can see details. Visual acuity is the highest in our foveal vision; that is the area where our vision is the sharpest. For interaction designers, visual acuity has a direct effect on the amount of detail we can reliably assume a user will be able to detect. Determinations concerning font size and graphic detail depend on the user's visual acuity, which is affected by factor such as the user's distance from the screen, age, and any disabling conditions. The greater the limitations, the larger must be the type to afford maximum detail detection.

Humans vary widely in terms of visual acuity; the norm has been identified as 20/20 vision. Normal vision is defined as the ability to perceive detail as small as 1 minute of arch. Total vision is calculated on 360 degrees, and each degree is divided into 60 minutes.

Human vision uses approximately 140 degrees, but we depend most on our fovea centralis, the area at the center of the retina that has the sharpest vision and highest color sensitivity. The fovea centralis covers about 15 degrees. Within that range 1 minute, or 1/60 degree, represents the smallest possible perceivable detail for normal vision.

Snellen tests are used to measure visual acuity. The characters on the test are created so that the smallest perceivable character is 5 minutes of arc and the smallest detail, the stroke widths and spaces, are one fifth of the whole character—1 minute of arc.

The actual size of the characters on the printed Snellen chart is calculated using a 20-foot distance or its virtual equivalent using mirrors. The E in Figure A.1, which is representative of the characters on the test, is measured at 5 minutes of arc, and the smallest detail is one fifth of the size of the whole character.

Identifying characters measuring 1 minute of arc from a 20-foot distance has been determined to be an adequate measure of normal visual acuity. That is, the retinal area affected by the image of the character contains, at least, the minimum

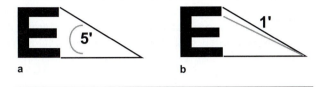

Figure A.1 (a) Smallest Snellen character. (b) Smallest Snellen detail.

number of cones required to distinguish the character's smallest detail. If the detail is smaller, it will not be perceived or will be perceived as a blur.

Visual Angle

If two colors are placed too close, they will merge into what will appear to be a third color created by mixing the two colors. For example, if a texture is created using black and white lines drawn closer than 1 minute of arc, the area will simply appear gray and no texture will be perceived. A brief look at the structure of the human eye will help to clarify this.

The retina contains two types of photoreceptors—rods and cones. Rods are sensitive to blue-green light and are mainly used for low-light vision. The cones are divided into red-sensitive, green-sensitive, and blue-sensitive groups and are predominantly situated at the center or foveal region of the retina. They diminish in number toward the periphery, where the rods become predominant.

When the eye receives visual stimuli the image passes through the lens and is projected upside down on the retina. The number of receptors involved depends on the visual angle of the projection. Figure A.2 shows that the relationship between the size of the stimuli and the distance to the lens is in direct proportion with the distance from the lens to the retina and the size of the projected image.

Given a particular distance and an acceptable visual angle (see the section Circle of Acuity), we can calculate an appropriate size for visual stimuli by using the formula

$$X/2 = d \tan(\theta/2)$$

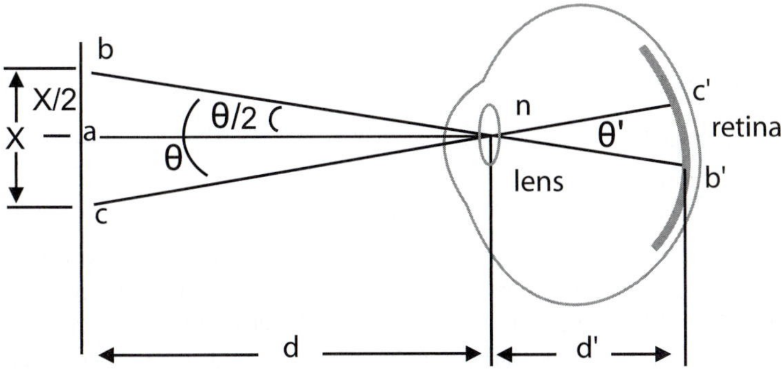

Figure A.2 Human eye.

By dividing the distance *cb* in half, we create a right triangle at point *a*. Through simple geometry we can calculate the smallest perceivable detail that can be distinguished with normal vision. This is how eye charts for visual acuity are calibrated.

Visual Acuity and Screen Design

Visual acuity decreases inversely with the distance from our center of focus—the center of fixation. The greater the distance a character is from the center of fix-ation, the lower is the visual acuity for that character. It has been shown that visual acuity is diminished by one half at a distance of 2.5 degrees from the cen-ter of fixation. This means that the area of highest visual acuity is a circle with a diameter of 5 degrees around the center of fixation (Tullis, 1984). This has implications for screen design, relating to the length of words and the grouping of screen elements.

Using the formula $X/2 = d \tan(\theta/2)$, we can determine the size of the circle of acuity around the center of fixation. Tullis suggests that a distance of 475 mm (approximately 18.7 inches) is the optimal distance from the screen. There is ev-idence, however, to suggest that 30 inches is preferable because of accommoda-tion and convergence, which cause eye strain and fatigue (Ankrum, 1996). Accommodation is the subtle reshaping of the lens to facilitate the different fo-cusing required for close-up and distance vision. Convergence occurs when ob-jects are close and the eyes converge toward each other to avoid seeing double.

It is difficult to make a concrete determination of screen distance. There are multiple issues involved such as possible vision impairments, environmental fac-tors, and personal preferences, so for the now we follow Tullis' calculations and use 475 mm for the screen distance. Thus we have

$$X/2 = d \tan(\theta/2)$$

$$X/2 = d \tan(5°/2)$$

$$X/2 = d (\tan 2.5°)$$

$$X/2 = 475(0.04366)$$

$$X/2 = 20.7389$$

$$X = 41.4779 \text{ mm (1.633 inches)}$$

Tullis makes some determinations of the average distance between characters—2.8 mm horizontally and 5.6 mm vertically based on "average dimensions of charac-ters displayed on three different vendors' CRT's" (Tullis, 1984, 30). Given a circle of acuity of 41.4779 mm, he calculates that 88 characters will be perceived clearly, rela-tive to their position on the radius.

		0	1	2	2	2	2	2	1	0				
	0	1	2	3	4	4	5	4	4	3	2	1	0	
0	2	3	4	5	6	7	7	7	6	5	4	3	2	0
1	2	3	5	6	7	9	10	9	7	6	5	3	2	1
0	2	3	4	5	6	7	7	7	6	5	4	3	2	0
	0	1	2	3	4	4	5	4	4	3	2	1	0	
		0	1	2	2	2	2	2	1	0				

Figure A.3 Circle of acuity.

Circle of Acuity

We depend predominantly on the fovea centralis, the area of the retina that affords the highest acuity. Consequently the characters nearer the center are weighted more heavily than the ones on the periphery due to the continuing reduction in visual acuity. Tullis uses a linear weighting scheme that weights the characters in inverse proportion to their distance from the center, which is arbitrarily assigned a value of 10.

The chart in Figure A.3 demonstrates the relative acuity of screen characters based on Tullis' calculations. To apply this procedure to screen design, certain statistics must be obtained, such as distance from the screen, screen resolution, and viewing area as well as the size of the font and the particular font face (not all 12-point fonts have the same-size characters).

Contrast Sensitivity

Contrast sensitivity is a measure of how well we can distinguish objects from their backgrounds. Whereas visual acuity can be considered a measure of visual quantity, contrast sensitivity can be considered a measure of visual quality.

Nature often uses visual contrast as a defense mechanism. Animals sometimes blend in with their surroundings by using colors and patterns that have low contrast with their environment. A polar bear would stand out in a pine forest but virtually disappears on a snow bank (Figure A.4).

In general, our sensitivity to contrast decreases in low-light environments, but it also decreases with age. The pupil gets smaller and the eye's optics become

Figure A.4 Natural camouflage.

less transparent, which means that less light reaches the photoreceptors. This causes contrast sensitivity to decline, reducing our ability to distinguish characters in a low-contrast situation such as white letters on a gray background or black letters on a blue background.

Design Ramifications

Currently the most common form of human–computer interaction is through a graphical user interface, which makes the human visual system the "gold standard" in contemporary interaction design. If an interface design does not conform to this standard, it will cause problems for the user.

The following list covers some of the factors that must be considered:

- People respond first to the physical intensity of visual stimuli such as size, shape, and color,
- Graphic screen elements can create associations with real-world objects and, therefore, increase comprehension.
- Learning can be facilitated by the proper use of visual elements.
- Color and detail perception are the strongest in our central vision.
- People are sensitive to motion in their peripheral vision.
- Distance directly affects our ability to see detail.
- Proper character size can be calculated according to the formula
  $X/2 = d \tan(\theta/2)$
- Clarity of screen elements can be calculated using the circle of acuity.
- Our sensitivity to contrast is affected by lighting conditions and age.

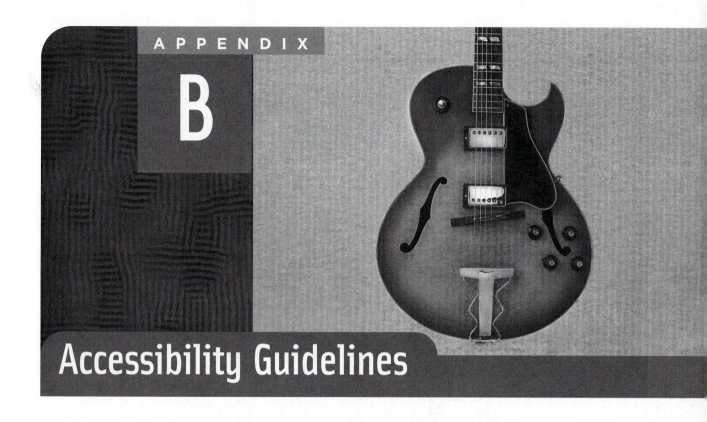

APPENDIX

B

Accessibility Guidelines

Good design enables, bad design disables.
(EIDD [European Institute for Design and Disability], 2006)

We live in an information society, and access to that information is filtered by the interfaces we design for computing devices. Human-centric design of these interfaces has become an essential part of the development process. Human-centric design involves understanding people's abilities and disabilities and strives to make information accessible to all people regardless of their condition. This has given rise to the concept of "design for all" (DFA).

There are a number of organizations and consortiums involved in the DFA movement. Each has its individual perspective on the concept, as can be seen by the following definitions they offer and the objectives they profess:

Dissemination Activities Supporting Design for All (DASDA)—"Design for all means creating products, services and systems to cater for the widest possible range of user abilities and circumstances for use" (DASDA, 2006).

European Design for All e-Accessibility Network (EDeAN)—"One of the objectives of the eEurope action plan is the integration of older people and people with disabilities into the information society. This will only come about as a result of designing mainstream products and services to be accessible by as broad a range of users as possible. This approach is termed Design for All.

"The term 'eAccessibility' stands for the access which new Information and Communication Technologies (ICTs) can provide to people—both access to the real world and to the growing Information Society world.

eAccessibility also implies a need for new technologies and systems themselves to be accessible—especially to users with functional impairments, older people and others who may be in danger of being left behind by the rapid advances of technology in all areas of society" (EDeAN, 2005).

Visual Information

Human–computer interaction in a GUI environment is predicated on human visual perception. GUIs comprise graphic components that represent system objects and functionality. To choose the appropriate command, the user must differentiate among various images and graphic representations.

Some users might have a visual impairment or be blind and therefore lack the perceptual abilities required for interaction with a GUI. The graphic nature of the contemporary GUI not only creates barriers for users who are visually impaired, it also has the potential to disenfranchise a large portion of the population.

Screen Readers and Audible Browsers

Users with visual impairments operate computers via screen readers and audible browsers. These are software programs that convert text into speech. Screen readers access the screen characters and use voice synthesizers to read the text on the screen.

Among the more popular applications are Jaws and Window Eyes. Audible browsers read HTML code and convert the plain text and some of the element attributes to audible stimuli. One of the more popular browsers is Home Page Reader from IBM.

Because audible browsers read the HTML code, it is important to write it properly so that visually impaired users will have equivalent access to information that is available to sighted users. Screen readers must also allow users access to system functionality in a manner that is equivalent to that available to sighted users. These requirements are clearly specified in the guidelines published by the W3C and the U.S. government as listed later.

Auditory Information

GUIs are, by definition, highly visual environments; however, auditory feedback is a significant component. Auditory feedback can take many forms, such as button clicks that provide confirmation that the event was registered, system beeps that signal errors or progress completions, sounds that accompany windows state changes, e-mail notifications, and alerts of all kinds.

Audio is increasingly being used on the Internet to make Web sites more engaging and informative. Web pages can include video clips with audio tracks radio stations offer live and archived news and music shows, and some sites use audio streaming for Web casts and live presentations.

Mobile computing has increased the focus on auditory interaction due to the limited screen sizes of many mobile devices. Ubiquitous computing is also an area in which audio can play a significant role.

Sound has many attractive qualities in a world in which visual overload is not uncommon. However, there are many users with different levels of auditory impairments who cannot fully take part in auditory interactions. Deaf users might be shut out entirely.

Governmental Regulation

A large segment of the population suffers, to one degree or another, from some form of perceptual impairment. These impairments can affect people's ability to access information, especially in an environment that is increasingly dependent on electronic information delivery. This fact has been recognized by many national governments and governmental regulatory agencies, such as the U.S. Federal Communications Commission.

Legislation has been passed in the United States with specific guidelines for the creation of electronic interfaces that address the needs of disabled communities:

> In 1998, Congress amended the Rehabilitation Act to require Federal agencies to make their electronic and information technology accessible to people with disabilities. Inaccessible technology interferes with an individual's ability to obtain and use information quickly and easily. Section 508 was enacted to eliminate barriers in information technology, to make available new opportunities for people with disabilities, and to encourage development of technologies that will help achieve these goals. The law applies to all Federal agencies when they develop, procure, maintain, or use electronic and information technology. Under Section 508 (29 U.S.C. '794d), agencies must give disabled employees and members of the public access to information that is comparable to the access available to others. (http://www.section508.gov/)

These guidelines require that public information be accessible to all people, regardless of their disabling condition, which can range from color blindness to complete loss of vision, from slight hearing impairment to complete deafness. Users with cognitive disabilities must also be afforded access to public information.

Similar legislation exists throughout the technologically developed world, and with the rapid evolution of the World Wide Web it has become essential for information to be accessible to as much of the population as possible.

The W3C, which manages Web standards and technology, has also addressed this issue. The W3C's Web Accessibility Initiative (WAI) published Web Content Accessibility Guidelines 1.0 (W3C Recommendation 5-May-1999), which are available at http://www.w3.org/TR/1999/WAI-WEBCONTENT-19990505*.

There are 14 general guidelines. Each guideline is categorized by a priority level (1 to 3, with 1 being the highest), and they are broken down into various checkpoints:

1. Provide equivalent alternatives to auditory and visual content.
2. Don't rely on color alone.
3. Use markup and style sheets, and do so properly.
4. Clarify natural language usage,
5. Create tables that transform gracefully.
6. Ensure that pages featuring new technologies transform gracefully.
7. Ensure user control of time-sensitive content changes.
8. Ensure direct accessibility of embedded user interfaces.
9. Design for device independence.
10. Use interim solutions.
11. Use W3C technologies and guidelines.
12. Provide context and orientation information.
13. Provide clear navigation mechanisms.
14. Ensure that documents are clear and simple.

Let's consider the Section 508 and W3C checkpoints in the context of the relevant interface issues—color, icons, text, and audio.

Guidelines and Checkpoints

One of the more general guidelines suggested by the W3C is to allow users the ability to choose the type and manner of information access:

> **11.3** Provide information so that users may receive documents according to their preferences (e.g., language, content type, etc.).

If, after all avenues have been explored, you cannot make your information accessible, the W3C makes the following recommendation:

> **11.4** If, after best efforts, you cannot create an accessible page, provide a link to an alternative page that uses W3C technologies, is accessible, has equivalent information (or functionality), and is updated as often as the inaccessible (original) page.

General Vision Impairment

Section 508 includes the following general guidelines in relation to vision impairments:

§ 1194.22 Web-based intranet and internet information and applications.

(b) Equivalent alternatives for any multimedia presentation shall be synchronized with the presentation.

§ 1194.24 Video and multimedia products.

(d) All training and informational video and multimedia productions which support the agency's mission, regardless of format, that contain visual information necessary for the comprehension of the content, shall be audio described.

§ 1194.31 Functional performance criteria.

(a) At least one mode of operation and information retrieval that does not require user vision shall be provided, or support for assistive technology used by people who are blind or visually impaired shall be provided.

(b) At least one mode of operation and information retrieval that does not require visual acuity greater than 20/70 shall be provided in audio and enlarged print output working together or independently, or support for assistive technology used by people who are visually impaired shall be provided.

The Web Content Accessibility Guidelines include the following checkpoint for general vision impairment:

1.4 For any time-based multimedia presentation (e.g., a movie or animation), synchronize equivalent alternatives (e.g., captions or auditory descriptions of the visual track) with the presentation.

Color

Humans not only differ in their cognitive approach to color recognition and meaning, they also differ in their relative ability to perceive color on a physical level. Human visual receptors vary greatly in their degree of sensitivity to changes in color.

Some people have limited abilities to differentiate between different colors. There are many types and degrees of color blindness. To make relationships and delineations clear to users with color vision deficiencies, it is essential that a system of redundant coding be used.

Section 508 includes the following guidelines for the application of color in electronic and information technology (EIT):

Subpart B—Technical Standards

§ 1194.21 Software applications and operating systems.

(g) Applications shall not override user selected contrast and color selections and other individual display attributes.

§ 1194.25 Self contained, closed products.

(i) Color coding shall not be used as the only means of conveying information, indicating an action, prompting a response, or distinguishing a visual element.

(j) When a product permits a user to adjust color and contrast settings, a variety of color selections capable of producing a range of contrast levels shall be provided.

Section 508 provides the following guideline for the use of color on Web pages:

§ 1194.22. Web-based intranet and internet information and applications.

(c) Web pages shall be designed so that all information conveyed with color is also available without color, for example from context or markup.

The Web Content Accessibility Guidelines include the following checkpoints for the application of color on the Web:

2.1 Ensure that all information conveyed with color is also available without color, for example from context or markup.

2.2 Ensure that foreground and background color combinations provide sufficient contrast when viewed by someone having color deficits or when viewed on a black and white screen.

Parsing these guidelines, we see that certain issues become clear:

- Users must be able to adjust their displays according to their individual needs. This might mean adjusting the screen contrast, changing the color of screen elements including backgrounds and text, or calibrating the brightness of the display.
- Color should be used to enhance an existing structure and not in isolation. This is important for people with color vision issues, blind users, and people with monochrome screens.

All designs must be tested on a variety of machines and in a variety of system configurations. When users have the ability to adjust screen elements, as is required by law, time must be allocated to testing the results of these adjustments. Unfortunate screen effects can be avoided by rigorously checking to see whether all possible combinations of system settings work with a particular interface design.

A decision to restrict an interface element in terms of color or size is an indicator of possible problems. These situations should be documented for later referral during the testing phase.

Color factors to consider include the following:

- Text color
- Background color
- Widget color (buttons, menus, etc.)
- Icon colors
- Dynamic system colors (highlighting, etc.)

Regulations require that people with cognitive deficiencies be afforded equal access to public information. This further emphasizes the need for a clear and logical structure that avoids ambiguity in the meaning of interface elements and their relationships.

Icons and Screen Components

Icons and screen components are graphic entities—they are images. It is important to ensure that all users have access to the functionality and information that these components provide.

Section 508 includes the following guidelines for the use of images in electronic and information technology.

Subpart B—Technical Standards

§ 1194.21 Software applications and operating systems.

(e) When bitmap images are used to identify controls, status indicators, or other programmatic elements, the meaning assigned to those images shall be consistent throughout an application's performance.

§ 1194.31 Functional performance criteria.

(a) At least one mode of operation and information retrieval that does not require user vision shall be provided, or support for assistive technology used by people who are blind or visually impaired shall be provided.

(b) At least one mode of operation and information retrieval that does not require visual acuity greater than 20/70 shall be provided in audio and enlarged print output working together or independently, or support for assistive technology used by people who are visually impaired shall be provided.

Section 508 provides the following guideline for the use of images on Web pages:

§ 1194.22 Web-based intranet and internet information and applications.

(a) A text equivalent for every non-text element shall be provided (e.g., via "alt", "longdesc", or in element content).

(e) Redundant text links shall be provided for each active region of a server-side image map.

The Web Content Accessibility Guidelines include the following checkpoints for the use of images on the Web:

1.1 Provide a text equivalent for every non-text element (e.g., via "alt", "longdesc", or in element content). *This includes*: images, graphical representations of text (including symbols), image map regions, animations (e.g., animated GIFs), applets and programmatic objects, ASCII art, frames, scripts, images used as list bullets, spacers, graphical buttons, sounds (played with or without user interaction), stand-alone audio files, audio tracks of video, and video.

1.2 Provide redundant text links for each active region of a server-side image map.

1.5 Until user agents render text equivalents for client-side image map links, provide redundant text links for each active region of a client-side image map.

3.1 When an appropriate markup language exists, use markup rather than images to convey information.

For example, use MathML to mark up mathematical equations, and style sheets to format text and control layout. Also, avoid using images to represent text—use text and style sheets instead.

Text

Text is arguably the most common format for information presentation. It is a powerful medium that has been influential in all aspects of human endeavor throughout history. It has also played an important role in human–computer interaction, from command-line input, to widget labels, to help files and Web page text.

It is essential that developers understand the implications this has for the communities of users with disabilities and what the proper methods are for using text in computer-based communication.

Section 508 includes the following guidelines for the application of text in electronic and information technology:

§ 1194.21 Software applications and operating systems.

(a) When software is designed to run on a system that has a keyboard, product functions shall be executable from a keyboard where the function itself or the result of performing a function can be discerned textually.

(f) Textual information shall be provided through operating system functions for displaying text. The minimum information that shall be made available is text content, text input caret location, and text attributes.

(k) Software shall not use flashing or blinking text, objects, or other elements having a flash or blink frequency greater than 2 Hz and lower than 55 Hz.

(l) When electronic forms are used, the form shall allow people using assistive technology to access the information, field elements, and functionality required for completion and submission of the form, including all directions and cues.

§ 1194.24 Video and multimedia products.

(e) Display or presentation of alternate text presentation or audio descriptions shall be user-selectable unless permanent.

Section 508 provides the following guideline for the use of text on framed Web pages:

§ 1194.22 Web-based intranet and internet information and applications.

(i) Frames shall be titled with text that facilitates frame identification and navigation.

The Web Content Accessibility Guidelines include the following checkpoints for the use of text on the Web:

1.3 Until user agents can automatically read aloud the text equivalent of a visual track, provide an auditory description of the important information of the visual track of a multimedia presentation.

3.3 Use style sheets to control layout and presentation.

For example, use the CSS 'font' property instead of the HTML FONT element to control font styles.

3.5 Use header elements to convey document structure and use them according to specification.

For example, in HTML, use H2 to indicate a subsection of H1. Do not use headers for font effects.

3.7 Mark up quotations. Do not use quotation markup for formatting effects such as indentation.

For example, in HTML, use the Q and BLOCKQUOTE elements to markup short and longer quotations, respectively.

4.1 Clearly identify changes in the natural language of a document's text and any text equivalents (e.g., captions).

4.2 Specify the expansion of each abbreviation or acronym in a document where it first occurs.

5.5 Provide summaries for tables.

5.6 Provide abbreviations for header labels.

> For example, in HTML, use the "abbr" attribute on the TH element.

6.1 Organize documents so they may be read without style sheets. For example, when an HTML document is rendered without associated style sheets, it must still be possible to read the document.

> When content is organized logically, it will be rendered in a meaningful order when style sheets are turned off or not supported.

7.1 Until user agents allow users to control flickering, avoid causing the screen to flicker.

Note. People with photosensitive epilepsy can have seizures triggered by flickering or flashing in the 4 to 59 flashes per second (Hertz) range with a peak sensitivity at 20 flashes per second as well as quick changes from dark to light (as with strobe lights).

Note. The BLINK and MARQUEE elements are not defined in any W3C HTML specification and should not be used.

9.5 Provide keyboard shortcuts to important links (including those in client-side image maps), form controls, and groups of form controls.

> For example, in HTML, specify shortcuts via the "accesskey" attribute.

10.5 Until user agents (including assistive technologies) render adjacent links distinctly, include non-link, printable characters (surrounded by spaces) between adjacent links.

11.3 Provide information so that users may receive documents according to their preferences (e.g., language, content type, etc.).

12.1 Title each frame to facilitate frame identification and navigation.

12.2 Describe the purpose of frames and how frames relate to each other if it is not obvious by frame titles alone.

12.3 Divide large blocks of information into more manageable groups where natural and appropriate.

13.1 Clearly identify the target of each link.

13.8 Place distinguishing information at the beginning of headings, paragraphs, lists, etc.

13.9 Provide information about document collections (i.e., documents comprising multiple pages).

14.1 Use the clearest and simplest language appropriate for a site's content.

14.2 Supplement text with graphic or auditory presentations where they will facilitate comprehension of the page.

Audio

The potential benefit of auditory interaction for users with disabilities is great, and computing technology is at a point at which tremendous strides can be made. It is therefore important that interaction design be infused with an understanding of the implications and ramifications of new technological developments.

Section 508 includes the following guidelines for the application of audio in electronic and information technology:

1194.22 Web-based intranet and internet information and applications.

(b) Equivalent alternatives for any multi-media presentation shall be synchronized with the presentation.

§ 1194.24 Video and multimedia products.

(c) All training and informational video and multimedia productions which support the agency's mission, regardless of format, that contain speech or other audio information necessary for the comprehension of the content, shall be open or closed captioned.

(e) Display or presentation of alternate text presentation or audio descriptions shall be user-selectable unless permanent.

§ 1194.25 Self contained, closed products.

(e) When products provide auditory output, the audio signal shall be provided at a standard signal level through an industry standard connector that will allow for private listening. The product must provide the ability to interrupt, pause, and restart the audio at anytime.

(f) When products deliver voice output in a public area, incremental volume control shall be provided with output amplification up to a level of at least 65 dB. Where the ambient noise level of the environment is above 45 dB, a volume gain of at least 20 dB above the ambient level shall be user selectable. A function shall be provided to automatically reset the volume to the default level after every use.

§ 1194.31 Functional performance criteria.

(b) At least one mode of operation and information retrieval that does not require user hearing shall be provided, or support for assistive technology used by people who are deaf or hard of hearing shall be provided.

(d) Where audio information is important for the use of a product, at least one mode of operation and information retrieval shall be provided in an enhanced auditory fashion, or support for assistive hearing devices shall be provided.

(e) At least one mode of operation and information retrieval that does not require user speech shall be provided, or support for assistive technology used by people with disabilities shall be provided.

Section 508 provides the following guideline for the use of audio on Web pages:

§ 1194.22 Web-based intranet and internet information and applications.

(k) A text-only page, with equivalent information or functionality, shall be provided to make a web site comply with the provisions of this part, when compliance cannot be accomplished in any other way. The content of the text-only page shall be updated whenever the primary page changes.

The Web Content Accessibility Guidelines include the following checkpoint for the use of audio on the Web:

1.1 Provide a text equivalent for every non-text element (e.g., via "alt", "longdesc", or in element content). *This includes*: images, graphical representations of text (including symbols), image map regions, animations (e.g., animated GIFs), applets and programmatic objects, ASCII art, frames, scripts, images used as list bullets, spacers, graphical buttons, sounds (played with or without user interaction), stand-alone audio files, audio tracks of video, and video.

We lives in an age in which much of the information we receive is disseminated digitally, and access to that information is obtained through digital user interfaces. We are just becoming aware how important it is for everyone to be able to access this information regardless of personal characteristics or handicapping conditions.

As we have seen in this appendix, industry guidelines and government legislation are evolving that strive to create a level playing field in the area of information accessibility. It is essential that these concerns be reflected in the design of digital information artifacts so that significant portions of society are not relegated to second class citizenship in this information age. The effort required to make user interfaces more accessible are not overwhelming and doing so will benefit not only people with disabilities but other users as well.

Input/Output Devices

Vision is our most highly developed sense and the most common channel of communication between people and computers. All methods of human–computer interaction, excluding certain forms of invisible computing, include some type of visual display. These can range from the common CRT or LCD screens found on desktop and laptop computers to the screenless virtual retinal display systems that use images projected onto the pupil with laser beams and are found in some immersive virtual reality environments.

Displays

There are many existing as well as emerging display configurations. Each technology has certain advantages and disadvantages; however, they all must adhere to the human visual system's capacities and limitations. To choose the most appropriate display solution for a particular design situation, a thorough knowledge of the various technologies and their characteristics and structural elements is required.

We now look at some of the more common displays, such as the CRTs and LCDs, and explore the emerging display technologies used in the ambient and wearable computing environments.

Resolution

Most screen-based displays are rated according to maximum pixel resolution: number of pixels per line, V, by number of lines per screen, H. The maximum resolution that is possible on a display depends on screen dimensions and graphic card memory.

Web authors are often interested in the screen resolution available to their prospective audience and try to design their Web sites to comply with the most common format. There are many resources that try to track this kind of information, but it is difficult to make clear determinations without actually putting a Web site online and tracking the users over time. However, it is clear that screen resolutions are increasing, and most users fall within the 800×600 to 1024×768 range.

Bit Depth

Each pixel on a display has a prescribed potential for the number of color variation levels it is capable of displaying; this is called color depth. Color depth is determined by the amount of memory on the graphics card and is designated by the number of bits that can be allocated to each pixel, or bit depth.

Higher screen resolutions require more pixels, increasing the number of overall pixels and, therefore, the amount of memory required to support the resolution and color depth.

Cathode Ray Tubes

The CRT screens used for most desktop computer stations are like television monitors. They require glass vacuum tubes that are deep enough to contain the necessary components such as anodes, cathodes, and the magnetic coils that direct the cathode rays (beams of high-speed electrons) to the phosphor-coated surface of the screen (Figure C.1).

Figure C.1 Cathode ray tube display.

CRTs have certain advantages: they have crisp, clear images that can easily handle the refresh rate requirements of high-speed video, and they are not subject to motion artifacts. They offer rich color and grayscale images as well as high resolutions and contrast levels and can represent pure black by stopping all electron emissions. They are generally used by graphic-intensive industries as the basic reference standard for color calibrations. Because they have been around for such a long time, they are also relatively inexpensive.

CRTs also have certain disadvantages. They are generally heavy and emit heat when in use. They consume a great deal of electricity and maintain an electrical charge for long periods after they are turned off. They also have a large footprint, requiring about as much depth as the diagonal tube size.

CRTs are also subject to glare, both direct and indirect. As a general rule, monitors of any sort should not be placed in front of a light source such as a lamp or window. The light emanating from a source directly in back of a monitor would cause the screen to fade and the colors to wash out.

However, a light source placed behind the user may reflect off the glass surface of a monitor, causing an indirect glare that would also diminish the visibility of the screen. Although the ambient lighting conditions might be beyond the control of the interaction designer, an understanding of the possible ambient conditions can help to avoid problematic interface designs.

Liquid Crystal Displays

Liquid crystal displays (LCDs) are thin and flat (Figure C.2). Their energy consumption is low, which makes them ideal for use in portable computing devices. The LCD pixel elements are made of liquid crystals suspended between two transparent glass layers with indium tin oxide (ITO) electrodes and two polarizing filters. When an electric charge is passed through the electrodes above the crystals, they twist, allowing light waves to either pass through the polarizing filters or causing them to be partially or completely blocked and therefore unlit.

Color LCDs divide each pixel into three subpixel cells that are colored with red, green, and blue filters. Microsoft's ClearType technology takes advantage of this subpixel resolution and affords finer-grained anti-aliasing.

LCDs are very bright and suitable for well-lit environments. They are lightweight, use little energy, do not give off heat, and have a small footprint so they save desk space, which can be a significant issue in cramped offices and work spaces.

LCD displays are not capable of representing pure black—they cannot technically eliminate all of the backlight from escaping. Lower-end displays also pose issues of limited viewing angle. These displays get darker and color reliability decreases when seen from a side angle, which may actually be beneficial for public

Figure C.2 Liquid crystal display.

displays such as ATMs where privacy is important. LCDs are also currently more expensive than CRTs; however, this may change as the technology matures.

Touchscreens

Touchscreens allow users to point to and manipulate screen objects directly, without using a mouse or other indirect manipulation device. They are found in ATMs and PDAs and are sometimes operated through the use of a stylus. Touchscreens are also popular in industrial environments in which keyboards and external mouse devices would be inappropriate.

Interactive Whiteboards

An interactive whiteboard (IW) is a whiteboard with computer functionality, or a large board connected to a computer and a digital projector. The screen image is projected on the board, and the user can manipulate the screen controls by touching the whiteboard.

The most common IWs are the SMART Boards from SMART Technologies. These devices come in front and rear projection models as well as overlays for existing plasma displays. The bundled software enables touch-based screen control and allows the user to write on the board using special pens or even a finger. The software also has the capacity for static and dynamic screen captures using standard graph and video formats. IWs are easy to set up and use and have been shown to be beneficial for collaborative work and educational environments.

Heads-Up Displays

Heads-up displays (HUDs) project computer-generated information directly to the user's visual field while allowing simultaneous normal viewing of the environment. This is important in mission-critical environments in which attention must be kept on critical objects within our foveal vision but we must also have access to information displayed at other locations in the environment.

HUDs have traditionally been fixed-screen displays located in front of the user's eyes. They were developed for military aviation to make critical aircraft information more accessible to the pilot and have been in use for more than 30 years. HUDs project related but not "visually registered" information about the pilot's actual environment or the state of the aircraft's controls.

SportVue produces a HUD for motorcyclists that uses two small, lightweight components: a wireless HMD that is mounted on the helmet visor and a motorcycle sending unit (MSU) that is mounted on the motorcycle. The system sends information such as speed, RPM, and gear position and presents it in real time to the rider's normal field of view (Figure C.3a).

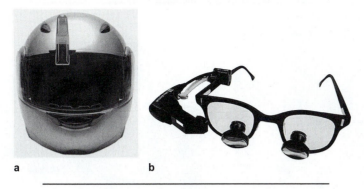

Figure C.3 (a) Sportvue MC1 motorcycle helmet heads-up display. (b) MicroOptical MD-6 Critical Data Viewer.

MicroOptical produces a number of HUD systems for various applications such as medical and military uses as well as for the portable video consumer market. The MD-6 Critical Data Viewer (Figure C.3b) works in conjunction with patient-monitoring equipment and displays vital signs, catheter lab images, or other critical data in a floating image within the clinician's field of vision, allowing him or her to monitor the patient without distraction.

Head-Mounted Displays

HMDs use small LCD or CRT screens mounted on a support that is worn on the head and situated a few centimeters from the user's eyes (Figure C.4). These displays are used by both augmented reality (AR) and virtual reality (VR) systems.

There are two ways in which virtual and real images can be blended to create an AR environment—video-see-through and optical-see-through. Video-see-through systems use video cameras to capture the real-world view and then feed it back to the user after it is combined with the virtual information. This can be

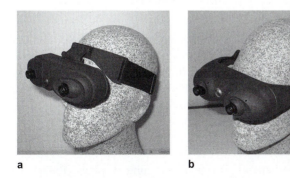

Figure C.4 (a) ARvision-3D_HMD by Trivisio. (b) ARvision-3D_Goggles by Trivisio.

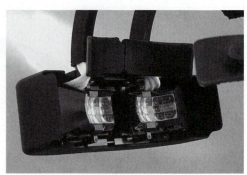

Figure C.5   piSight Virtual Reality (VR) system.

done by using color keying (traditional blue screen techniques) in which the background of the virtual scene is made transparent so the real view shows through or by using depth information to mix the two scenes.

Optical-see-through systems use optical combiners to mix the computer-generated information with the real-world view the user has through the HMD. Both systems use head tracking to align (register) the virtual and real-world objects.

The ARvision-3D HUD (and Goggle version) shown in Figure C.4 is a video see-through system. It uses two liquid-crystal-on-silicon (LCOS) displays that offer 800/600 resolution and 18-bit display colors. The ARvision-3D HUD has a real field of view of 40 degrees diagonally, which, according to the manufacturer, is like watching a 57-inch screen from a distance of 2 meters. Trivisio offers HMDs for mixed reality, virtual reality, and augmented reality environments. Suggested applications for these systems range from 3D visualizations of new designs (cars, buildings, boats, etc.) to design and visualization of architectural projects, to reconstruction of ancient ruins and monuments. Trivisio is currently prototyping optical see-through systems.

The piSight system by Sensics (Figure C.5) offers full 3D immersion from 82 to 180 degrees diagonally with an effective 2400/1720 resolution and 24-bit color. The system uses a microdisplay array forming a concave display that wraps around the user's eyes. Due to the system's panoramic immersion, it can be compared with CAVE environments (see later discussion).

Virtual Retinal Displays

Virtual retinal displays (VRDs) or retinal scanning displays (RSDs) use laser technology to scan light directly onto the retina. The Virtual Retinal Display Group at Hit Lab at the University of Washington developed two versions of their system, a bench-mounted unit that displays a full-color VGA (640 × 480) image with a

a   b

Figure C.6 **(a) CAVE automated virtual environment at the National Center for Supercomputing Applications (NCSA). (b) Sketching a virtual world in the VR design tool ShadowLight.**
Photographs and ShadowLight application courtesy of Kalev Leetaru.

60-Hz refresh rate, and a portable unit, housed in a briefcase, that is capable of displaying a monochrome VGA image.

CAVE

The CAVE by Fakespace Systems is a small room with three walls and a floor (Figure C.6). The CAVE system uses four CRT/DLP projectors placed 10 feet behind the walls, which display high-resolution images onto the four surfaces.

The user wears special infrared Crystal Eyes active stereo LCD shutter glasses that create a stereoscopic impression of the images. The computer sends two images of the walls to the user, one for the left eye and one for the right eye each at 48 frames per second (fps), providing a combined 96-fps image. The glasses are designed to distinguish between the images, causing one eye shutter to go opaque when an image is projected on the other eye. This happens so fast that the images are reconciled by the user's mind as a 3D representation of the projected object.

Because the user's head is tracked in six DOF the computer can generate images that respond to his or her position as well as orientation. The user, therefore, can examine a virtual object from any angle.

There are a number of CAVE systems. They range from reconfigurable systems to six-sided systems that create a seamless cube after the user enters. A comprehensive list can be found on the Fakespace Web site at http://www.fakespacesystems. com/displays.htm.

Pointing Devices

There are a number of different pointing devices, each with its own attributes and limitations. They generally do not obscure the user's view of the screen, and, although they involve movement on a separate plane (the desk as opposed to the screen), they follow a close mapping between the hand's movements and the cursor's position.

For beginners and people with motor disabilities, however, the required movement may be difficult or even impossible, and, as with most handheld devices, prolonged use of any of these can cause fatigue or discomfort.

Let's look at some of the more common pointing devices and see what issues are involved in their use.

Mouse

The original and still most common pointing device is the mouse (Figure C.7). There are different types of mouse devices, such as the optical or cordless mouse, however, these all function in more or less the same way. These devices are used to control the cursor that is used to select and activate particular screen elements. The mouse is not an isomorphic device, in that the cursor moves proportionally to the movement of the mouse and not in a one-to-one relationship.

Mouse devices can have one to three buttons that offer preprogrammed or user-programmable functionality. They might also have a scroll wheel, which makes scrolling more efficient because the user does not have to first locate the scrollbar, access it with the cursor, and activate it by moving the mouse.

Mouse pointers require a clean, flat, dedicated work space, and their operation requires the user to remove his or hands from the keyboard. This can become tedious for someone who must do a great deal of typing. This is why most typists learn the keyboard shortcuts for the most common pointing operations, such as selection, copy and paste, save, and others.

Because these devices are peripheral to the computer, they are not well suited to public environments in which supervision is not possible. Their mechanisms are relatively simple, yet they do break and are subject to theft.

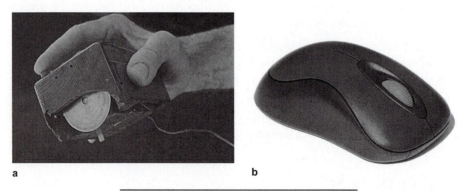

a   b

**Figure C.7 (a) The first mouse, created by D. Engelbart.
(b) A wireless laser mouse with scroll wheel.**

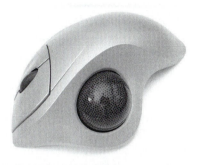

Figure C.8 Trackball with two buttons and a scroll wheel.

Trackballs

Trackballs are basically inverted mouse devices (Figure C.8). Instead of moving the mouse on the desktop, the user rotates a small ball that is built into the device. It is difficult for users, however, to relate distances on the screen to the amount of rotation of the ball.

Trackballs do not need much desk space because the ball is embedded. These devices can also be easily built into the computer's console, eliminating the risk of theft in public spaces.

Touchpads

A touchpad is a pointing device more commonly found on portable computers (Figure C.9). It is a small, depressed area just below the keyboard, which usually has a few associated buttons above or below with the same functionality as standard mouse buttons. Single- and double-clicking can also be accomplished by tapping on the pad.

Figure C.9 Touchpad.

Figure C.10 Logitech Freedom 2.4-GHz cordless joystick.

A touchpad is not easily damaged or stolen when it is embedded in the computer. Its proximity to the keys means that the user does not have to move too far to use it. It is also relatively small and does not require large finger movements.

Joysticks

Joystick controllers were originally used in aircraft to control the ailerons and elevators. They became popular during the 1980s for use with computer games. A joystick is basically a stick that pivots on one end and sends coordinates to the computer. Most joysticks have two axes, but some have three (Figure C.10).

Digital joysticks are limited to four coordinate directions with the addition of up and down movements. Analog joysticks are capable of continuous-state coordinate movement and are becoming more popular. Some joysticks are also capable of delivering haptic feedback, a feature that is gaining popularity in computer gaming environments.

Pointing Sticks

The pointing stick is a small isometric joystick used in some laptop computer models (Figure C.11). It is usually located in the middle of the keyboard and is combined with two "mouse" buttons located below the spacebar. It senses applied force and direction to determine the speed and location of the cursor.

The pointing stick is convenient for typists who find it cumbersome to lift their hands from the keyboard; however, it is becoming less common in recent laptop models.

Stylus

A stylus is a thin, pen-shaped plastic stick that is used with PDAs to point at and click screen controls, such as buttons, checkboxes, and hyperlinks. It is generally used to avoid the deleterious effects of the skin's natural oils on the screen that would occur from using a finger to point and click. It is also used on digitizing tablets to produce brush strokes and control screen elements.

Figure C.11 Pointing stick.

Figure C.12 Graphic tablet, stylus, and screen.

Graphic Tablet

A graphic tablet is a pressure-sensitive pad that is used with a stylus (Figure C.12). It is generally used with drawing and painting programs and is designed to create a more natural interaction for the creation of hand-drawn images.

The stylus controls the cursor during line creation or brush strokes and translates the pressure according to settings within the program, for example, varying the width or density of the brush stroke. The Wacom tablet devices manufactured by the Wacom Company are some of the more common devices used by graphics professionals.

Eye Tracking

A novel approach to pointing and clicking interaction is eye-gaze tracking. This is done by using sensors to track the user's eye and translate its movement to the screen controls. The user can move the cursor to any location on the screen and activate custom controls by fixating his or her gaze for a prescribed duration. These systems can be used in common OS environments and have significant implications for people with limited functionality in their arms or hands.

They can also be used by search engine optimizers to analyze how a Web site visitor explores a Web page. The user's focus and duration of attention can be recorded and later displayed as a color-coded map showing the areas of high or low interest.

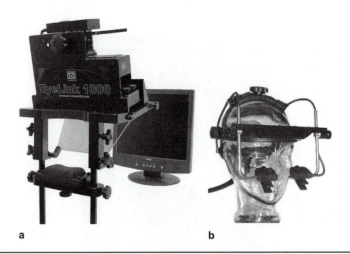

a   b

Figure C.13   (a) EyeLink® 2K, Tower Mount. (b) EyeLink® II Head Mounted Binocular Video-based Eye Tracking Systems.

Copyright © SR Research, Ltd.

SR Research produces various eye-tracking systems such as the EyeLink II shown in Figure C.13. This system uses three miniature head-mounted high-speed cameras to capture corneal reflections in combination with pupil tracking. It also contains an optical head-tracking camera that allows tracking of the subject's point of gaze.

Head Tracking

A related technology to eye tracking is head tracking. The user wears a small reflective wafer on his or head that is tracked by a receiver placed on top of the computer screen. The software uses the position of the wafer to manipulate the position of the cursor. Duration can be interpreted as a click when the user fixates on one screen location.

The SmartNAV™ is a head-tracking system by NaturalPoint® (Figure C.14). It plugs into a USB port and uses an infrared (IR) camera to track the user's head movements. The wafer can be worn on the forehead, glasses or hat. The system provides up to 120-fps tracking and a pixel precise resolution of 101,000 pixels. This type of hands-free cursor control system can be beneficial for people with carpal tunnel syndrome, repetitive strain injury or assistive technology needs.

NaturalPoint also makes the TrackIR™, which is a head-tracking system that enables hands-free control of PC game interfaces and simulation applications. This system is gaining popularity among game players who want to free their hands to manipulate many of the game controls while letting the TrackIR™ system control navigation and viewer perspective within the virtual environment.

Figure C.14   NaturalPoint® head-tracking system.

Keyboards

The keyboard is one of the most common I/O peripherals. It is a descendent of the typewriter and presents an almost universally understandable interface. The basic functions of a keyboard are for the most part completely intuitive: the user presses the keys, and text appears on the screen. Keyboards were a natural choice for the early alphanumeric display technologies, and in modified formats are even appropriate for wearable computing systems.

Keyboard Layout

The most common layout of keys is the QWERTY format, which was created in the late nineteenth century and named after the first six keys of the top left row of alphabetic keys. Most QWERTY keyboards use the same layout for the alphanumeric keys, but they often differ from country to country in terms of the location of the special characters.

The Dvorak Simplified Keyboard was designed by August Dvorak and William Dealey in the 1920s and 1930s (Figure C.15). It is based on studies of letter frequencies and the physiology of the human hand and took approximately 12 years to design. The Dvorak system is purported to be superior to the QWERTY layout in terms of speed and fatigue, although studies have not proven this to be true.

There are a few versions of the Dvorak layout; some are designed for one-hand typing (an important feature for users with disabilities or people who need to use a mouse while they type), and others are designed to address different national variations based on the letter frequencies of those languages.

Number Pads

Number pads can be found on many devices, such as calculators, cell phones, PDAs, and ATM machines. There are two configurations: the calculator format

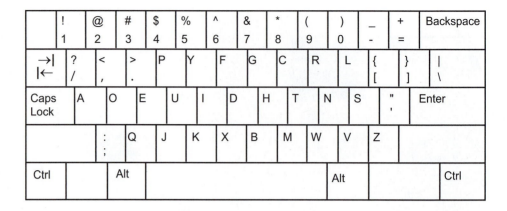

Figure C.15 Dvorak keyboard layout.

with the numbers starting on the bottom row and then proceeding upward left to right (Figure C.16a), and the telephone configuration with the numbers going left to right, starting at the top row and progressing downward (Figure C.16b).

Telephone number pads should really be considered alphanumeric because they also contain the letters of the alphabet. There are three letters assigned to each number starting with the number two. This configuration has become a common way to enter text due to the popularity of the short message service (SMS) or text messaging (texting) on cell phones.

Chorded Keyboards

Chorded keyboards (also called chording or chord keyboards) are used by pressing more than one key simultaneously (Figure C.17). The most common type of chorded keyboard is the stenograph machine used to transcribe court proceedings. It is a two-handed device that uses key combinations to represent a

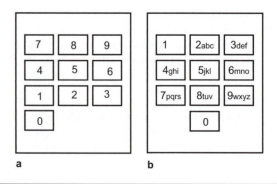

Figure C.16 (a) Calculator number pad. (b) Telephone alphanumeric pad.

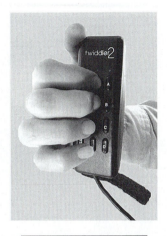

Figure C.17 Handykey Twiddler.

special type of shorthand. Chorded keyboards such as the Twiddler by the Handykey Corporation (Figure C.17) or the Bellaire Cykey are ideal for wearable computing environments.

The basic concept behind chorded keyboards is that each keystroke represents a prescribed entity, and that vocabularies can be created by combining any number of keystrokes. The only limitation on the vocabulary is the number of possible key combinations, which is restricted by the number of keys and the number of fingers used.

Chorded keyboards have certain advantages:

- They are small, which makes them appropriate for wearable and mobile Computing environments.
- They can be used with one hand, which is advantageous for disabled users or people who need to use other devices simultaneously.
- Their information throughput is high—one stroke can represent a great deal of information.
- The hand remains in a fixed position, which reduces the need to locate keys that do not fall under the fingers and eliminates reaching.
- They can be used in any posture—while standing, sitting, or walking—and they do not have to be placed on a flat, horizontal surface.
- They can be placed at any location, and do not have to be placed in front of the monitor.

Chorded keyboards have certain disadvantages:

- They are not self-referential—they do not provided cues for operation; the user must be able to touch-type.

Figure C.18 The virtual keyboard by VKB Inc.

- There is a high cognitive overhead—key combinations must be memorized, and symbol representations must be learned.
- There is a steep learning curve—it can take time to become proficient.

Virtual Keyboards

A novel approach to keyboard design is the virtual keyboard by VKB Inc. (Figure C.18). The virtual keyboard is used with wireless handhelds and projects a full-size, fully functional keyboard on any flat surface. It affords touch-typing at normal speeds.

As we have seen in Chapter 1, the 5W + H heuristic of computing paradigms involves interdependencies that can help interaction designers make choices about interface characteristics and components. To choose the proper I/O devices for an interface requires a knowledge of the user's abilities and limitations as well as other factors such as computing environment and user tasks to name a few.

Choosing the proper I/O device also requires a knowledge of the devices themselves. We need to understand the tasks and environments for which they are the most appropriate. This is an area, however, of ongoing and continual progress. As new computing innovations enter the market place there arise new opportunities to make our interaction designs more effective and efficient.

References

Abowd, G. and Beale, R. 1991. Users, systems and interfaces: A unifying framework for interaction. In Proceedings of HCI '91: People and Computers VI, D. Diaper and N. Hammond, Eds. 73-87.

Accot, J., & Zhai, S. (2003, April). *Refining Fitts' law models for bivariate pointing.* Paper presented at Human Factors in Computing Systems, Ft. Lauderdale, FL.

Adler, M. J., & van Doren, C. (1972). *How to read a book.* New York: Simon & Schuster.

Alhalabi, M. O., & Horiguchi, S. (2001, May). *Tele-handshake: Cooperative haptic shared virtual environment.* Paper presented at Eurohaptics 2001, Birmingham, England.

Amara, F., & Portaneri, F. (1996). Arabization of graphical user interfaces. In E. del Galdo & J. Nielsen (Eds.), *International user interfaces.* New York: Wiley.

Ankrum, D. R. (1996). Viewing distance at computer workstations. *WorkPlace Ergonomics, 2*(5), 10–12.

Apple Computer Inc. (2007). *Apple Human Interface Guidelines.* Retrieved January 12, 2007, from http://developer.apple.com/documentation/UserExperience/Conceptual/OSXHIGuidelines/index.html.

Arons, B. (1991). *Hyperspeech: Navigating in speech-only hypermedia.* Paper presented at the Proceedings of the Third Annual ACM Conference on Hypertext, San Antonio, TX.

Arons, B. (1997). SpeechSkimmer: A system for interactively skimming recorded speech. *ACM Transactions on Human–Computer Interaction (TOCHI), 4*(1), 3–38.

Asakawa, C., Takagi, H., Ino, S., & Ifukube, T. (2002). *Auditory and tactile interfaces for representing the visual effects on the Web.* Paper presented at the Proceedings of the Fifth International ACM SIGCAPH Conference on Assistive Technologies, Edinburgh, Scotland.

Bailey, R. W. (2002, December). Optimal line length: Research supporting how line length affects usability. *User Interface Design Monthly Update, Web Usability.* Retrieved October 21, 2005, from http://www.webusability.com/article_line_length_12_2002.htm.

Baker, J. R. (2003). The impact of paging vs. scrolling on reading online text sassages [Electronic Version]. *Usability News, 5.* Retrieved December 23, 2006, from http://psychology.wichita.edu/surl/usabilitynews/51/paging_scrolling.htm.

Barnum, C. M. (2002). *Usability testing and research.* New York: Pearson Education.

Baumeister, L. K., John, B. E., & Byrne, M. D. (2000, April). *A comparison of tools for building GOMS models.* Paper presented at the SIGCHI Conference on Human Factors in Computing Systems, The Hague, Netherlands.

Baxter, W., Scheib, V., Lin, V. M. C., & Manocha, D. (2001). DAB: Interactive Haptic Painting with 3D Virtual Brushes. *Proceedings of ACM SIGGRAPH 01,* 461–468.

Beaudouin-Lafon, M., & Conversy, S. (1996). Auditory illusions for audio feedback. In *Conference companion on human factors in computing systems: common ground* (pp. 299–300). Vancouver, Canada: Conference on Human Factors in Computing Systems.

Beaudouin-Lafon, M., & Mackay, W. (2002). Prototyping tools and techniques. In *The human–computer interaction handbook: Fundamentals, evolving technologies and emerging applications* (pp. 1006–1031). Mahwah, NJ: Lawrence Erlbaum Associates.

Bejczy, A., & Salisbury, K. (1980). Kinematic coupling between operator and remote manipulator. *Advances in Computer Technology, 1*, 197–211.

Bernard, M., Fernandez, M., & Hull, S. (2002). The effects of line length on children and adults' online reading performance. *Usability News, 4*(2). Available: http://psychology. wichita.edu/surl/usabilitynews/42/text_length.htm.

Beyer, H., & Holzblatt, K. (1998). *Contextual design: Defining customer-centered systems.* San Francisco: Morgan-Kaufmann.

Biederman, I. (1987). Recognition by components: A theory of human image understanding. *Psychological Review, 94*, 115–147.

Blattner, M. M., Sumikawa, D. A., & Greenberg, R. (1989). Earcons and icons: Their structure and common design principles. *Human–Computer Interaction, 4*, 11–44.

Bliss, C. K. (1965). *Semantography (Blissymbolics).* Sidney: Semantography Press.

Bohem, B. W. (1988). A spiral model of software development and enhancement. *IEEE Computer Graphics and Applications, 21*(5), 61–72.

Bouma, H. (1980). Visual reading processes and the quality of text displays. In E. Grandjean & E. Vigliani (Eds.), *Ergonomic aspects of visual display terminals* (pp. 101–114). London: Taylor & Francis.

Brewster, S. (2000, October). Final report: principles for improving interaction in telephone-based interfaces. Retrieved November 4, 2005, from http://www.dcs.gla.ac.uk/ ~stephen/research/telephone/Telephone_project_final_report.pdf.

Brewster, S. A. (2003). Nonspeech auditory output. In J. Jacko & A. Sears (Eds.), *The human–computer interaction handbook: Fundamentals, evolving technologies and emerging applications* (pp. 221–237). Mahwah, NJ: Lawrence Erlbaum Associates.

Brooks, F. P., Jr., Ouh-Young, M., Batter, J. J., & Kilpatrick, P. J. (1990). GROPE-I haptic displays for scientific visualization. *Computer Graphics, 24*(4), 759–763.

Bruce, M., & Foster, J. J. (1982). The visibility of colored characters on colored backgrounds in viewdata displays. *Visible Language, 16*, 382–390.

Burdea, G. C. (1996). *Force and touch feedback for VR.* New York: Wiley.

Bush, V. (1945). As we may think. *Atlantic Monthly, 176*(1), 101–108.

Buxton, W. A. S. (1990). A three-state model of graphical input. In D. Diaper, D. J. Gilmore, G. Cockton & B. Shackel (Eds.), *Human–computer interaction—INTERACT '90* (pp. 449–456). Amsterdam: Elsevier Science.

Byrne, M. D. (1993). *Using icons to find documents: Simplicity is critical.* Paper presented at the ACM INTERCHI'93 Conference on Human Factors in Computing Systems, Amsterdam.

Card, S. K., Moran, T. P., & Newell, A. (1983). *The psychology of human–computer interaction.* Mahwah, NJ: Lawrence Erlbaum Associates.

Carello, C., & Turvey, M. T. (2000). Rotational invariants and dynamic touch. In M. Heller (Ed.), *Representation and blindness.* London: Oxford University Press.

Carlin, A. S., Hoffman, H. G., & Weghorst, S. (1997). Virtual reality and tactile augmentation in the treatment of spider phobia: A case study. *Behavior Research and Therapy, 35*, 153–158.

Castelhano, M. S., & Muter, P. (2001). Optimizing the reading of electronic text using rapid serial visual presentation. *Behaviour & Information Technology, 20*(4), 237–247.

Chen, L., & Jin, W. (1996). A Chinese text display supported by an algorithm for Chinese segmentation. In E. del Galdo & J. Nielsen (Eds.), *International user interfaces* (pp. 151–177). New York: Wiley.

Cherry, E. C. (1953). Some experiments on the recognition of speech, with one and two ears. *Journal of the Acoustic Society of America, 25*, 975–979.

CMS. (2003). *The Chicago manual of style* (15th ed.). Chicago: University of Chicago Press.

Cohen, B., & Kirman, J. H. (1986). Vibrotactile frequency discrimination at short durations. *Journal of General Psychology, 113*(2), 179–186.

Comber, T., & Maltby, J. R. (1997). *Layout complexity: Does it measure usability?* Paper presented at the INTERACT'97, Atlanta, GA.

Conversy, S. (1998, April). *Wind and wave auditory icons for monitoring continuous processes.* Paper presented at the CHI 98 Conference Summary on Human Factors in Computing Systems, Los Angeles.

Cooper, A., & Reimann, R. M. (2003). *About Face 2.0: The essentials of interaction design.* New York: Wiley.

Craik, K. J. W. (1943). *The nature of exploration.* London: Cambridge University Press.

DASDA. (2006). Design-for-all.info. Retrieved December 11, 2006, from http://www.design-for-all.info.

del Galdo, E., & Nielsen, J. (1996). *International user interfaces.* New York: Wiley.

Dix, A., Finlay, J., Abowd, G., & Beale, R. (1998). *Human–computer interaction* (2nd ed.). Upper Saddle River, NJ: Prentice Hall.

Dosher, J., Lee, G., & Hannaford, B. (2001). Detection thresholds for small haptic effects. In M. L. McLaughlin, J. P. Hespanha, & G. S. Sukhatme (Eds.), *Touch in virtual environments.* Upper Saddle River, NJ: Prentice Hall.

Dreyfuss, H. (1972). *Symbol sourcebook—An authoritative guide to international graphic symbols.* New York: McGraw-Hill.

DSO. (2006, November 4). About collaborative computing: About this area. *IEEE Distributed Systems Online.* Available http://dsonline.computer.org/portal/site/dsonline/menuitem. 9ed3d9924aeb0dcd82ccc6716bbe36ec/index.jsp?&pName=dso_level1&path=dsonline/ topics/collaborative&file=about.xml&xsl=article.xsl&.

Duchnicky, J. L., & Kolers, P. A. (1983). Readability of text scrolled on visual display terminals as a function of window size. *Human Factors, 25*, 683–692.

Dumas, J., & Redish, J. (1999). *A practical guide to usability testing* (Rev. ed.). Exeter, England: Intellect.

Dyson, M. C., & Haselgrove, M. (2001). The influence of reading speed and line length on the effectiveness of reading from a screen. *International Journal of Human–Computer Studies, 54*, 585–612.

Dyson, M. C., & Kipping, G. J. (1998). The effects of line length and method of movement on patterns of reading from screen. *Visible Language, 32*, 150–181.

EDeAN. (2005). European Design for All e-Accessibility Network. Retrieved July 8, 2005, from http://www.e–accessibility.org/design–for–all.htm.

EIDD. (2006). European Institute for Design and Disability. Retrieved December 11, 2006, from http://www.design-for-all.org.

Engelbart, D. (1968). The mother of all demos. Retrieved Sept. 12, 2005, from http://sloan.stanford.edu/MouseSite/1968Demo.html.

Ergonomics Society. (2005). Retrieved July 31, 2005 from http://www.ergonomics.org.uk/index.htm.

Faineteau, H., Gentaz, E., & Viviani, P. (2003). The kinaesthetic perception of Euclidean distance: a study of the detour effect. Exp Brain Res., Sep; 152 (2): 166–72. Epub 2003 Jul 29.

Foner, L. N. (1999). Artificial synesthesia via sonification: A wearable augmented sensory system. *Mobile Networks and Applications, 4*(1), 75–81.

Forlines, C., Shen, C., & Buxton, B. (2005, April). *Glimpse: A novel input model for multi-level devices* (extended abstract). Paper presented at the CHI 05, Portland, OR.

Fraser, B. (1996). Color in mind. *Adobe Magazine,* 1996(November):42–48.

Freed, M., Matessa, M., Remington, R., & Vera, A. (2003). *How Apex automates CPM-GOMS.* Paper presented at the Fifth International Conference on Cognitive Modeling, Bamberg, Germany.

FusionGRID. (2005). Retrieved June 24, 2005 from http://www.fusiongrid.org/projects/

Galitz, W. O. (2002). *The essential guide to user interface design* (2nd ed.). New York: Wiley.

Gaver, W. W. (1989). The SonicFinder: An interface that uses auditory icons. *Human–Computer Interaction 4*(1), 67–94.

Gentaz, E., & Hatwell, Y. (2003). Haptic processing of spatial and material object properties. In Y. Hatwell, A. Streri, and E. Gentaz (Eds.), *Touching for knowing* (pp. 123–159). Amsterdam: John Benjamin.

Gentry, S., Wall, S., Oakley, I., & Murray-Smith, R. (2003, July). *Got rhythm? Haptic-only lead and follow dancing.* Paper presented at Eurohaptics 2003, Dublin, Ireland.

Gilkey, R. H., Simpson, B. D., & Weisenberger, J. M. (2001). Creating auditory presence. In M. J. Smith, G. Salvendy, D. Harris, & R. J. Koubek (Eds.), *Usability evaluation and interface design: Cognitive engineering, intelligent agents, and virtual reality* (Vol. 1, pp. 609–613). Mahwah, NJ: Lawrence Erlbaum Associates.

Goetz, J. P., & LeCompte, M. D. (1984). *Ethnographic and qualitative design in Educational Research.* Orlando, FL: Academic Press.

Goff, G. D. (1967). Differential discrimination of frequency of cutaneous mechanical vibration. *Journal of Experimental Psychology, 74*(2), 294–299.

Gomez, D., Burdea, G., & Langrana, N. (1995). *Integration of the Rutgers Master II in a virtual reality simulation.* Paper presented at the Proceedings of Virtual Reality Annual International Symposium '95, Research Triangle Park, NC.

Hale, K. S., & Stanney, K. M. (2004). Deriving haptic design guidelines from human physiological, psychophysical, and neurological foundation. *IEEE Computer Graphics and Applications, 24*(2), 33–39.

Hannaford, B., Wood, L., Guggisberg, B., McAffee, D., & Zak, A. (1989). *Performance evaluation of a six-axis generalized force-reflecting teleoperator.* Pasadena, CA: JPL, California Institute of Technology.

Haramundanis, K. (1996). Why icons cannot stand alone. *ACM SIGDOC Asterisk Journal of Computer Documentation, 20*(2), 1–8.

Hartson, H. R., & Hix, D. (1989). Toward empirically derived methodologies and tools for human–computer interface development. *International Journal of Man–Machine Studies, 31,* 477–494.

Hass, E. (2001). Perceptual and performance issues in the integration of virtual technologies in demanding environments. In M. J. Smith, G. Salvendy, D. Harris, & R. J. Koubek (Eds.), *Usability evaluation and interface design: Cognitive engineering, intelligent agents, and virtual reality* (pp. 843–847). Mahwah, NJ: Lawrence Erlbaum Associates.

Helbing, K. G., Jenkins, J., Kim, Y. S., & Miller, M. E. (1993). Influence of icon detail, color, and perspective on preference, recognition time, and search time. In *Proceedings of Interface '93.* Raleigh, NC: The Human Factors and Ergonomics Society.

Hoadley, E. D. (1990). Investigating the effects of color. *Communications of the ACM, 33*(2), 120–125.

Horton, W. (1994). *The icon book: Visual symbols for computer systems and documentation.* New York: Wiley.

Hutchins, E. L., Hollan, J. D., & Norman, D. A. (1986). Direct manipulation interfaces. In D. A. Norman & S. W. Draper (Eds.), *User centered system design* (pp. 87–124). Mahway, NJ: Lawrence Erlbaum Associates.

IBM. (2006). What is user-centered design? Retrieved November 4, 2006, from http://www–03.ibm.com/easy/page/2.

Jacobson, I., Christerson, M., Jonsson, P., & Övergaard, G. (1992). *Object-oriented software engineering: A use case driven approach.* Reading, MA: Addison-Wesley.

John, B. E., & Kieras, D. E. (1996). Using GOMS for user interface design and evaluation. Which technique? *ACM Transactions on Human–Computer Interaction (TOCHI), 3*(4), 287–319.

Juola, J. F., Ward, N. J., & McNamara, T. (1982). Visual search and reading of rapid, serial presentation of letter strings, words, and text. *Journal of Experimental Psychology: General, 111*, 208–227.

Kandinsky, W. (1977). *Concerning the Spiritual in Art.* New York: Dover.

Kang, J. T., & Muter, P. (1989). Reading dynamically displayed text. *Behaviour & Information Technology, 8, 1*, 33–42.

Kappers, A. M. L. (1999). Large systematic deviations in the haptic perception of parallelity. *Perception, 28*, 1001–1012.

Karat, C.-M., Vergo, J., & Nahamoo, D. (2002). Conversational interface technologies. In *The human–computer interaction handbook: Fundamentals, evolving technologies and emerging applications* (pp. 170–184). Mahwah, NJ: Lawrence Erlbaum Associates.

Kawai, Y., & Tomita, F. (2001). A support system for visually impaired persons using acoustic interface-recognition of 3-D spatial information. In M. J. Smith, G. Salvendy, D. Harris, & R. J. Koubek (Eds.), *Usability evaluation and interface design: Cognitive engineering, intelligent agents, and virtual reality* (Vol. 1, pp. 203–207). Mahwah, NJ: Lawrence Erlbaum Associates.

Kemeny, J. G. (1979). *Report of the President's Commission on the Accident at Three Mile Island. The need for change: The legacy of TMI.* Washington, DC: U.S. Government Printing Office.

Kieras, D. (2006). A guide to GOMS model usability evaluation using GOMSL and GLEAN4. Retrieved November 4, 2006, from ftp://www.eecs.umich.edu/people/kieras/GOMS/GOMSL_Guide_v4c.pdf.

Kieras, D. E. (2004). GOMS models and task analysis. In D. Diaper & N. A. Stanton (Eds.), *The handbook of task analysis for human–computer interaction* (pp. 83–116). Mahwah, NJ: Lawrence Erlbaum Associates.

Kolers, P. A., Duchnicky, R. L., & Ferguson, D. C. (1981). Eye movement measurement of readability of CRT displays. *Human Factors, 23*, 517–527.

Krug, S. (2006). *Don't make me think: A common sense approach to Web usability* (2nd ed.). Berkeley, CA: New Riders.

Krugman, H. E. (1986). Low recall, high recognition of ads. *Journal of Advertising Research, 1986* (February/March), 79–86.

Kurniawan, S. H. (2000). *A rule of thumb of icons' visual distinctiveness.* Paper presented at the Proceedings on the 2000 ACM Conference on Universal Usability, Arlington, VA.

Lai, J., & Srinivasan, S. (2001). Designed for enablement or disabled by design? Choosing the path to effective speech application design. In M. J. Smith, G. Salvendy, D. Harris, and R. Koubek (Eds.), *Usability evaluation and interface design: Cognitive engineering, intelligent agents and virtual reality* (Vol. 1, pp. 380–384). Mahwah. NJ: Lawrence Erlbaum Associates.

Lass, N. J., & Leeper, H. A. (1977). Listening rate preference: Comparison of two time alteration techniques. *Perceptual Motor Skills*, 44:1163–1168.

Licklider, J. C. R. (1968). The computer as a communication device. *Science and Technology, 76*, 21–31.

Lodding, I., & Kenneth, N. (Eds.). (1990). *Iconic interfacing, visual programming environments: Applications and issues.* Los Alamitos, CA: IEEE Computer Society Press.

Luciano, C., Banerjee, P., Florea, L., & Dawe, G. (2005, July). *Design of the ImmersiveTouch: A high-performance haptic augmented virtual reality system.* Paper presented at the 11th International Conference on Human–Computer Interaction, Las Vegas, NV.

MacKenzie, I. S. (2003). Motor behaviour models for human–computer interaction. In J. M. Carroll (Ed.), *Toward a multidisciplinary science of human–computer interaction* (pp. 27–54). San Francisco: Morgan Kaufmann.

MacKenzie, I. S., & Buxton, W. (1992, May). *Extending Fitts' law to two-dimensional tasks.* Paper presented at the SIGCHI Conference on Human Factors in Computing Systems, Monterey, CA.

MacKenzie, I. S., & Oniszczak, A. (1997). *The tactile touchpad* (extended abstract). Paper presented at the Conference on Human Factors in Computing Systems, Atlanta, GA.

Marcus, A. (1995). Principles of effective visual communication for graphical user interface design. In R. M. Baecker, R. M. Buxton, W. Grudin, & J. Grudin (Eds.), *Readings in human–computer interaction: Toward the year 2000.* San Francisco, CA: Morgan Kaufmann.

Marcus, A. (1996). Icon and symbol design issues for graphical user interfaces. In E. DelGaldo & J. Nielsen (Eds.), *International User Interfaces* (pp. 257–270). New York: Wiley.

Marcus, A. (1998). Metaphor design in user interfaces. *Journal of Computer Documentation, ACM/SIGDOC, 22*(2), 43–57.

Masson, M. E. J. (1983). Conceptual processing of text during skimming and rapid sequential reading. *Memory & Cognition, 11*, 262–274.

Mayers, B., Hudson, S. E., & Pausch, R. (2002). Past, present, and future of user interface software tools. In J. M. Carroll (Ed.), *Human–computer interaction in the new millennium* (pp. 213 – 233). Reading, MA: Addison-Wesley.

McLaughlin, M. L., Hespanha, J., & Sukhatme, G. (Eds.). (2002). *Introduction to haptics.* Upper Saddle River, NJ: Prentice Hall.

Microsoft Co. (2006). Official guidlines for user interface developers and designers [Electronic Version]. Retrieved August 30, 2006m from http://msdn.microsoft.com/library/default.asp?url=/library/en–us/dnwue/html/ch14f.asp.

Mills, C. B., & Weldon, L. J. (1987). Reading text from computer screens. *ACM Computing Surveys (CSUR), 19*(4), 329–357.

Morley, S., Petrie, H., O'Neill, A., & McNally, P. (1998, April). *Auditory navigation in hyperspace: design and evaluation of a no—visual hypermedia system for blind users.* Paper presented at the Proceedings of the Third International ACM Conference on Assistive Technologies, Marina del Rey, CA.

Moyes, J. (1994, April). *When users do and don't rely on icon shape.* Paper presented at Human Factors in Computing Systems, Boston.

Murch, G. M. (1987). Color graphics: Blessing or ballyhoo? In R. M. Baecker, J. Grudin, W. A. S. Buxton, & S. Greenberg (Eds.), *Readings in human–computer interaction: Toward the year 2000* (2nd ed., pp. 442–443). San Mateo, CA: Morgan Kaufmann.

Murray, C. D., Arnold, P., & Thornton, B. (2000). Presence accompanying induced hearing loss: Implications for immersive virtual environments. *Presence: Teleoperators and Virtual Environments, 9,* 137–148.

Mynatt, E. D. (1994). Designing with auditory icons: how well do we identify auditory cues? *Conference companion to the ACM conference on human factors in computing systems* (pp. 269–270). Boston: ACM Press.

Nakamura, N., & Fukui, Y. (2003). *Development of human navigation system "HapticNavi" using GyroCube.* Paper presented at the XVth Triennial Congress of the International Ergonomics Association, Seoul, South Korea.

Neurath, M. (1972). ISOTYPE education through the eye. In H. Dreyfuss (Ed.), *Symbol sourcebook—An authoritative guide to international graphic symbols* (pp. 24–25). New York: McGraw-Hill.

Nielsen, J. (1994). Guerrilla HCI: Using discount usability engineering to penetrate the intimidation barrier. Retrieved May 5, 2006, from http://www.useit.com/papers/guerrilla_hci.html.

Nielsen, J. (2003). Usability 101: Introduction to usability. *Alertbox.* Retrieved April 26, 2006, from http://www.useit.com/alertbox/20030825.html.

Nielsen, J. (2004). Guidelines for visualizing links. *Alertbox.* Retrieved December 22, 2006, from http://www.useit.com/alertbox/20040510.html.

Norman, D. (1990). *The design of everyday things.* New York: Doubleday/Currency.

Norman, D. (1997). How might people interact with agents? In J. Bradshaw (Ed.), *Software agents.* Menlo Park, CA: AAAI Press/Cambridge, MA: MIT Press.

Norman, D. A. (1998). *The invisible computer.* Cambridge, MA: MIT Press.

O'Hara, K., Sellen, A. J., & Bentley, R. (1999). Supporting memory for spatial location while reading from small displays. In *Proceedings of CHI '99 Conference on Human Factors in Computing Systems*, Pittsburgh, PA.

Ohlsson, K., Nilsson, L., & Ronnberg, J. (1981). Speed and accuracy in scanning as a function of combinations of text and background colors. *International Journal of Man–Machine Studies, 14,* 215–222.

Olson, J. R., & Olson, G. M. (1990). The growth of cognitive modeling in human–computer interaction since GOMS. *Human–Computer Interaction, 5,* 221–265.

O'Modhrain, S., & Gillespie, R. B. (1997, April). *The Moose: A haptic user interface for blind persons.* Paper presented at the Proceedings of the WWW6, Santa Clara, CA.

Ouh-Young, M., Pique, M., Hughes, J., Srinivasan, N., & Brooks, F. P., Jr. (1988, April). *Using a manipulator for force display in molecular docking.* Paper presented at the IEEE Robotics and Automation Conference, Philadelphia.

Packard, E. (2006). A closer look at Division 21: Human error or designer error? *APA Monitor on Psychology, 37*(2), 76.

Pasquero, J., & Hayward, V. (2003). *STReSS: A practical tactile display with one millimeter spatial resolution and 700 Hz refresh rate.* Paper presented at EuroHaptics 2003, Dublin, Ireland.

Peirce, C. S. (1991). *Peirce on signs.* Chapel Hill, NC: University of North Carolina Press.

Pierotti, D. (1995). Heuristic evaluation—A system checklist [Electronic Version]. Retrieved July 17, 2006, from http://www.stcsig.org/usability/topics/articles/he–checklist.html.

Potter, M. C., Kroll, J. F., & Harris, C. (1980). Comprehension and memory in rapid sequential reading. In R. Nickerson (Ed.), *Attention and performance VIII* (pp. 395–418). Hillsdale, NJ: Lawrence Erlbaum Associates.

Proust, M. (1982). *Remembrance of things past. Volume III: The captive, The fugitive and Time regained.* New York: Vintage.

Radl, G. W. (1980). Experimental investigations for optimal presentation-mode and colours of symbols on the CRT-screen. In E. Grandjean & E. Vigliani (Eds.), *Ergonomic aspects of visual display terminals* (pp. 127–136). London: Taylor & Francis.

Ramey, J. (1989). Escher effects in on–line text. In E. Barrett (Ed.), *The society of text: Hypertext, hypermedia, and the social construction of information* (pp. 388–402). Cambridge, MA: MIT Press.

Ramos, G., Boulos, M., & Balakrishnan, R. (2004, April). *Pressure widgets.* Paper presented at the CHI 2004, Vienna.

Raskin, J. (2000). *The human interface: New directions for designing interactive systems.* Reading, MA: Addison-Wesley.

RCSB. (2005). Welcome to the RCSB PDB. Retrieved December 23, 2006, from http://www.rcsb.org/index.html.

Repokari, L., Saarela, T., & Kurkela, I. (2002). *Visual search on a mobile phone display.* Paper presented at the SAICSIT 2002 Enablement Through Technology Annual Conference of the South African Institute of Computer Scientists and Information Technologists, Port Elizabeth, South Africa.

Royce, W. W. (1970). *Managing the development of large software systems.* Paper presented at the IEEE WESCON, Monterey, CA. Reprinted in (1987) *Proceedings of the 9th International Conference on Software Engineering* (pp. 328–338). New York: ACM Press.

Rubens, P., & Krull, R. (1988). *Communicating with icons as computer commands.* Paper presented at the ACM Special Interest Group for Design of Communications, Ann Arbor, MI.

Rubin, J. (1994). *Handbook of usability testing: How to plan, design, and conduct effective tests.* New York: Wiley.

Russo, P., & Boor, S. (1993). *How fluent is your interface? Designing for international users.* Paper presented at CHI '93, Amsterdam.

Ryan, T. A., & Schwartz, C. B. (1956). Speed of perception as a function of mode of representation. *American Journal of Psychology, 69,* 60–69.

Sato, M. (2002, Sept. 25). Development of string–based force display. Paper presented at the Eighth International Conference on Virtual Reality and Multimedia, Gyeongju, Korea.

Schmandt, C., & Mullins, A. (1995). AudioStreamer: Exploiting simultaneity for listening. In *CHI '95 conference companion on human factors in computing systems* (pp. 218–219). Denver, CO.

Schneider, G., & Winters, J. P. (2001). *Applying use cases: A practical guide* (2nd ed.). Reading, MA: Addison-Wesley.

Schwarz, E., Beldie, I. P., & Pastoor, S. A. (1983). A comparison of paging and scrolling for changing screen contents by inexperienced users. *Human Factors, 25,* 279–282.

Sekey, A., & Tietz, J. (1982). Text display by "saccadic scrolling." *Visible Language, 17,* 62–77.

Shannon, C. E., & Weaver, W. (1949). *The mathematical theory of communication.* Urbana: University of Illinois Press.

Sherrick, C. E., & Craig, J. C. (Eds.). (1982). *The psychophysics of touch*: Cambridge: Cambridge University Press.

Shneiderman, B. (1982). The future of interactive systems and the emergence of direct manipulation. *Behavior and Information Technology, 1*(3), 237–256.

Shneiderman, B., & Plaisant, C. (2005). *Designing the user interface: Strategies for effective human–computer interaction* (4th ed.). Reading, MA: Addison-Wesley.

Siewiorek, D. P., & Smailagic, A. (2003). User-centered interdisciplinary design of wearable computers. In J. A. Jacko & A. Sears (Eds.), *The human–computer interaction handbook*. Mahwah, NJ: Lawrence Erlbaum Associates.

SPARC. (2005). What is SPARC? Retrieved June 24, 2005, from http://www.si.umich.edu/sparc/background.htm.

Stone, R.J. (2000, August–September). *Haptic feedback: A potted history, from telepresence to virtual reality*. Paper presented at the Proceedings of the First International Workshop on Haptic Human–Computer Interaction, Glasgow, Scotland.

Sukaviriya, P., & Moran, L. (1990). User interfaces for Asia. In J. Nielsen (Ed.), *Designing user interfaces for international use* (pp. 189–217). Amsterdam: Elsevier.

Sutherland, I. (1965). *The ultimate display*. Paper presented at the Proceedings of the International Federation of Information Processing Congress 65, New York City.

The Chimpanzee Collaboratory. (2005). The Chimpanzee Collaboratory. Retrieved June 24, 2005, from http://www.chimpcollaboratory.org/

Thorell, L. G., & Smith, W. J. (1990). *Using computer color effectively: An illustrated reference*. Upper Saddle River, NJ: Prentice Hall.

Tsukada, K., & Yasumrua, M. (2004). *ActiveBelt: Belt-type wearable tactile display for directional navigation*. Paper presented at UbiComp 2004, Nottingham, England.

Tullis, T. S. (1984). *Predicting the usability of alphanumericdisplays*. Unpublished doctoral dissertation, Rice University, Houston, TX.

Ulrich, I., & Borenstein, J. (2001). The GuideCane—Applying mobile robot technologies to assist the visually impaired. *IEEE Transactions on Systems, Man, and Cybernetics, Part A, 31*(2), 131–136.

Unicode Consortium (2006). Glossary of Unicode terms. Retrieved December 23, 2006, from http://www.unicode.org/glossary.

Usability.gov. (2006). Usability basics. Retrieved April 26, 2006, from http://www.usability.gov/basics/index.html.

van Erp, J. B. F. (2002). *Guidelines for the use of vibro–tactile displays in human–computer interaction*. Paper presented at Eurohaptics 2002, University of Edinburgh, Edinburgh, Scotland.

van Erp, J. B. F., & Spapé, M. M. A. (2003). *Distilling the underlying dimensions of tactile melodies*. Paper presented at EuroHaptics 2003, Dublin, Ireland.

van Erp, J. B. F., & van Veen, H. A. H. C. (2003). *A multi–purpose tactile vest for astronauts in the International Space Station*. Paper presented at Eurohaptics 2003, Dublin, Ireland.

Vartabedian, A. G. (1971). The effects of letter size, case, and generation method on CRT display search time. *Human Factors, 13*, 363–368.

Velázquez, F., Maingreaud, & Pissaloux, E. (2003). *Intelligent glasses: A new man–machine interface concept integrating computer vision and human tactile perception*. Paper presented at EuroHaptics 2003, Dublin, Ireland.

Vera, A., Tollinger, I., Eng, K., Lewis, R., & Howes, A. (2005). *Architectural building blocks as the locus of adaptive behavior selection*. Paper presented at the 27th Annual Meeting of the Cognitive Science Society, Stresa, Italy.

Weinschenk, S., & Schaffer, E. (2003). UI Design Update Newsletter: Insights from Human Factors International. Retrieved December 23, 2006, from http://www.humanfactors.com/downloads/feb03.htm.

Weiser, M. (1991). The computer for the 21st century. *Scientific American, 265*(3), 94–104.

Williamson, D. T., & Barry, T. P. (2001). Speech recognition in the Joint Air Operations Center—A human-centered approach. In M. J. Smith, G. Salvendy, D. Harris, & R. J. Koubek (Eds.),

Usability evaluation and interface design: Cognitive engineering, intelligent agents, and virtual reality (Vol. 1, pp. 843–847). Mahwah, NJ: Lawrence Erlbaum Associates.

Wolfe, J. L. (2000). Effects of annotations on student readers and writers. In K. Anderson (Ed.), *Proceedings of the Fifth ACM Conference on Digital Libraries* (pp. 19–26). New York: ACM Press.

Wong, W. (1997). *Principles of color design—Designing with electronic color.* New York: Van Nostrand Reinhold.

Youngman, M., & Scharff, L. (1998). *Text width and margin width influences on readability of GUIs.* Paper presented at SWPA 1998. Retrieved December 18, 2006, from http://hubel.sfasu.edu/research/textmargin.html.

Yu, W., Ramloll, R., Brewster, S. A., & Riedel, B. (2001). *Exploring computer-generated line graphs through virtual touch.* Paper presented at the 6th International Symposium on Signal Processing and Its Applications, Kuala-Lumpur, Malaysia.

Credits

Figure 1.2(a) and (b), p. 6: Courtesy of Douglas Engelbart and Bootstrap Alliance.

Figure 1.4(a) and (b), p. 14: Courtesy IBM Corporate Archives.

Figure 1.5, p. 16: Courtesy Palo Alto Research Center.

Figures 1.6, p. 18; 1.7(a) and (b), p. 21; 1.8(a) and (b), p. 22; and 1.9, p. 23: © BigStockPhoto.

Figure 1.10(a) and (b), p. 25: © 2001–2007 SMART Technologies Inc. All rights reserved.

Figure 1.12, p. 30: © BigStockPhoto.

Figures 2.1, p. 42; and 2.2, p. 44: © Donald Norman.

Figure 2.3, p. 46: © British Informatics Society Ltd 1991. Reprinted with the permission of Cambridge University Press.

Figure 2.16, p. 73: Courtesy of AZA Raskin, President, Humanized Inc.

Figure 3.3, p. 89: © Barry Bohem.

Figure 3.4, p. 91: Reproduced by kind permission of the DSDM Consortium. DSDM and **DSDM** are registered trademarks of Dynamic Systems Development Method Limited.

Figure 6.2, p. 196: © British Informatics Society Ltd 1991. Reprinted with the permission of Cambridge University Press.

Figures 6.4, p. 200; 6.15, p. 213; 6.17, p. 214; 6.19, p. 215; and 6.21, p. 215: © Adobe® product screen shots reprinted with permission from Adobe® Systems Incorporated.

Figure 6.5, p. 201: © Google Inc. Used with permission.

Figure 6.10, p. 207: Courtesy of Pearson Education.

Figure 6.23, p. 216: Courtesy of the Museum of Modern Art.

Figure 6.24(a), p. 217: Courtesy of the Metropolitan Museum of Art.

Figure 6.26, p. 218: © 2006 XM Satellite Radio Inc. All rights reserved.

Figure 6.35(a) and (b), p. 224: Courtesy of T. S. Tullis.

Tables 7.3, p. 241; and 7.4, p. 242: Reprinted with permission from Card, S. K., Moran, T. P., and Newell A., *The Psychology of Human–Computer Interaction* (New ed.): Lawrence Erlbaum Associates (1983).

Table 7.5, p. 243: Reprinted from *Human–Computer Interaction, 5,* Olson, J. R., & Olson, G. M., The growth of cognitive modeling in human–computer interaction since GOMS, 221–265, 1990, with permission from Elsevier.

Figures 7.6, p. 256; and 7.7, p. 257: Reprinted from *Human–computer interaction—INTERACT '90,* Buxton, W. A. S., A three-state model of graphical input., 449–456, 1990, with permission from Elsevier.

Figure 7.8, p. 257: Reprinted from *Toward a multidisciplinary science of human–computer interaction,* MacKenzie, I. S., Motor behaviour models for human–computer interaction., 27–54, 2003, with permission from Elsevier.

Figure 7.11, p. 259: Reprinted with permission from MacKenzie, I. S., & Oniszczak, A. (1997). *The tactile touchpad* (extended abstract). Paper presented at the Conference on Human Factors in Computing Systems, Atlanta, GA.

Figures 7.12, p. 259; and 7.13, p. 260: Reprinted with permission from Forlines, C., Shen, C., & Buxton, B. (2005, April). *Glimpse: A novel input model for multilevel devices* (extended abstract). Paper presented at the CHI 05, Portland, OR.

Figure 9.5(a) and (b), p. 324: © Jim Nilsen (www.jimnilsen.com). Used with permission.

Figure 9.21(b), (d), and (f), p. 346: © BigStockPhoto.

Figure 9.28 (a), (b), and (c), p. 351: © Adobe® product screen shot reprinted with permission from Adobe® Systems Incorporated.

Figures 10.3, p. 366; 10.5, p. 370; 10.8, p. 374; 10.10, p. 382; 10.22, p. 392; 10.26, p. 396: © Adobe® product screen shot reprinted with permission from Adobe® Systems Incorporated.

Figure 11.9, p. 418: © 2006 Amazon.com, Inc. or its affiliates. All Rights Reserved.

Figure 12.11, p. 481: © Jakob Nielsen. Used with permission.

Figure 12.12, p. 482: Courtesy of the W3C (World Wide Web Consortium).

Figure 12.13, p. 483: © 2006 Amazon.com, Inc. or its affiliates. All Rights Reserved.

Figure 14.8, p. 573: Courtesy of ImmersiveTouch.

Figure 14.9, p. 574: Reproduced by permission of Immersion Corporation. © 2006 Immersion Corporation. All rights reserved.

Figure 14.10, p. 576: © Johann Borenstein. Reprinted with permission from Ulrich, I., & Borenstein, J. (2001). The GuideCane—Applying mobile robot technologies to assist the visually impaired. *IEEE Transactions on Systems, Man, and Cybernetics, Part A, 31*(2), 131–136.

Figure 14.14, p. 578: Courtesy of CYBERDYNE Inc. (www.cyberdyne.jp).

Figure 14.15(a), p. 579: © SensAble Technologies, Inc.® Used with permission. The SenSitus molecular docking software package shown is courtesy of Stefan Birmanns, Ph.D., of the Laboratory for Structural Bioinformatics, University of Texas Health Science Center at Houston.

Figure 14.18, p. 588: © ACM, Reprinted by permission.

Figure 14.19(a) and (b), p. 589: Courtesy of Kraft Telerobotics Inc.

Figure 14.20(a), (b), and (c), p. 590: Reproduced by permission of Immersion Corporation. © 2006 Immersion Corporation. All rights reserved.

Figure 14.21(a) and (b), p. 591: © SensAble Technologies, Inc®. Used with permission.

Figure 14.22, p. 592: © Makoto Sato.

Figures A.4, p. 606; C.1, p. 620; and C.2, p. 621: © BigStockPhoto.

Figure C.3(a), p. 623: Courtesy of Sport Vue™.

Figure C.3(b), p. 623: Courtesy of MicroOptical Corporation.

Figure C.4(a) and (b), p. 623: Courtesy of Trivisio Technologies.

Figure C.5, p. 624: Courtesy of Sensics Inc.

Figure C.6(a) and (b), p. 625: Photographs and ShadowLight application courtesy of Kalev Leetaru.

Figure C.7(a), p. 626: Courtesy of Douglas Engelbart and Bootstrap Alliance.

Figures C.7(b), p. 626; C.8, p. 627; C.9, p. 627; C.10, p. 628; C.11, p. 628; and C.12, p. 629: © BigStockPhoto.

Figure C.13(a) and (b), p. 630: © SR Research, Ltd.

Figure C.14, p. 631: © NaturalPoint® Inc.

Figure C.17, p. 633: Courtesy of Handykey Corp. (www.handykey.com).

Figure C.18, p. 634: © Lumio Corp.

Index